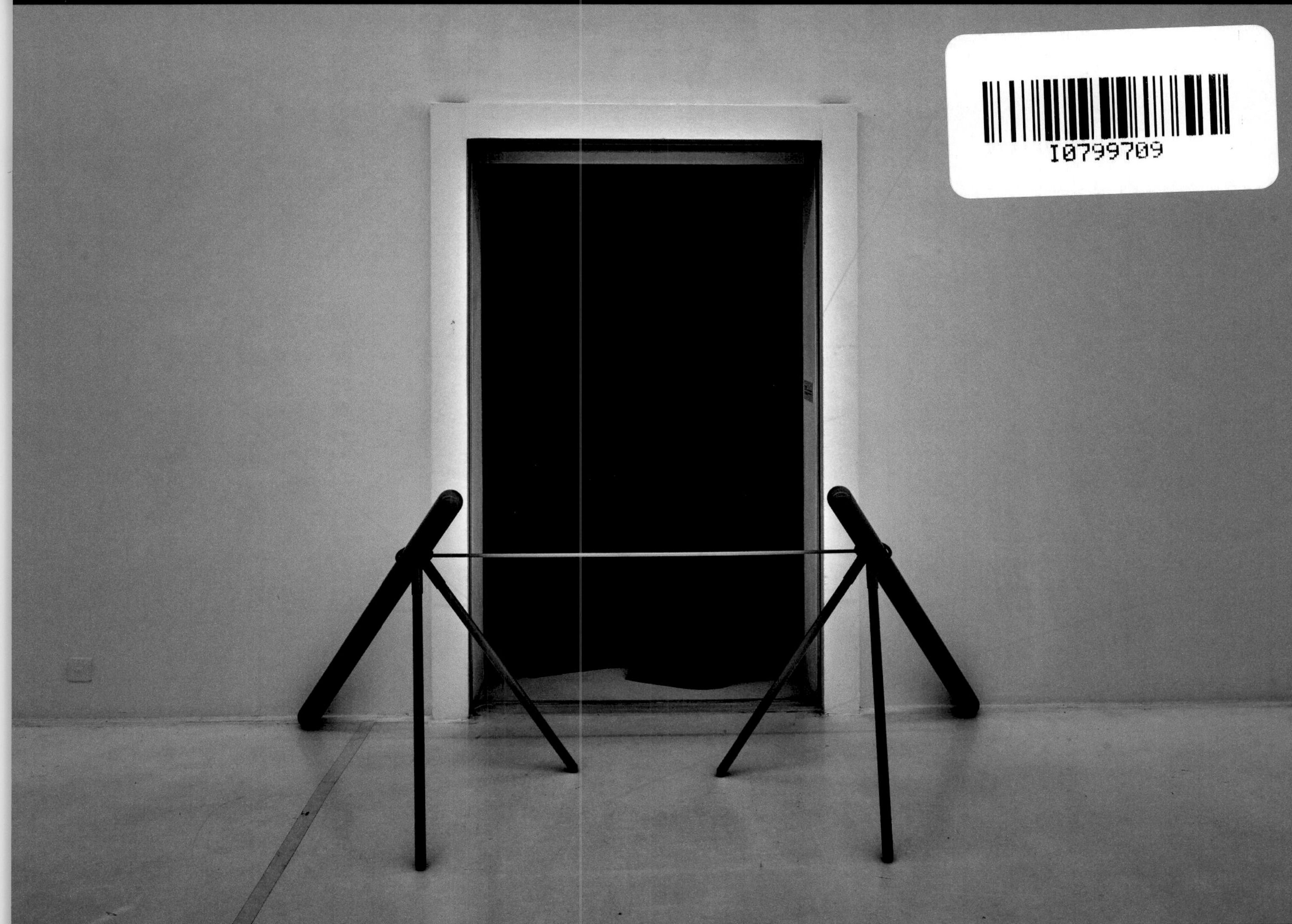

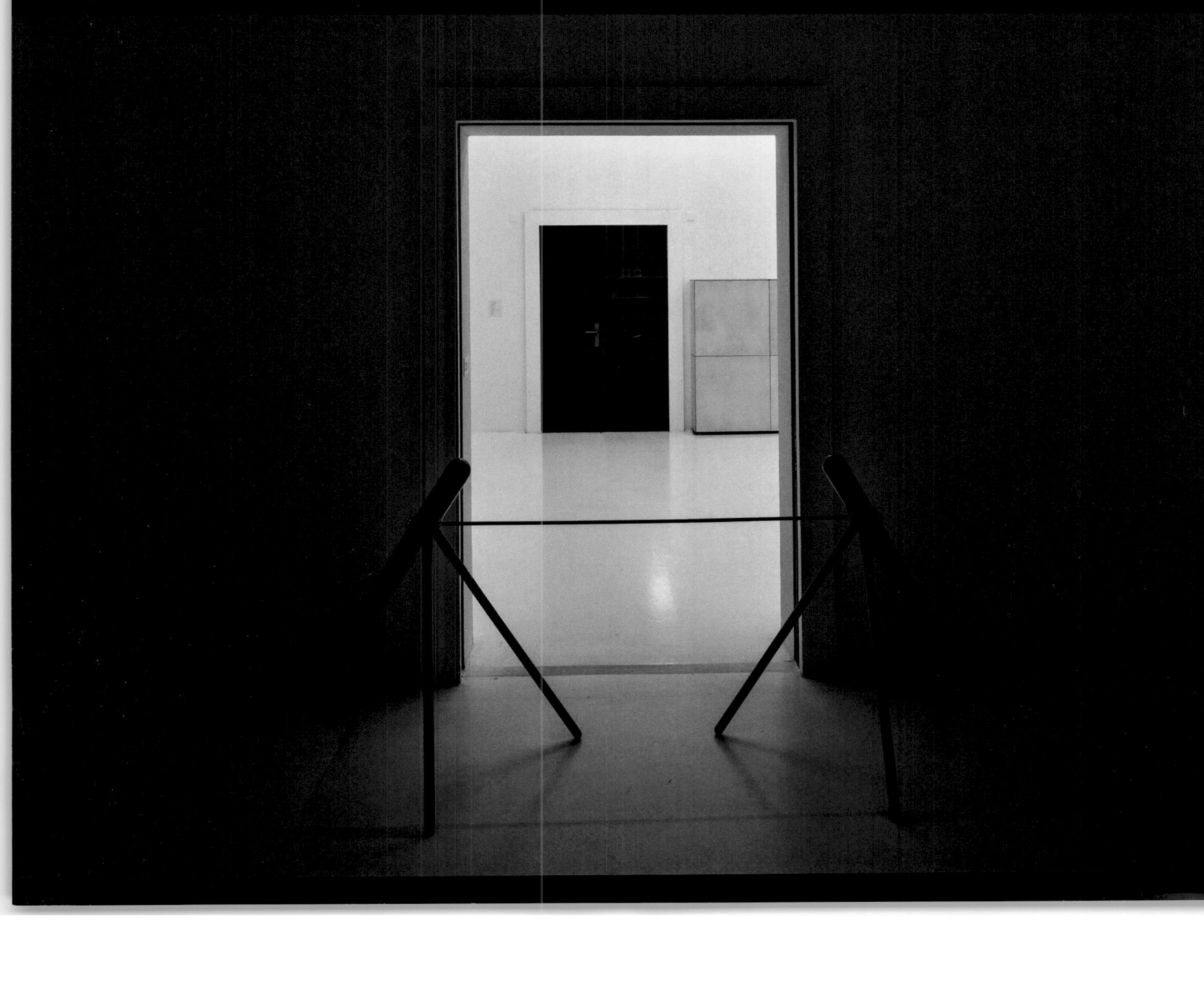

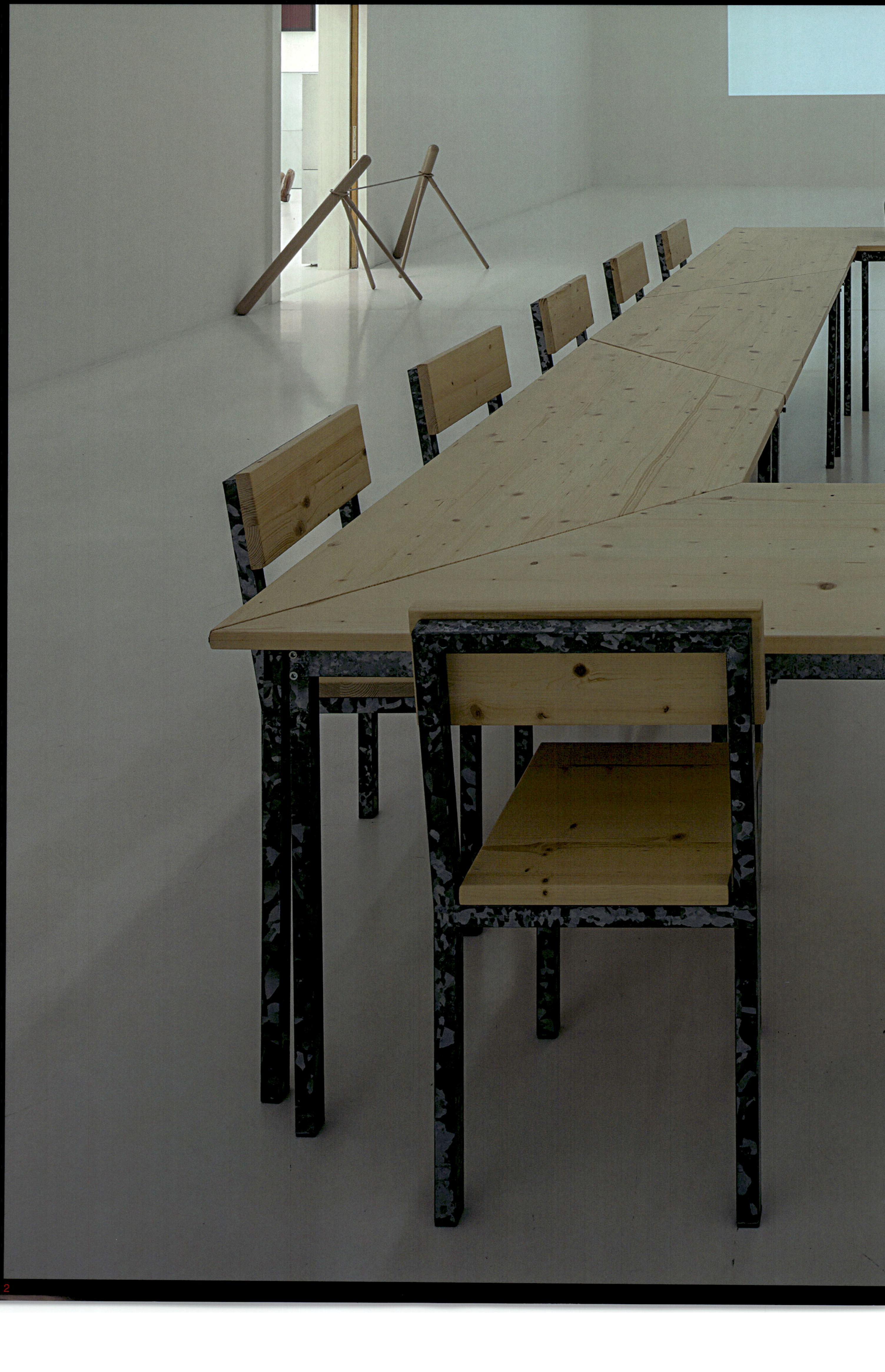

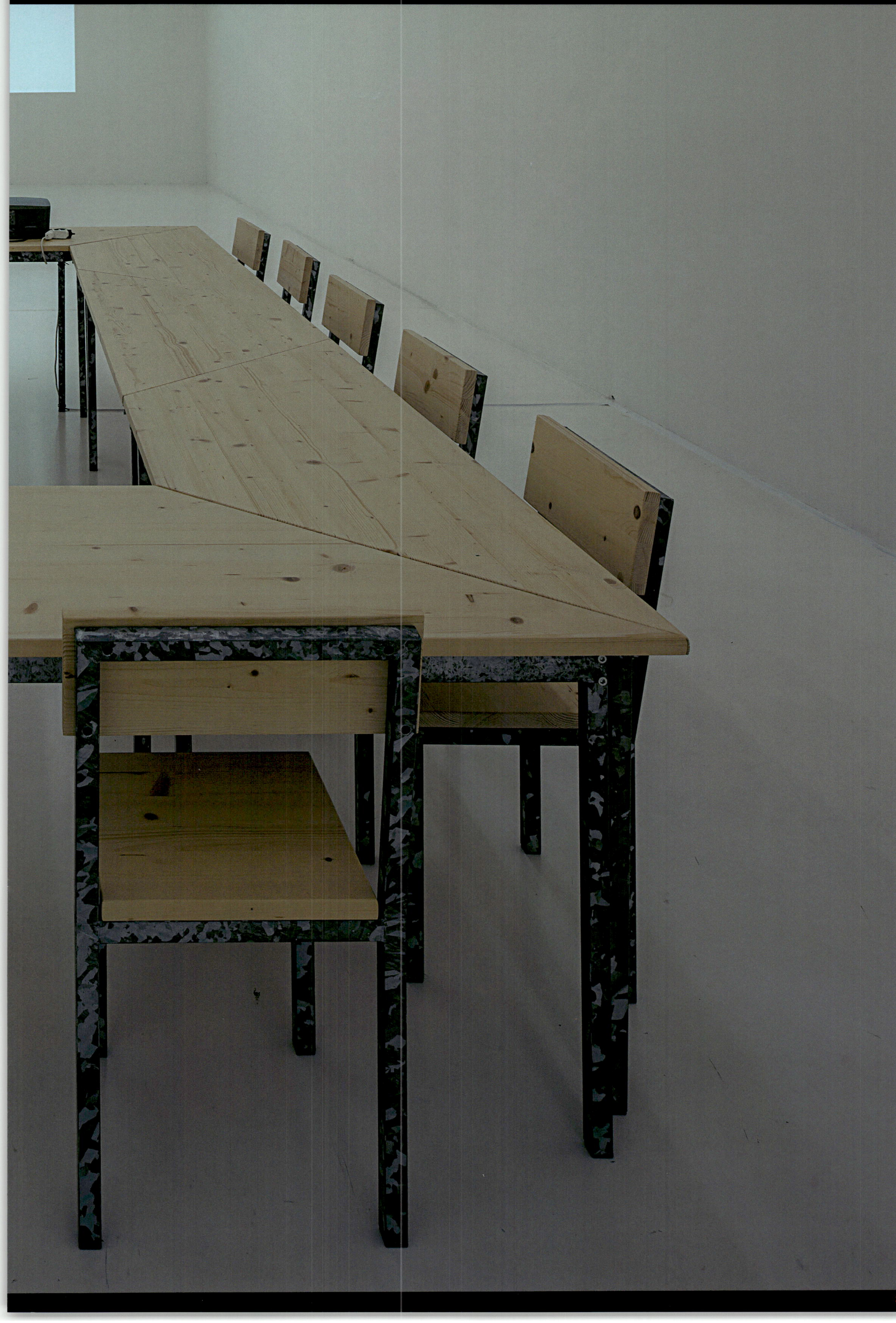

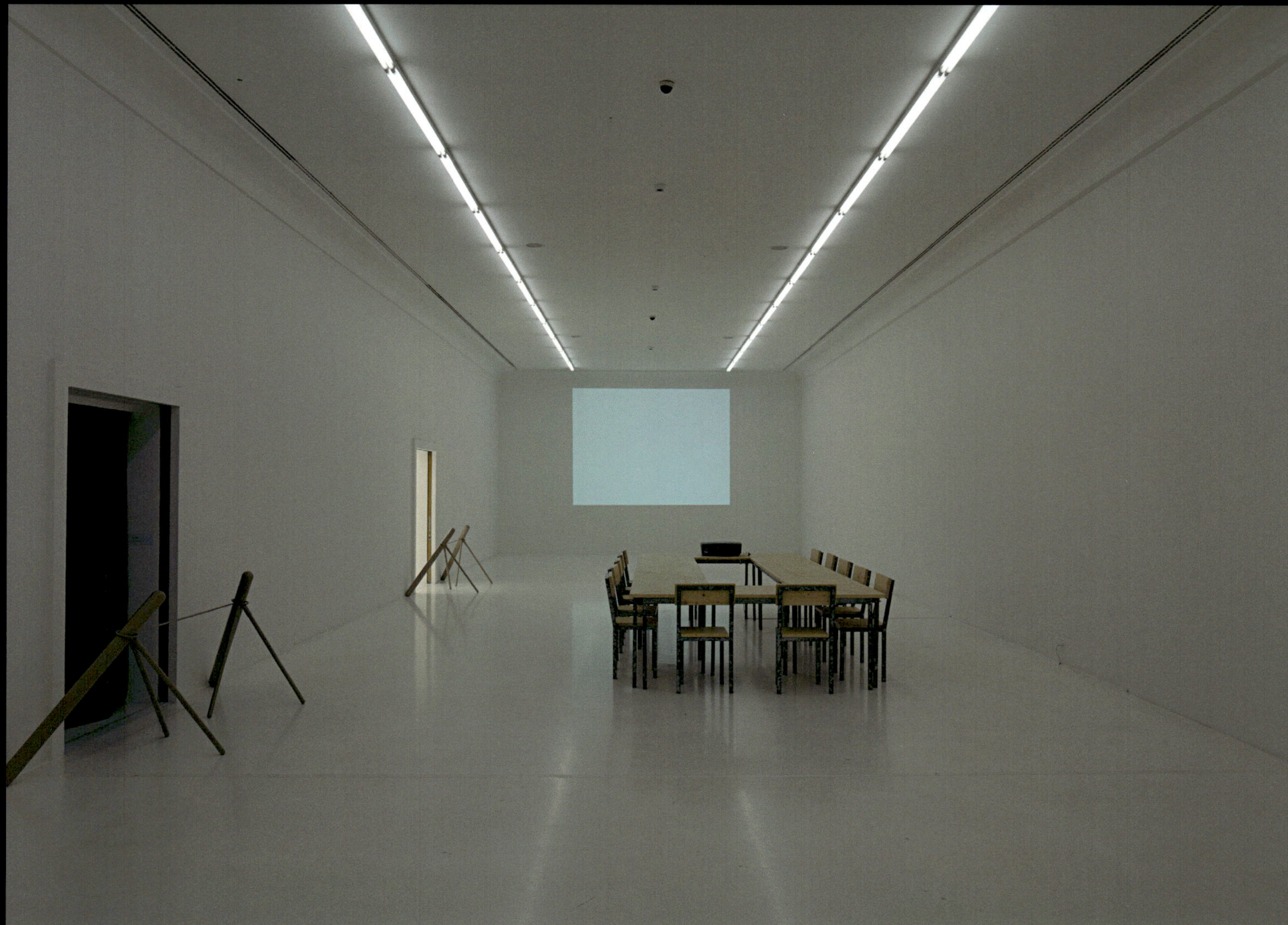

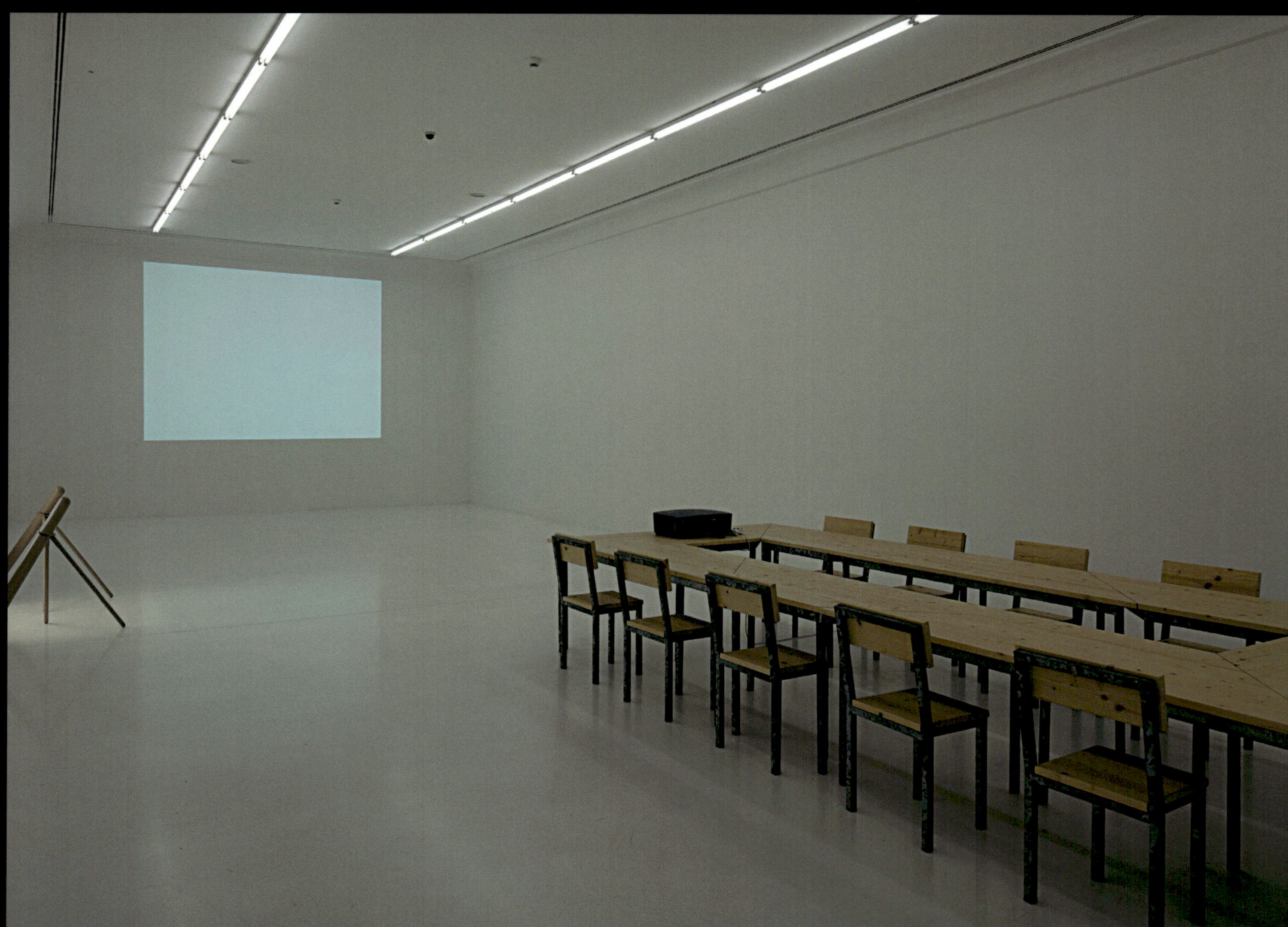

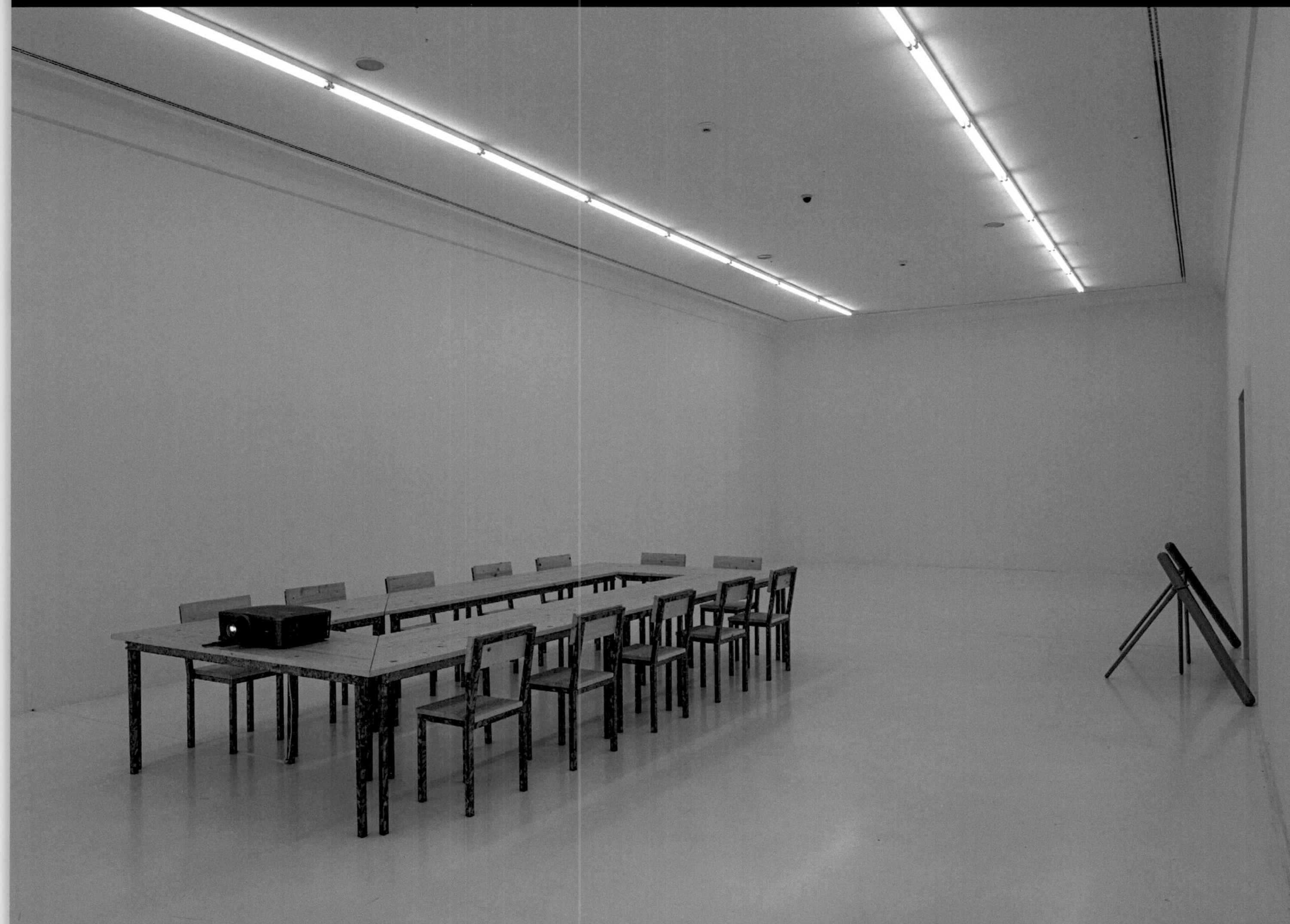

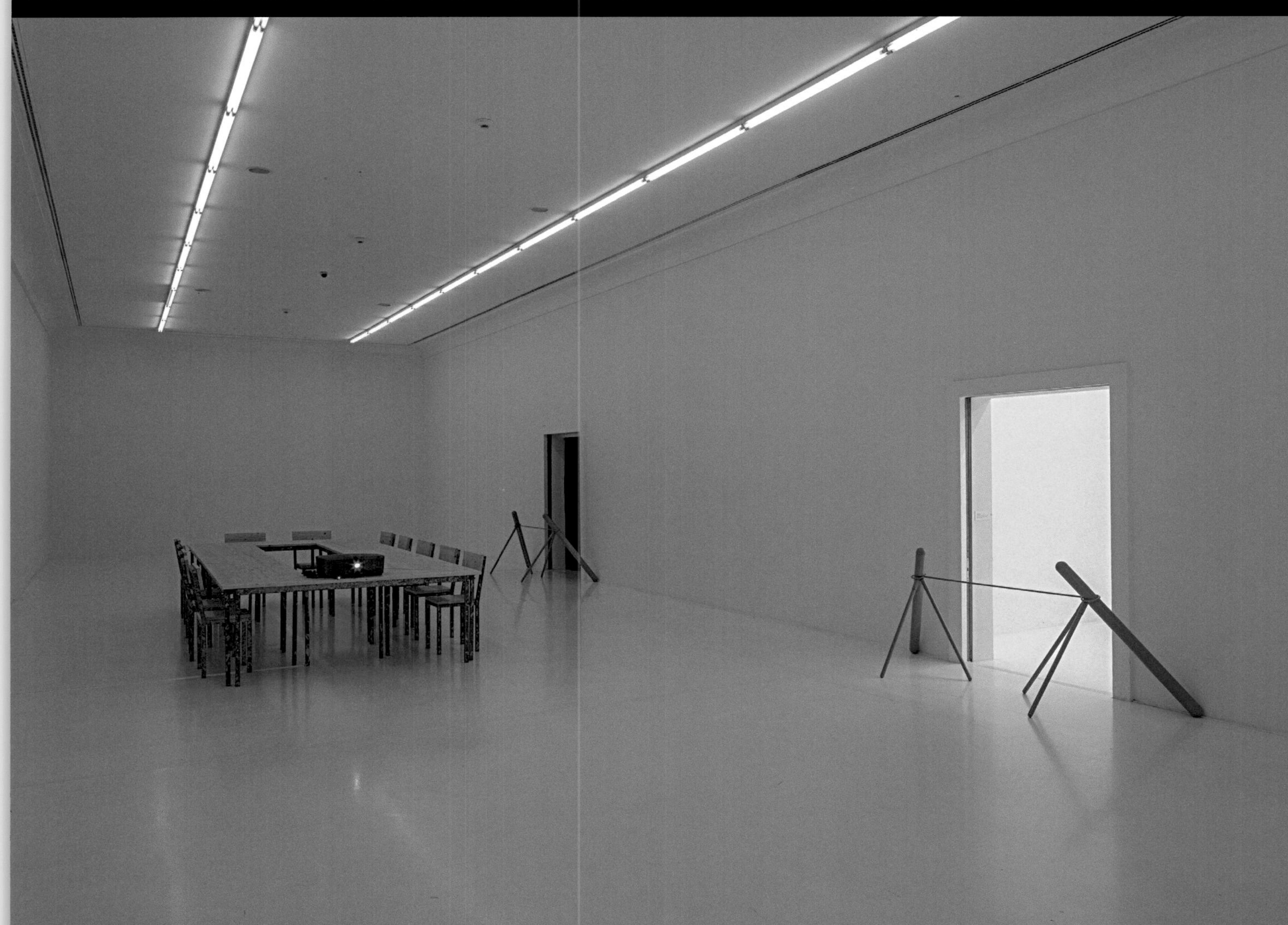

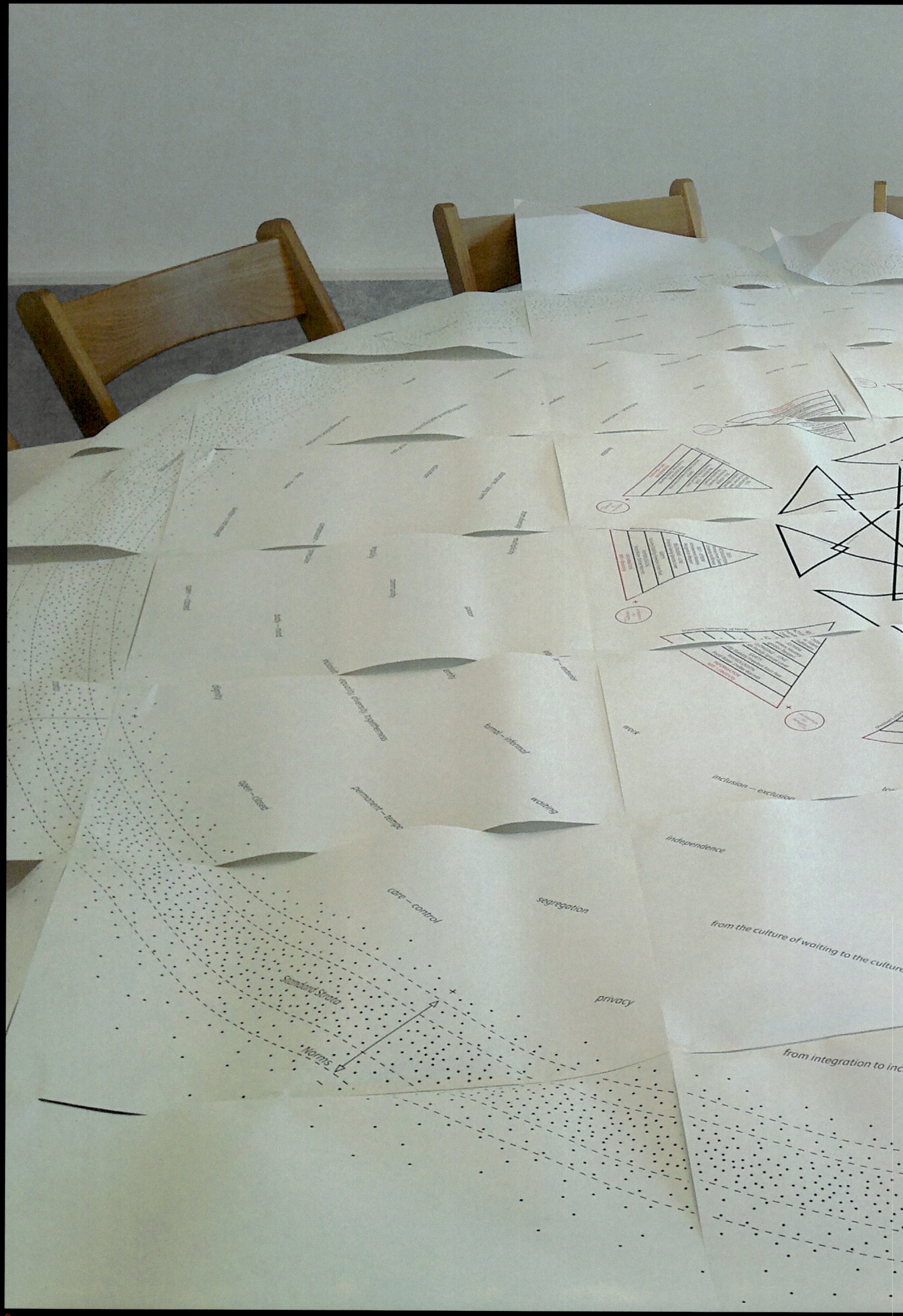

inclusion – exclusion
independence
care – control
segregation
from the culture of waiting to the culture o
privacy
from integration to inclu
Standard Strata
Norms
formal – informal
permanent – tempo
waiting

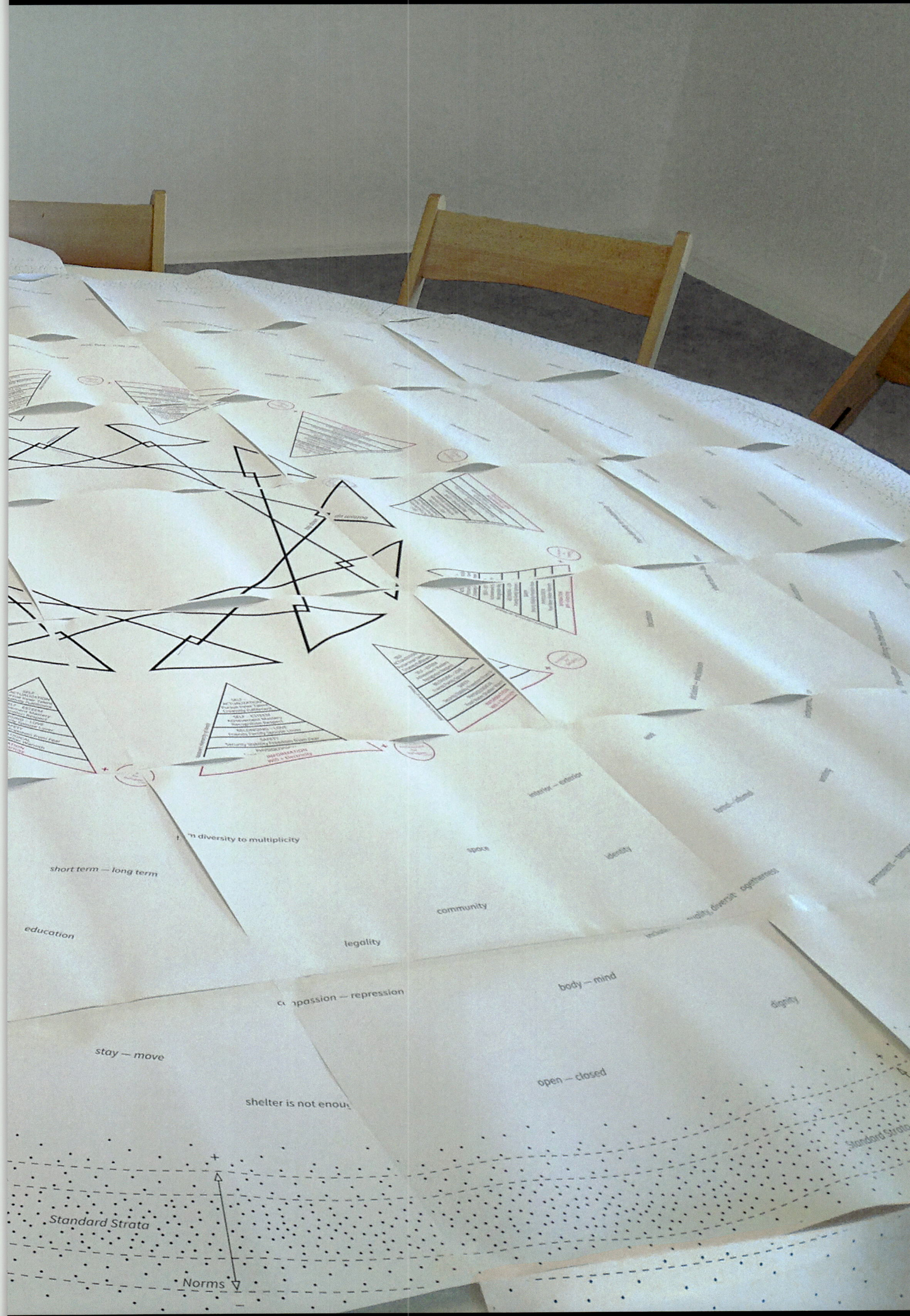
short term — long term
education
legality
community
space
identity
interior — exterior
compassion — repression
body — mind
dignity
stay — move
open — closed
Standard Strata
Norms
Standard Strata

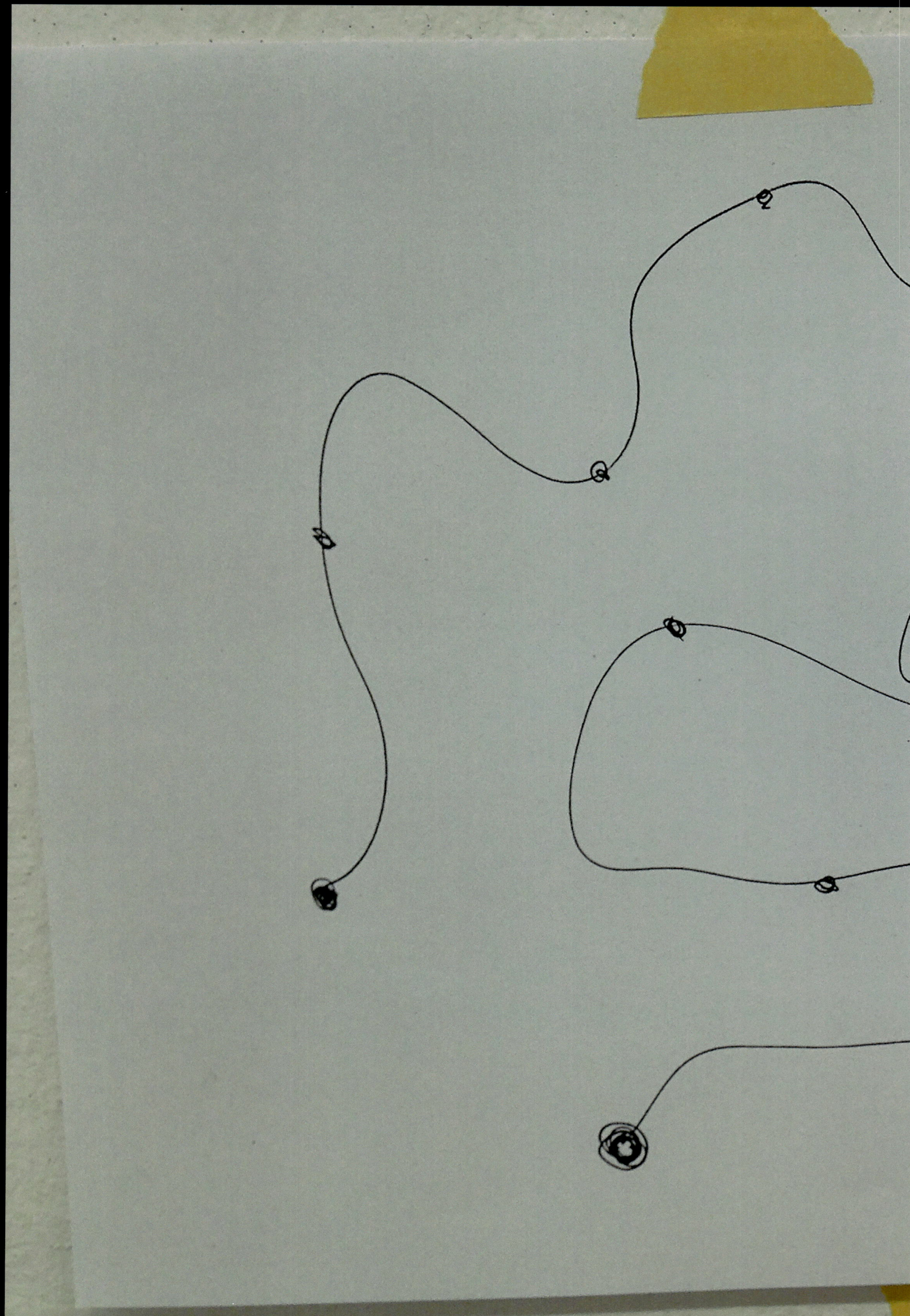

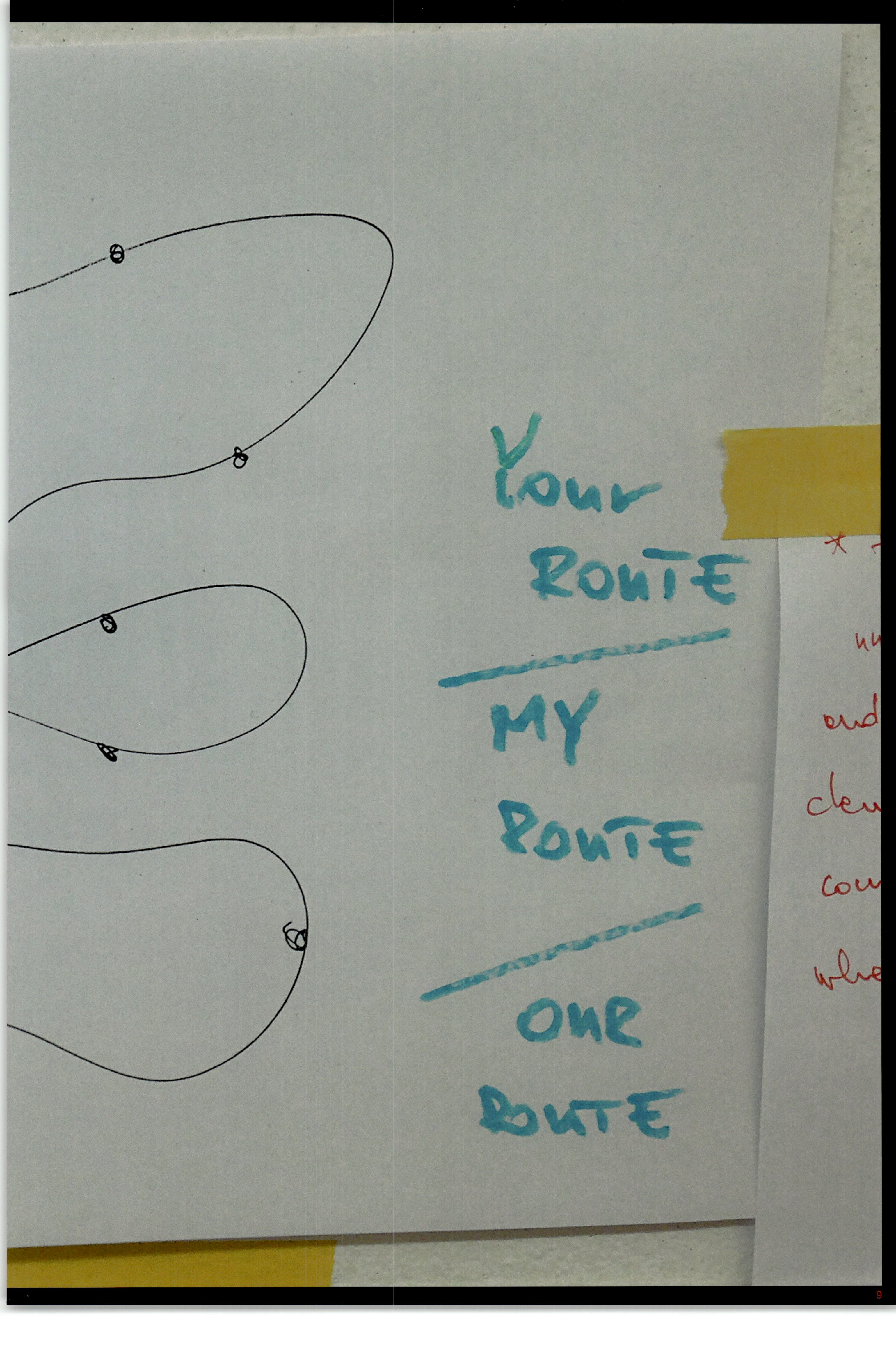
YOUR
ROUTE
MY
ROUTE
OUR
ROUTE

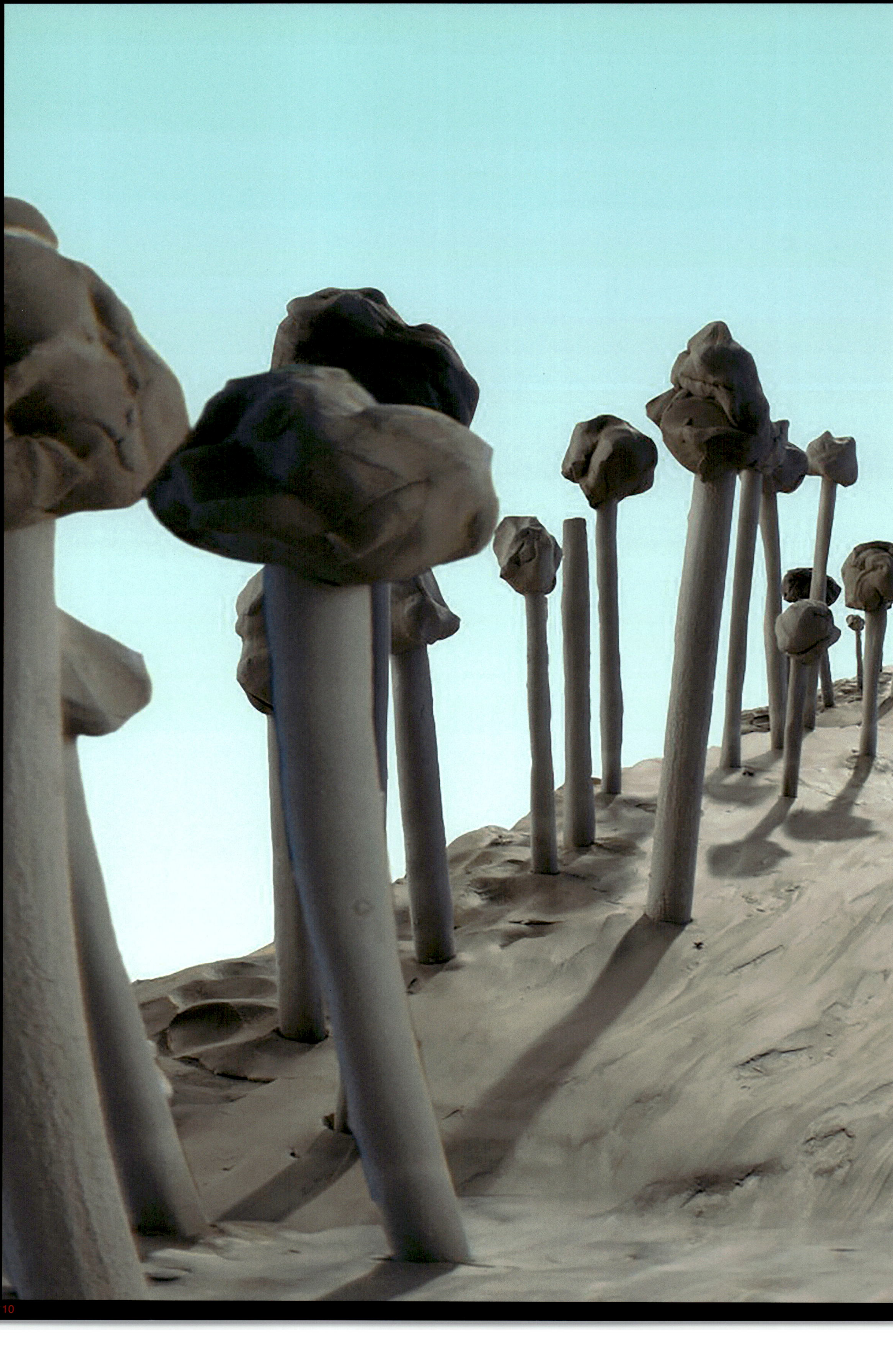

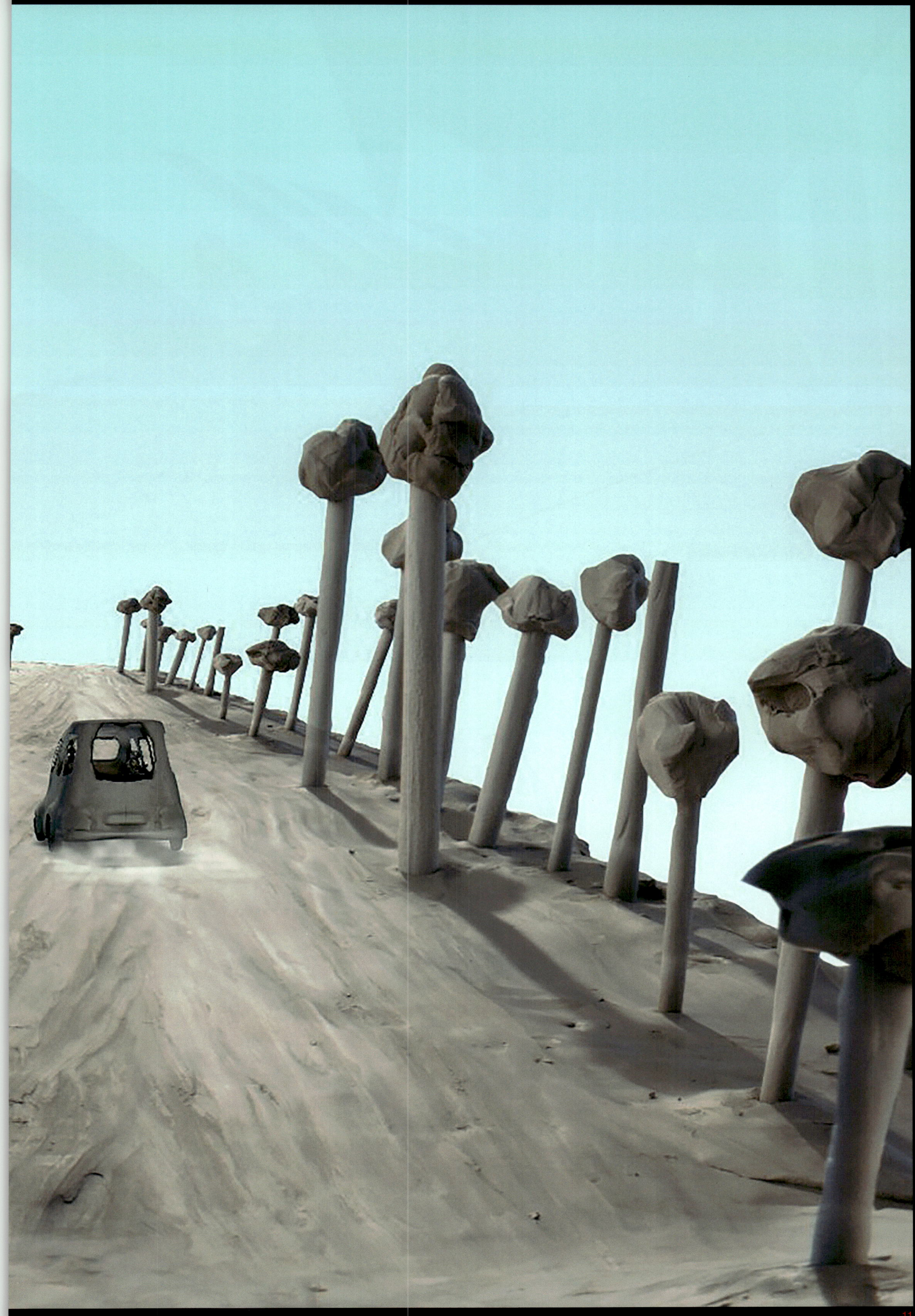

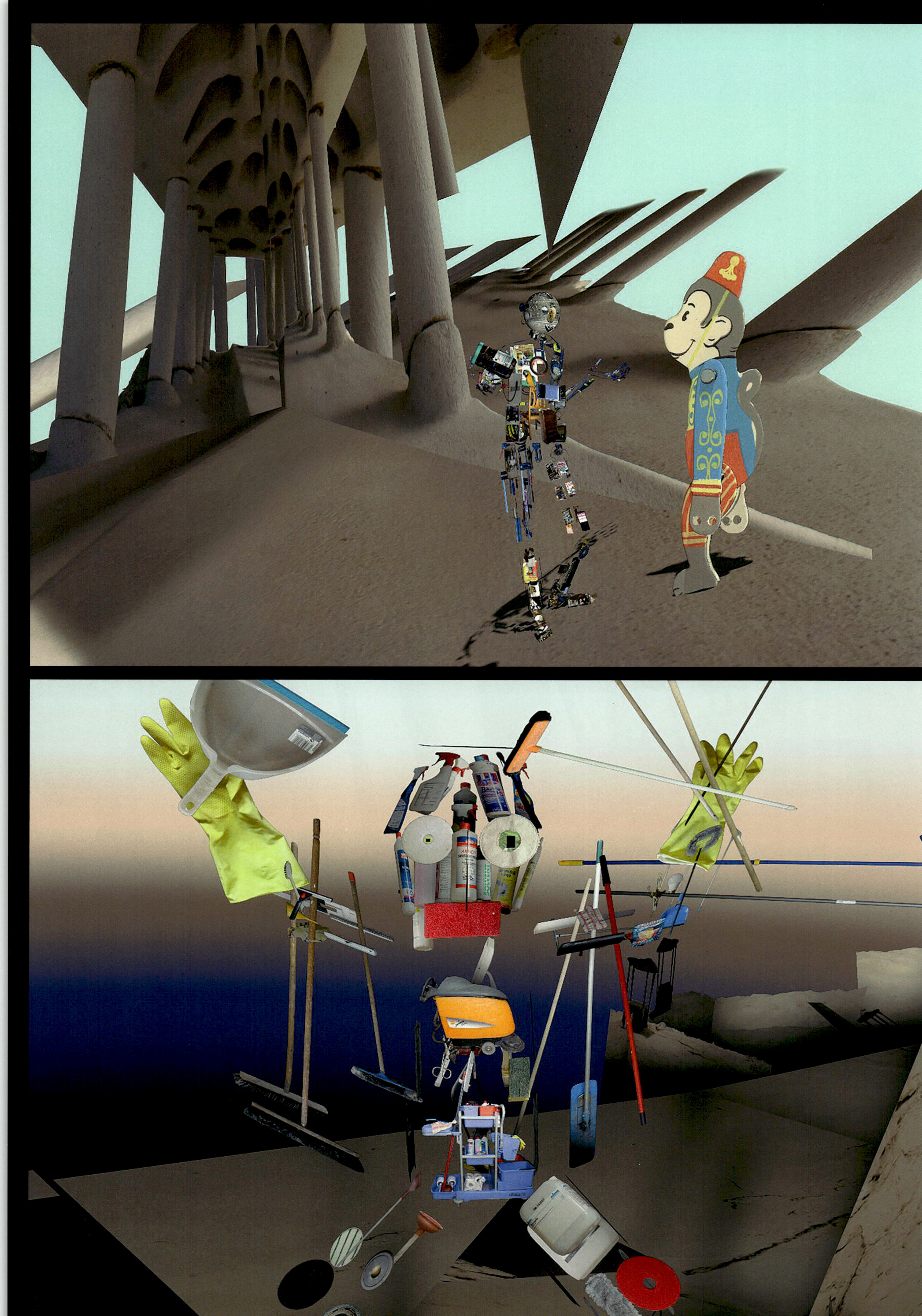

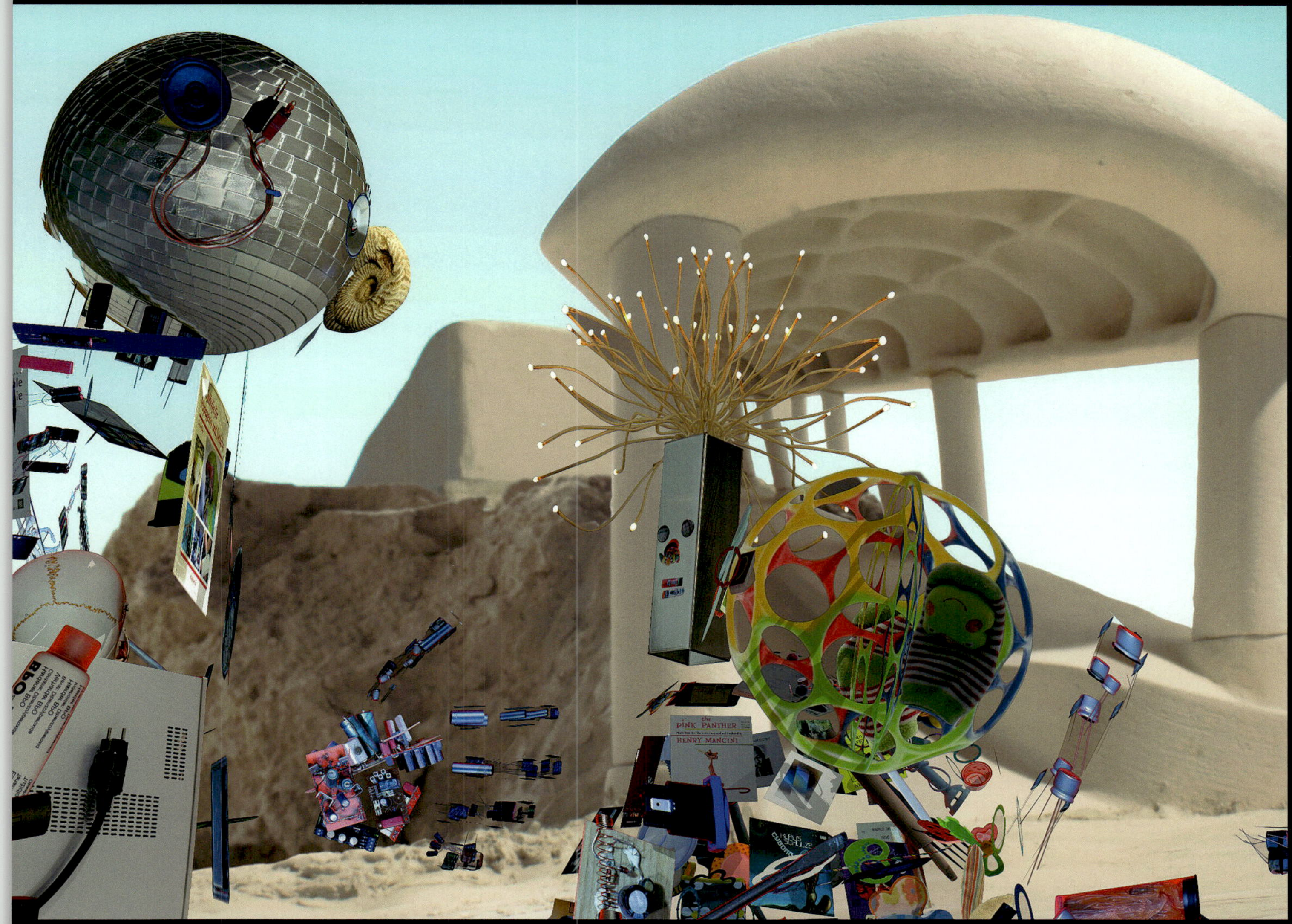

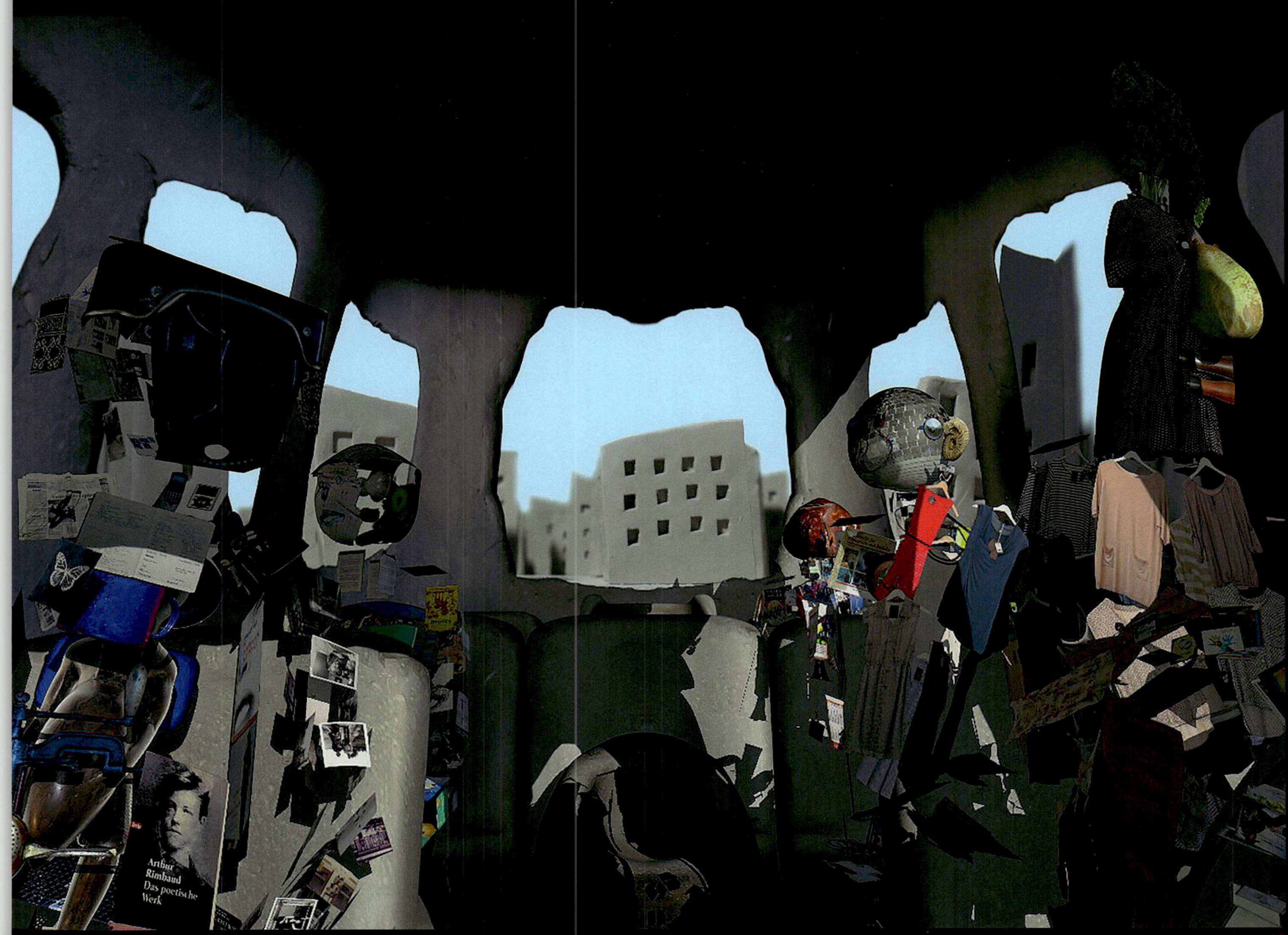
Arthur
Rimbaud
Das poetische
Werk

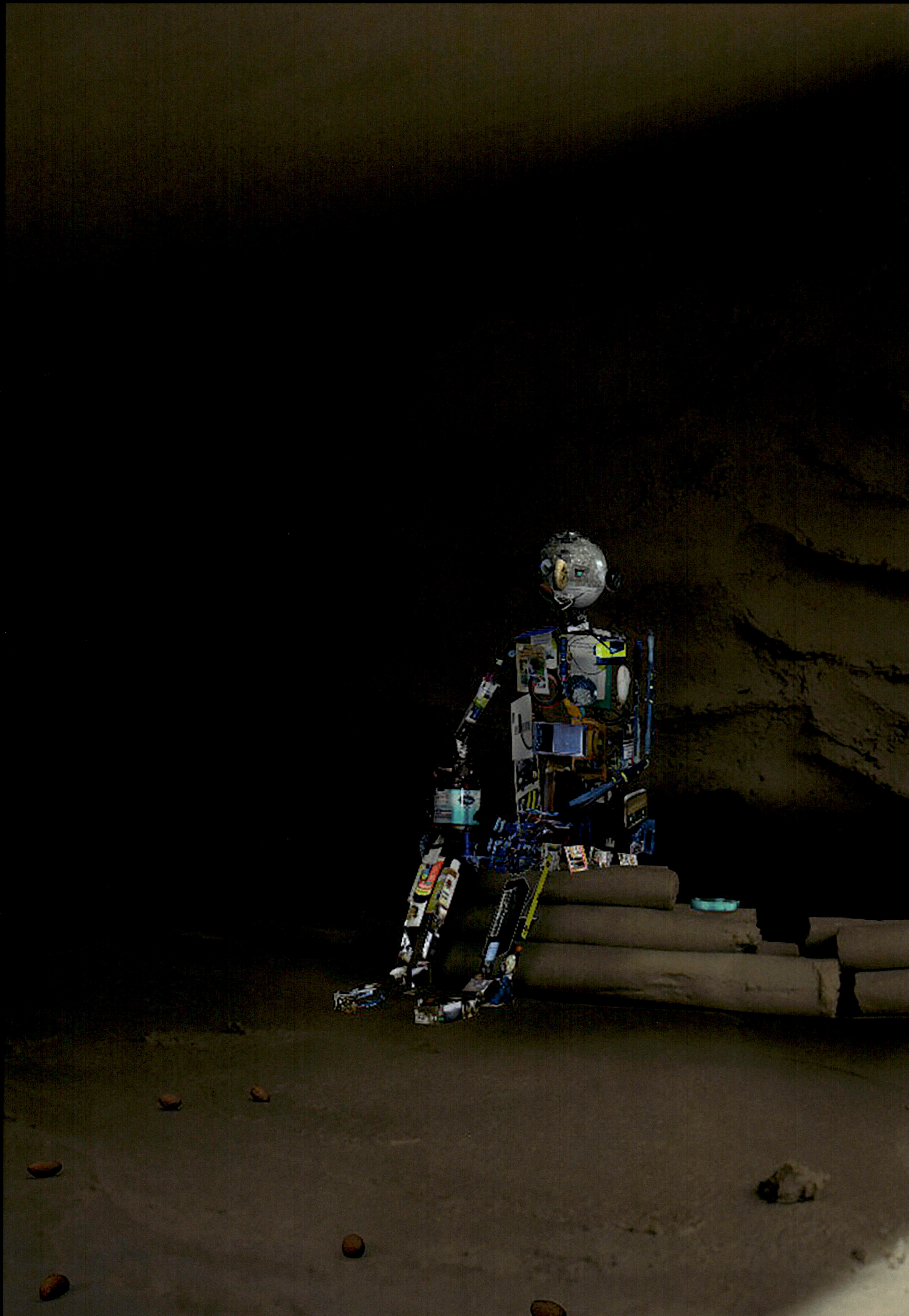

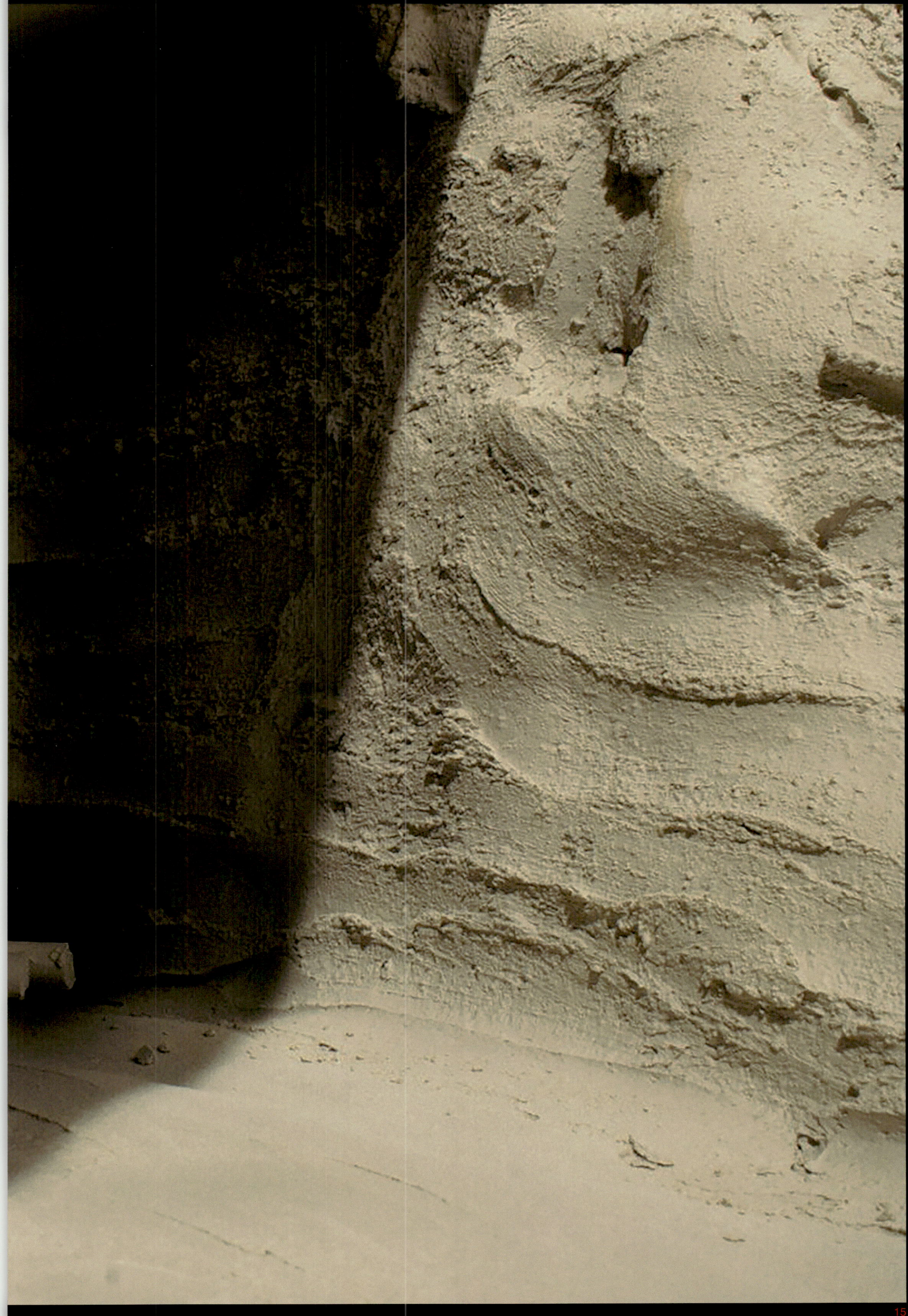

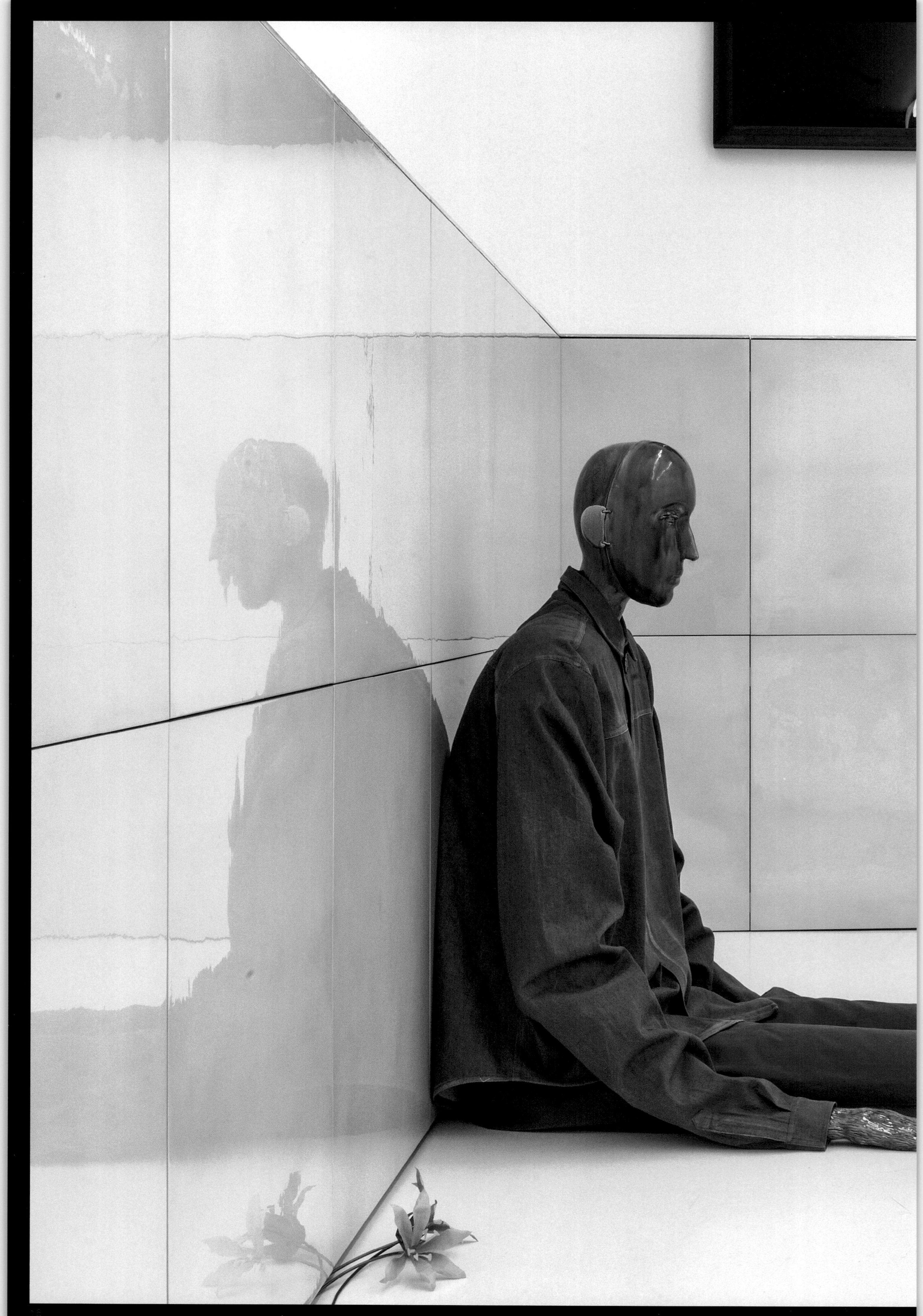

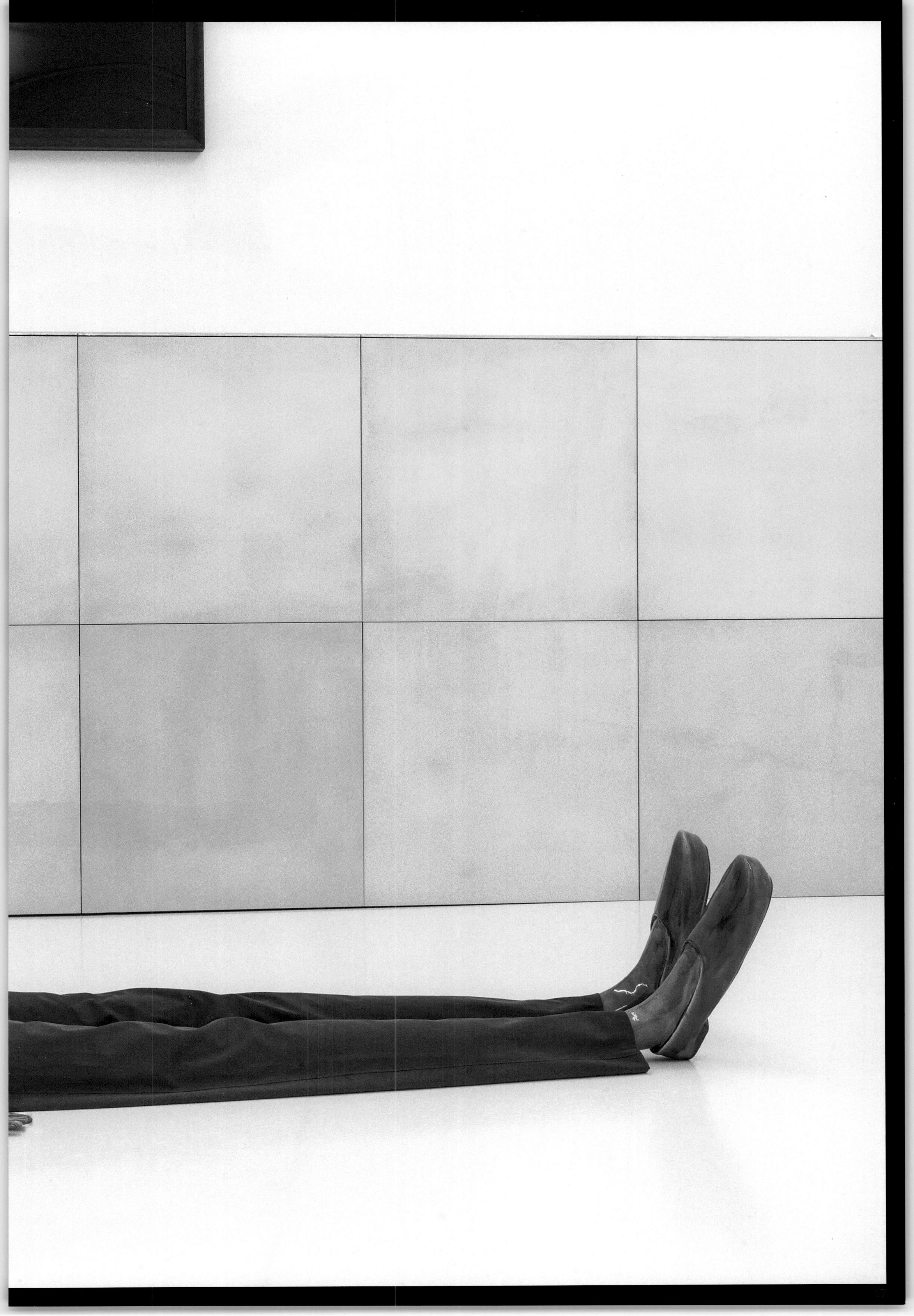

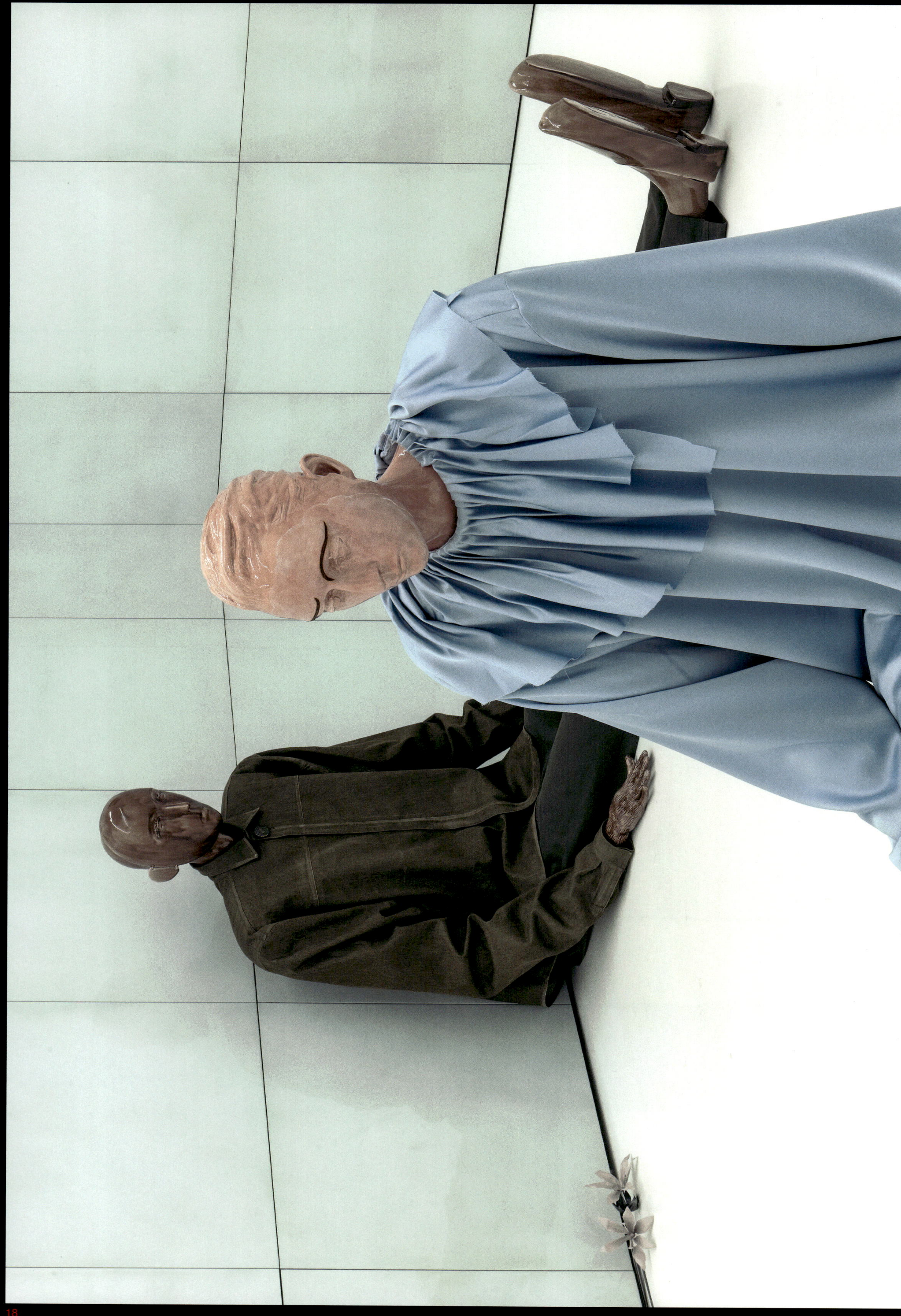

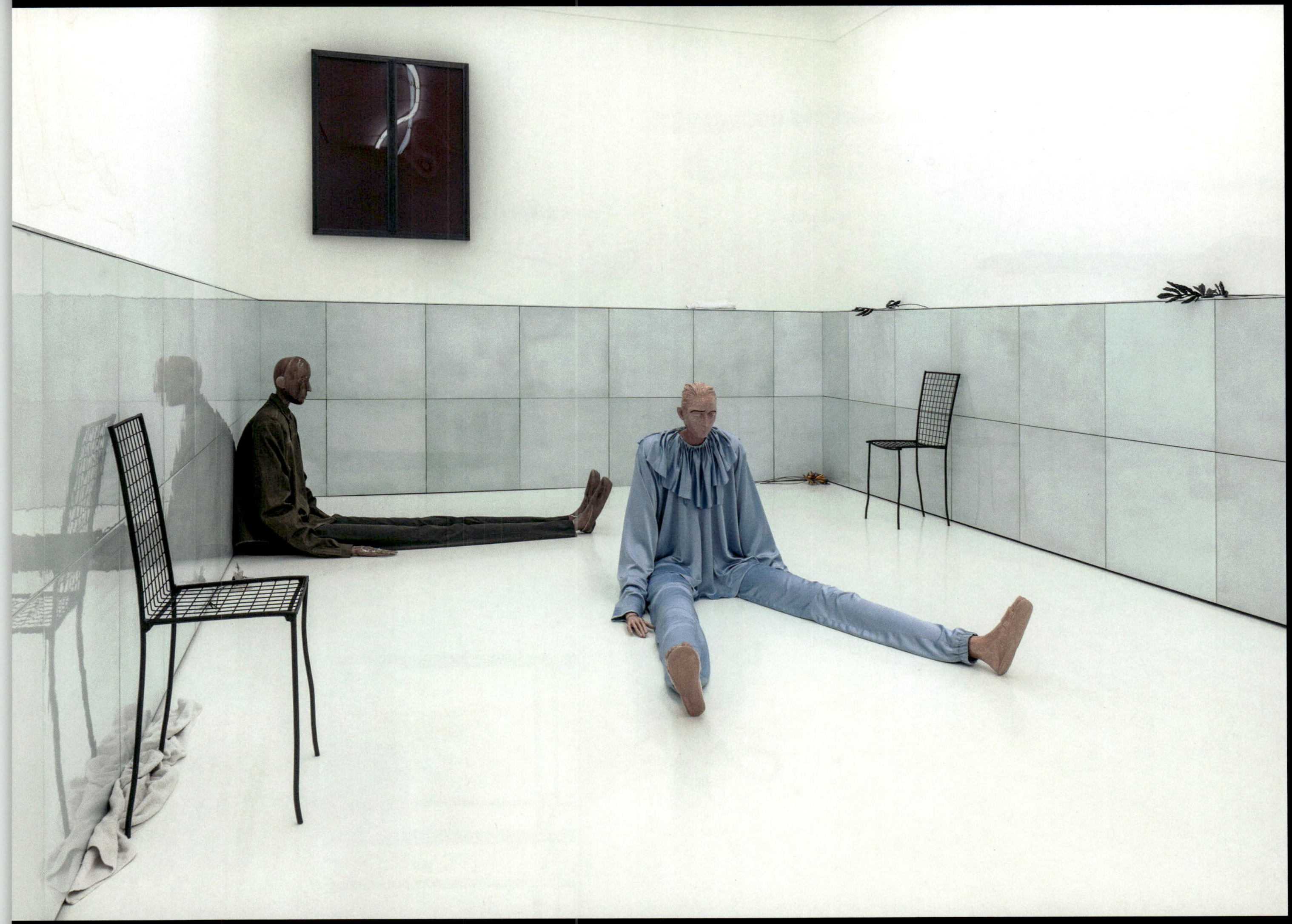

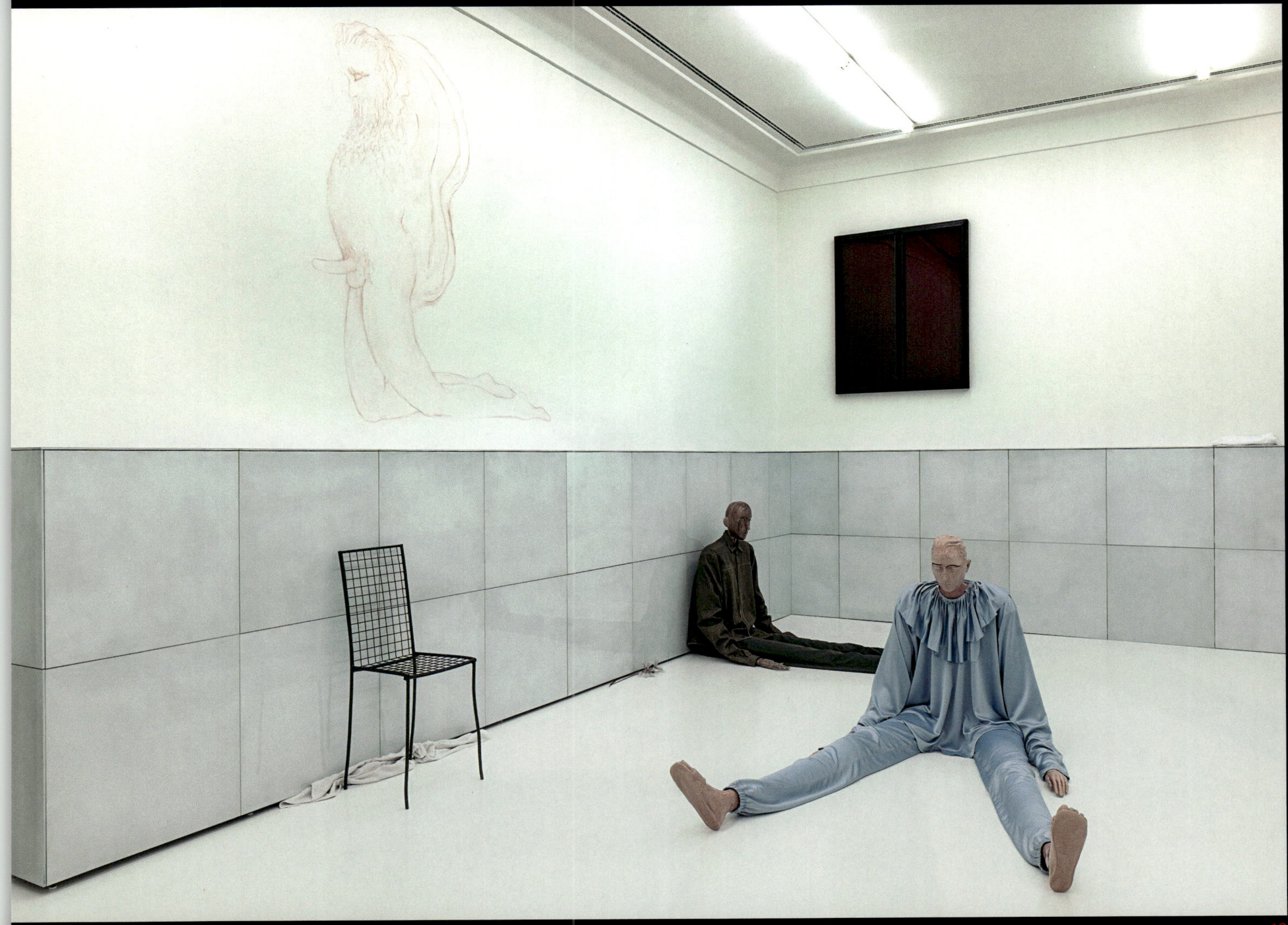

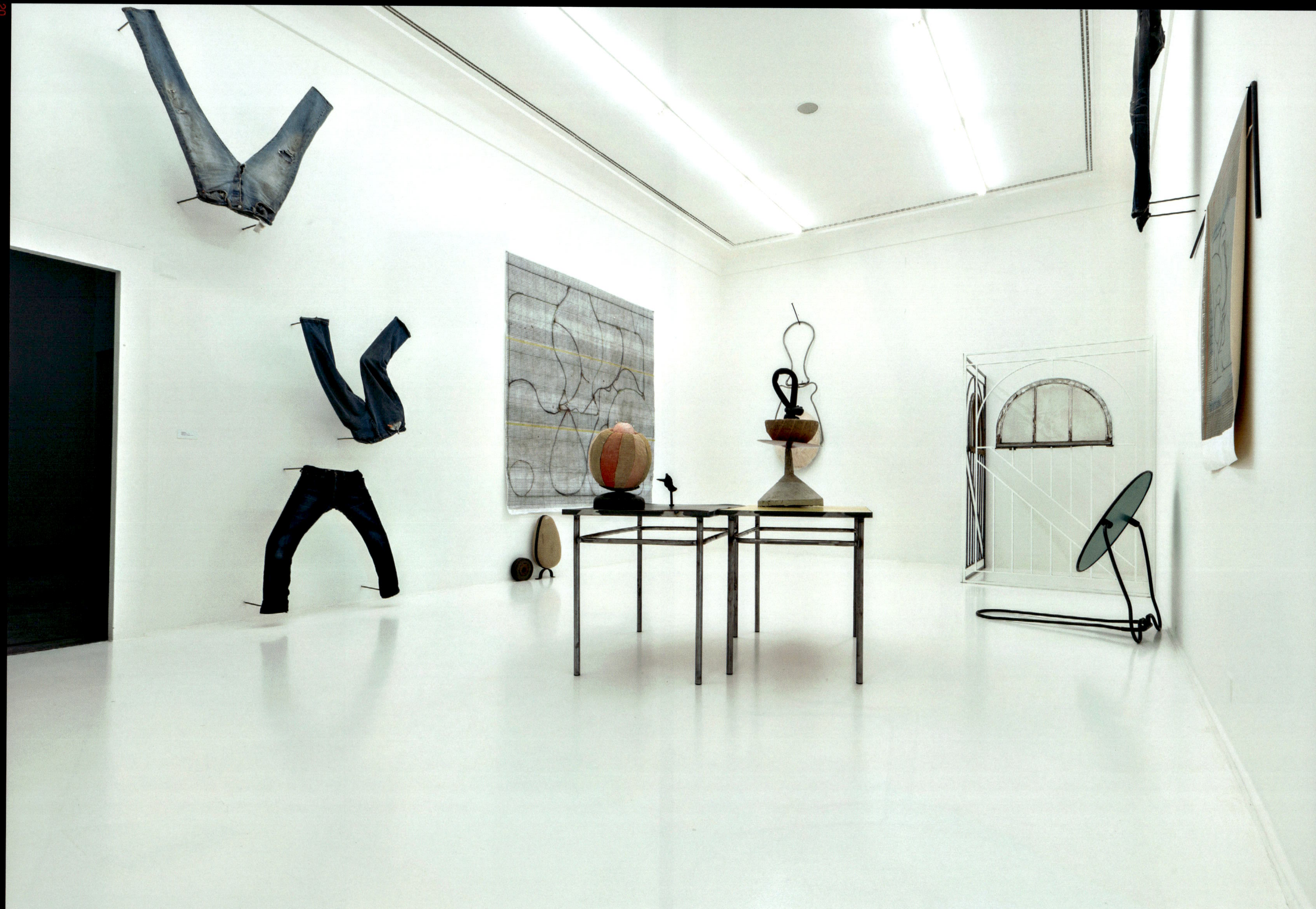

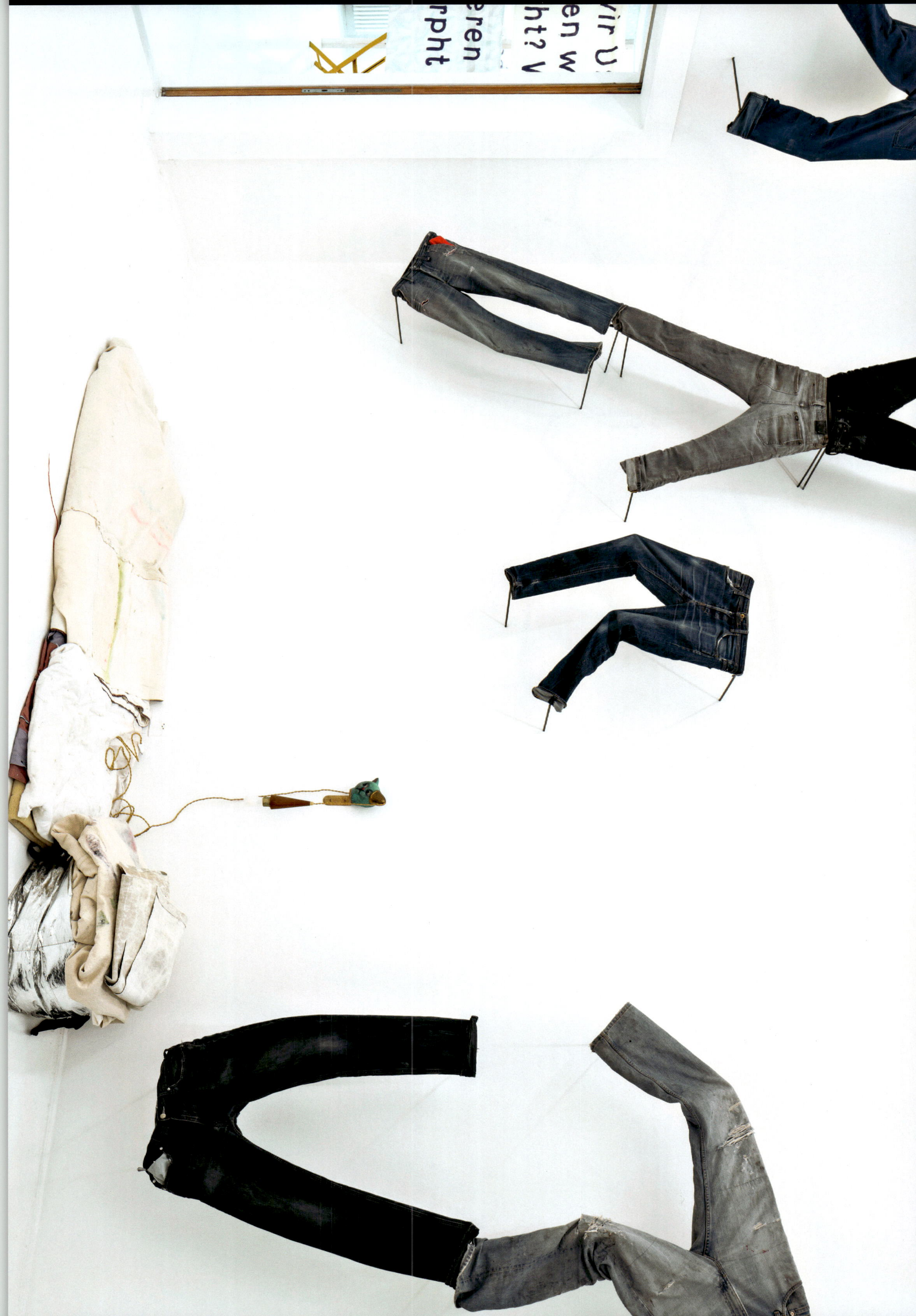

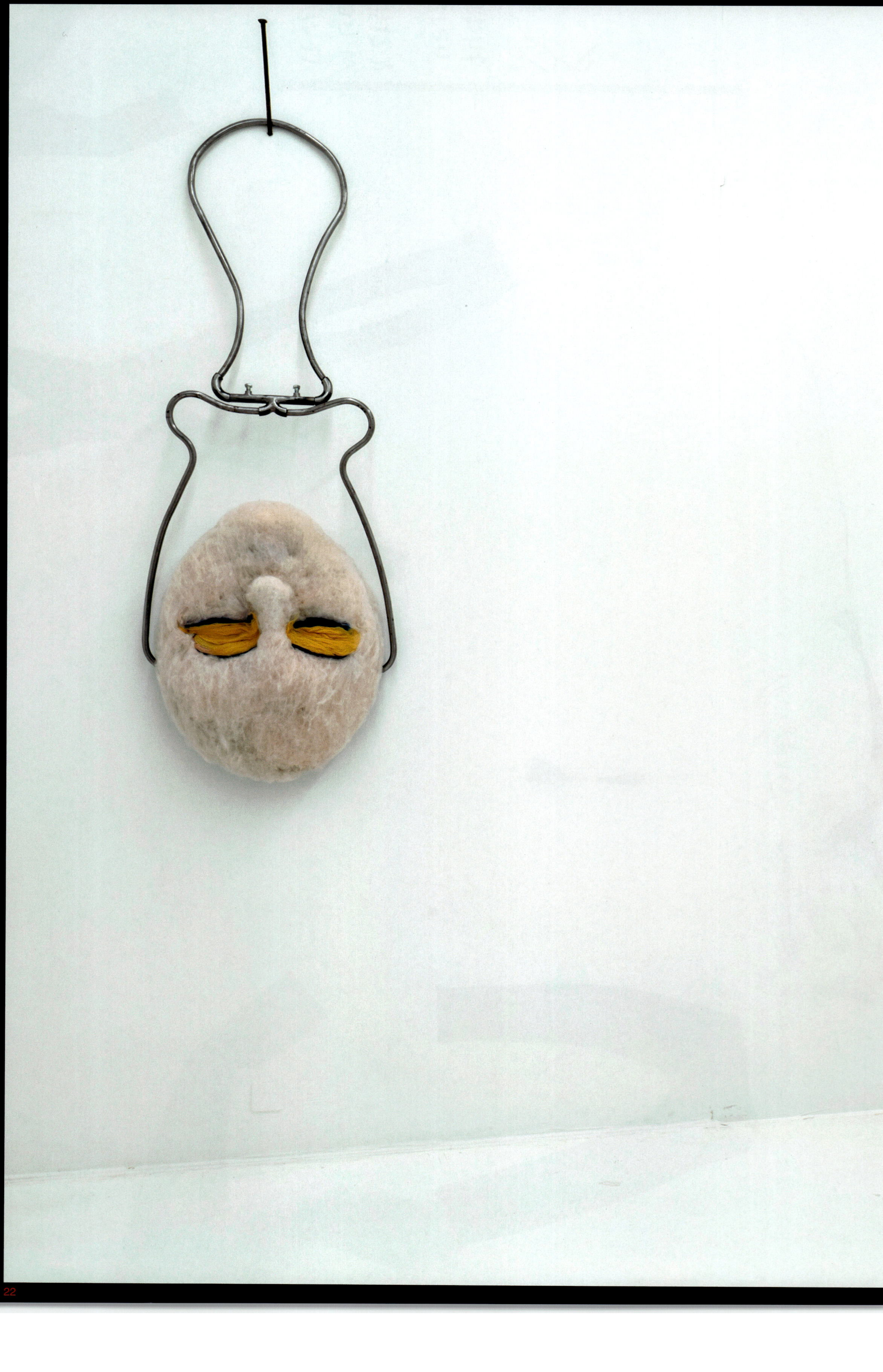

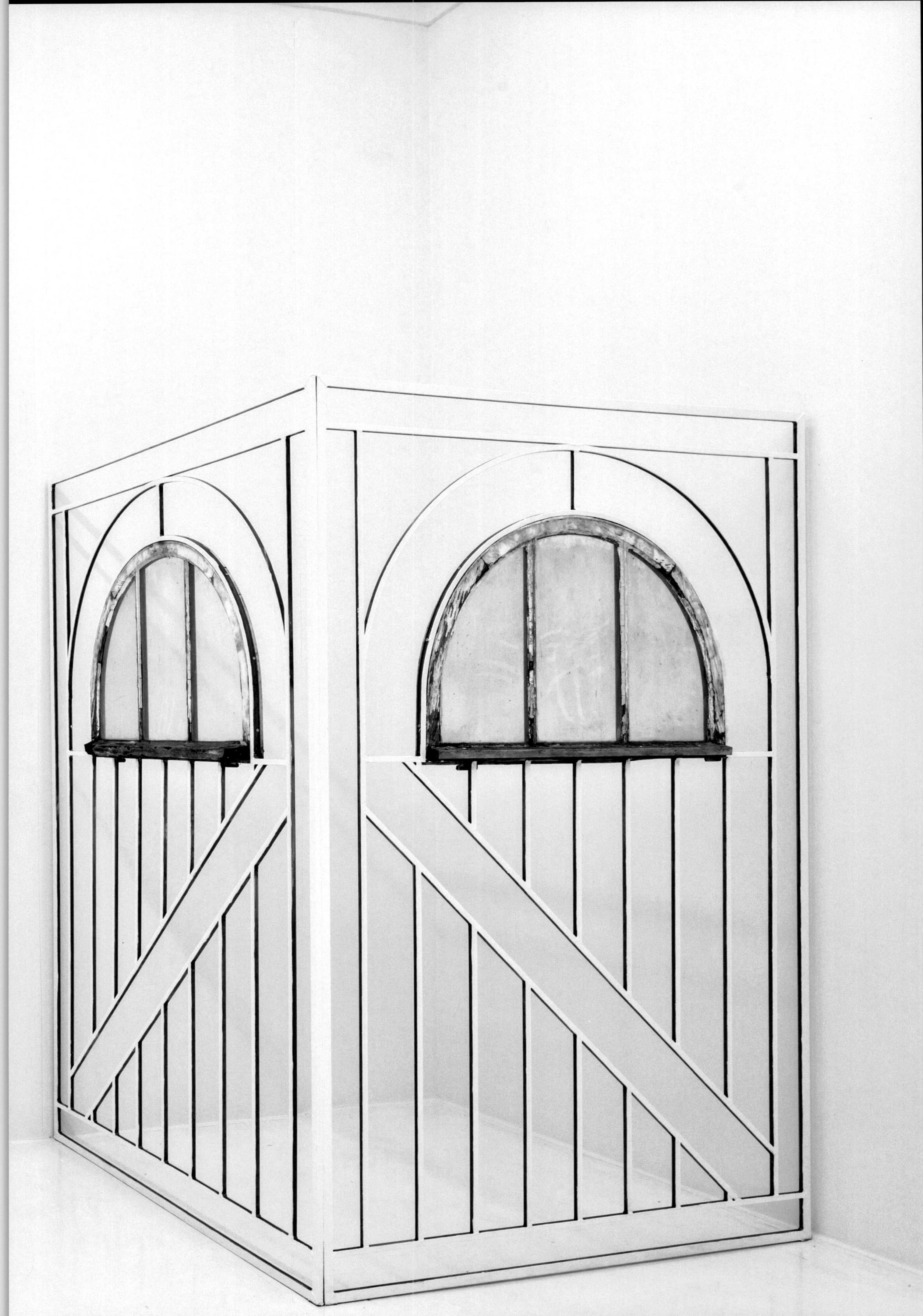

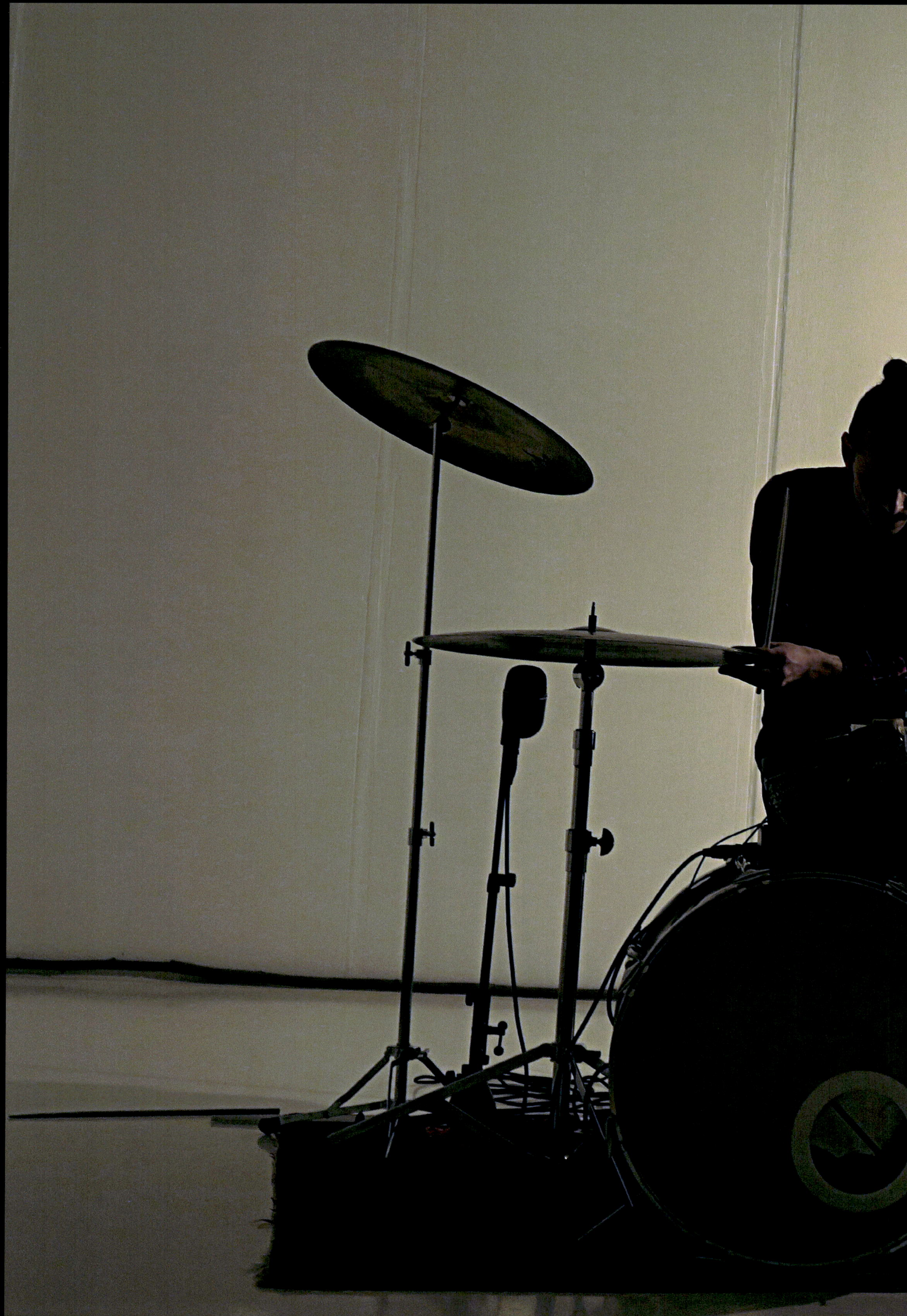

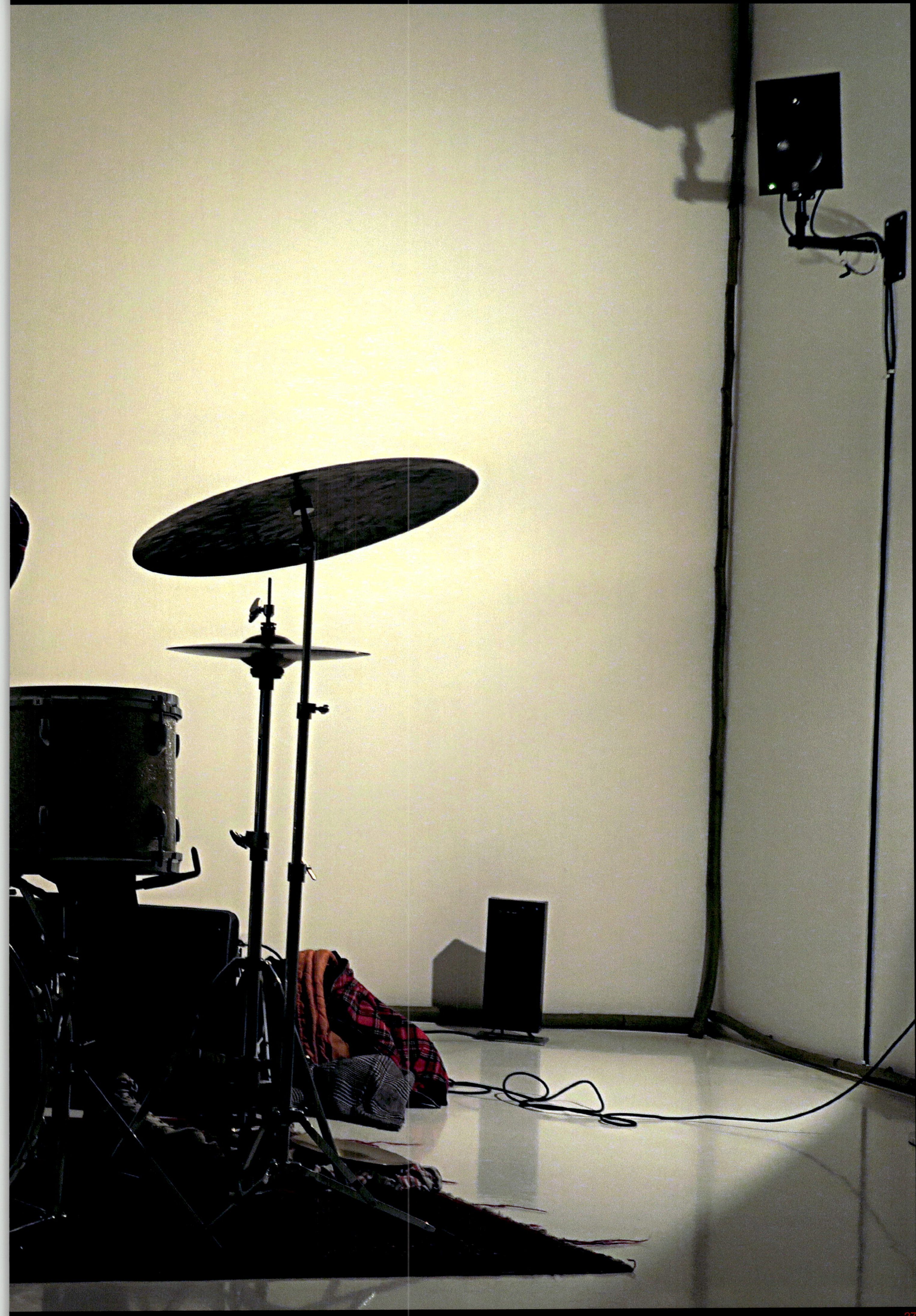

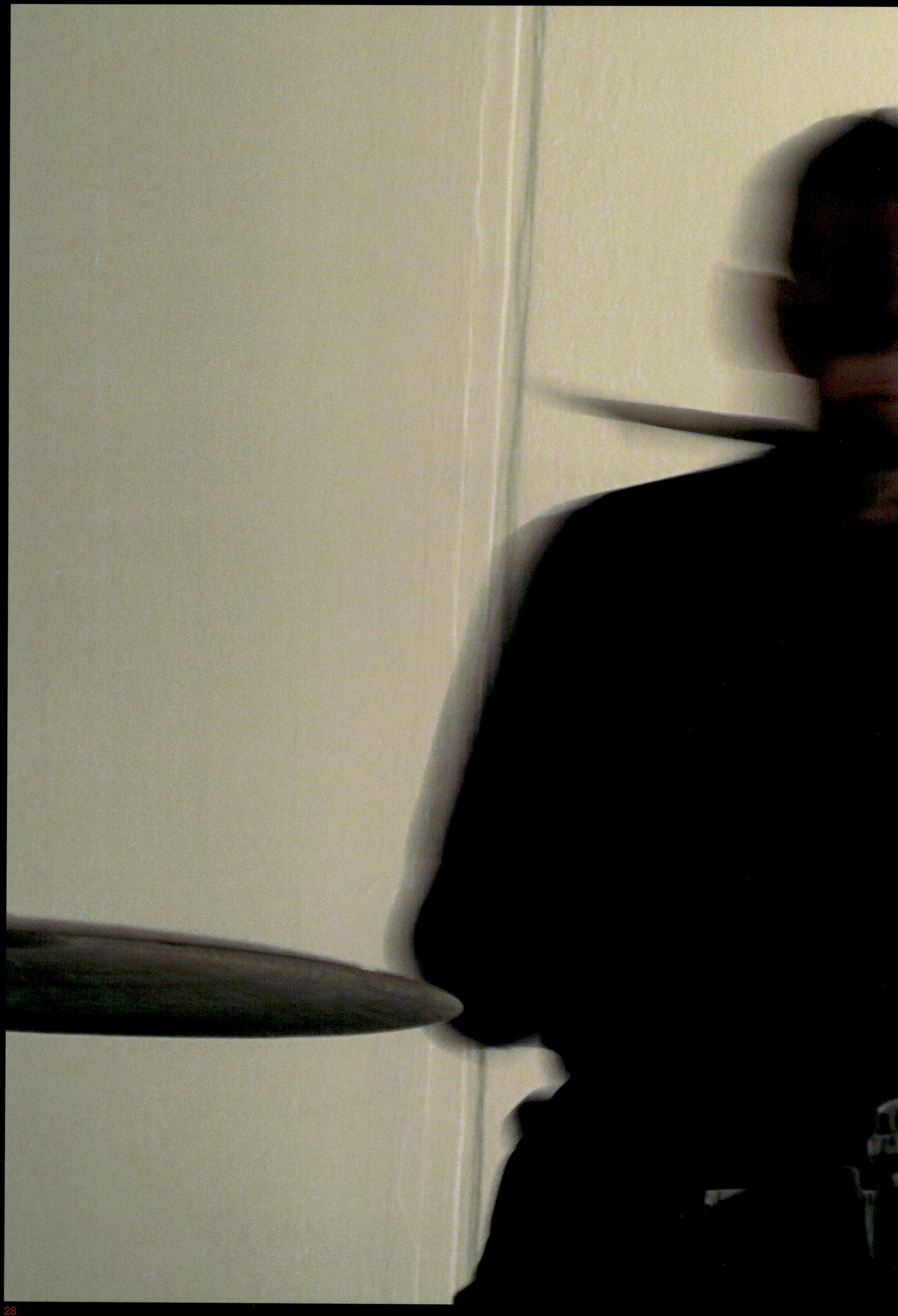

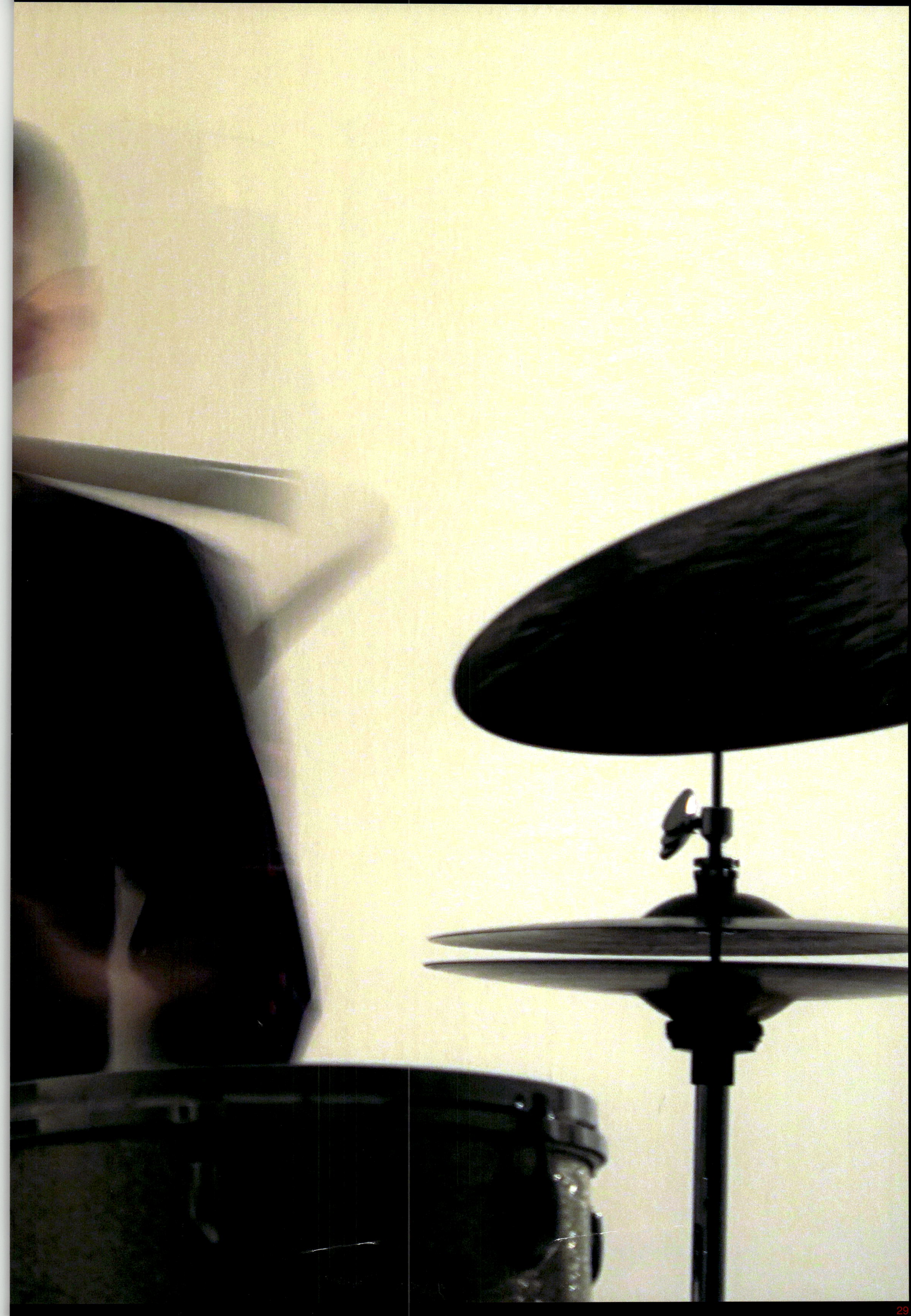

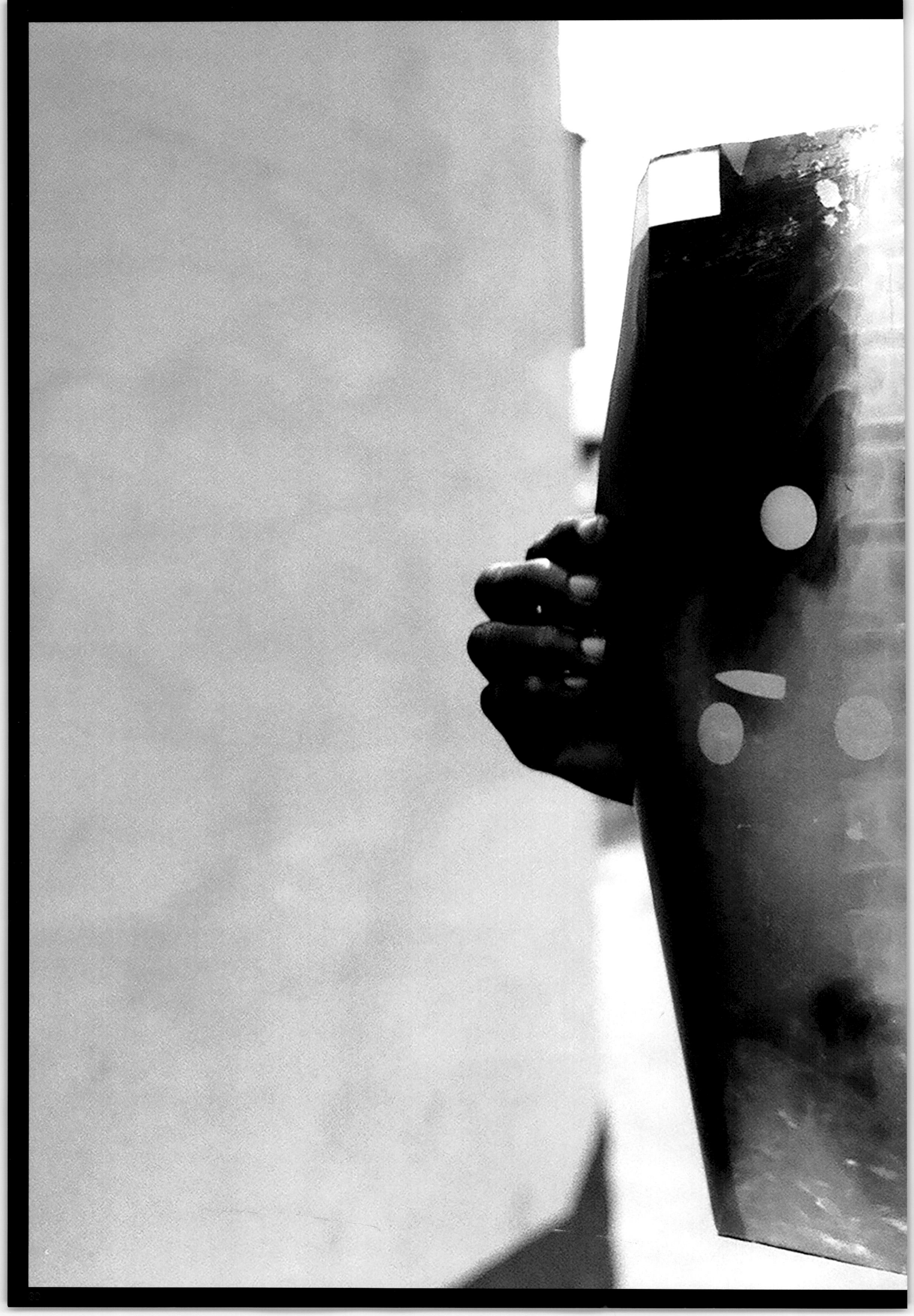

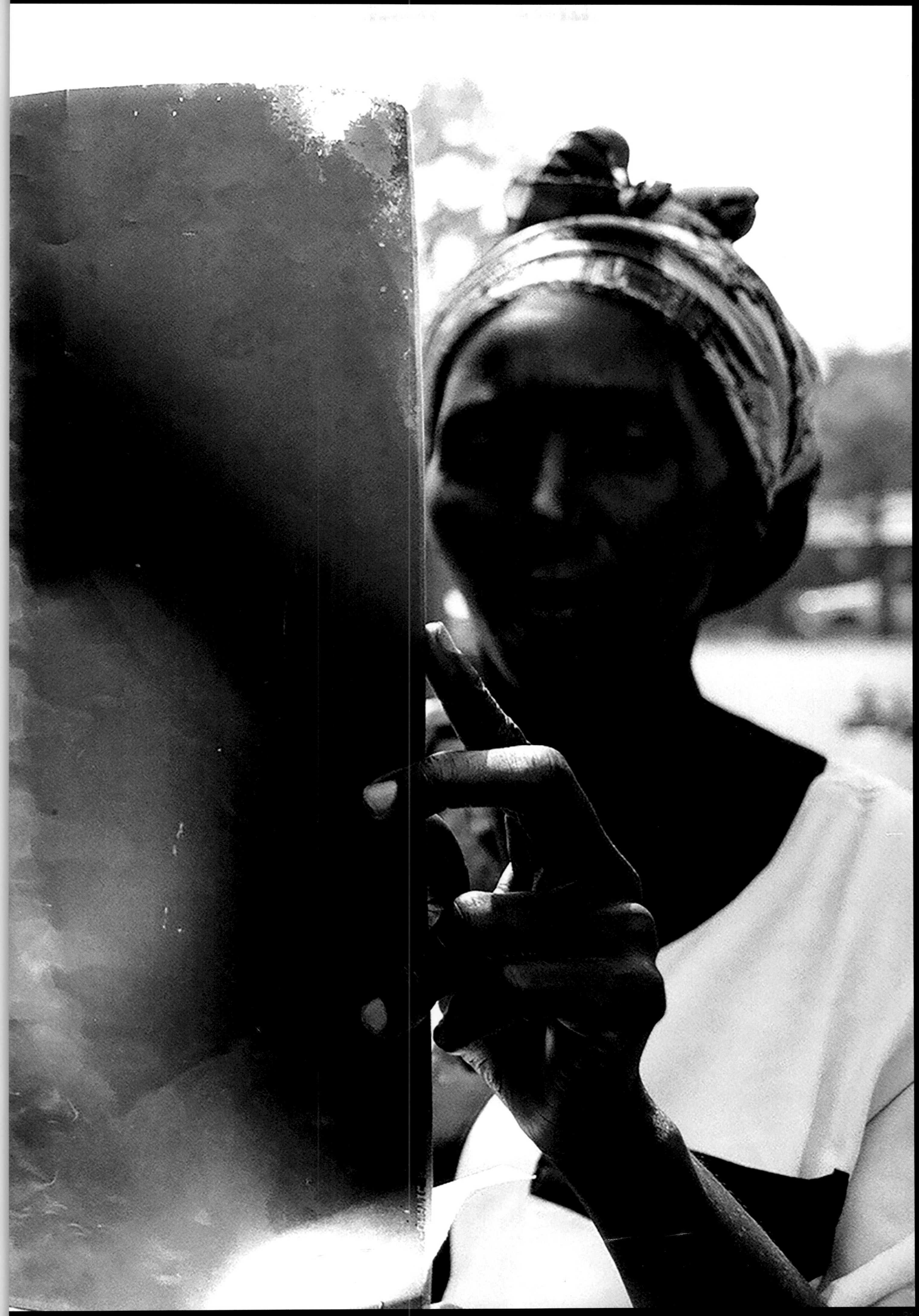

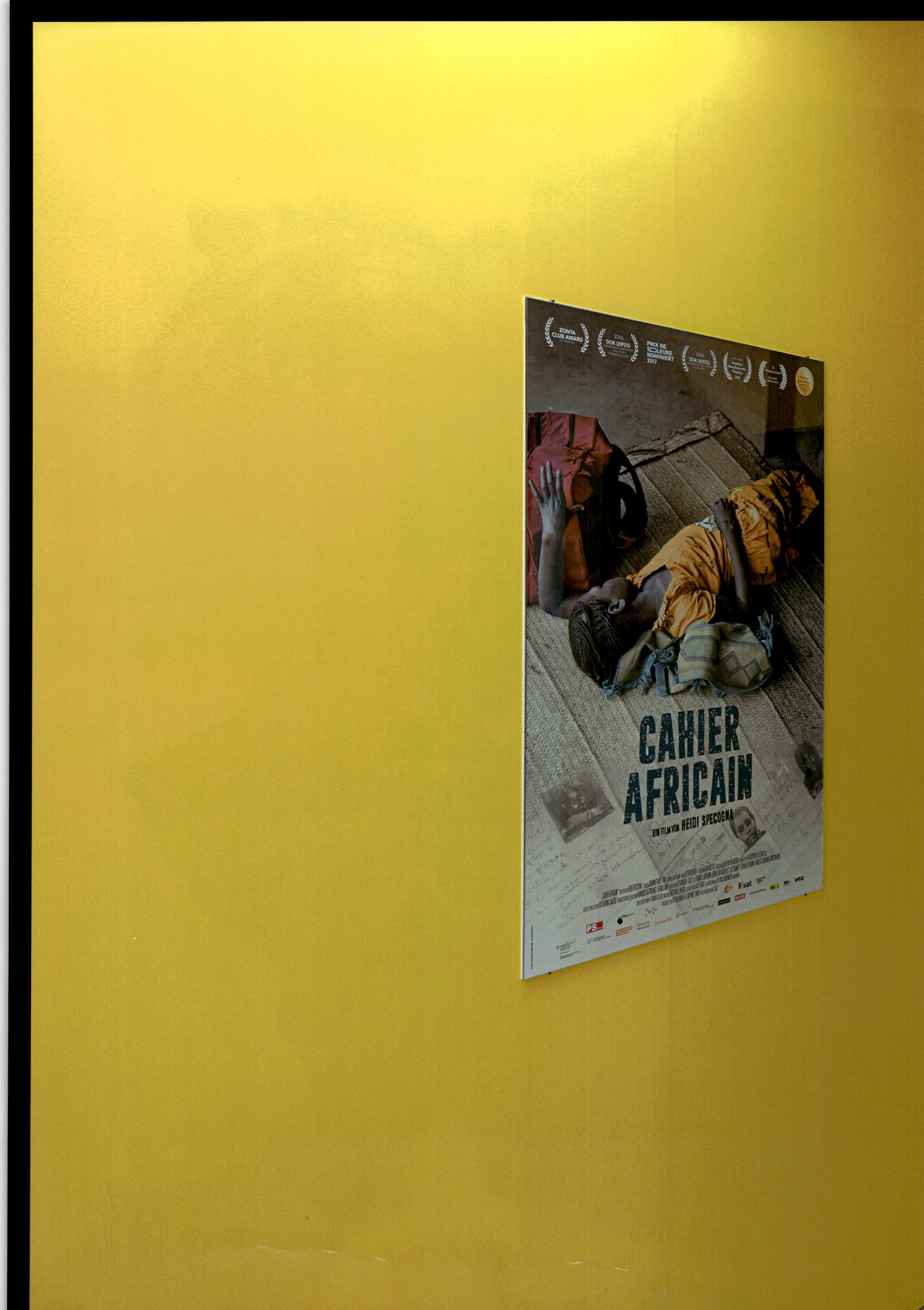
ZONTA CLUB AWARD
2016 DOK LEIPZIG
PRIX DE SOLEURE NOMINIERT 2017
CAHIER AFRICAIN
EIN FILM VON HEIDI SPECOGNA

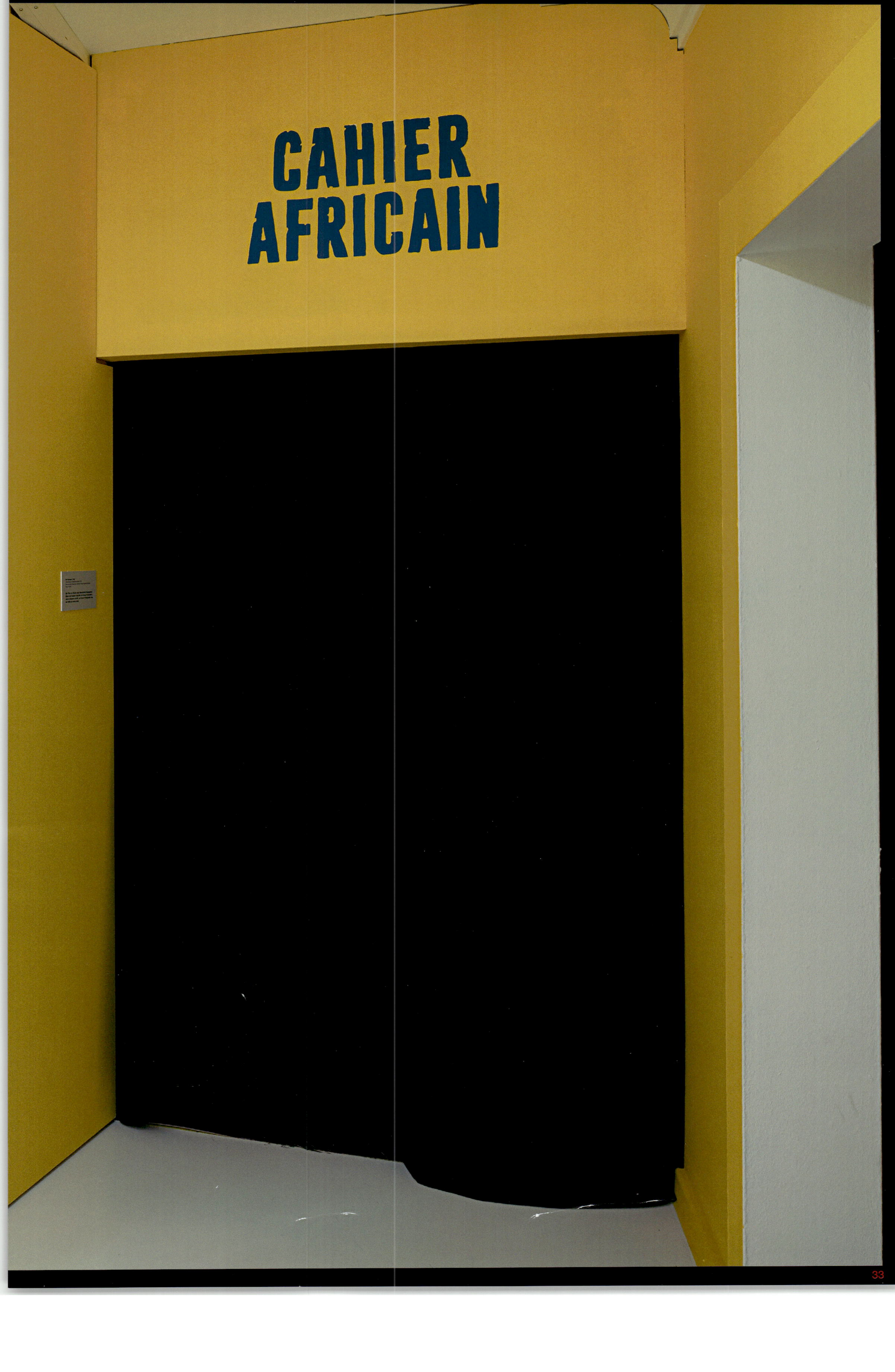
CAHIER
AFRICAIN

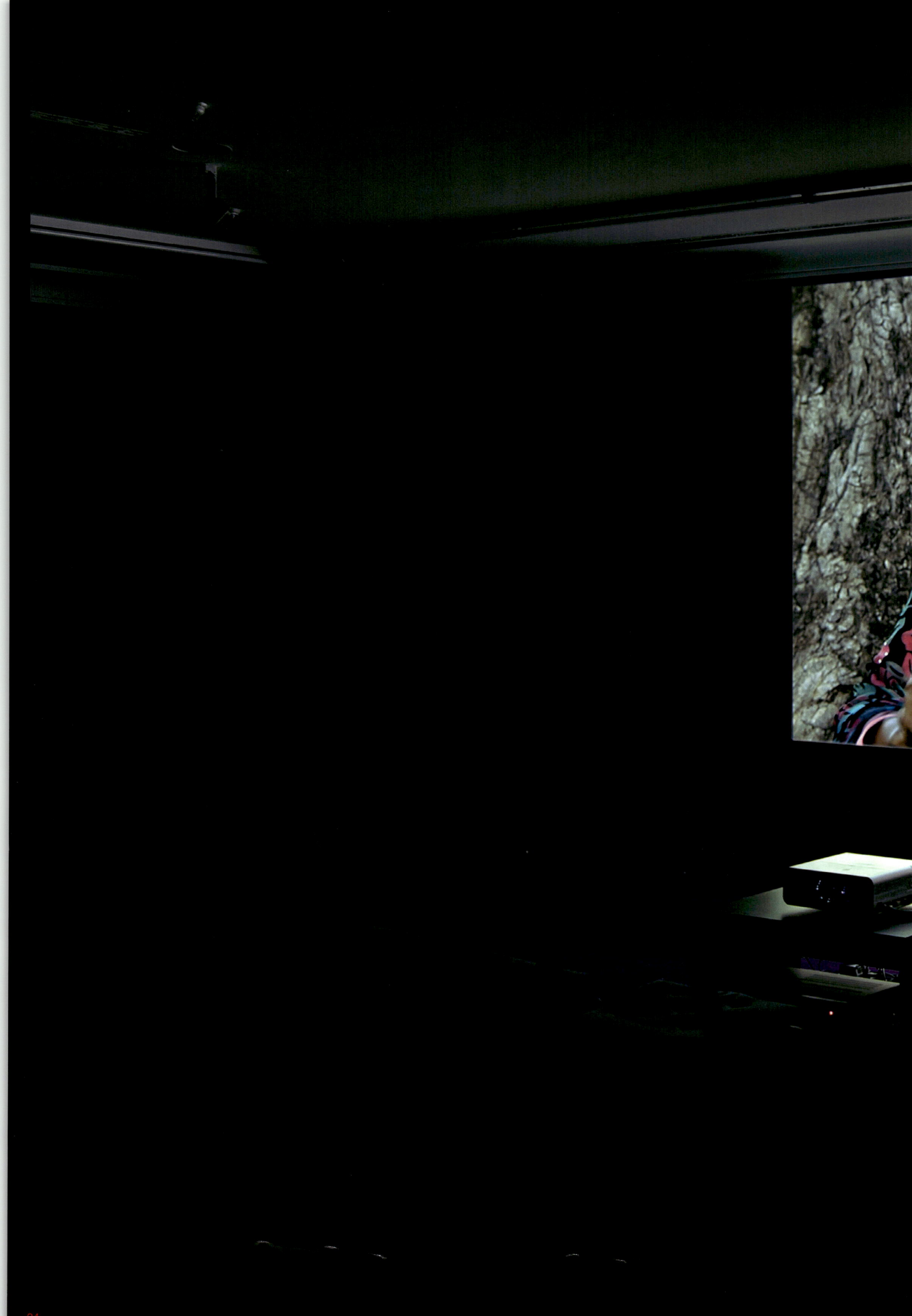

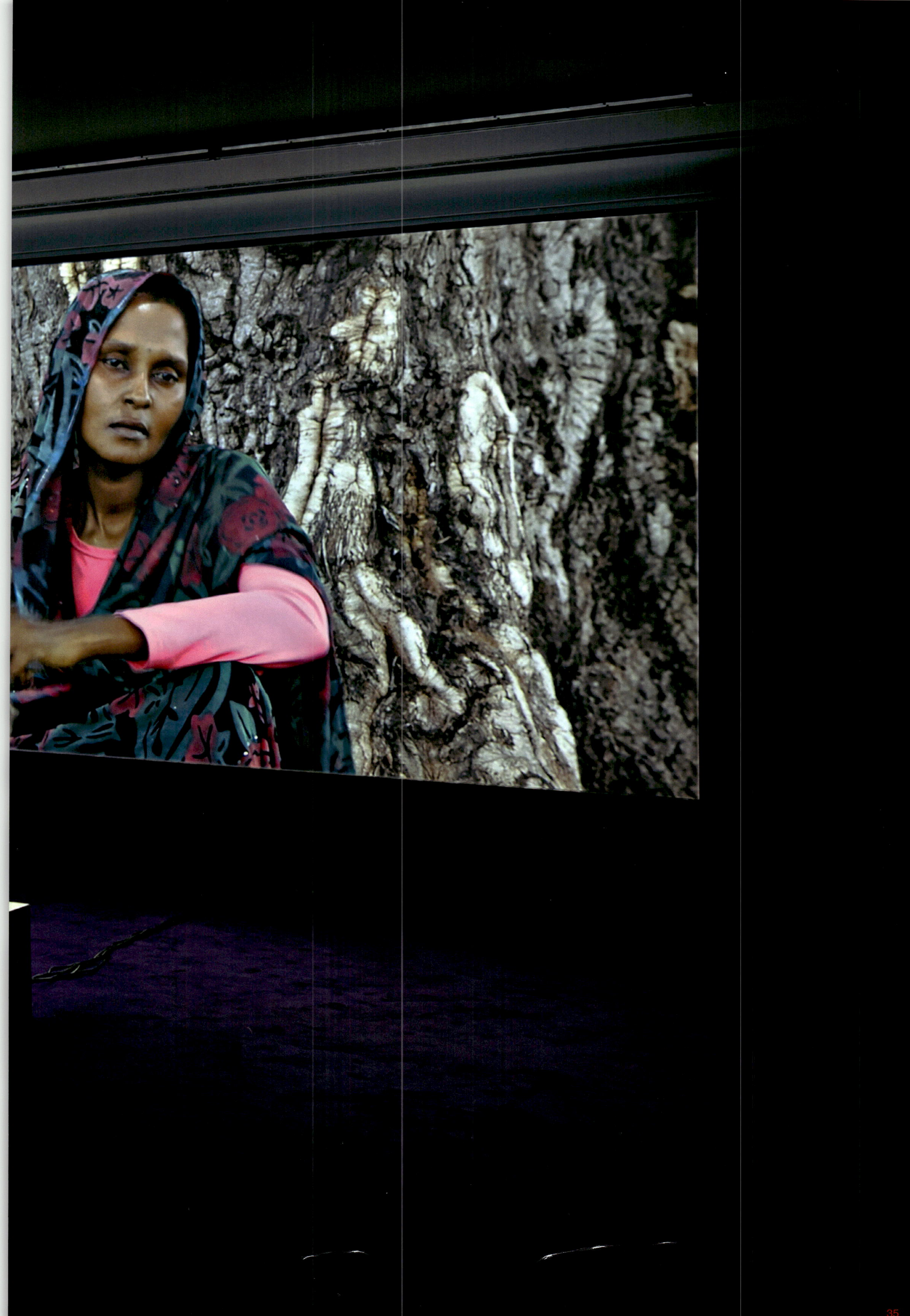

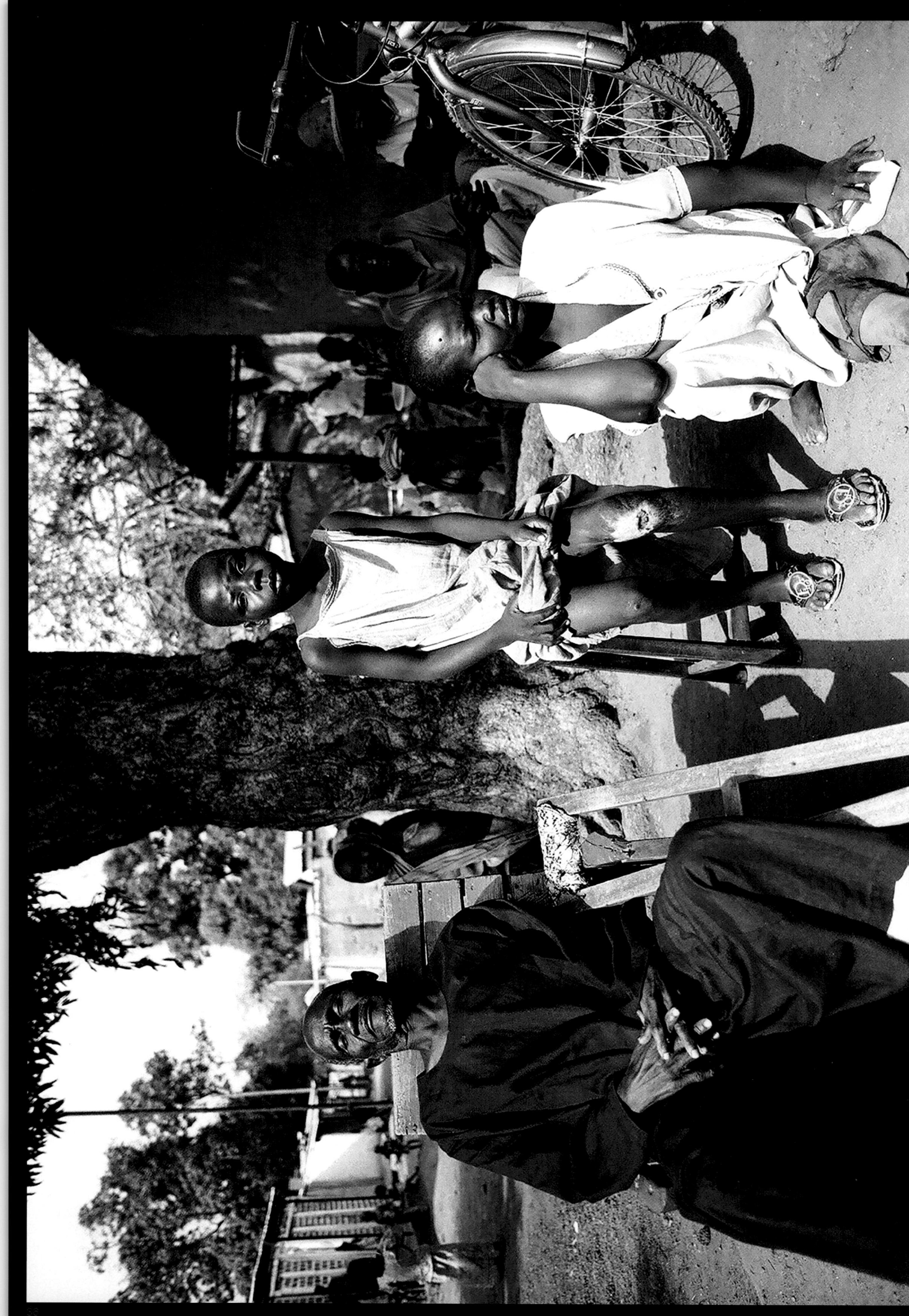

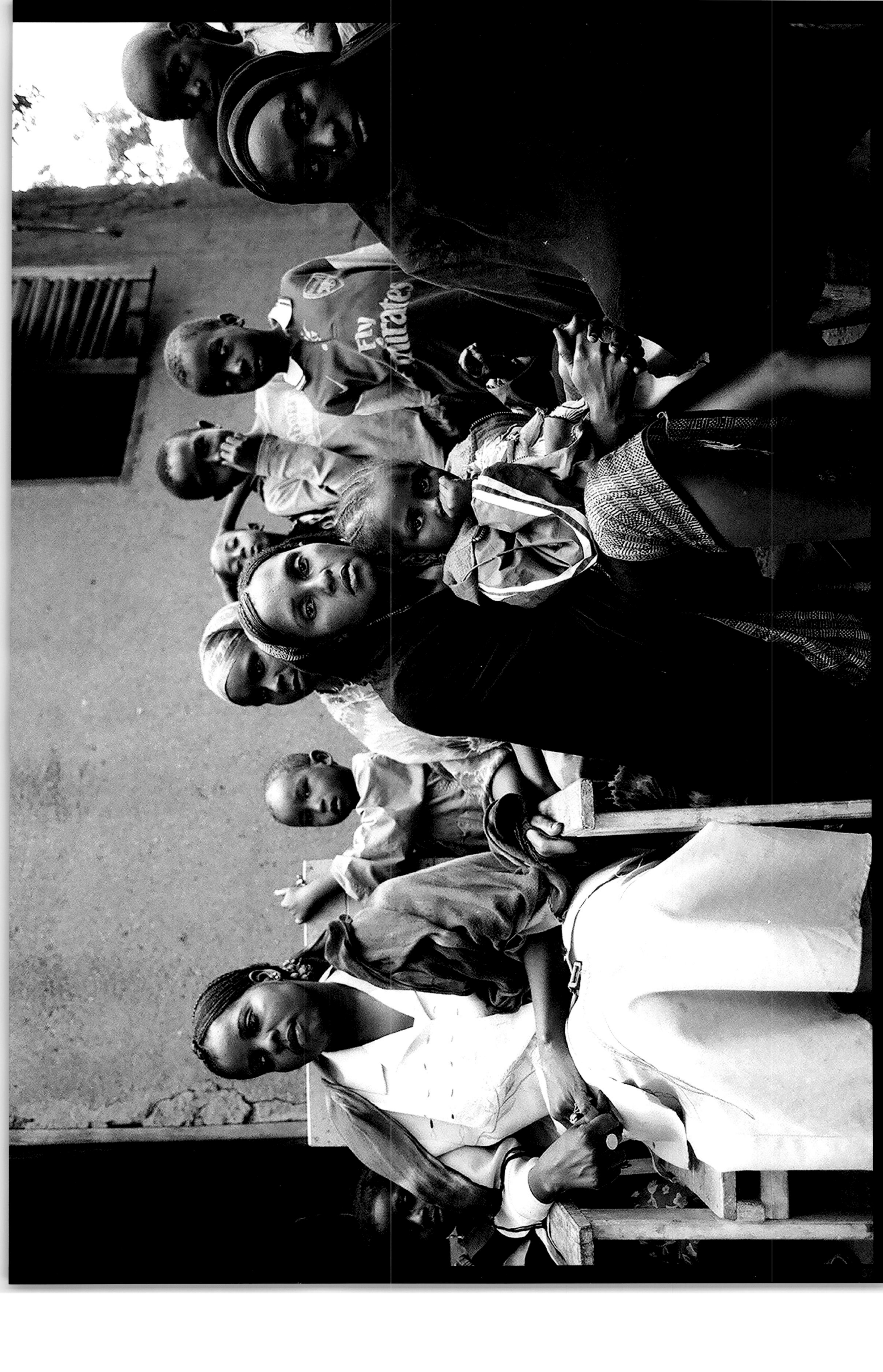

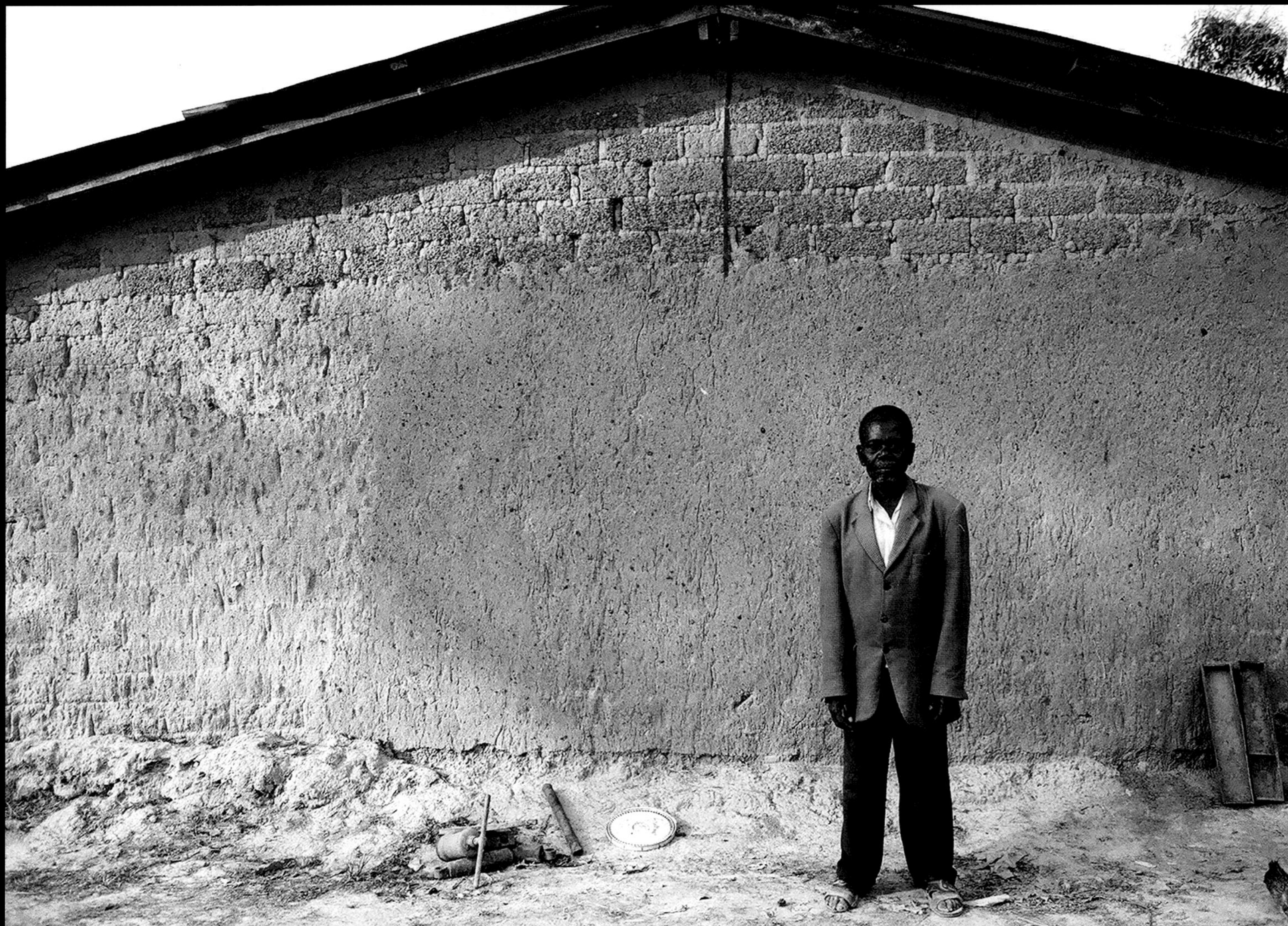

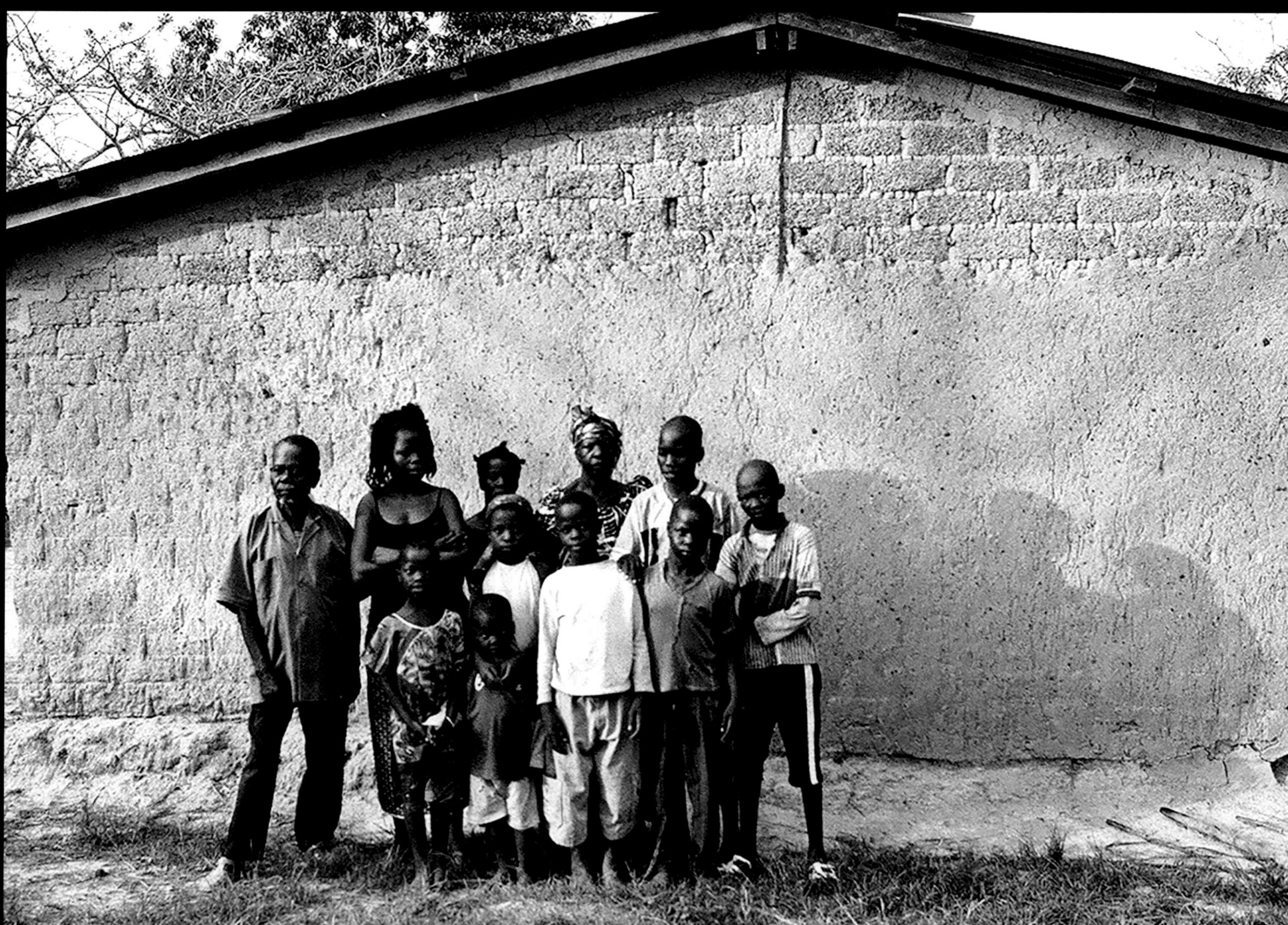

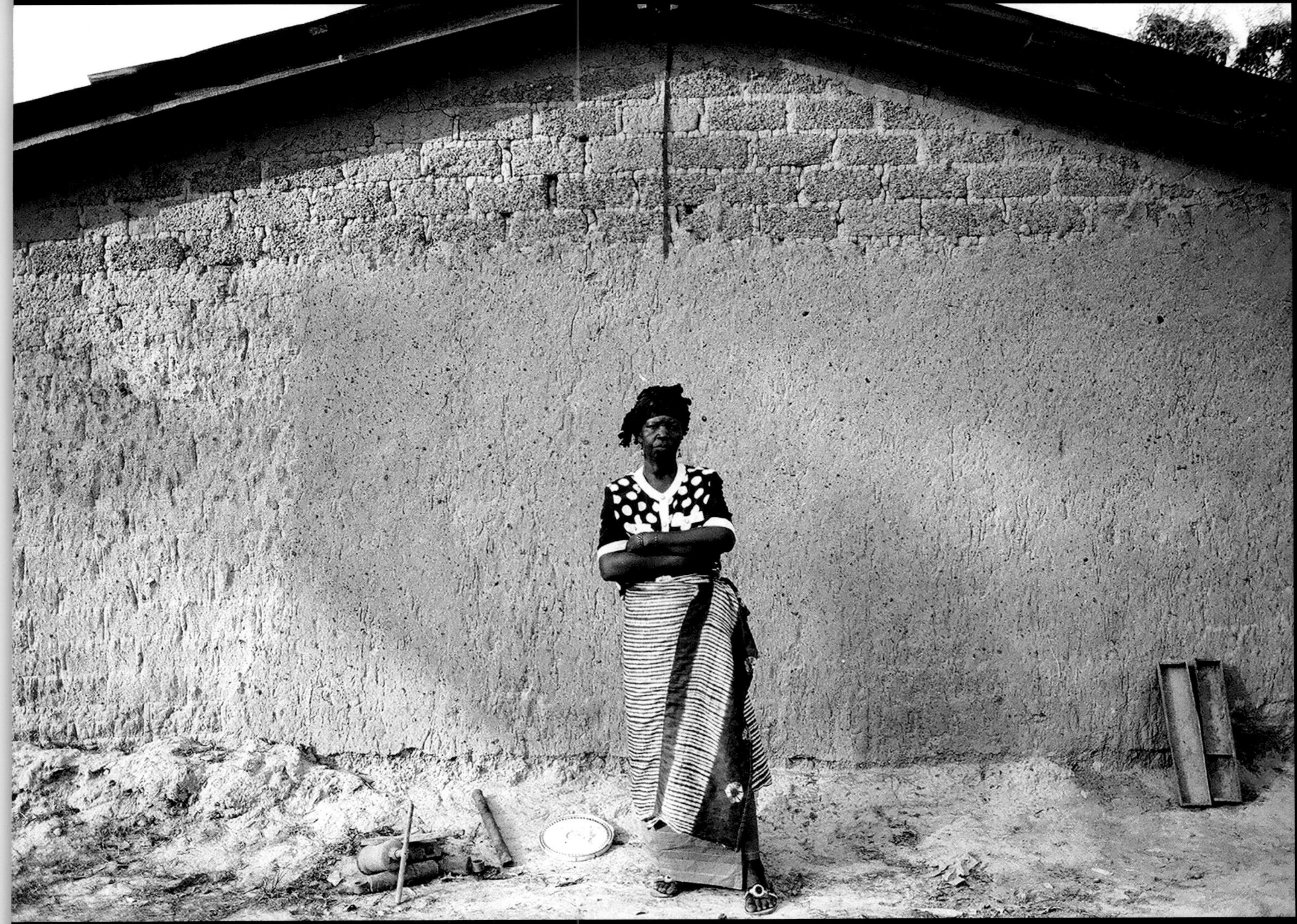

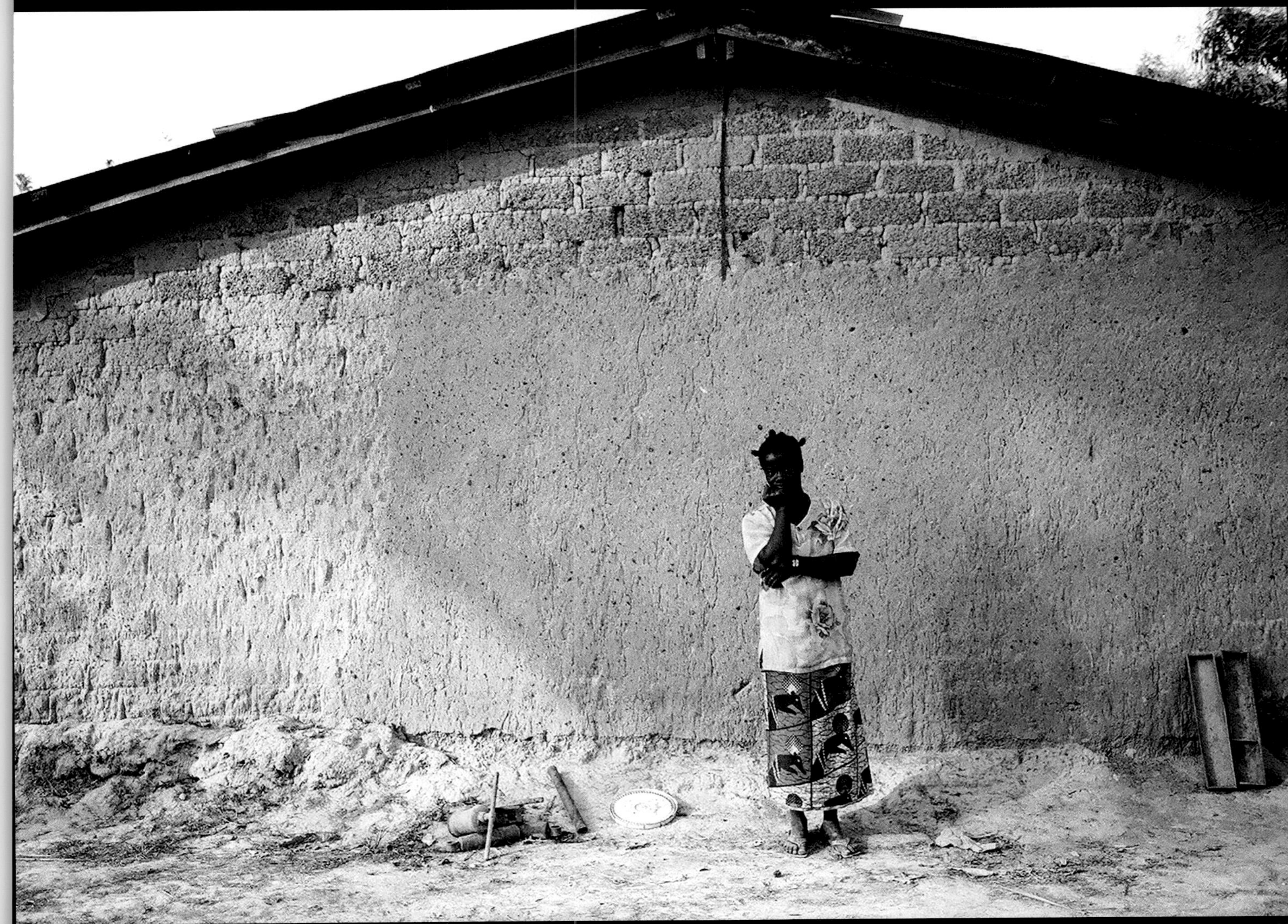

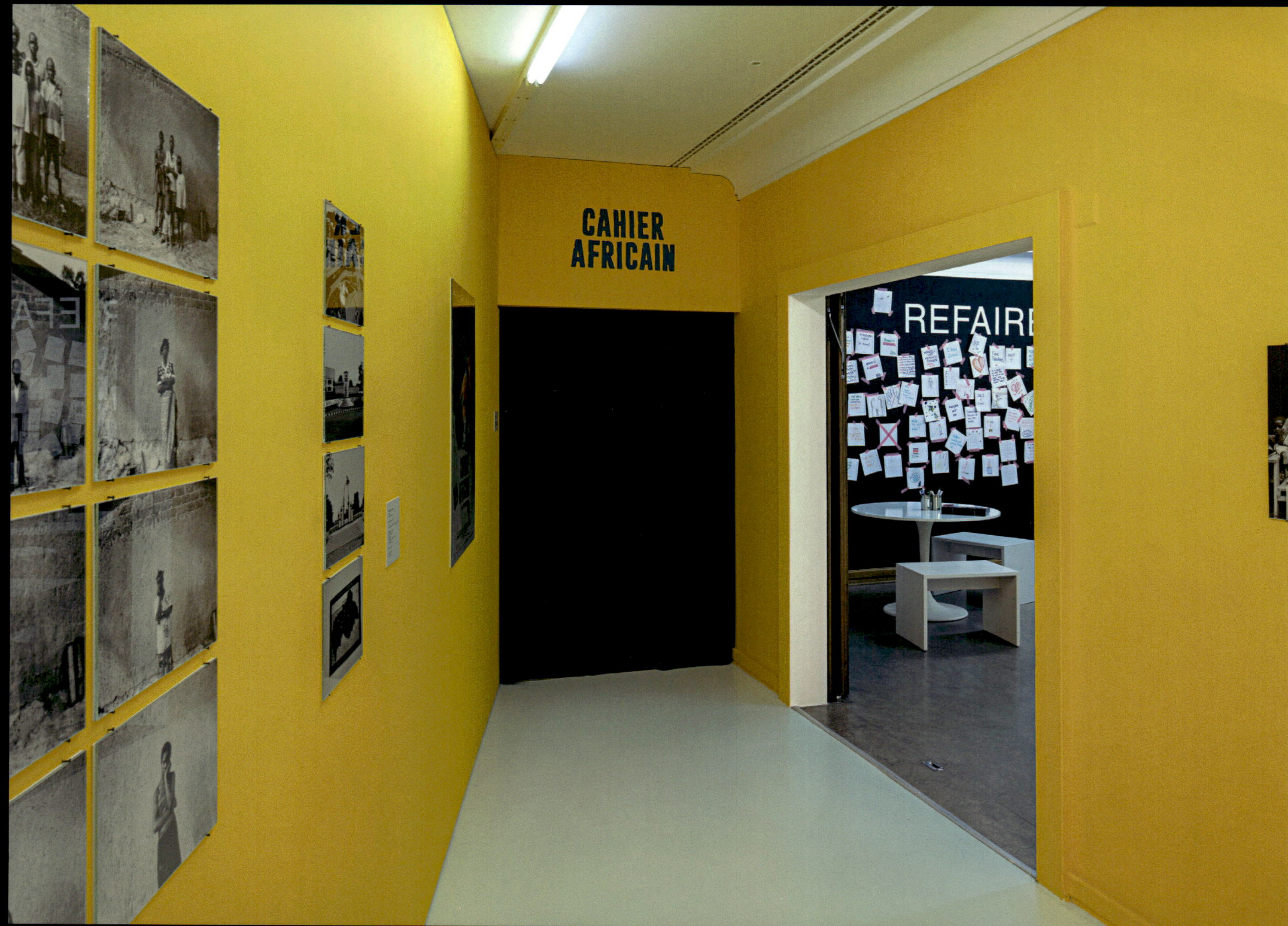
CAHIER
AFRICAIN
REFAIRE

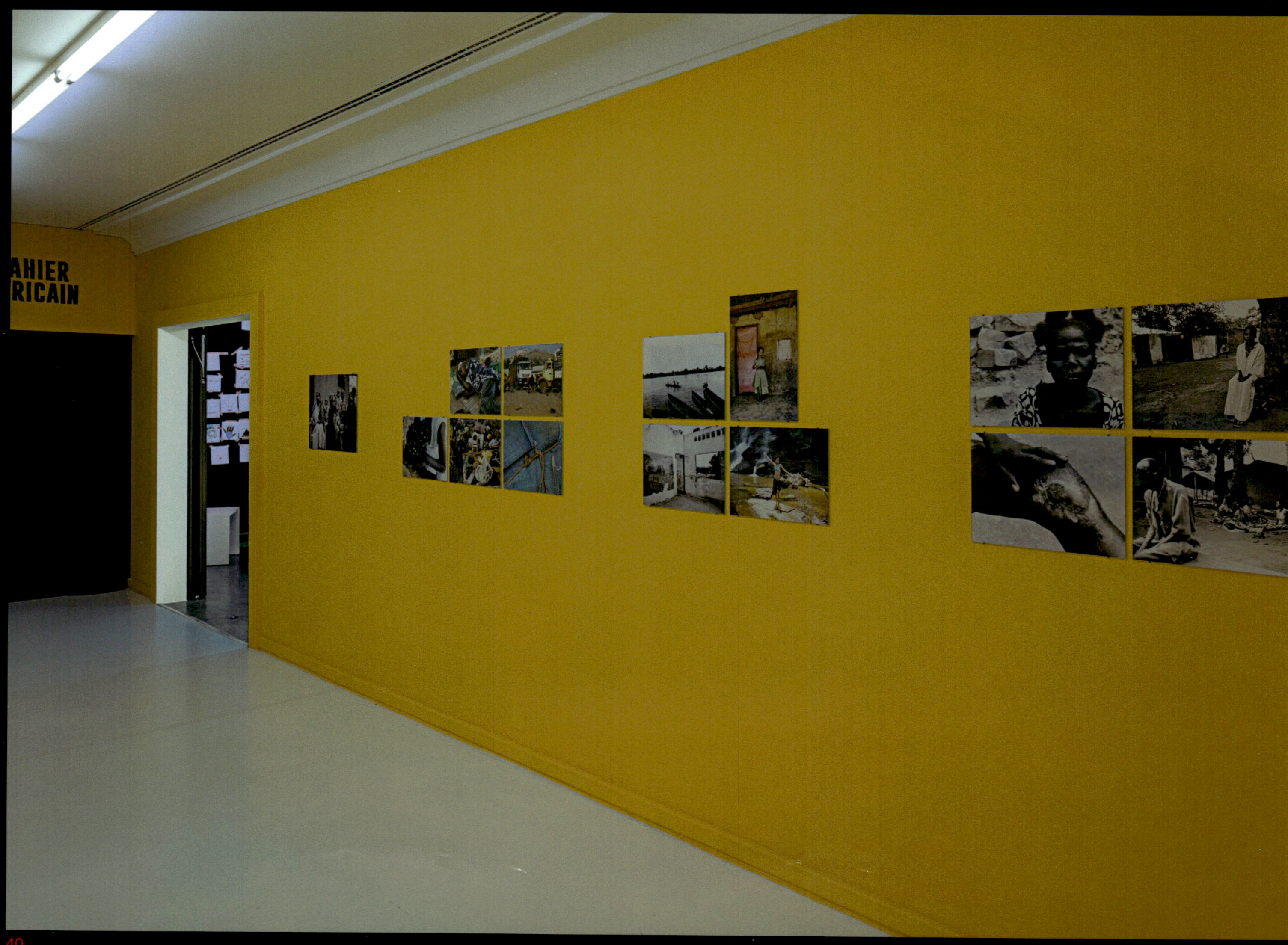
AHIER
RICAIN

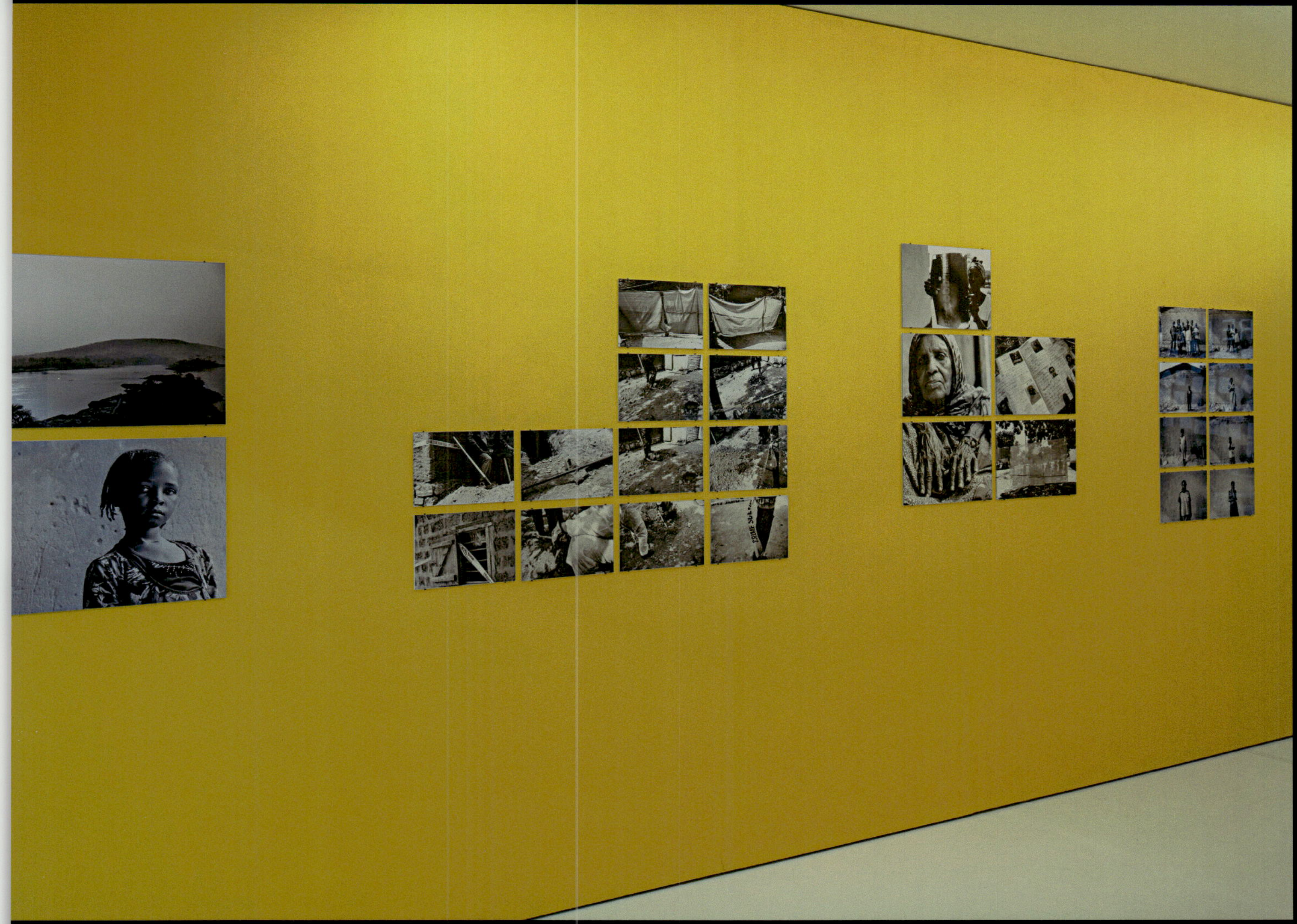

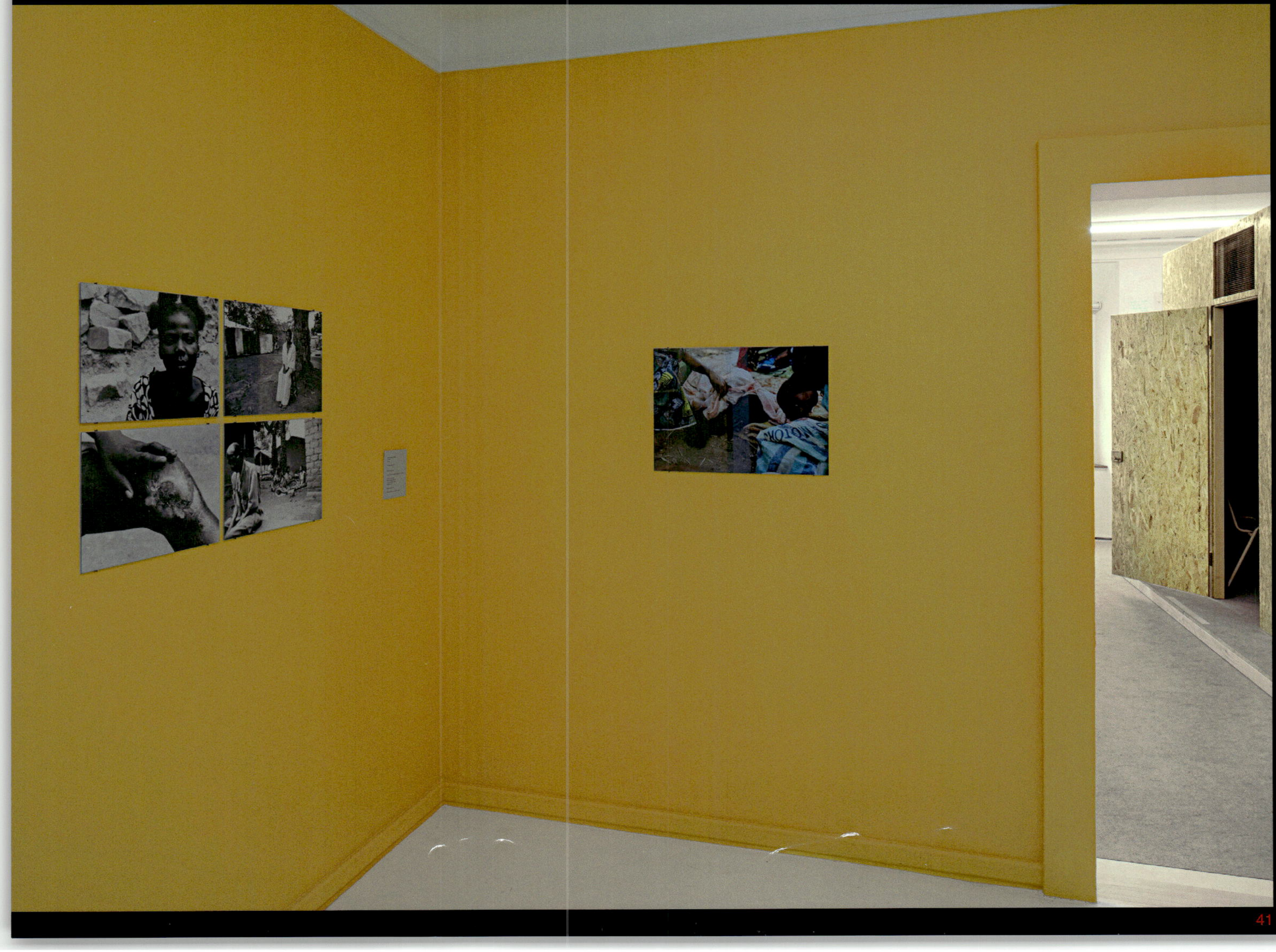

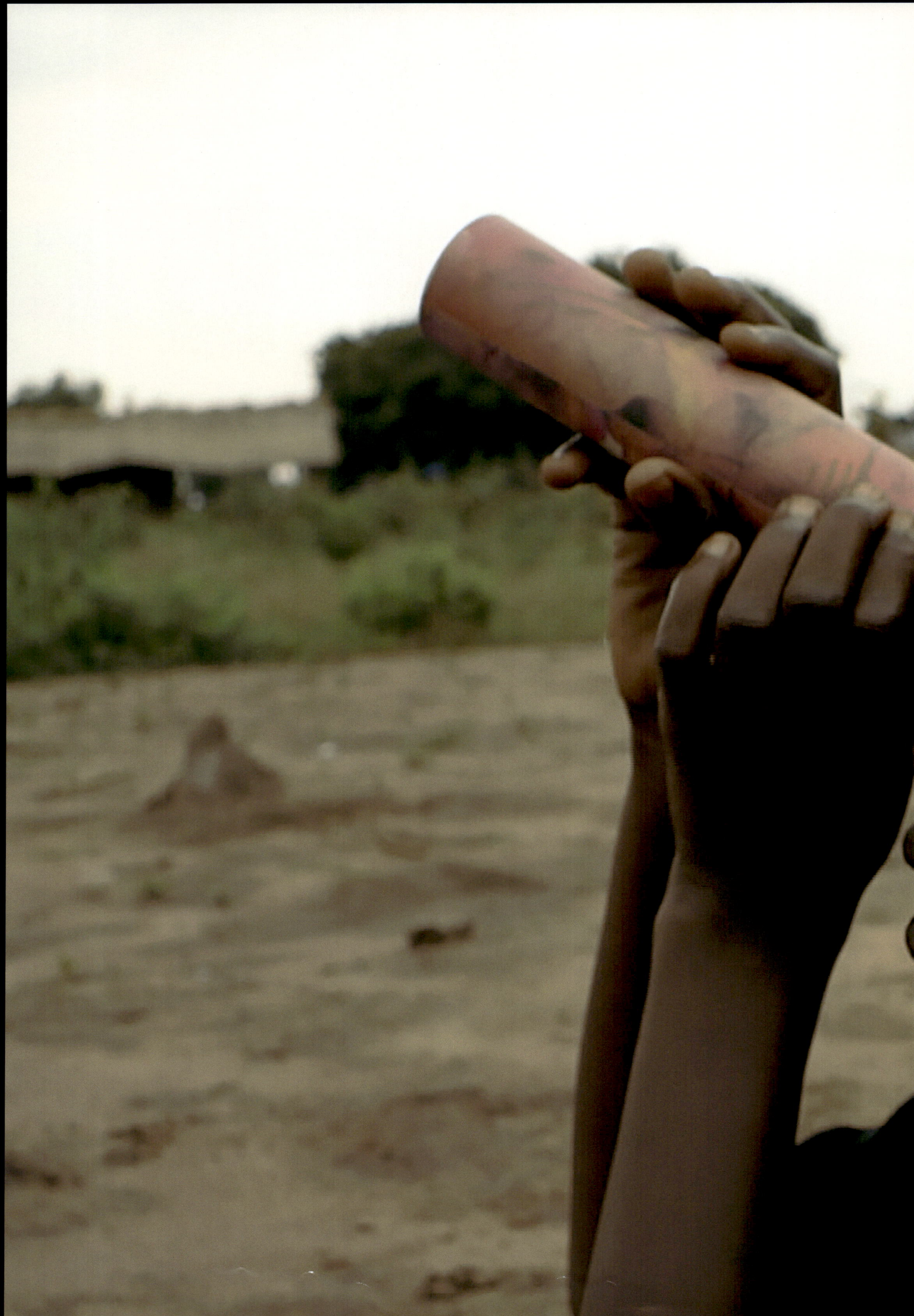

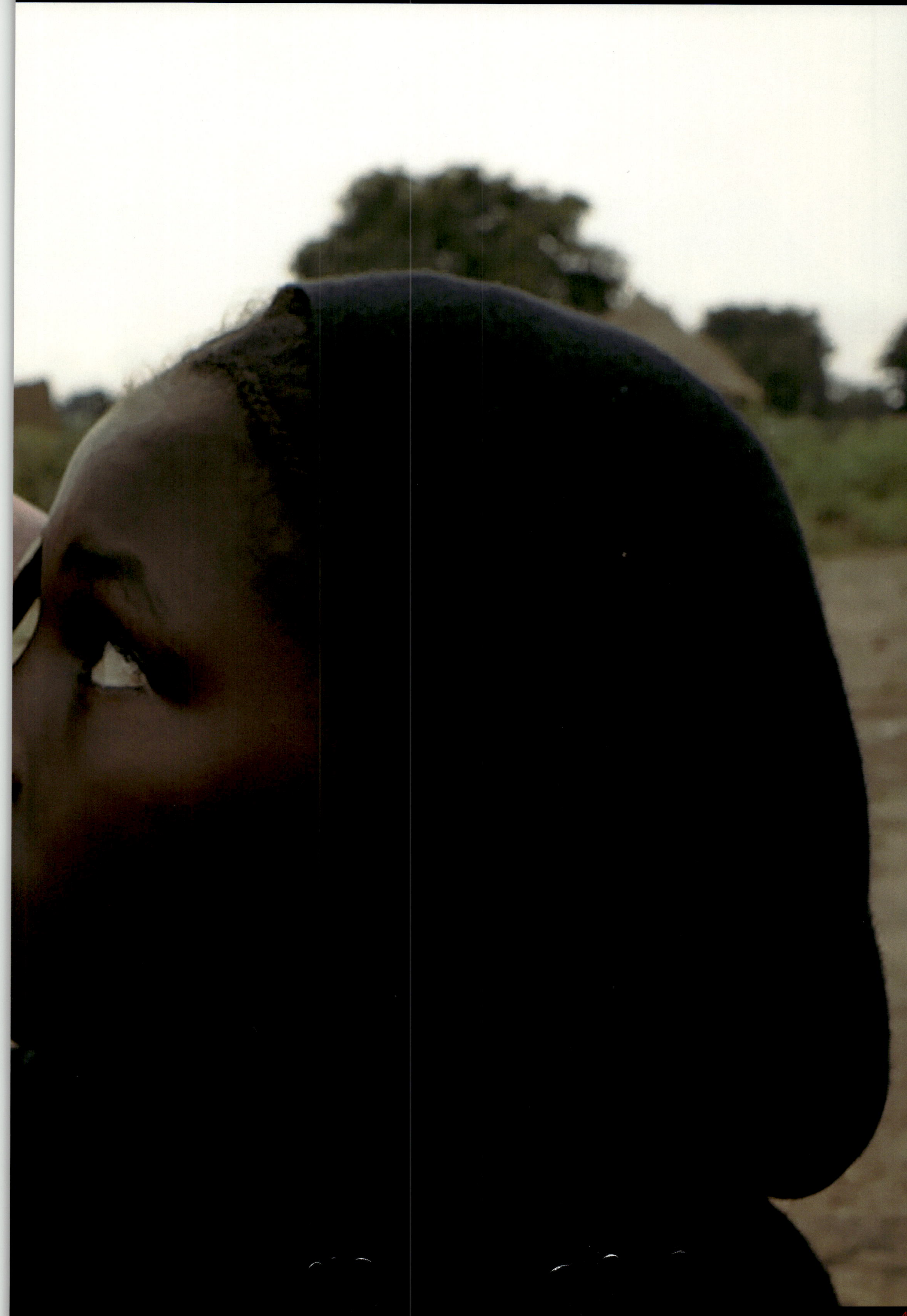

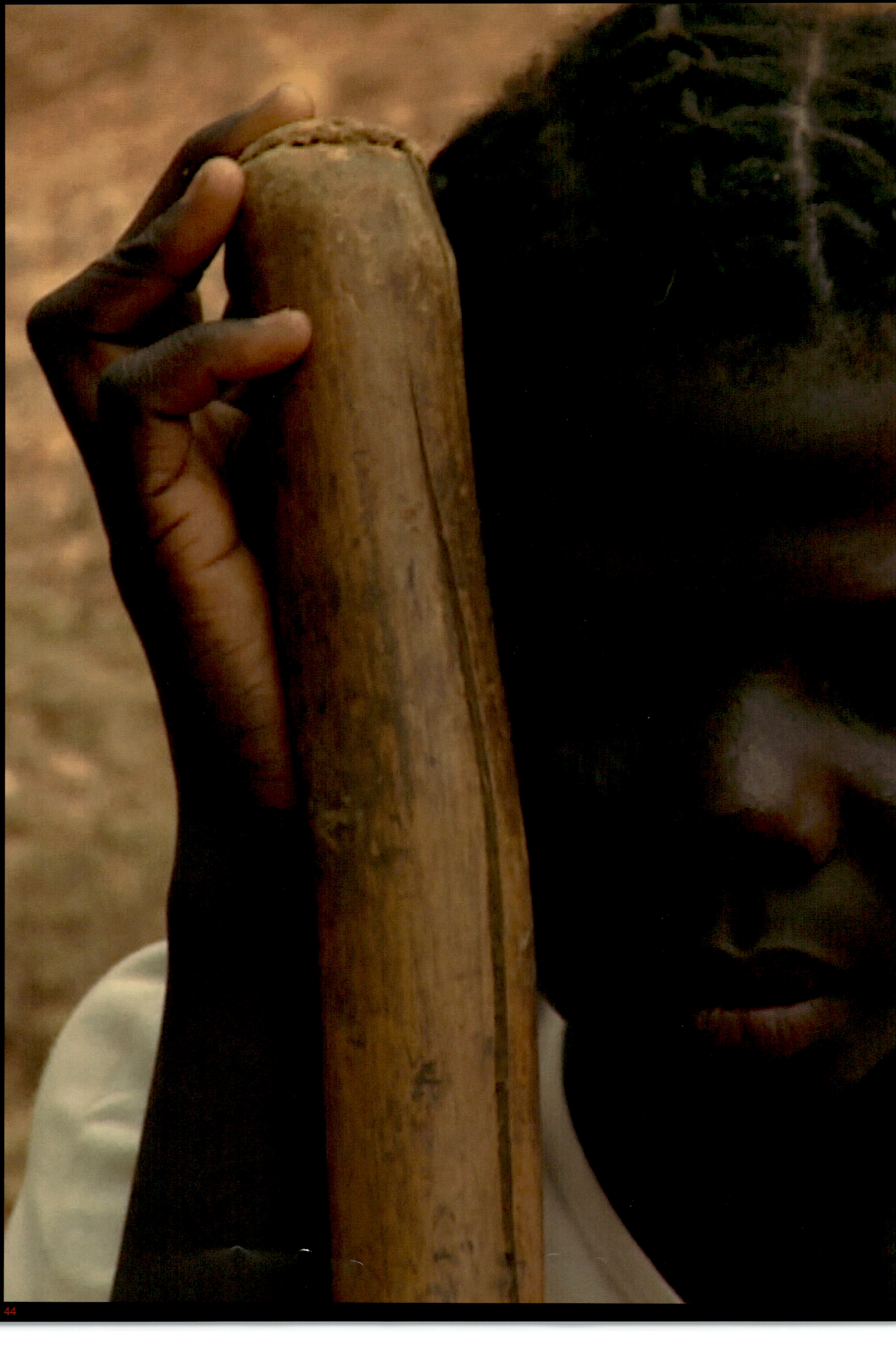

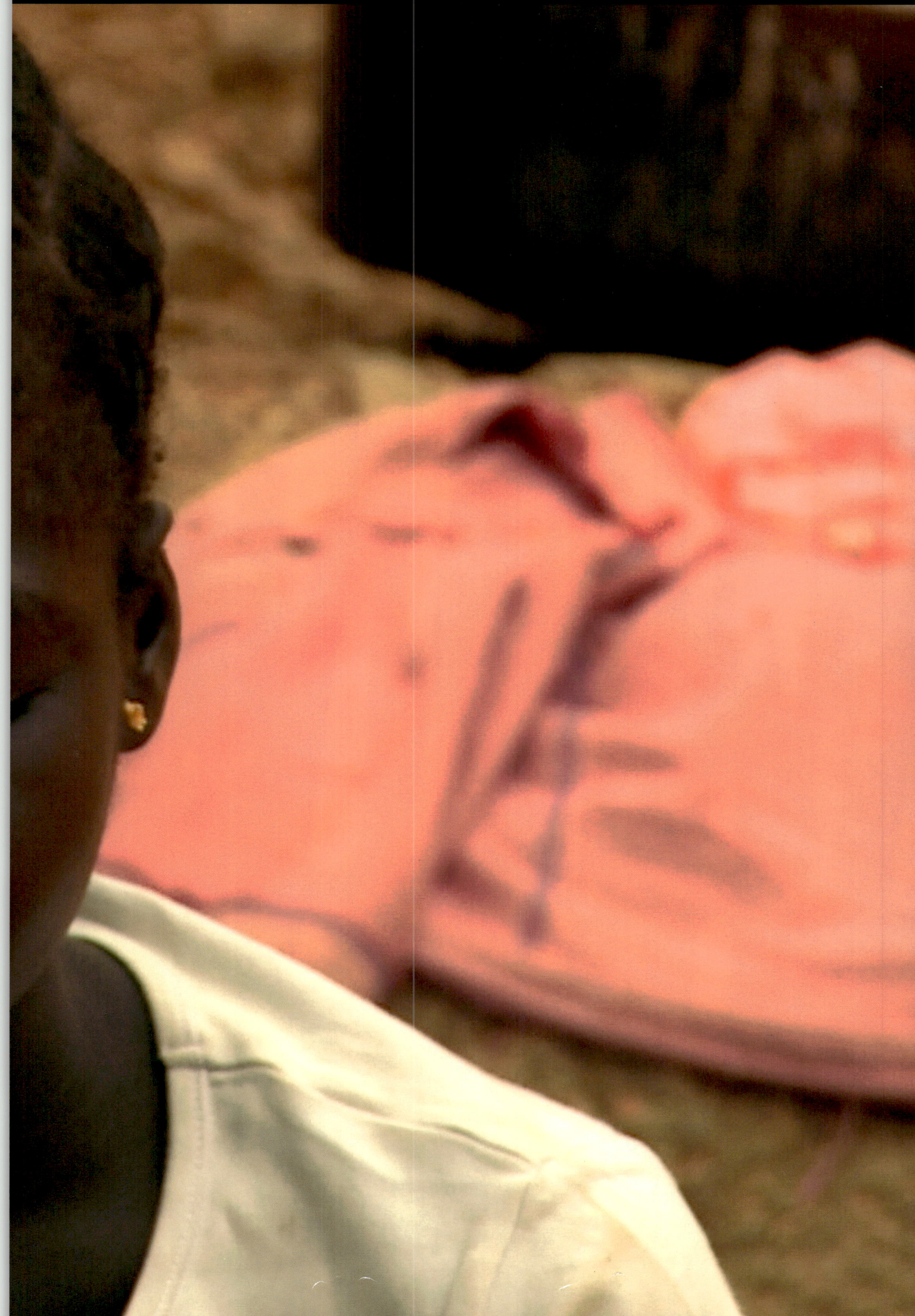

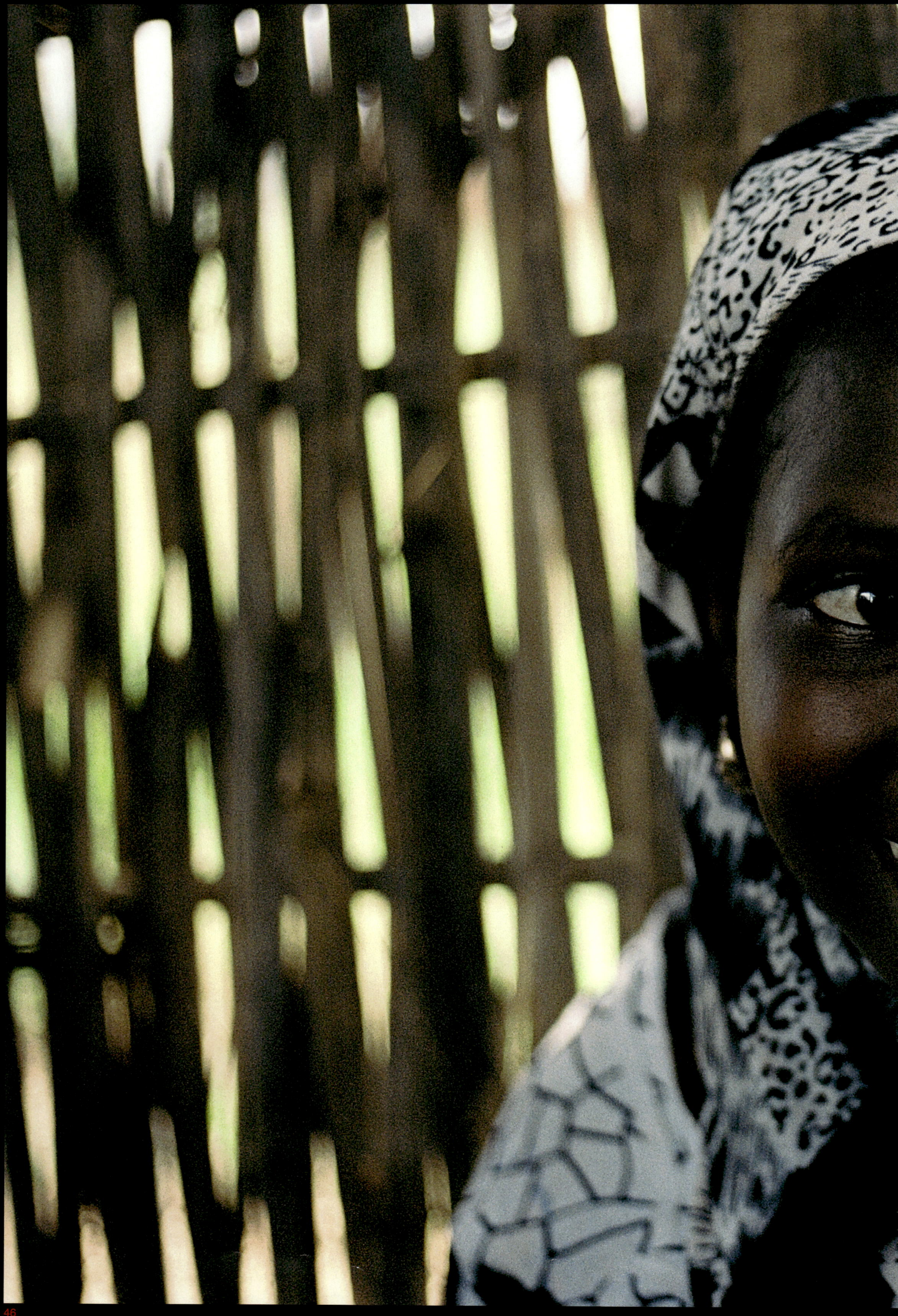

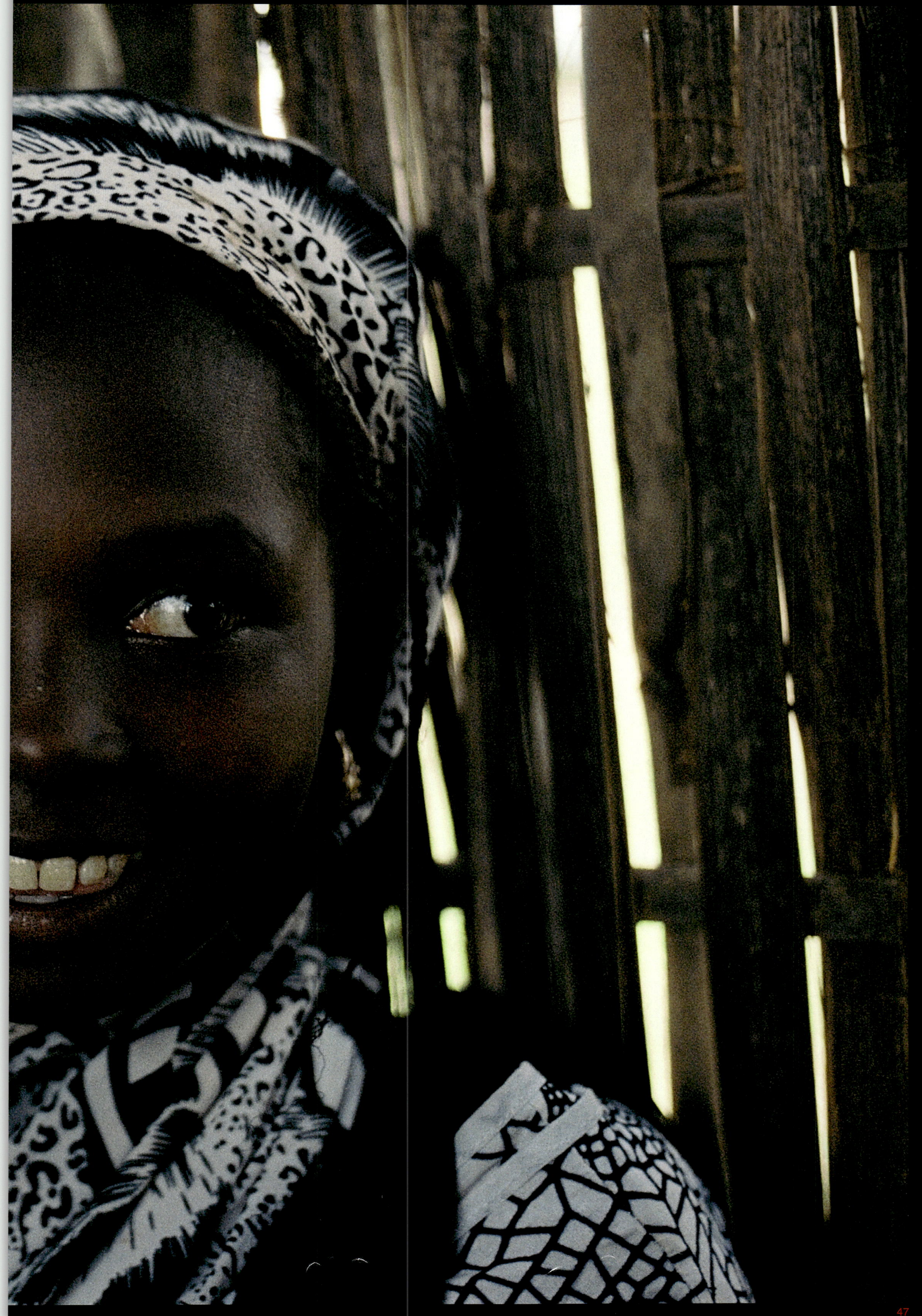

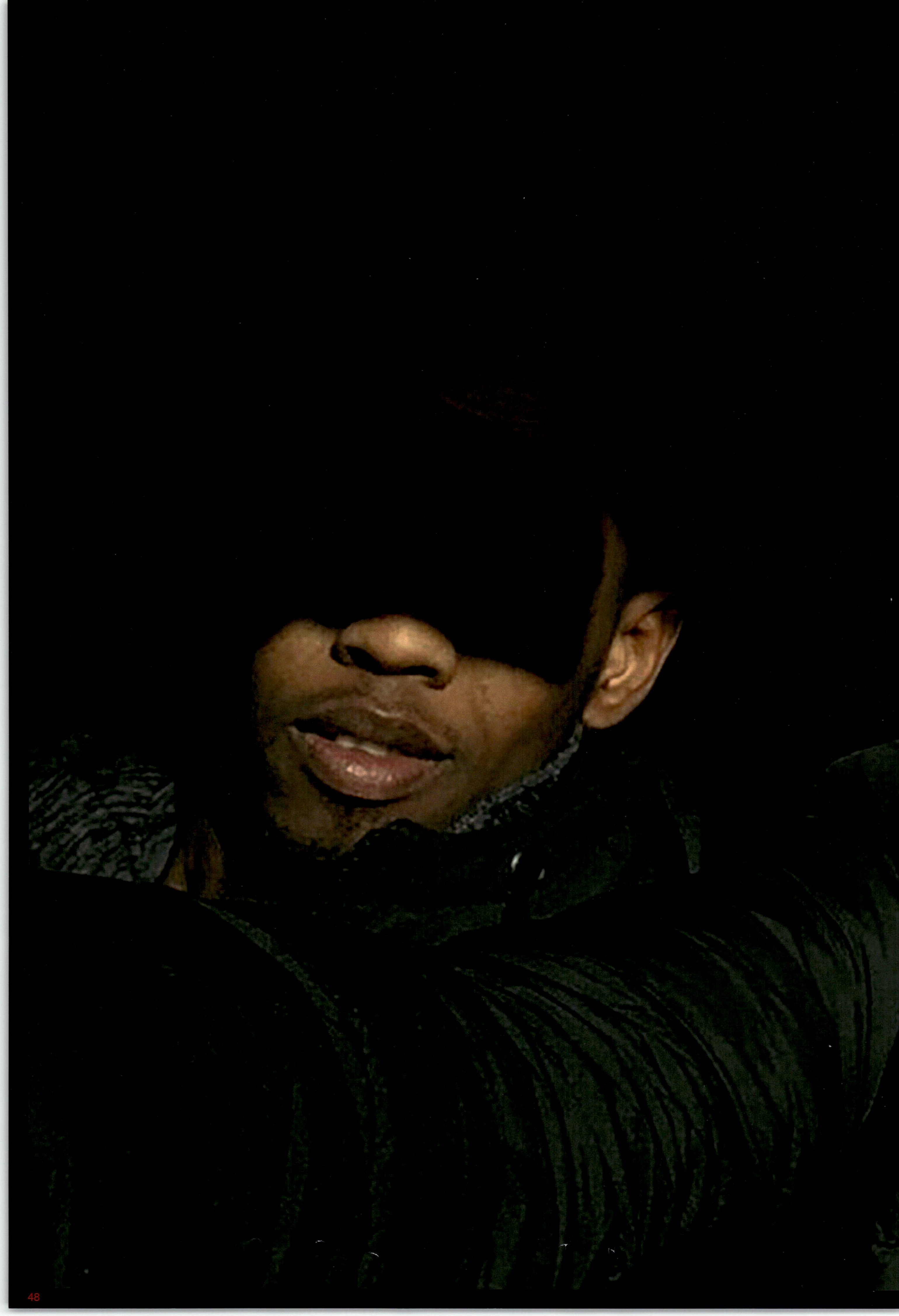

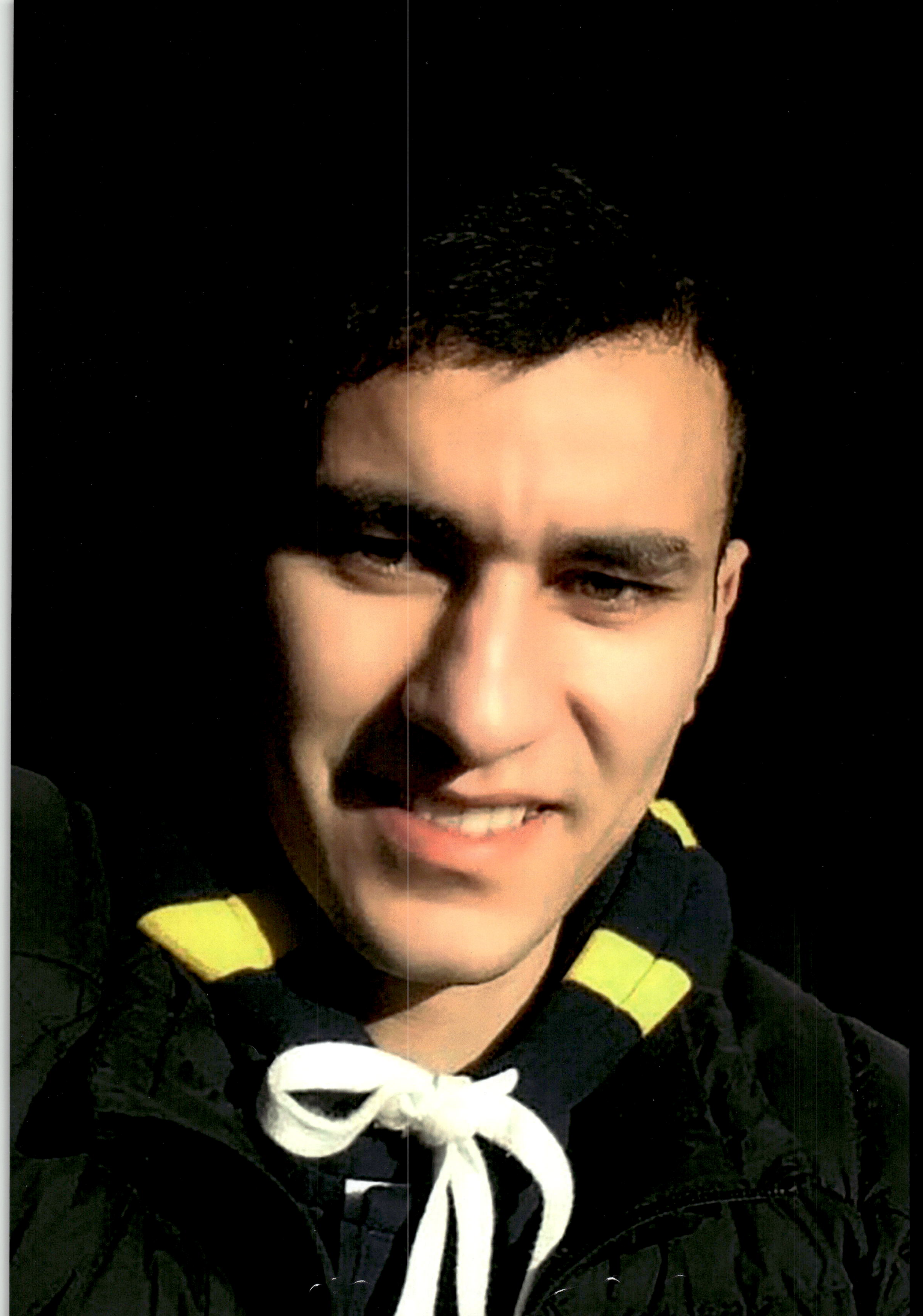

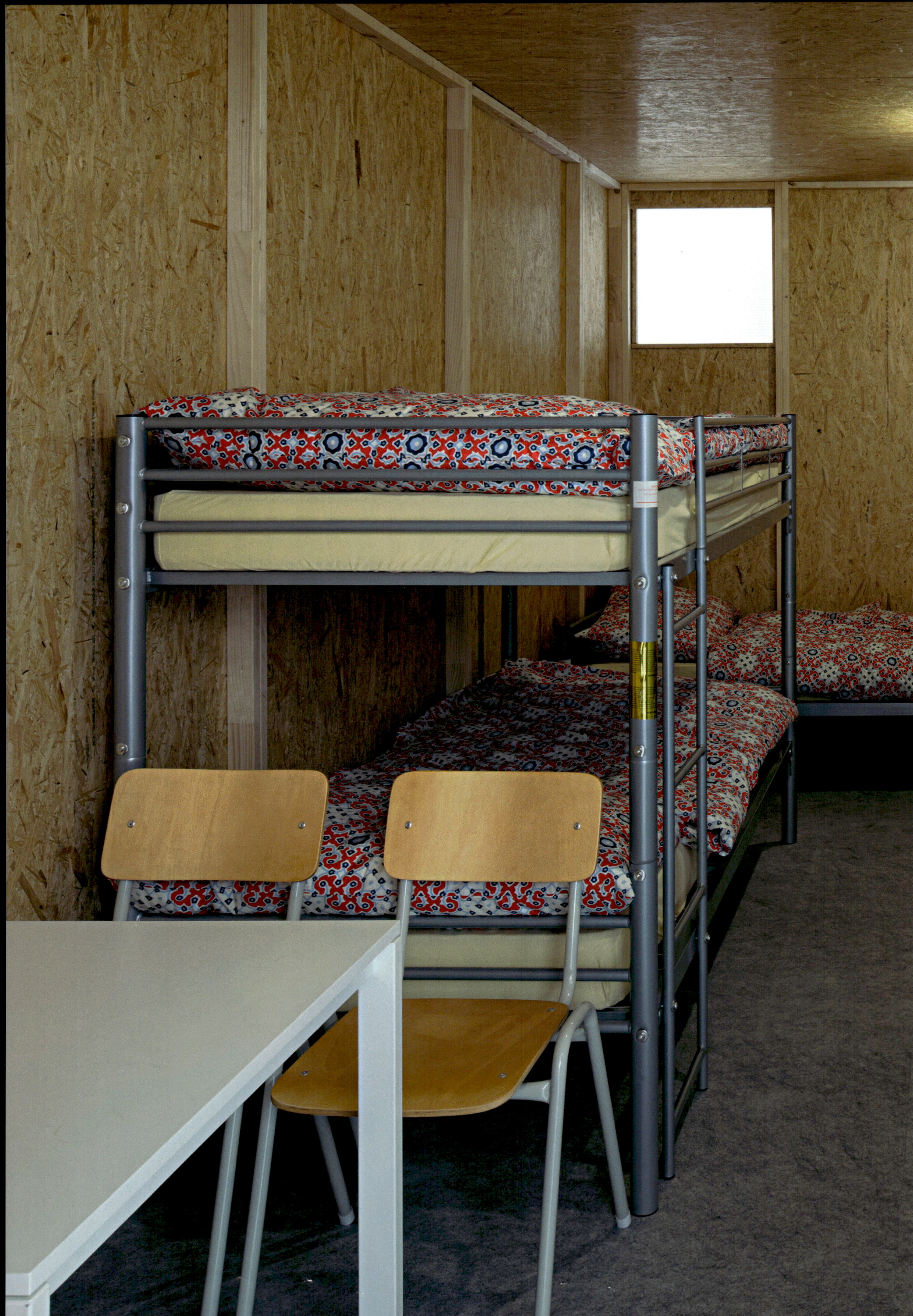

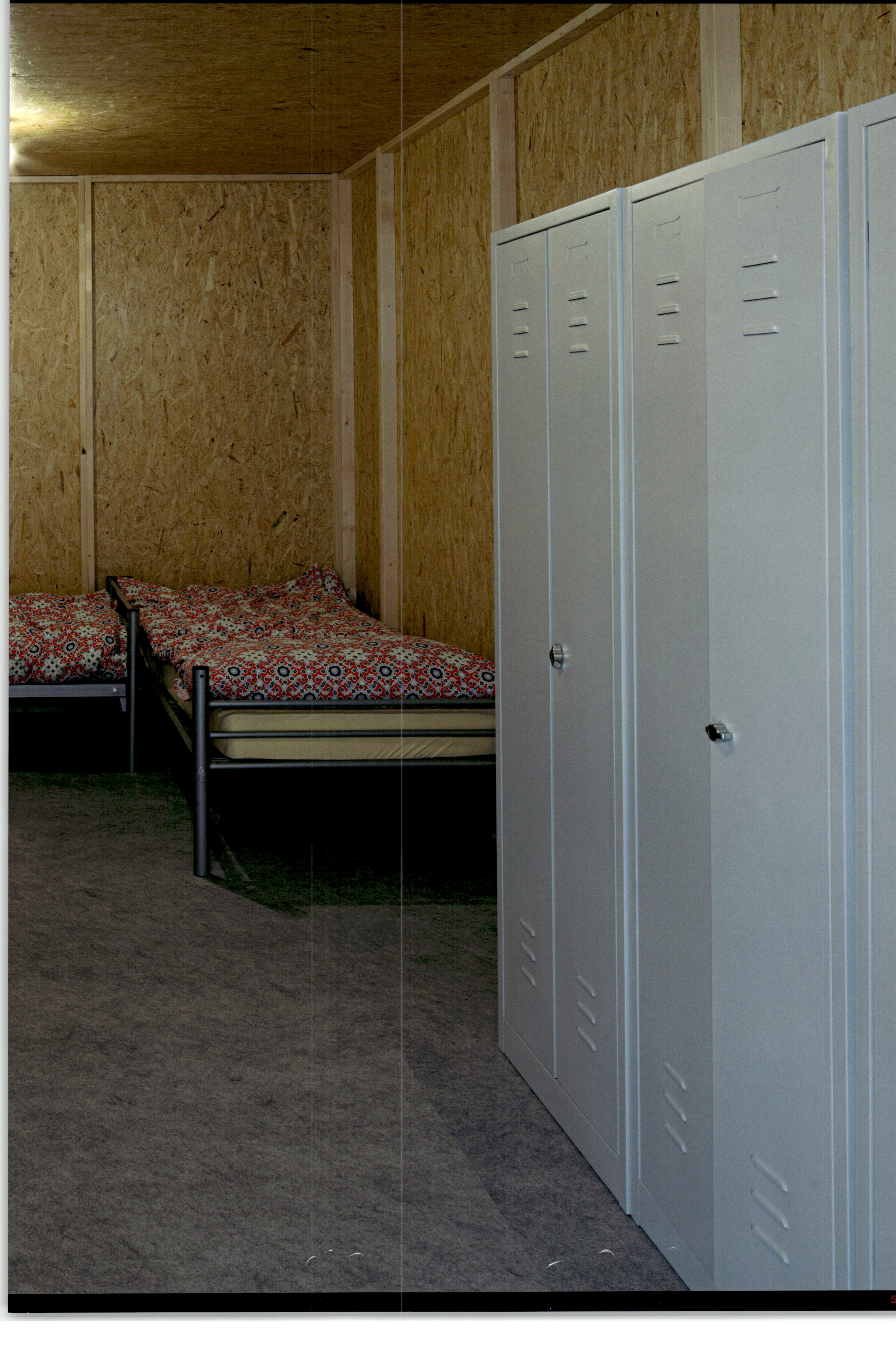

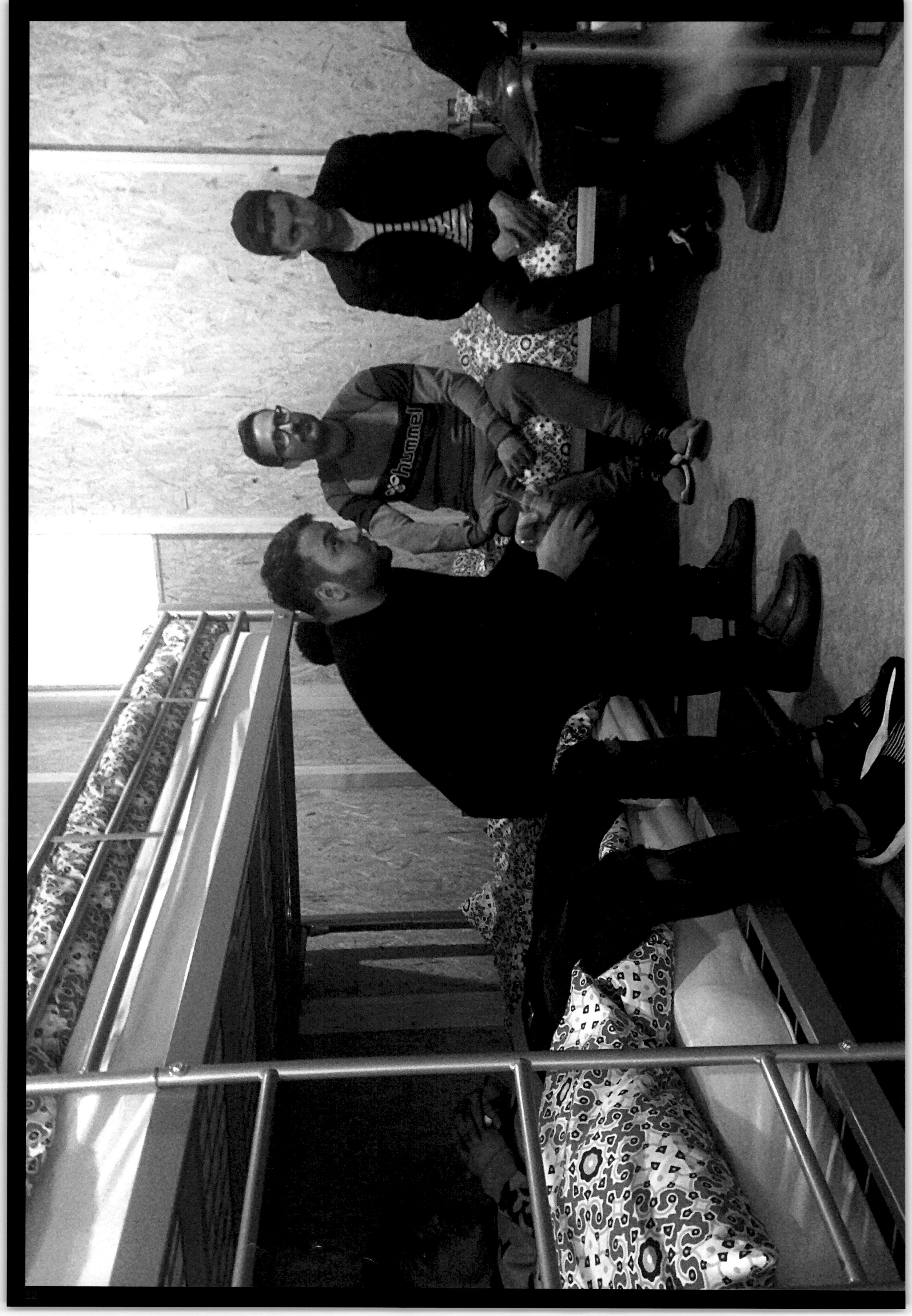
hummel

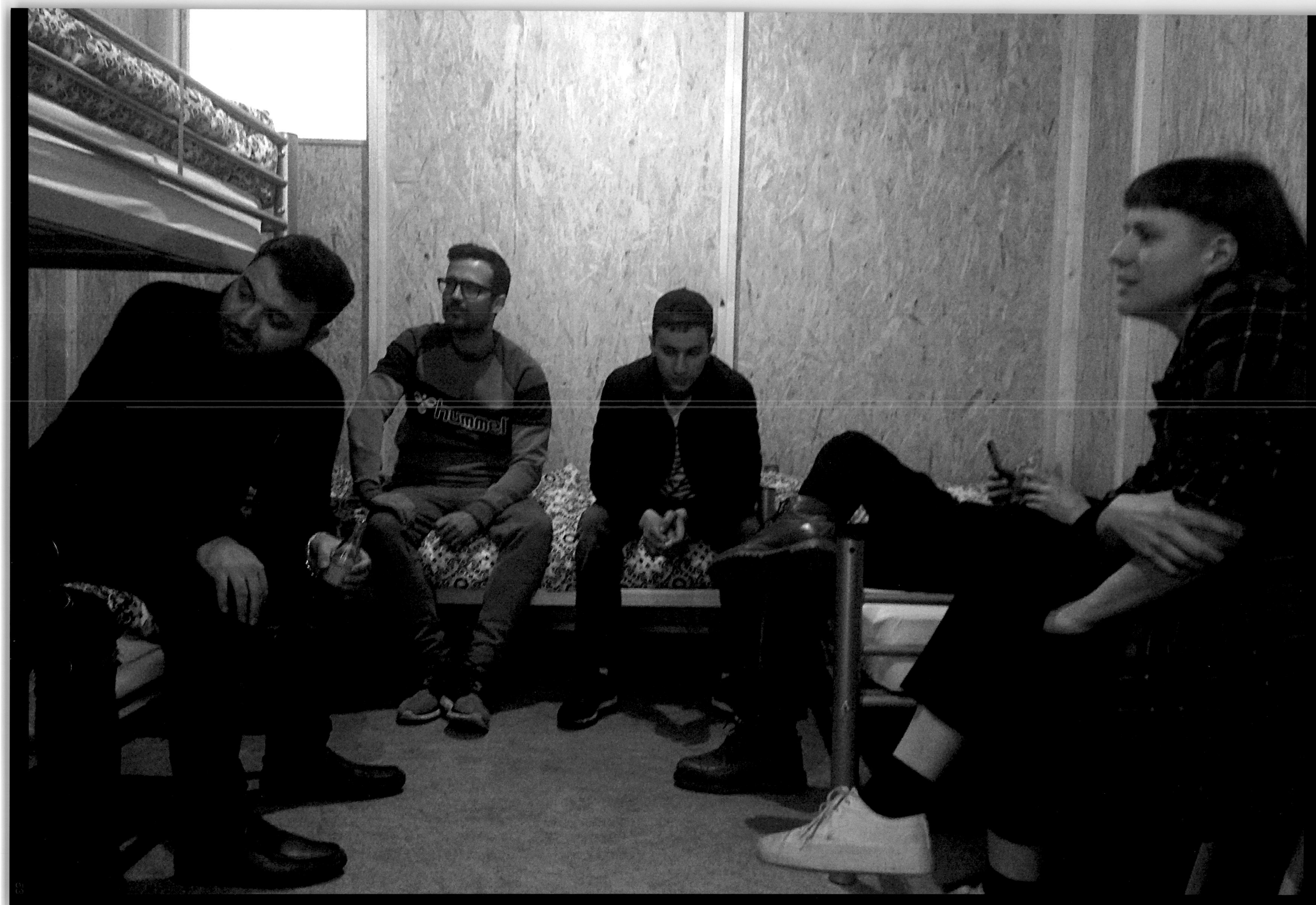
hummel

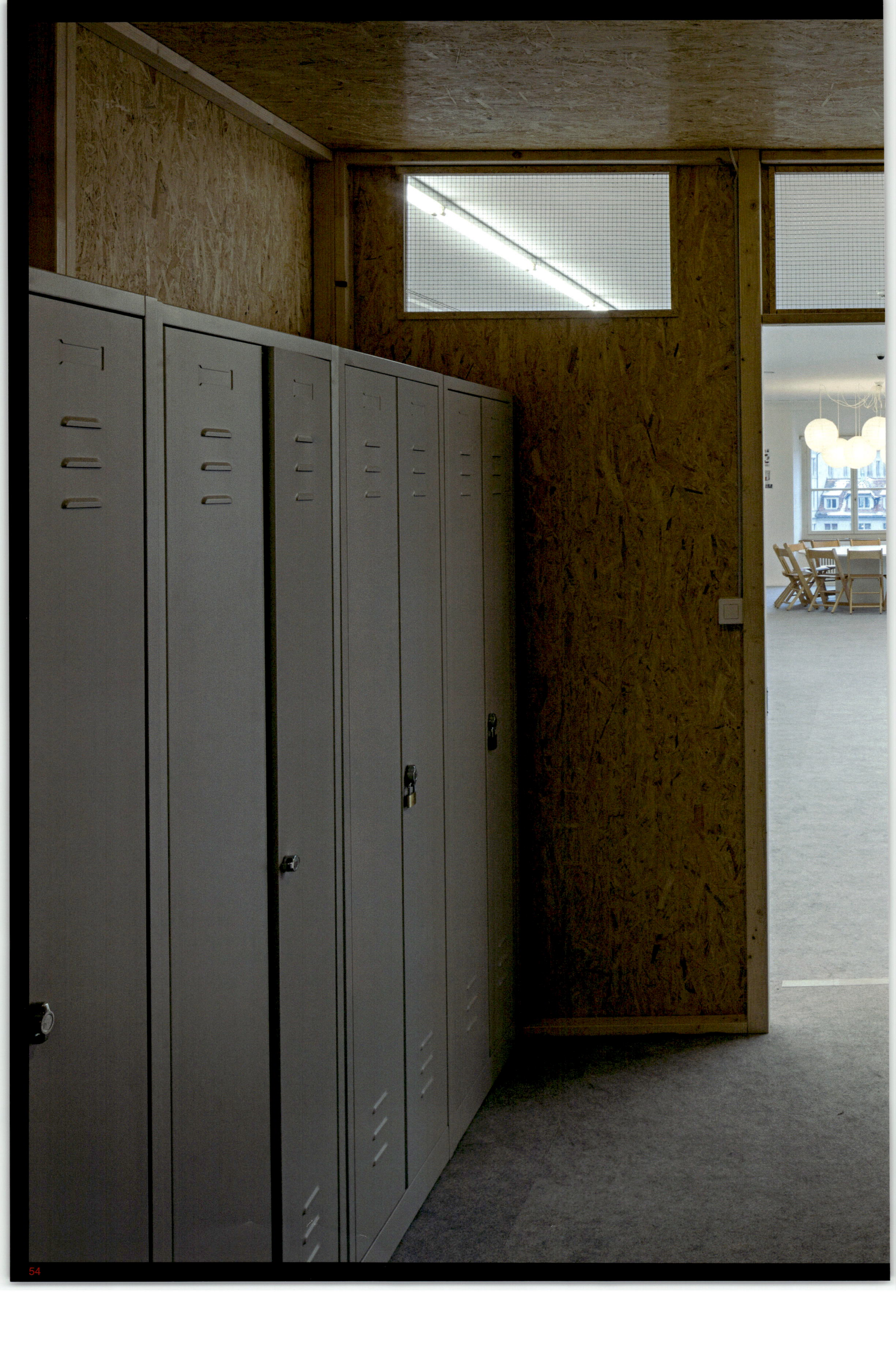

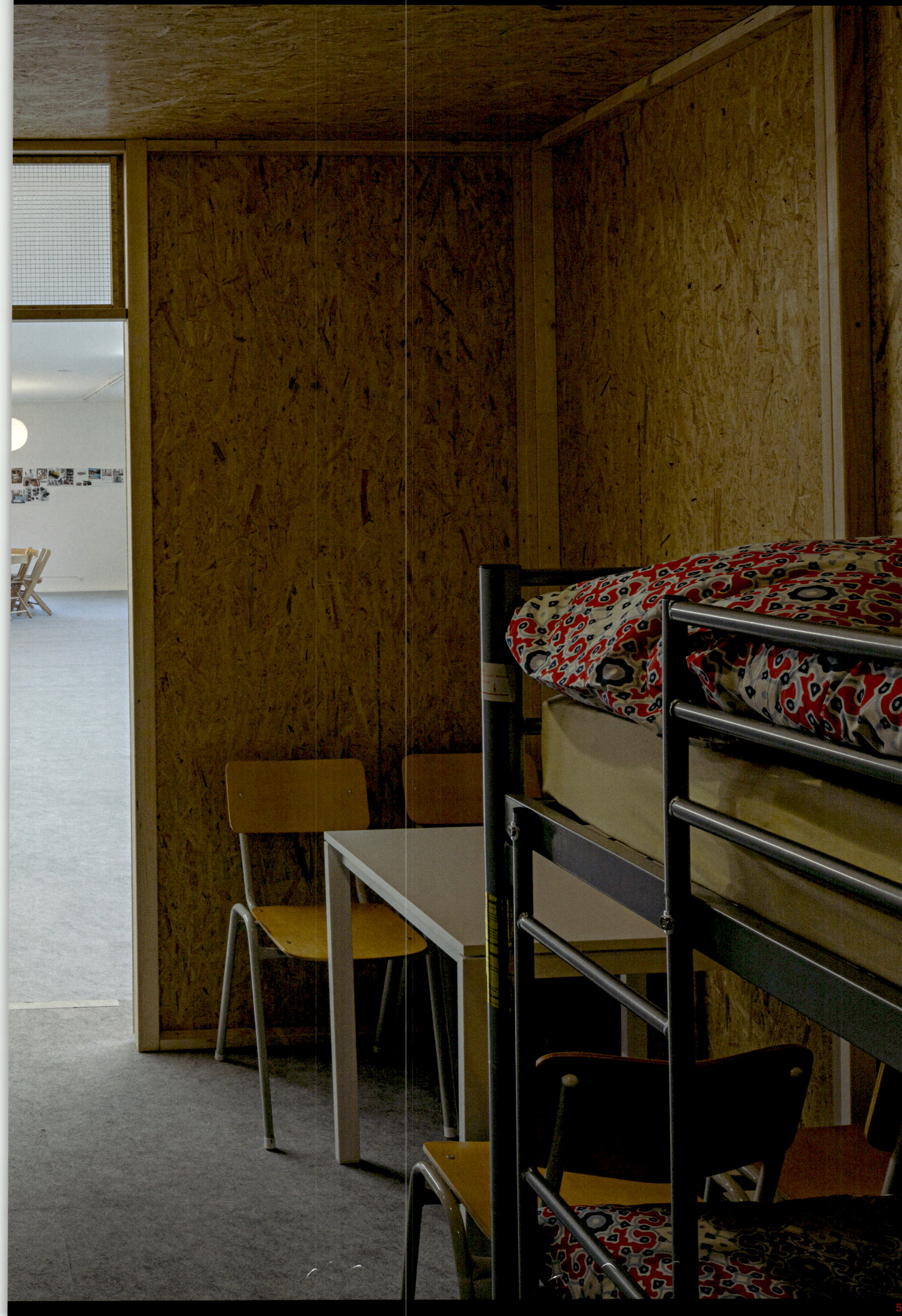

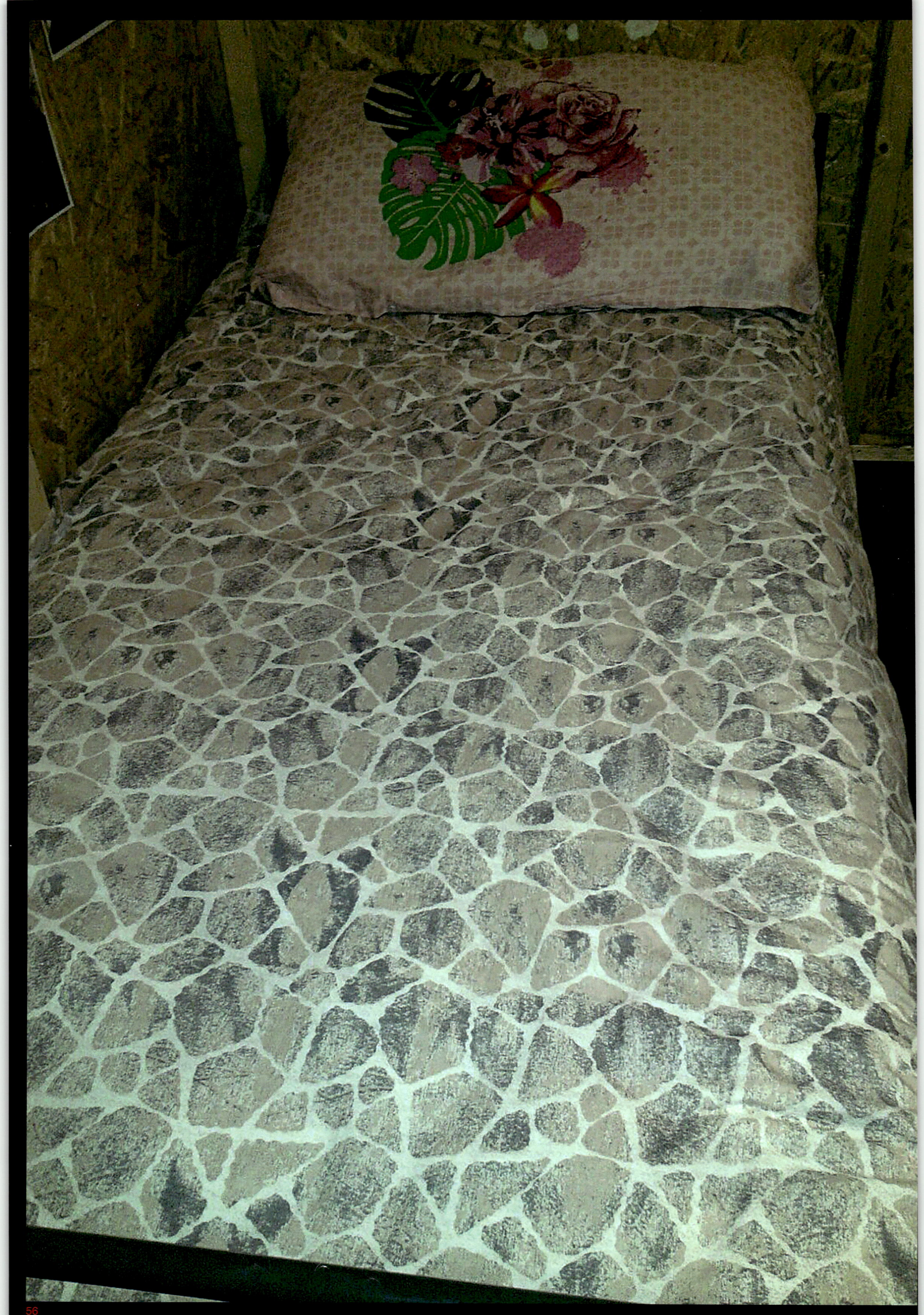

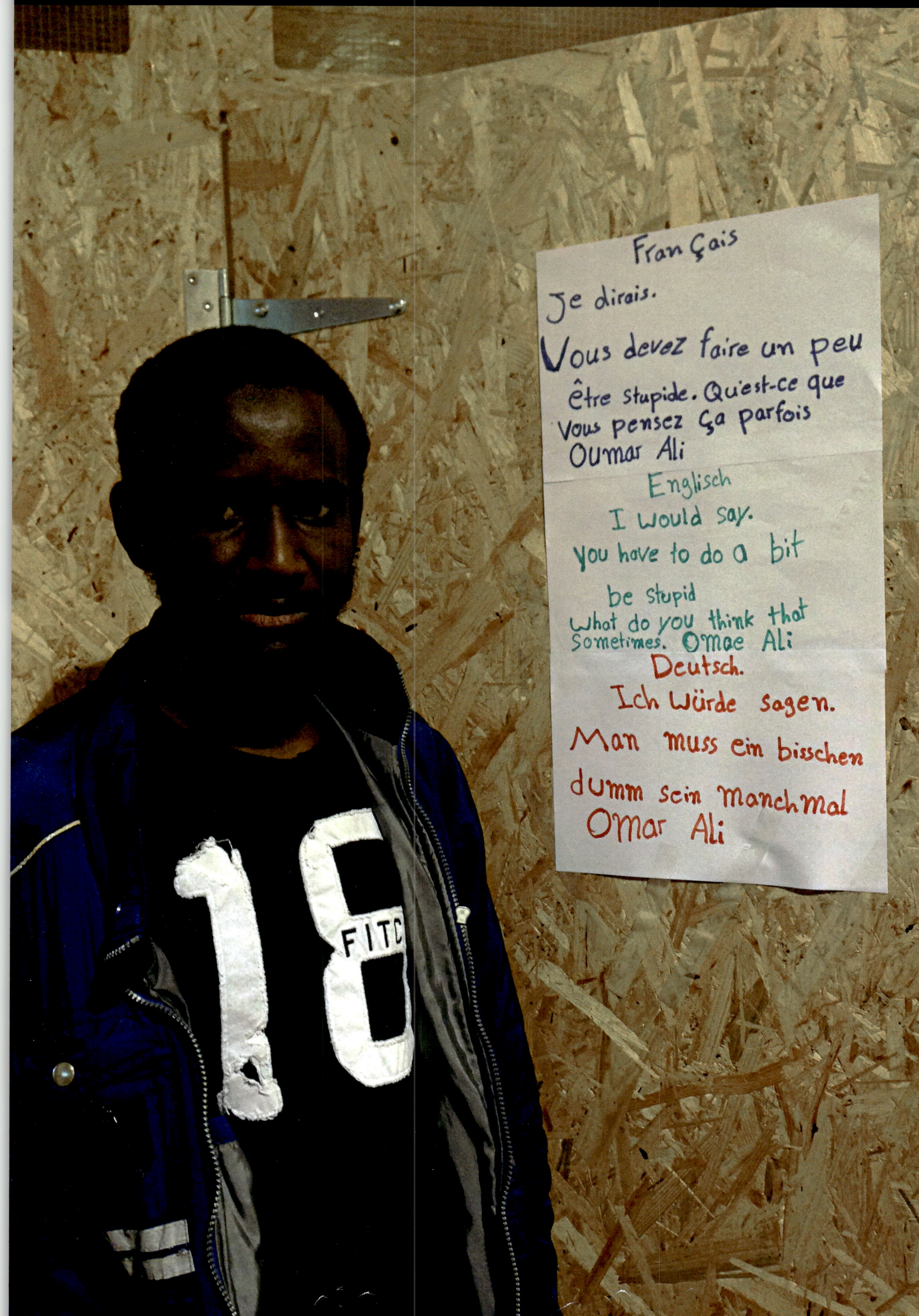
Fran Çais
Je dirais.
Vous devez faire un peu
être stupide. Qu'est-ce que
Vous pensez Ça parfois
Oumar Ali
Englisch
I would say.
you have to do a bit
be stupid
what do you think that
Sometimes. Omae Ali
Deutsch.
Ich Würde sagen.
Man muss ein bisschen
dumm sein manchmal
Omar Ali

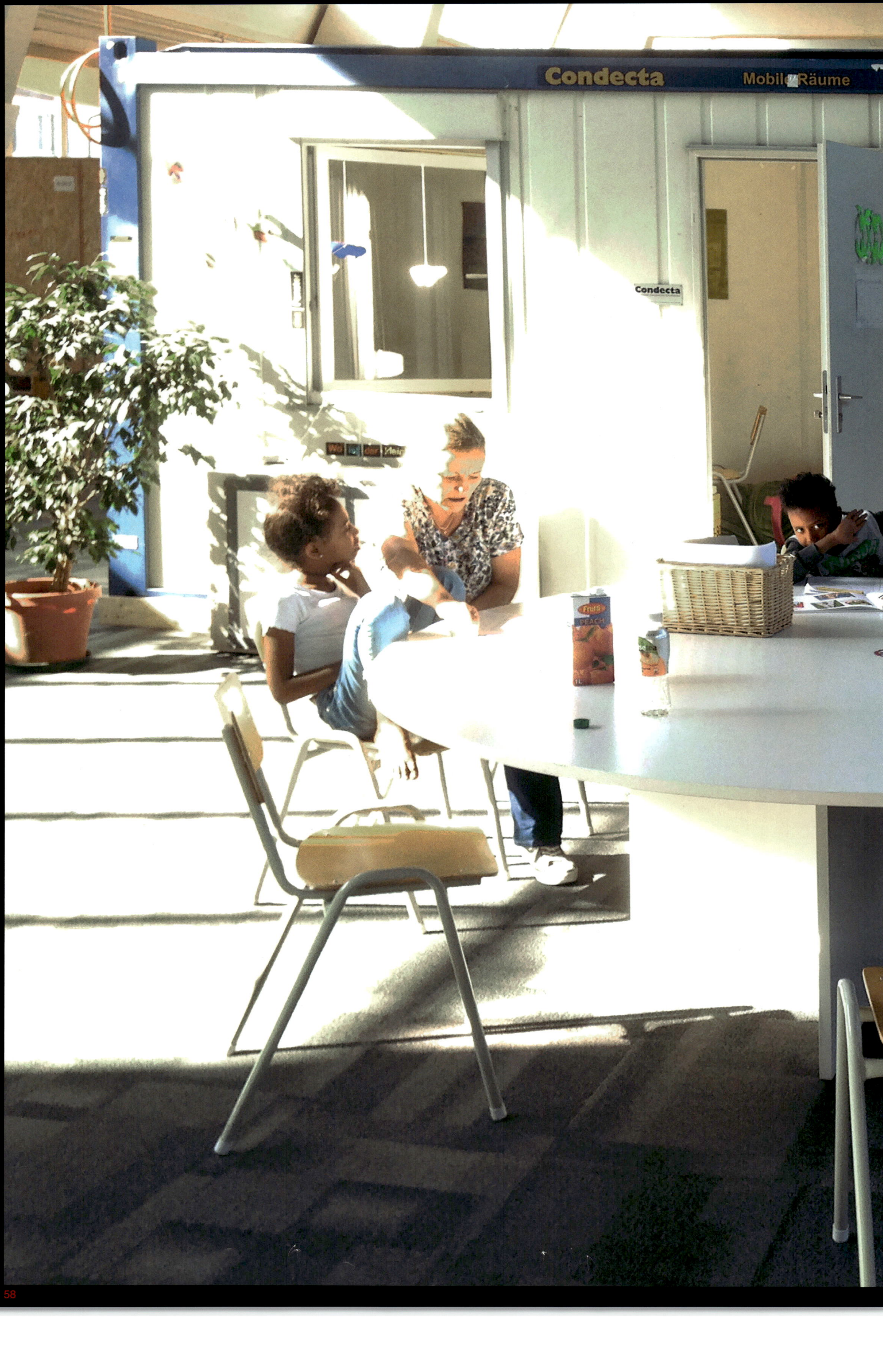
Condecta
Mobile Räume
Condecta

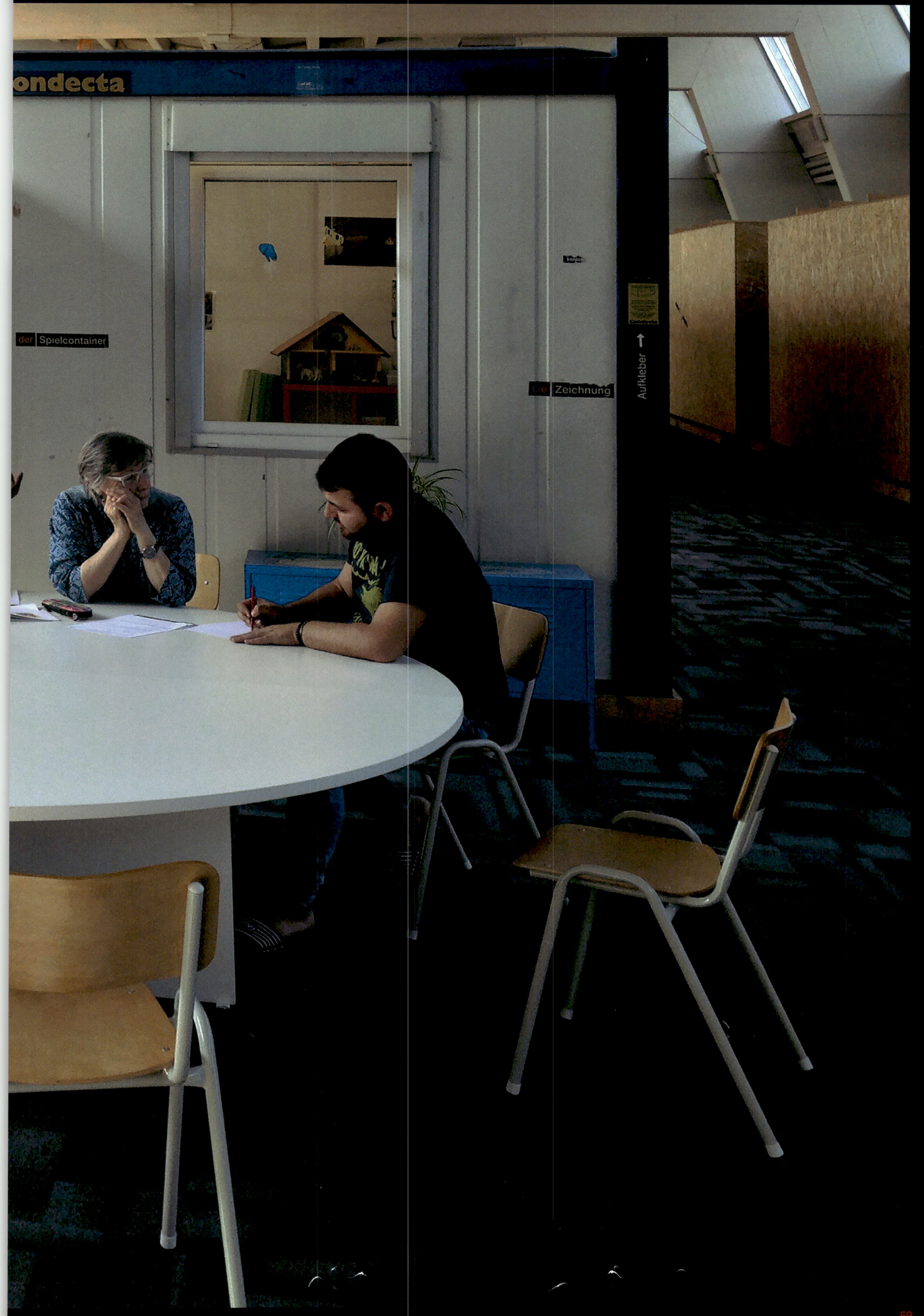
ondecta
der Spielcontainer
die Zeichnung
Aufkleber

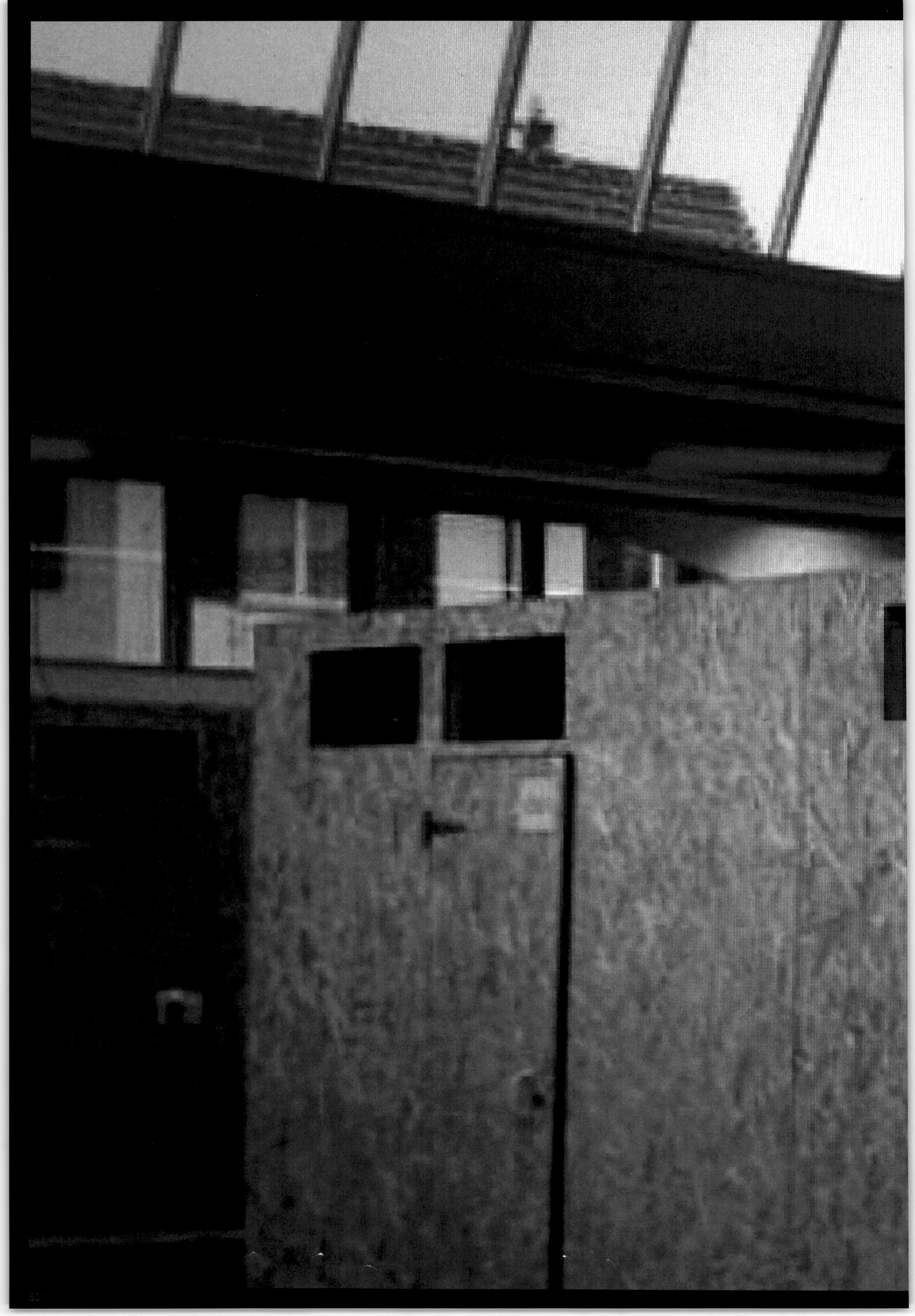

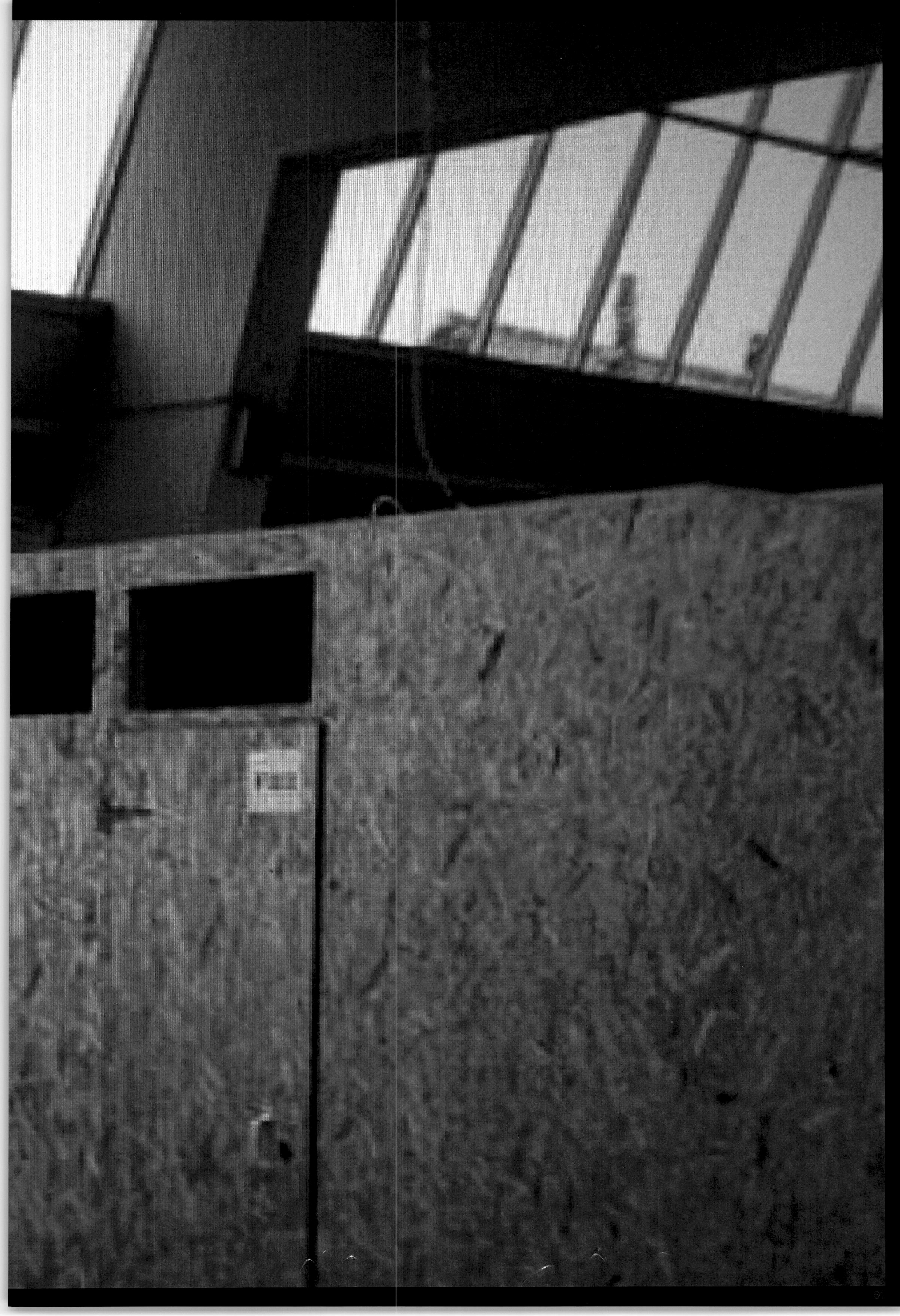

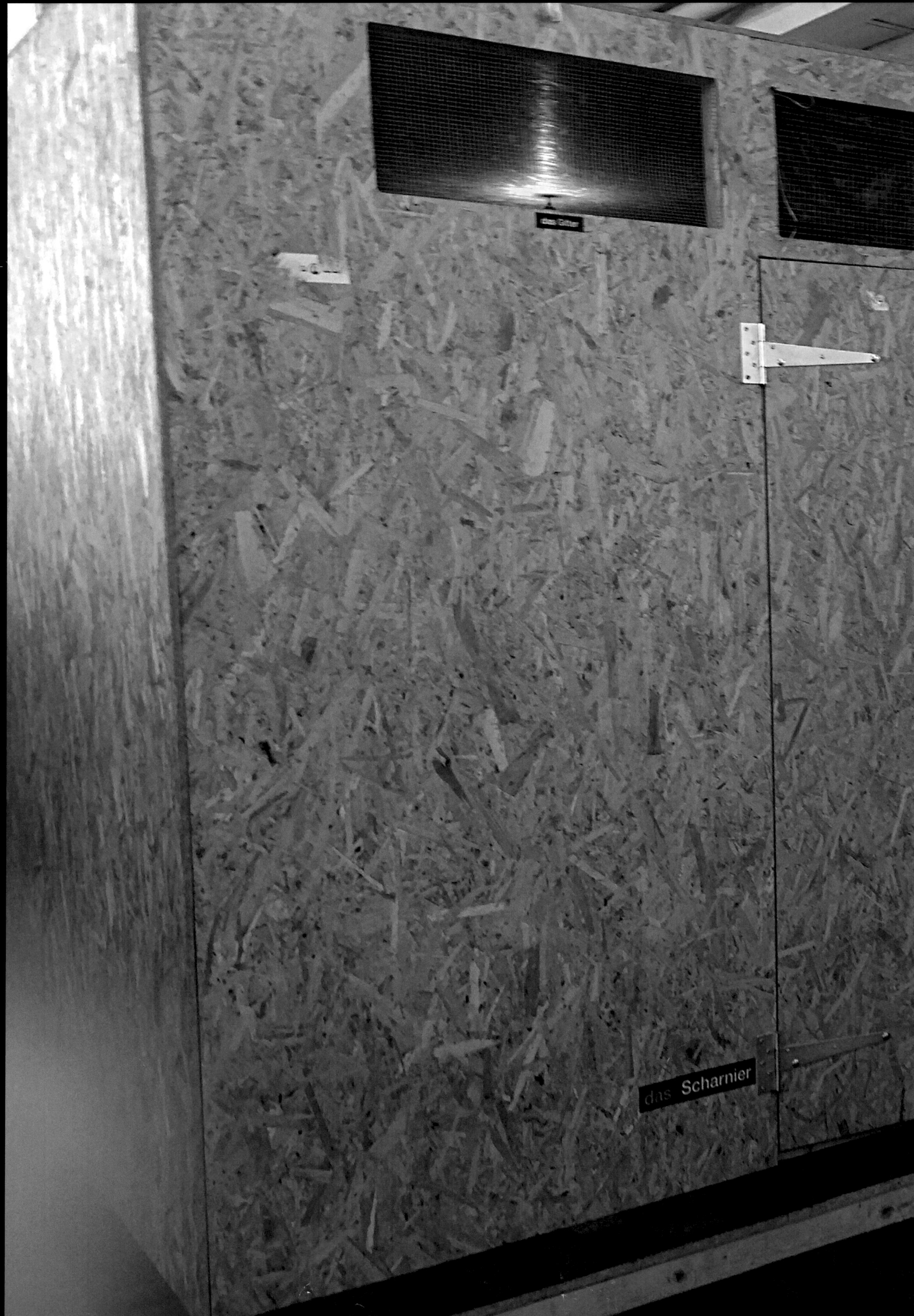
das Gitter
das Scharnier

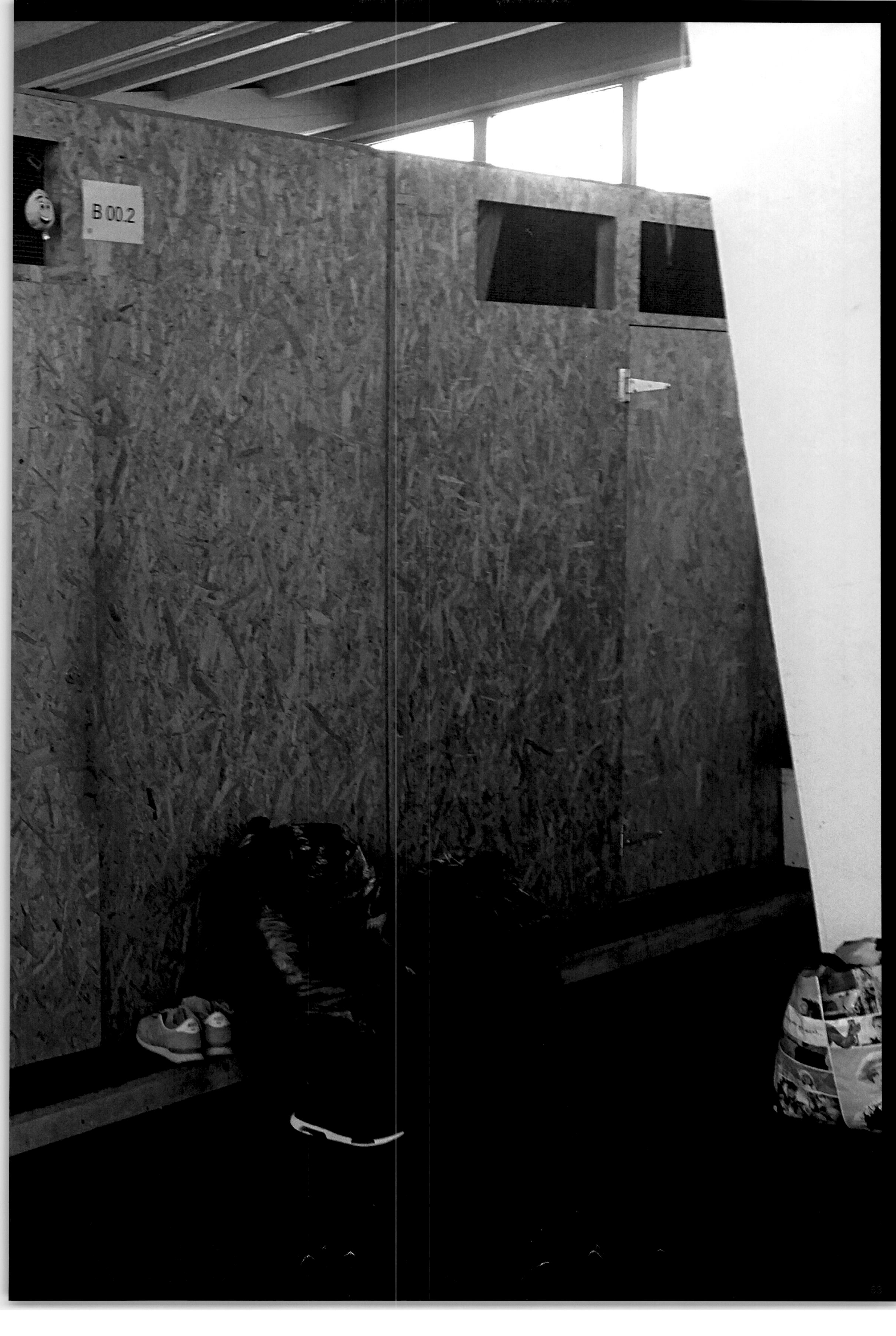
B 00.2

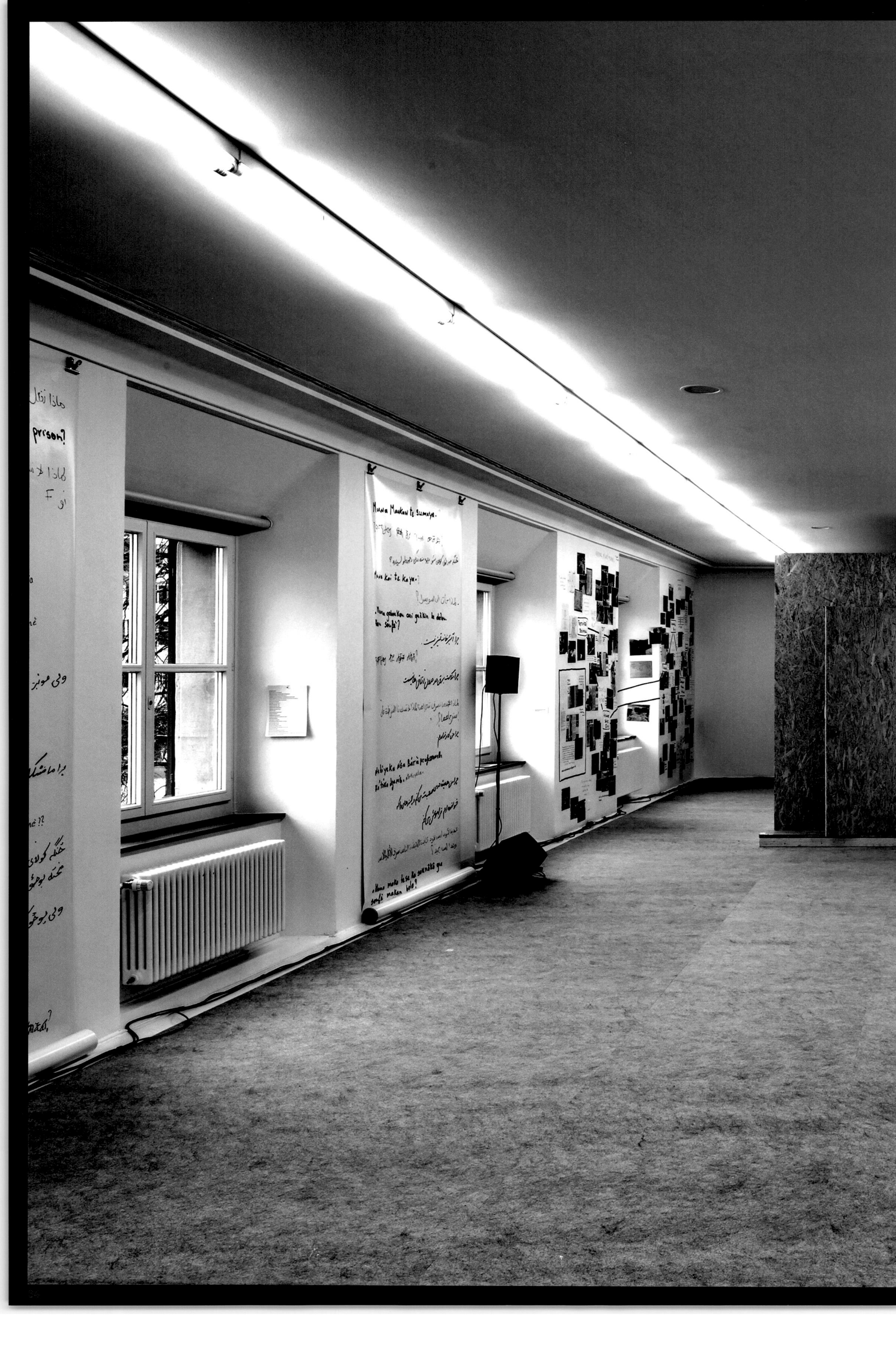

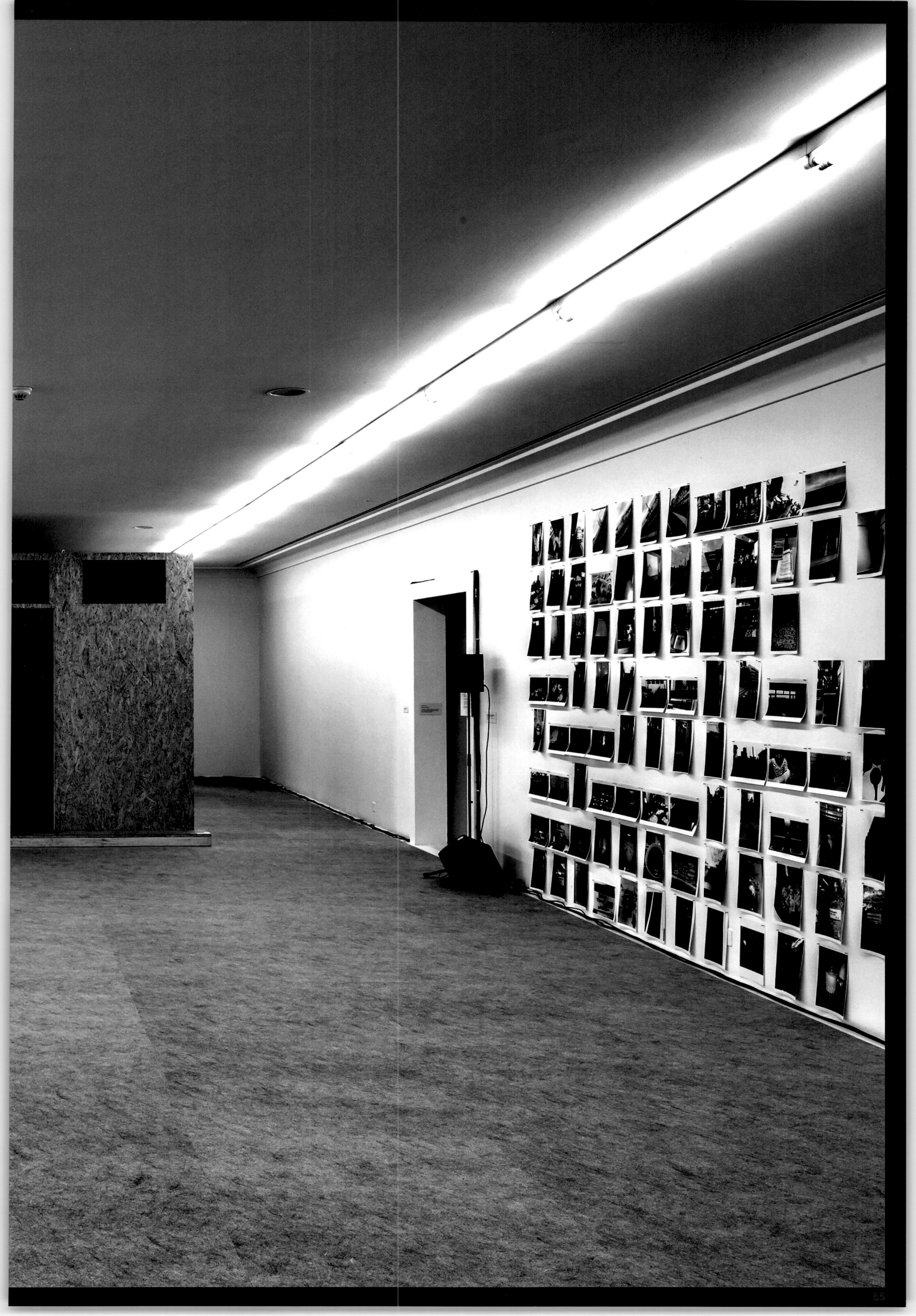

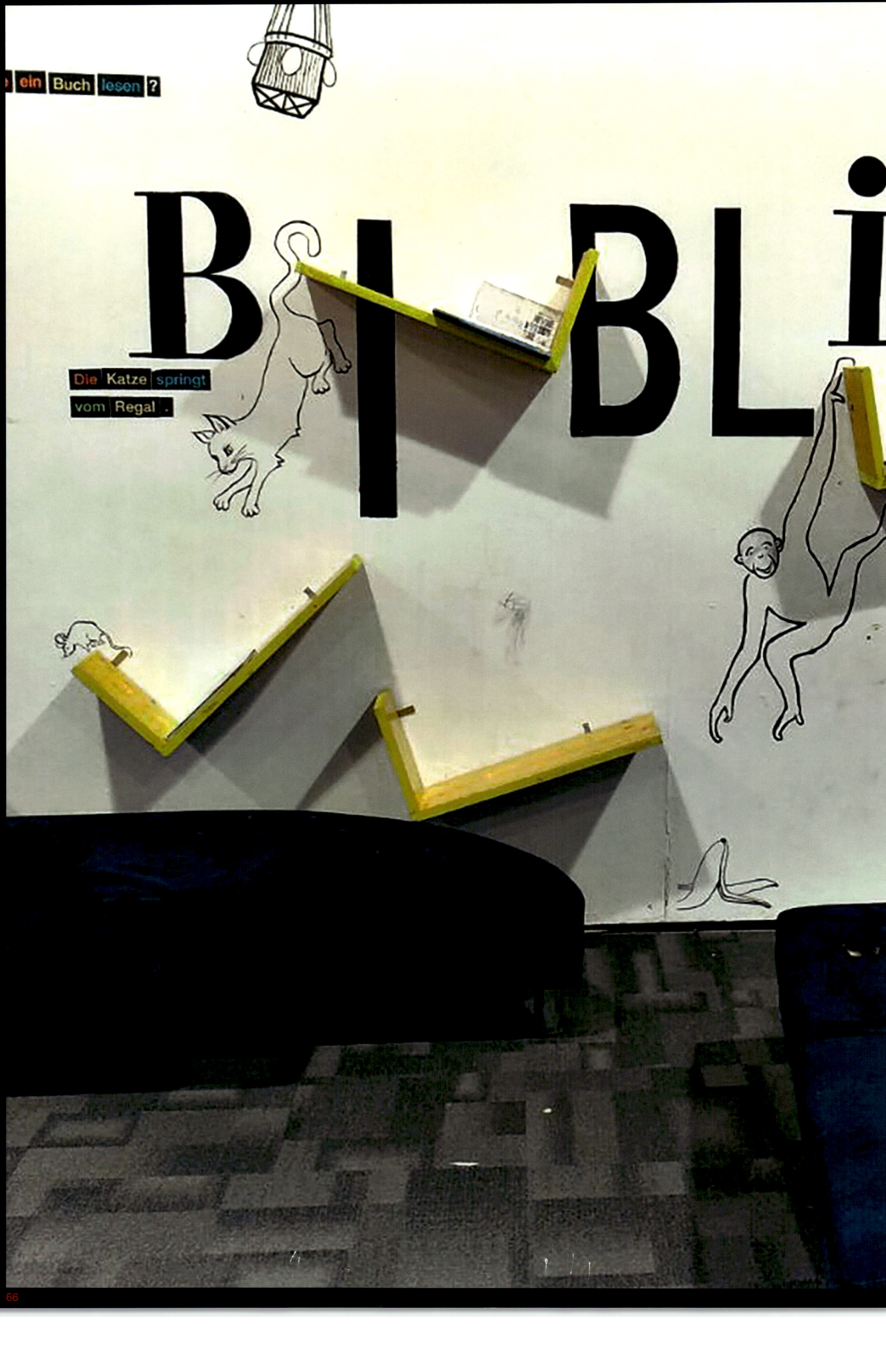
ein Buch lesen ?
Die Katze springt
vom Regal .

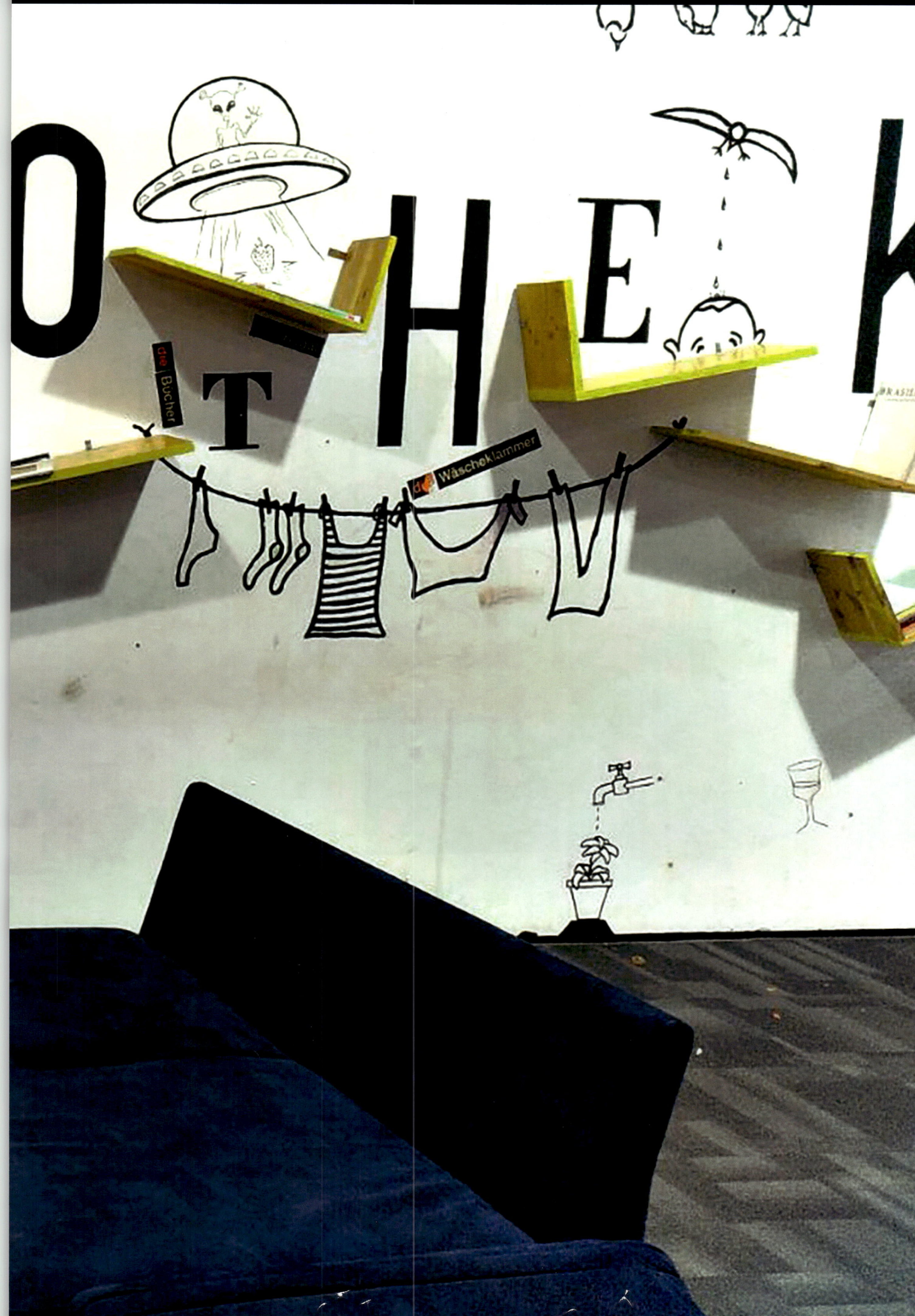
Bücher
Wäscheklammer

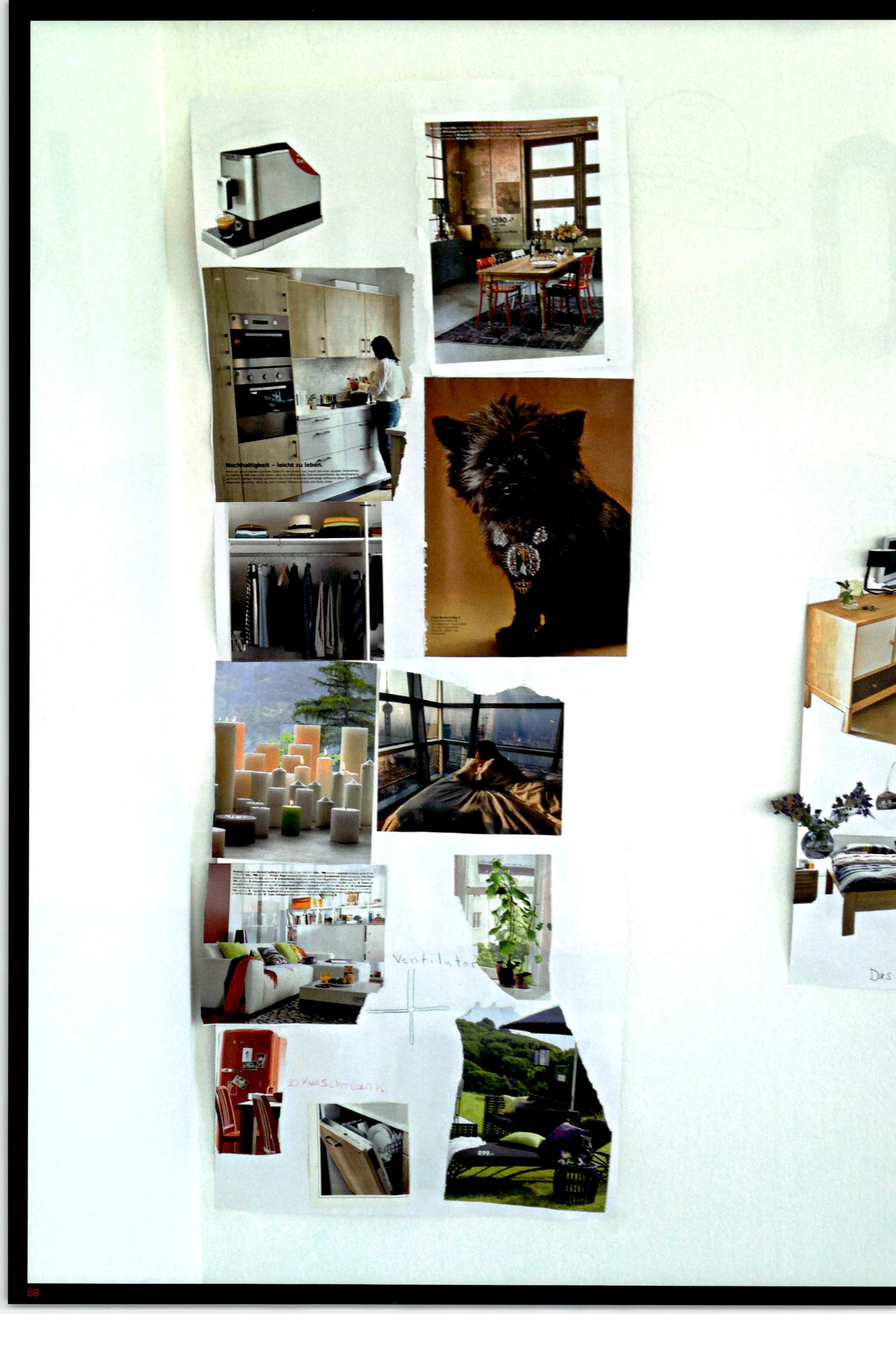
Nachhaltigkeit – leicht zu leben.
Ventilator

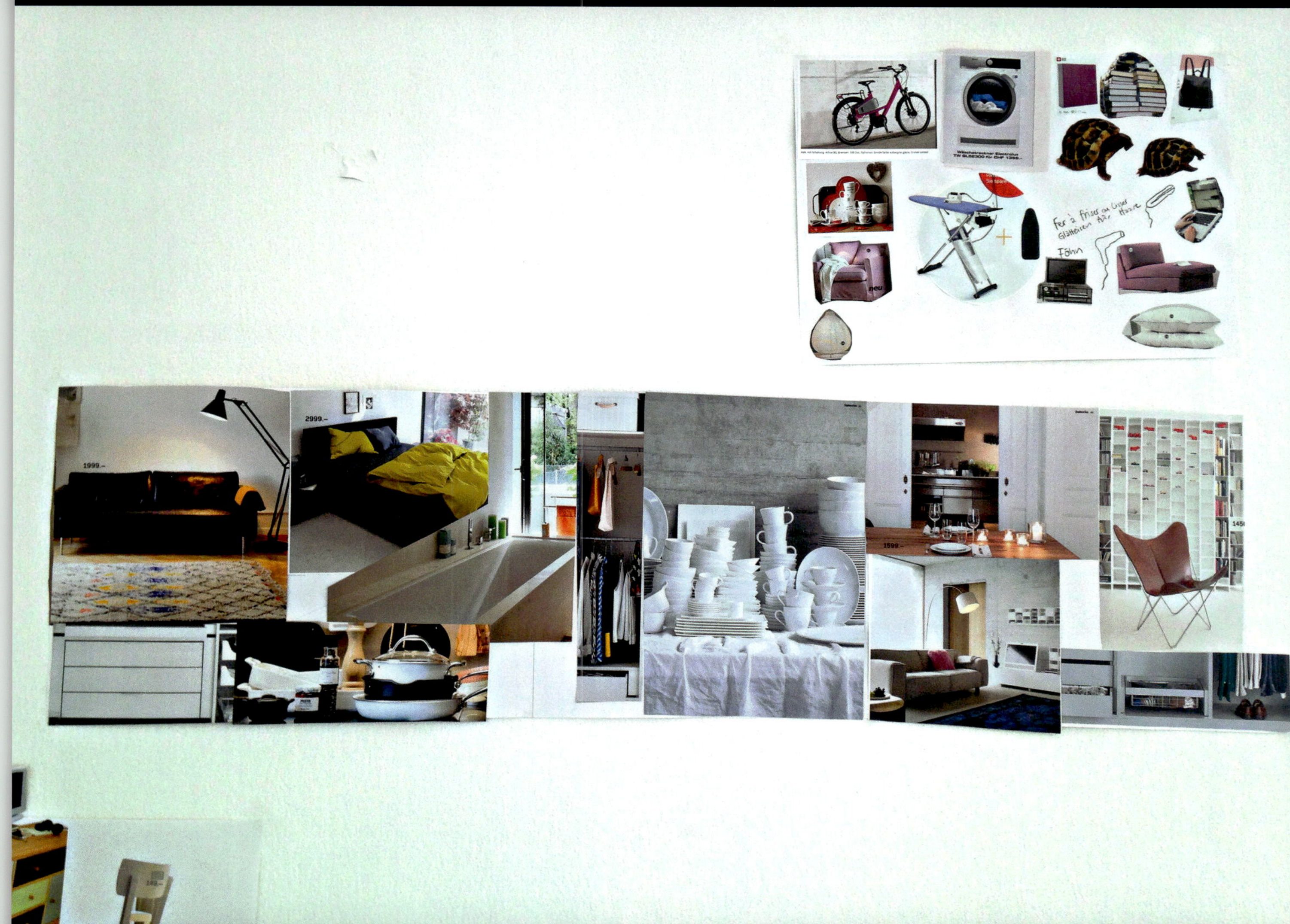

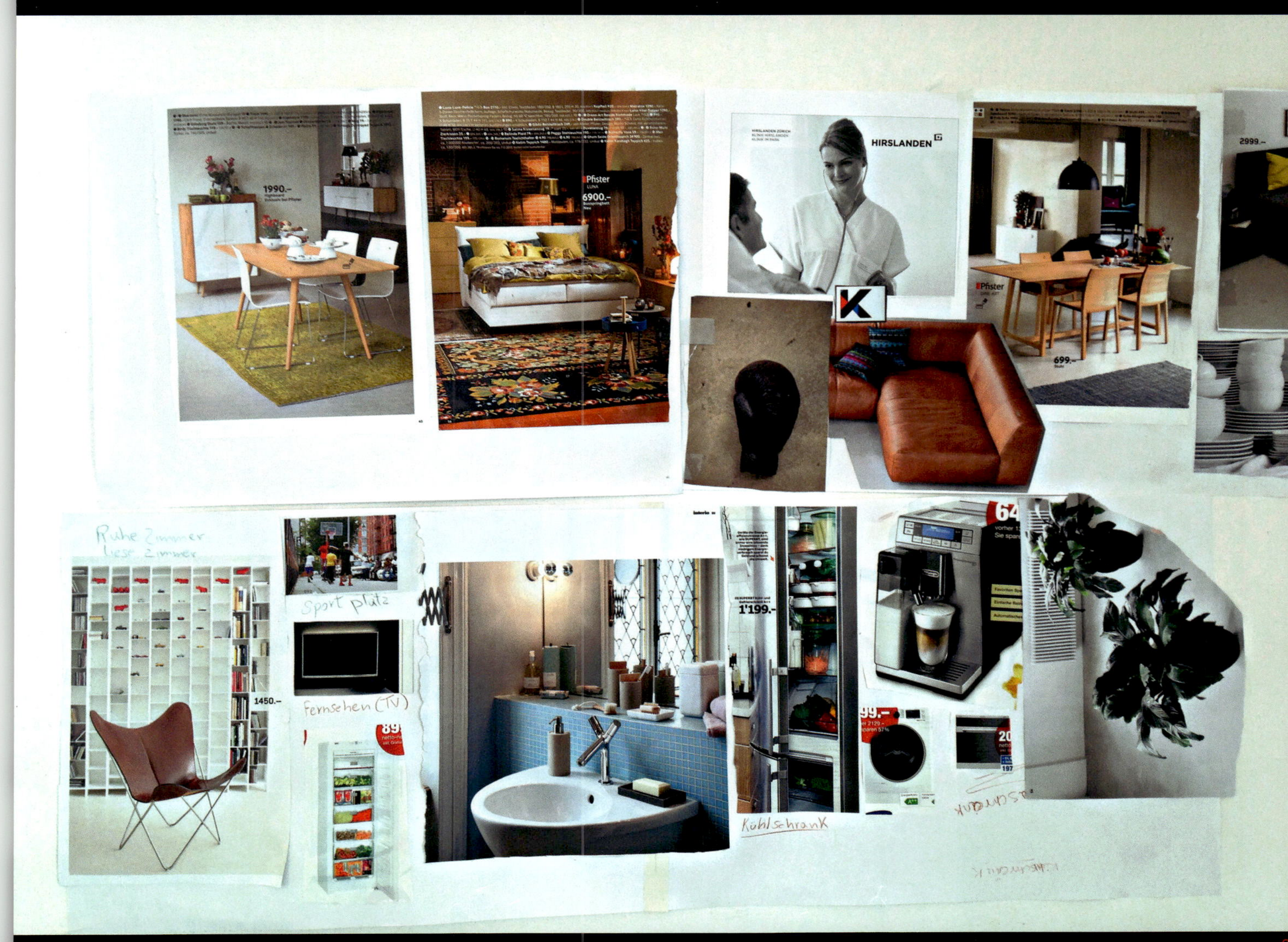
HIRSLANDEN
Pfister
Ruhe Zimmer
Lese Zimmer
Sport plätz
Fernsehen (TV)
Kühlschrank

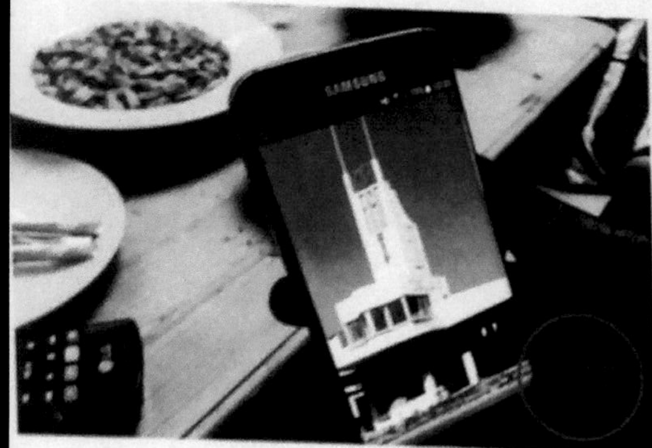

«Ohne postitiven Bescheid
ich nicht arbeiten - wir
eben wie Hunde.»

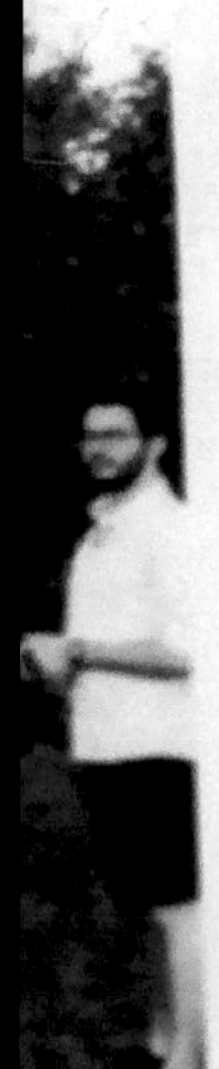

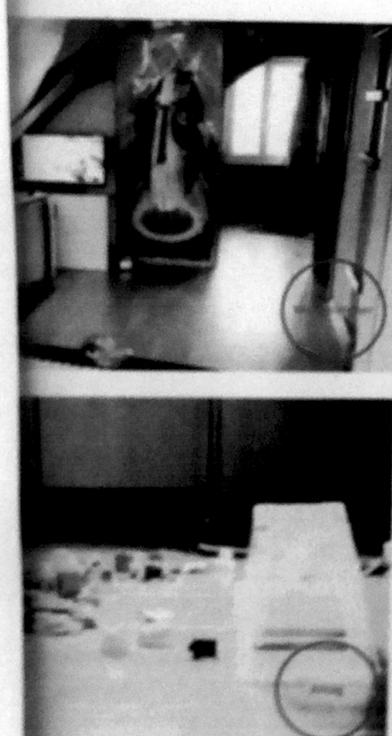

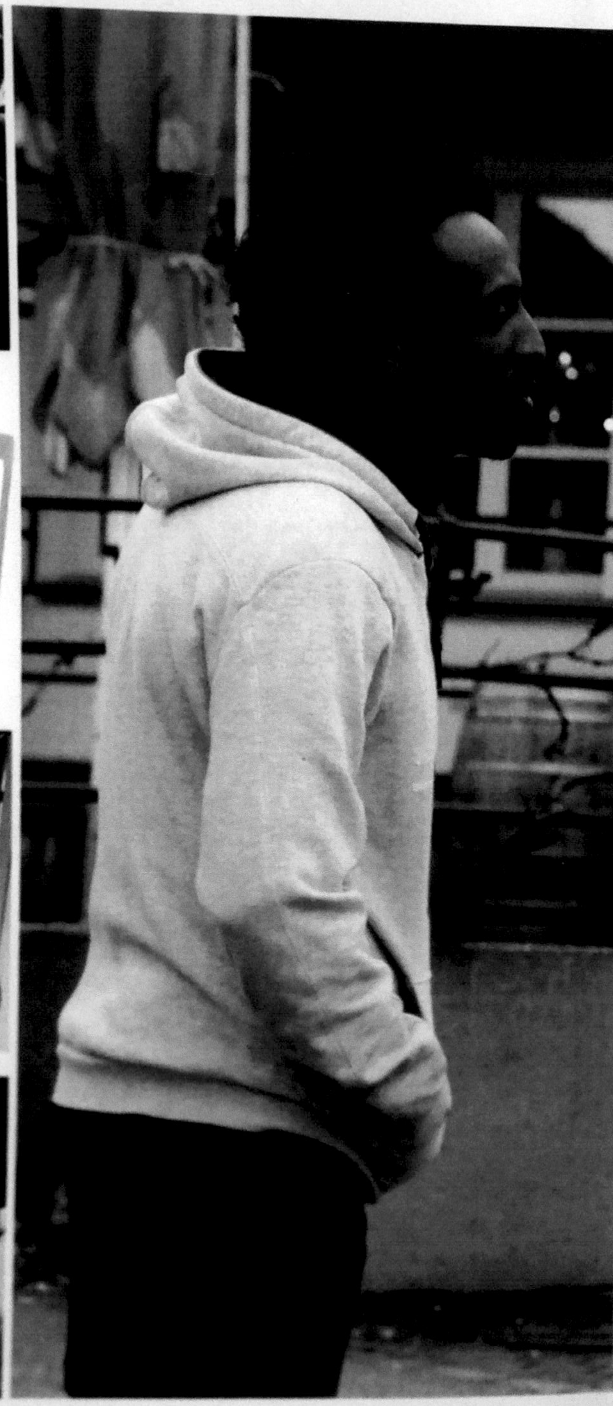

Filmon H. aus Eritrea

Hallo! Ich heisse Filmon H. und bin 28 Jahre alt. Ich komme aus Asmara, der Hauptstadt von Eritrea. Ich habe eine Frau und eine Tochter. Ich lebe mit meiner Familie seit 2014 in Neftenbach. Meine Frau ist in der selben Strasse wie ich in Asmara aufgewachsen. Als ich von Italien in die Schweiz gekommen bin, gab es einen Konflikt zwischen den beiden Ländern, deshalb musste ich 17 Monate ins Gefängnis. Ich habe mein neugeborenes Kind erst gesehen, nachdem ich aus dem Gefängnis entlassen wurde. Im Gefängnis wollte ich arbeiten, aber dies war nicht möglich. Es ist nicht einfach, im Gefängnis einen Job zu bekommen. Am Ende konnte ich doch ein bisschen arbeiten, das war sehr gut. Ohne Arbeit und Aktivitäten lebt man dort wie ein Hund – man isst und schläft nur.

In Asmara...

...habe ich mit zwei Brüdern, zwei Schwestern und meiner Mutter gelebt. Morgens haben wir viel geredet und meine Mutter erzählte uns gerne Witze. Wir haben immer viel gelacht. Ich lebte mit meiner Familie in einem kleinen Haus. Wir hatten zwei Schlafzimmer, eins für die Jungen und eins für die Mädchen. Dazwischen hatten wir ein Wohnzimmer und eine Küche, eine Toilette und ein kleines Haus für den Hund. Zwischen der Strasse und dem Gebäude war ein Garten. Eritrea war eine italienische Kolonie, was einen grossen Einfluss auf die Architektur in Asmara hatte.
Ich ging zur Schule bis ich 17 Jahre alt war, also bis in die 11. Klasse. Dann begann ich als Händler zu arbeiten. Mein Arbeitstag startete um 4 Uhr morgens und endete etwa um 5 Uhr abends, montags bis freitags. Ich reiste oft zwischen den Städten hin und her. An den Wochenenden gingen wir ins Kino, schauten Fussballspiele oder gingen einfach in die Stadt. Es gibt verschiedene Religionen in Eritrea, aber es gibt keine religiösen Konflikte. Jeder lebt neben jedem. Die Frauen müssen auch ins Militär gehen, diese Pflicht mag niemand. Ich habe Eritrea 2011 verlassen, um nicht Militärdienst leisten zu müssen. Ich bin viel herumgereist, habe versucht, in verschiedenen Nachbarländern zu arbeiten, aber ich habe nie ein Visum bekommen. Nach mehreren Jahren der Anstrengung und vielen Monaten im Gefängnis - wegen meines illegalen Status - habe ich entschieden, nach Europa zu kommen.

In Neftenbach...

...leben wir in einer Attika-Wohnung. Die Wohnung ist super. Der offene Dachstuhl ist für uns ungewohnt, daran müssen wir uns noch gewöhnen. Am Tag spiele ich mit meiner Tochter, da ich nichts anderes zu tun habe. Wir essen, schlafen, essen, schlafen - wir leben wie Hunde. Ich frage Herrn Wuffli (Sozialvorsteher Gemeinde Neftenbach) immer nach Arbeit - sogar ohne Lohn, aber es gibt nichts zu tun. Es ist nicht möglich. Ich warte immer noch auf den Asylbescheid. Ohne positiven Bescheid darf ich nicht arbeiten. Ich liebe die Liebe und nicht das Geld.

Du kannst die Zukunft...

...nicht sehen, wenn du keine Gegenwart hast! Meine Gegenwart hier ist ungewiss. Ich warte immer noch auf die Entscheidung: JA oder NEIN. Diese Ungewissheit, beeinflusst mein tägliches Leben. Diese Antwort könnte ich jeden Tag bekommen, aber ich warte jetzt schon seit Monaten.

Filmon H. from Eritrea

Hello! My name is Filmon H., I am 28 years old. I'm from Asmara, the capital city of Eritrea. I have a wife and a daughter. I have been living with my family in Neftenbach since 2014. My wife grew up in the same street in Asmara like me. When I came from Italy to Switzerland, there was a conflict between these two countries, so I had to go to jail for 17 months. I first got to see my newborn child when I was discharged from jail. In the jail I wanted to work, but this was not possible. It is not easy to get a job in the jail. At the end I managed to get some job and work, this was very good. Without work and activities you live there like a dog - you only eat and sleep.

In Asmara...

...I lived with two brothers, two sisters, and my mother. In the morning we talked a lot and my mother used to tell us jokes. We always laughed a lot. I lived with my family in a small house. We had two bedrooms, one for the boys and one for the girls. In between we had a living room and a kitchen, a toilette and a small house for the dog. Between the street and the house there was a garden. Eritrea was an Italian colony which had a great impact on the architecture in Asmara.
I went to school until I was 17 years old, so until 11th grade. Then I began to work as a merchant. My workday started at 4 o'clock in the morning and ended around 5 o'clock in the evening, Monday to Friday. I often traveled from city to city. On the weekend we went to cinemas, watched soccer matches, or simply went to the city. There are different religions in Eritrea, but there are no religious conflicts. Everybody lives in peace next to the other. Women also have to give military service, nobody likes this duty. I left Eritrea in 2011, to not have to go to the army. I traveled around, tried to find work in various neighboring countries, but I never got a visa. After several years of effort and many months in jail -because of my illegal status-, I decided to come to Europe.

In Neftenbach...

...We live in an attic-flat. The flat is great, the only unfamiliar thing that we have to get used to is the open roof framework. During the day I play with my daughter, as I do not have anything else to do. We eat, sleep, eat, sleep - we live like dogs. I always ask Mr. Wuffli (Social Management Neftenbach) for work -even without salary-, but there is nothing to do. It is not possible. I am still waiting for my asylum report. Without a positive report I am not allowed to work. I love the love and not the money.

You cannot see the future...

...if you do not have a present! My status here is uncertain. I am still waiting for the decision: YES or NO. This uncertainty influences my everyday life. The answer can arrive any day but I have already been waiting for it for months now.

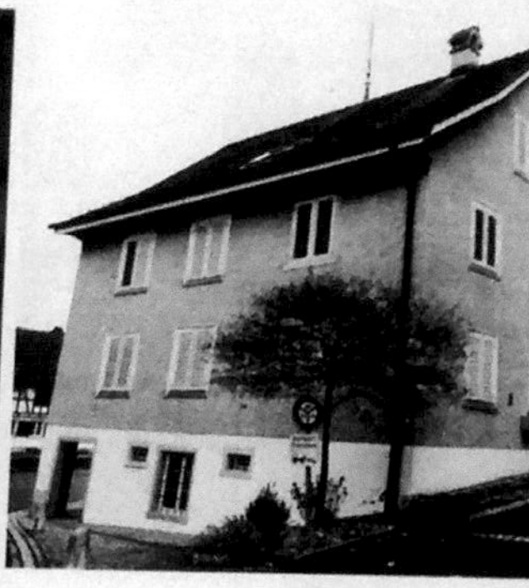

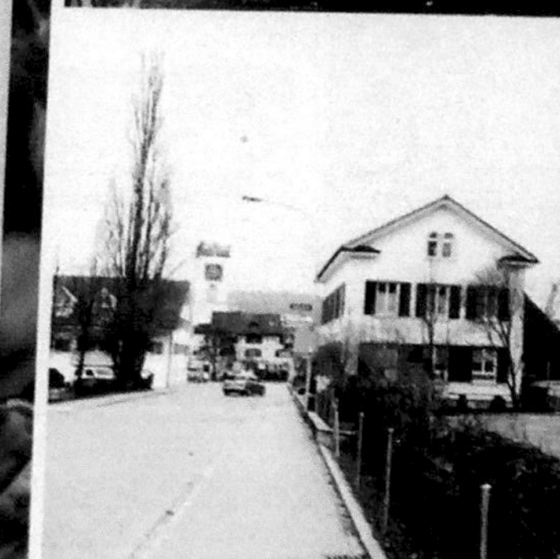

«Ich liebe die Lieb
und
nicht das Geld.»

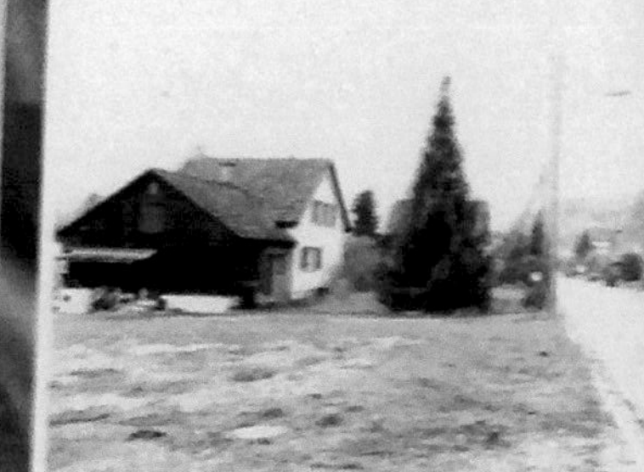

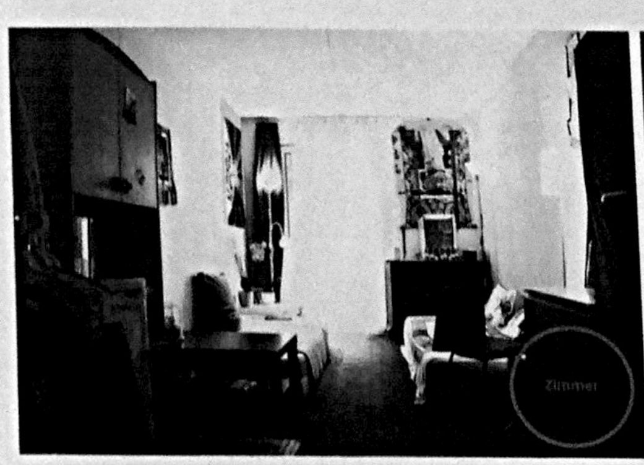

«Heimat bedeutet für mich die Beziehung zu Menschen. Es bedeutet, sich umeinander zu kümmern und füreinander da zu sein.»

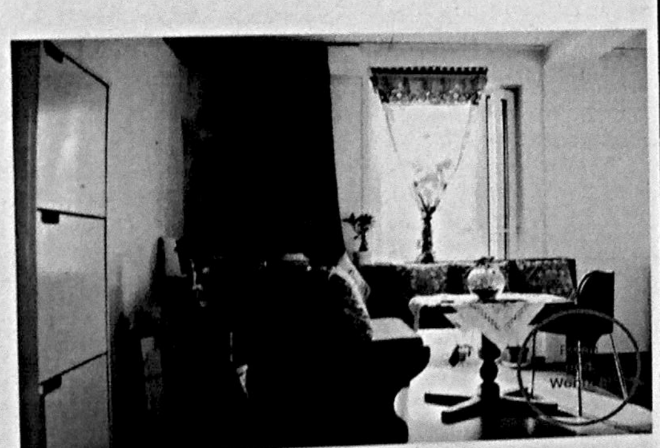

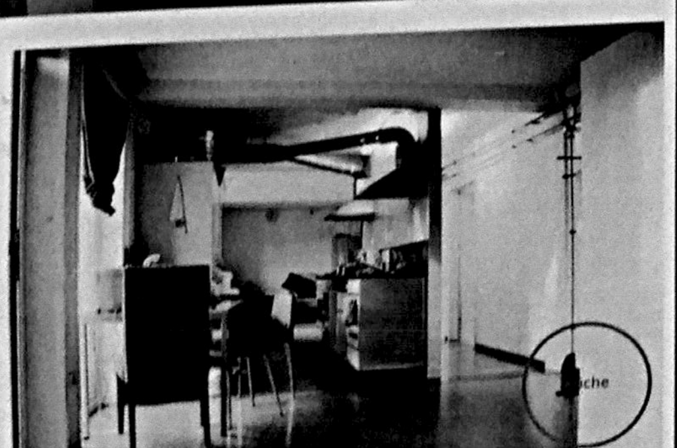

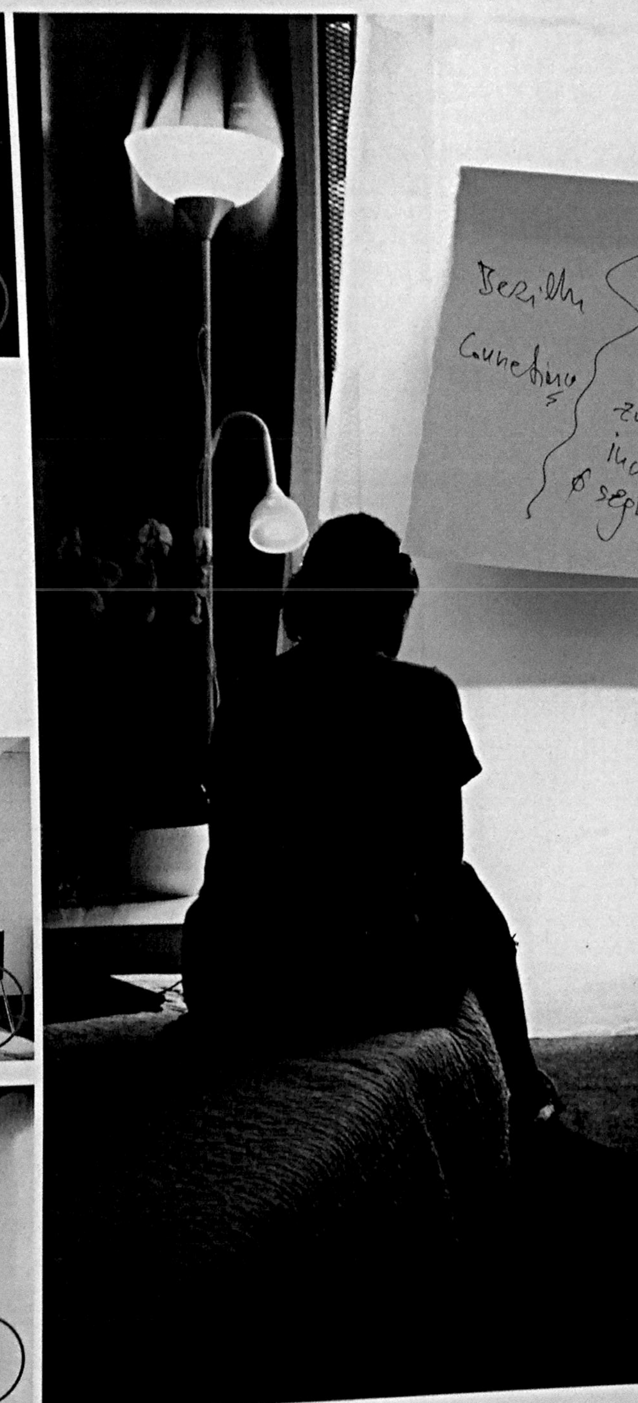

Tashi Lhamo aus Tibet

Hallo, mein Name ist Tashi Lhamo, ich bin 24 Jahre alt und komme aus einem kleinen Dorf aus Tibet. Ich bin 2015 alleine in die Schweiz ausgewandert. Anfangs war … ver, in der Asylunterkunft mit so … hen Kulturen zusammenzuleben, … rstand man sich immer besser, ak… tierte sich gegenseitig. Wir merkten … neinsame Bedürfnisse haben und … r näher gebracht. Mittlerweile woh… ren Asylunterkunft; zu den neuen … e ich ebenfalls eine gute Beziehung … sellige Person, die gerne Menschen … paar Monaten arbeite ich in einem … rich und bin fleissig am Deutsch ler… ht die B2 Deutschprüfung an. Ich … regt und hoffe, dass ich sie bestehen

… m mit meiner Familie in einem … d Umschwung gelebt. Die Nach… nicht in unmittelbarer Nähe, trotz… Kontakt. Wir haben uns oft … en gegessen, kümmerten uns umeinander und waren füreinander da. Der Kontakt war unkompliziert. Man hat sich besucht, ohne einen Termin zu vereinbaren, ging einfach ins Haus ohne zu klopfen oder klingeln. Ich bin es nicht gewohnt, alleine zu leben. Mir sind eine gute Nachbarschaft und das Zusammenleben wichtig.

In den ersten drei Monaten...

...wohnte ich an der Regensbergstrasse in Oerlikon in einem Asylheim. Im August 2016 bin ich in die Asylunterkunft hier an der Aargauerstrasse nach Zürich gezogen. Es sind mehrere Container mit je 4 Zimmern, die unterschiedlich belegt sind. In meiner Wohnung leben neben mir noch drei Familien. Mit ihnen teile ich die Küche, den Wohn- und Essbereich sowie das Bad und WC. Mein Zimmer teile ich mir mit einer weiteren Person. Viel Platz habe ich nicht, aber ich verstehe mich sehr gut mit meinen Nachbarn, wir kümmern uns umeinander und sind für einander da. Ich habe auch Kontakt zur restlichen Nachbarschaft der Asylunterkunft. Im Sommer spielen wir hin und wieder Tischtennis oder man trifft sich in der Waschküche und unterhält sich. Es ist wichtig, solche Orte zu haben, an denen man sich spontan und zufällig treffen kann ohne sich verabreden zu müssen.
Bisher beschränkt sich meine neue Heimat auf die Aargauerstrasse, ich wünsche mir aber, dass sich dies ändert. Es ist schwierig, Kontakt zu Einheimischen zu knüpfen, da hier viele nur zur Arbeit gehen und nicht hier wohnen. Man trifft viel seltener Menschen auf der Strasse, als es in Oerlikon der Fall war.

Für meine Zukunft...

...wünsche ich mir, hier bleiben zu dürfen. Dann würde ich gerne in einer gemeinschaftlichen Nachbarschaft wohnen. In einer Nachbarschaft, in der man sich gegenseitig umeinander sorgt, wo man Beziehungen aufbauen kann und füreinander da ist. Ich hätte gerne eine eigene Wohnung, ohne das Gefühl zu haben, dass ich alleine bin.

Tashi Lhamo from Tibet

Hello. My name is Tashi Lhamo, I am 24 years old and I come from a small town in Tibet. In 2015, I migrated to Switzerland on my own. In the beginning, at the asylum centre, I found it very difficult to live together with so many different cultures, but over time we were getting along better and better and started accepting and respecting each other. We soon realized that we have the same needs and that brought us closer to each other. Nowadays I live in another asylum centre and I have a good relationship with my new housemates, too. I am a very sociable person and like having people around me. For a couple of months I have been working at a home for the elderly and I am busy studying German. Soon I will be taking the B2-level test. I am already quite nervous and hope I will pass it successfully.

Tibet...

Back in my hometown, I used to live with my family in a big house on a large land. Our neighbours were not within close distance, but we had a good relationship with them. We used to get together often and share meals, we cared about and supported each other. The relationship with them was uncomplicated. We would visit each other without previously setting an appointment; we would just go into the house without ringing the bell or knocking on the door. I am not used to living alone. A good neighbourhood and a community are very important to me.

In the first three months...

When I came to Switzerland in 2015, I lived the first three months at an asylum centre at the Regensbergstrasse in Oerlikon. In August 2016, I moved to Zurich to the asylum centre at the Aargauerstrasse. There are several shared flats, each one with four rooms, which are diversely occupied. Families as well as single people from different cultures are living together. I live in my shared flat with three families. We share the kitchen, the living room and dining area, as well as the bathroom and the toilet. I share my room with another single person. I do not have much space, but I get along very well with my flatmates. We care about and support each other. I have good relationships within the neighbourhood at the centre. During the summer, we play ping-pong, meet at the community laundry and chat. It is important to have such spaces where people meet spontaneously or bump into each other, without having to pre-arrange.
So far now, my new home has been limited to the center on Aargauerstrasse, but I wish this changed. It is difficult to get in touch with locals, because when they come here, it is for work and they do not live here. Around the centre there are not many people in the streets as it was the case in Oerlikon.

What comes next?...

If I was allowed to stay here I could choose how to live in the future. I would like to be able to live in a community. In a neighbourhood built upon close relationships, where everyone cares about and helps each other. I would like to have my own flat without feeling lonely.

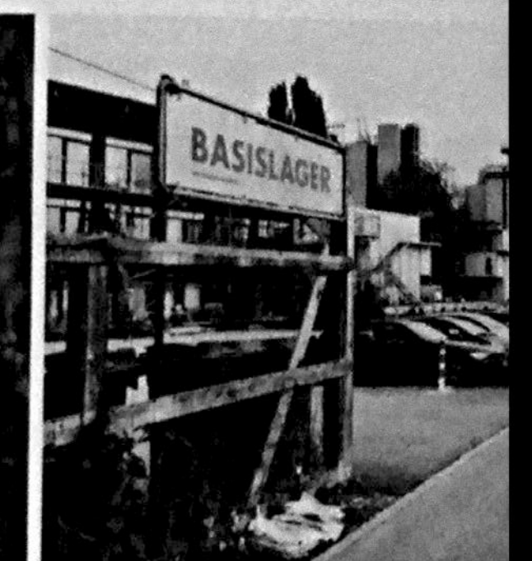

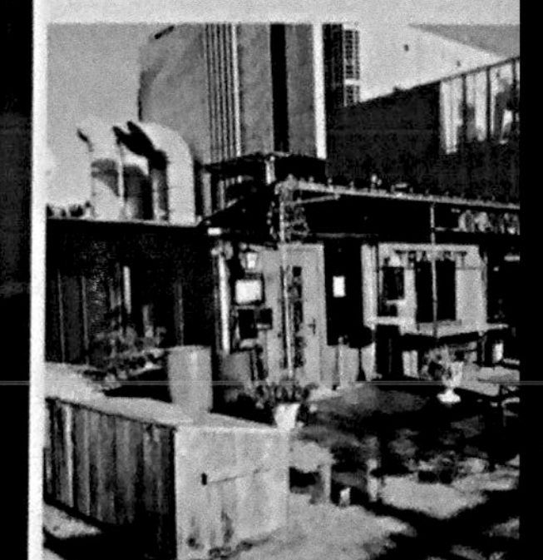

«Dort zu wo…
wo auch andere w…
nicht nur zur Arbeit…
wäre mein Wu…

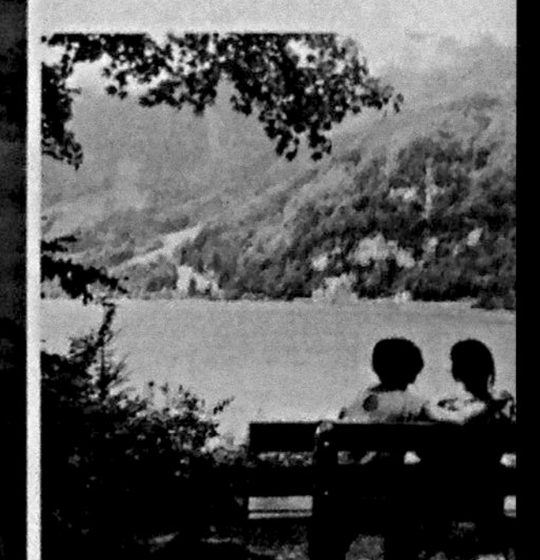

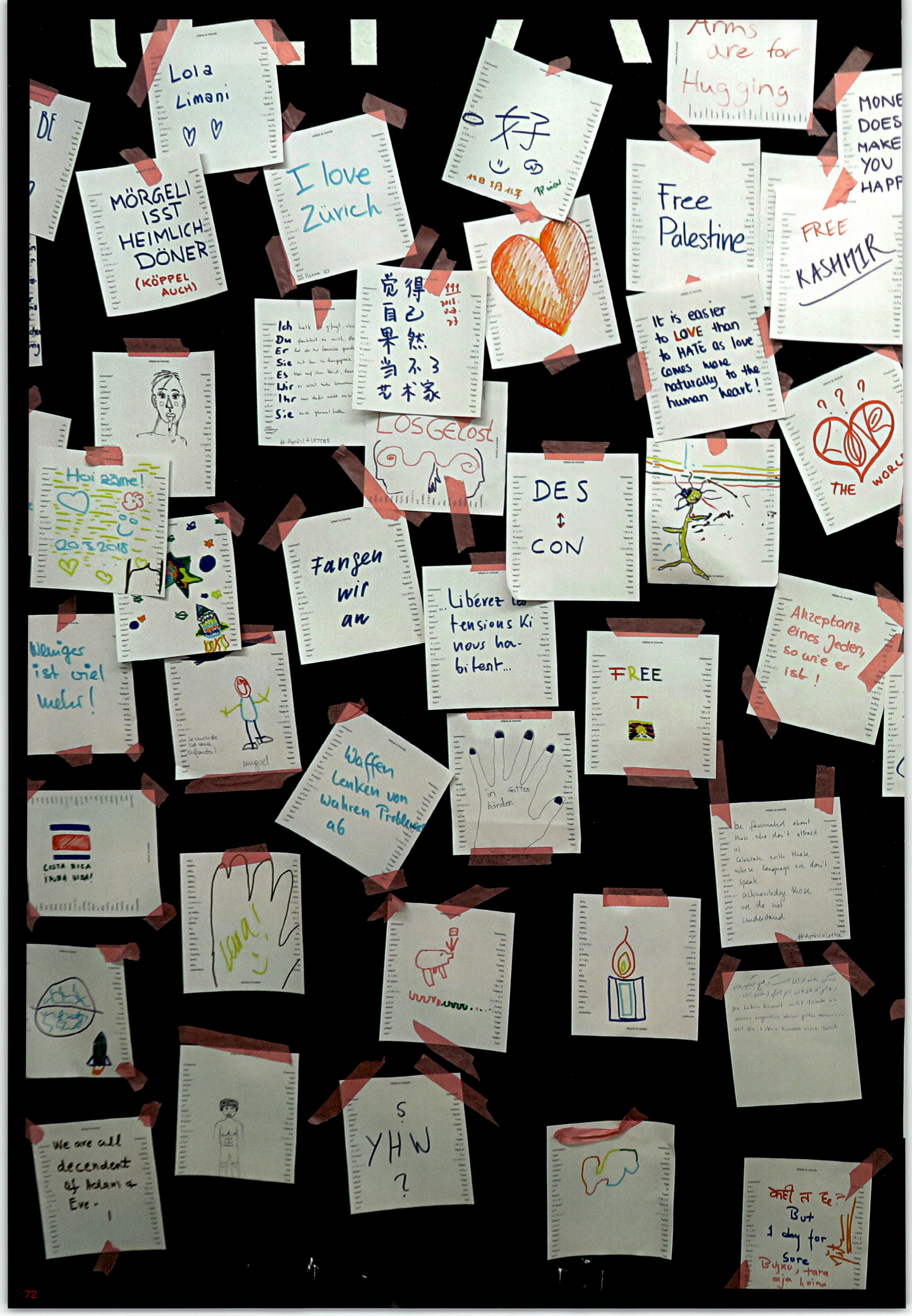
Lola Limani
I love Zürich
Arms are for Hugging
MÖRGELI ISST HEIMLICH DÖNER (KÖPPEL AUCH)
Free Palestine
FREE KASHMIR
It is easier to LOVE than to HATE as love comes more naturally to the human heart!
LOSGELÖST
DES ↕ CON
Hoi zäme!
Fangen wir an
Libérez les tensions Ki nous ha-bitent...
Akzeptanz eines Jeden, so wie er ist!
Weniger ist viel mehr!
FREE T
Waffen lenken von wahren Problemen ab
in Gottes händen
COSTA RICA PURA VIDA!
We are all decendent of Adam & Eve.
YHW ?
But 1 day for sore

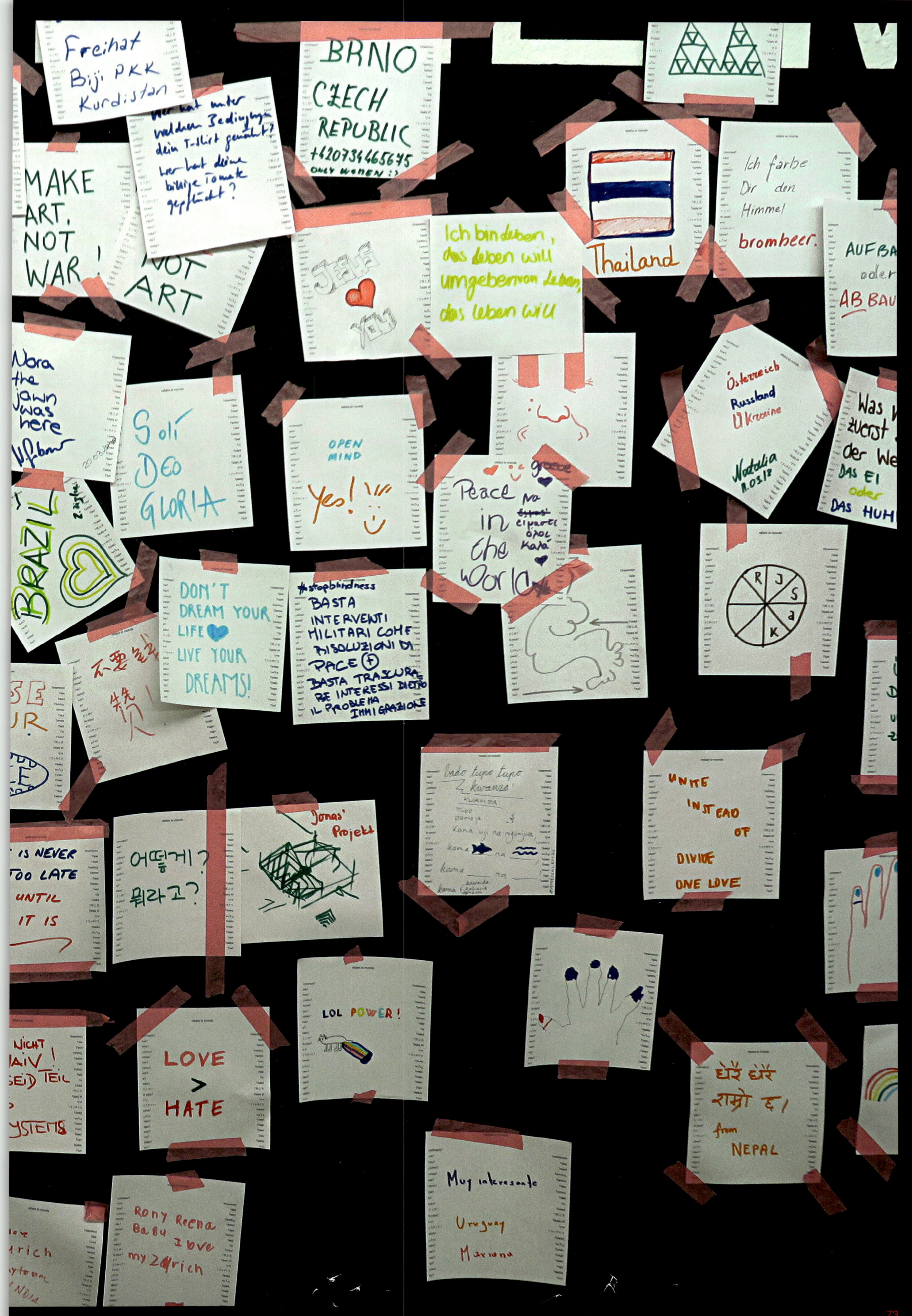
Freihat
Biji PKK
Kurdistan
BRNO
CZECH
REPUBLIC
MAKE
ART,
NOT
WAR!
NOT
ART
Ich farbe
Dir den
Himmel
brombeer.
Thailand
Ich bin das Leben,
das leben will
umgeben von Leben,
das Leben will
AUFBAU
oder
ABBAU
Soli
Deo
Gloria
OPEN
MIND
Yes!
Österreich
Russland
Ukraine
Natalia
Peace
in
the
World
greece
BRAZIL
DON'T
DREAM YOUR
LIFE
LIVE YOUR
DREAMS!
#stopblindness
BASTA
INTERVENTI
MILITARI COME
RISOLUZIONI DI
PACE
BASTA TRASCURARE INTERESSI DIETRO
IL PROBLEMA IMMIGRAZIONE
UNITE
INSTEAD
OF
DIVIDE
ONE LOVE
IT IS NEVER
TOO LATE
UNTIL
IT IS
어떻게?
뭐라고?
Jonas' Projekt
LOL POWER!
LOVE
>
HATE
from
NEPAL
Muy interesante
Uruguay
Mariana
Rony Reena
Babu I love
my Zürich

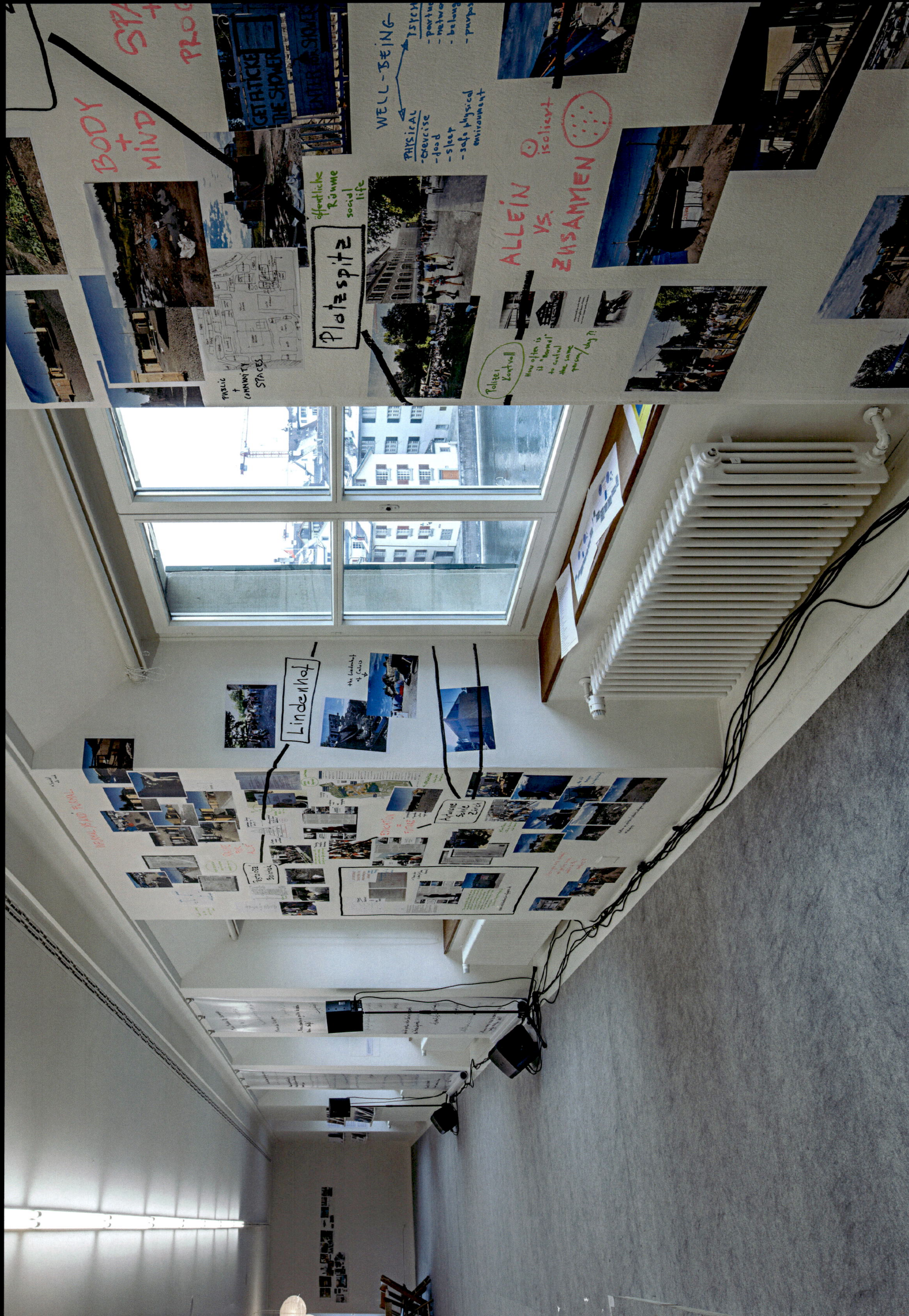
BODY + MIND
WELL-BEING
ALLEIN VS. ZUSAMMEN
Platzspitz
Lindenhof

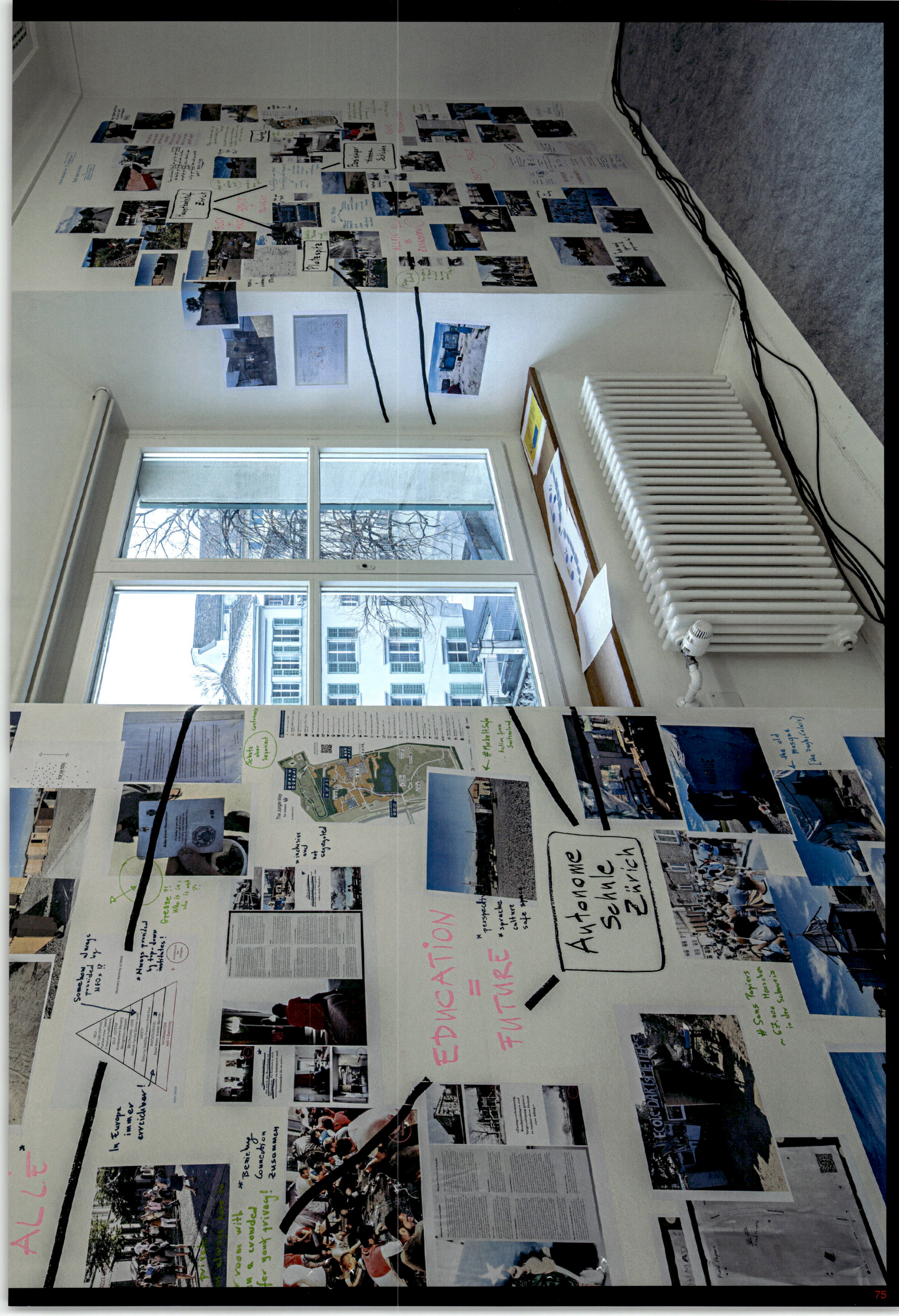
Autonome Schule Zürich
EDUCATION = FUTURE

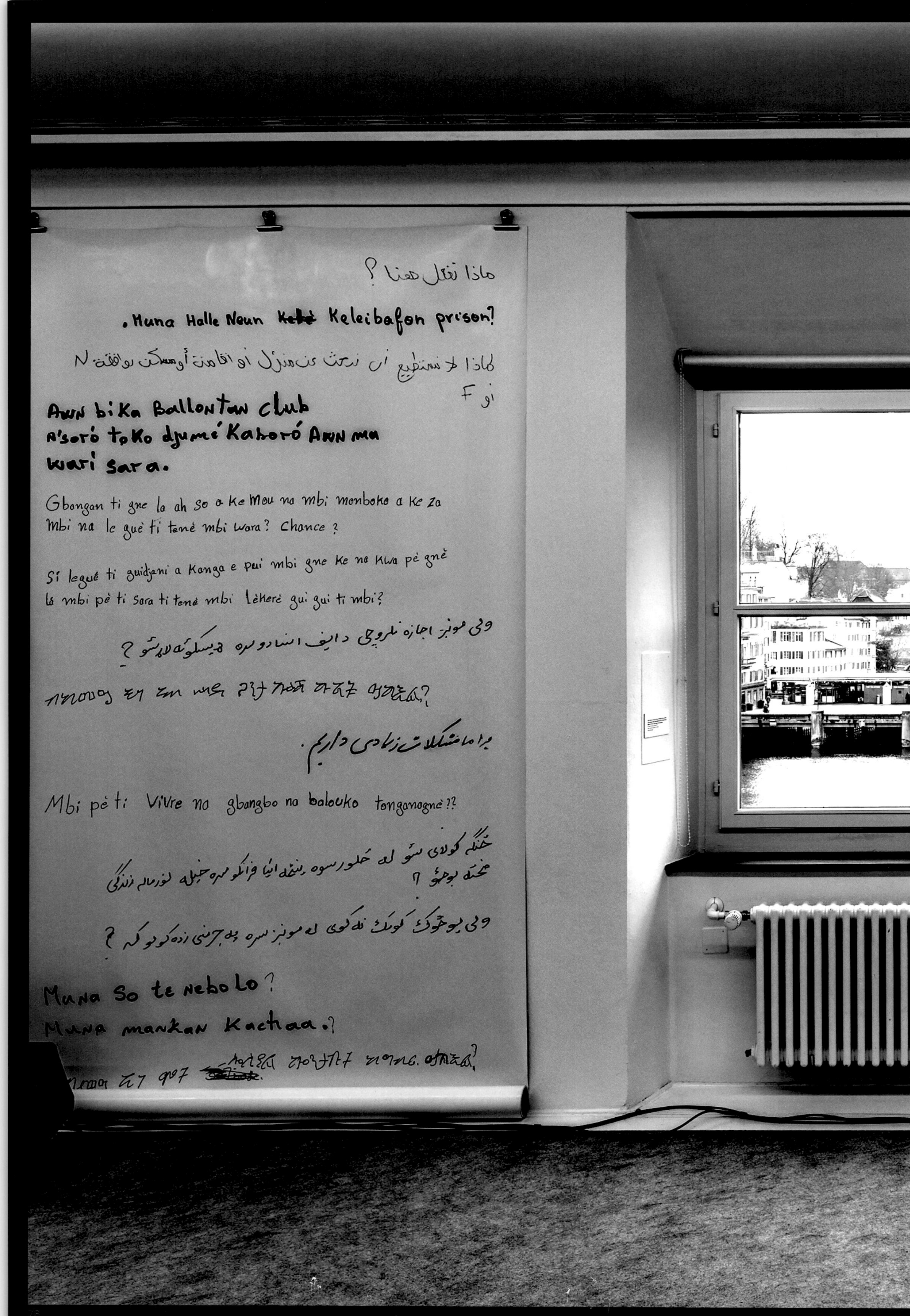
ماذا تفعل هنا ؟
Muna Halle Neun Keleibafon prison?
Gbongan ti gne la ah so a ke Mou na mbi monboko a ke za
Mbi na le guè ti tené mbi wara? Chance?
Si legué ti guidjani a Konga e pui mbi gne ke na kwa pè gnè
la mbi pè ti sara ti tené mbi lèkere gui gui ti mbi?
Mbi pè ti vivre na gbangbo na balouko tonganognè??
Muna so te nebo lo?
Muna mankan kachaa.?

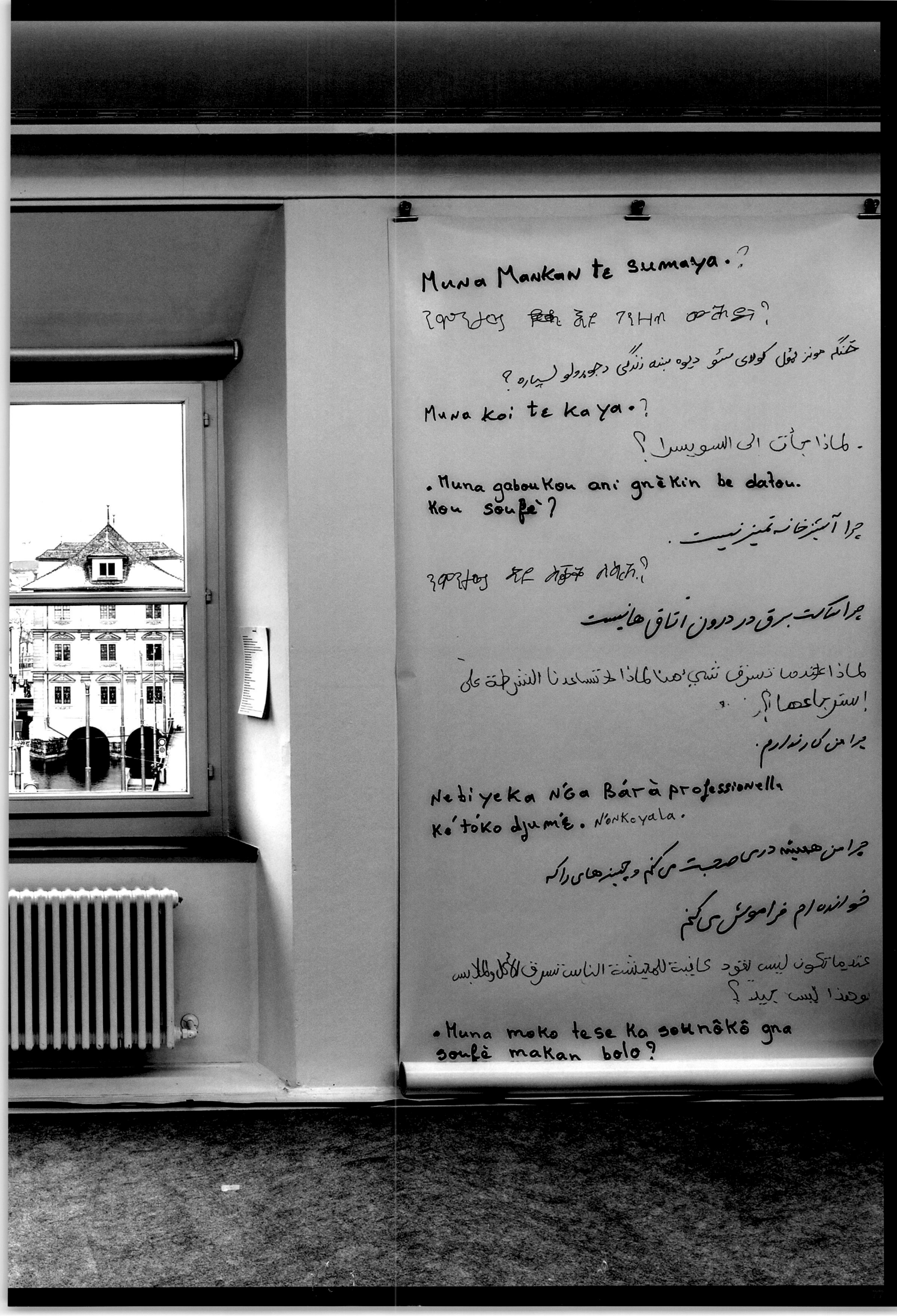
Muna Mankan te sumaya.?
چرا آشپزخانه تمیز نیست.
Muna koi te kaya.?
لماذا جئت الى السويسرا؟.
. Muna gaboukou ani gnèkin be datou.
Kou soufè?
چرا من کار ندارم.
Nebiyeka N'Ga Bárà professionella
Ko'toko djumè. N'onkoyala.
. Muna moko tese ka sounôkô gna
soufè makan bolo?

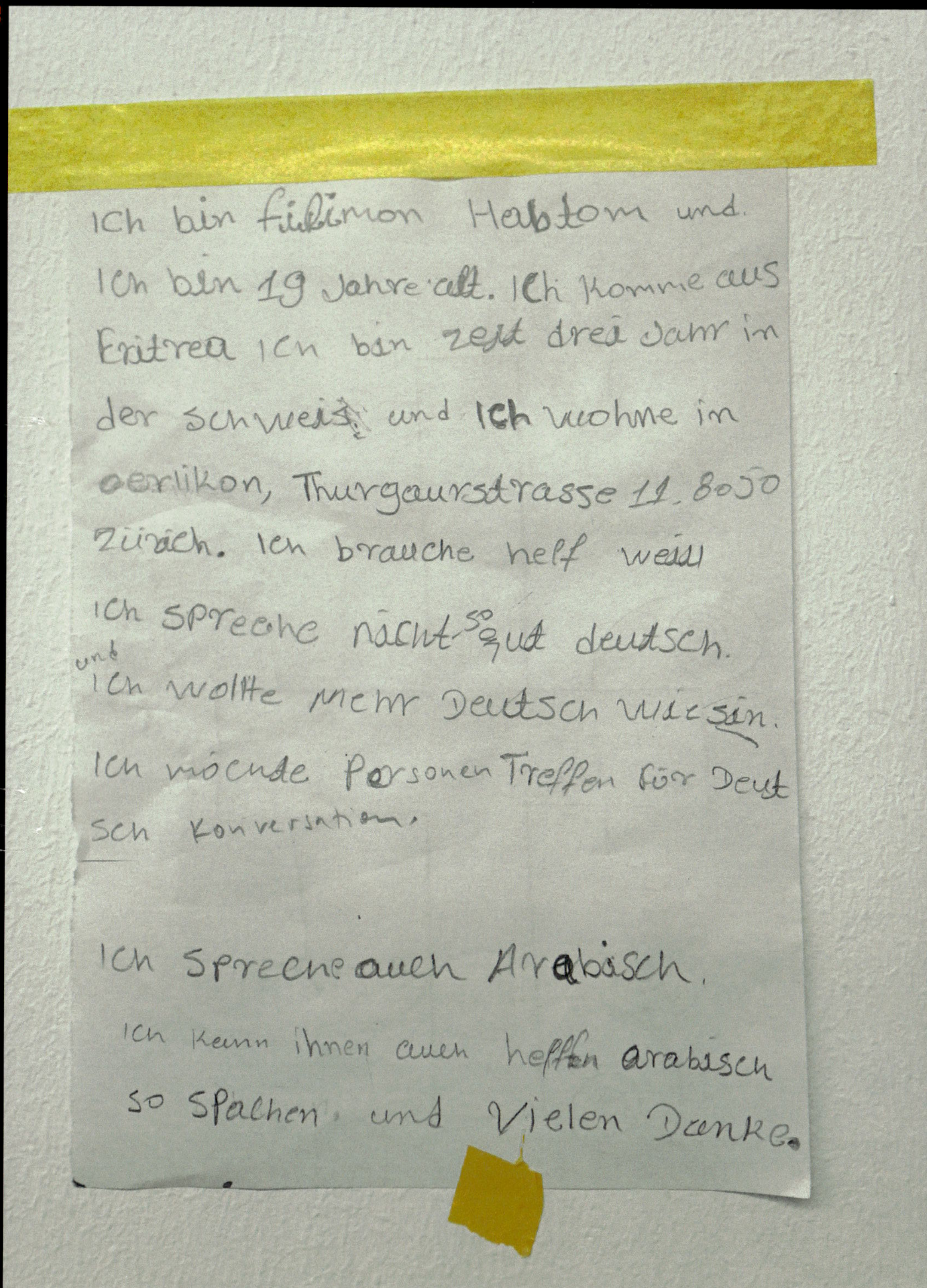
Ich bin fiilimon Habtom und.
Ich bin 19 Jahre alt. Ich komme aus
Eritrea Ich bin zeit drei Jahr in
der schweis und Ich wohne in
oerlikon, Thurgauerstrasse 11. 8050
Zürich. Ich brauche helf weill
Ich spreche nicht so gut deutsch.
und Ich wollte mehr Deutsch wissin.
Ich möchde Personen Treffen für Deut
sch Konversation.
Ich Sprecheauch Arabisch.
Ich Kenn ihnen auch helffen arabisch
so Spachen. und Vielen Danke.

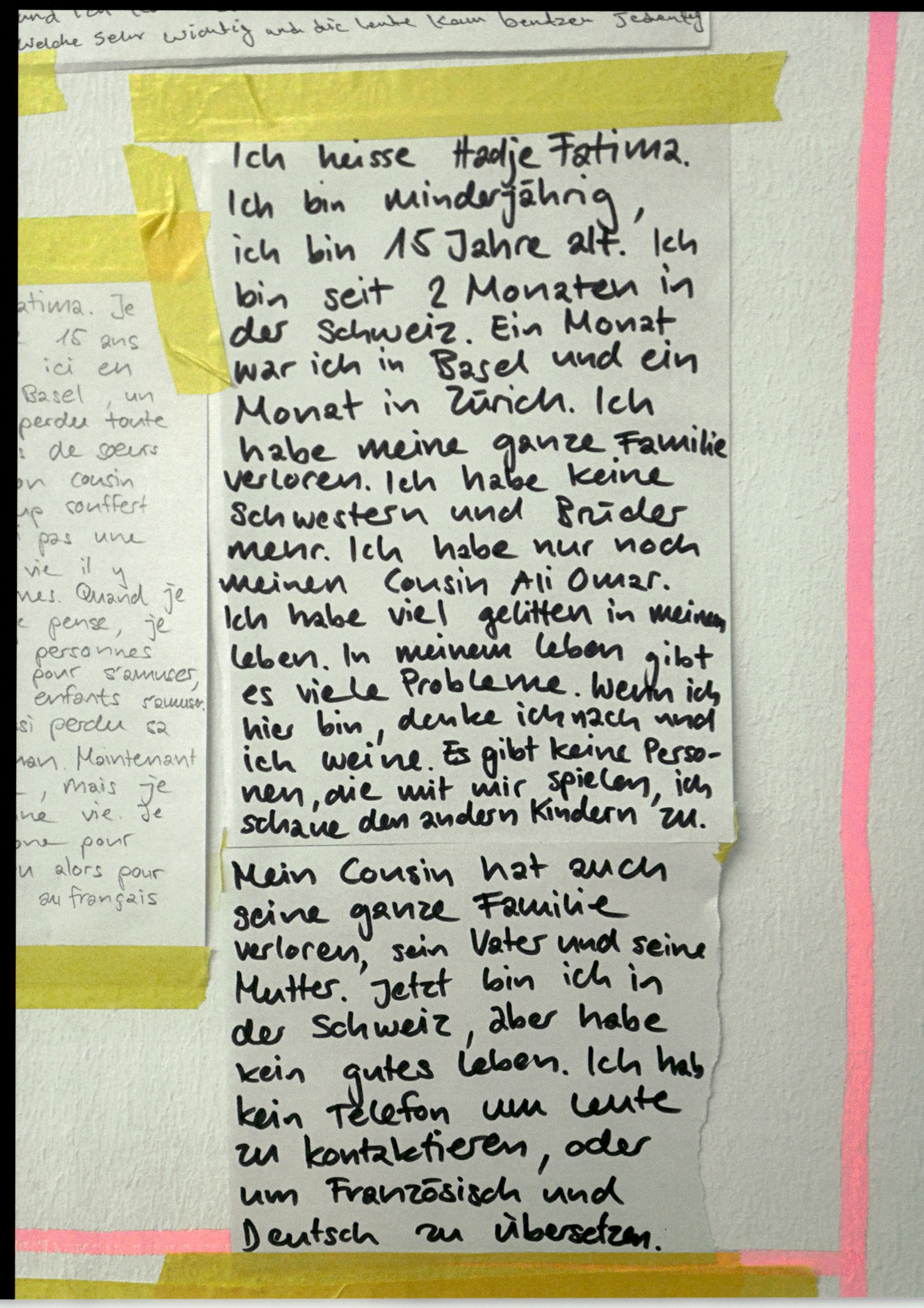
Ich heisse Hadje Fatima.
Ich bin minderjährig,
ich bin 15 Jahre alt. Ich
bin seit 2 Monaten in
der Schweiz. Ein Monat
war ich in Basel und ein
Monat in Zürich. Ich
habe meine ganze Familie
verloren. Ich habe keine
Schwestern und Brüder
mehr. Ich habe nur noch
meinen Cousin Ali Omar.
Ich habe viel gelitten in meinem
leben. In meinem leben gibt
es viele Probleme. Wenn ich
hier bin, denke ich nach und
ich weine. Es gibt keine Perso-
nen, die mit mir spielen, ich
schaue den andern Kindern zu.
Mein Cousin hat auch
seine ganze Familie
verloren, sein Vater und seine
Mutter. Jetzt bin ich in
der Schweiz, aber habe
kein gutes leben. Ich hab
kein Telefon um Leute
zu kontaktieren, oder
um Französisch und
Deutsch zu übersetzen.

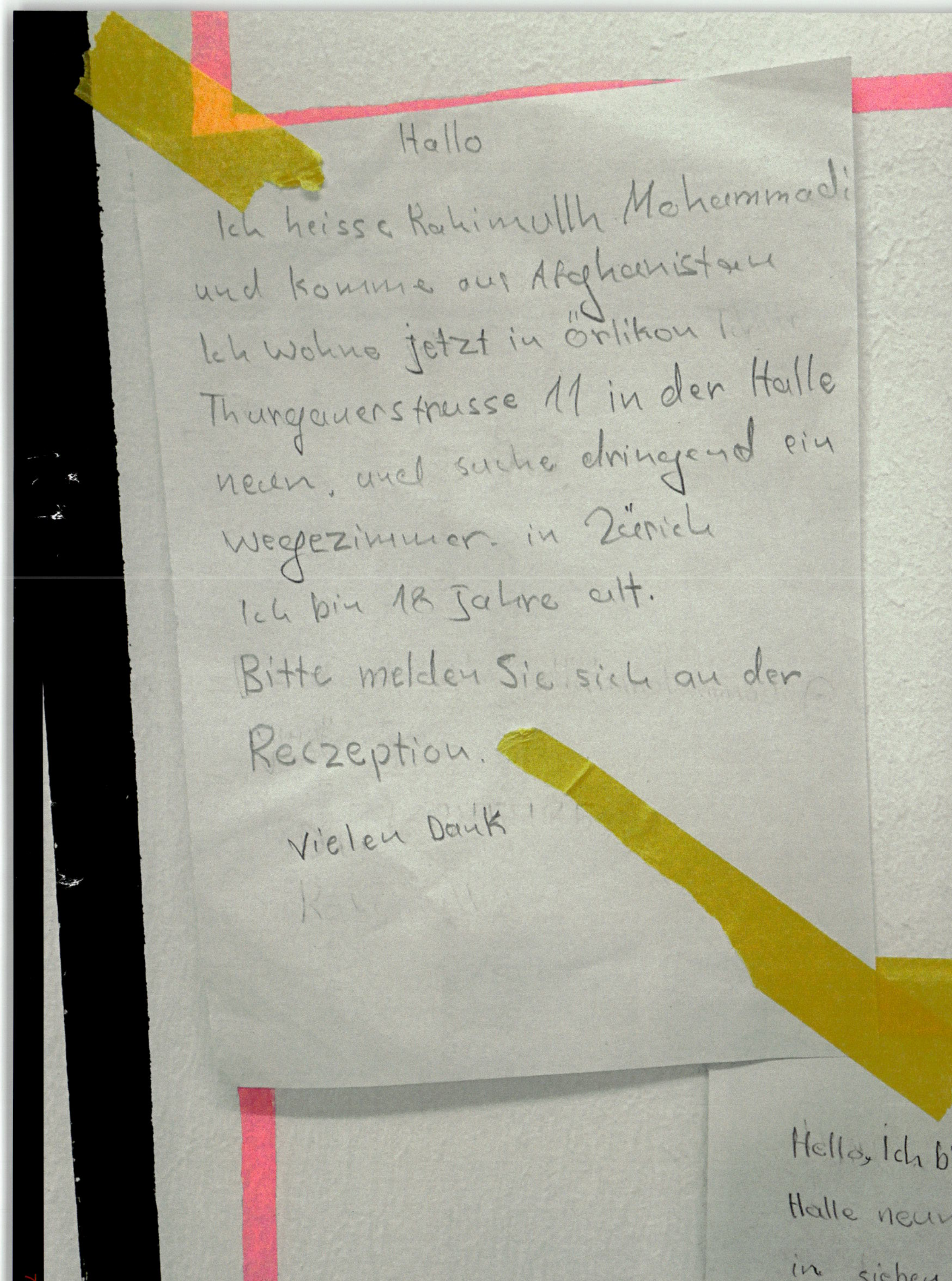
Hallo
Ich heisse Rahimullh Mohammadi
und komme aus Afghanistan
Ich wohne jetzt in Örlikon
Thurgauerstrasse 11 in der Halle
neun, und suche dringend ein
wegezimmer. in Zürich
Ich bin 18 Jahre alt.
Bitte melden Sie sich an der
Reczeption.
Vielen Dank
Hallo, Ich bi
Halle neun
in sieben

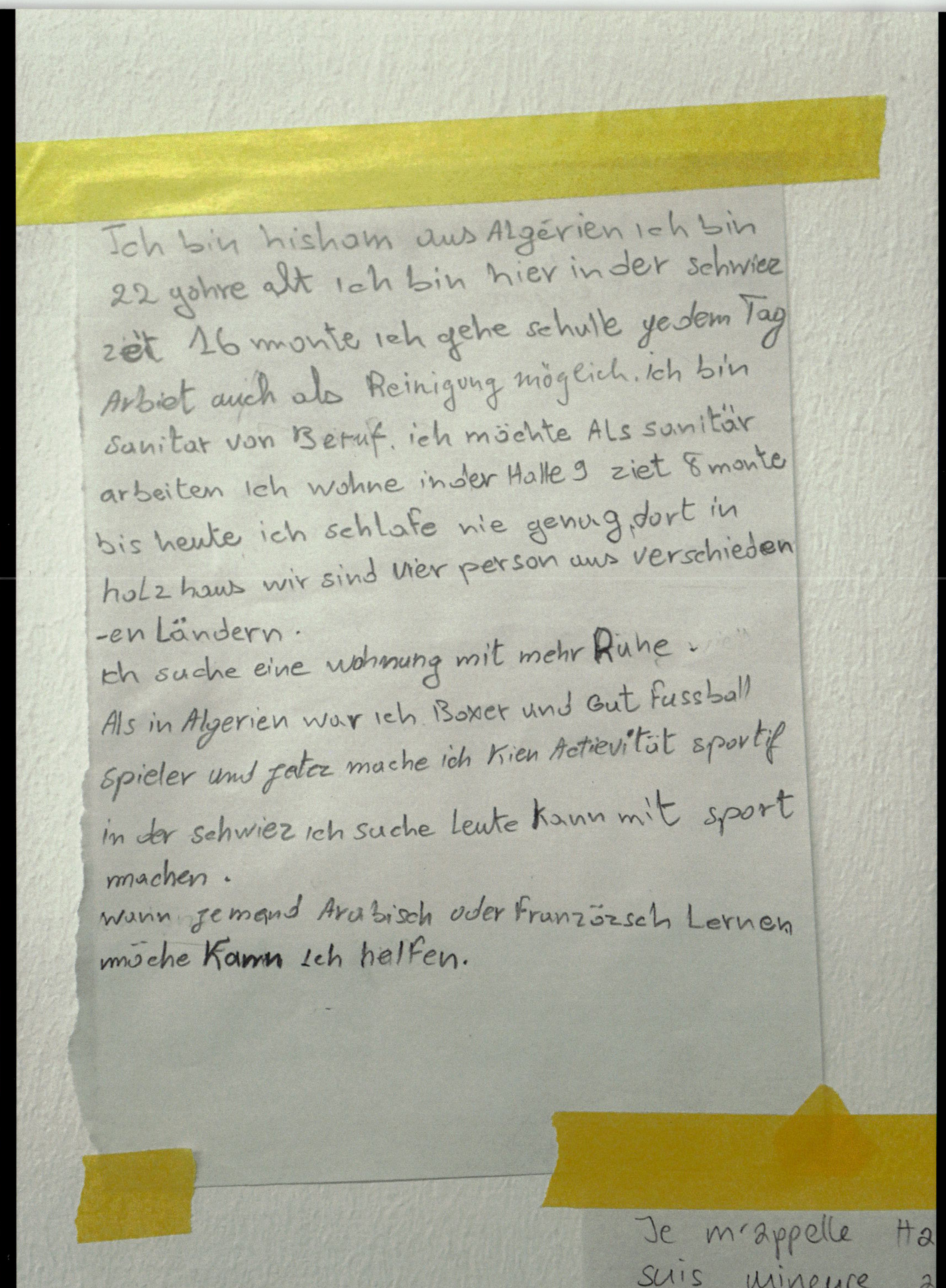
Ich bin hisham aus Algérien ich bin
22 yohre alt ich bin hier in der schwiez
zëit 16 monte ich gehe schulle yedem Tag
Arbiet auch als Reinigung mögeich. Ich bin
Sanitar von Beruf. ich möchte Als sanitär
arbeiten ich wohne in der Halle 9 ziet 8 monte
bis heute ich schlafe nie genug, dort in
holz haus wir sind vier person aus verschieden
-en Ländern.
Ich suche eine wohnung mit mehr Ruhe.
Als in Algerien war ich Boxer und Gut fussball
spieler und jetzt mache ich kien Actievität sportif
in der schwiez ich suche leute kann mit sport
machen.
wann jemand Arabisch oder Französch Lernen
möche Kann ich helfen.
Je m'appelle Ha
suis mineure

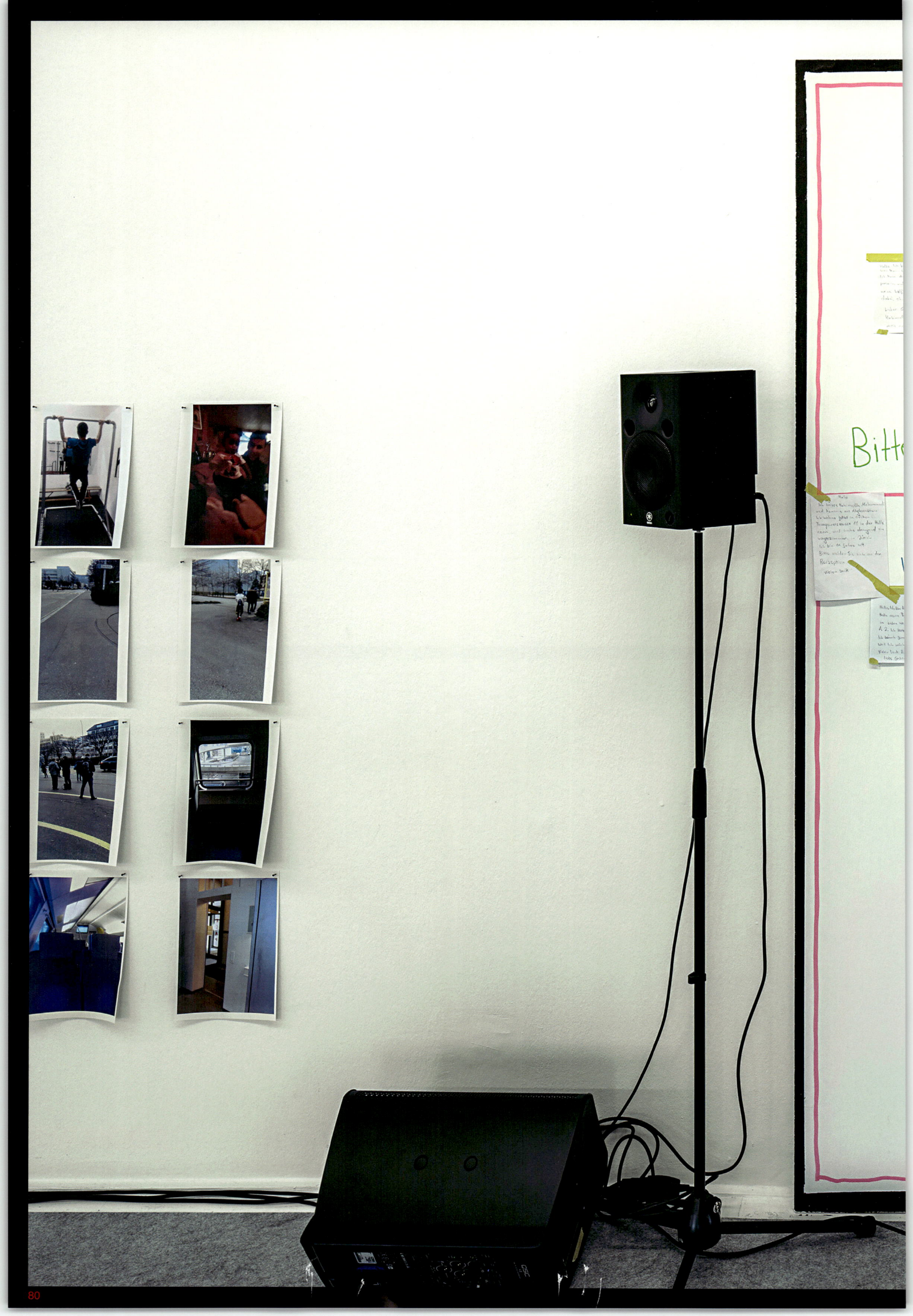

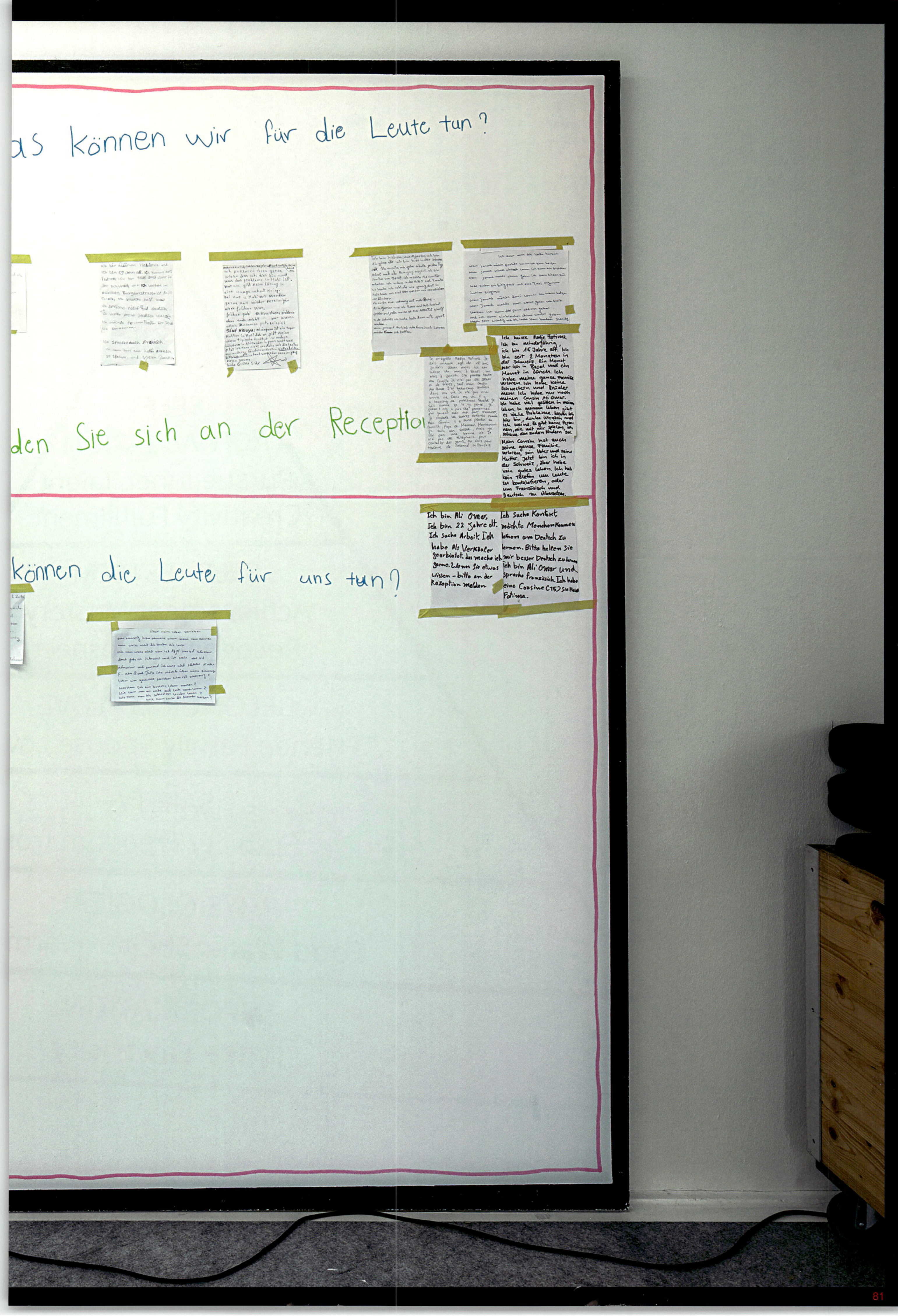
as können wir für die Leute tun?
den Sie sich an der Receptio
können die Leute für uns tun?

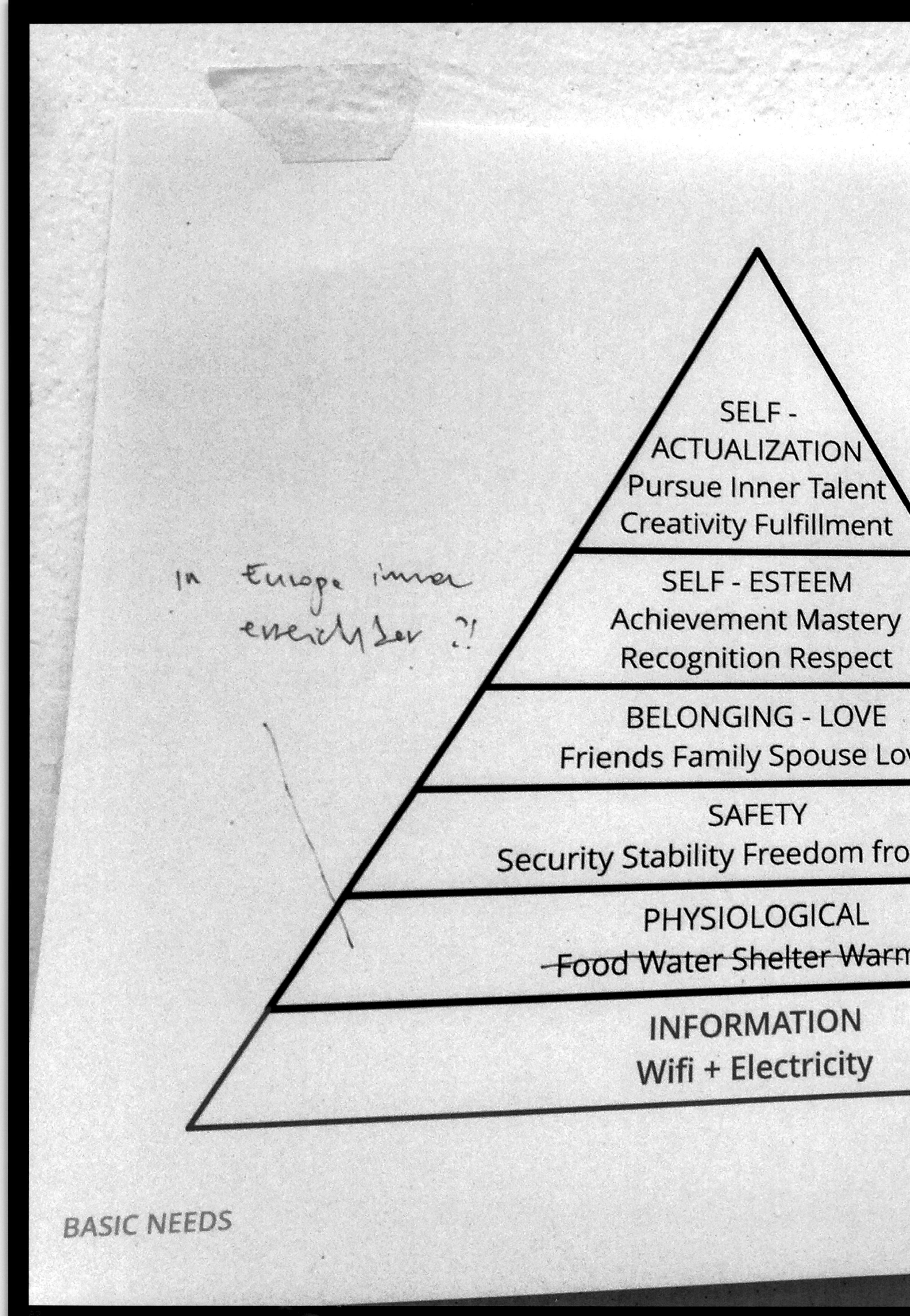
SELF - ACTUALIZATION
Pursue Inner Talent
Creativity Fulfillment
SELF - ESTEEM
Achievement Mastery
Recognition Respect
BELONGING - LOVE
Friends Family Spouse
SAFETY
Security Stability Freedom
PHYSIOLOGICAL
Food Water Shelter Warm
INFORMATION
Wifi + Electricity
In Europe immer
erreichbar ?!
BASIC NEEDS

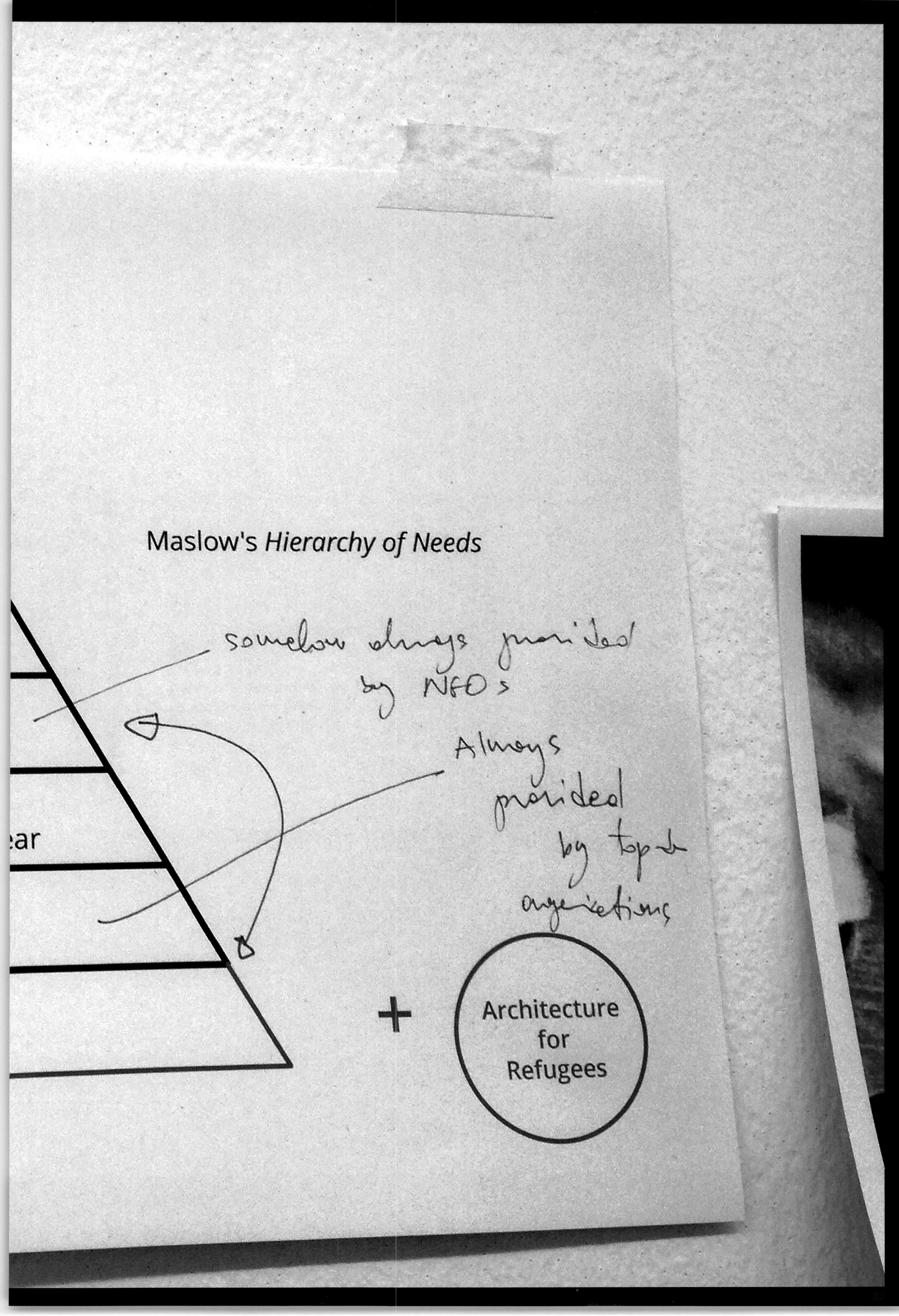
Maslow's *Hierarchy of Needs*
ear
+
Architecture for Refugees

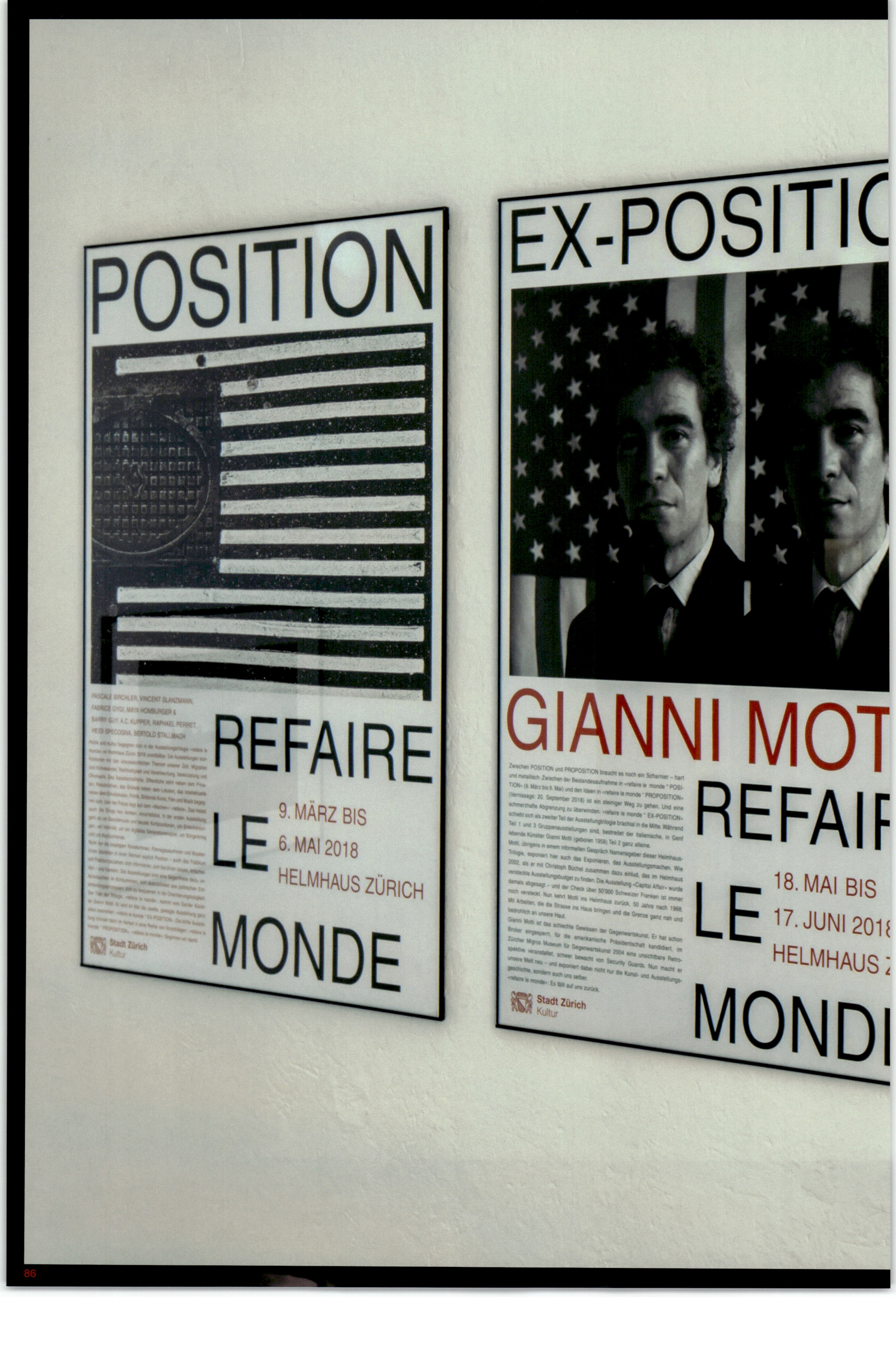
POSITION
REFAIRE
LE
MONDE
9. MÄRZ BIS
6. MAI 2018
HELMHAUS ZÜRICH
Stadt Zürich
Kultur
EX-POSITIO
GIANNI MOT
REFAIR
LE
MONDI
18. MAI BIS
17. JUNI 2018
HELMHAUS Z
Stadt Zürich
Kultur

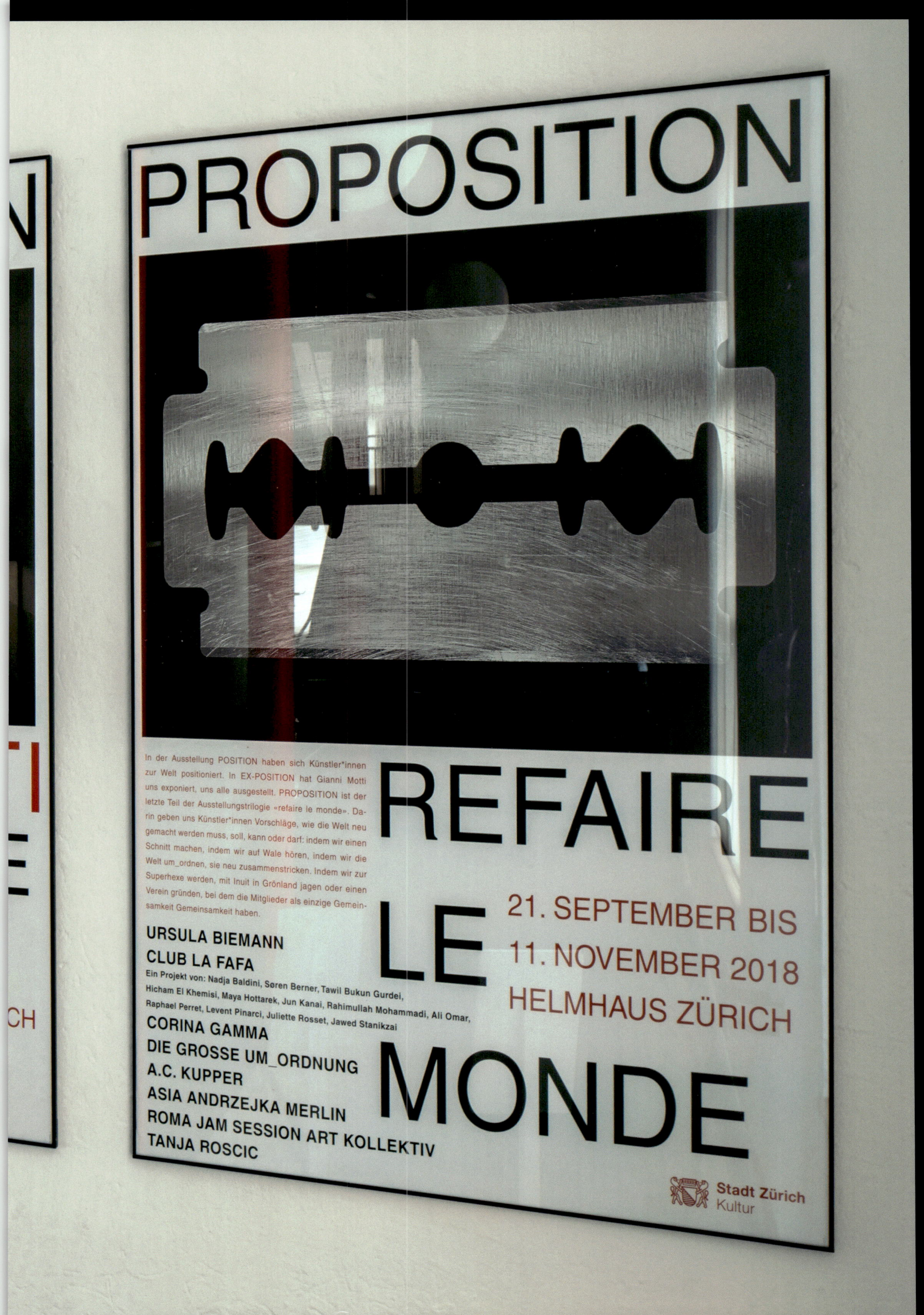
PROPOSITION
In der Ausstellung POSITION haben sich Künstler*innen zur Welt positioniert. In EX-POSITION hat Gianni Motti uns exponiert, uns alle ausgestellt. PROPOSITION ist der letzte Teil der Ausstellungstrilogie «refaire le monde». Darin geben uns Künstler*innen Vorschläge, wie die Welt neu gemacht werden muss, soll, kann oder darf: indem wir einen Schnitt machen, indem wir auf Wale hören, indem wir die Welt um_ordnen, sie neu zusammenstricken. Indem wir zur Superhexe werden, mit Inuit in Grönland jagen oder einen Verein gründen, bei dem die Mitglieder als einzige Gemeinsamkeit Gemeinsamkeit haben.
URSULA BIEMANN
CLUB LA FAFA
Ein Projekt von: Nadja Baldini, Søren Berner, Tawil Bukun Gurdei, Hicham El Khemisi, Maya Hottarek, Jun Kanai, Rahimullah Mohammadi, Ali Omar, Raphael Perret, Levent Pinarci, Juliette Rosset, Jawed Stanikzai
CORINA GAMMA
DIE GROSSE UM_ORDNUNG
A.C. KUPPER
ASIA ANDRZEJKA MERLIN
ROMA JAM SESSION ART KOLLEKTIV
TANJA ROSCIC
REFAIRE
LE
MONDE
21. SEPTEMBER BIS
11. NOVEMBER 2018
HELMHAUS ZÜRICH
Stadt Zürich
Kultur

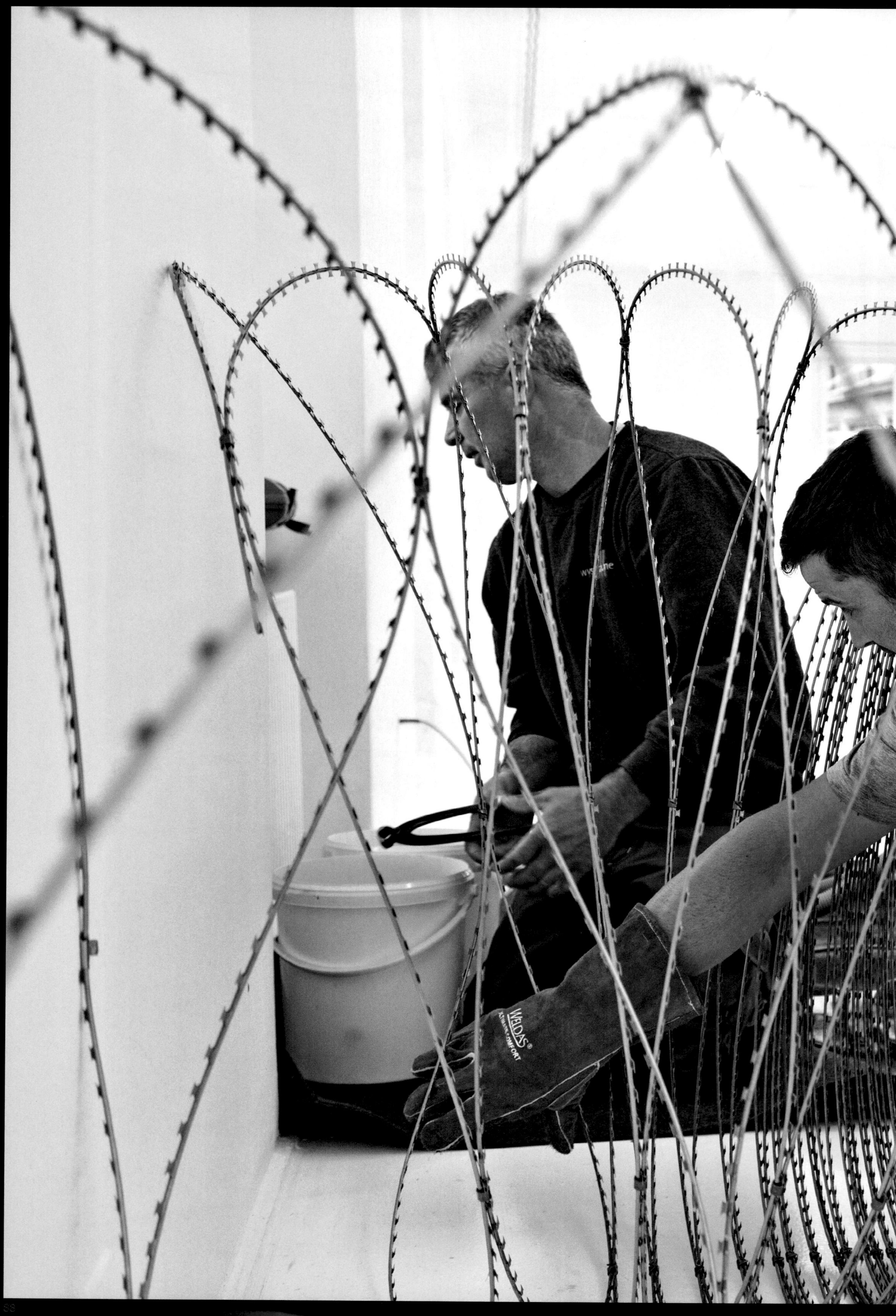
WELDAS®

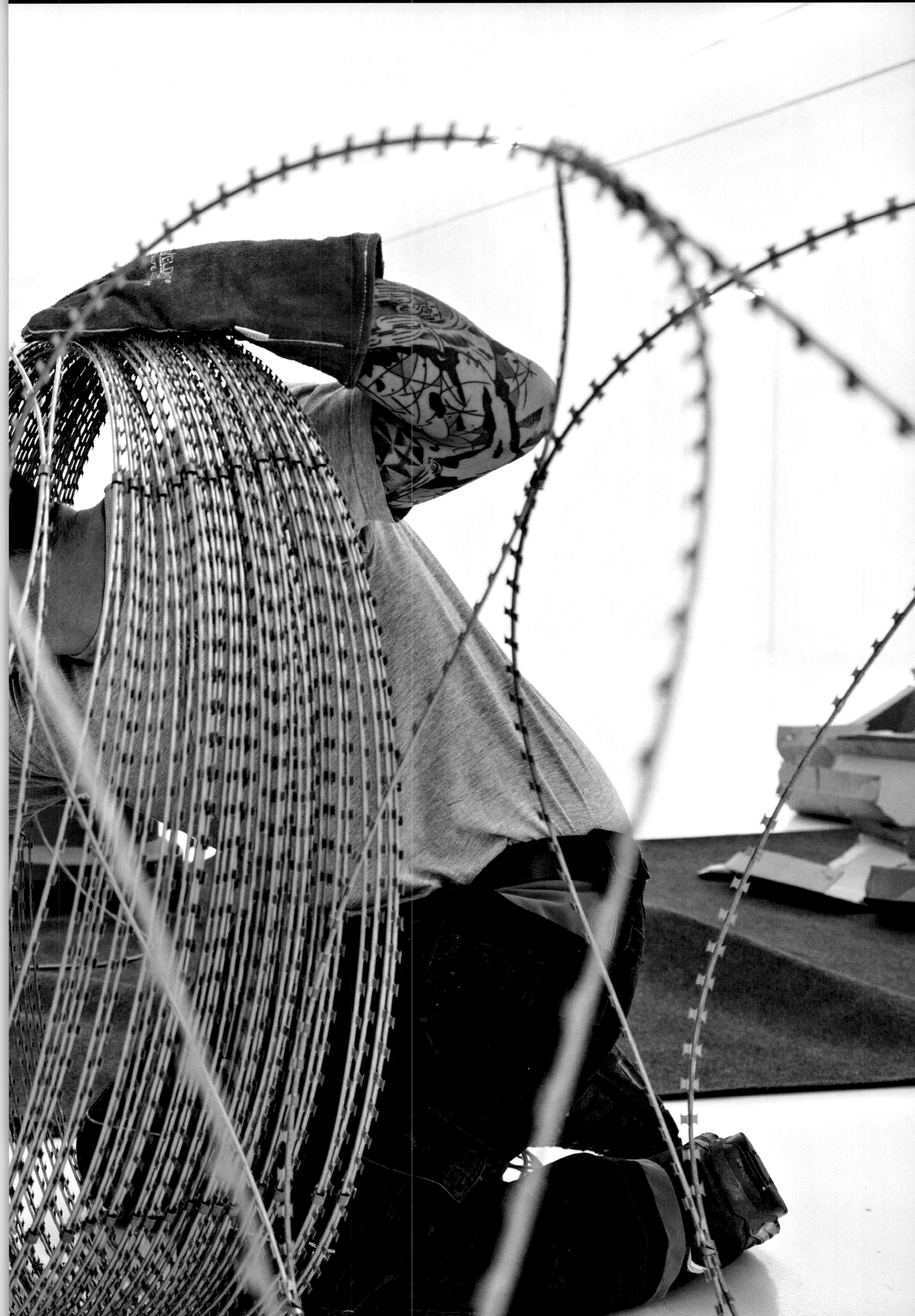

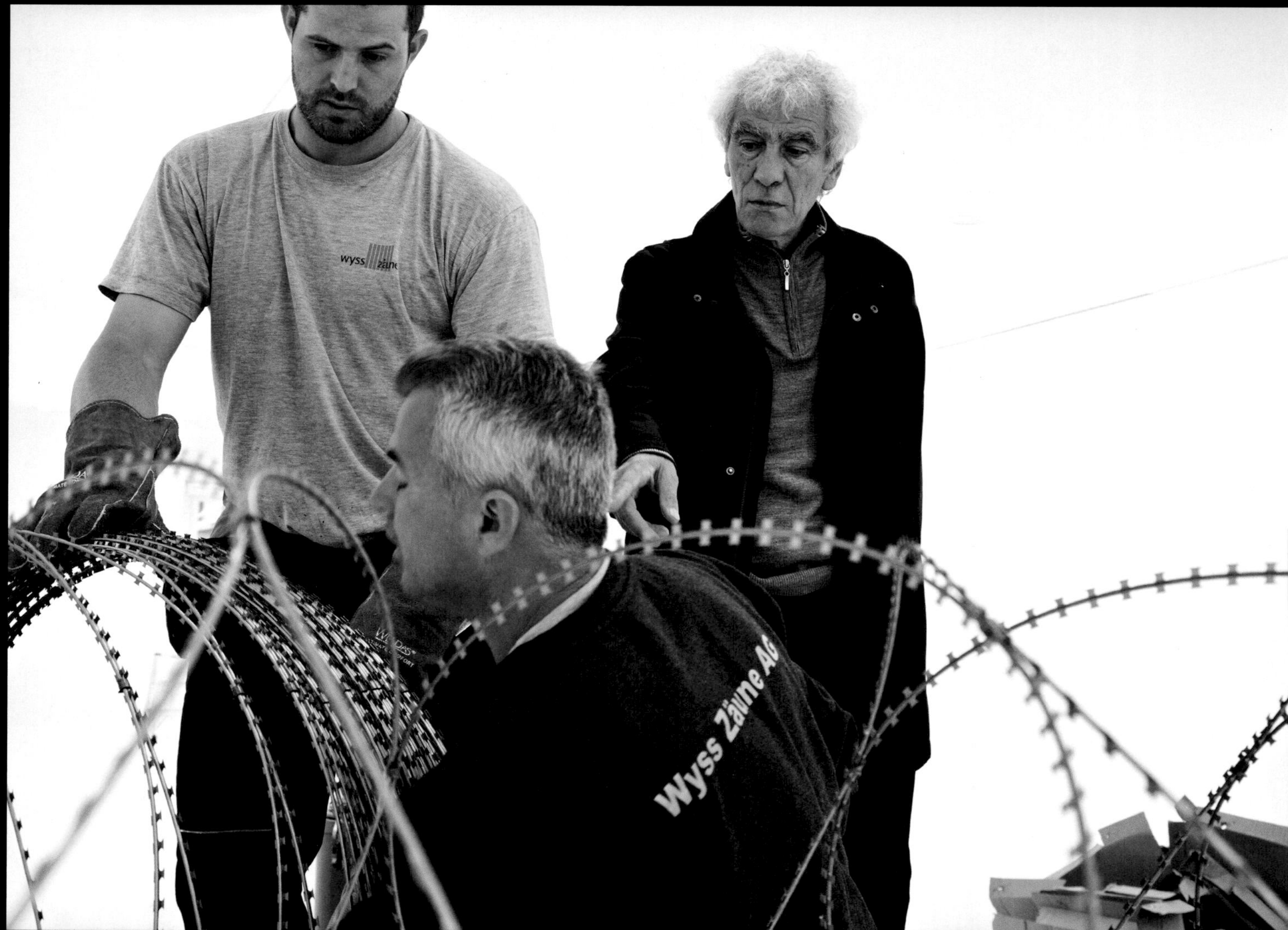
Wyss Zäune AG

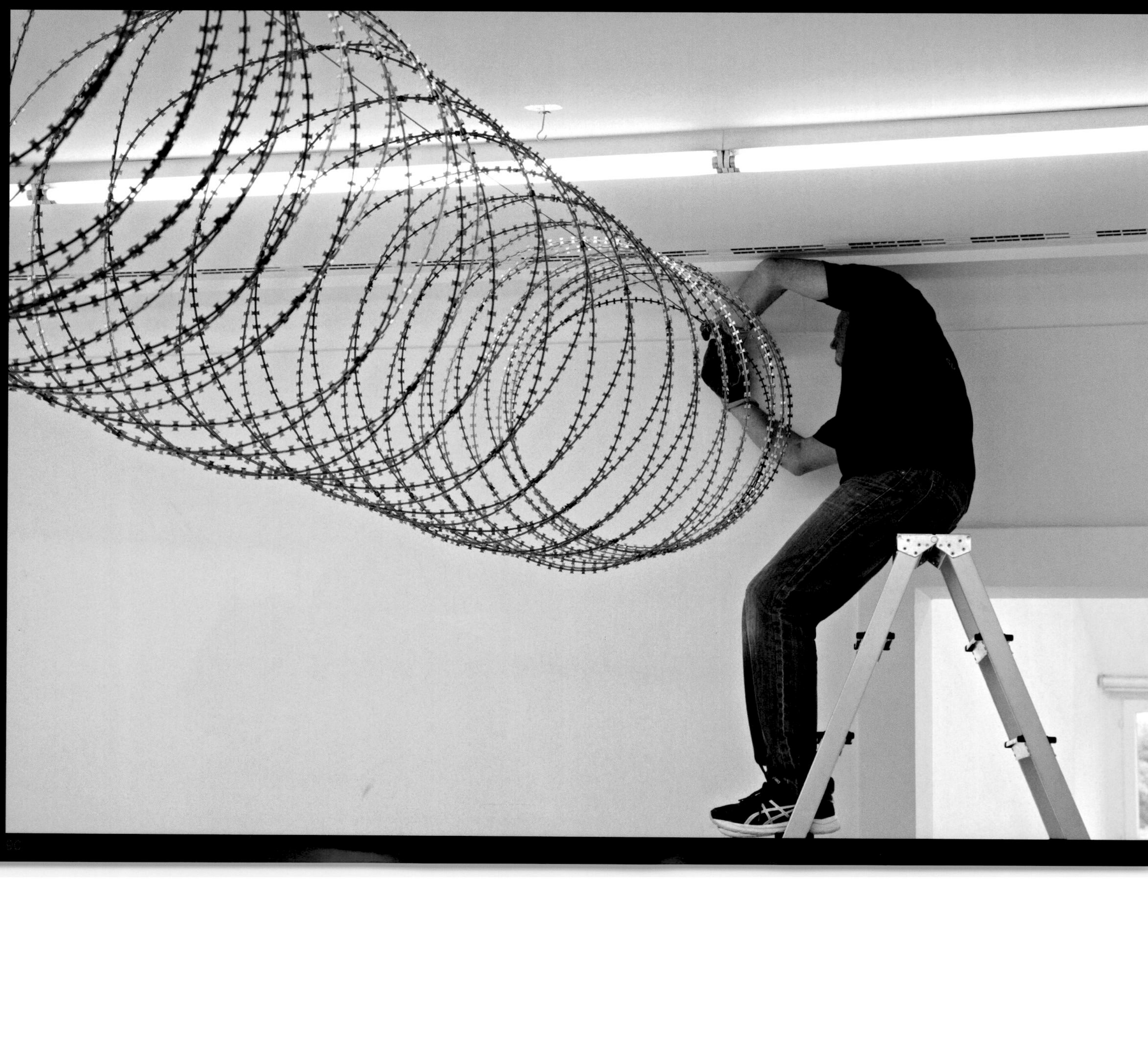

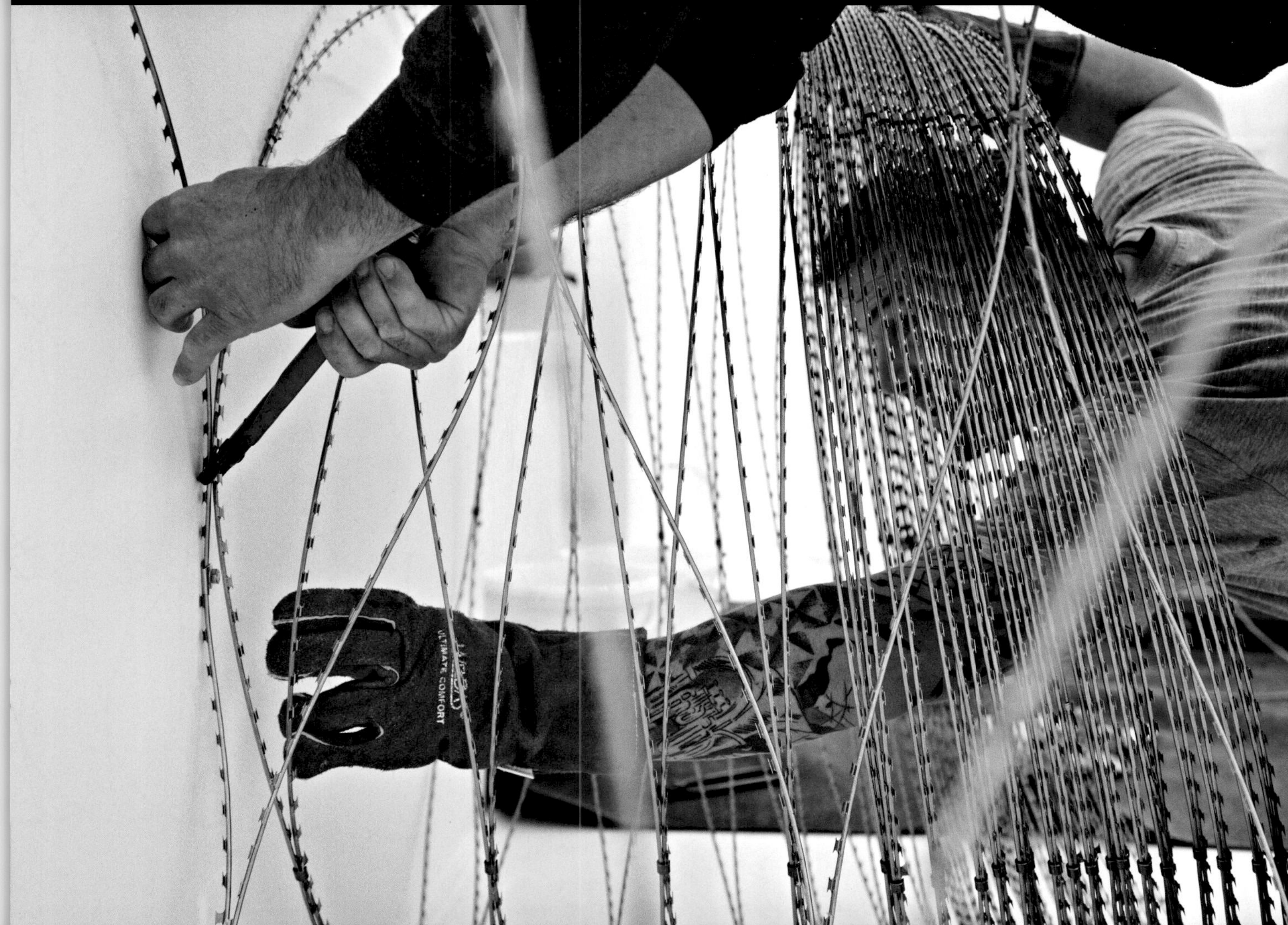
ULTIMATE COMFORT

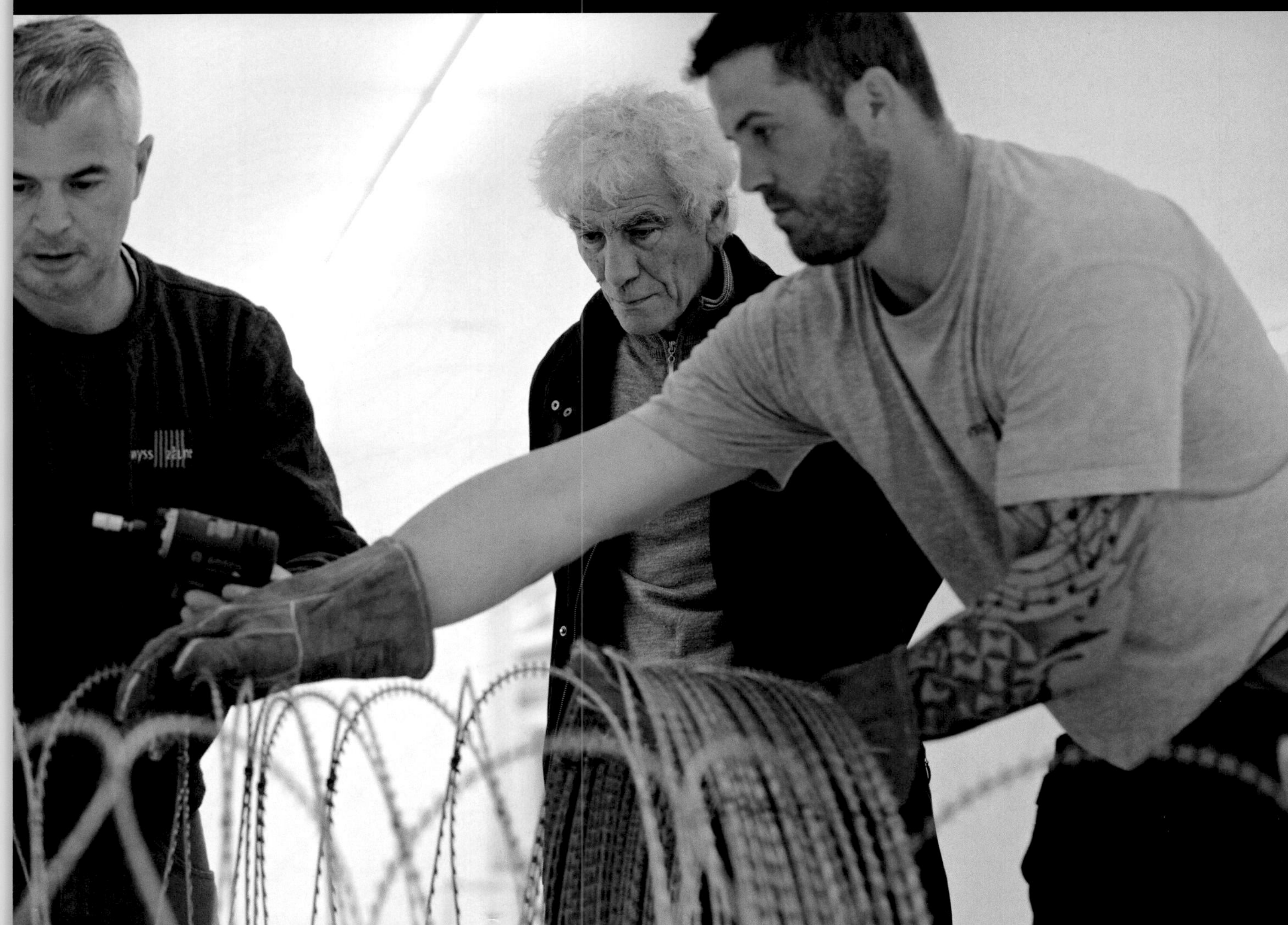

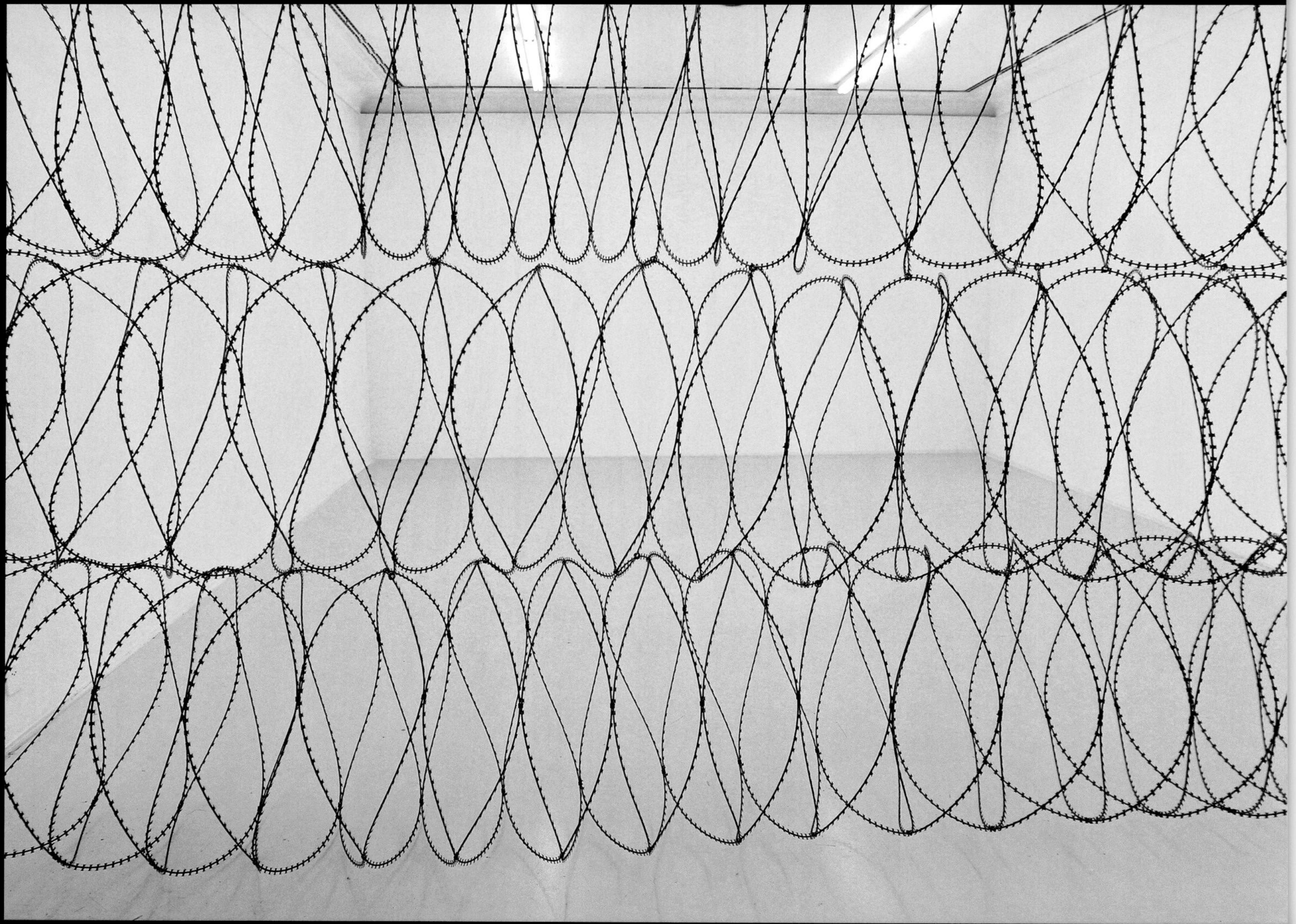

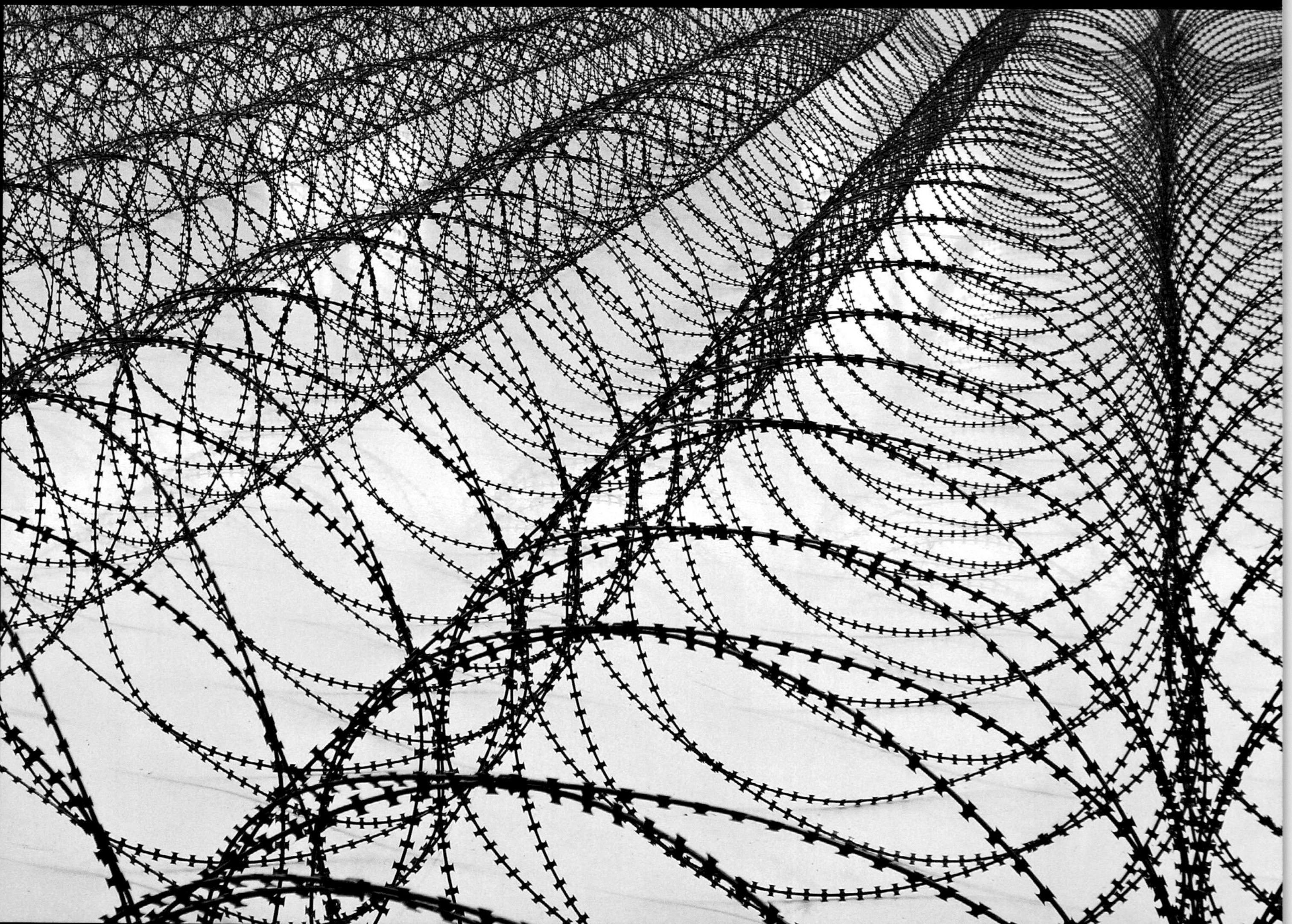

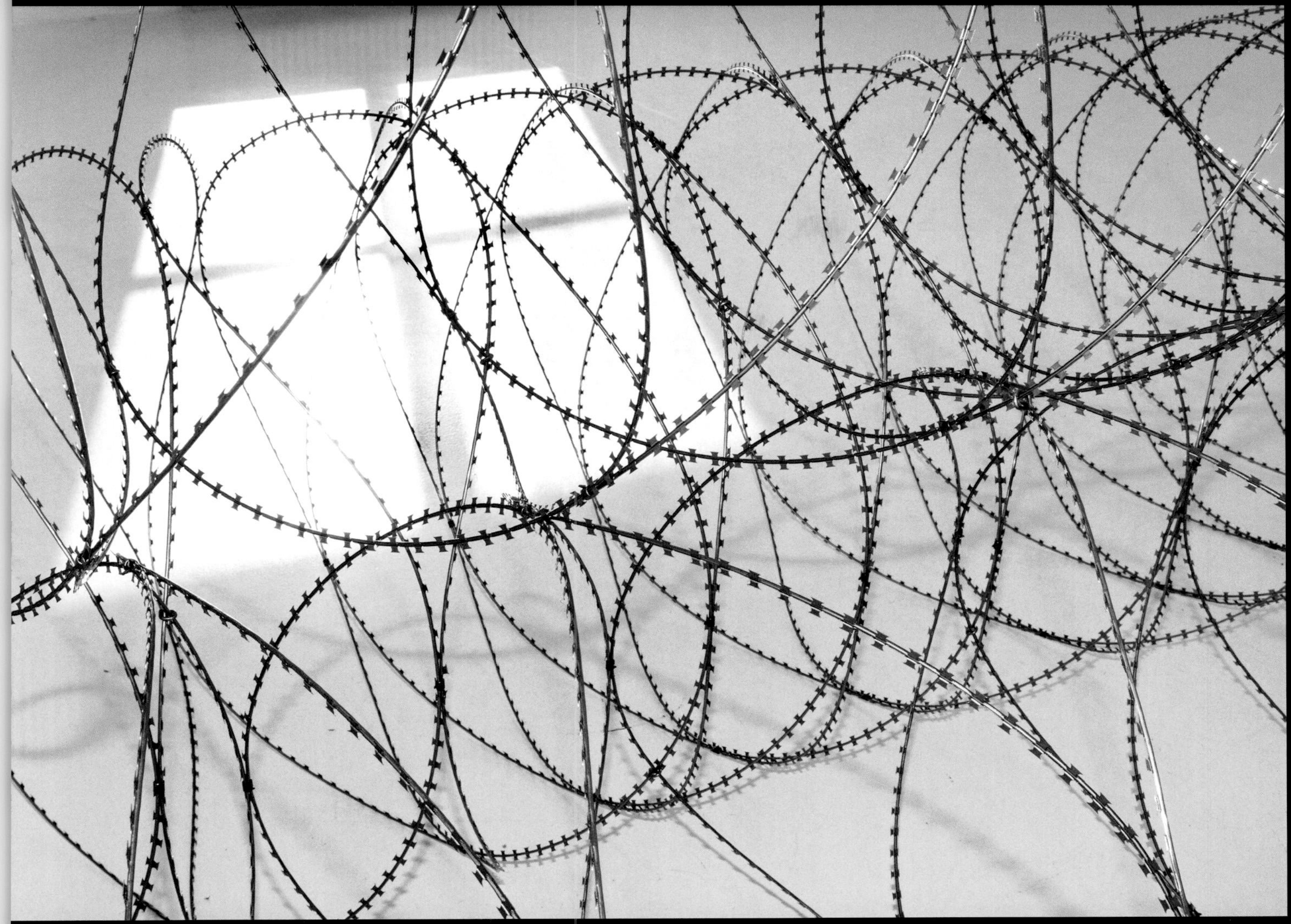

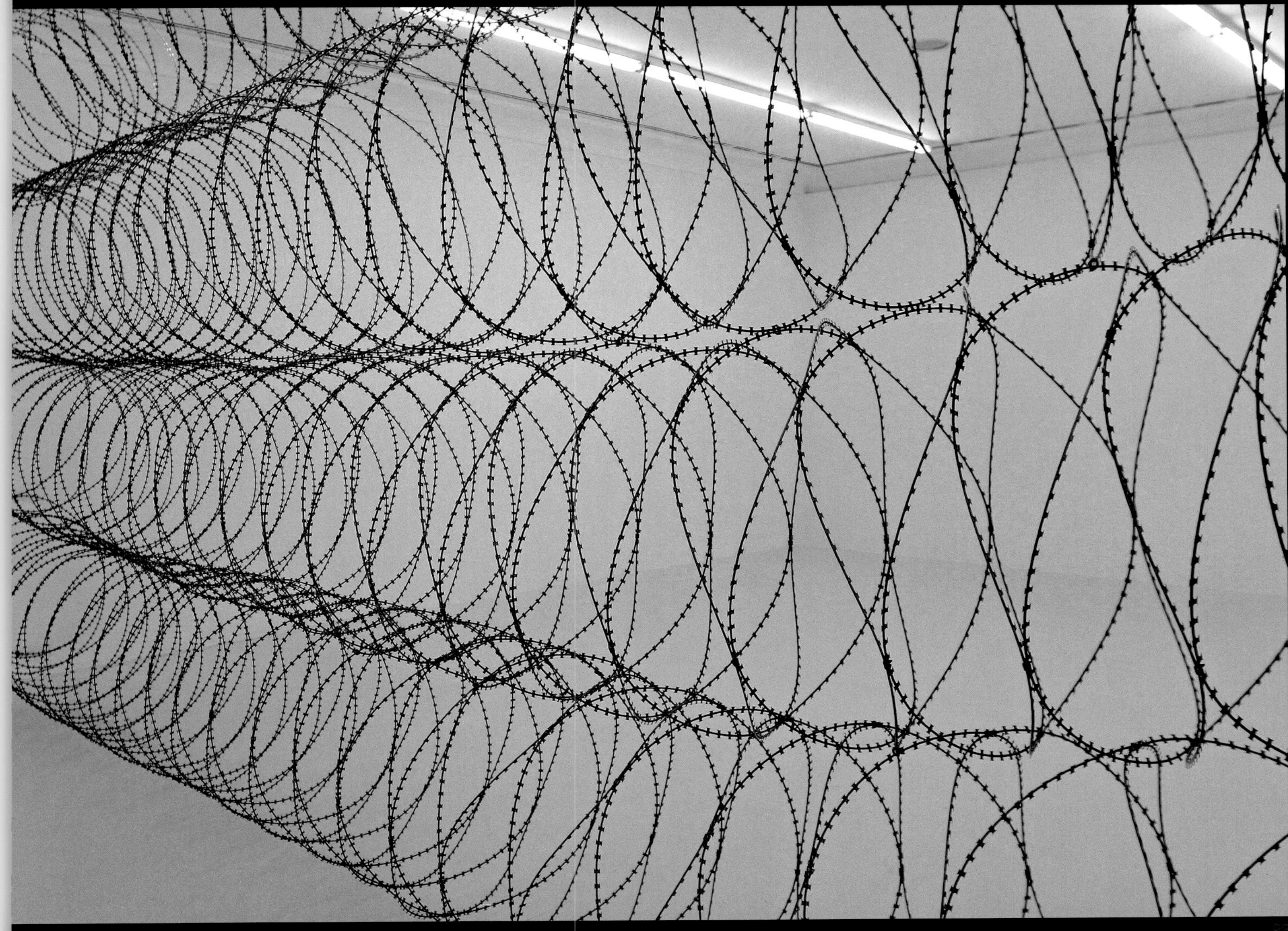

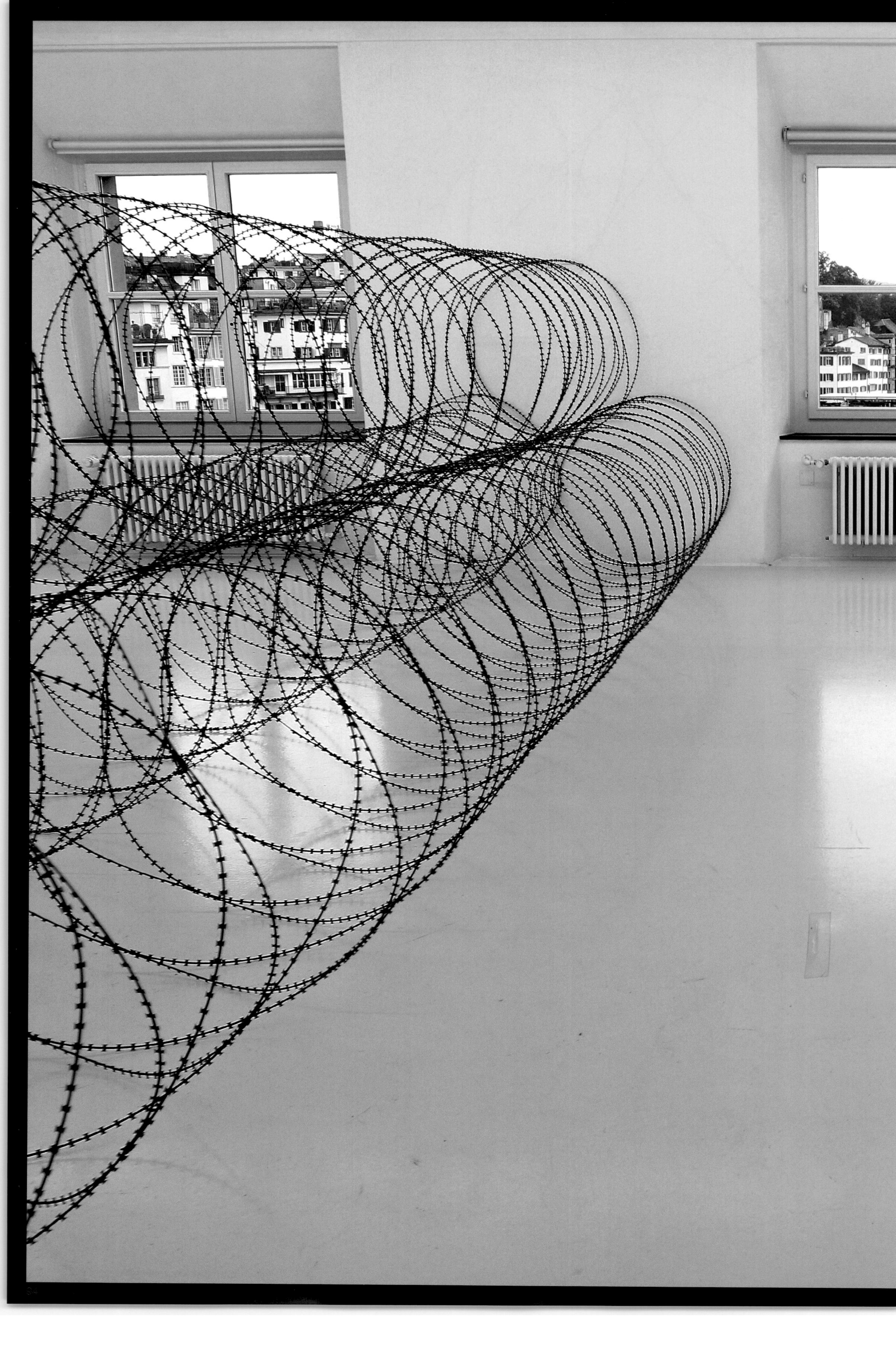

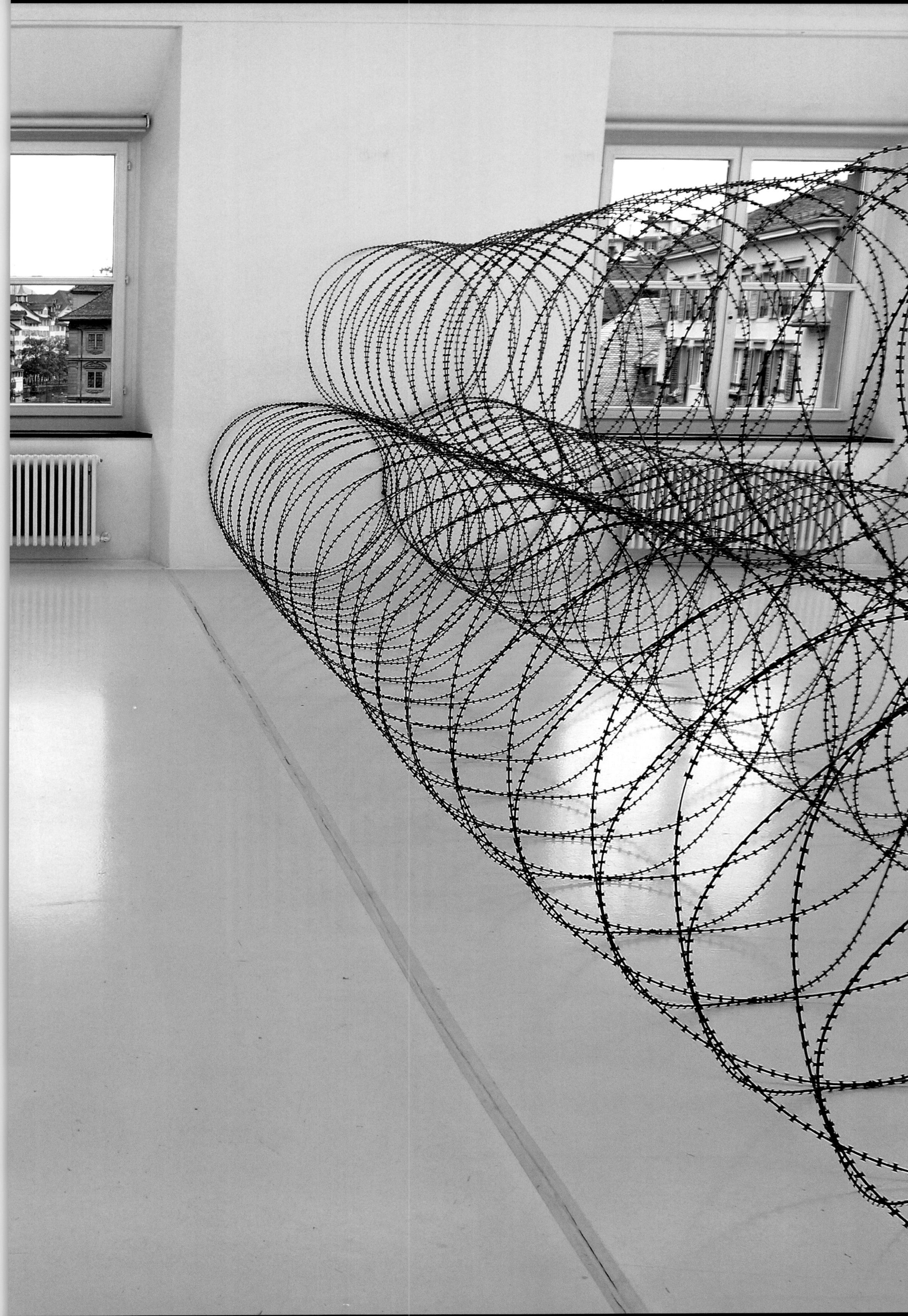

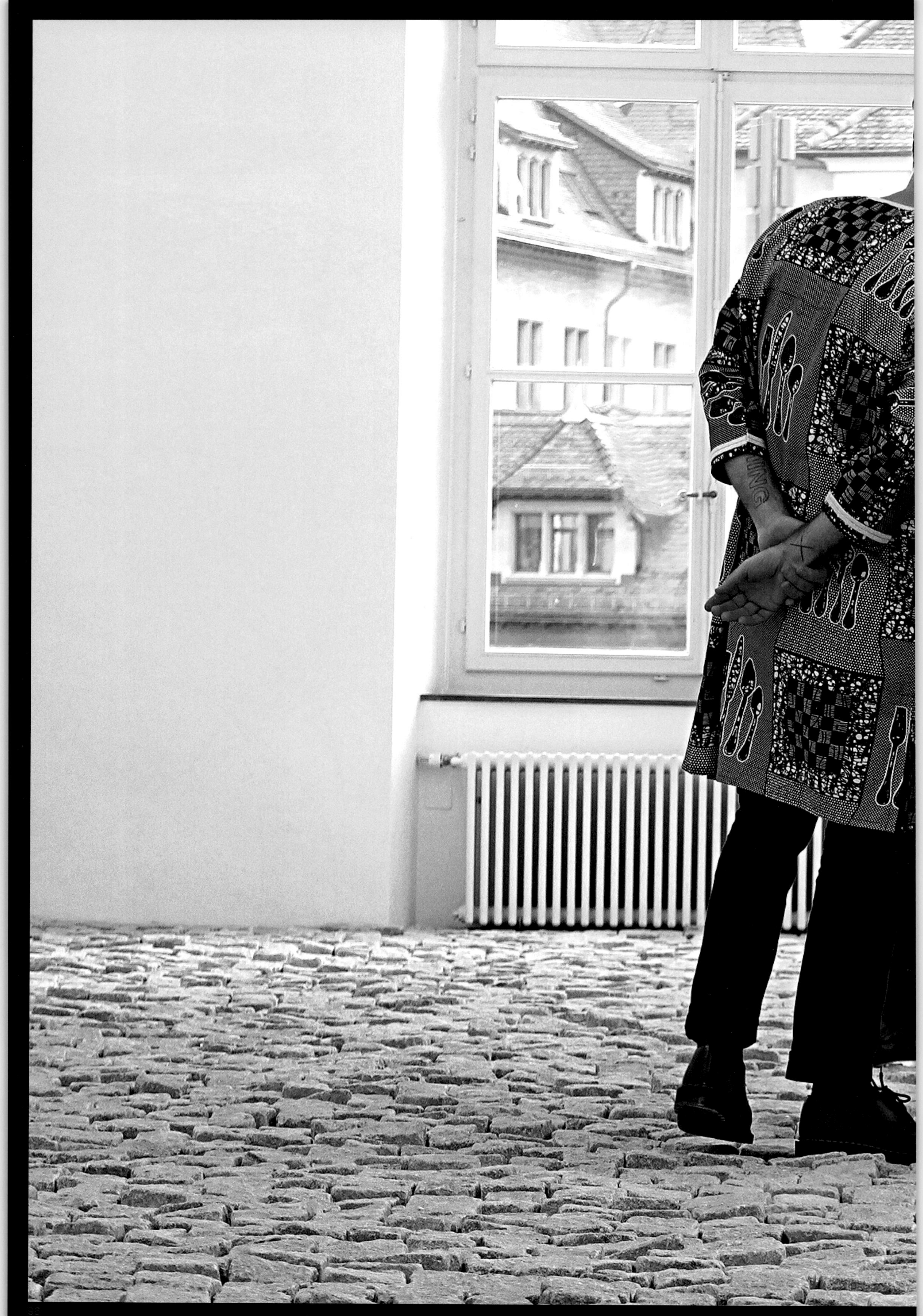

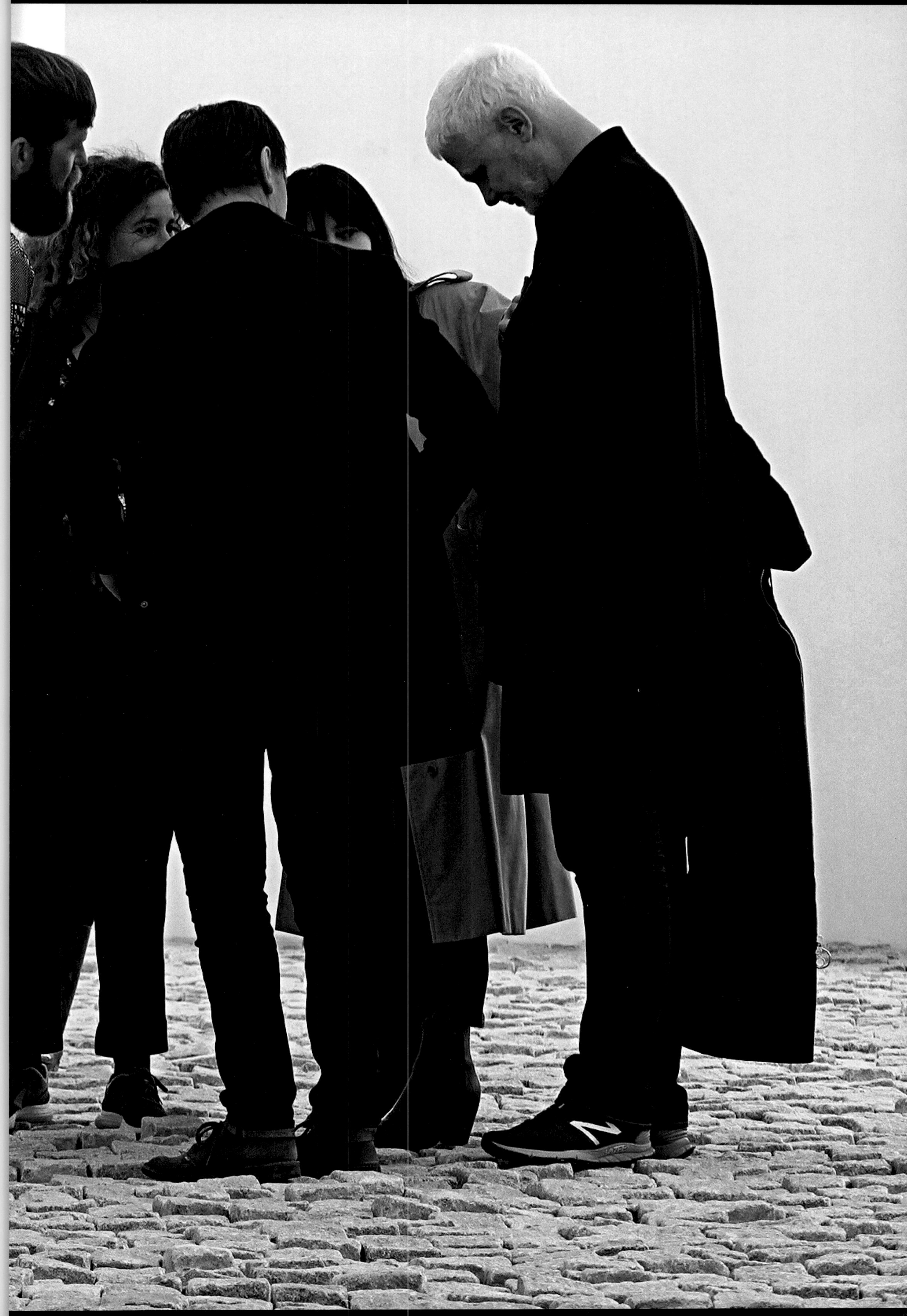

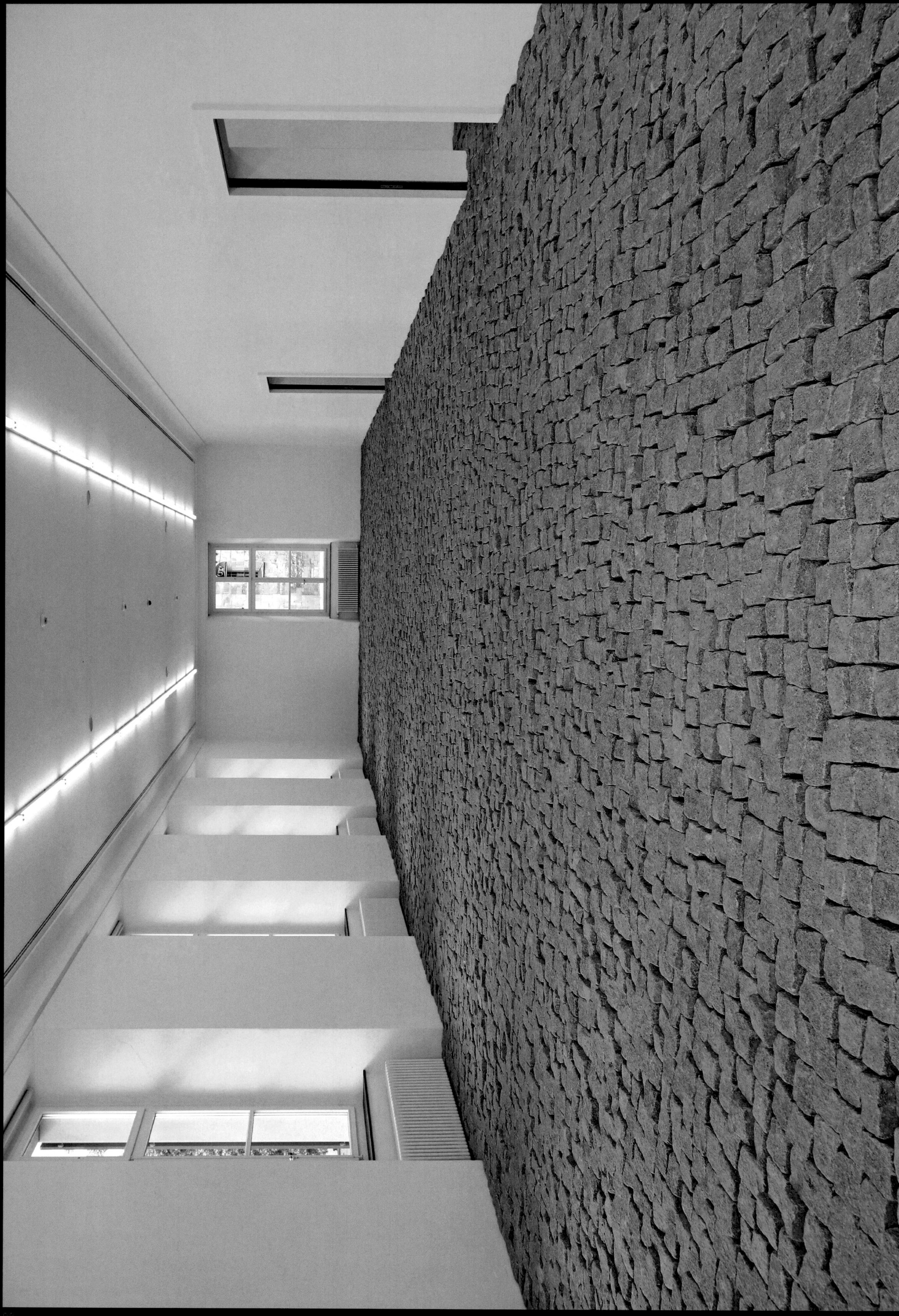

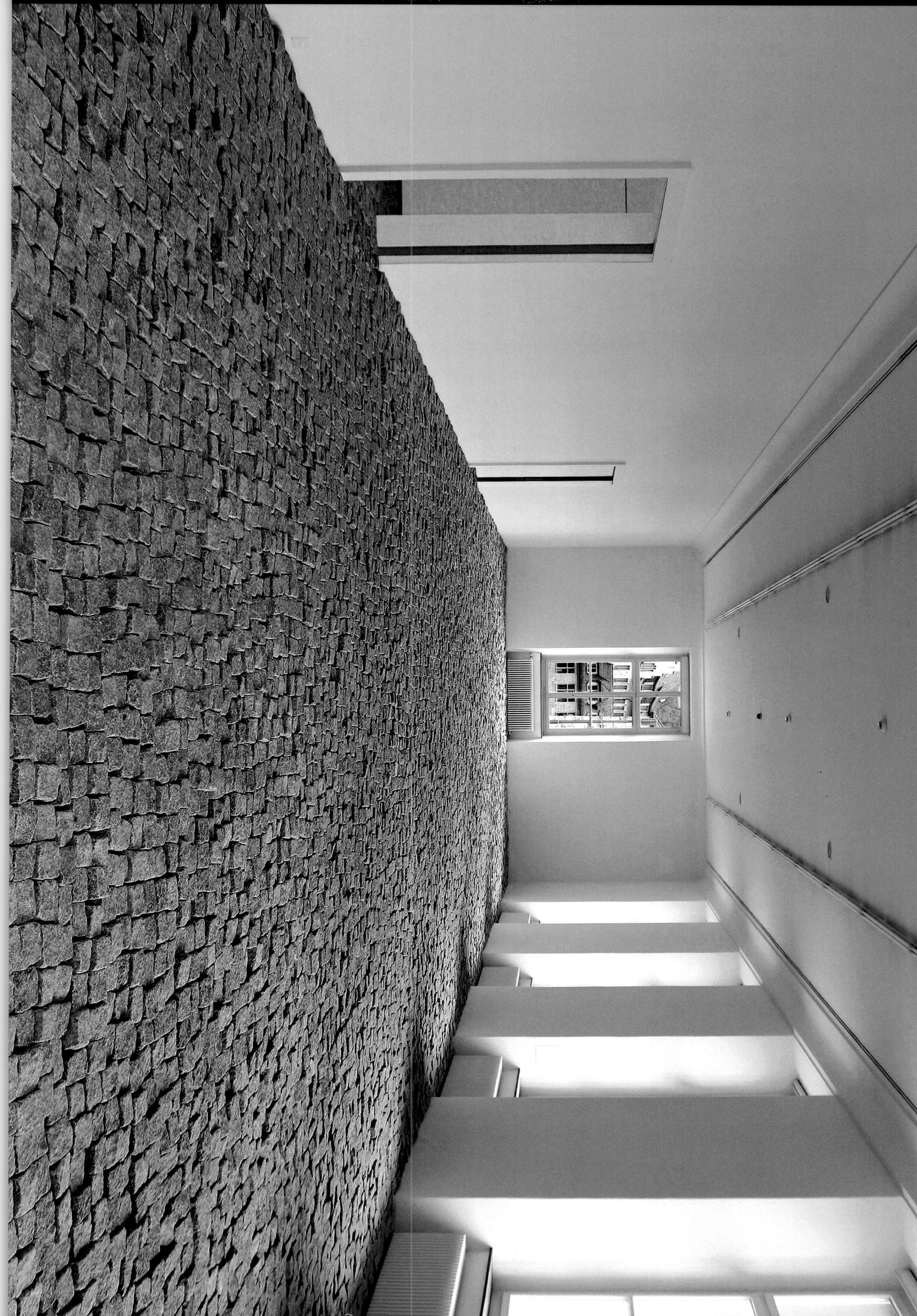

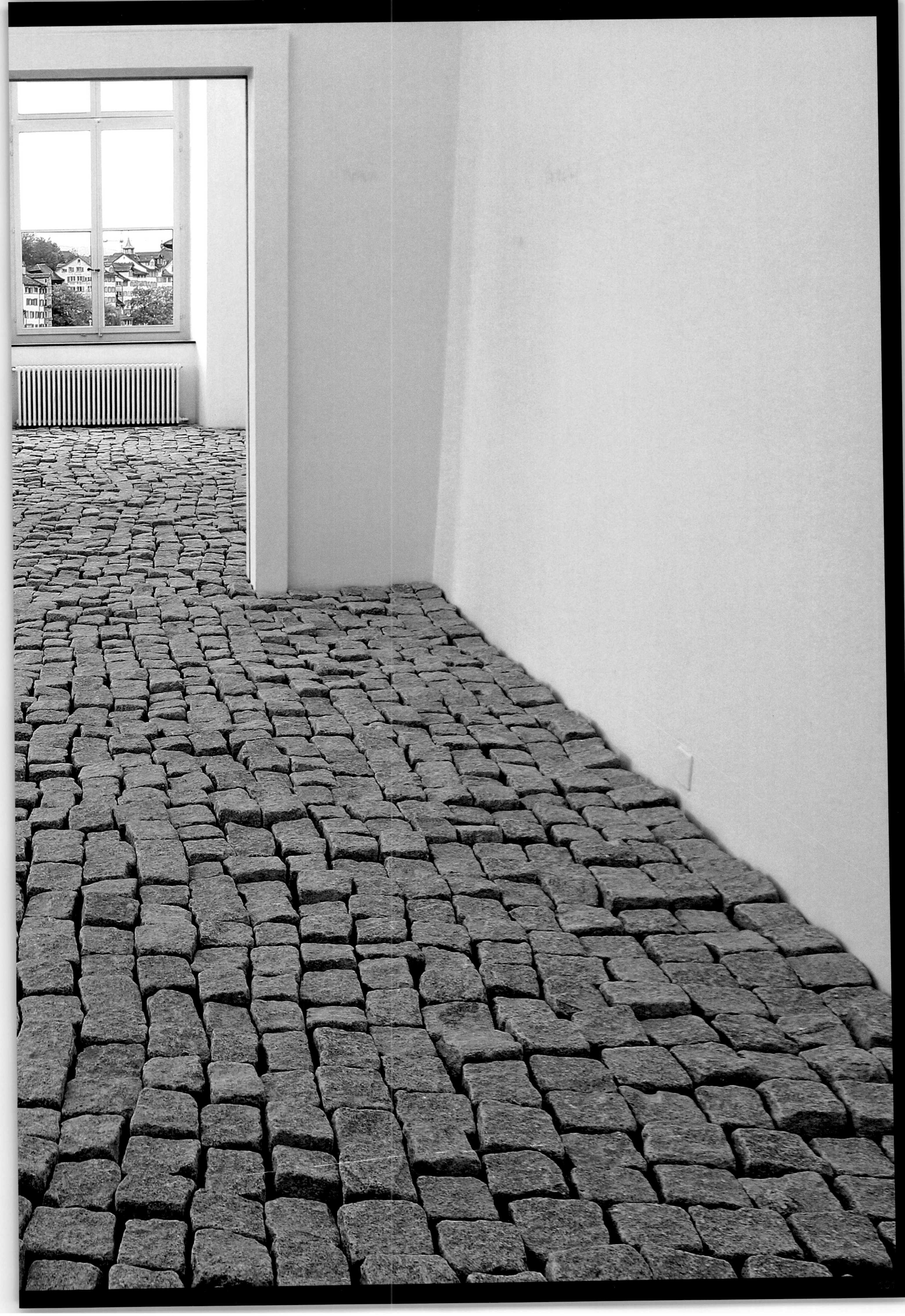

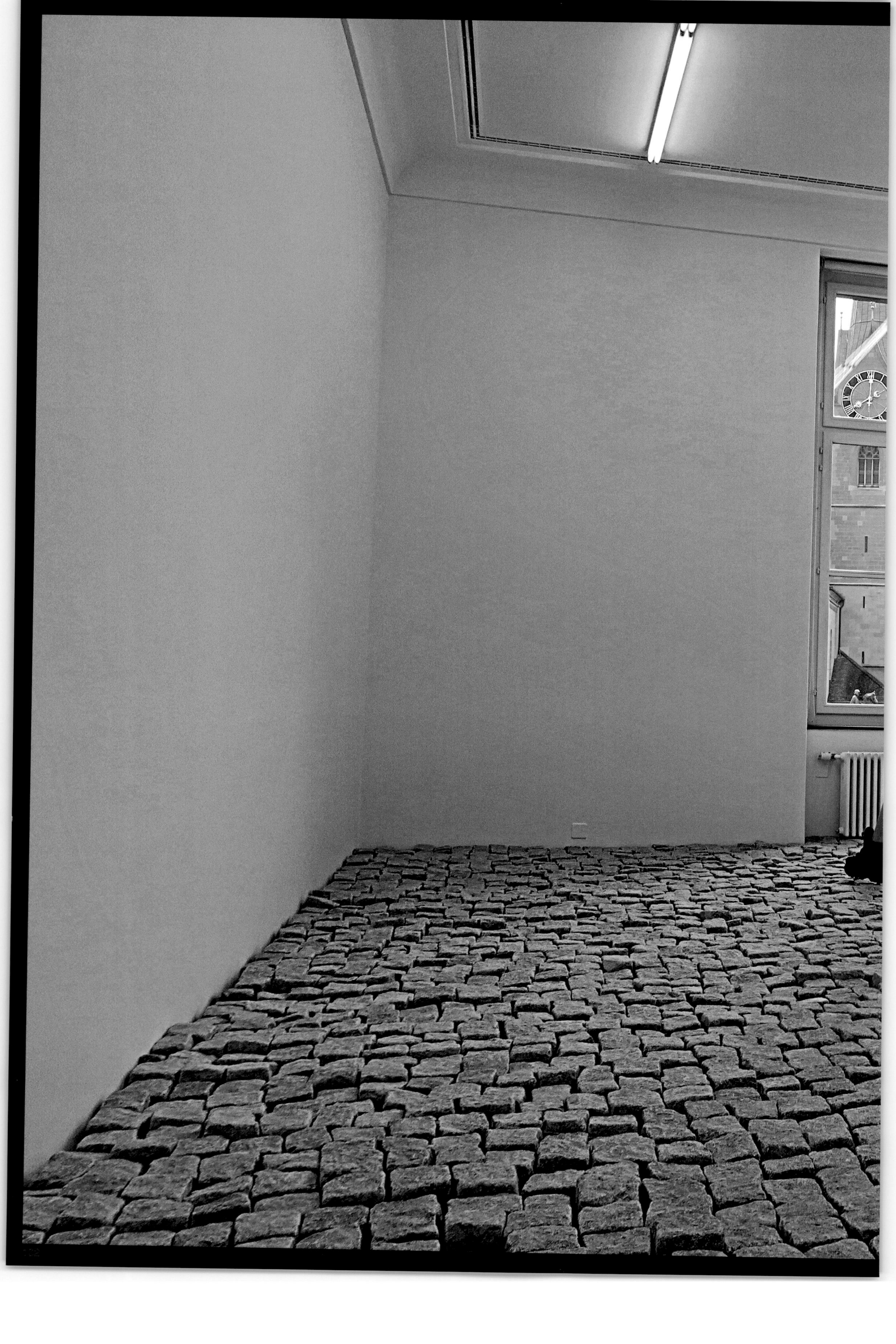

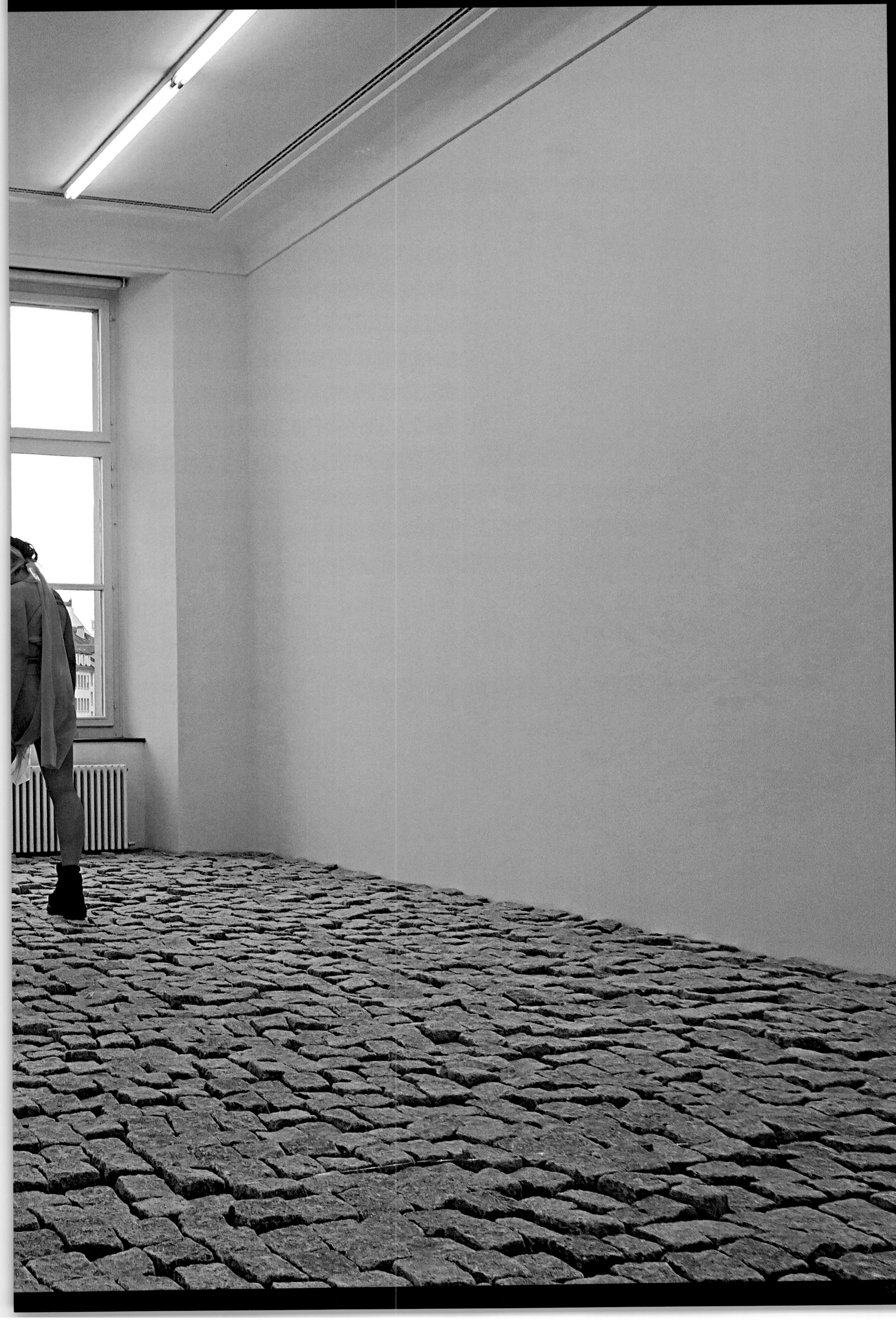

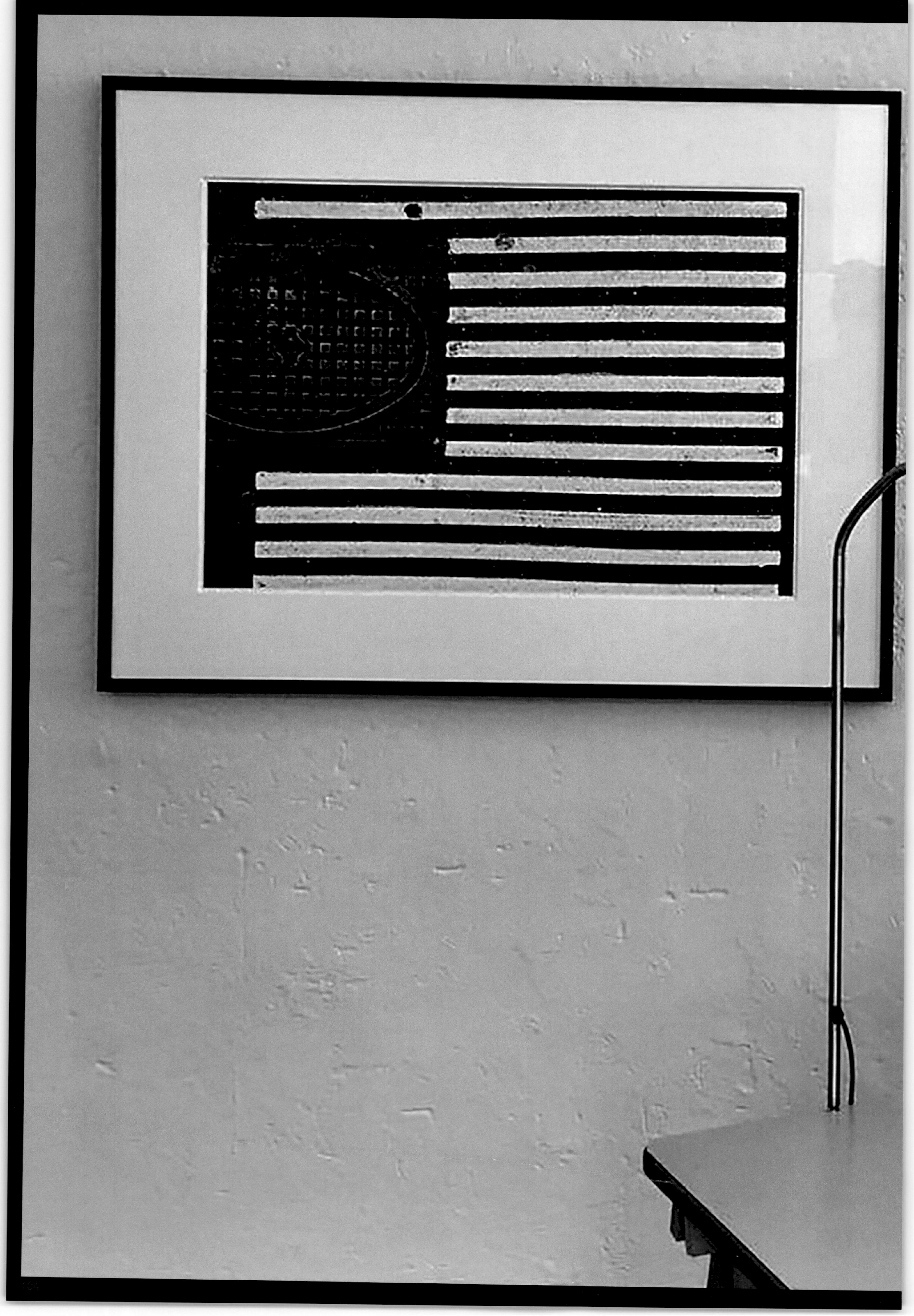

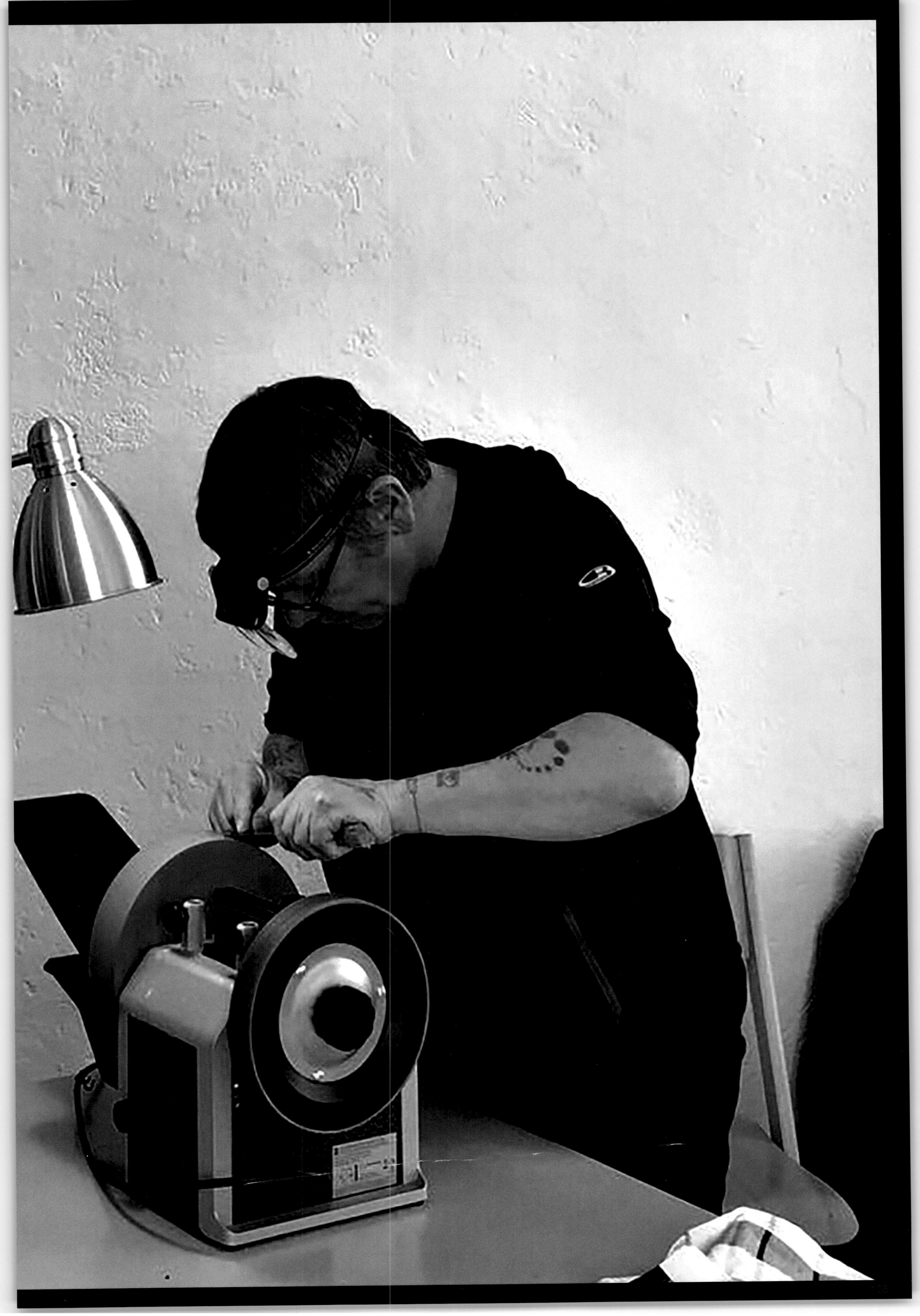

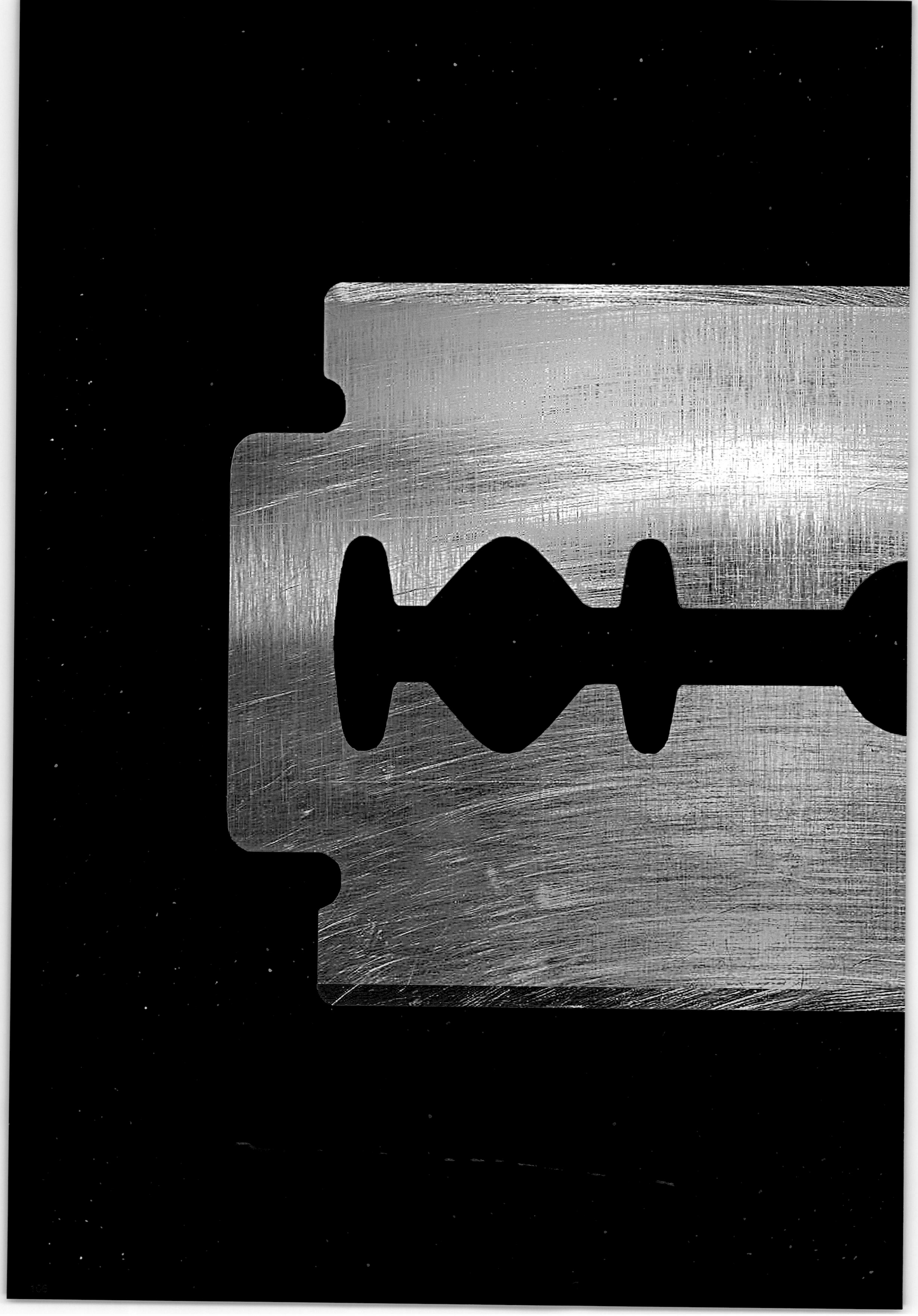

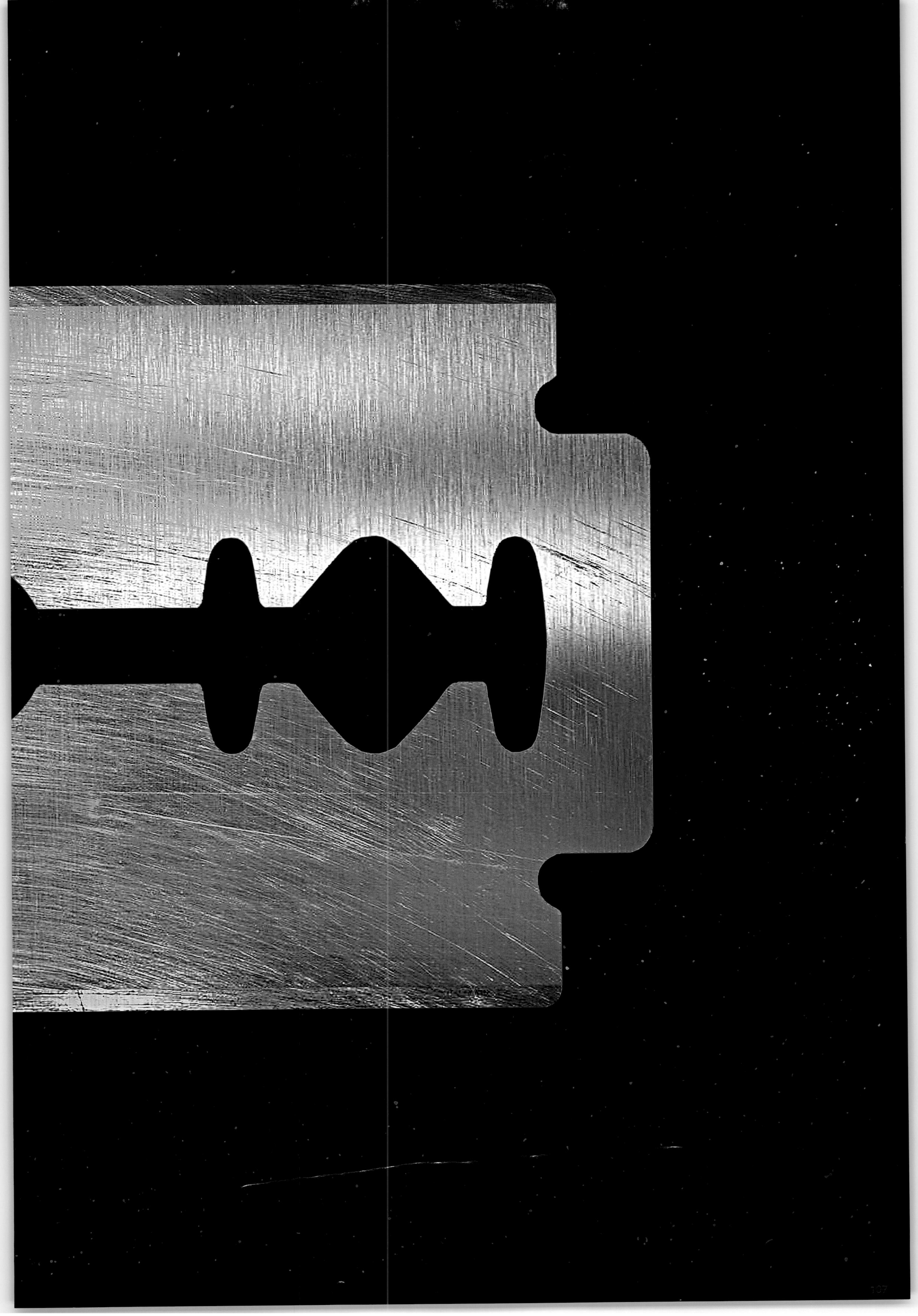

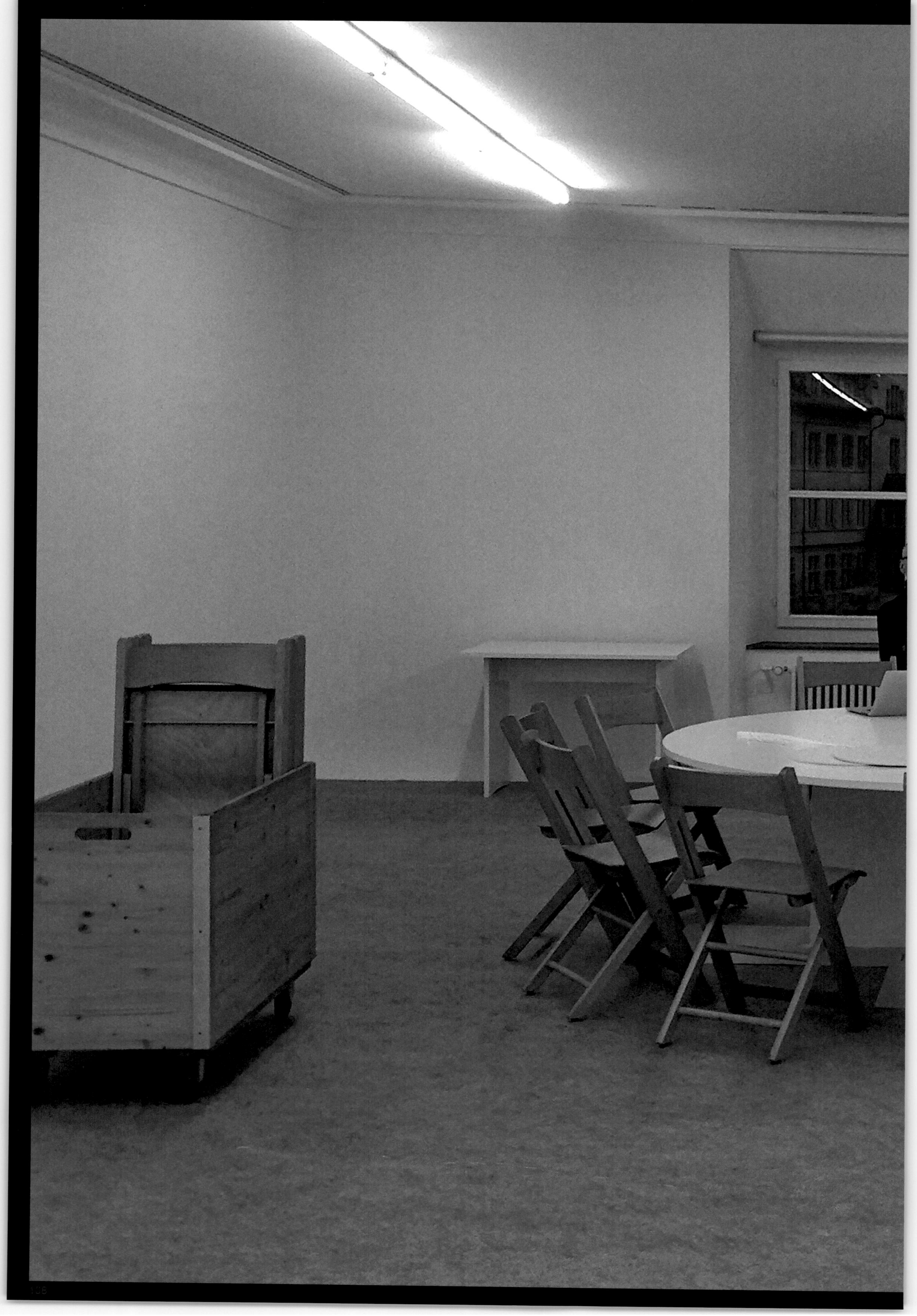

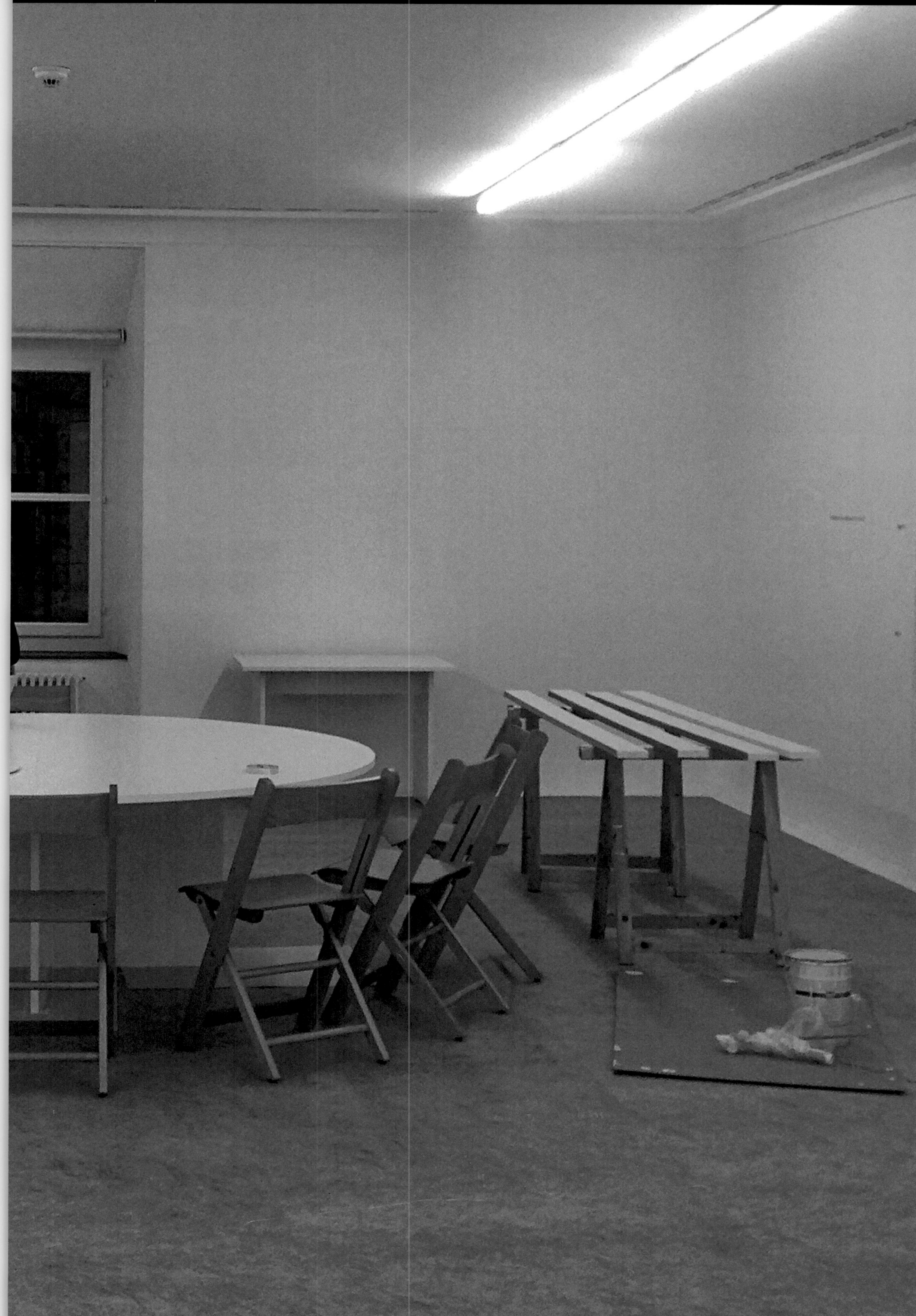

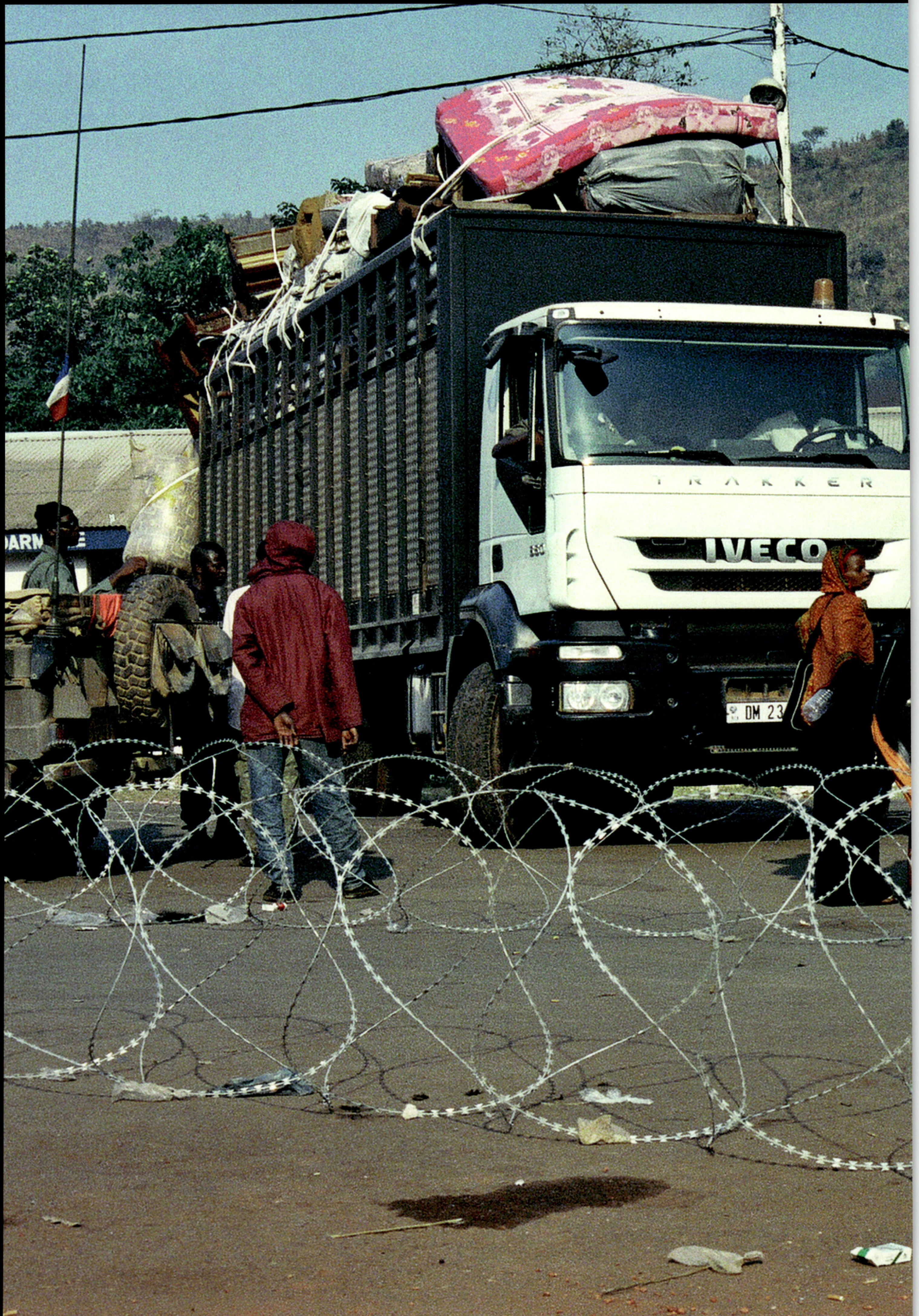
TRAKKER
IVECO
DM 23

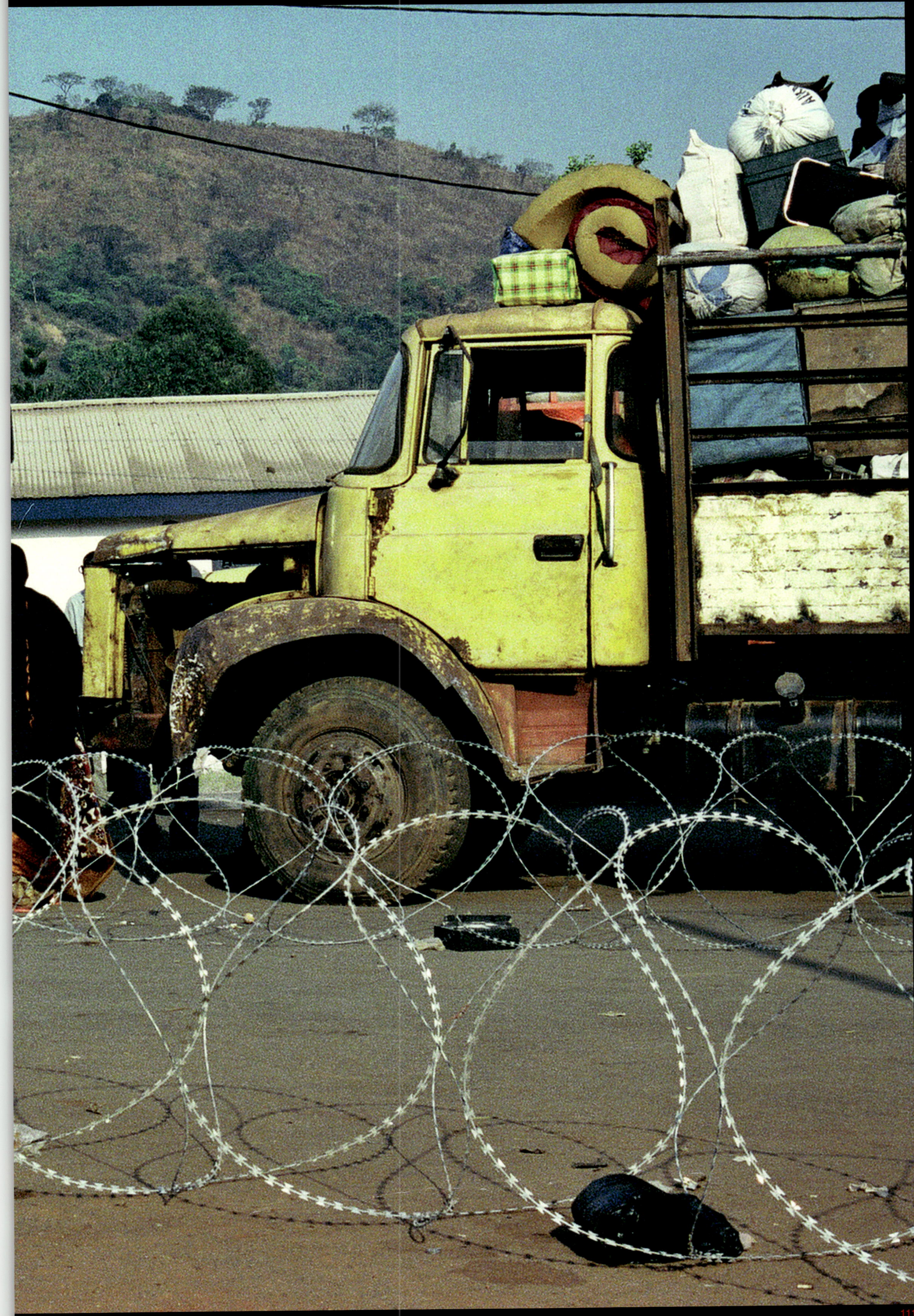

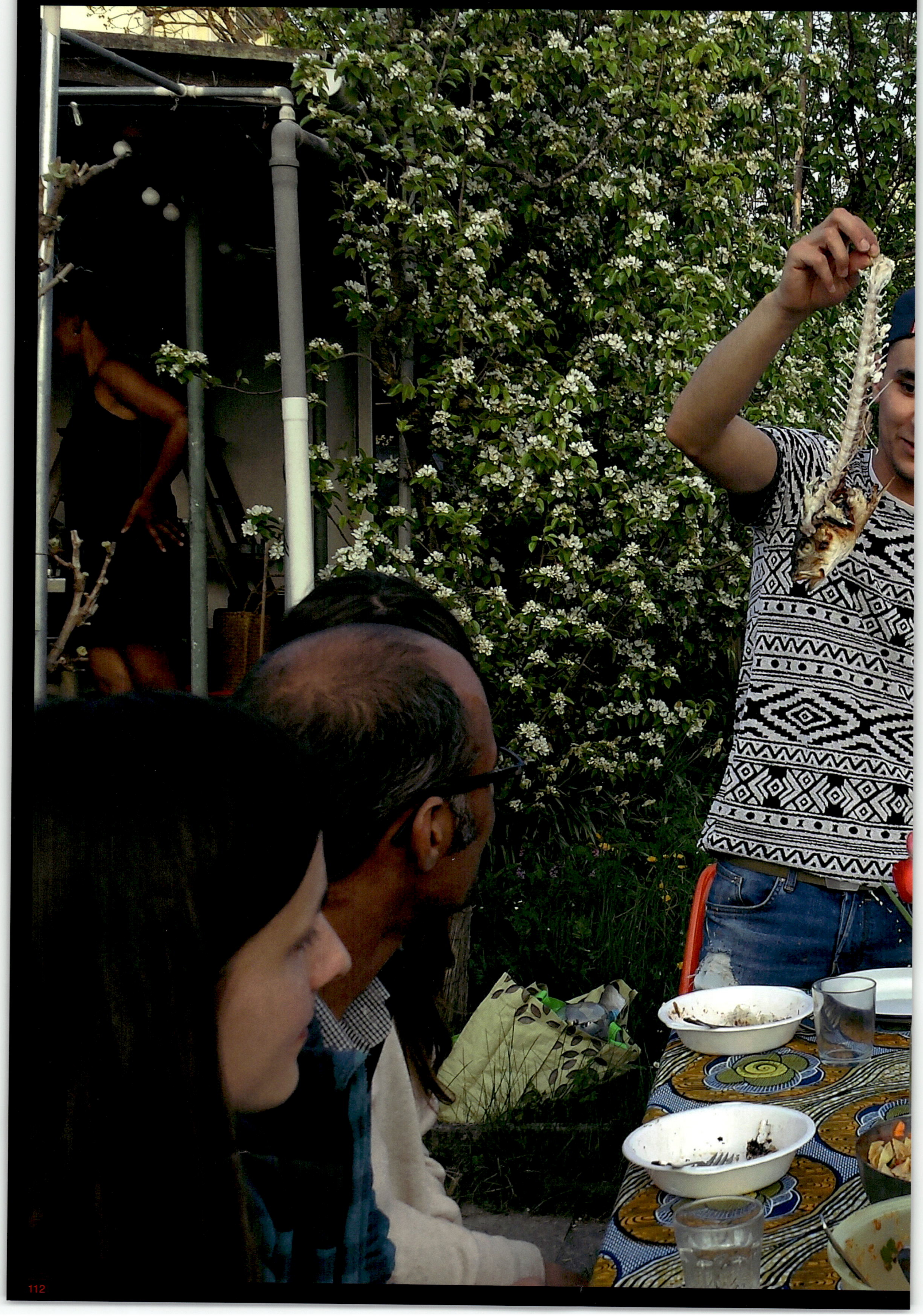

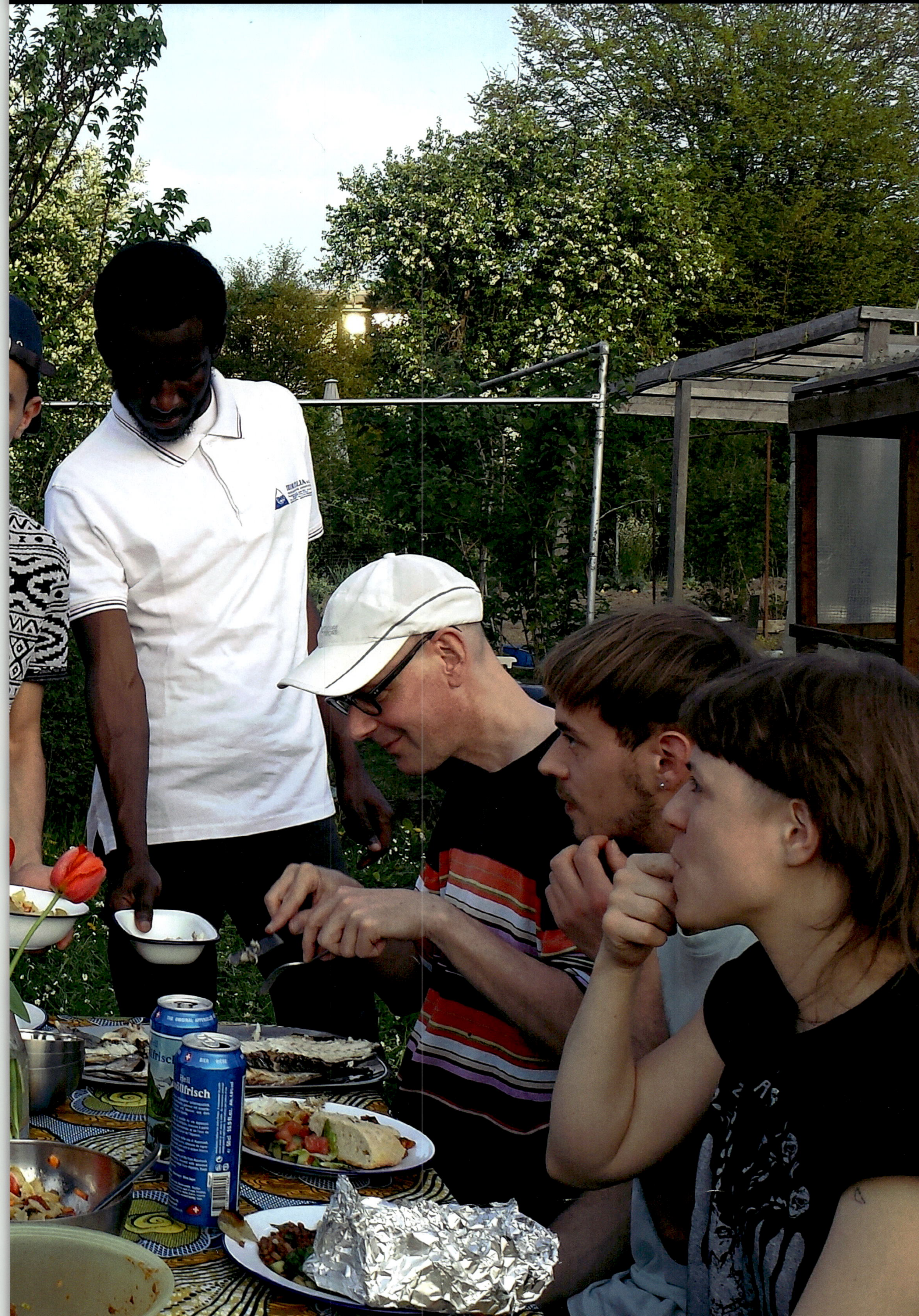

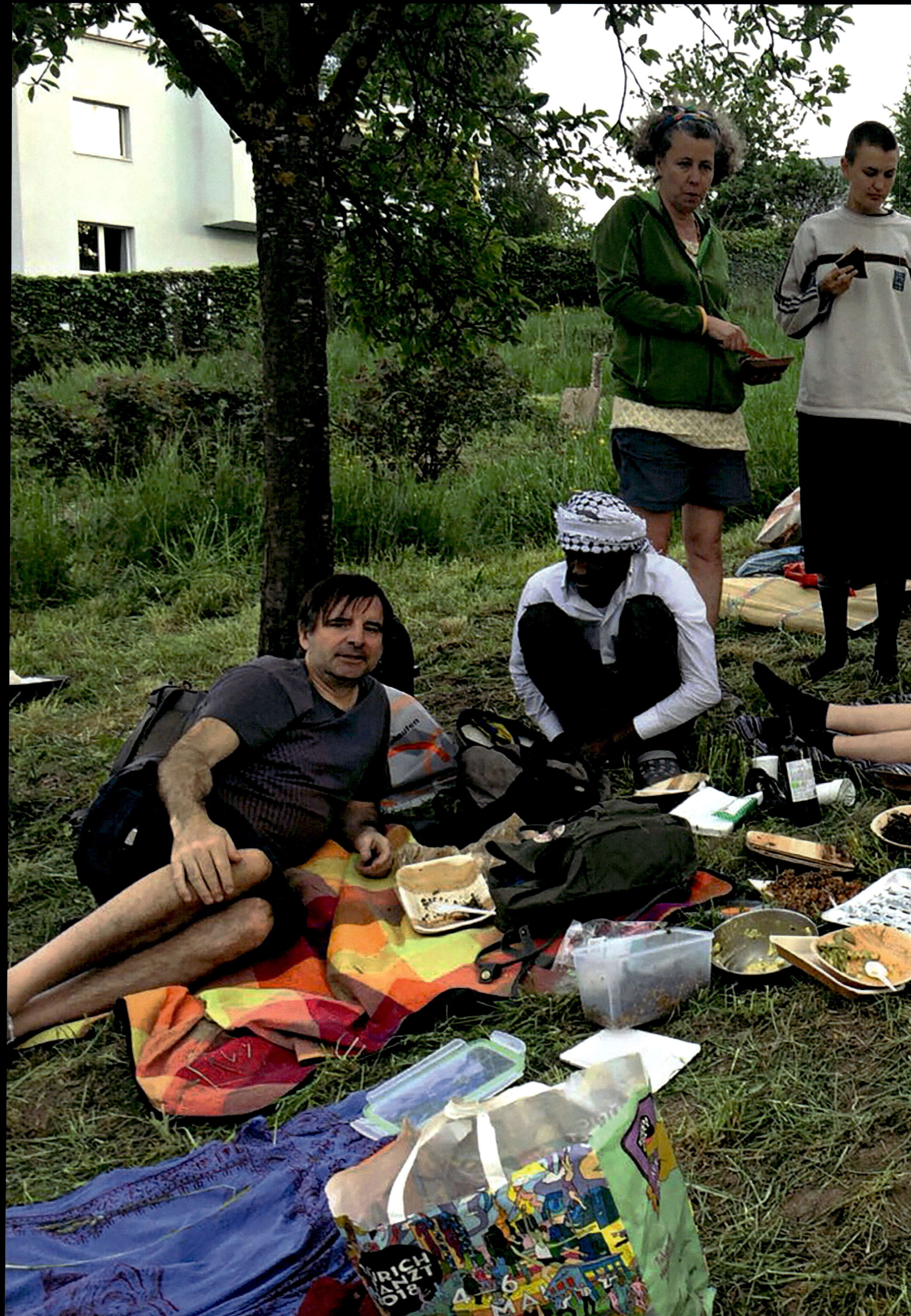

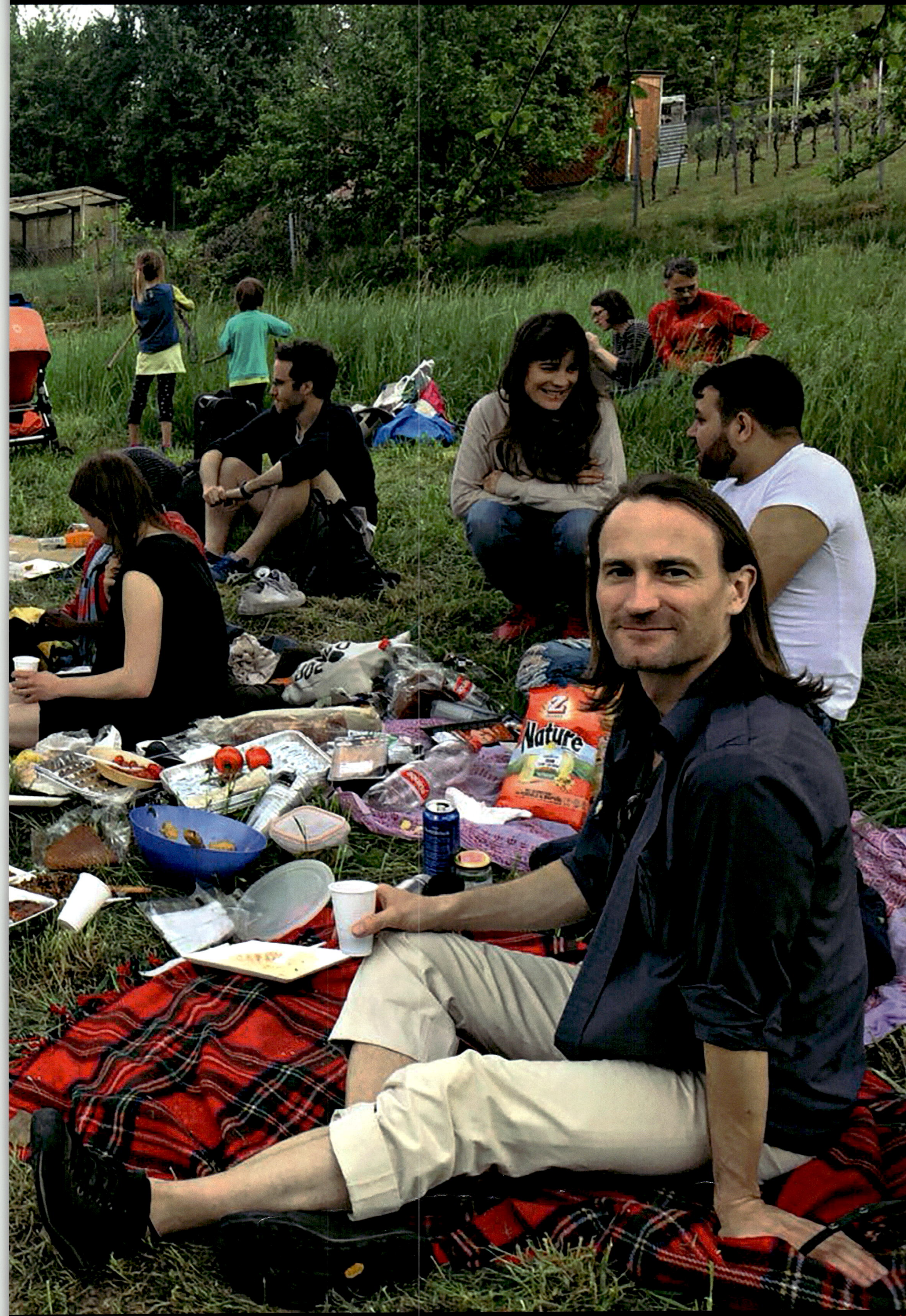
Nature

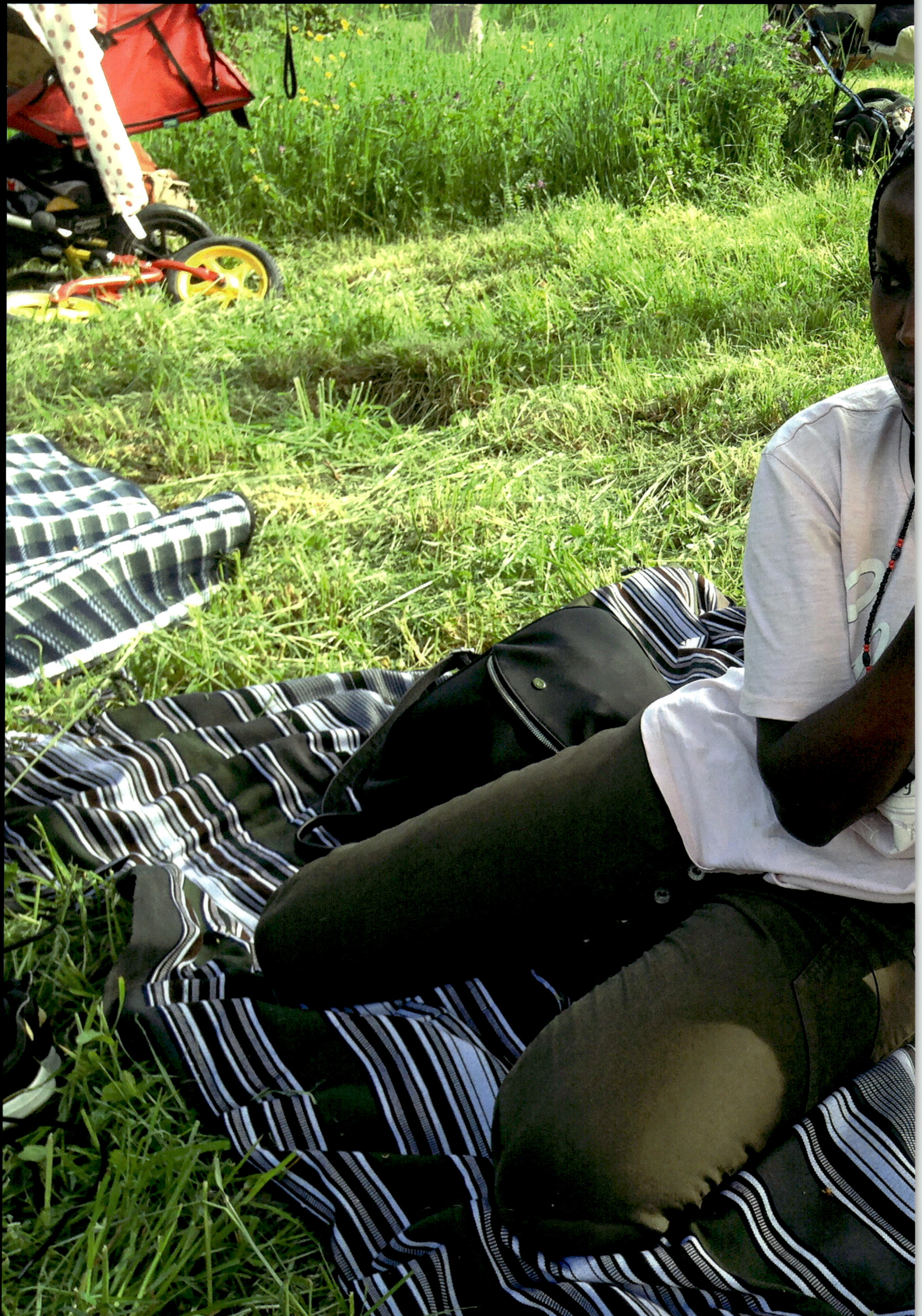

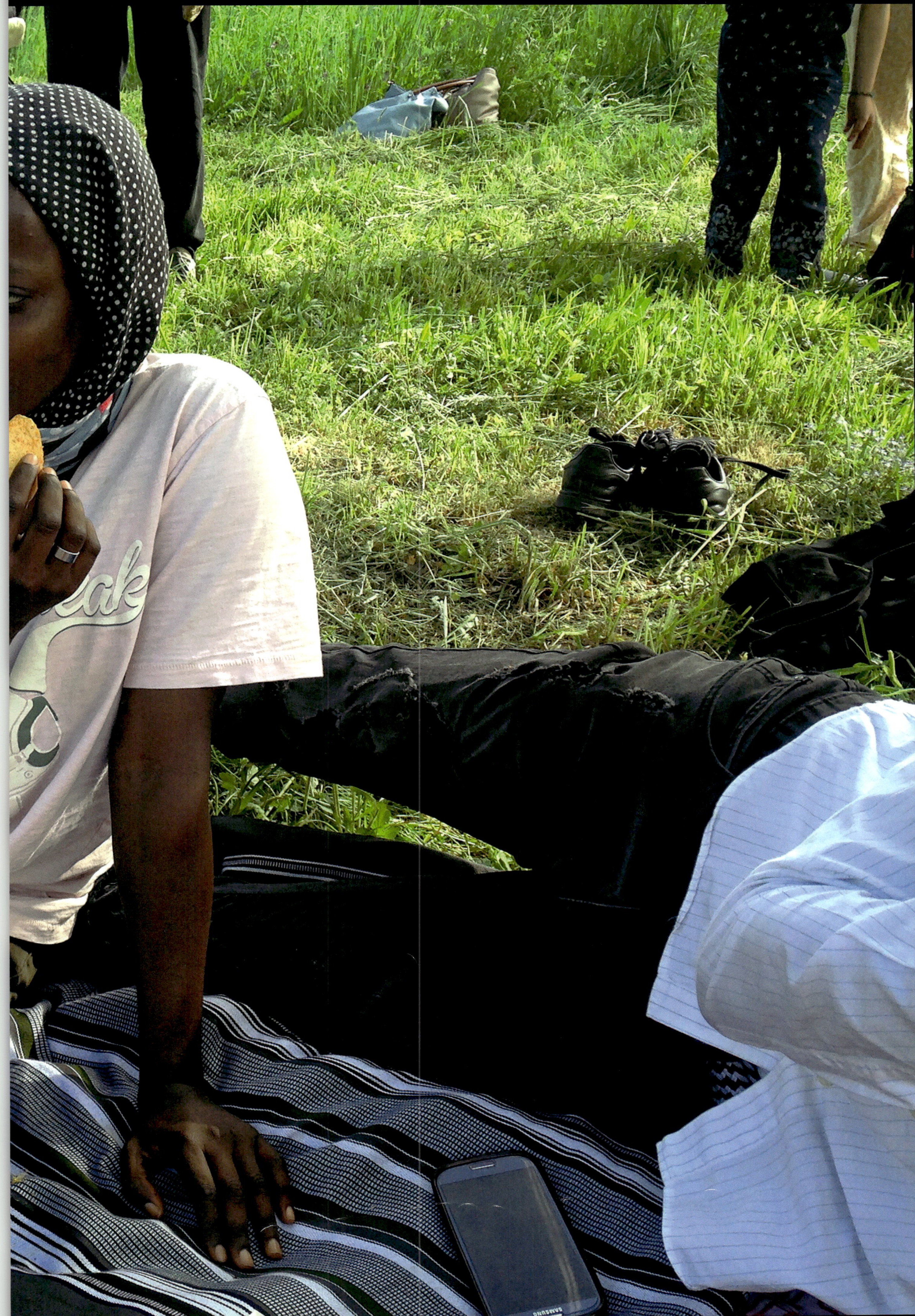

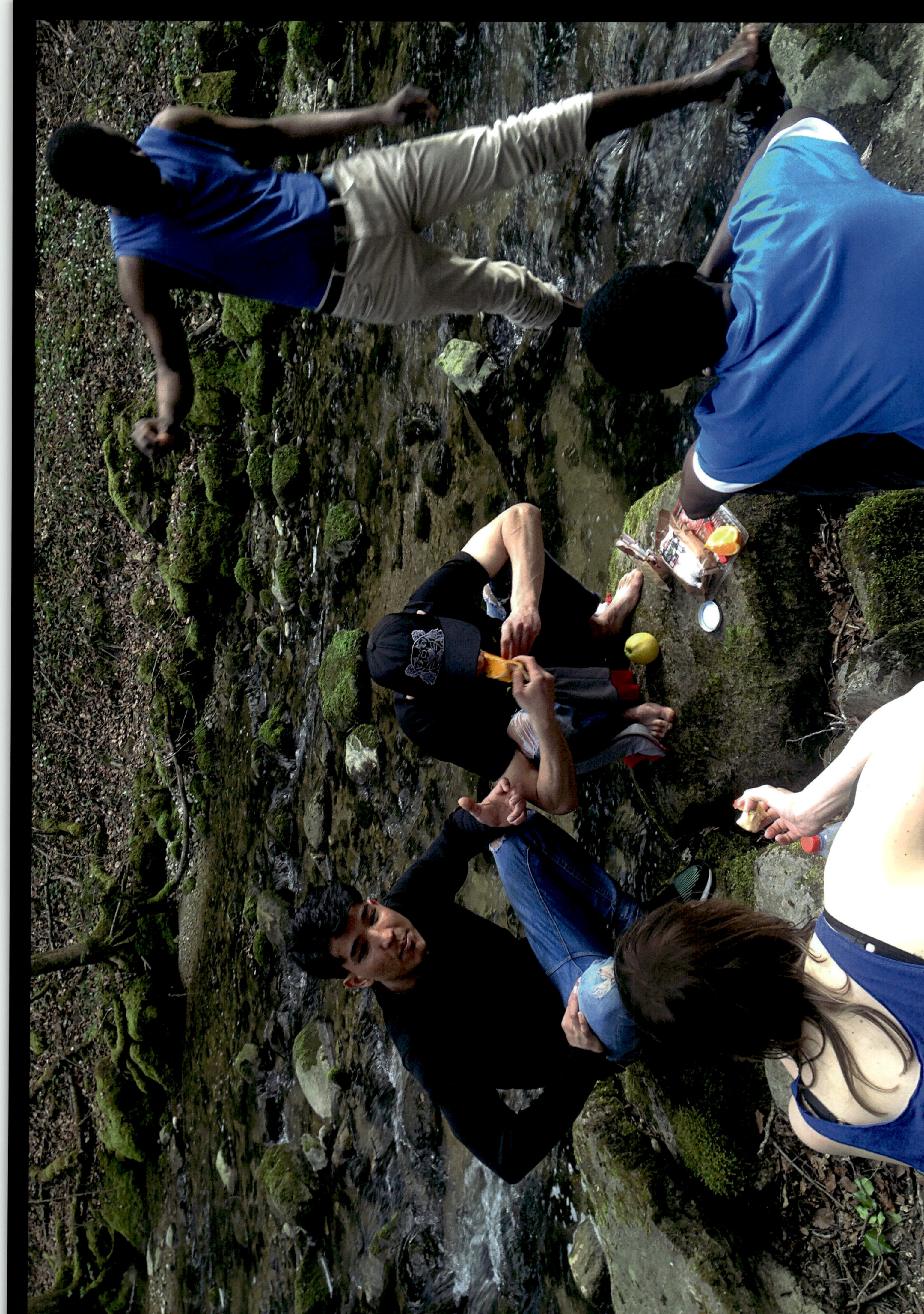

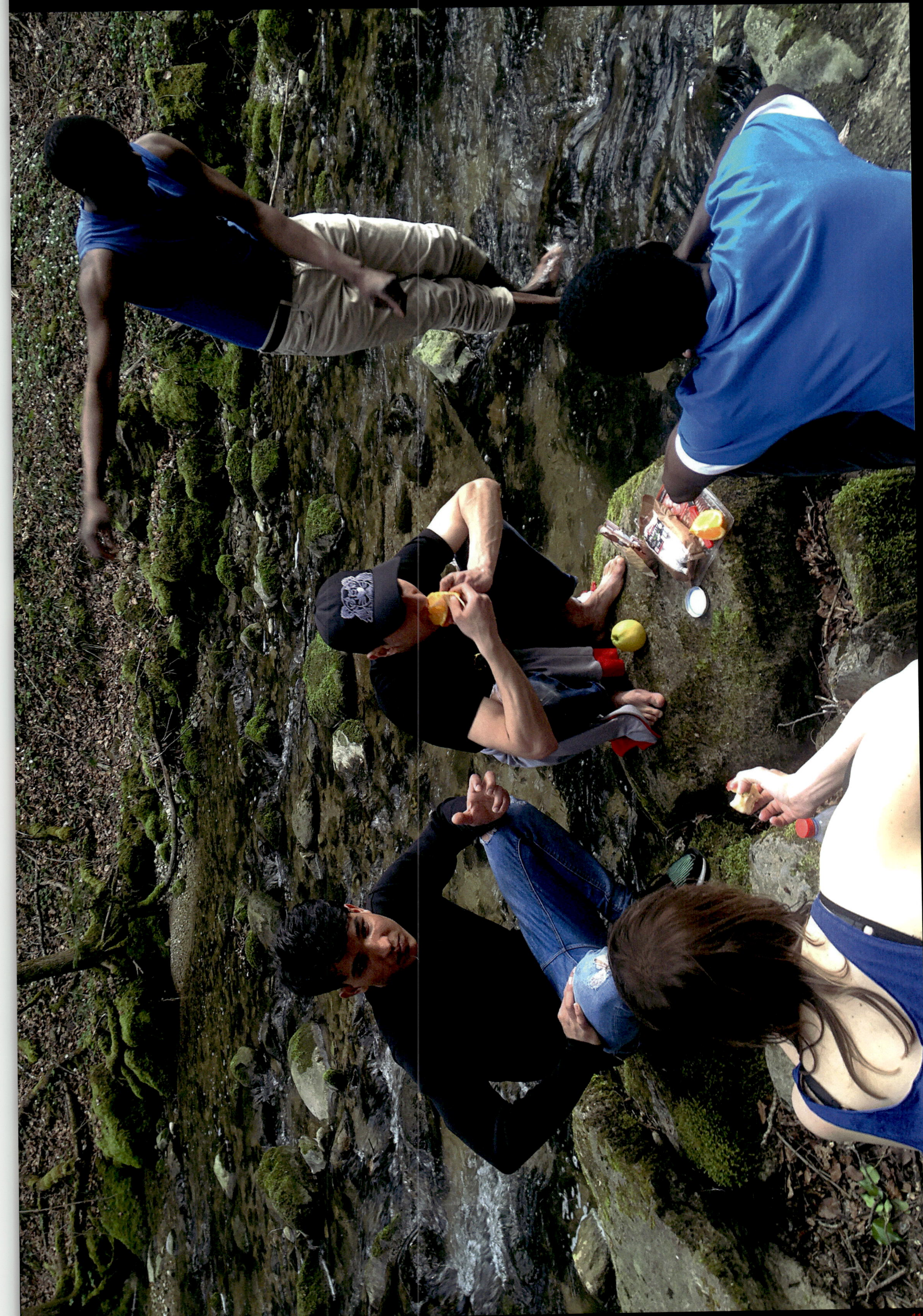

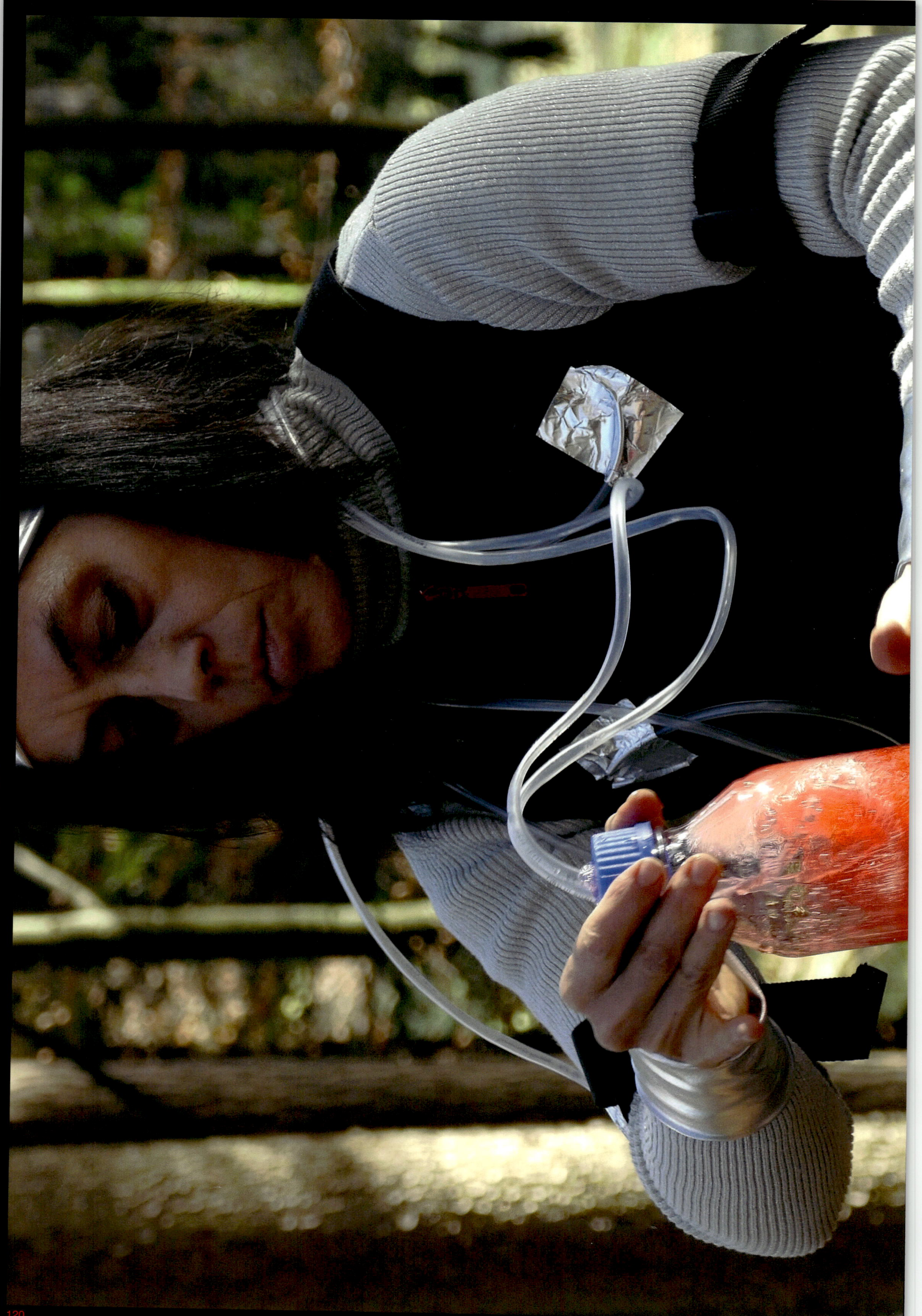

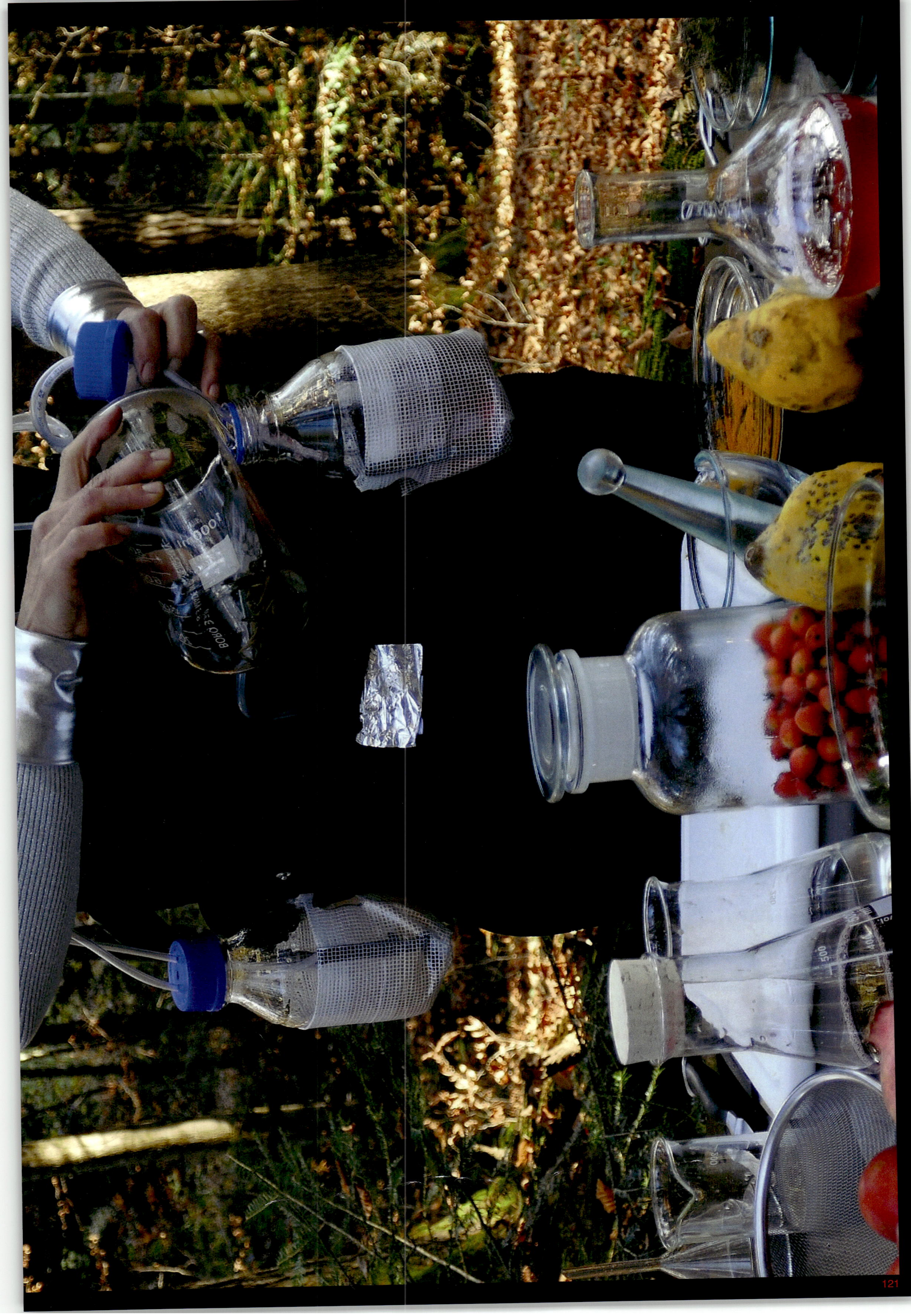

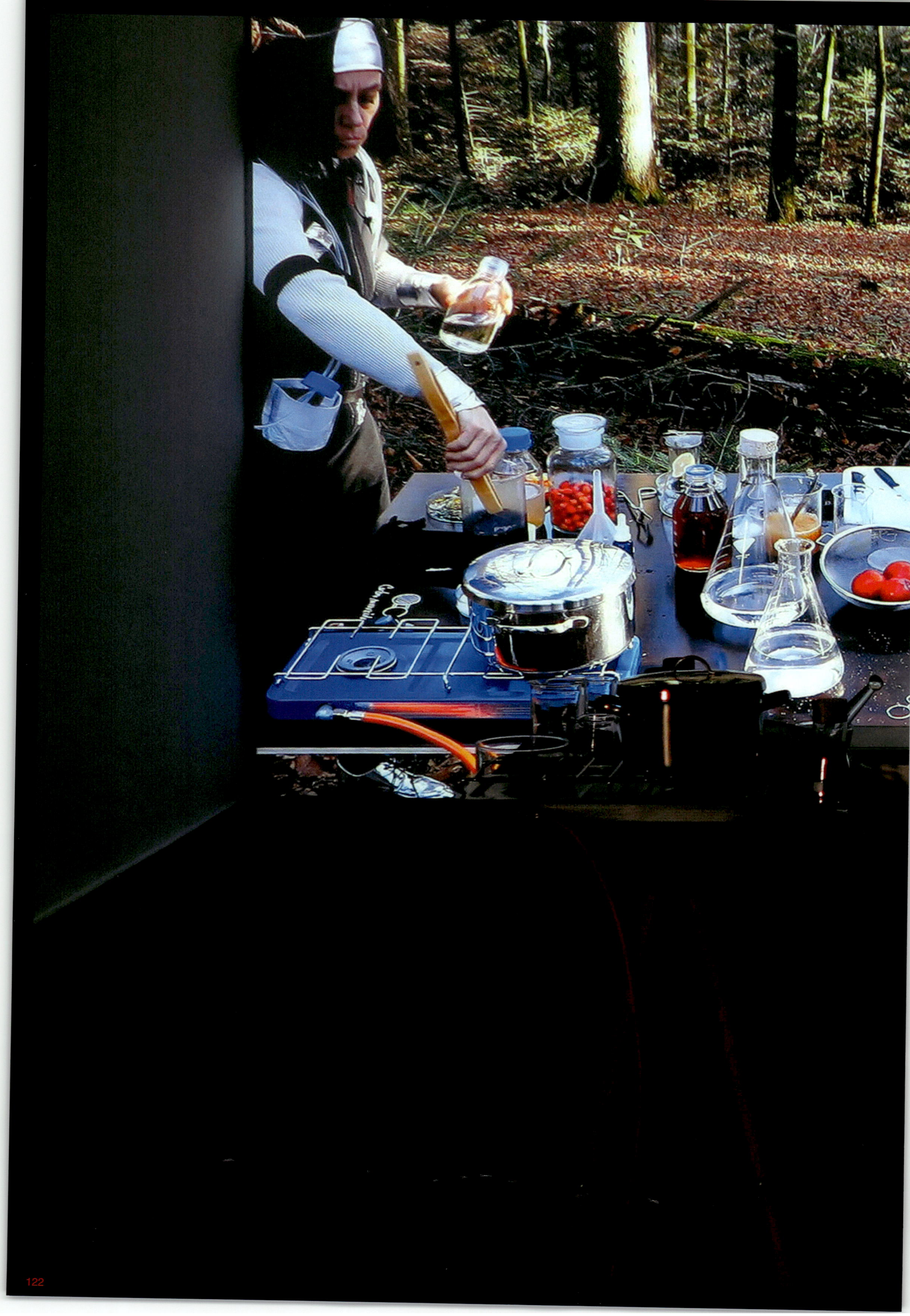

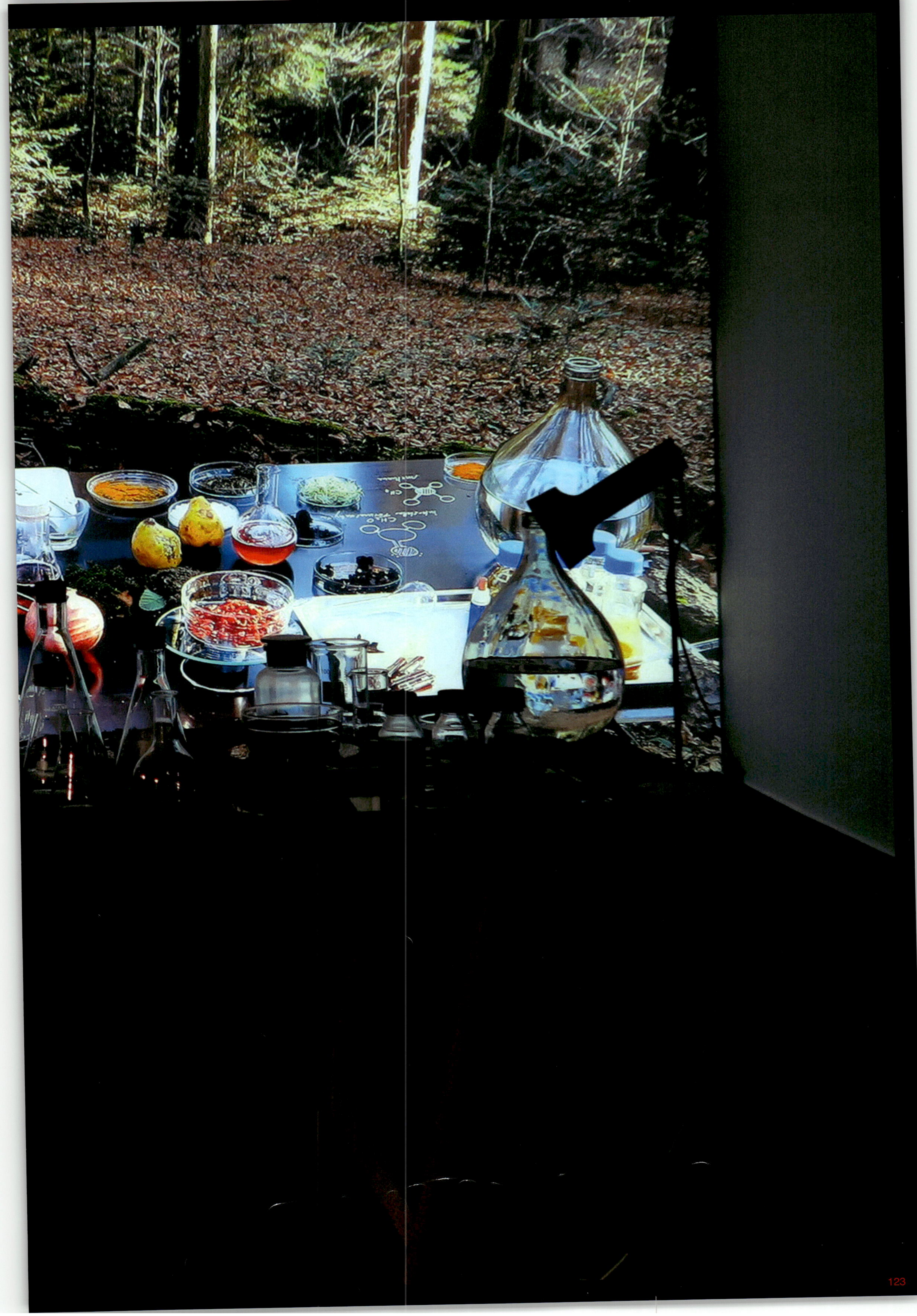

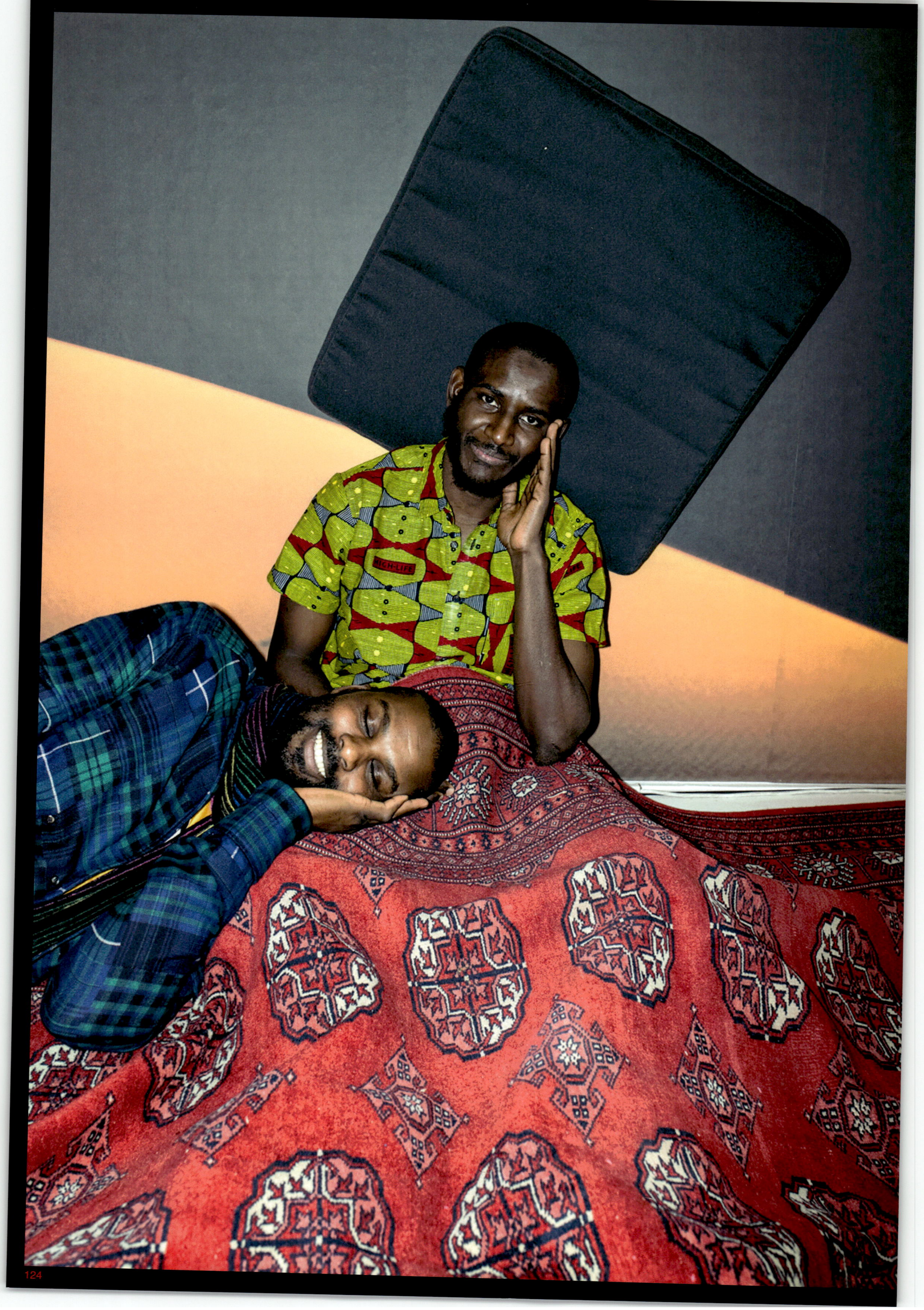

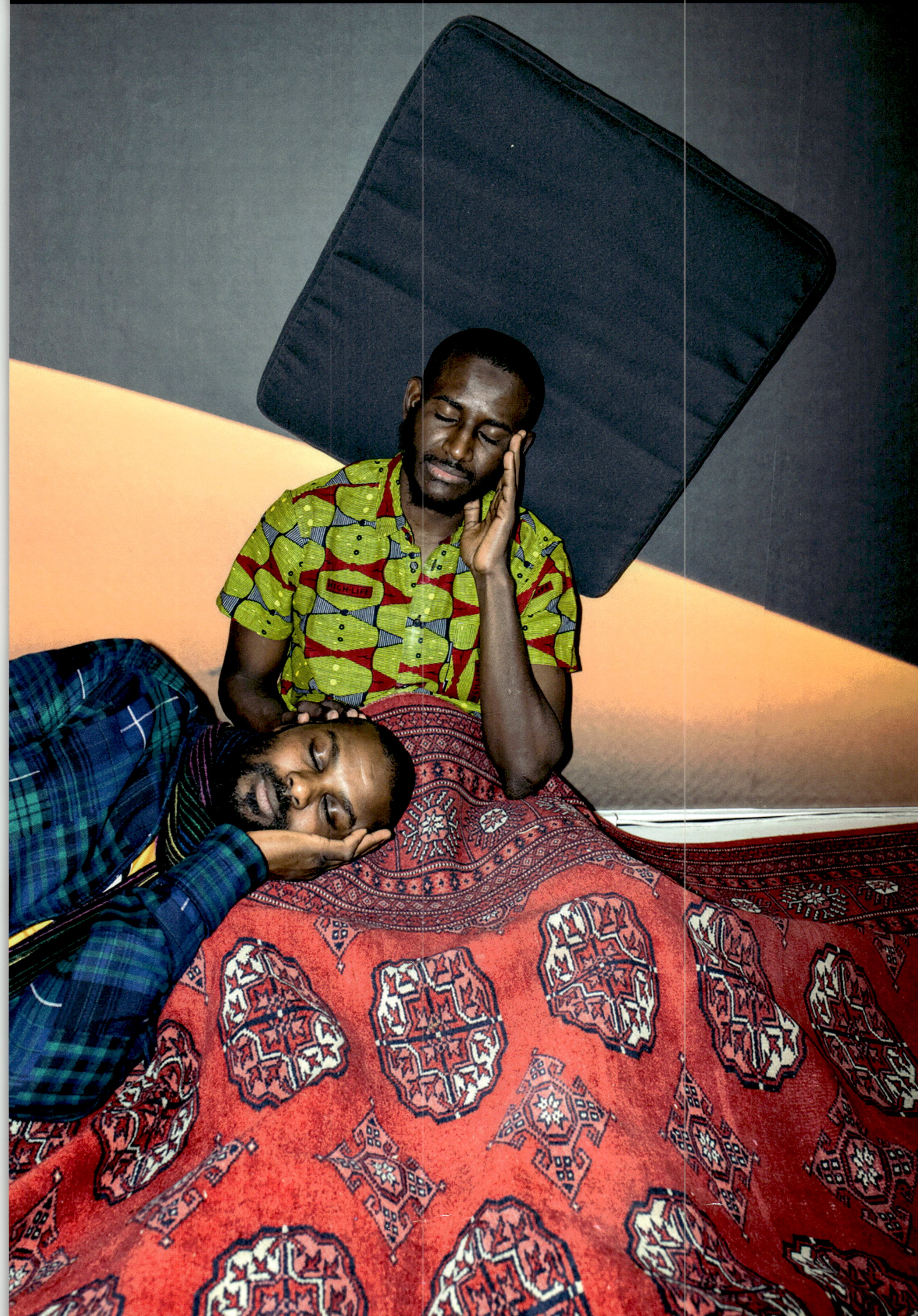

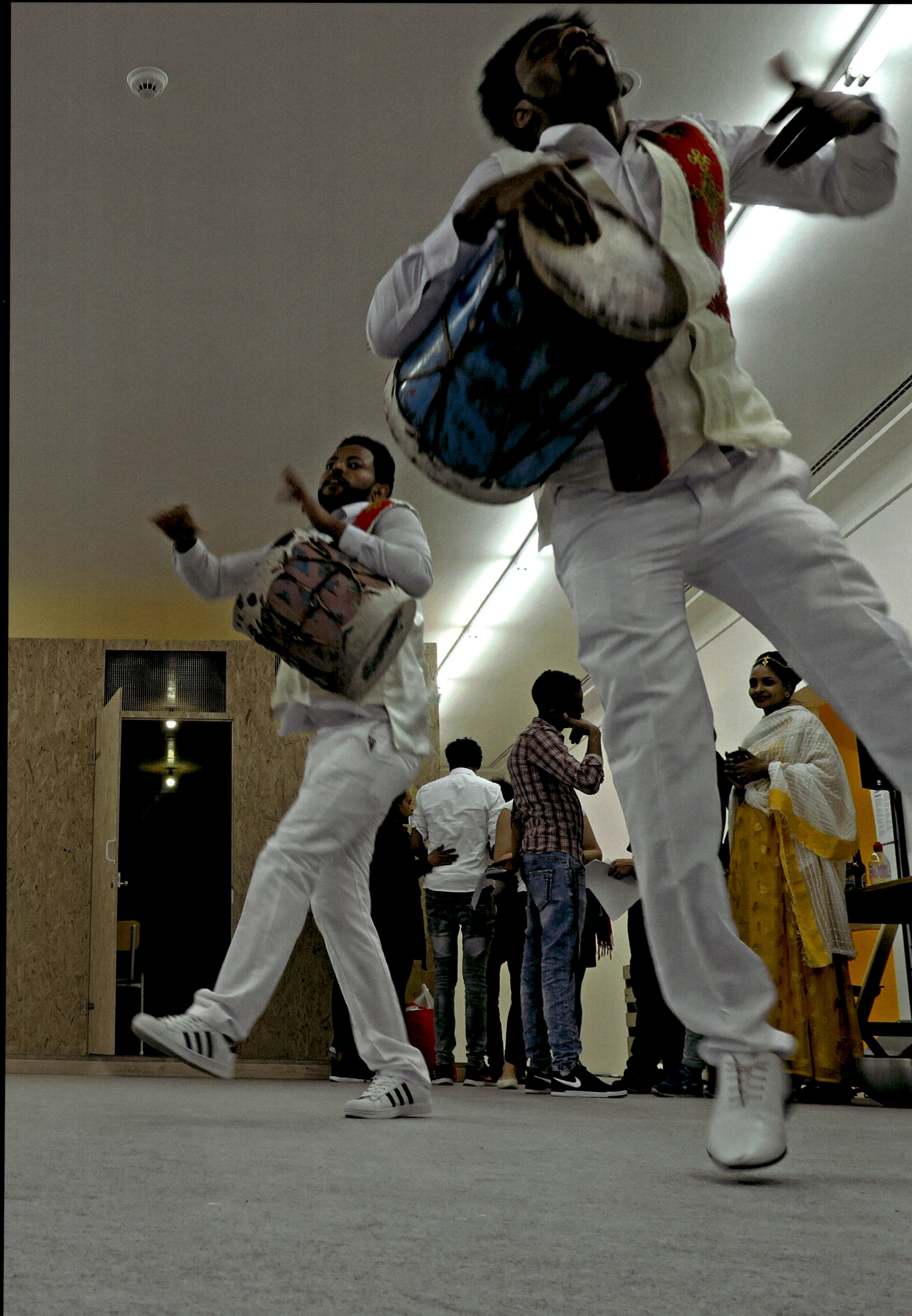

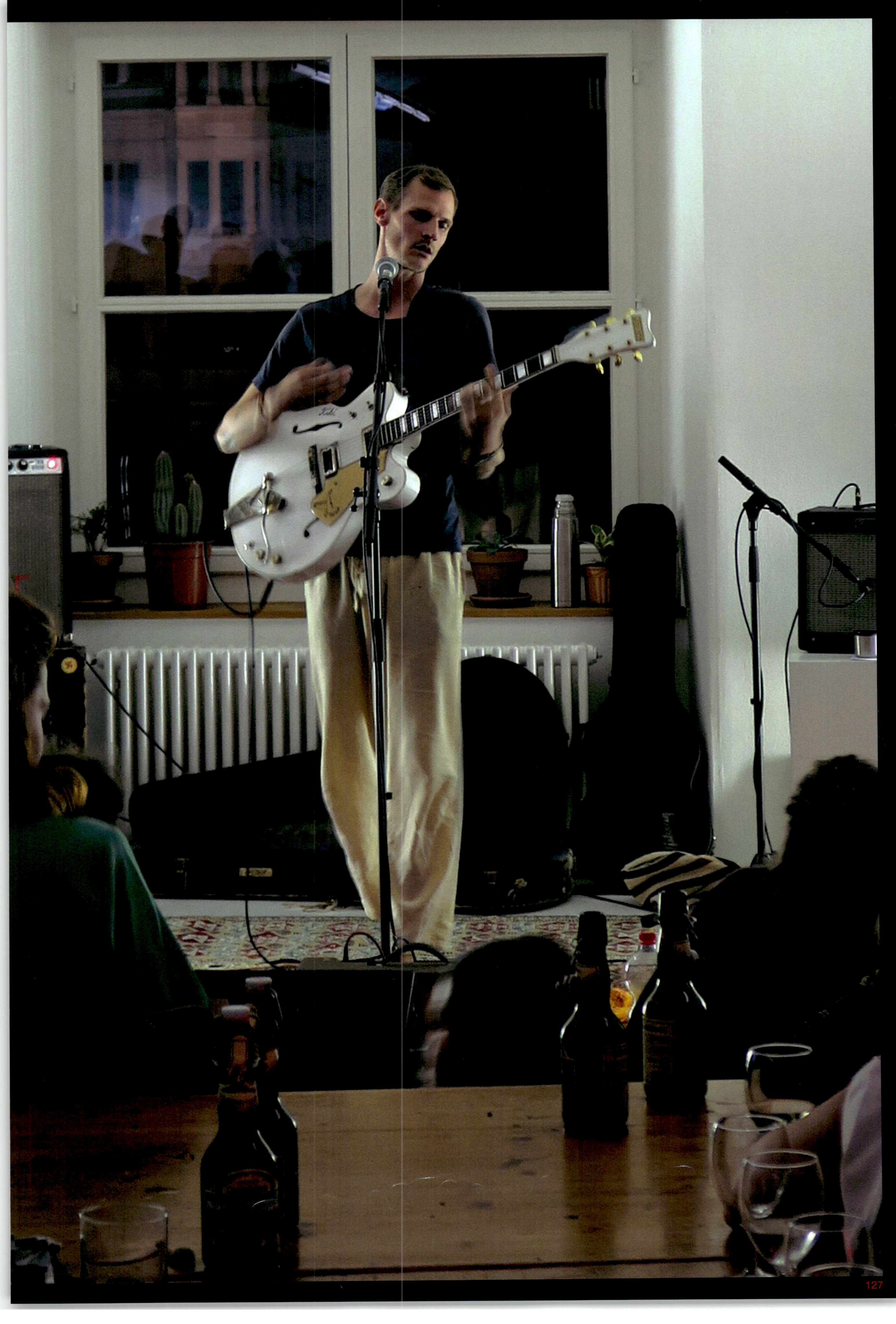

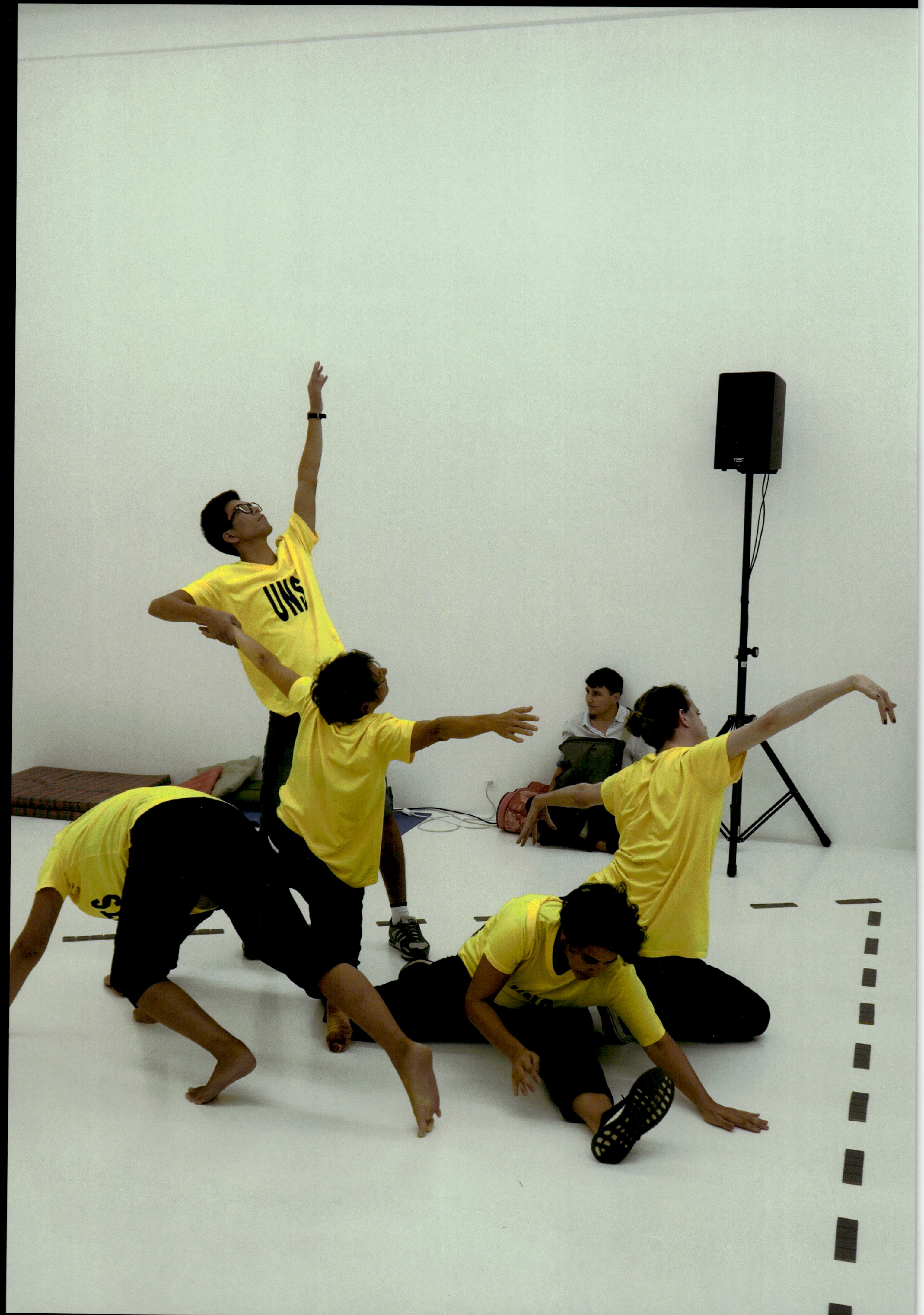
UNS

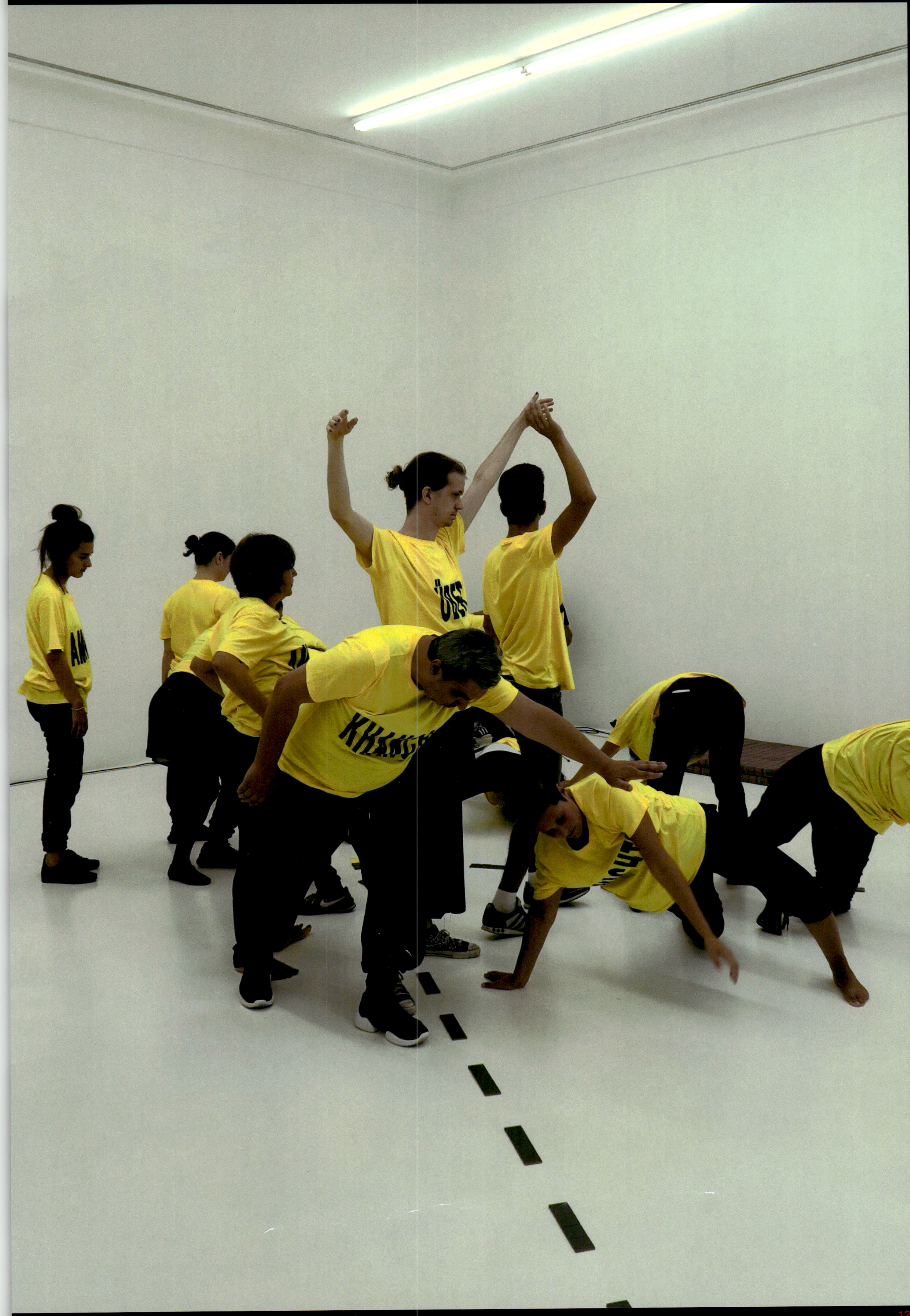

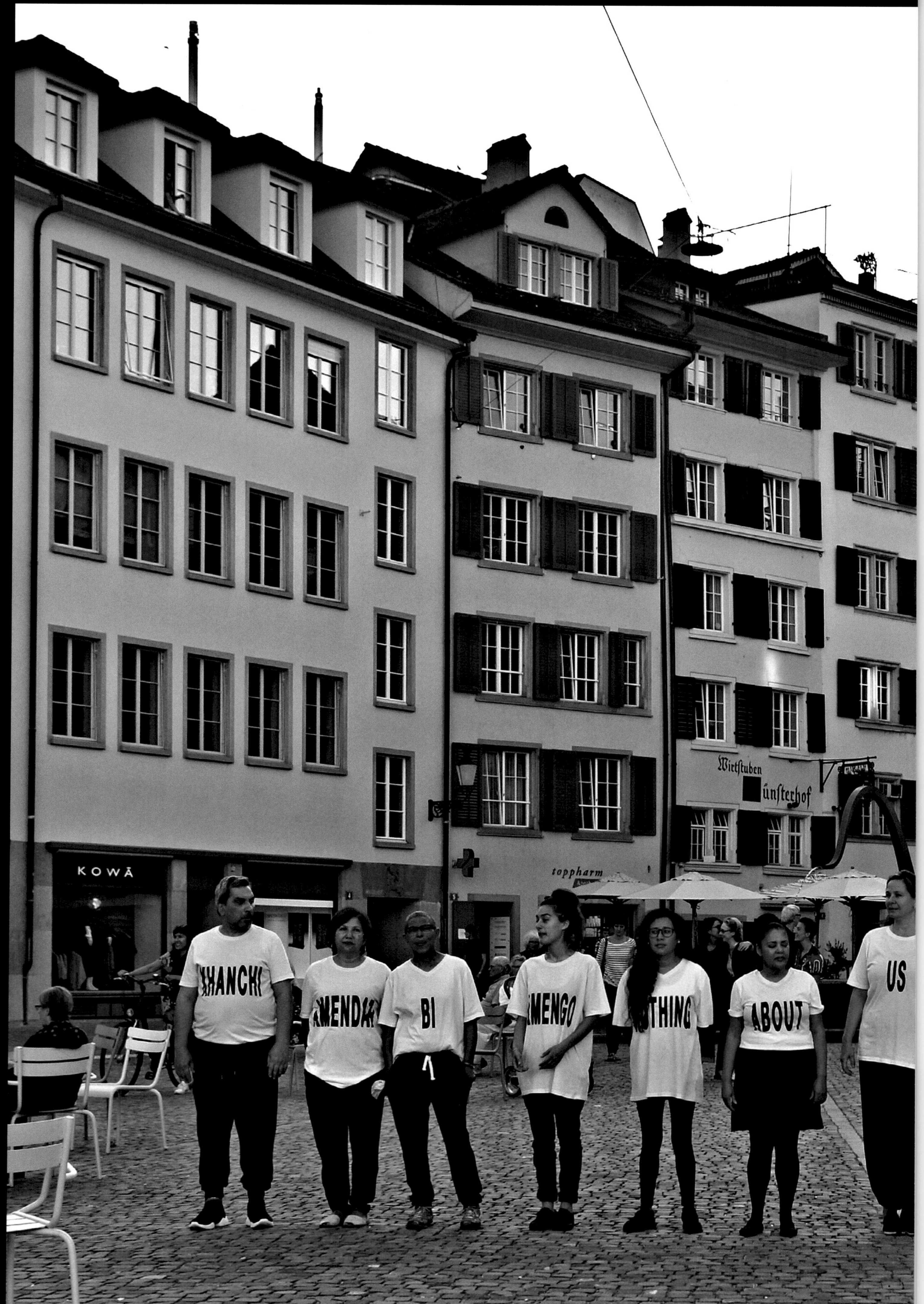
KOWĀ
toppharm
Wirtstuben
BI
ABOUT
US

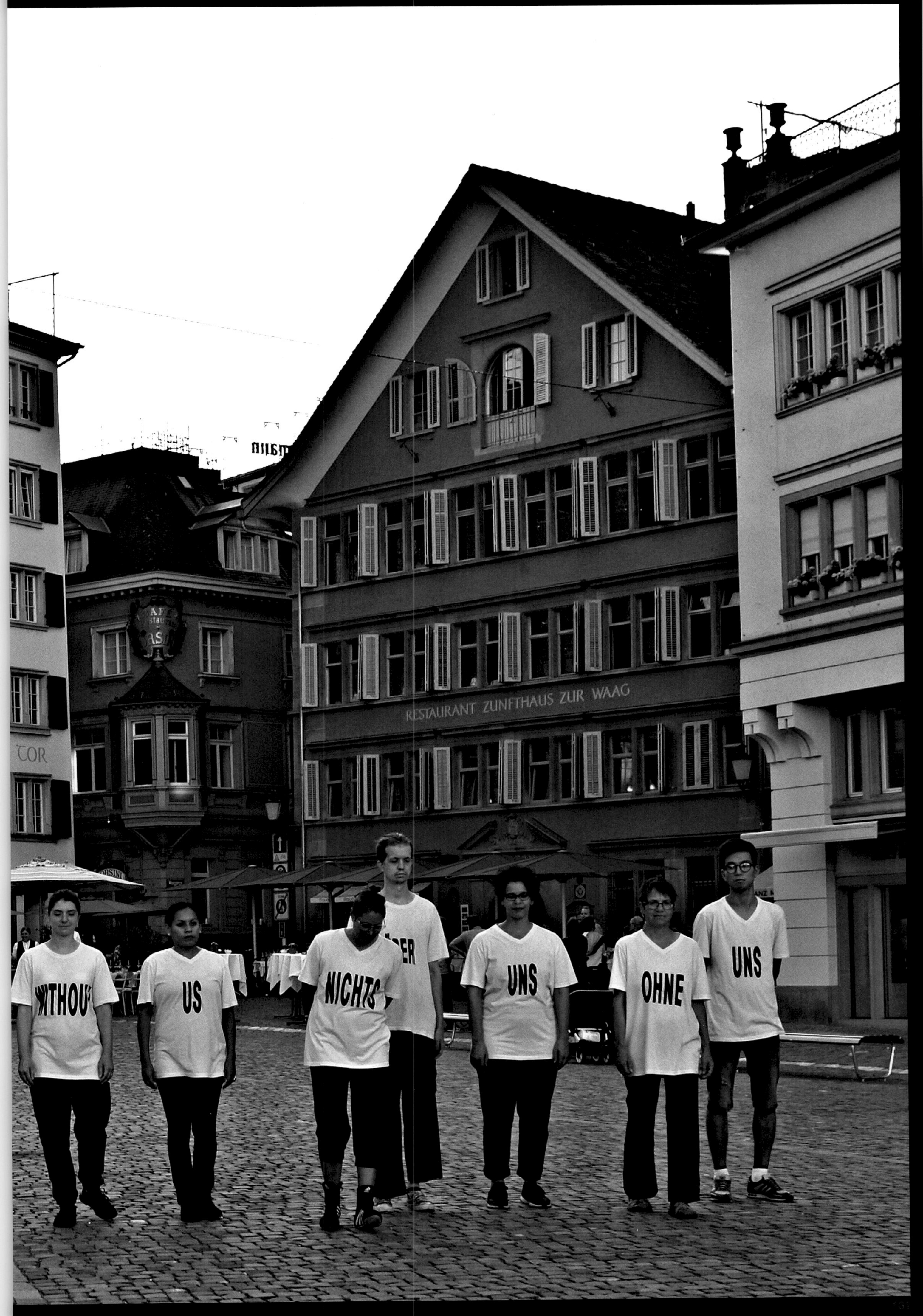
RESTAURANT ZUNFTHAUS ZUR WAAG
TOR
US
NICHTS
UNS
OHNE
UNS

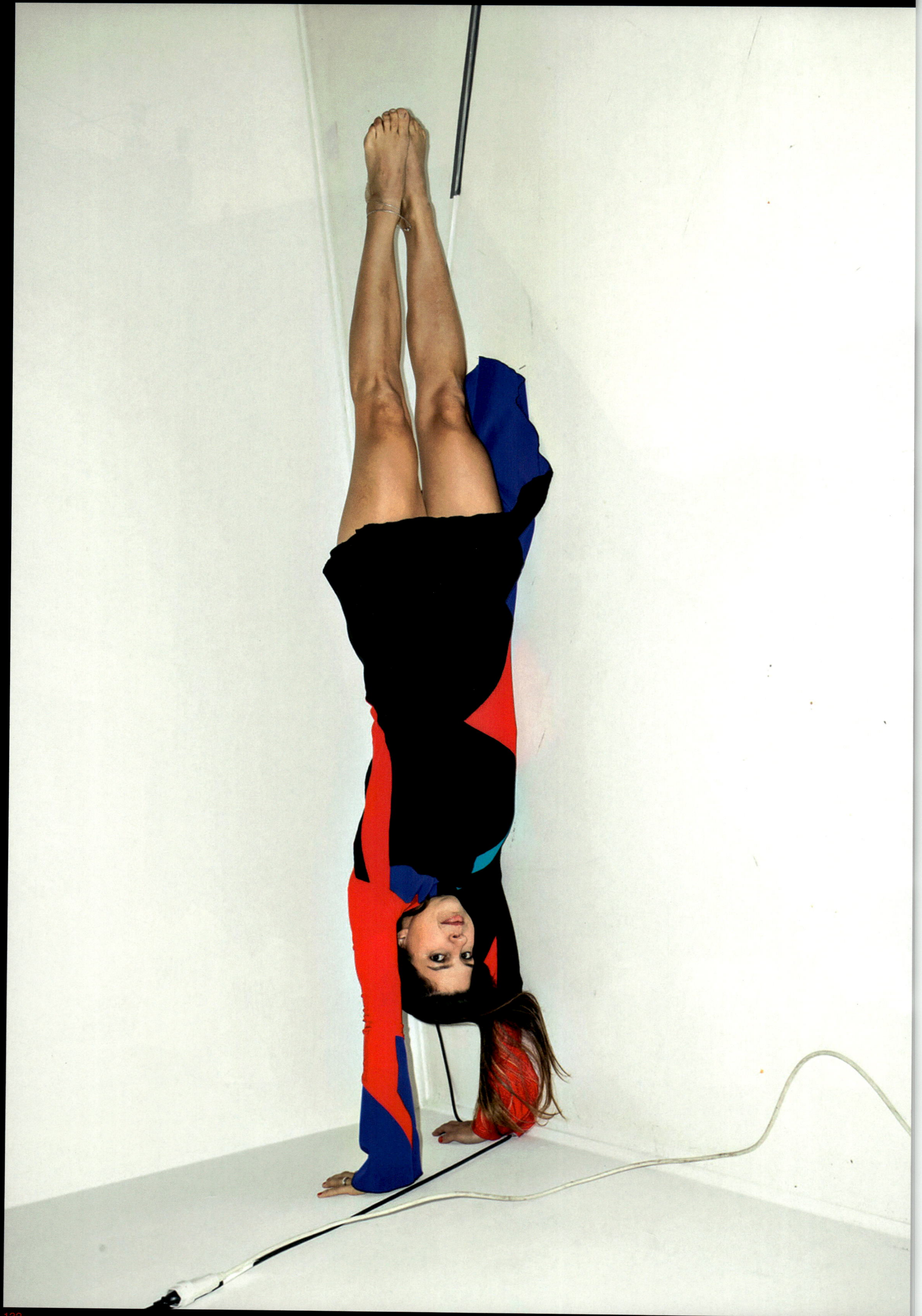

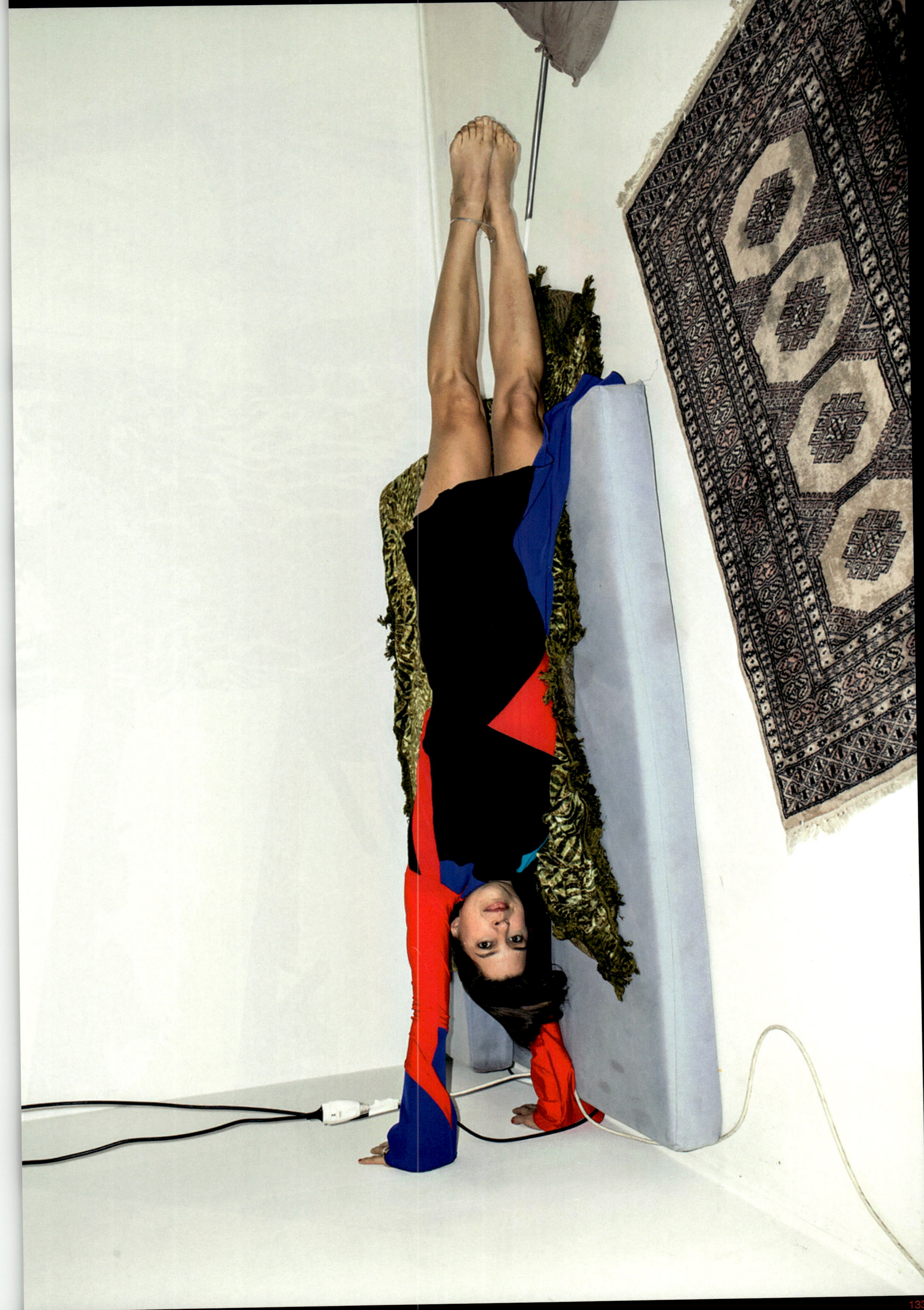

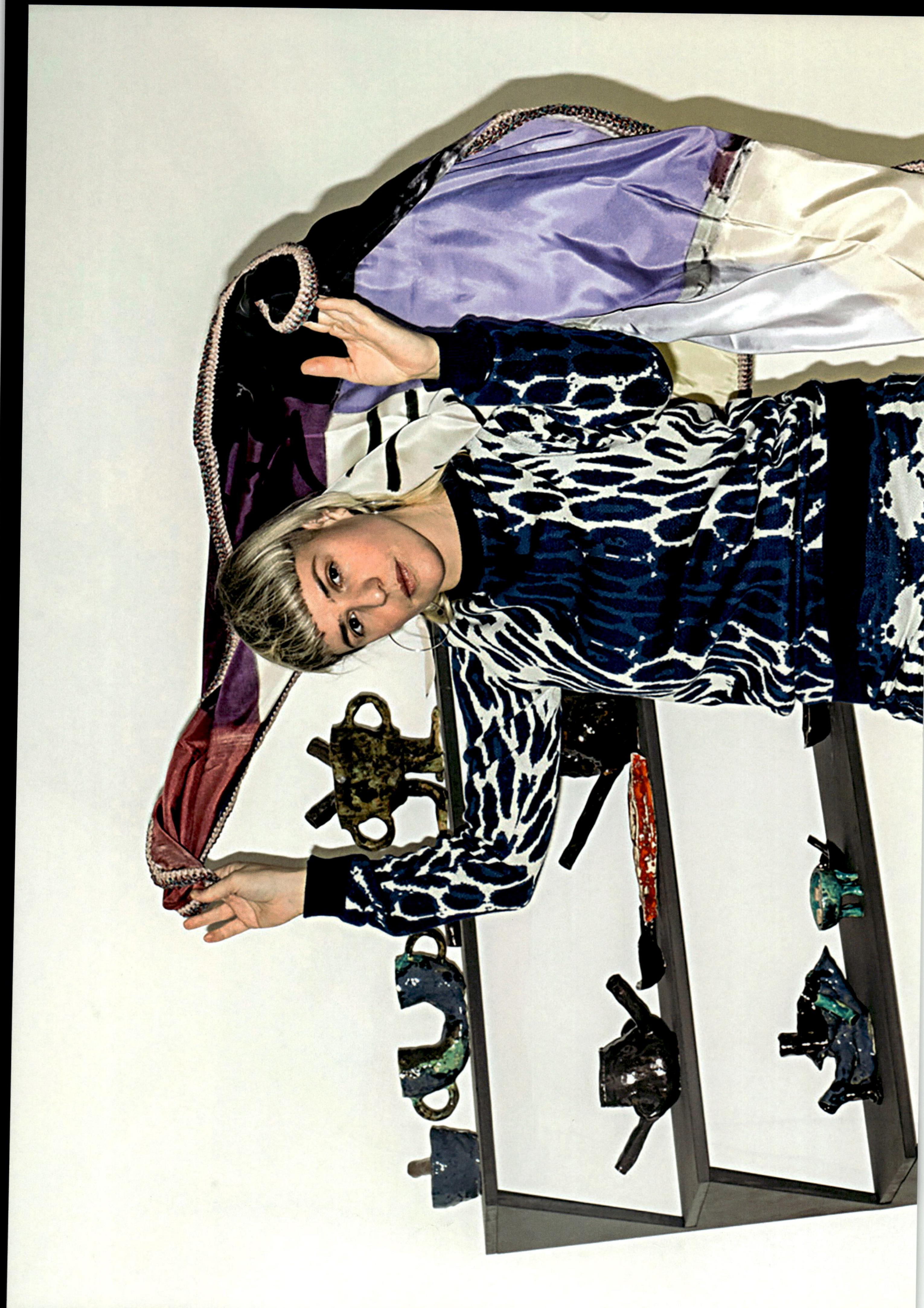

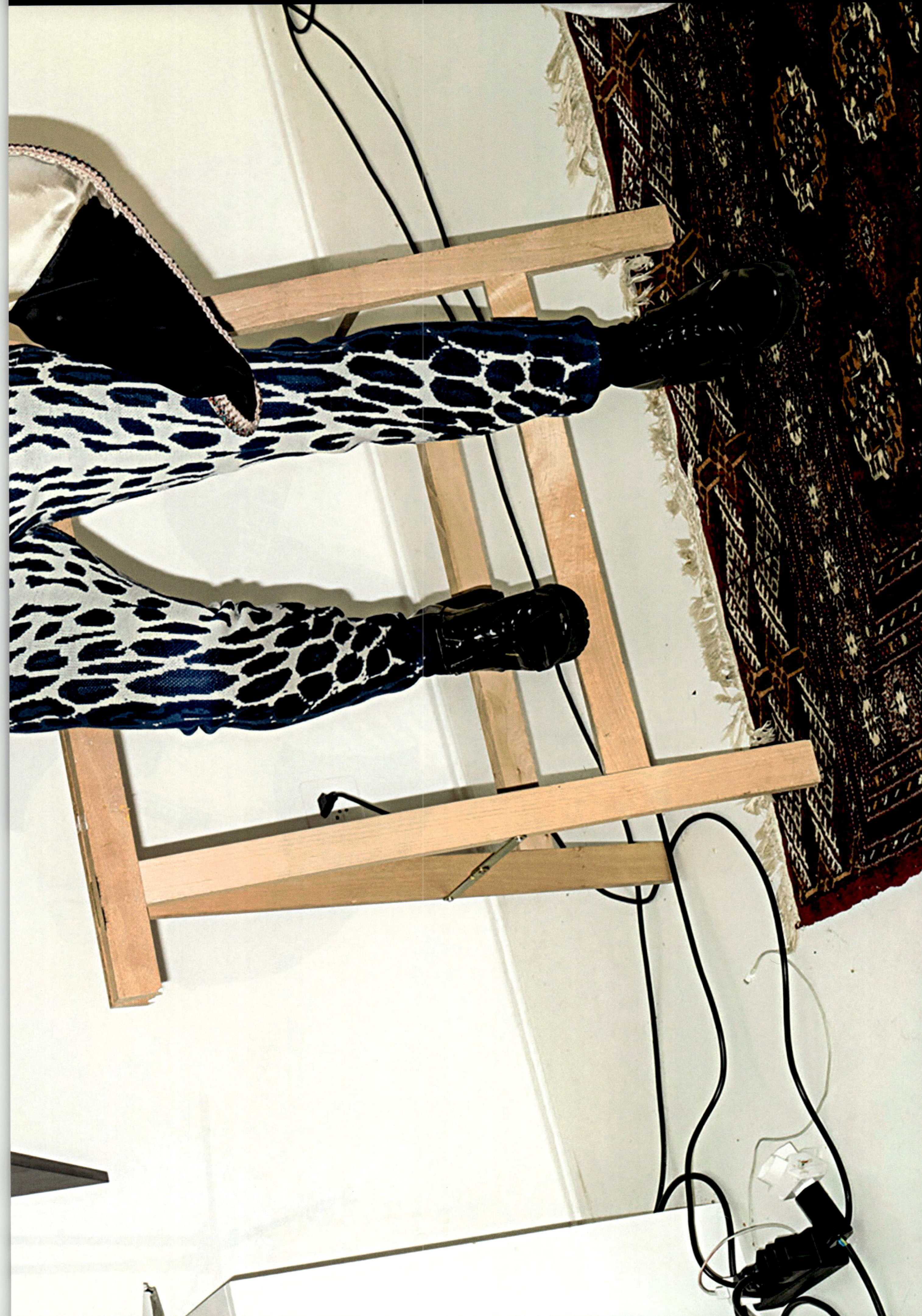

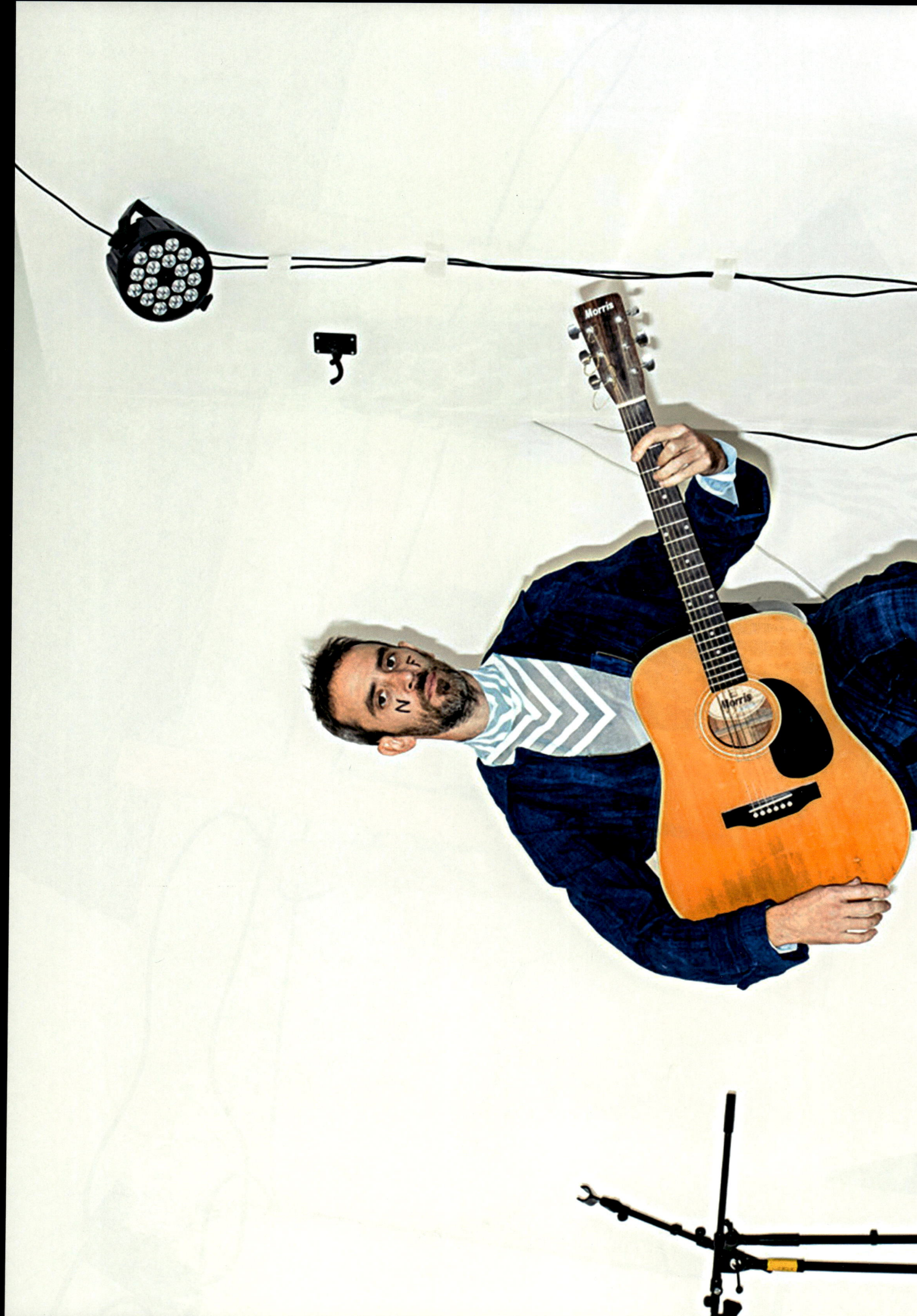
Morris
Morris

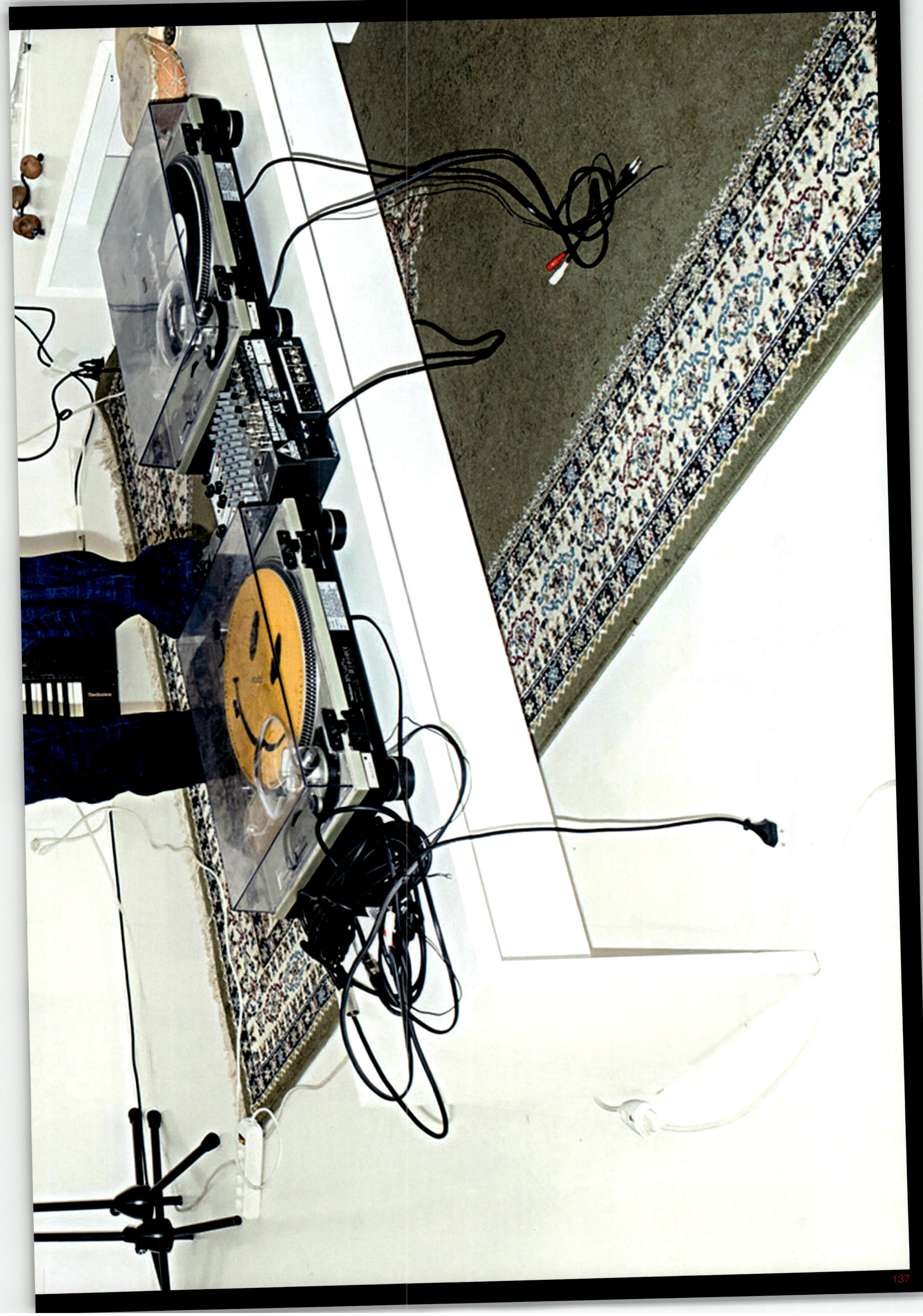

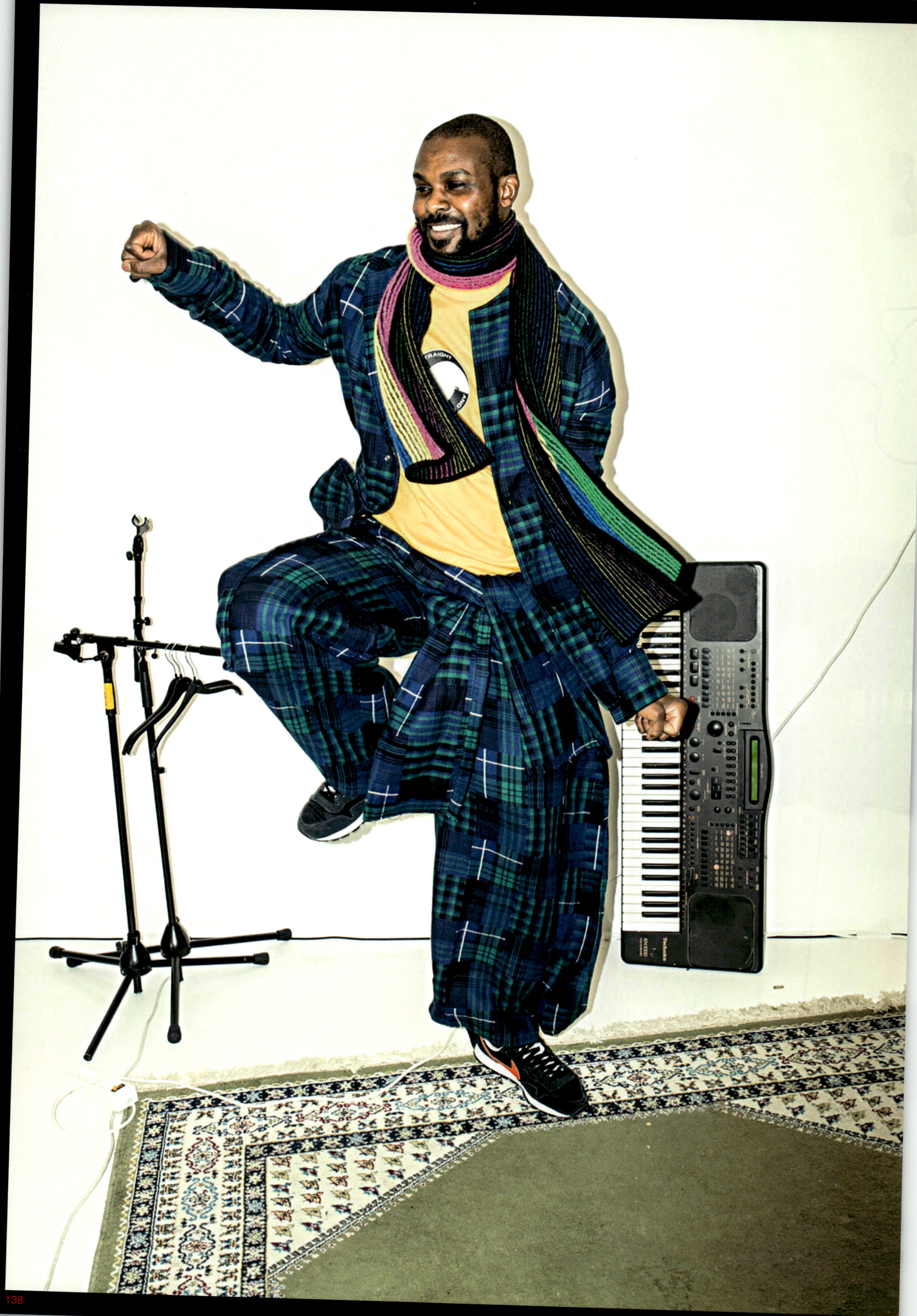

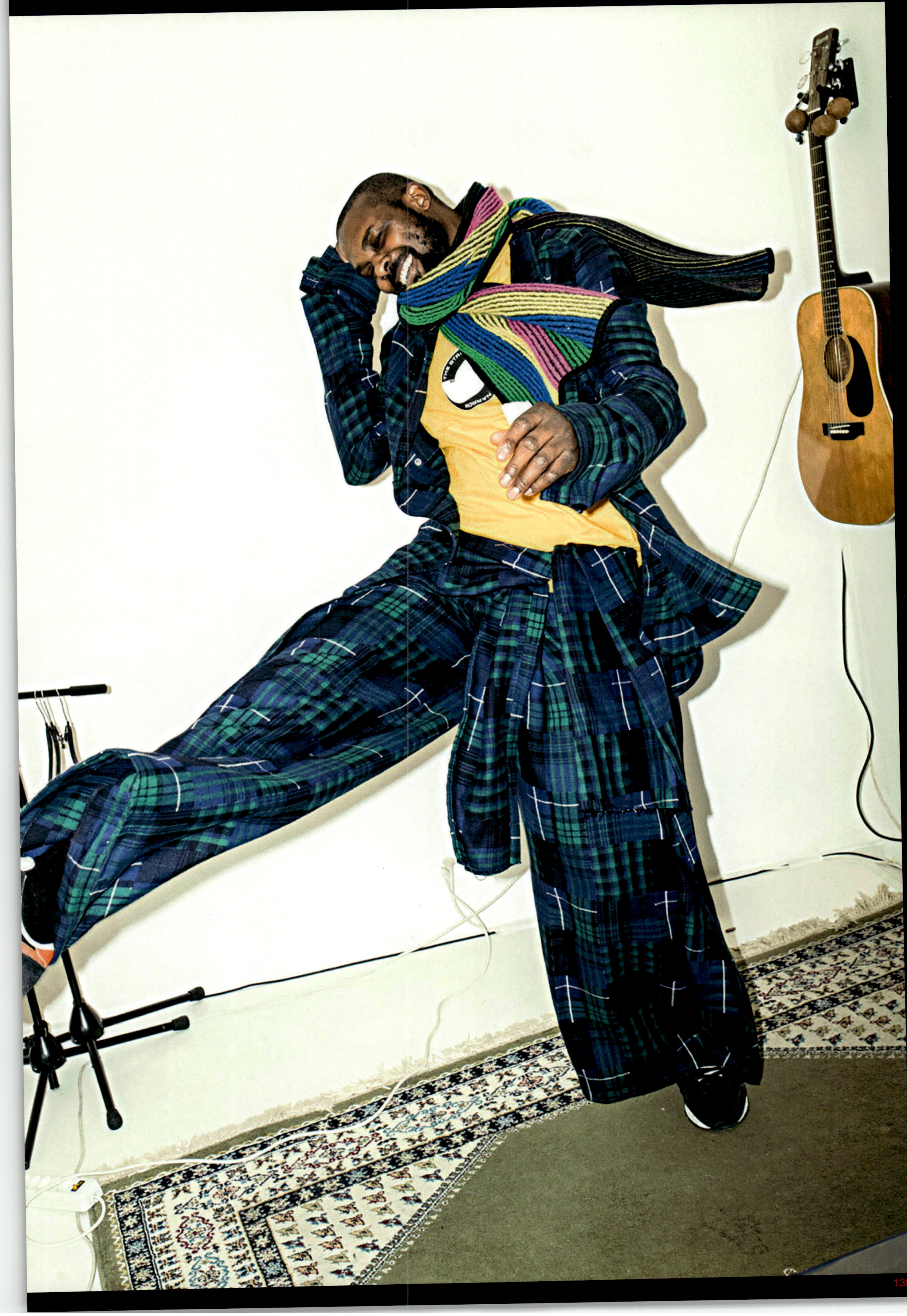

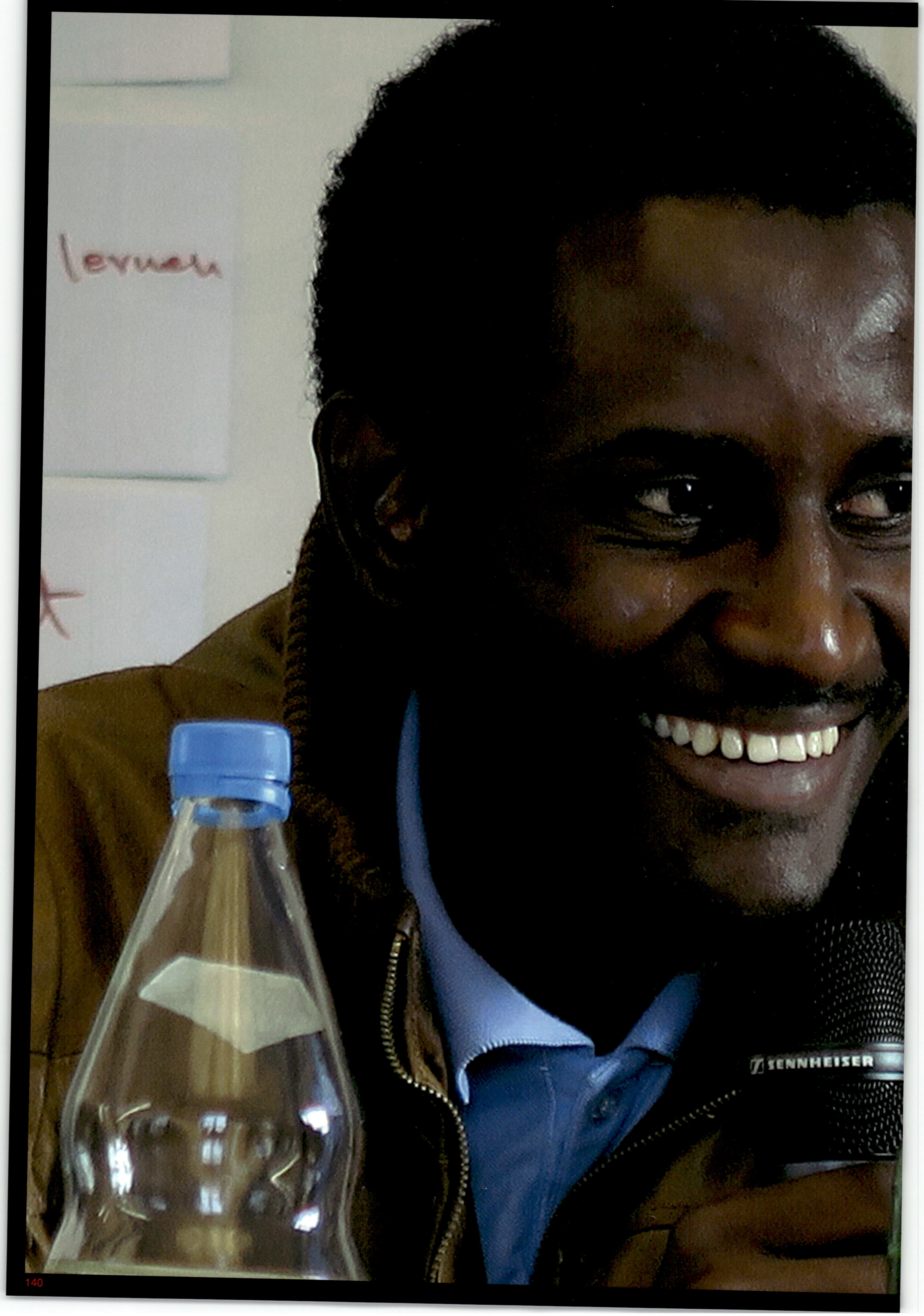
SENNHEISER

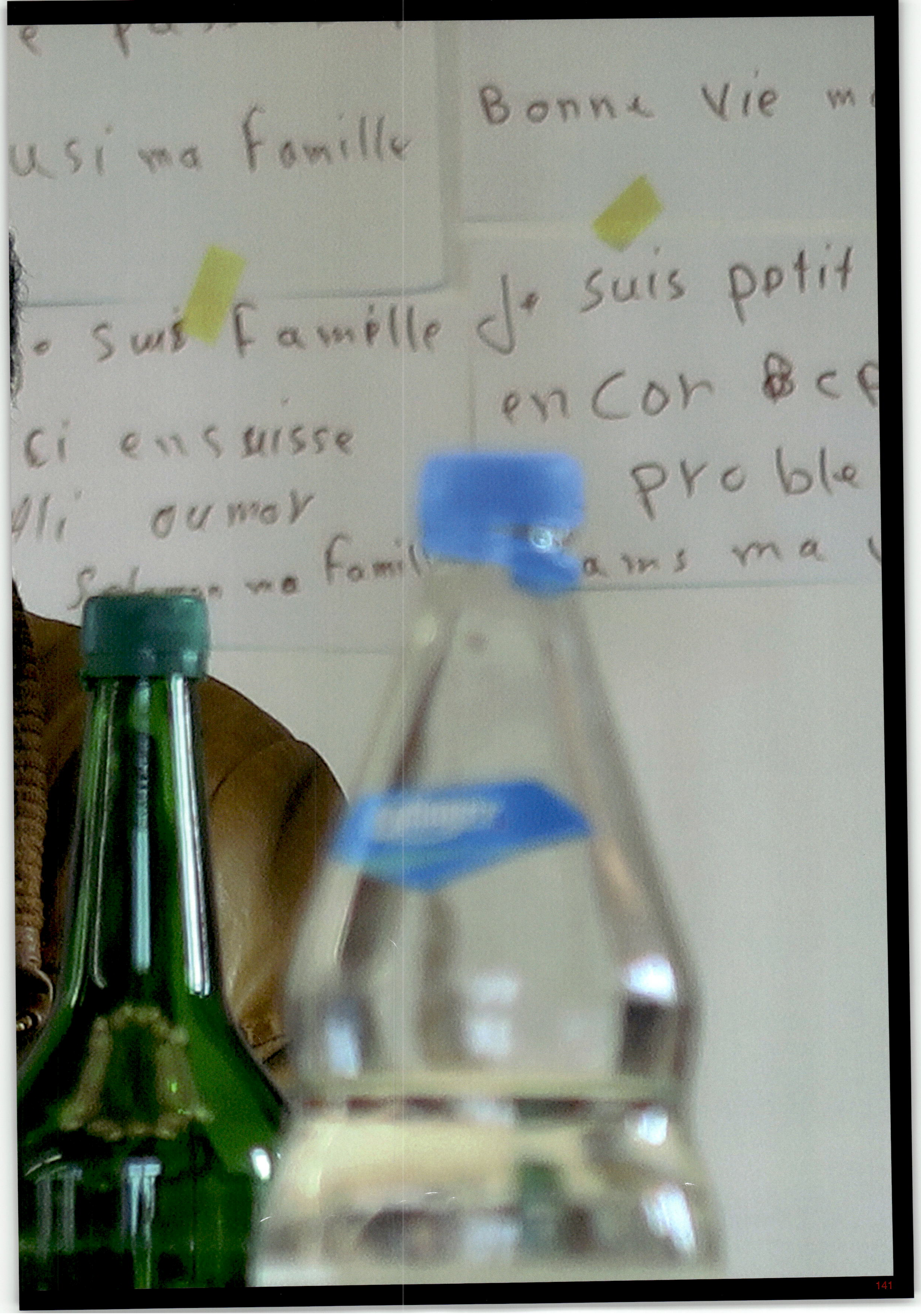
Bonne vie
usi ma famille
Je suis potit
e suis famille
encor
si enssuisse
proble
oumor
ams ma

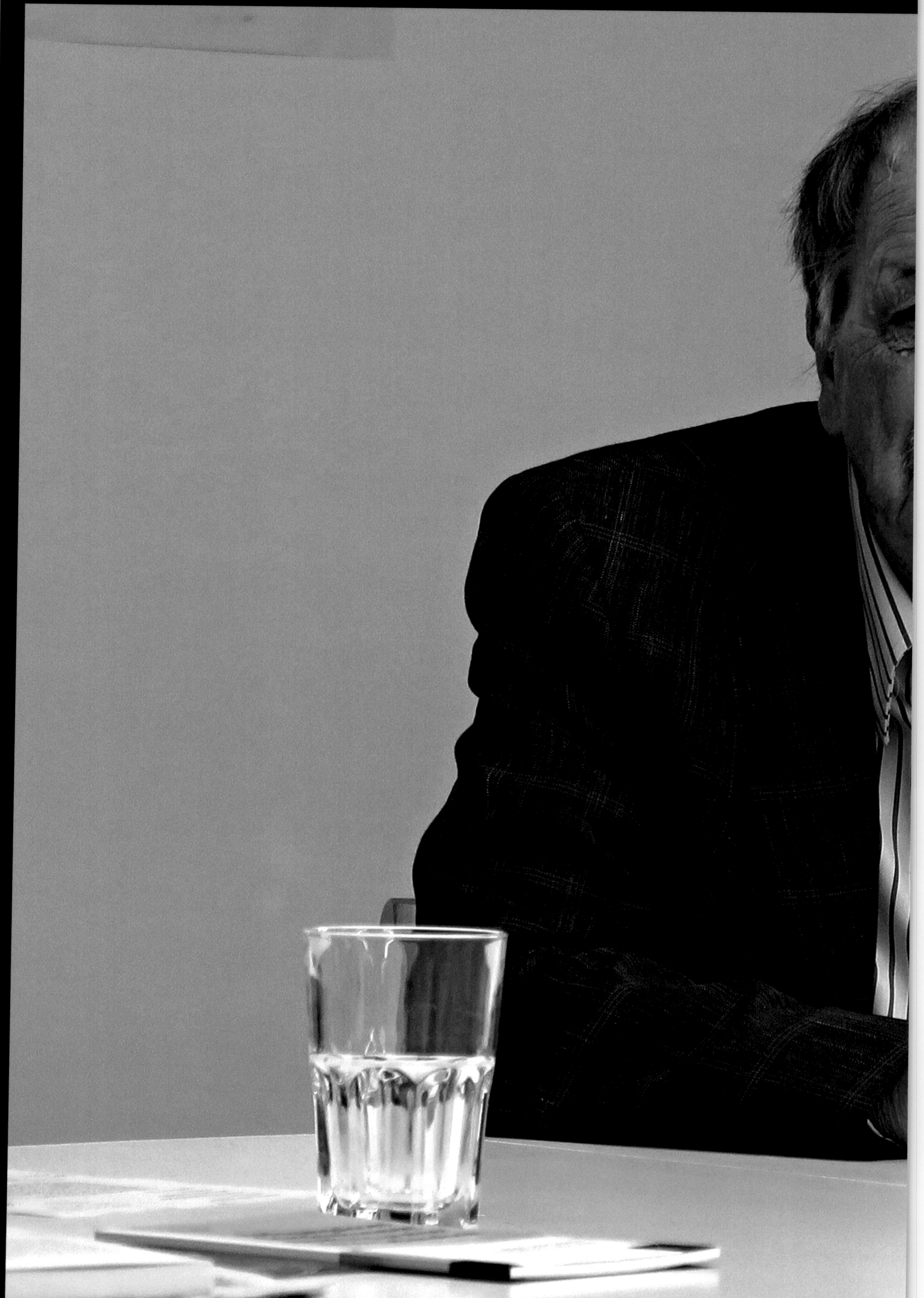

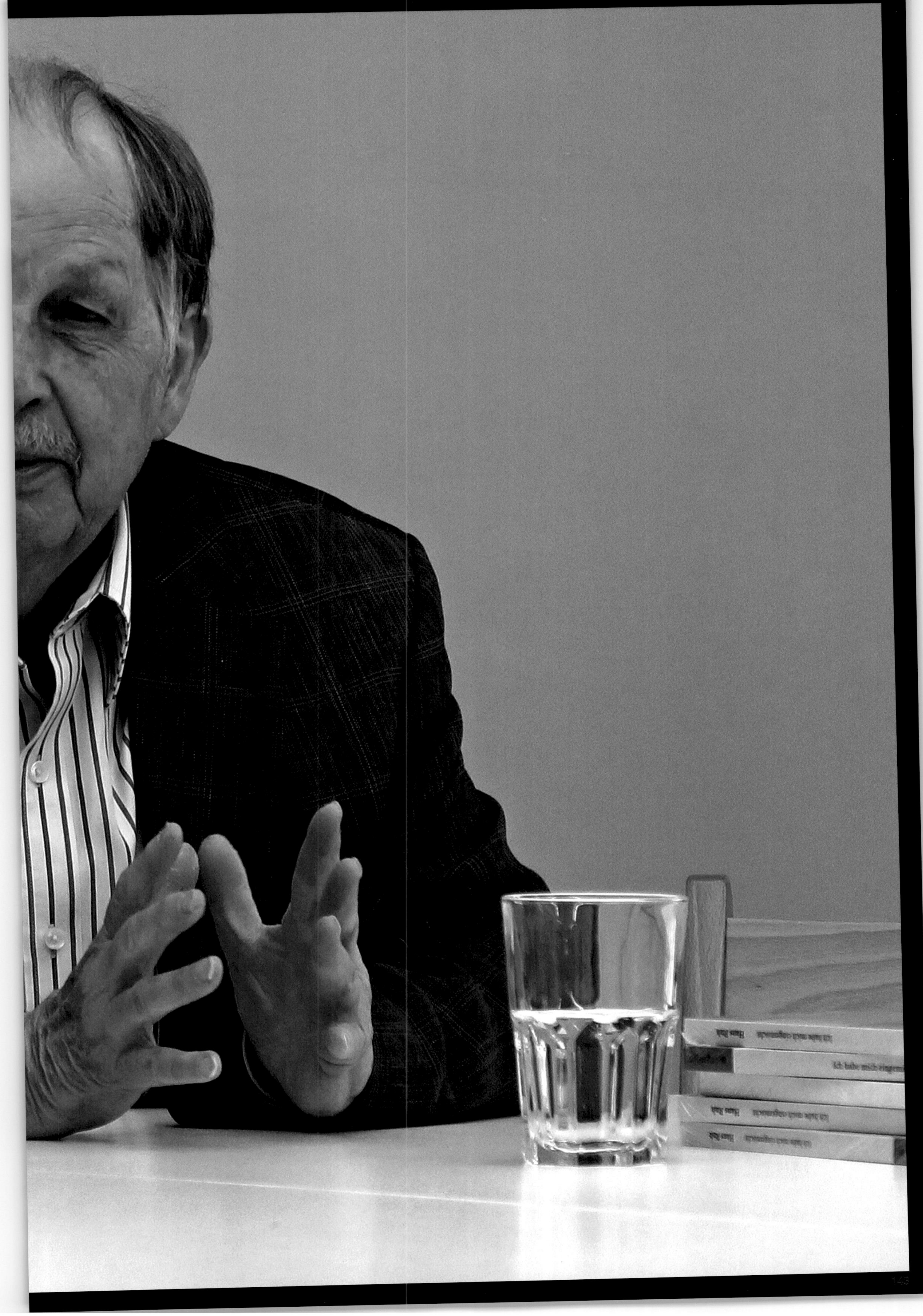

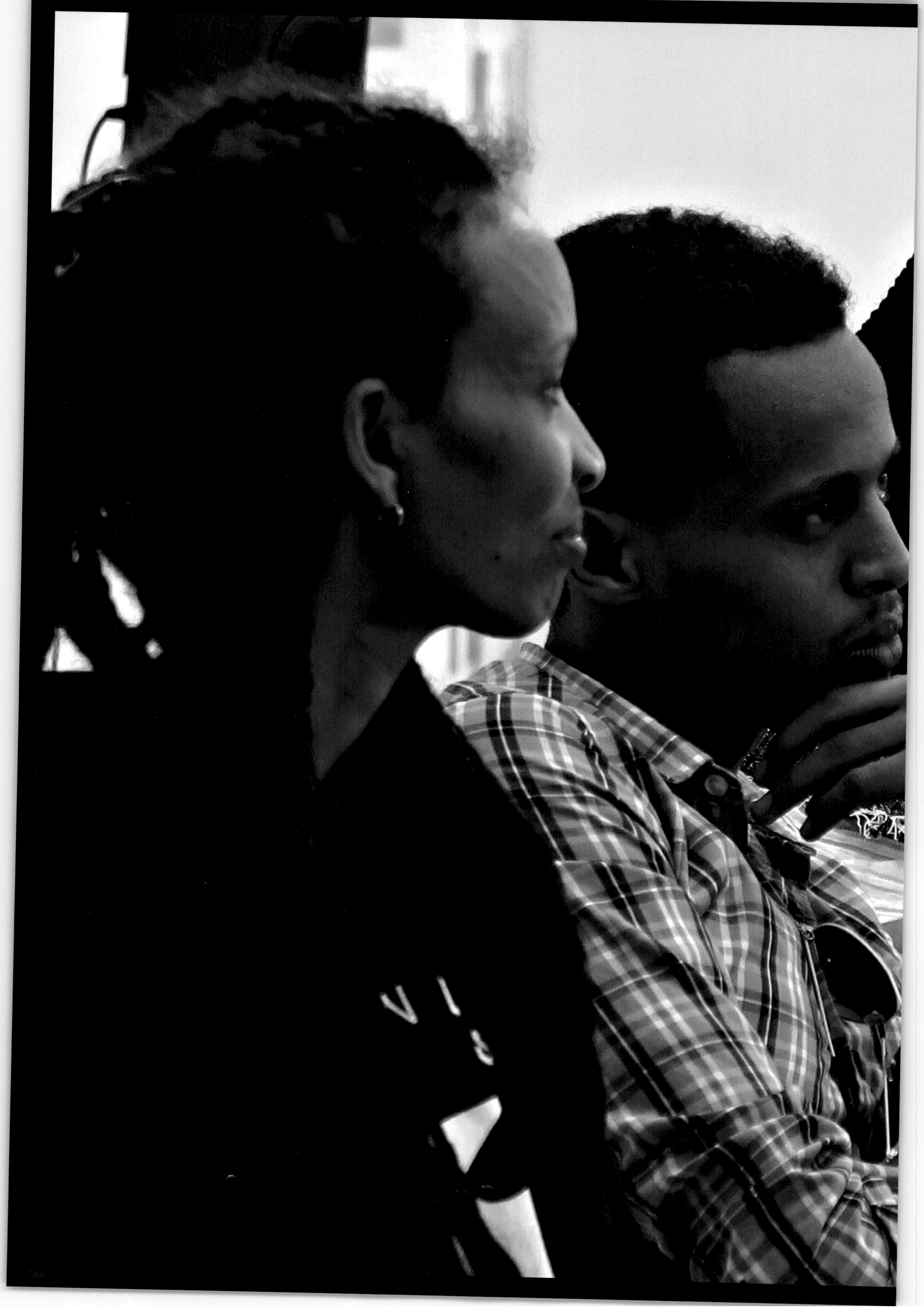

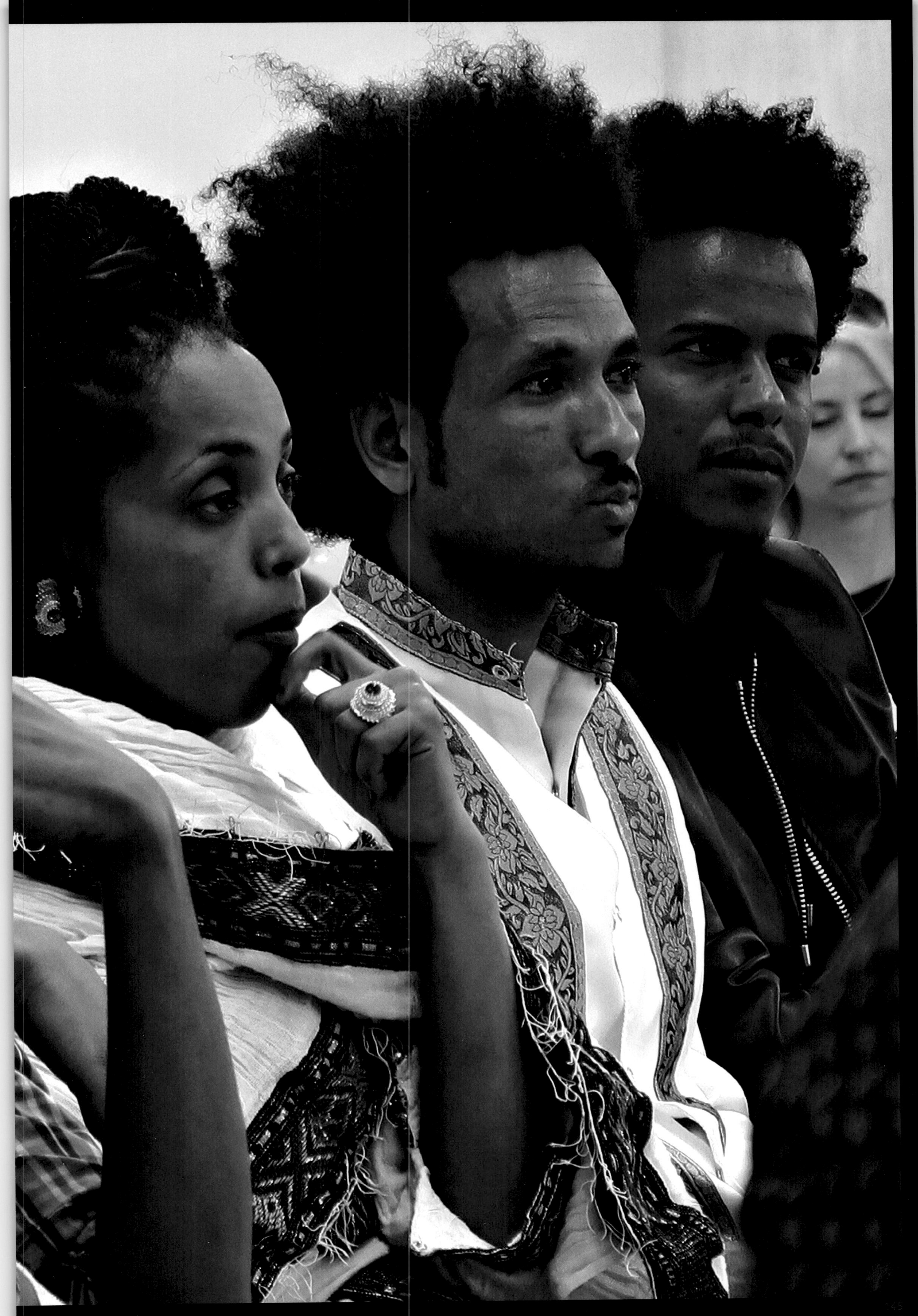

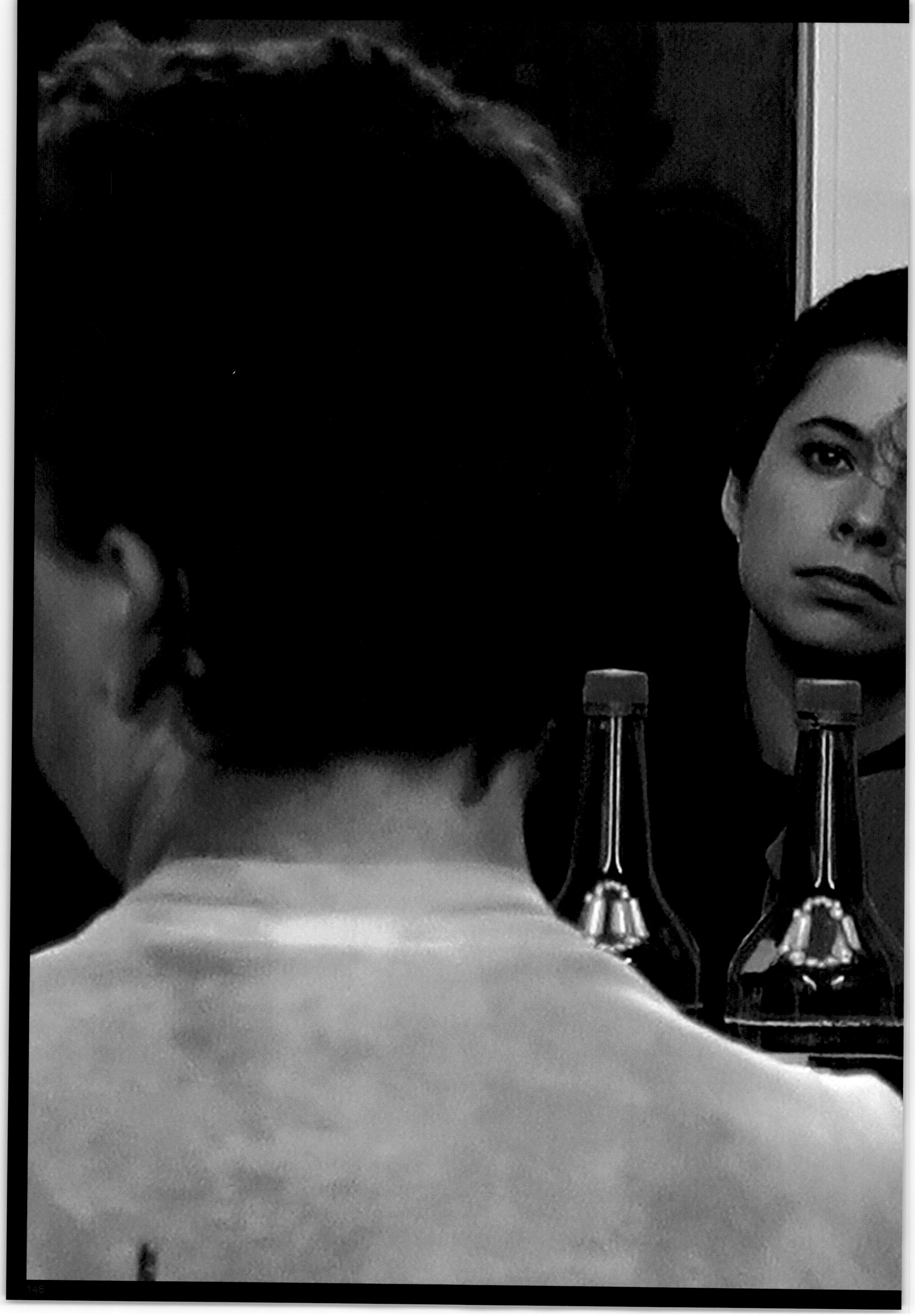

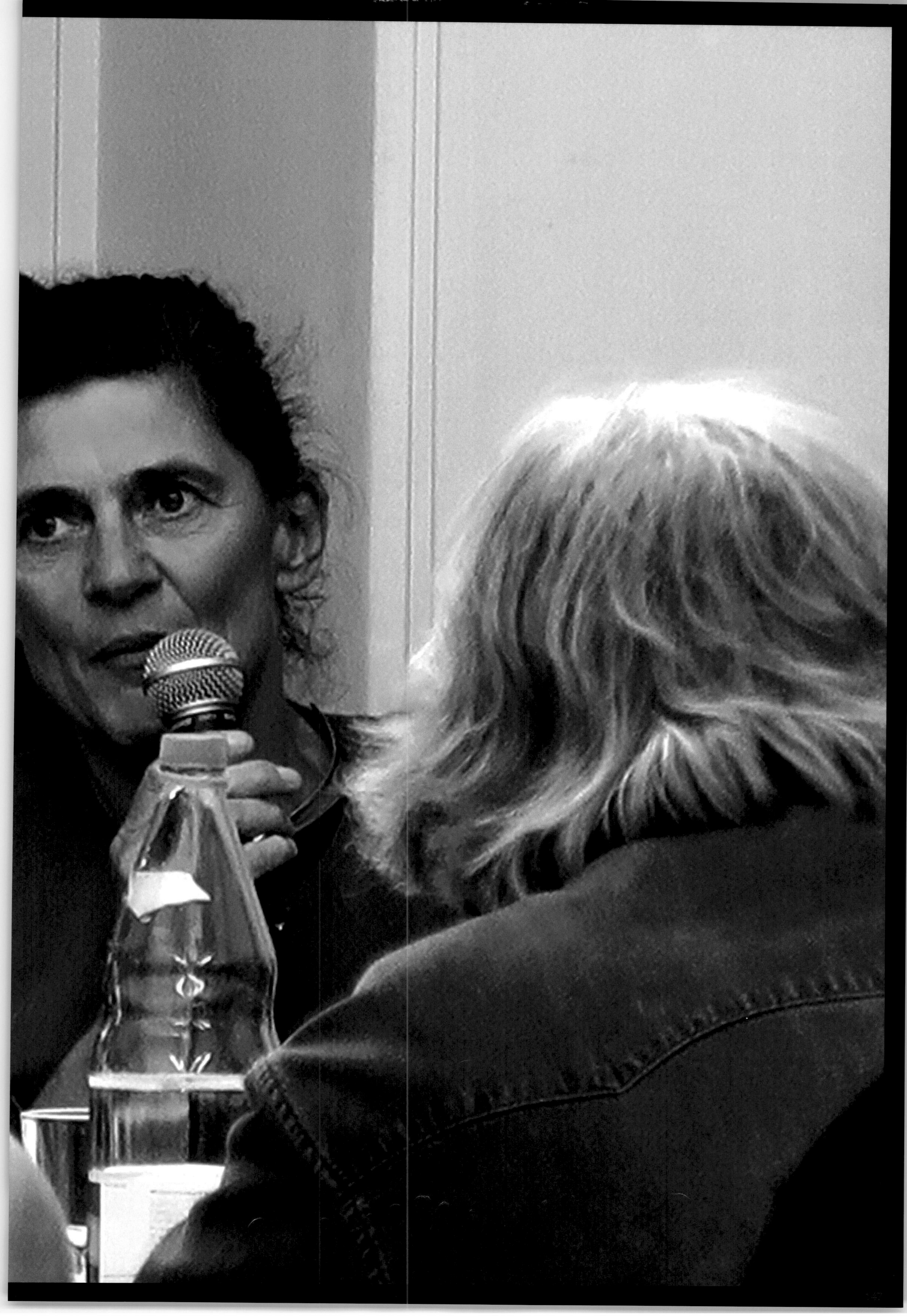

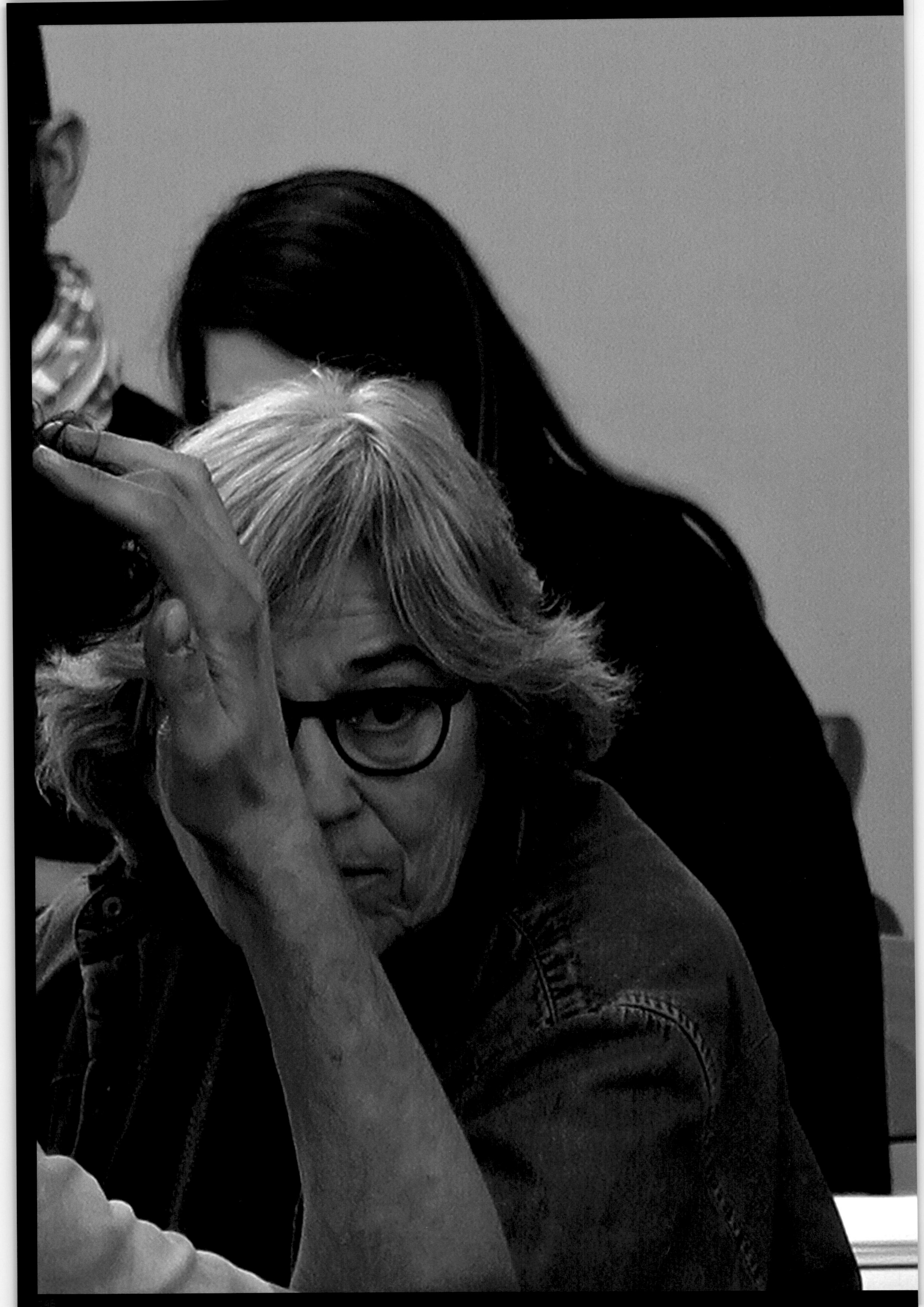

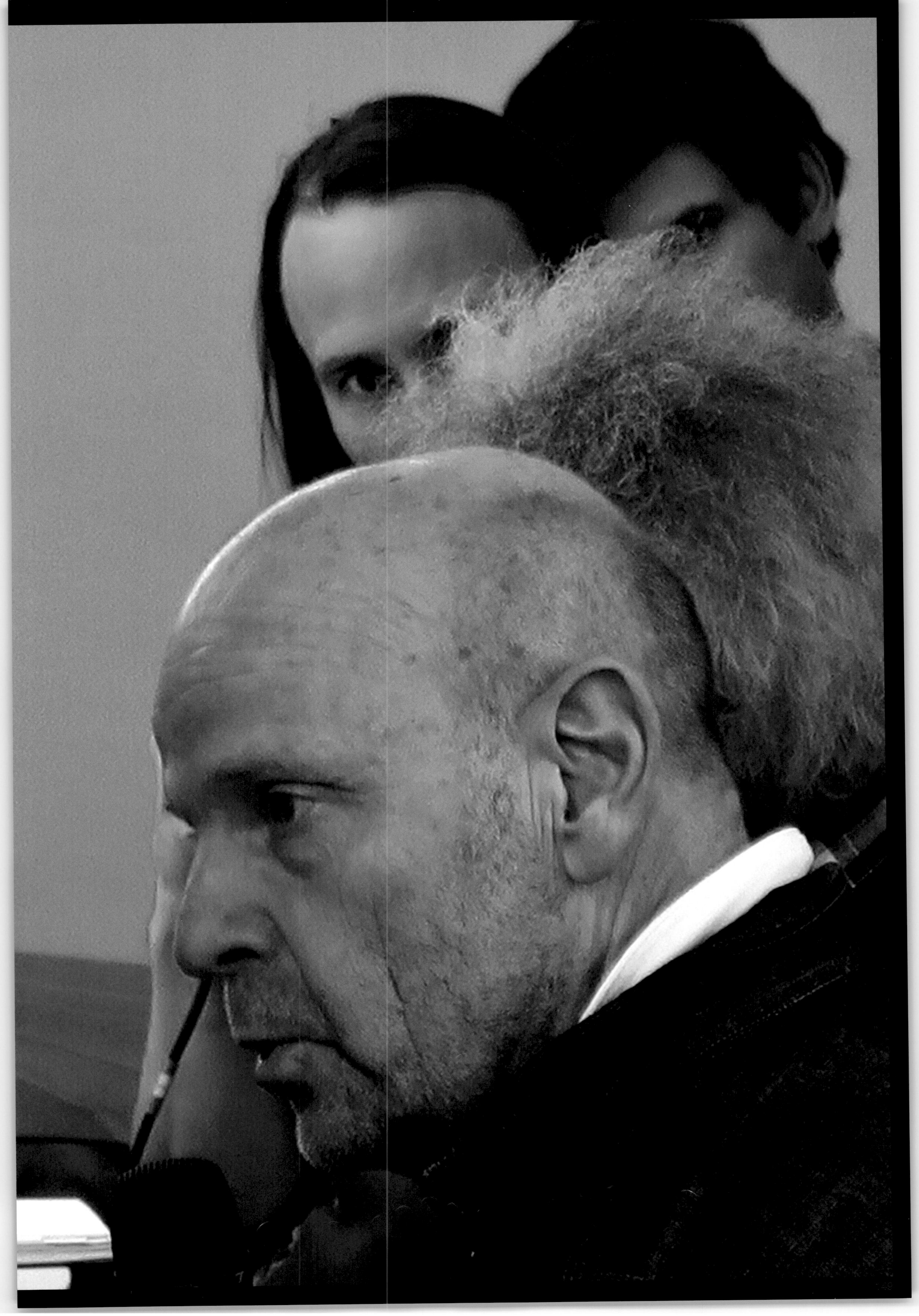

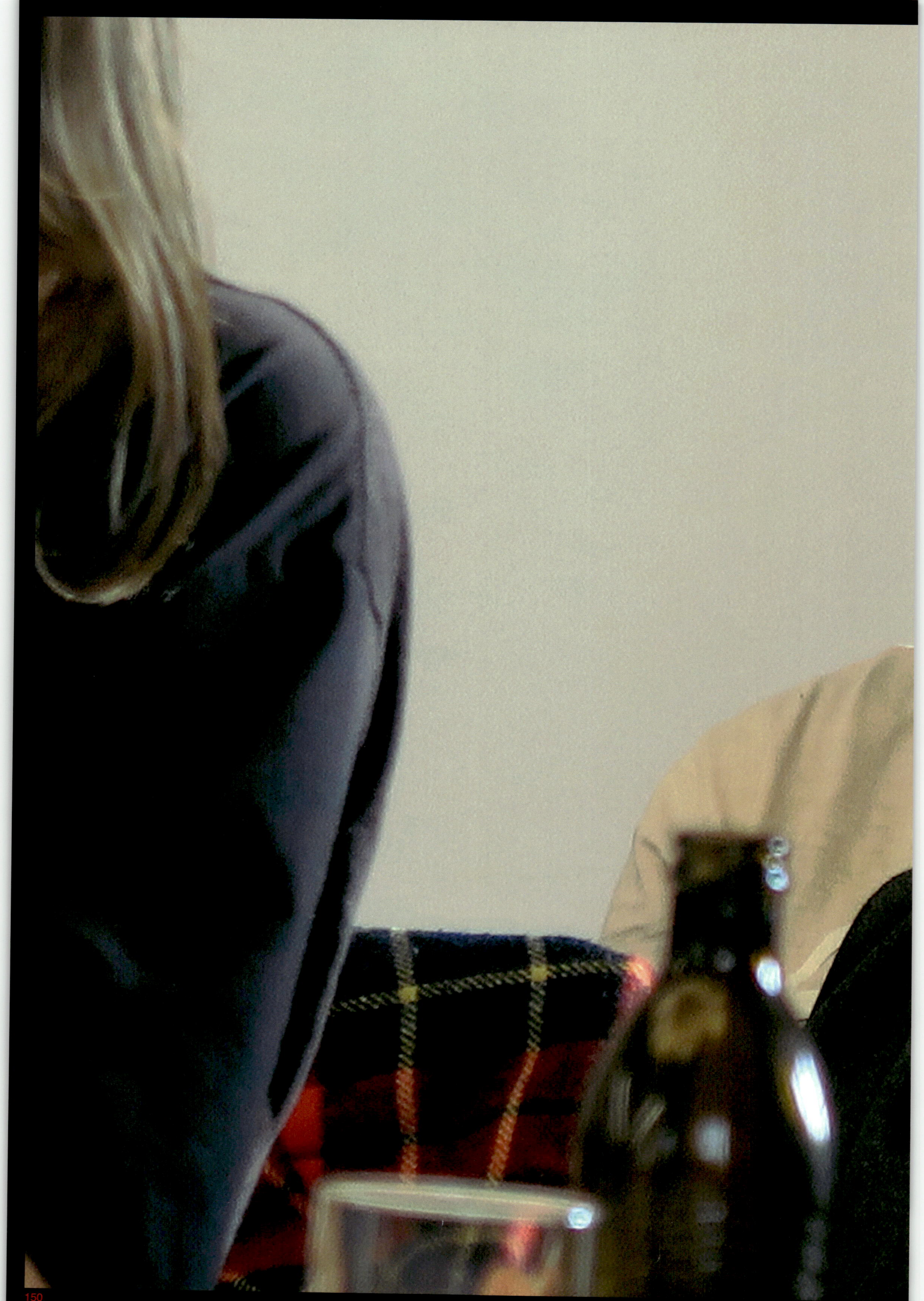

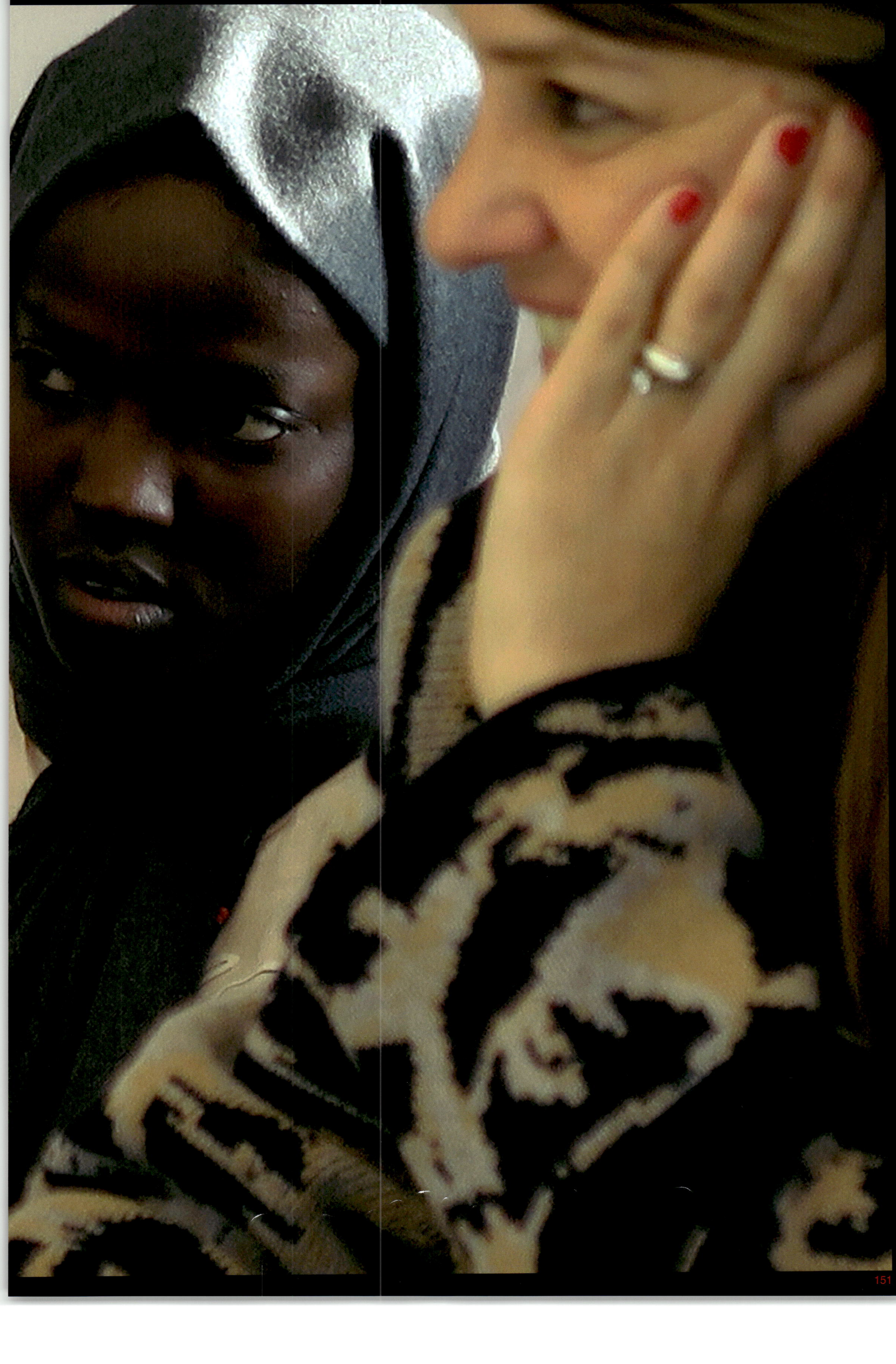

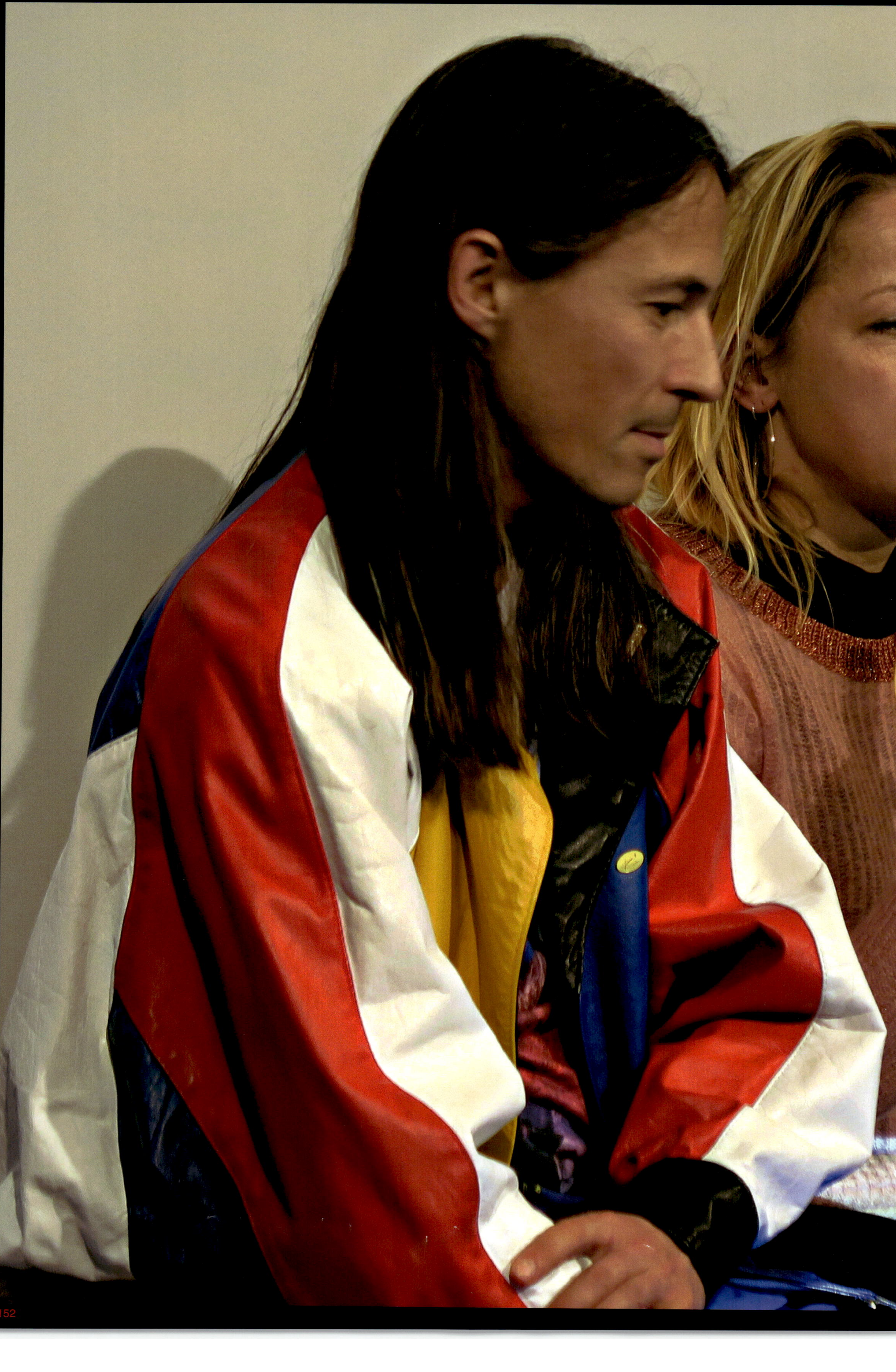

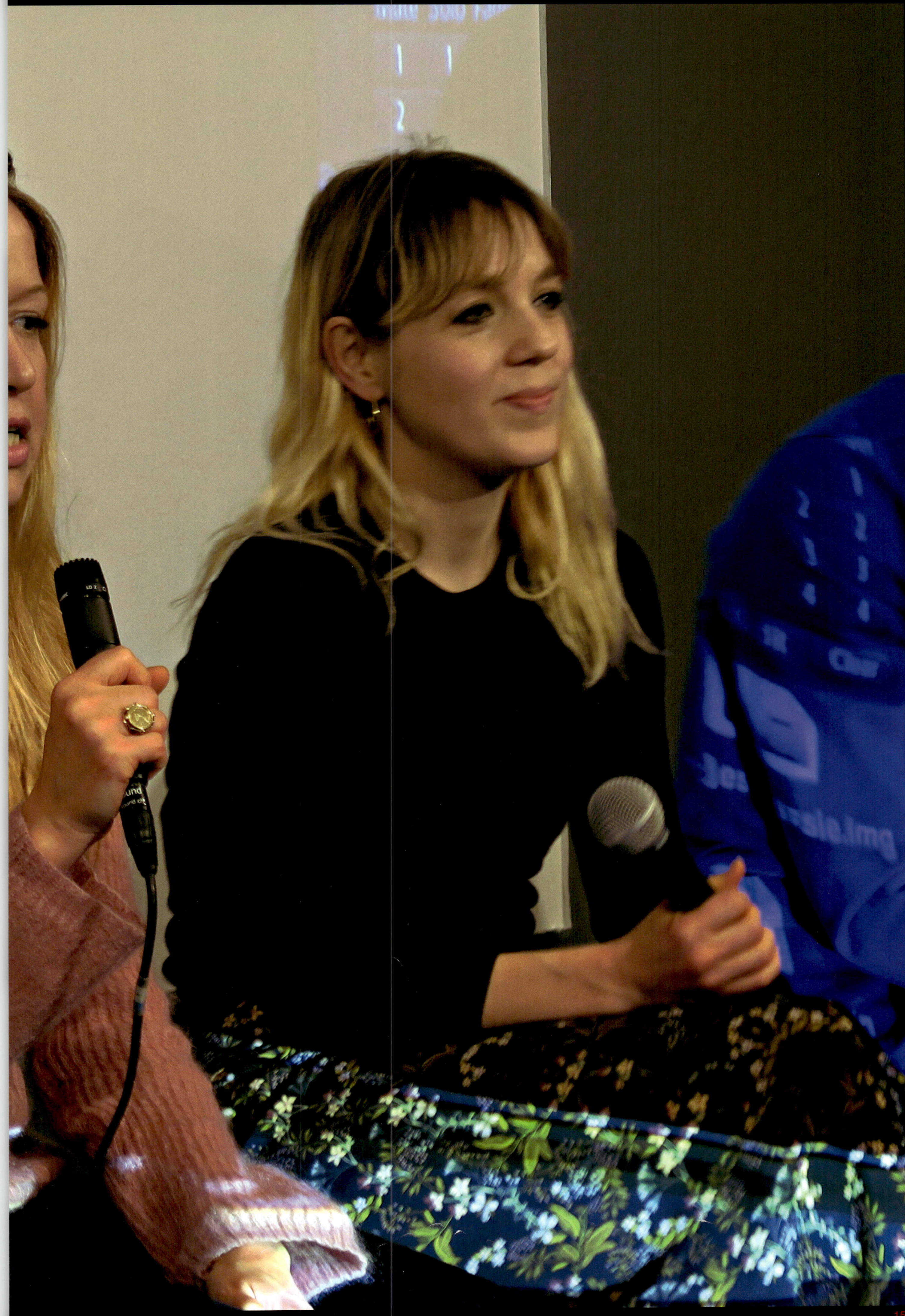

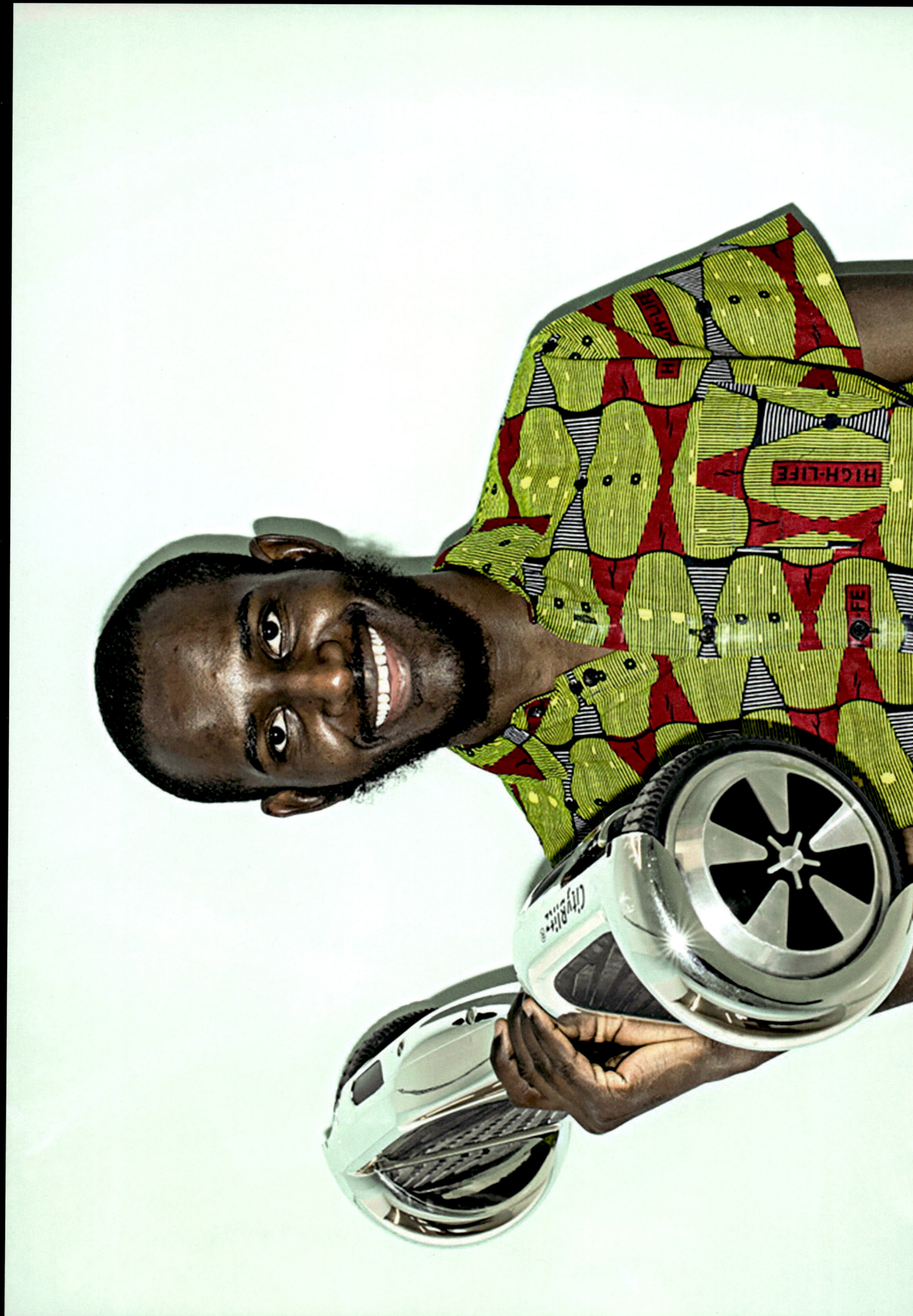
HIGH-LIFE

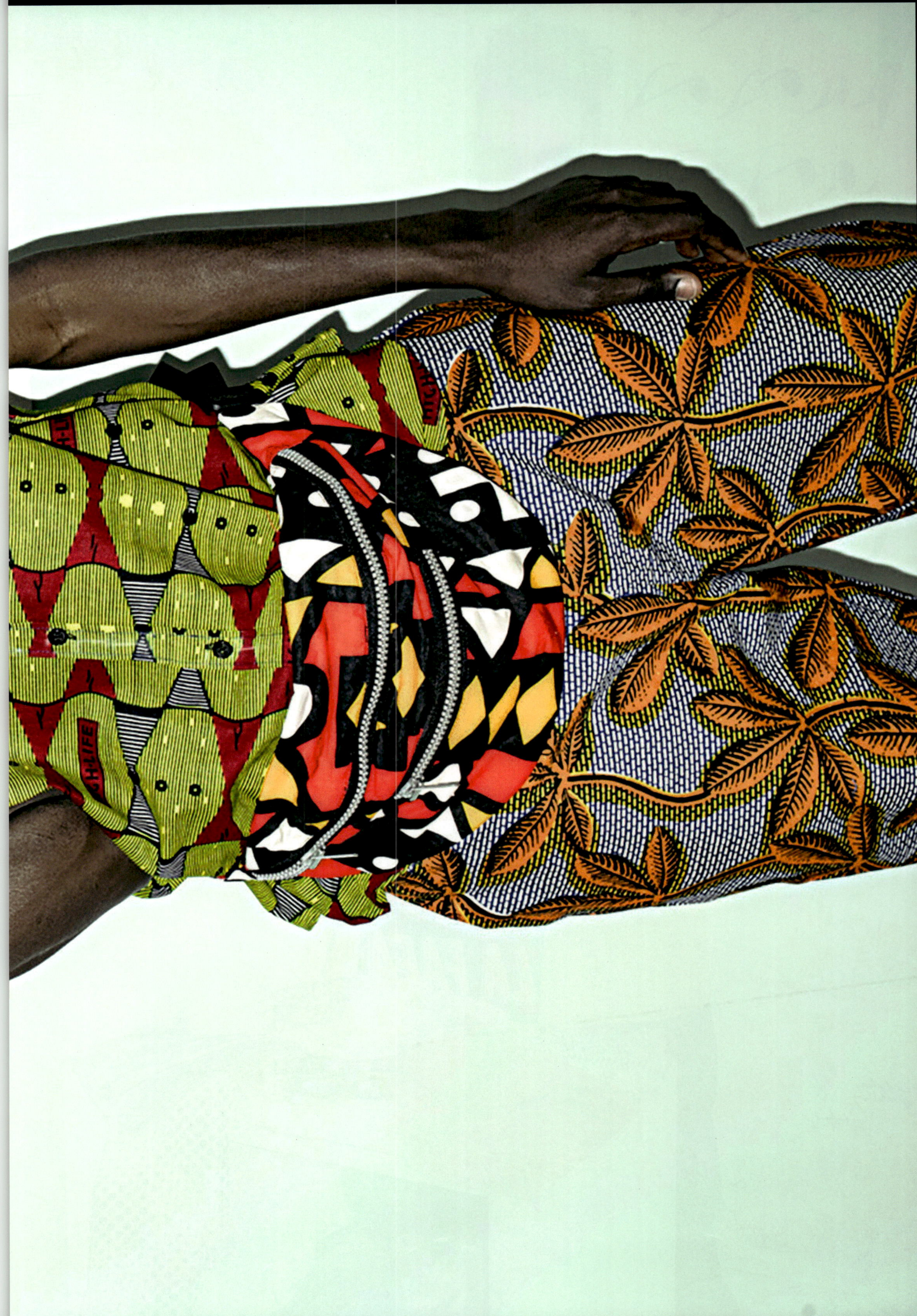

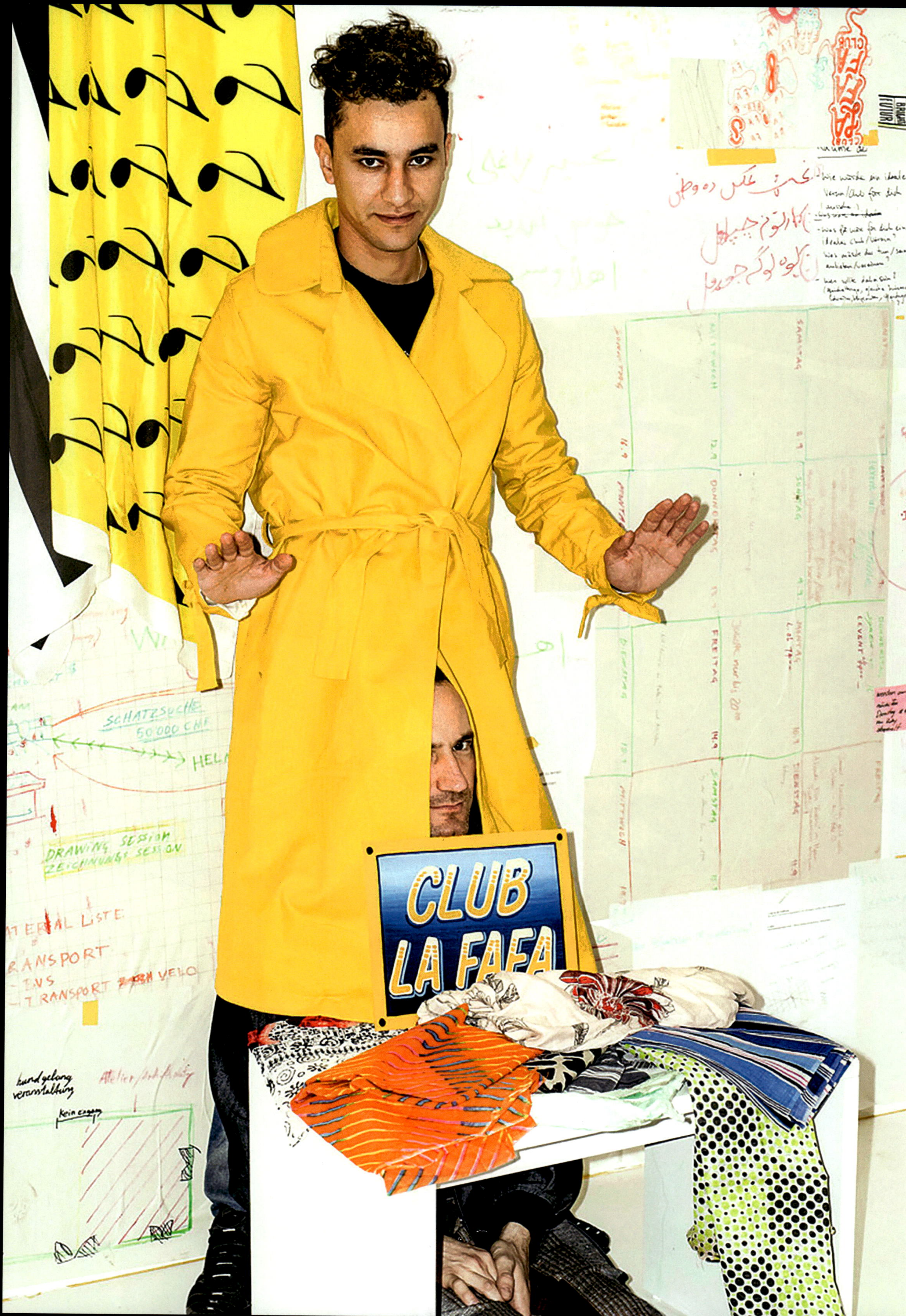
CLUB
LA FAFA
SCHATZSUCHE
50 000 CHF
DRAWING SESSION
ZEICHNUNGS SESSION

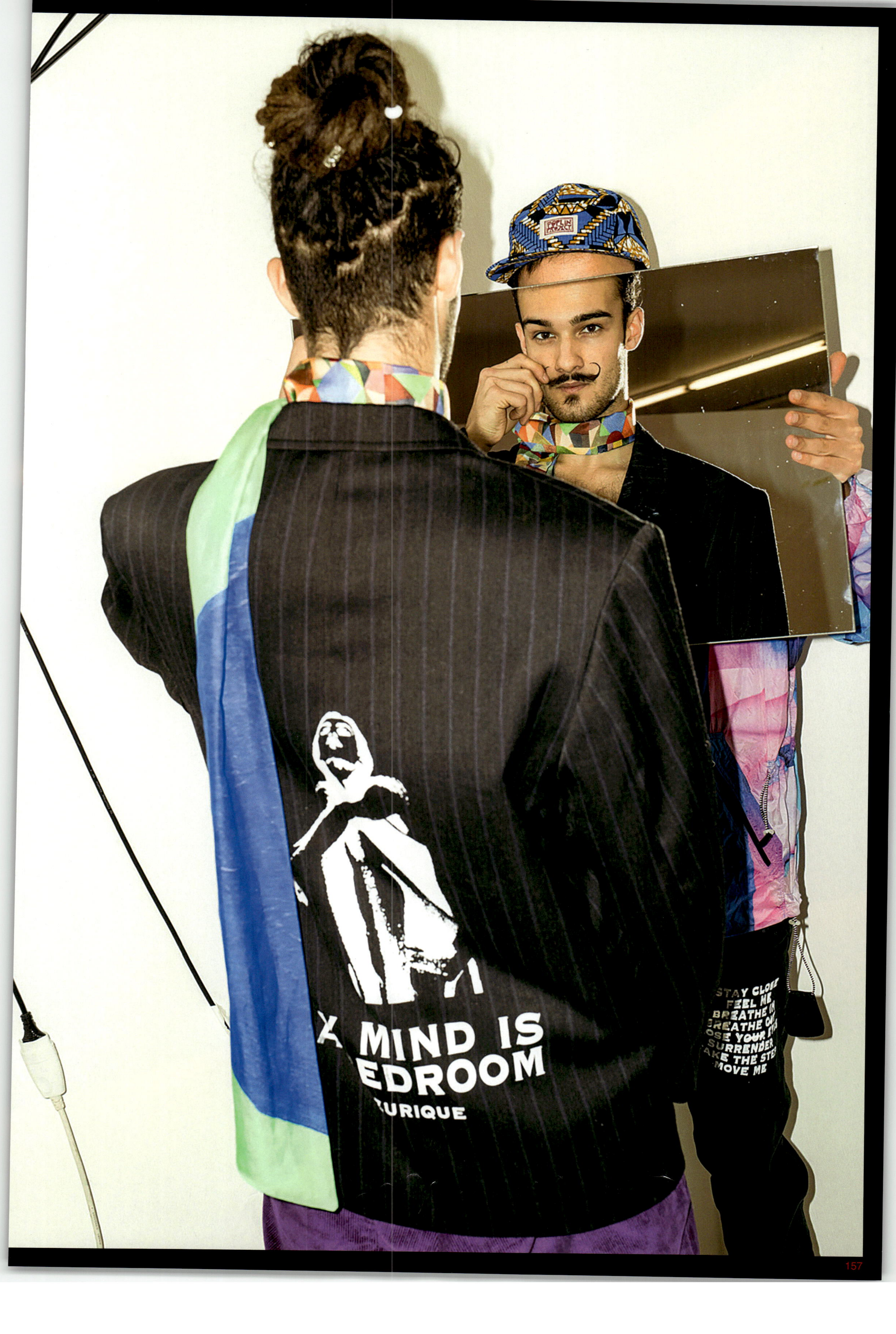
MIND IS

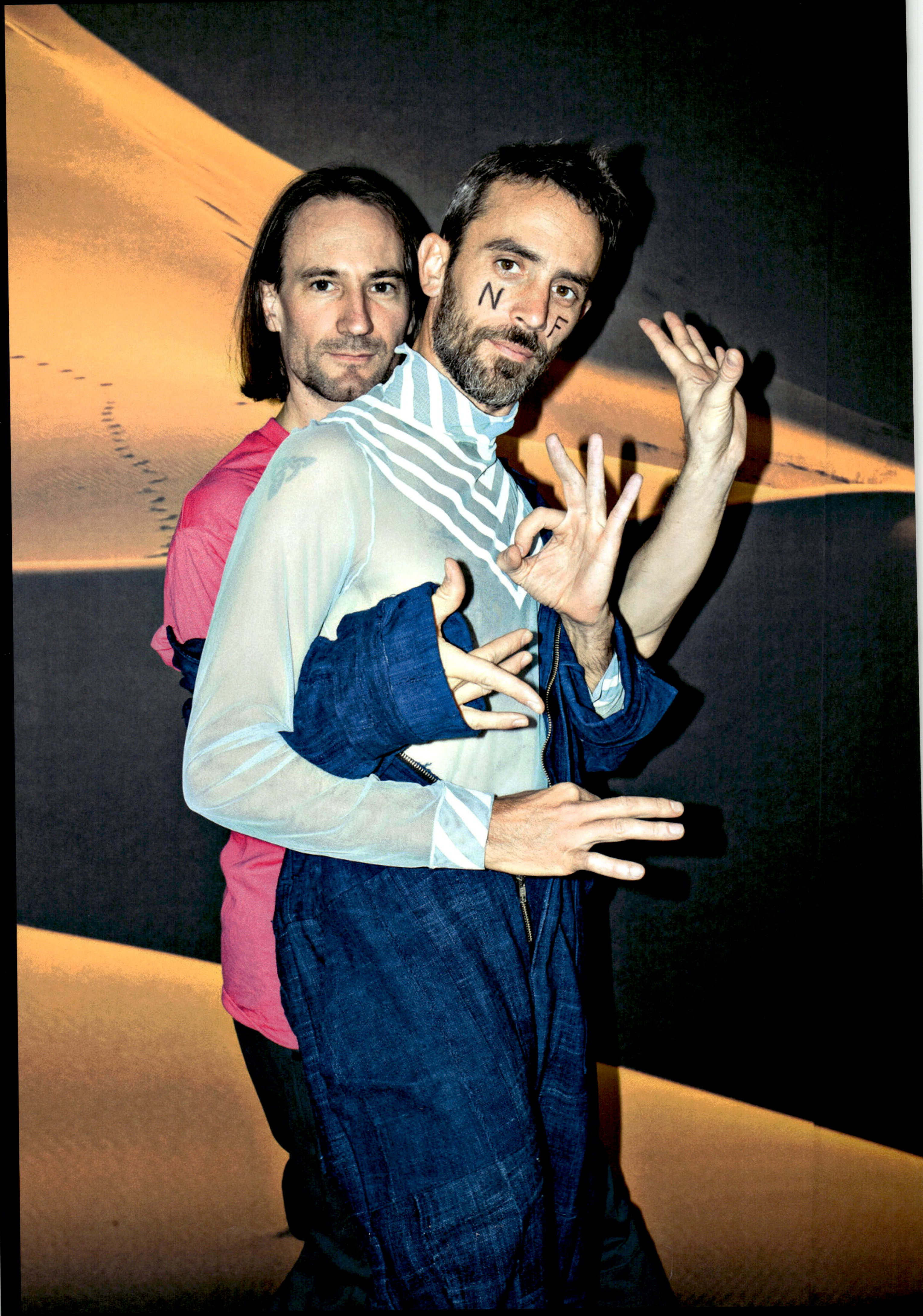

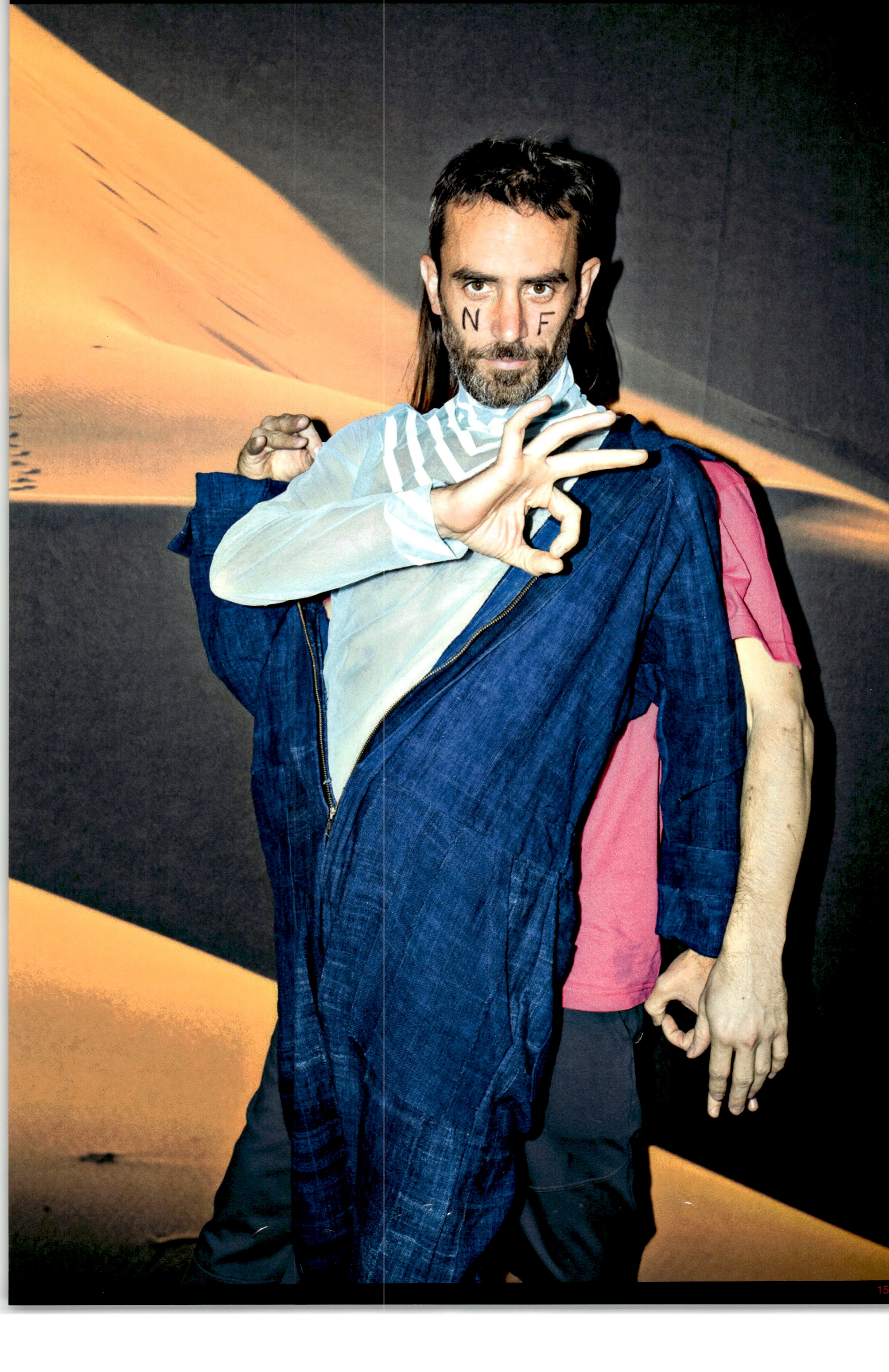
N F

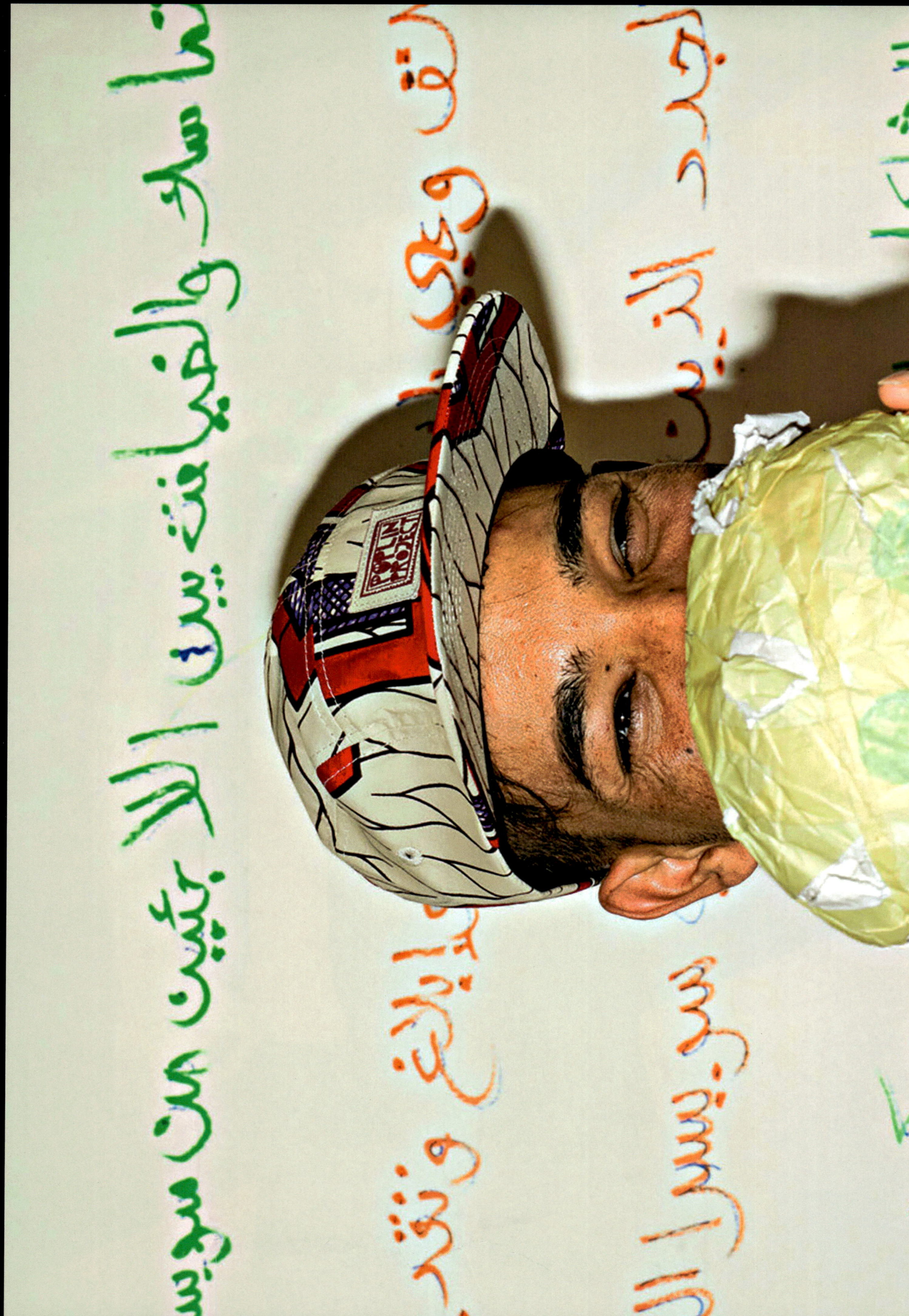

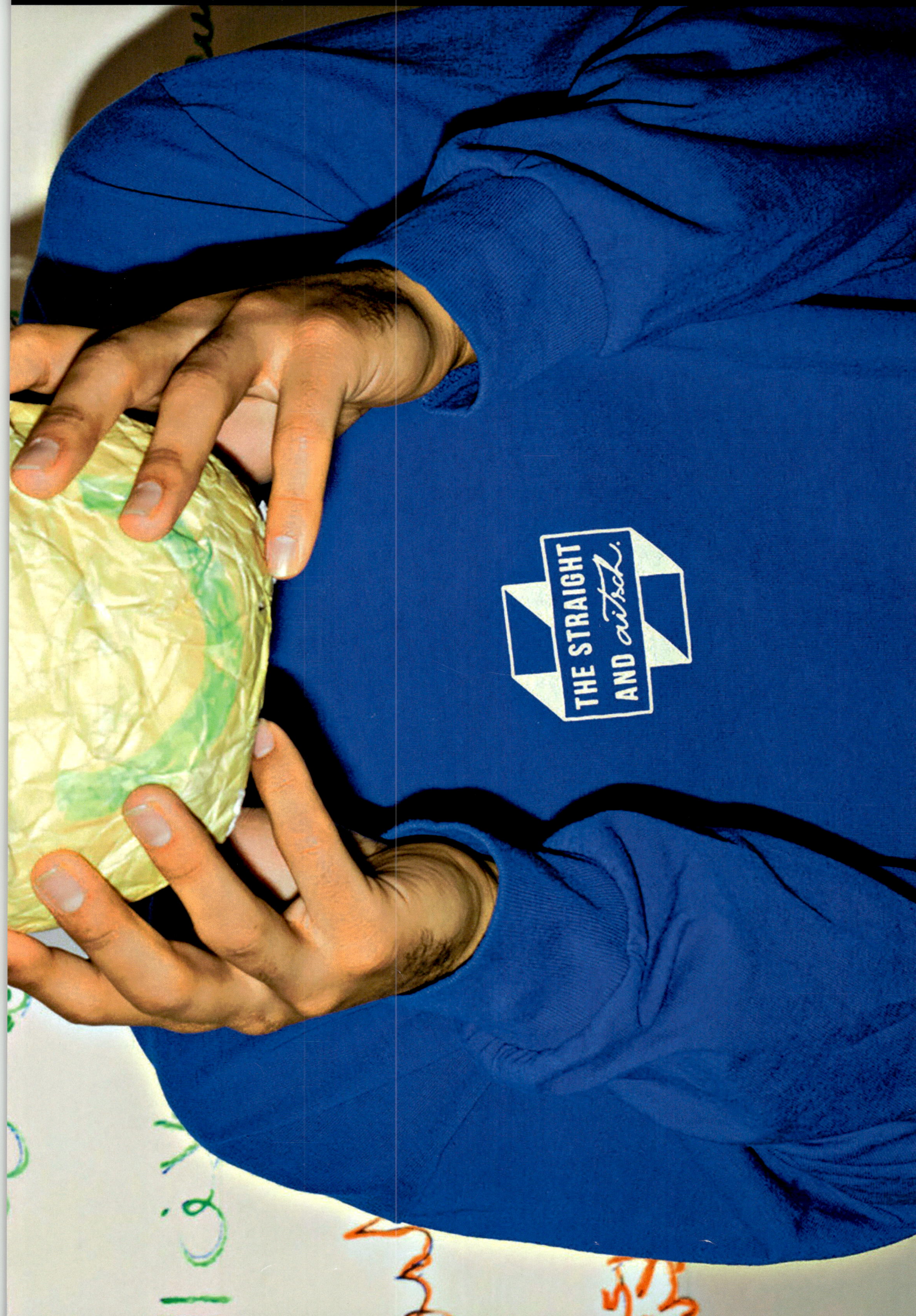
THE STRAIGHT
AND aitsch.

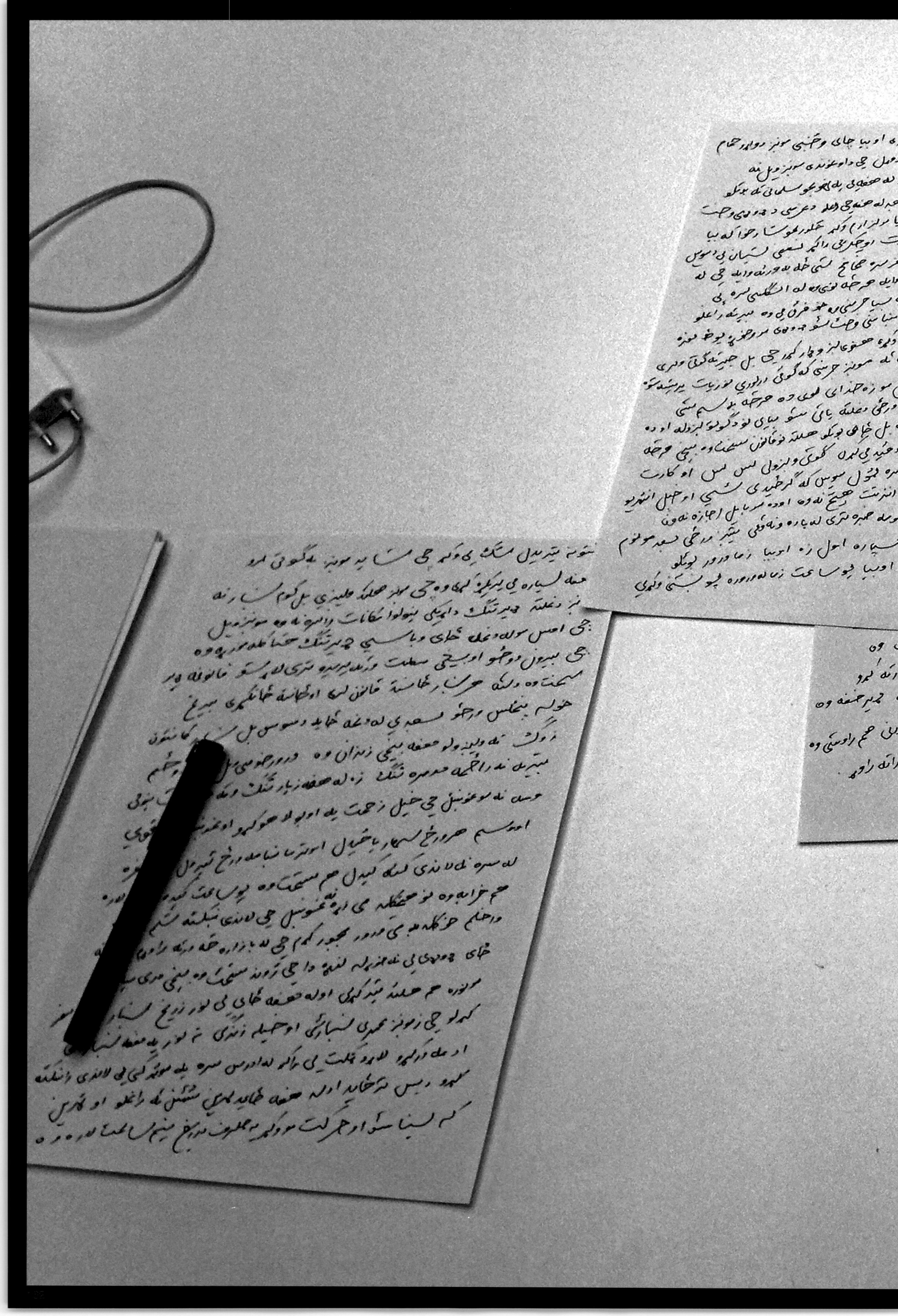

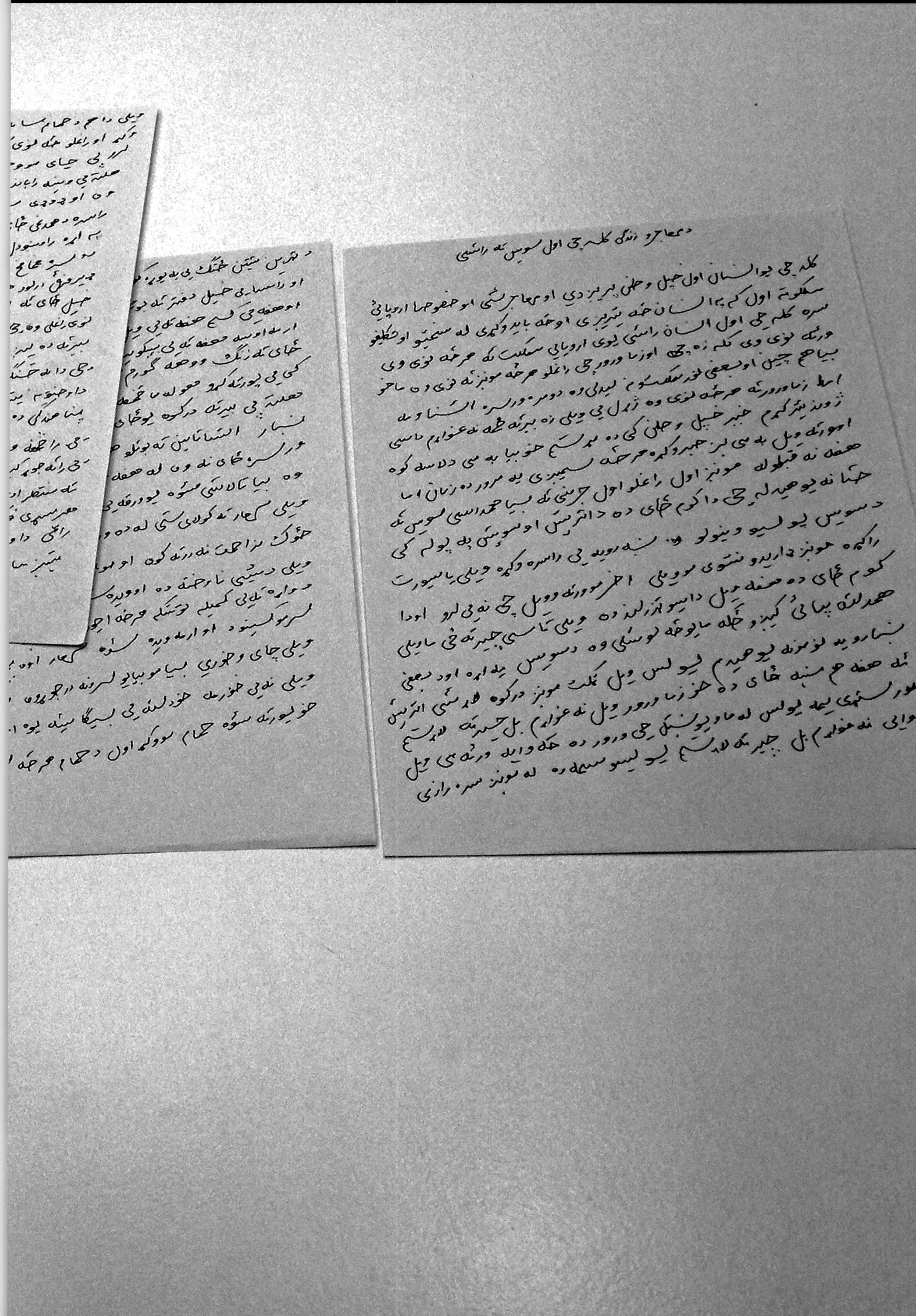
د مهاجرو ژوندی کله چی اول سویس ته راشی

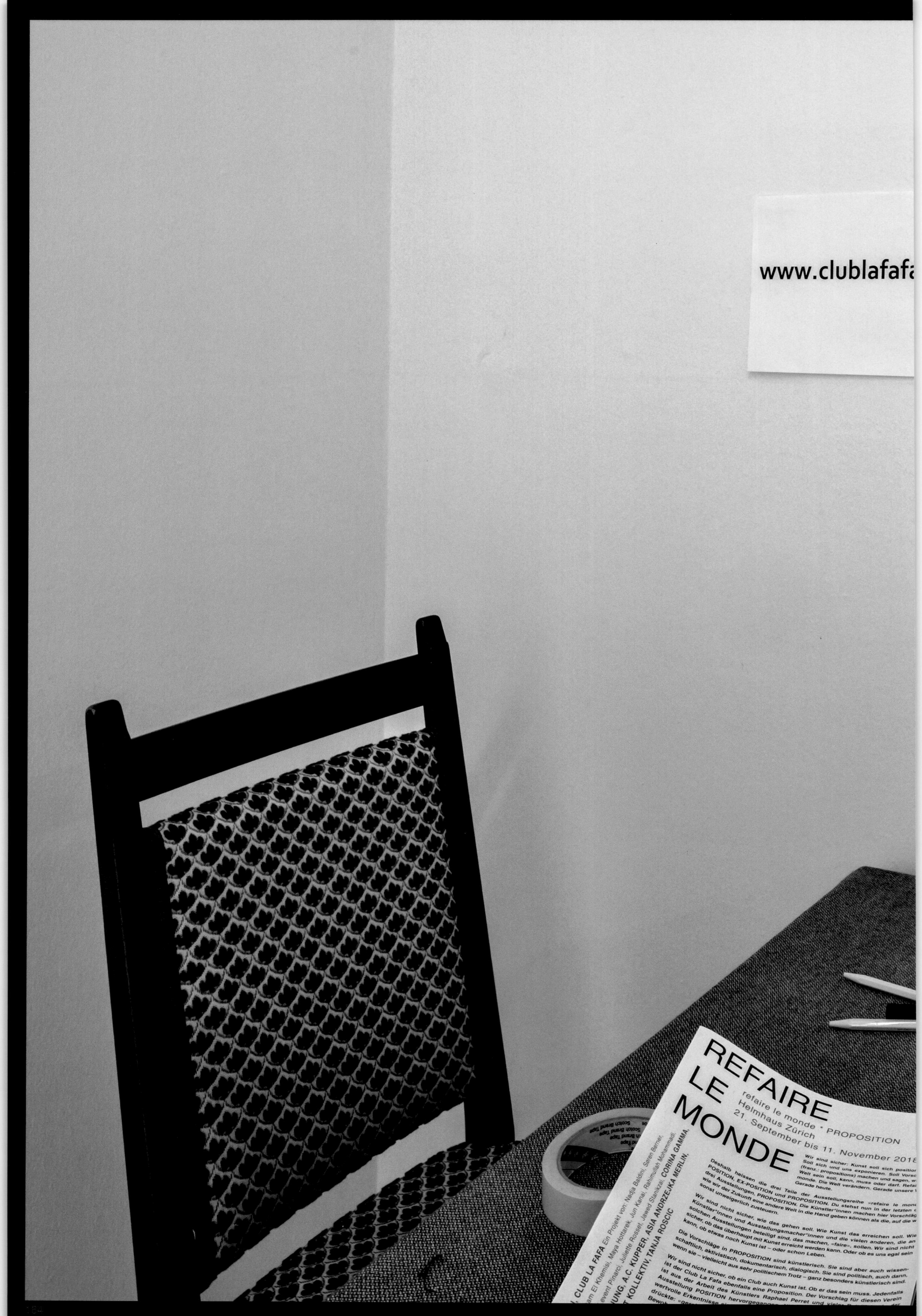
www.clublafafa
REFAIRE
LE
MONDE
refaire le monde · PROPOSITION
Helmhaus Zürich
21. September bis 11. November 2018

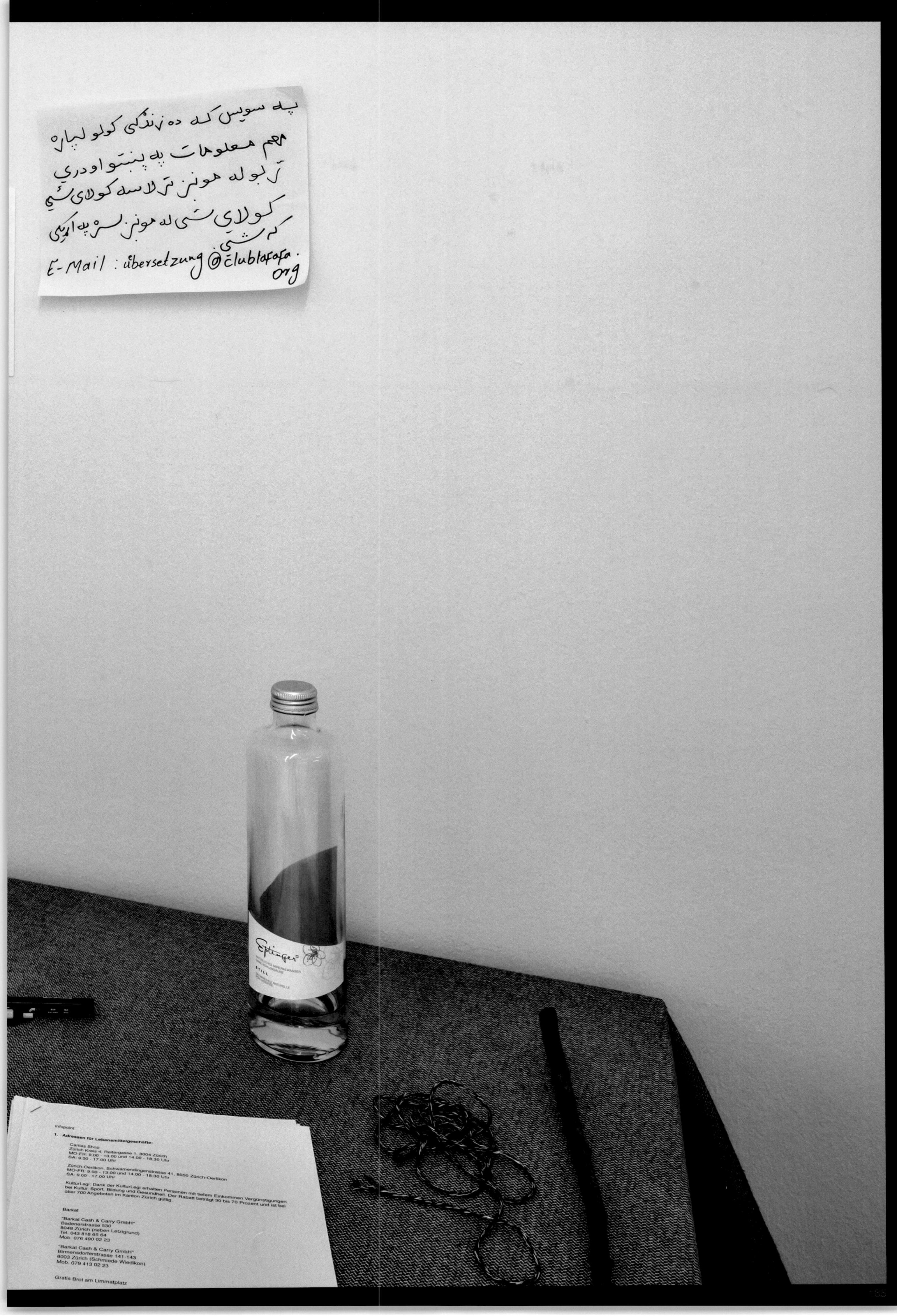
E-Mail : übersetzung@clublafafa.org
Infopoint
1. Adressen für Lebensmittelgeschäfte:
Caritas Shop
Zürich Kreis 4, Reitergasse 1, 8004 Zürich
MO-FR: 9.00 - 13.00 und 14.00 - 18.30 Uhr
SA: 9.00 - 17.00 Uhr
Zürich-Oerlikon, Schwamendingenstrasse 41, 8050 Zürich-Oerlikon
MO-FR: 9.00 - 13.00 und 14.00 - 18.30 Uhr
SA: 9.00 - 17.00 Uhr
KulturLegi: Dank der KulturLegi erhalten Personen mit tiefem Einkommen Vergünstigungen bei Kultur, Sport, Bildung und Gesundheit. Der Rabatt beträgt 30 bis 70 Prozent und ist bei über 700 Angeboten im Kanton Zürich gültig.
Barkat
"Barkat Cash & Carry GmbH"
Badenerstrasse 530
8048 Zürich (neben Letzigrund)
Tel. 043 818 65 64
Mob. 076 490 02 23
"Barkat Cash & Carry GmbH"
Birmensdorferstrasse 141-143
8003 Zürich (Schmiede Wiedikon)
Mob. 079 413 02 23
Gratis Brot am Limmatplatz

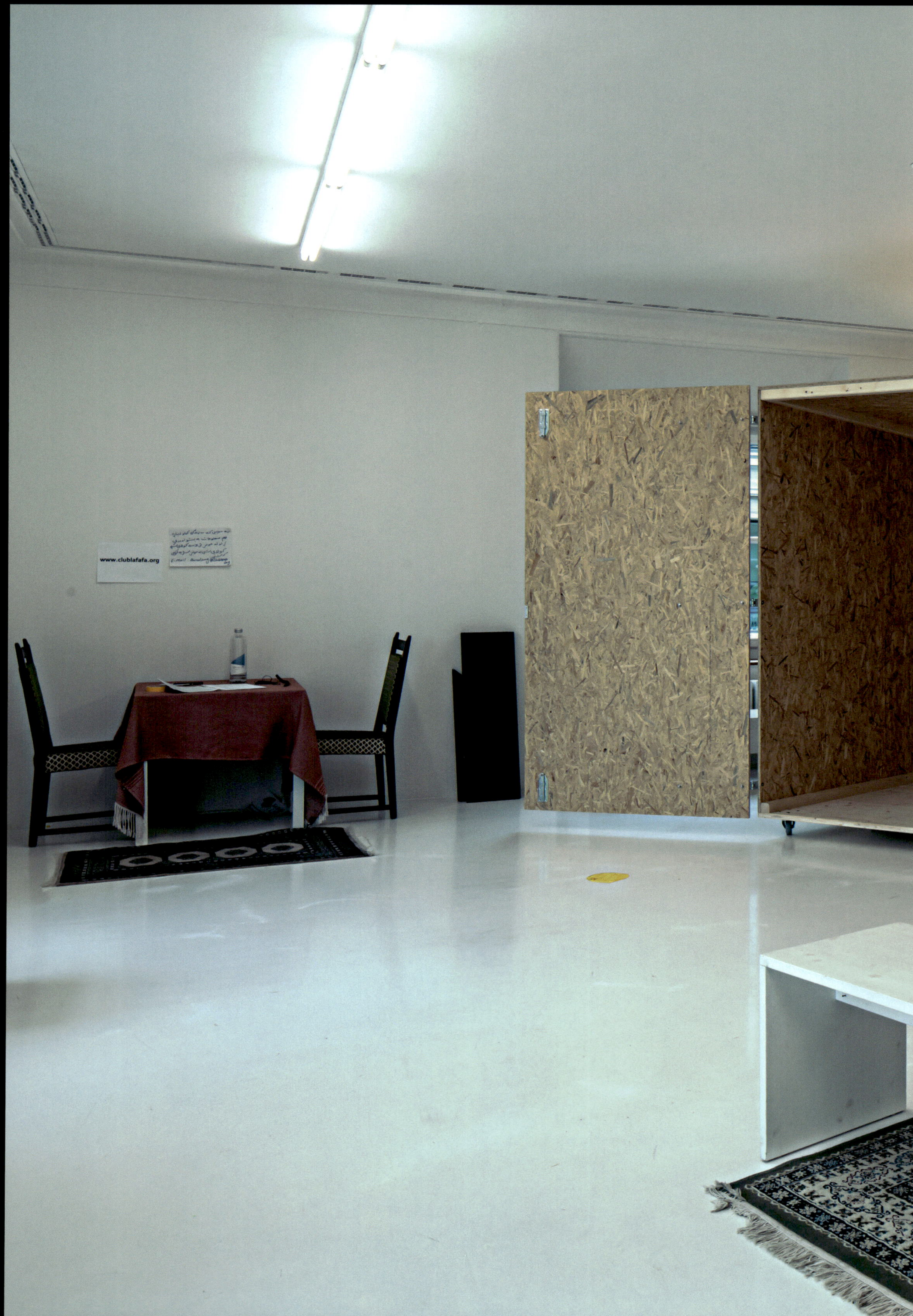
www.clublafafa.org

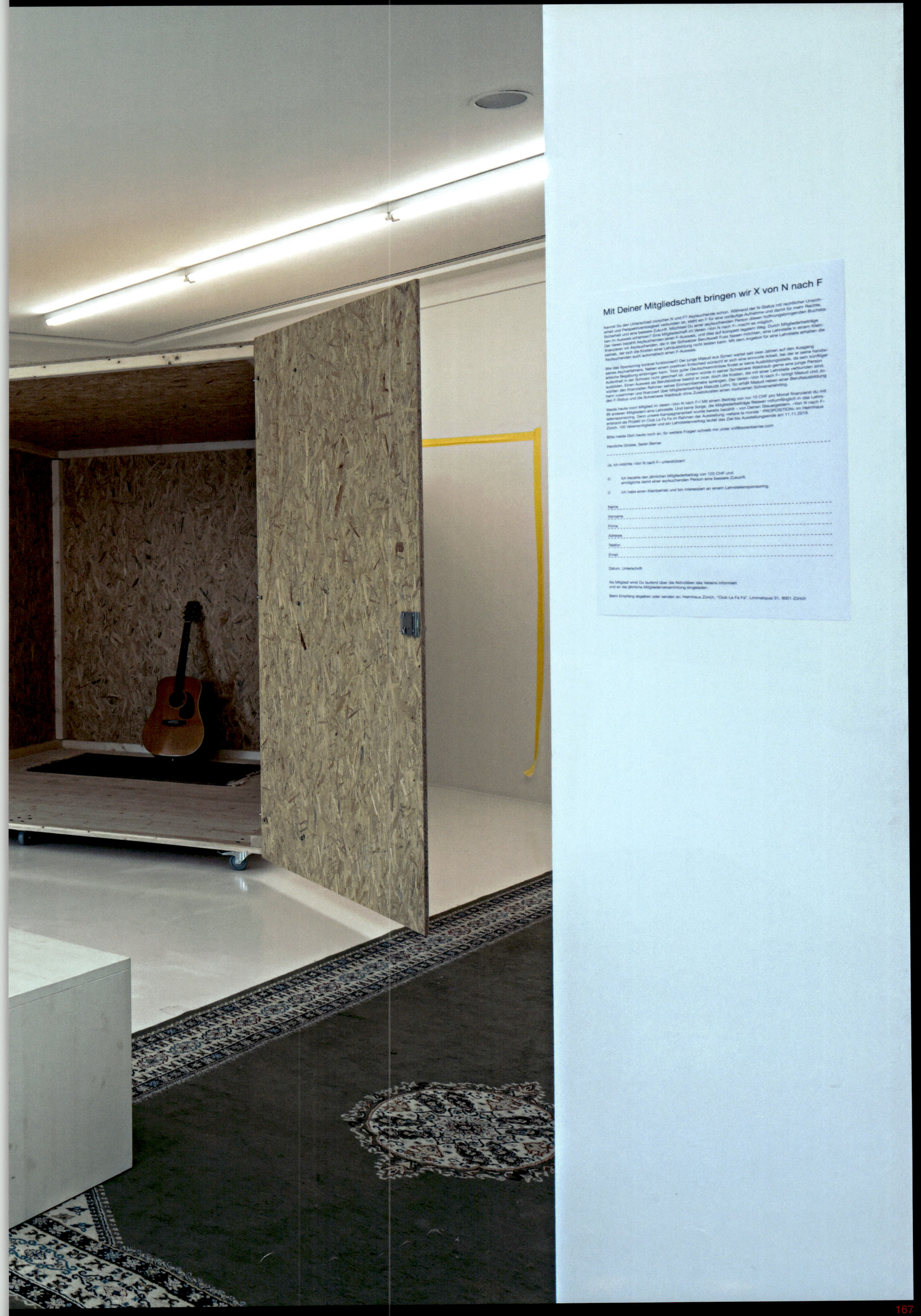
Mit Deiner Mitgliedschaft bringen wir X von N nach F

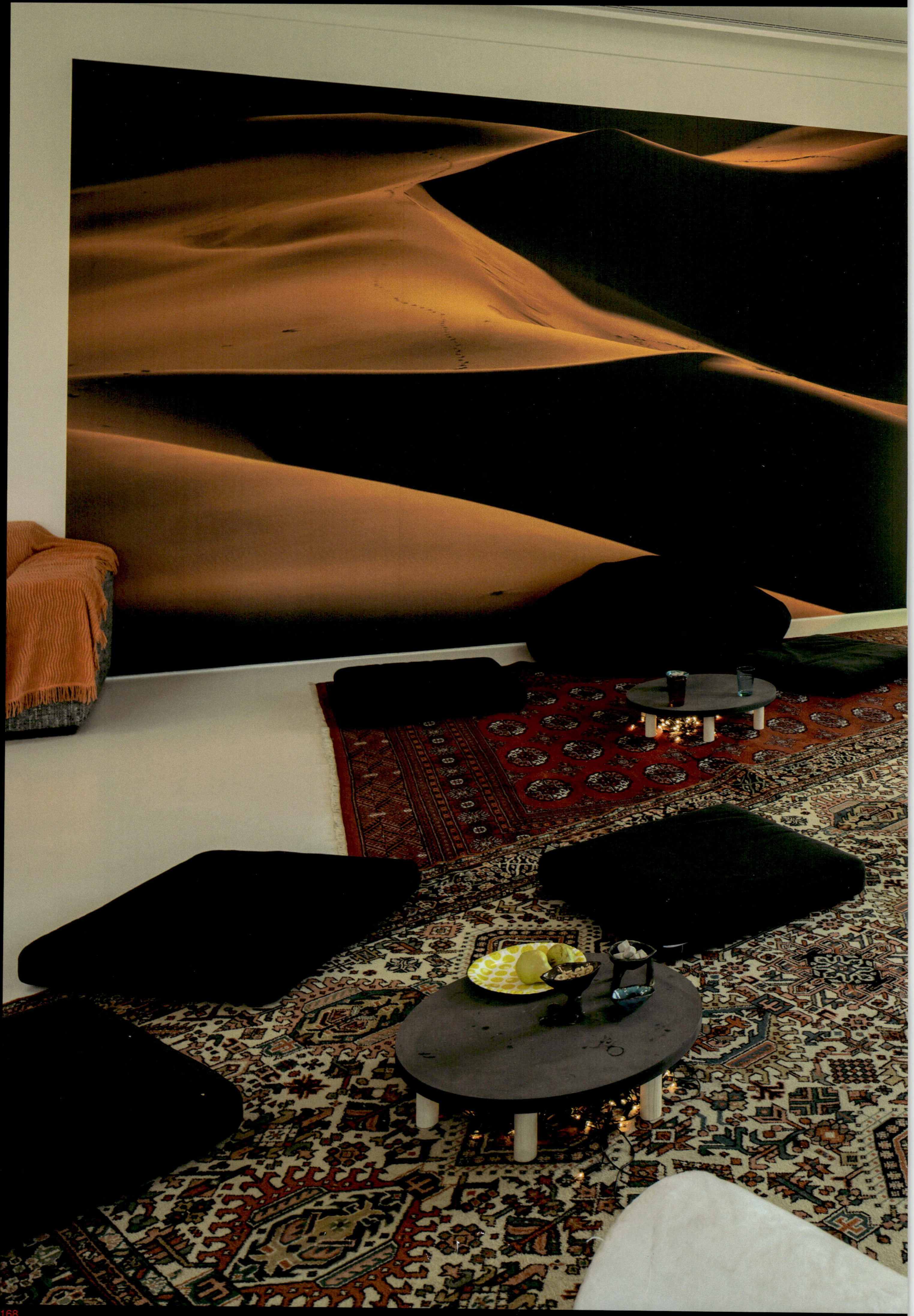

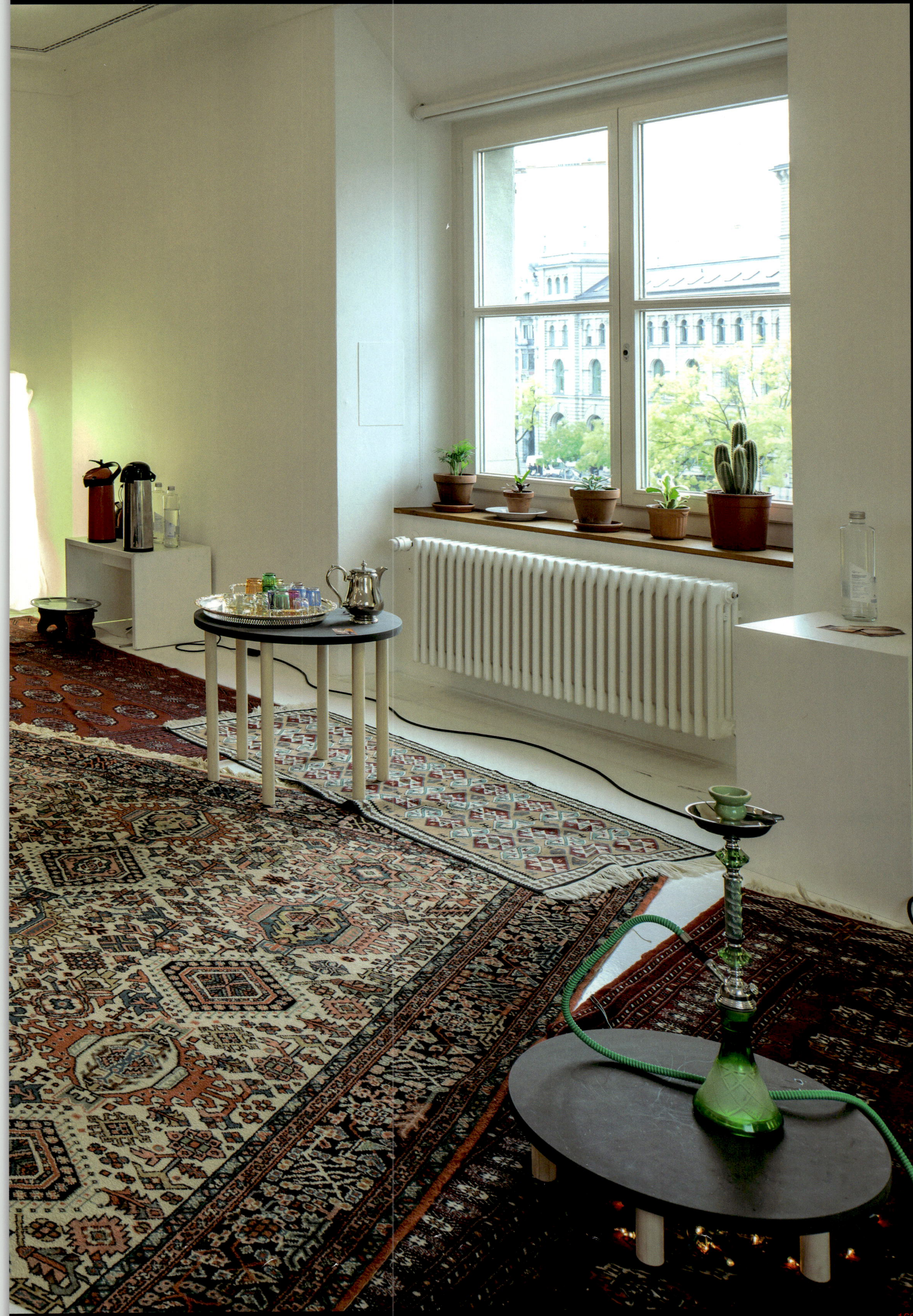

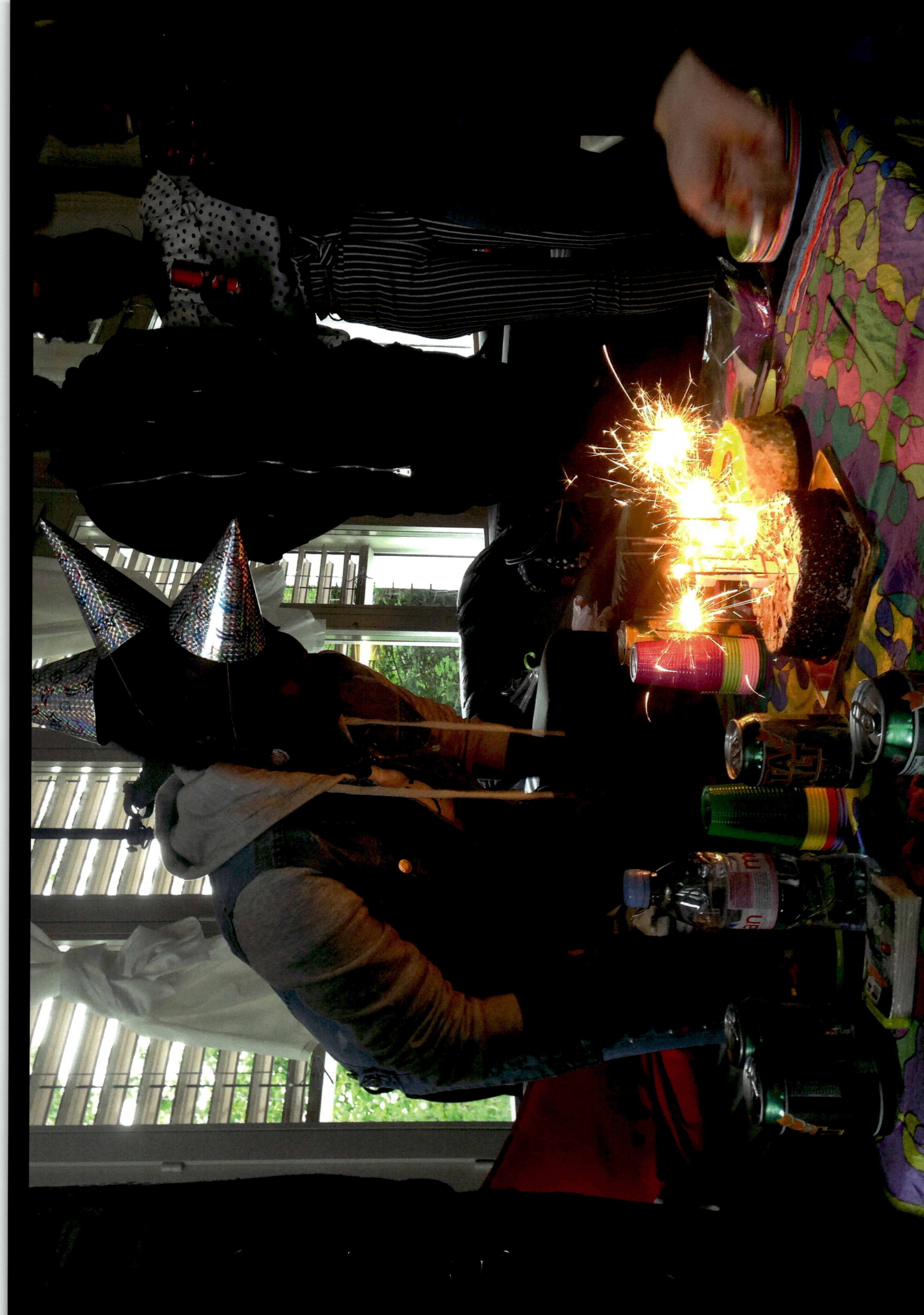

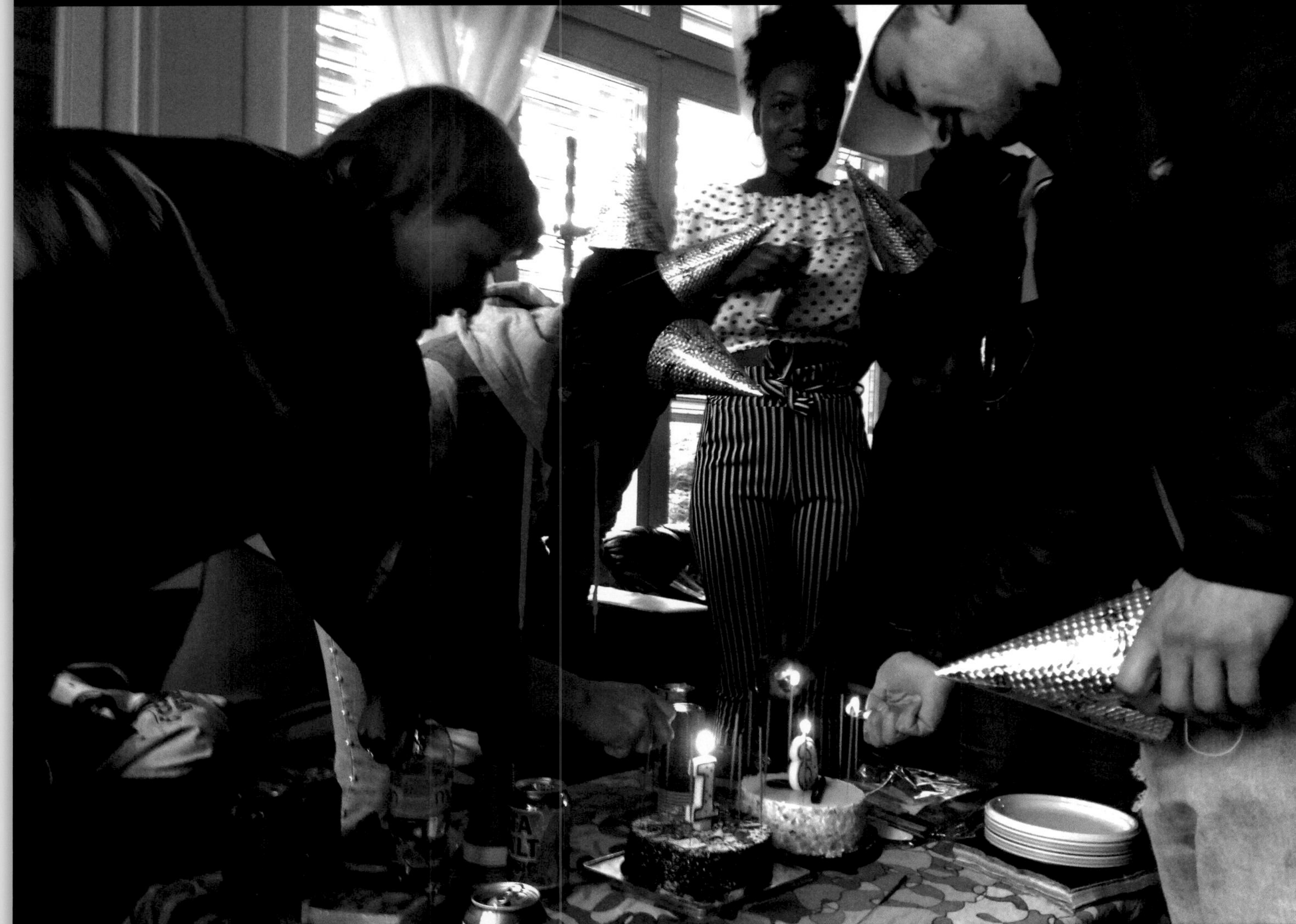

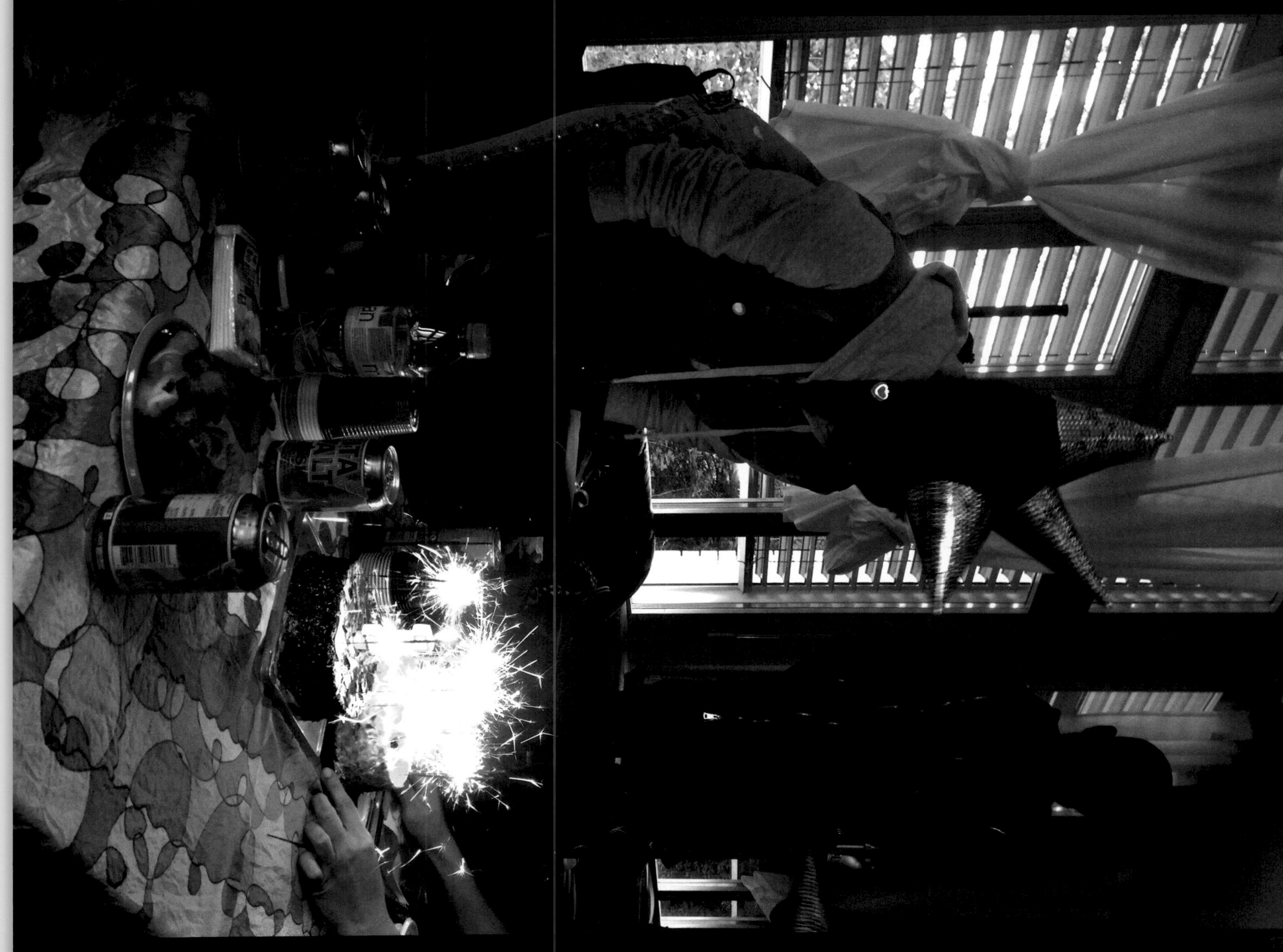

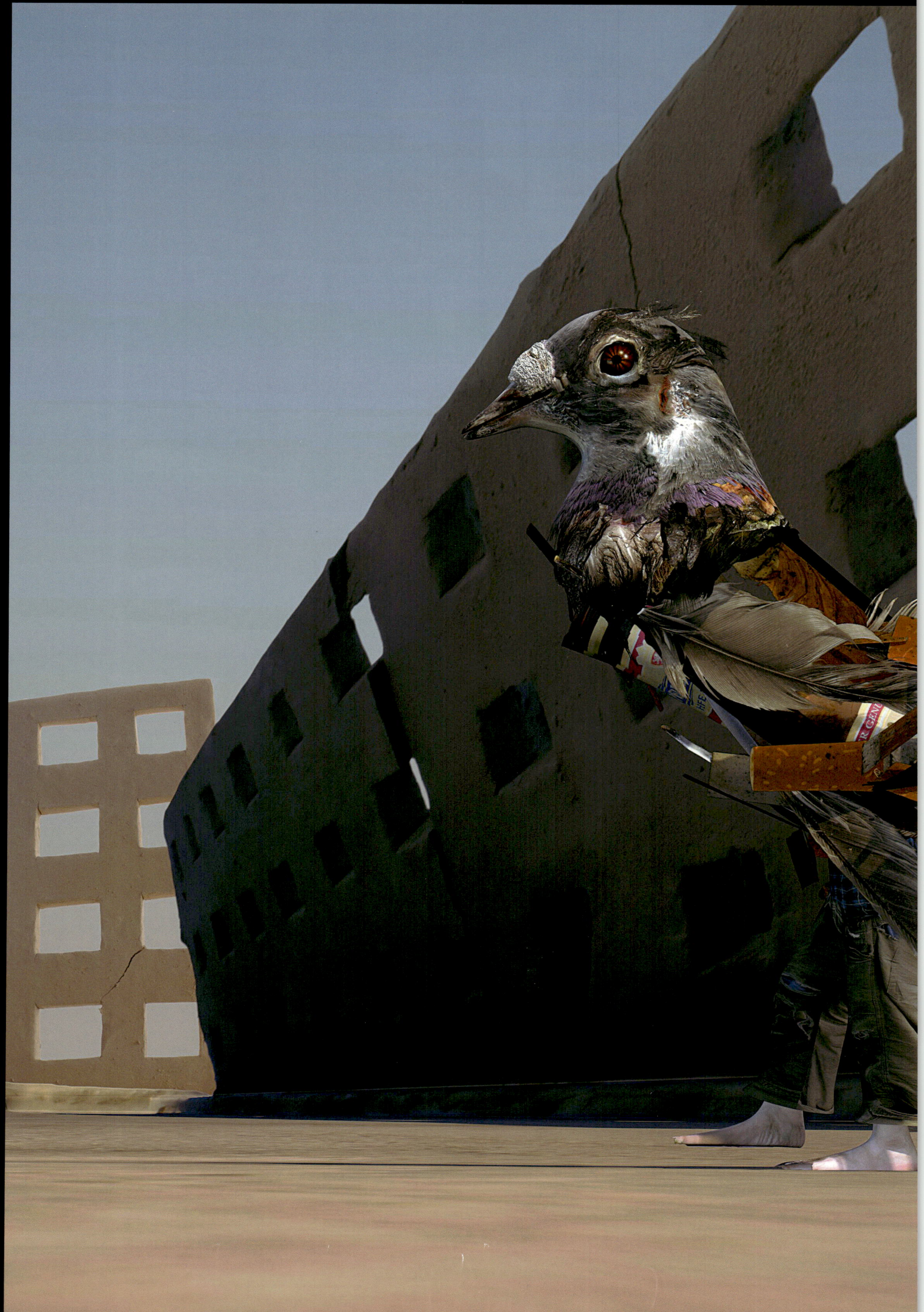

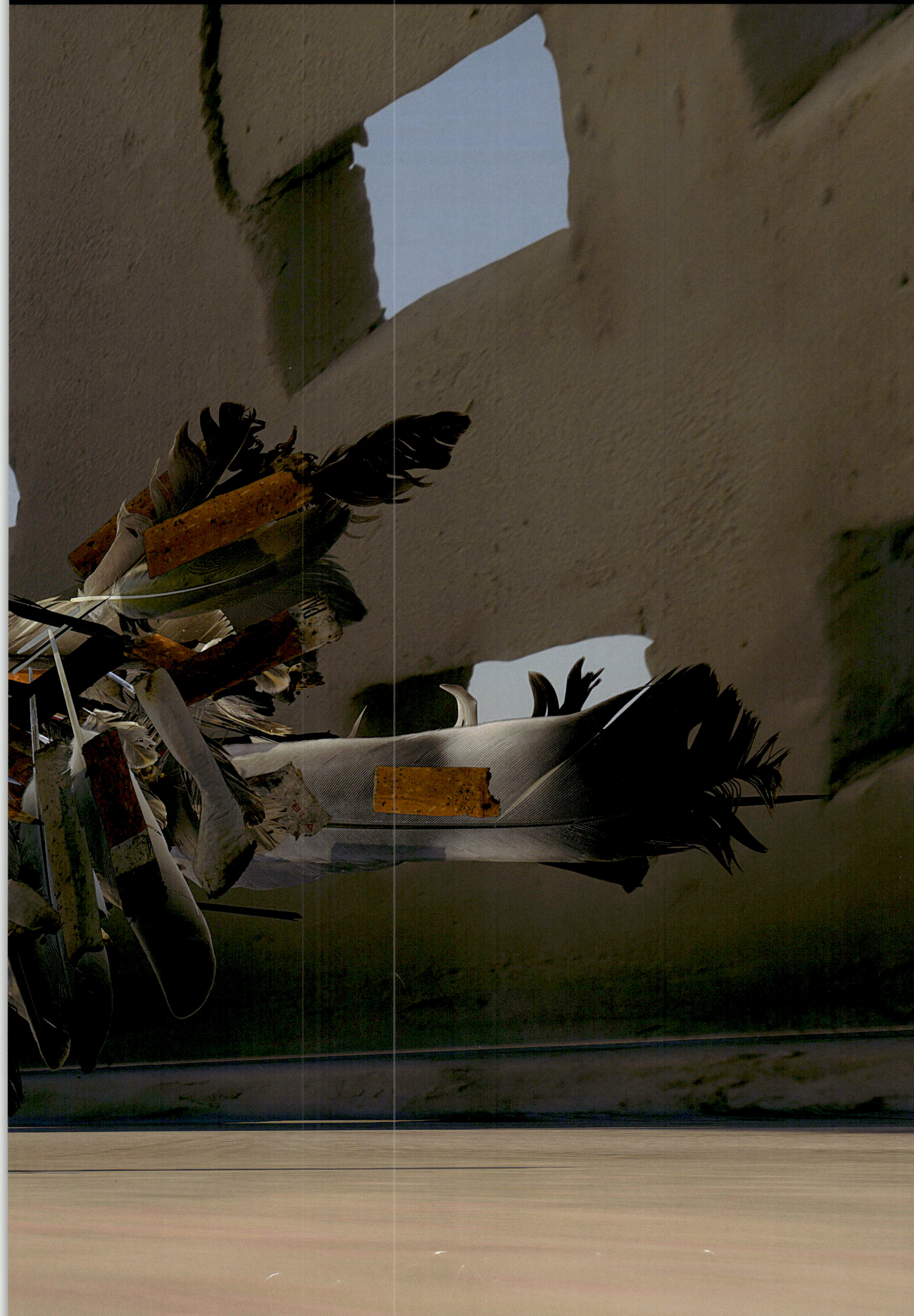

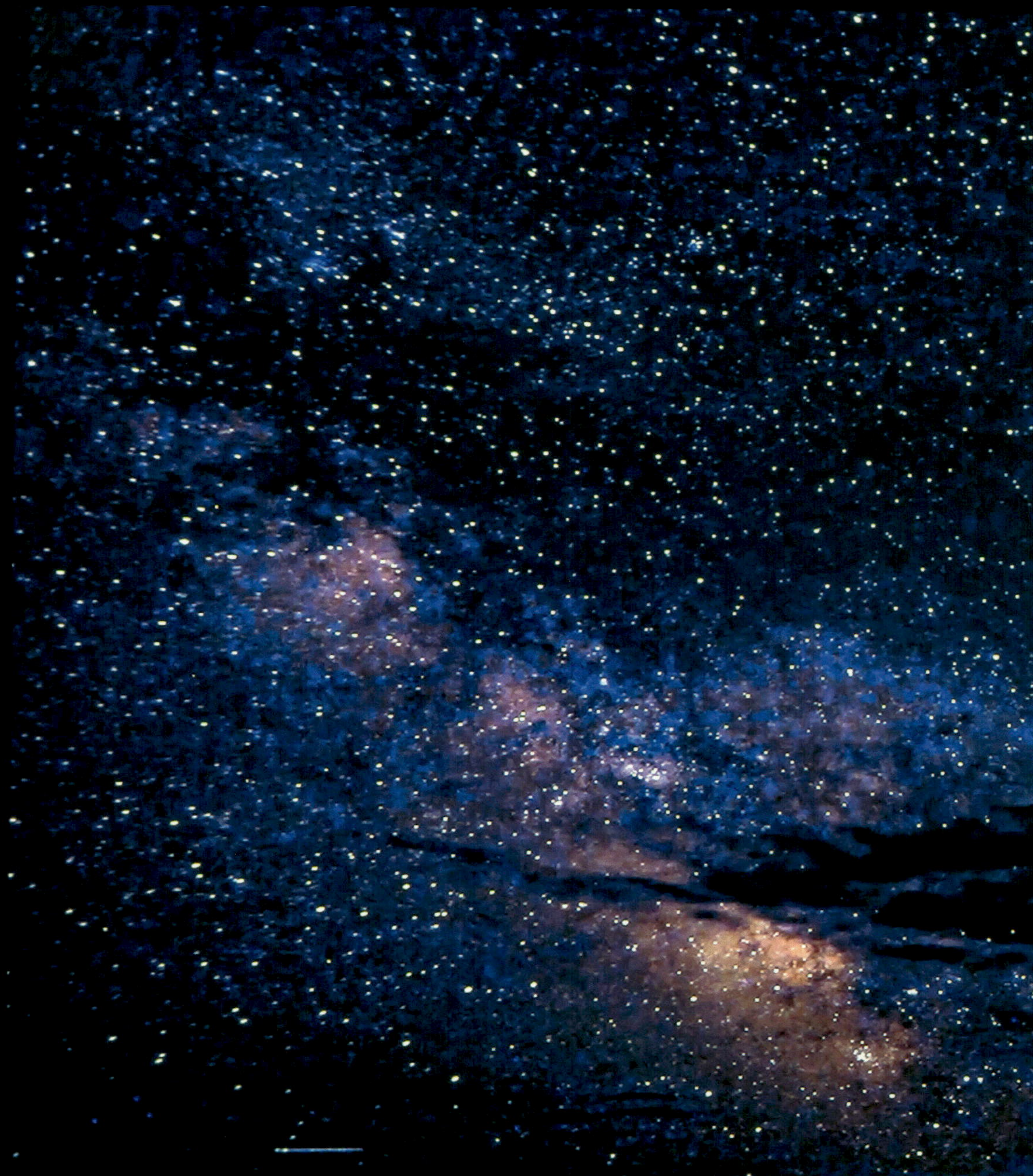

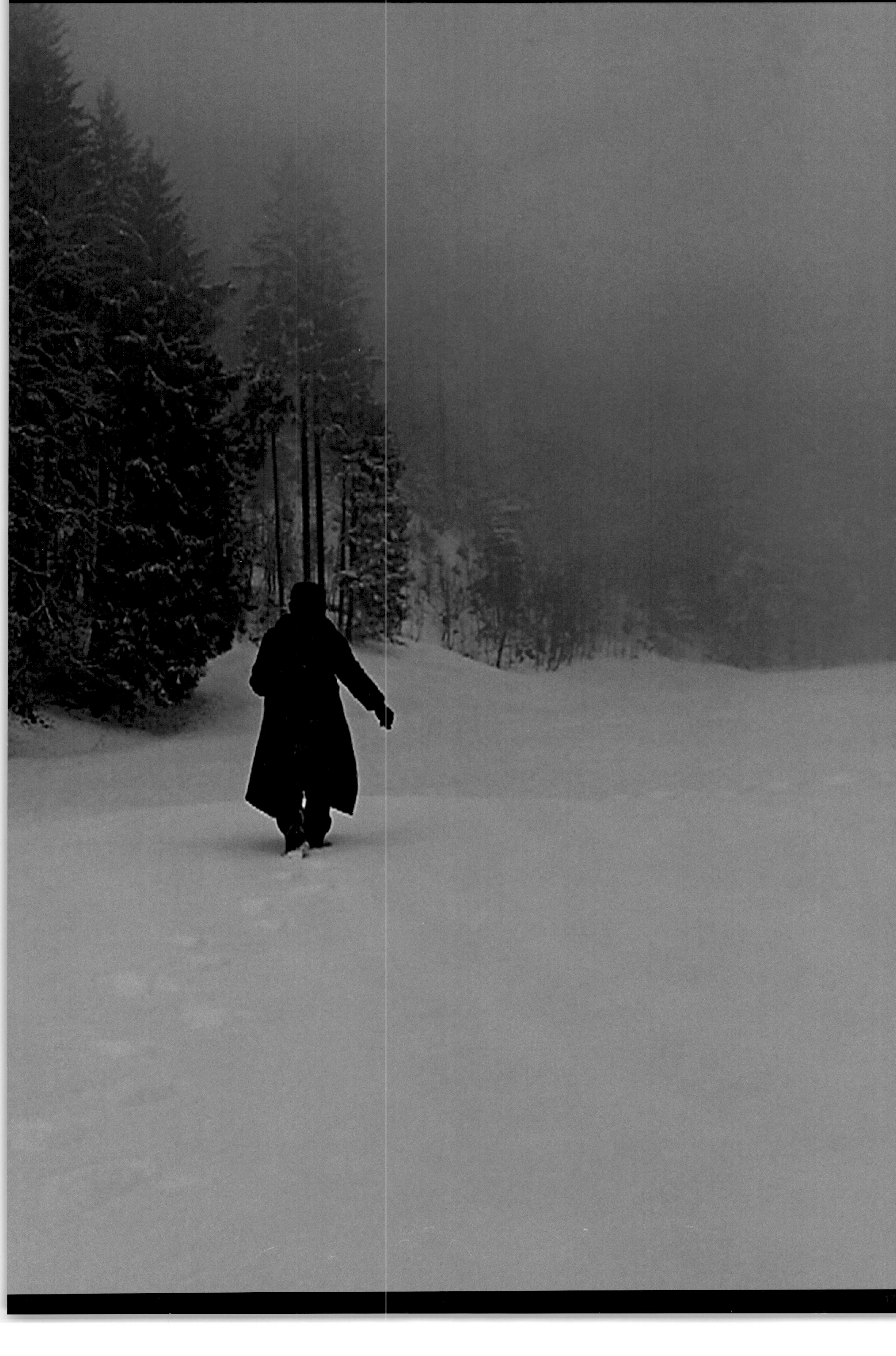

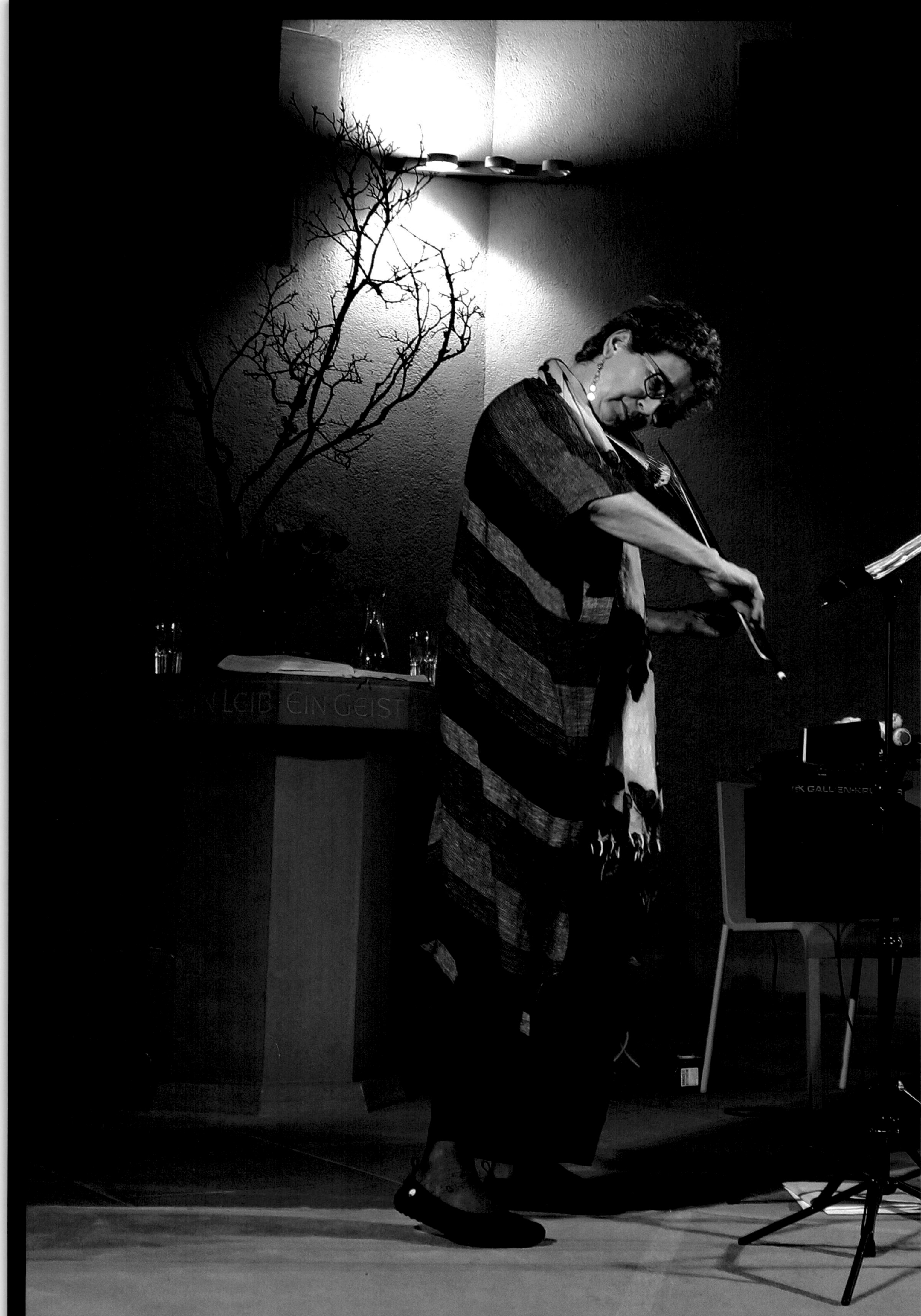
N LEIB · EIN GEIST

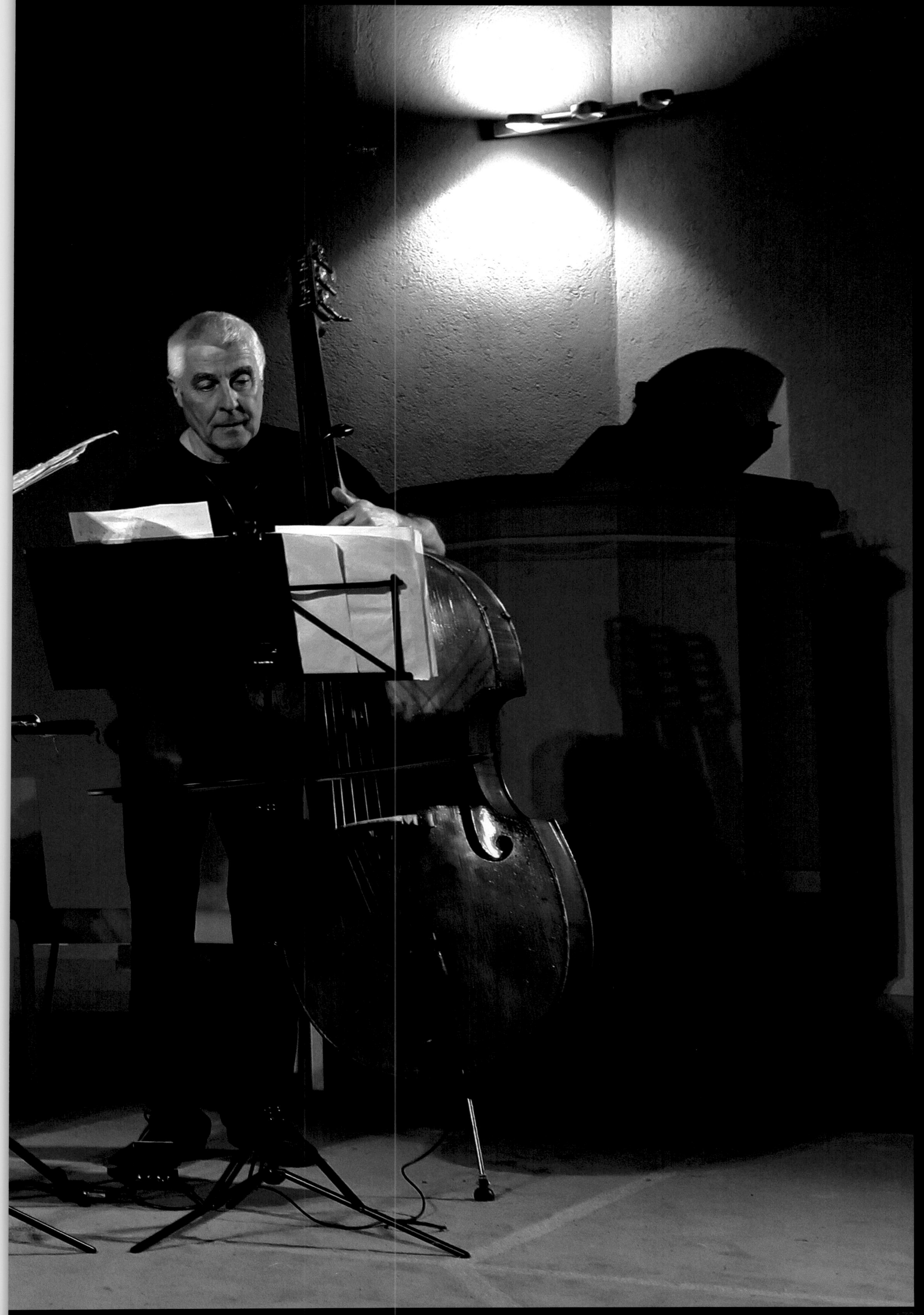

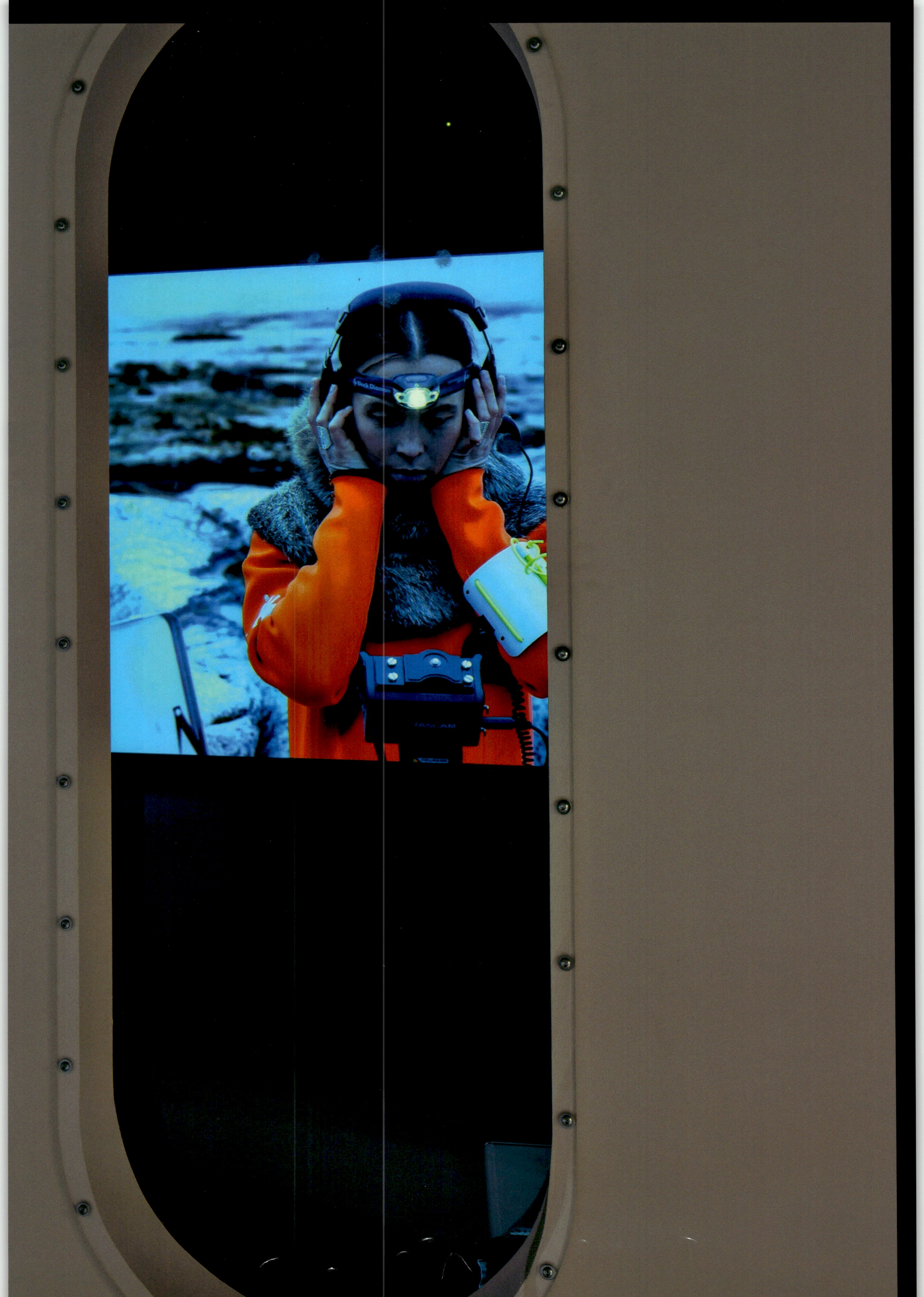

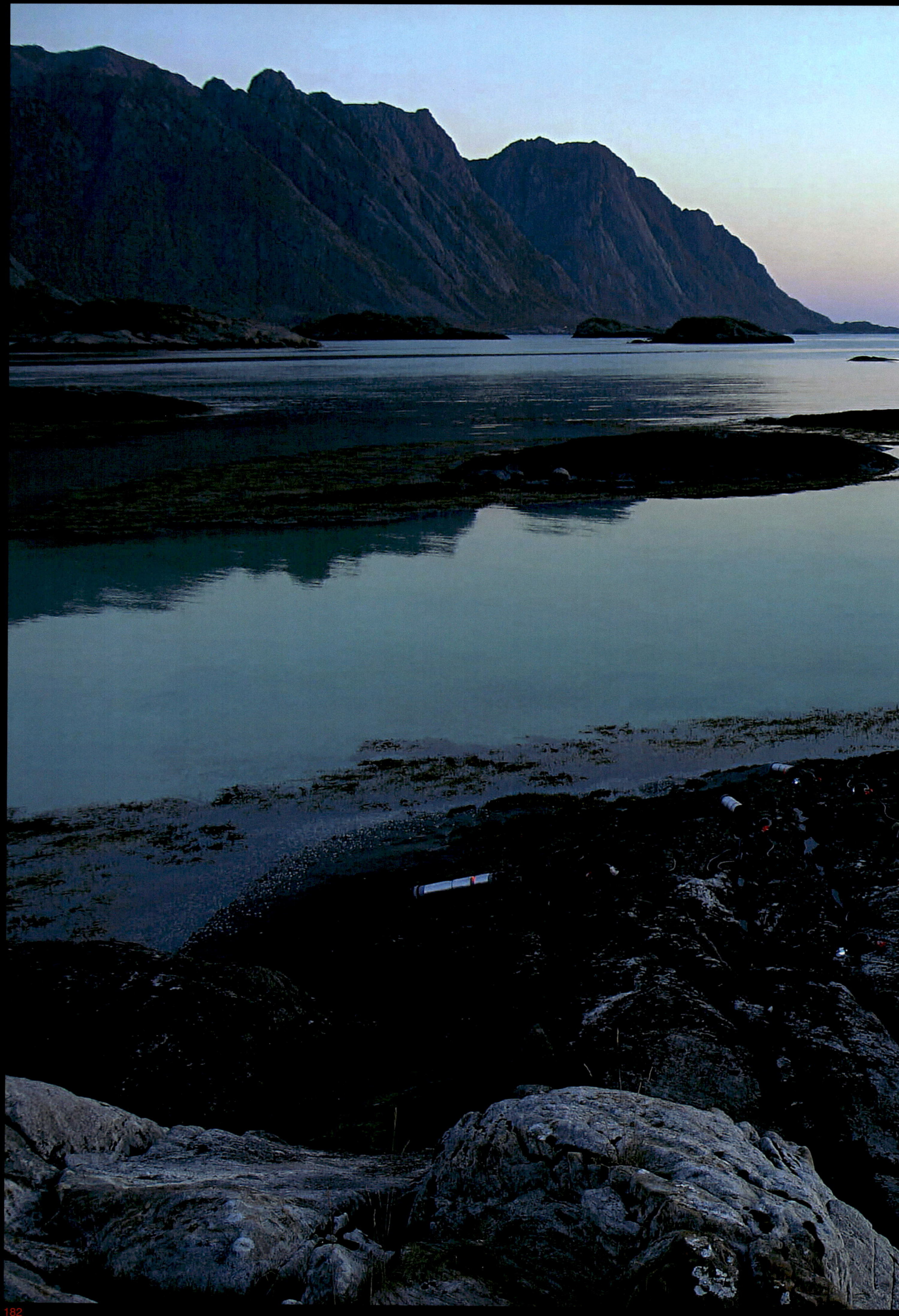

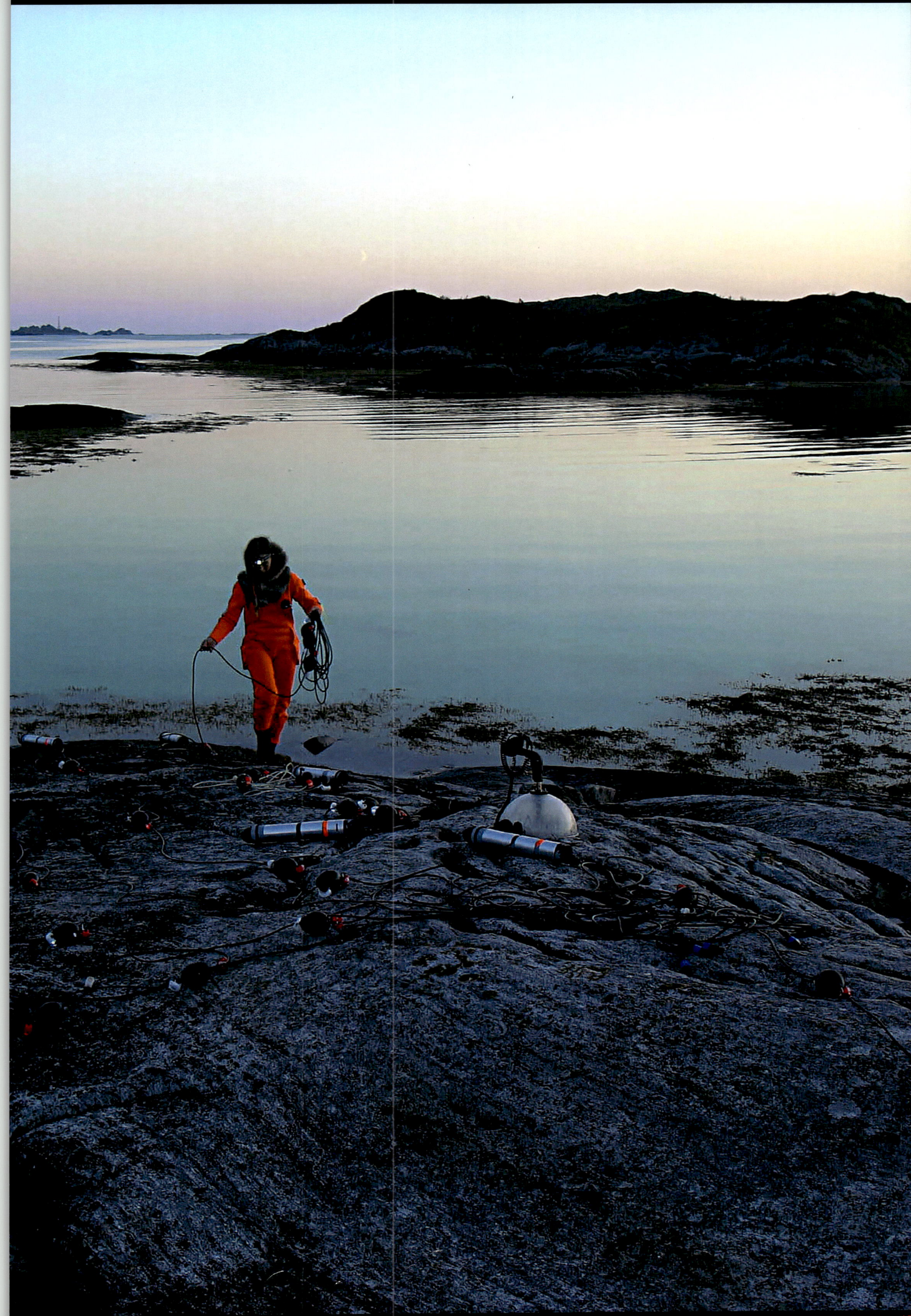

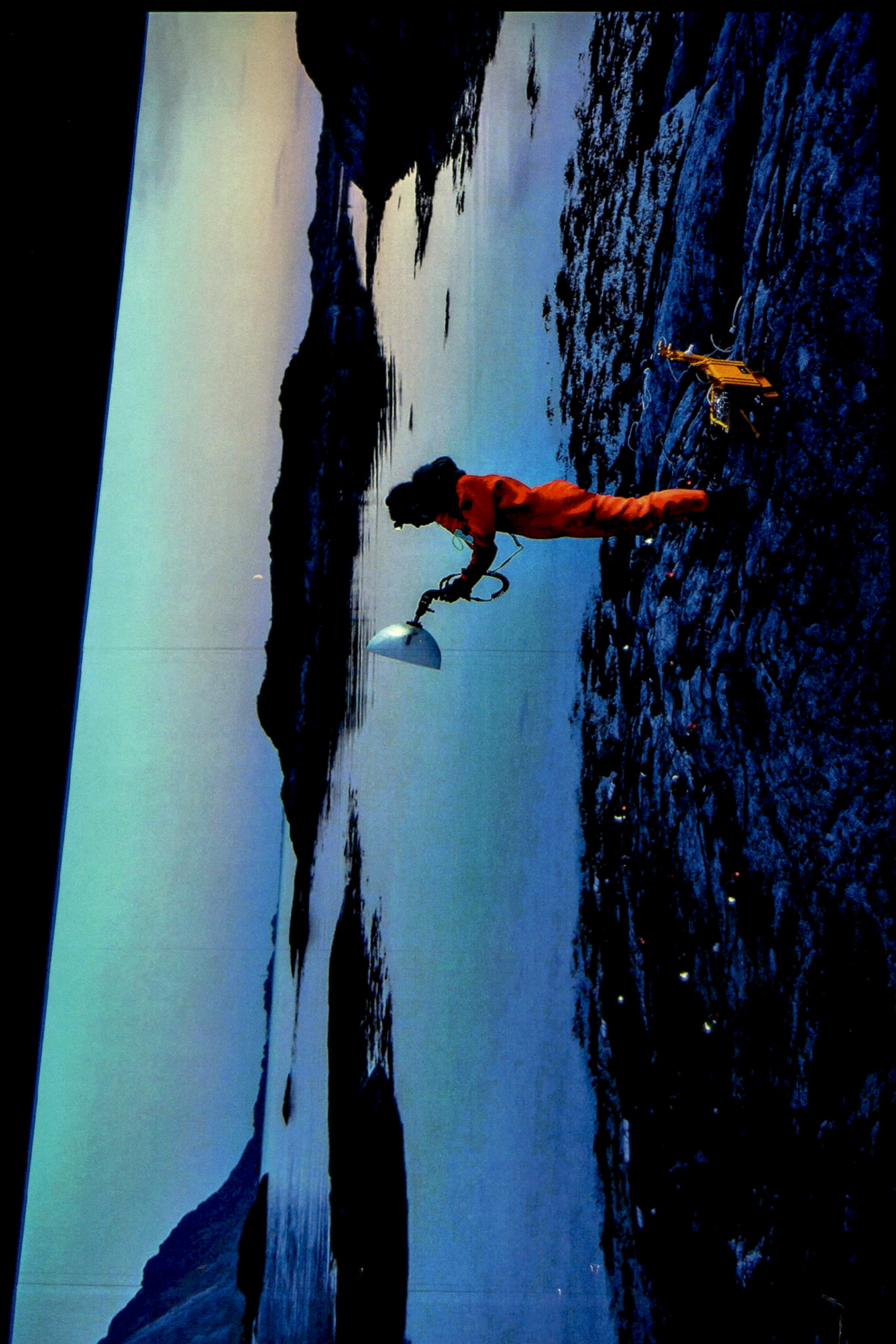

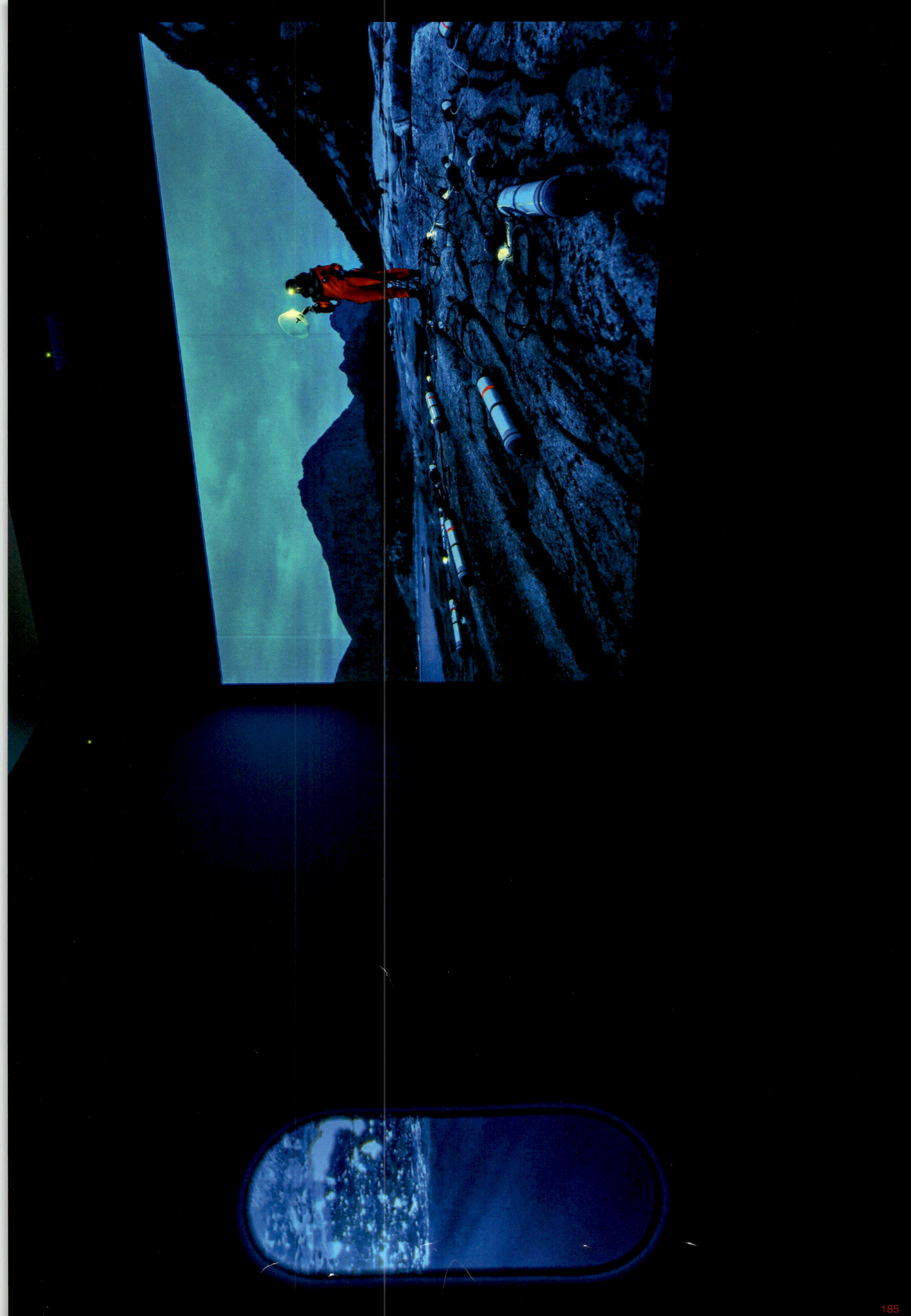

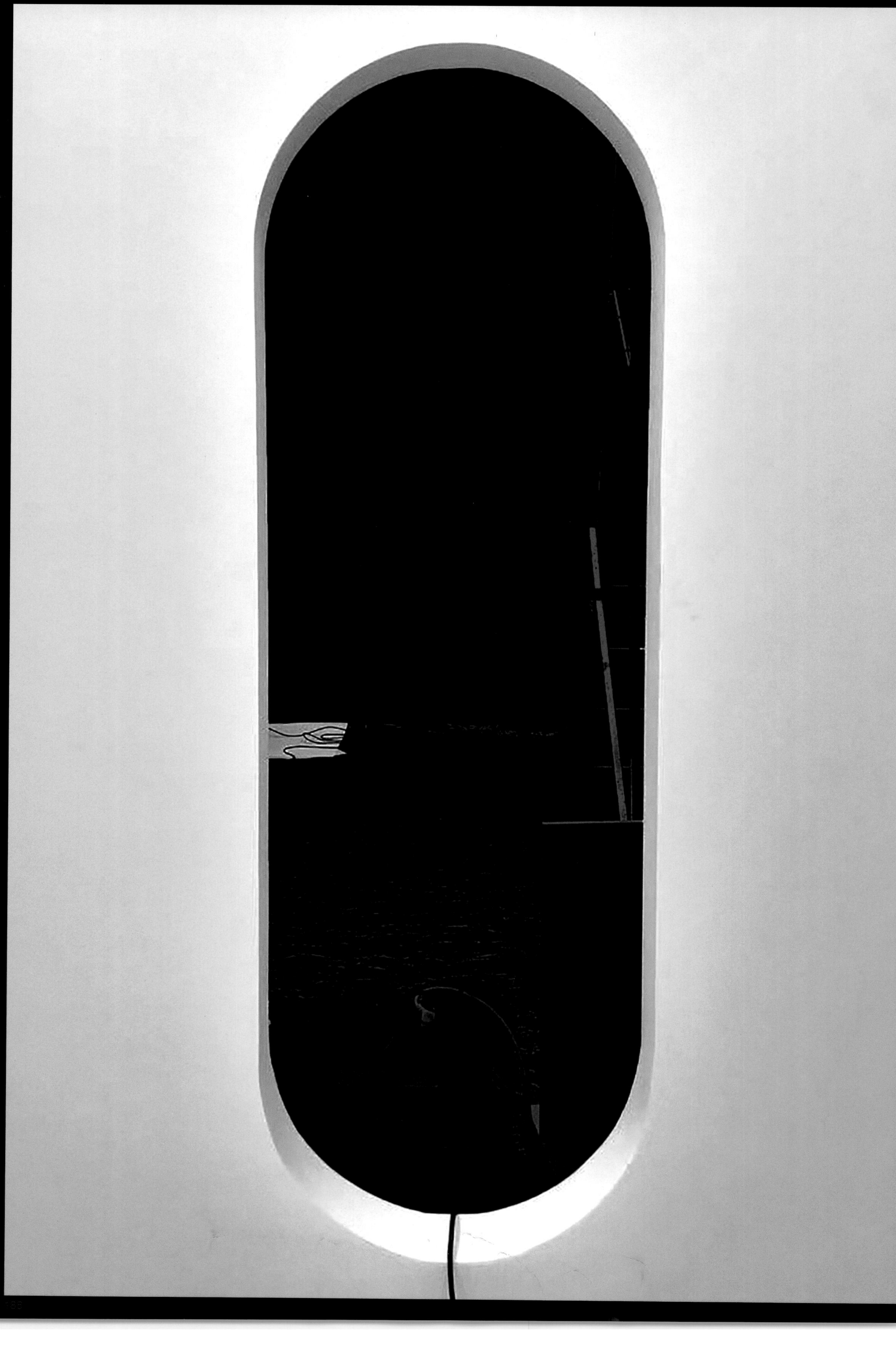

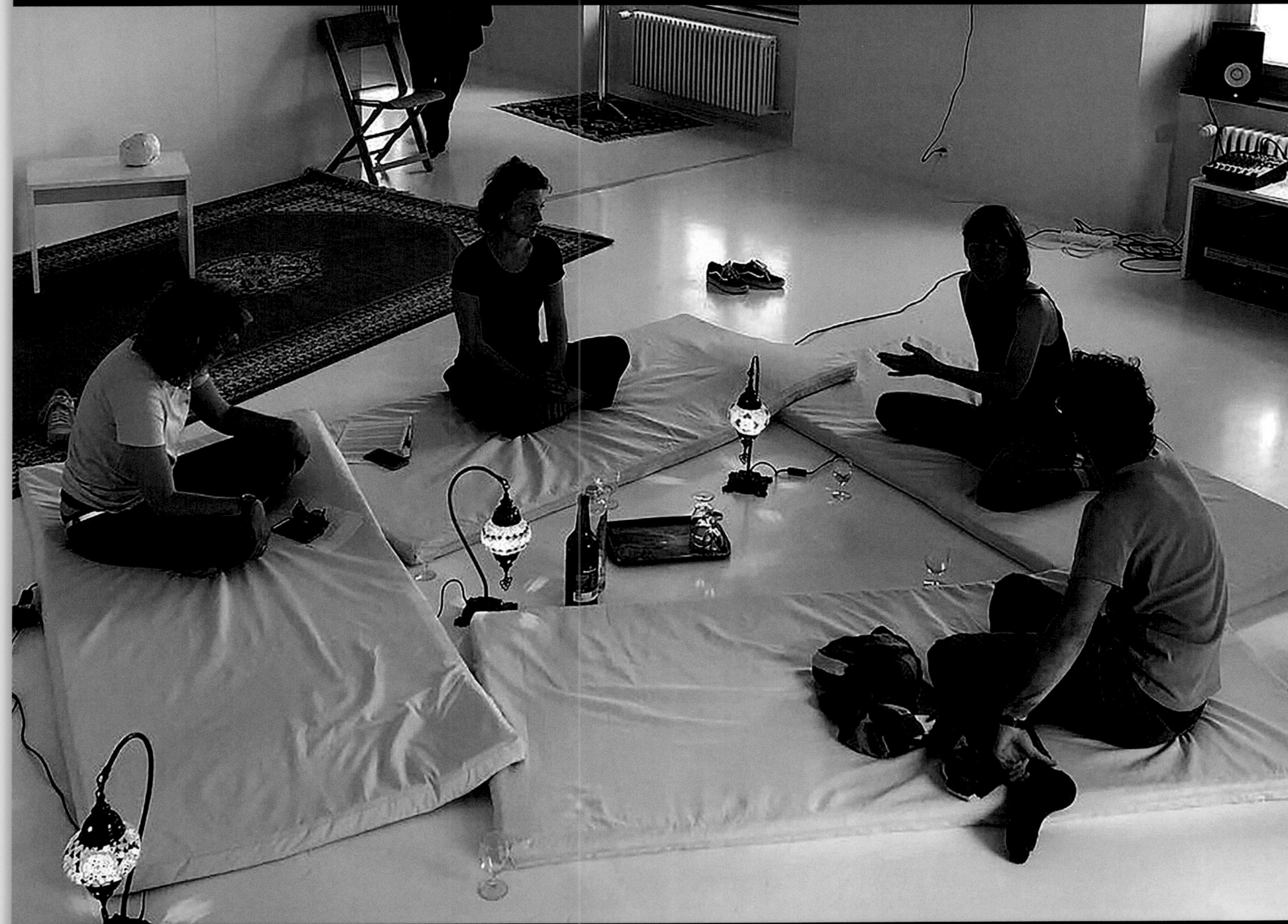

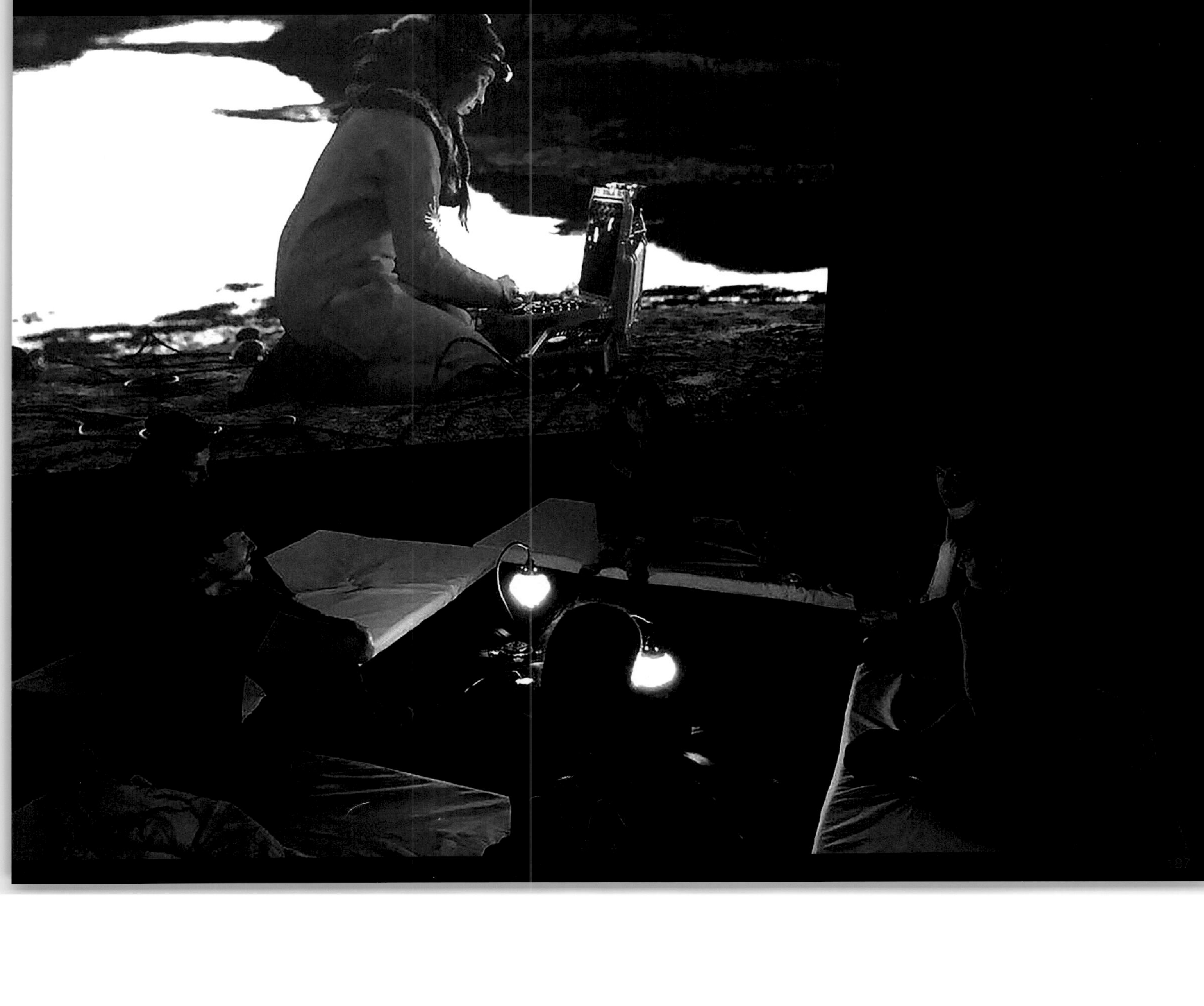

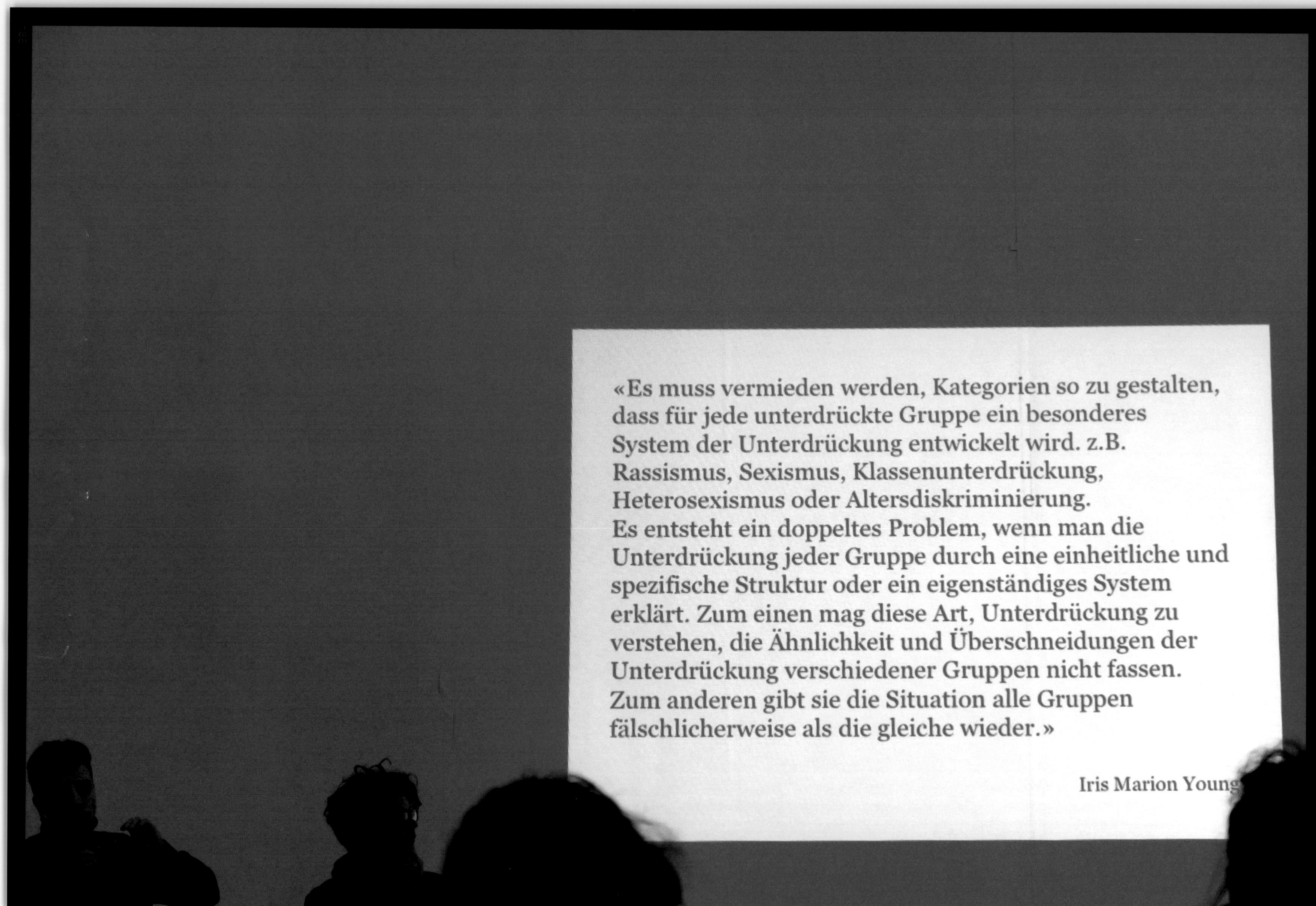
«Es muss vermieden werden, Kategorien so zu gestalten, dass für jede unterdrückte Gruppe ein besonderes System der Unterdrückung entwickelt wird. z.B. Rassismus, Sexismus, Klassenunterdrückung, Heterosexismus oder Altersdiskriminierung.
Es entsteht ein doppeltes Problem, wenn man die Unterdrückung jeder Gruppe durch eine einheitliche und spezifische Struktur oder ein eigenständiges System erklärt. Zum einen mag diese Art, Unterdrückung zu verstehen, die Ähnlichkeit und Überschneidungen der Unterdrückung verschiedener Gruppen nicht fassen. Zum anderen gibt sie die Situation alle Gruppen fälschlicherweise als die gleiche wieder.»
Iris Marion Young

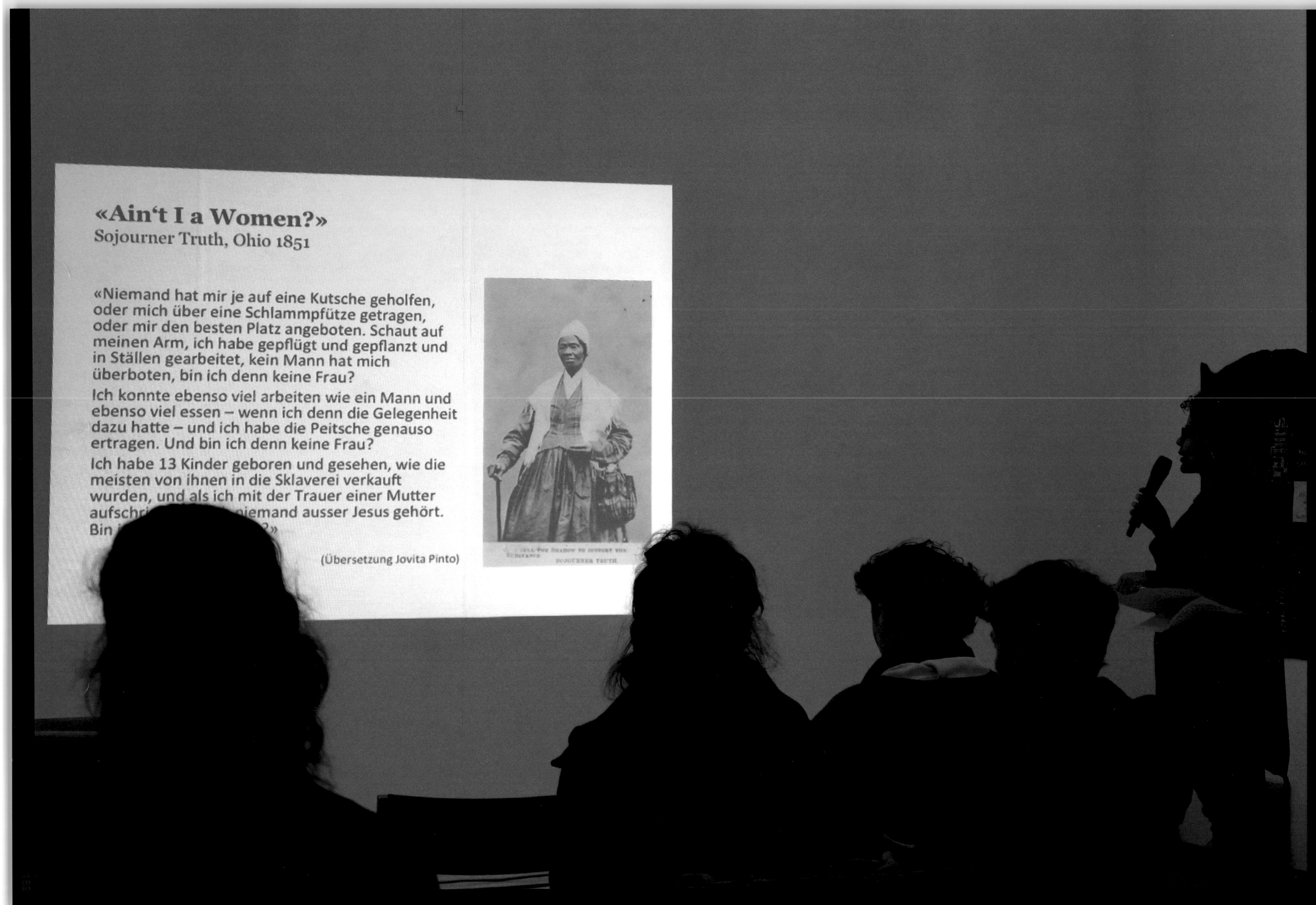
«Ain‘t I a Women?»
Sojourner Truth, Ohio 1851
«Niemand hat mir je auf eine Kutsche geholfen, oder mich über eine Schlammpfütze getragen, oder mir den besten Platz angeboten. Schaut auf meinen Arm, ich habe gepflügt und gepflanzt und in Ställen gearbeitet, kein Mann hat mich überboten, bin ich denn keine Frau?
Ich konnte ebenso viel arbeiten wie ein Mann und ebenso viel essen – wenn ich denn die Gelegenheit dazu hatte – und ich habe die Peitsche genauso ertragen. Und bin ich denn keine Frau?
Ich habe 13 Kinder geboren und gesehen, wie die meisten von ihnen in die Sklaverei verkauft wurden, und als ich mit der Trauer einer Mutter
niemand ausser Jesus gehört.
(Übersetzung Jovita Pinto)
SOJOURNER TRUTH.

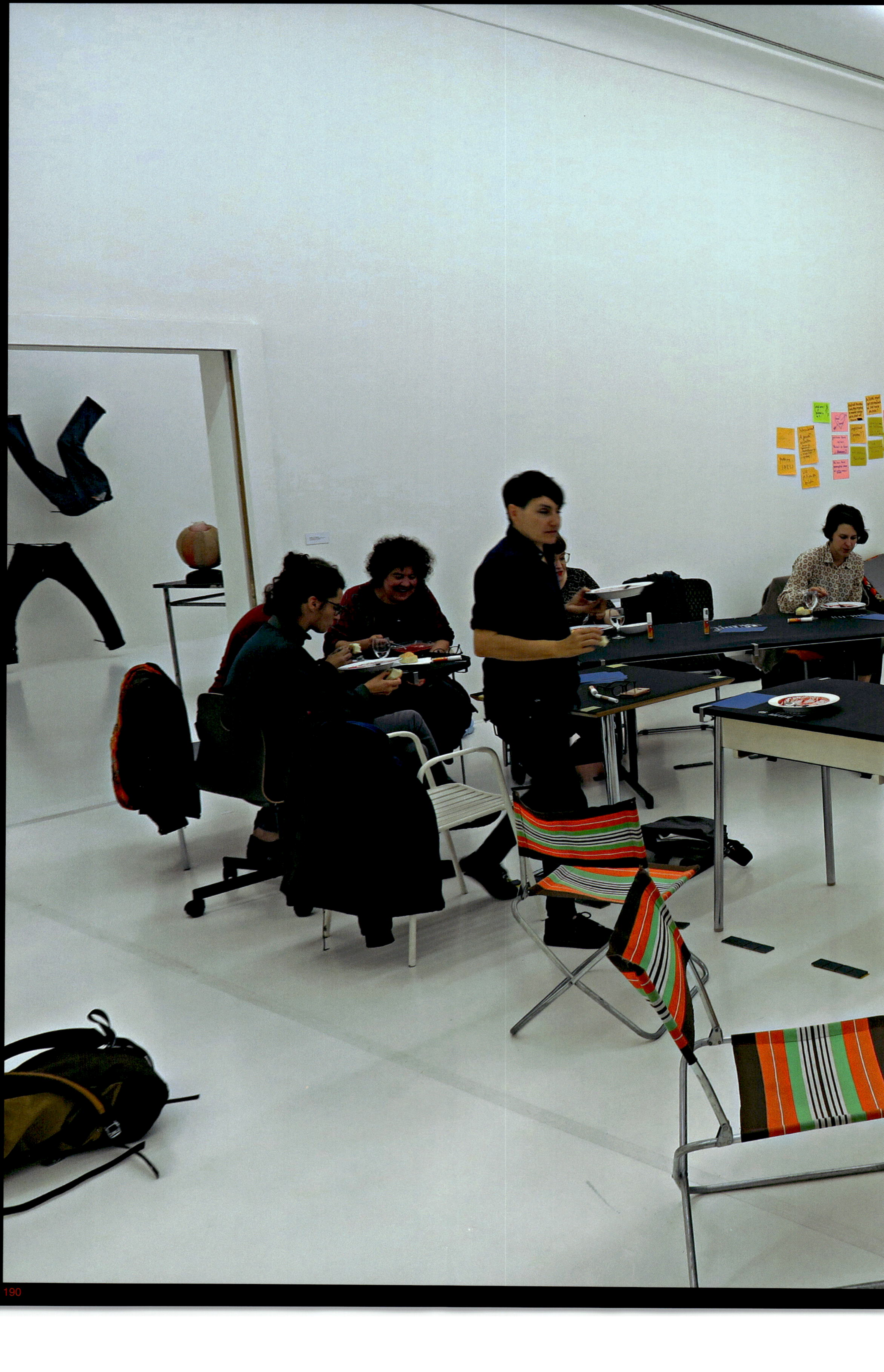

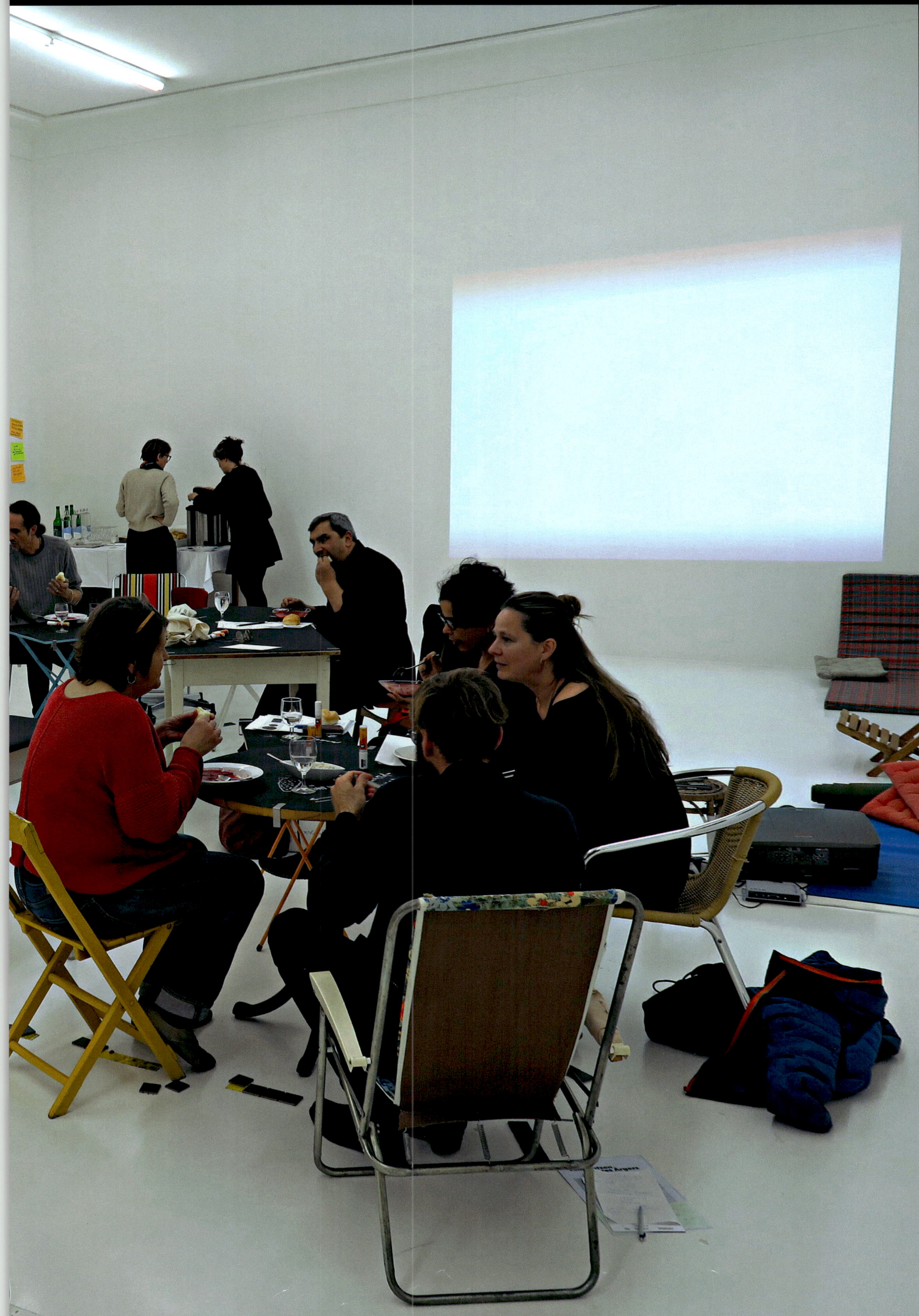

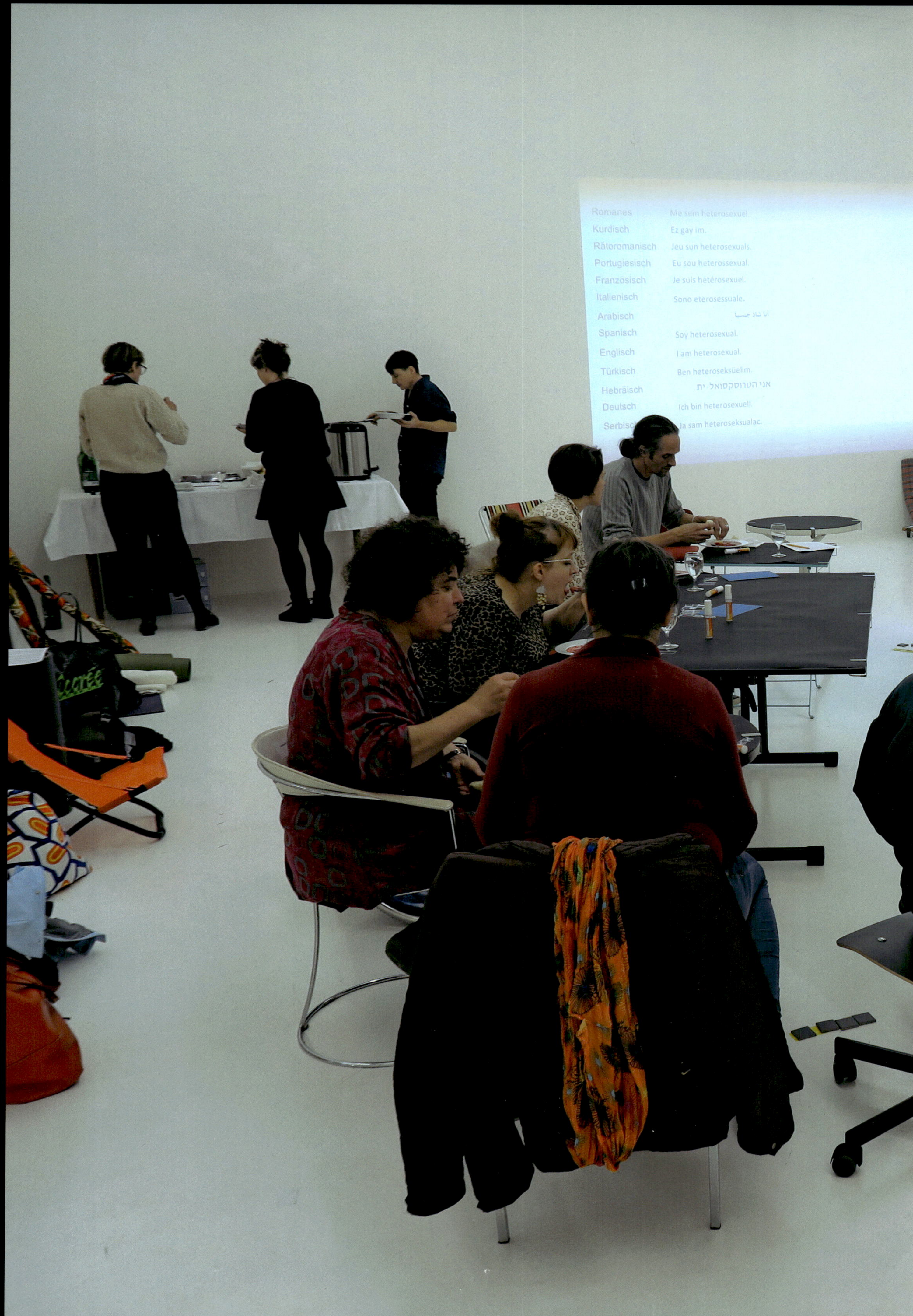
Romanes Me sem heterosexuel.
Kurdisch Ez gay im.
Rätoromanisch Jeu sun heterosexuals.
Portugiesisch Eu sou heterossexual.
Französisch Je suis hétérosexuel.
Italienisch Sono eterosessuale.
Arabisch
Spanisch Soy heterosexual.
Englisch I am heterosexual.
Türkisch Ben heteroseksüelim.
Hebräisch אני הטרוסקסואל ית
Deutsch Ich bin heterosexuell.
Serbisc Ja sam heteroseksualac.

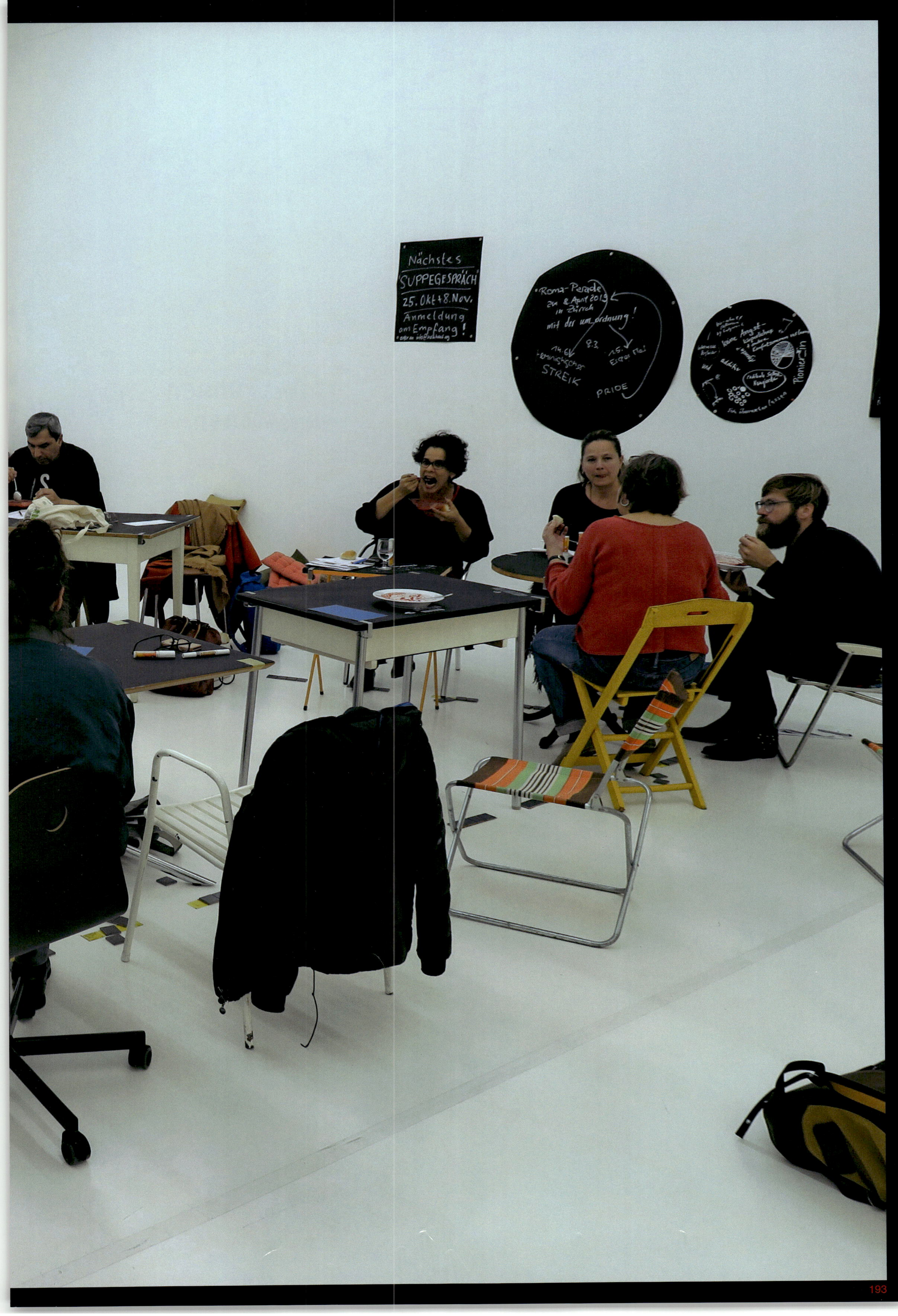
Nächstes
SUPPEGESPRÄCH
25. Okt + 8. Nov.
Anmeldung
am Empfang!
Roma-Parade
mit der um_ordnung!
STREIK
PRIDE
keine Angst
Pionier_in

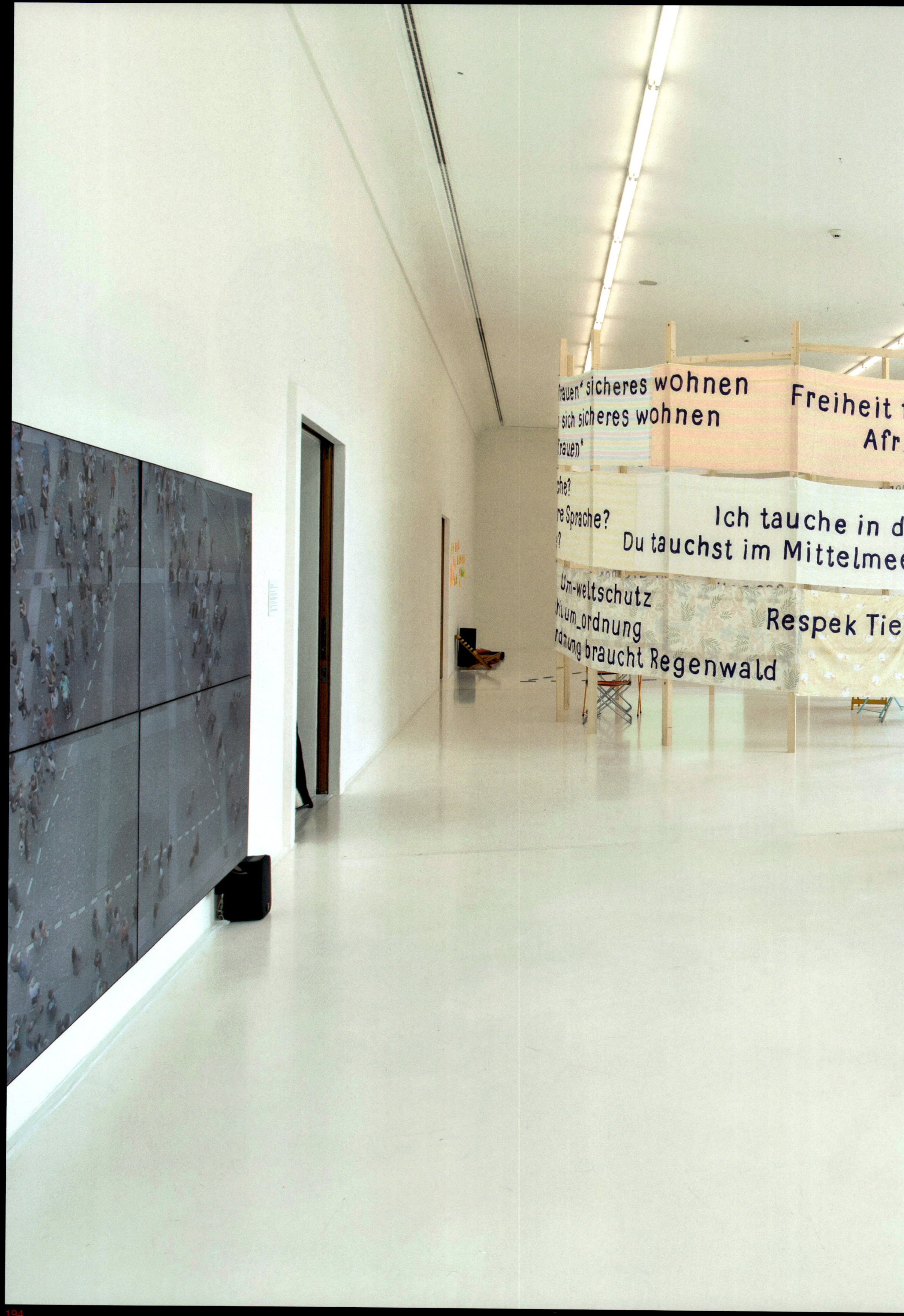
sicheres wohnen
sich sicheres wohnen
Freiheit
Ich tauche in
Du tauchst im
Um-weltschutz
um_ordnung
Respek
braucht Regenwald

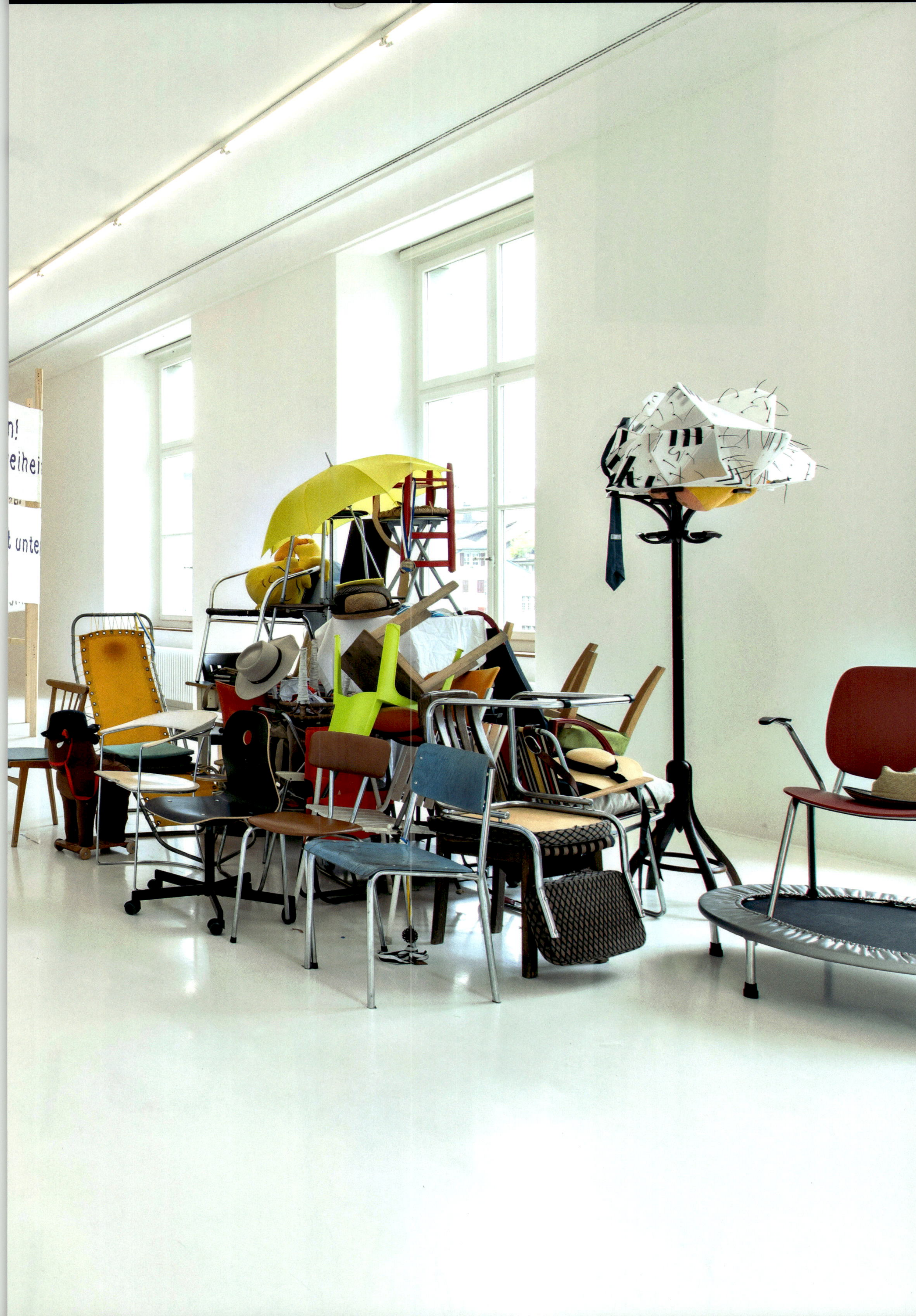

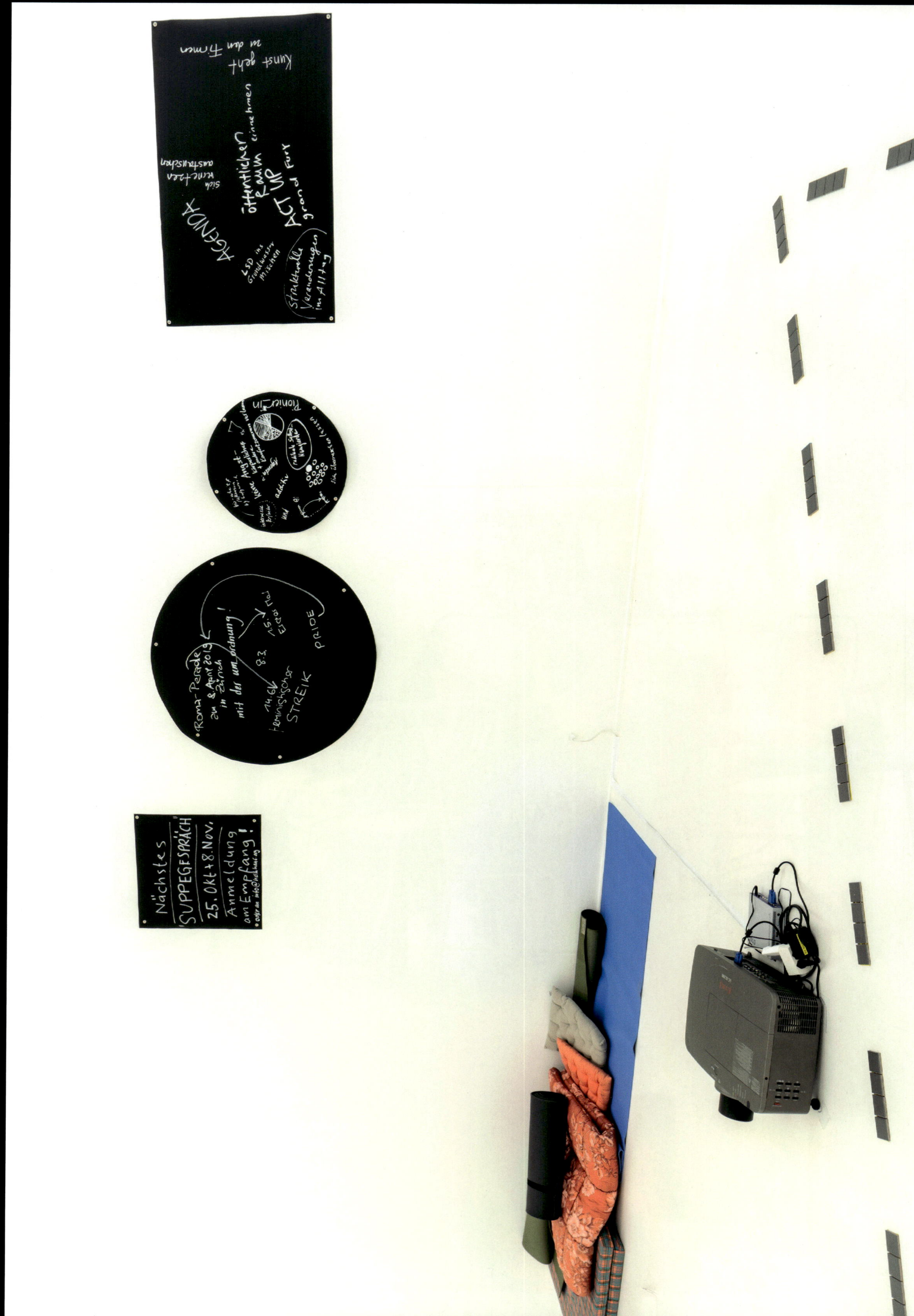
AGENDA
ACT UP
Nächstes
SUPPEGESPRÄCH
25. Okt + 8. Nov.
Anmeldung
am Empfang!
STREIK
PRIDE

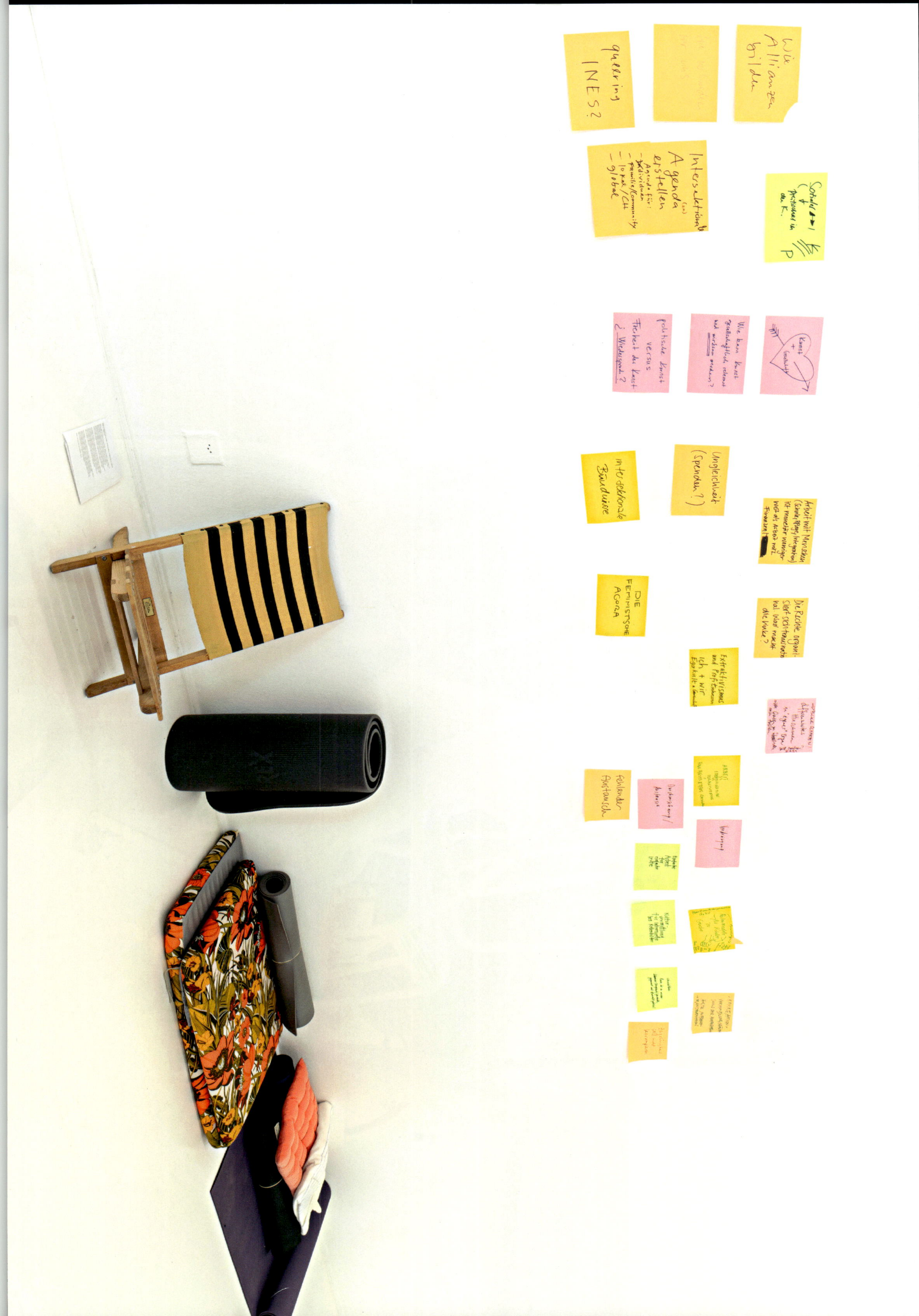

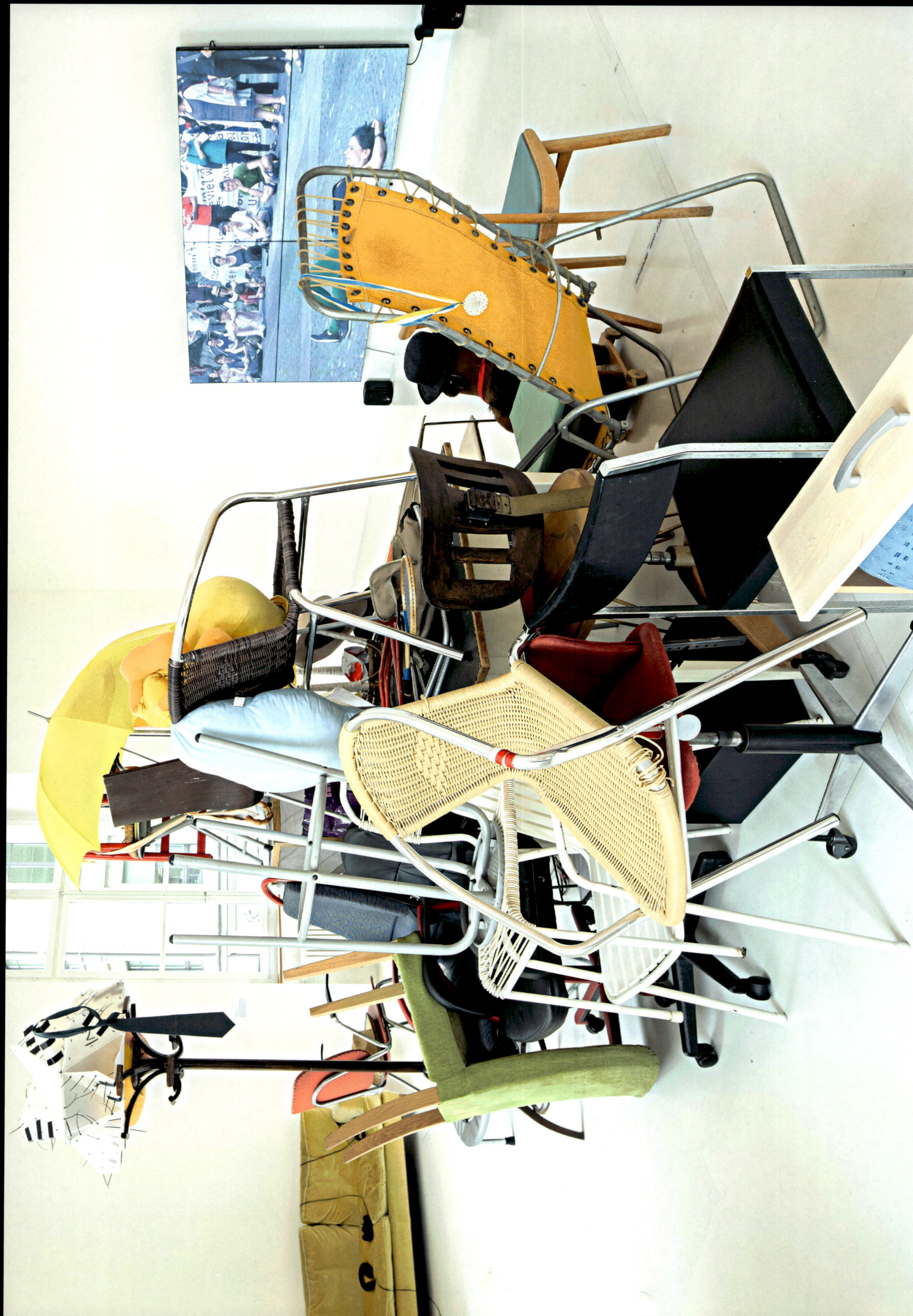

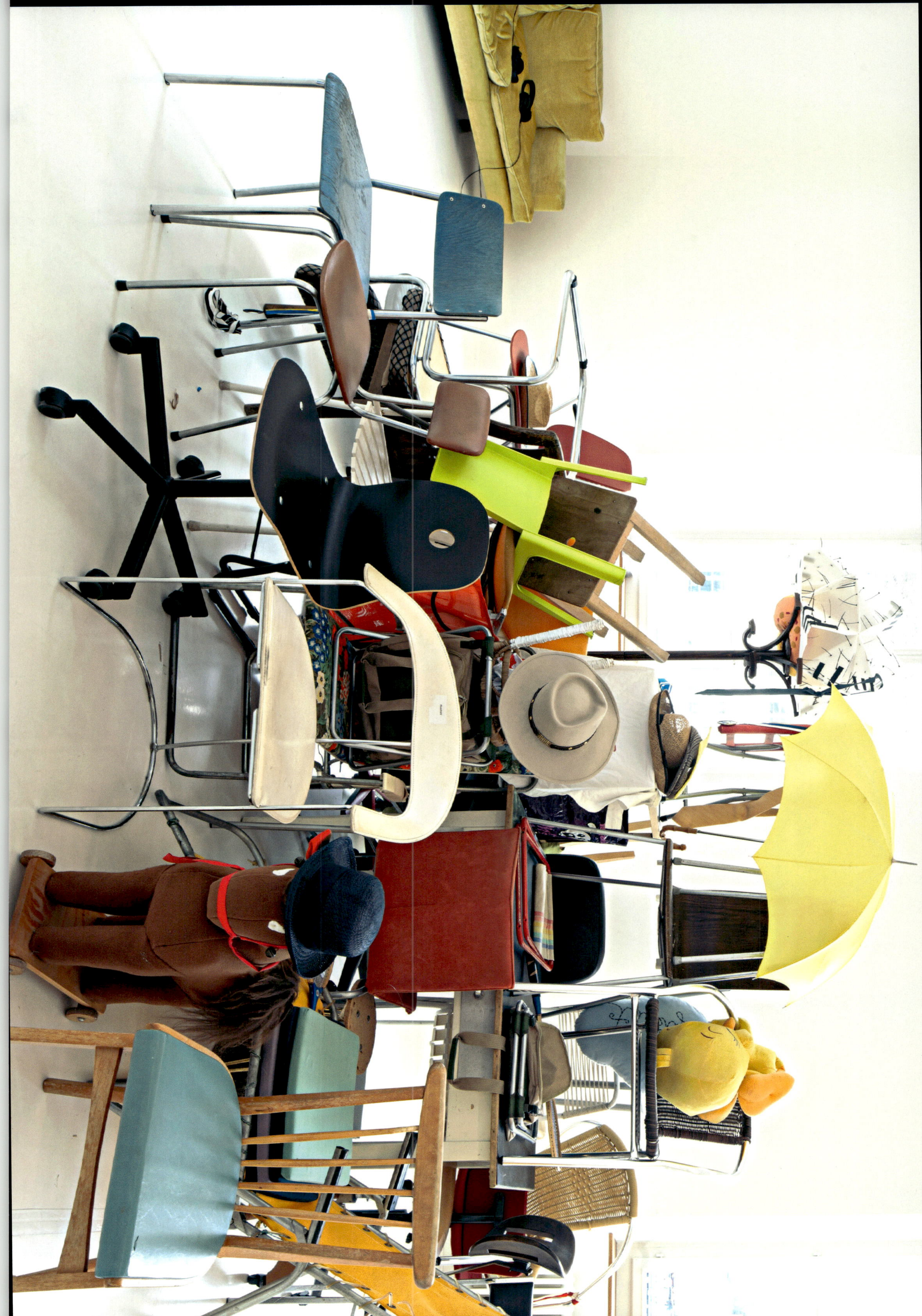

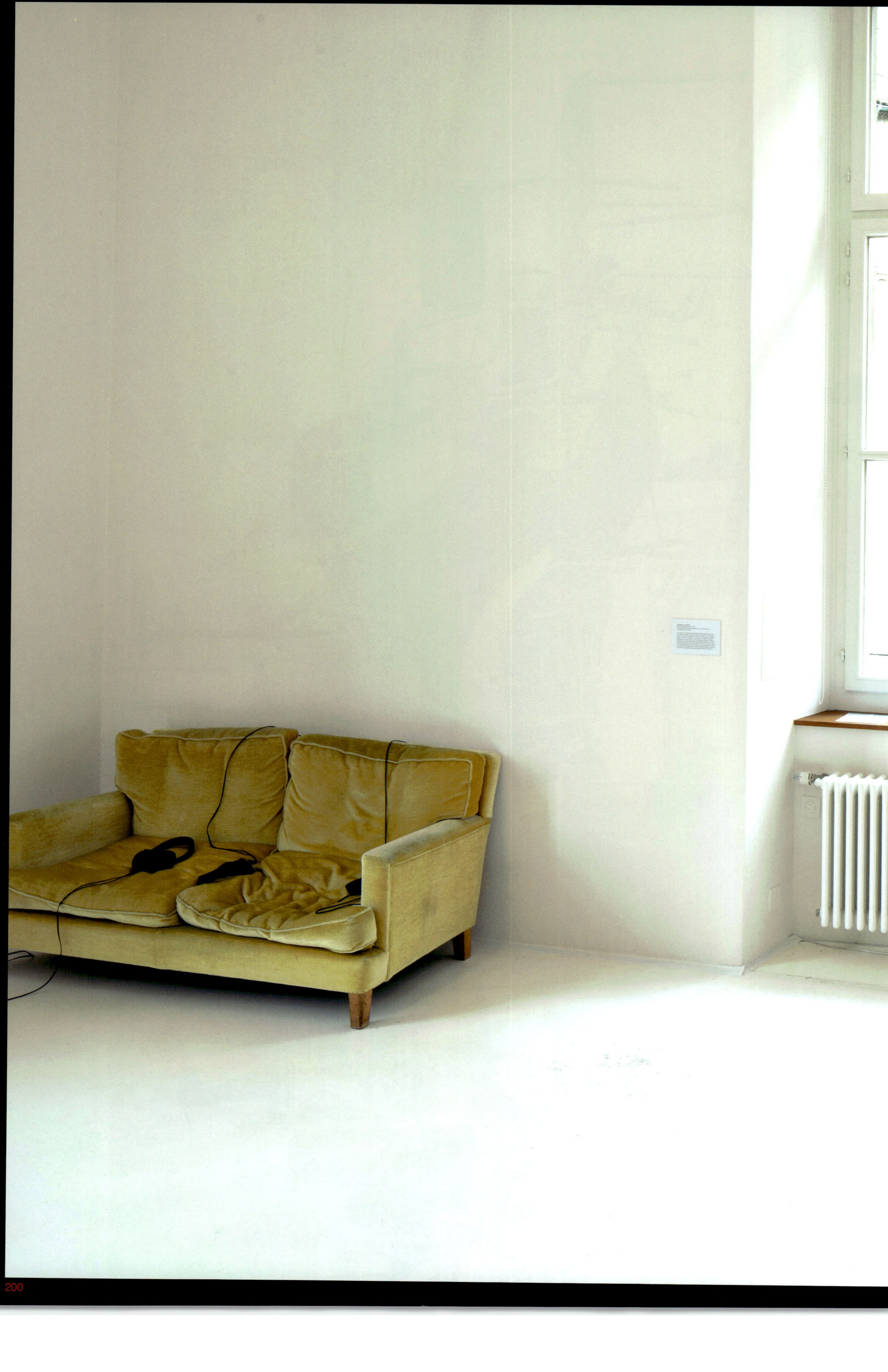

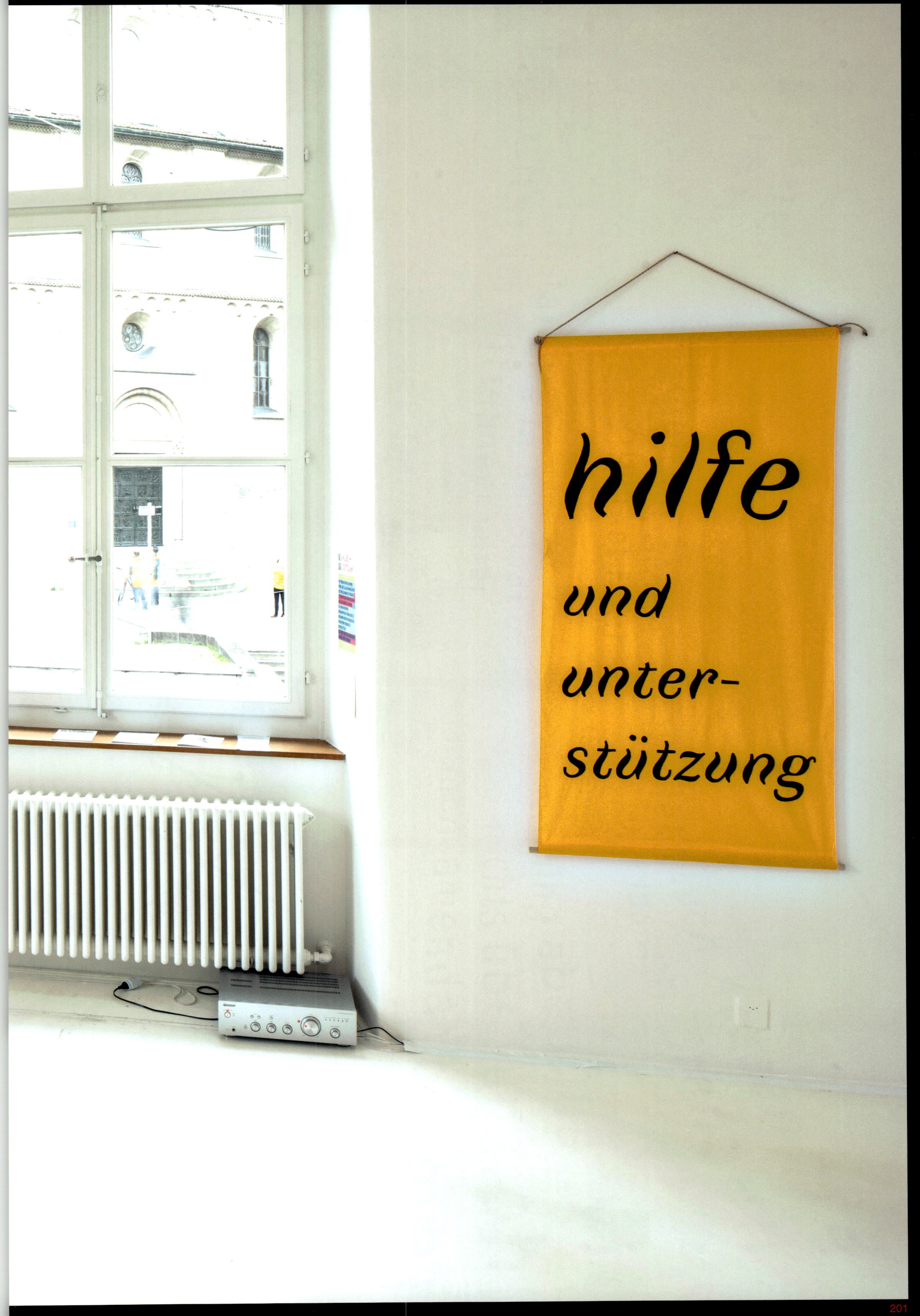
hilfe
und
unter-
stützung

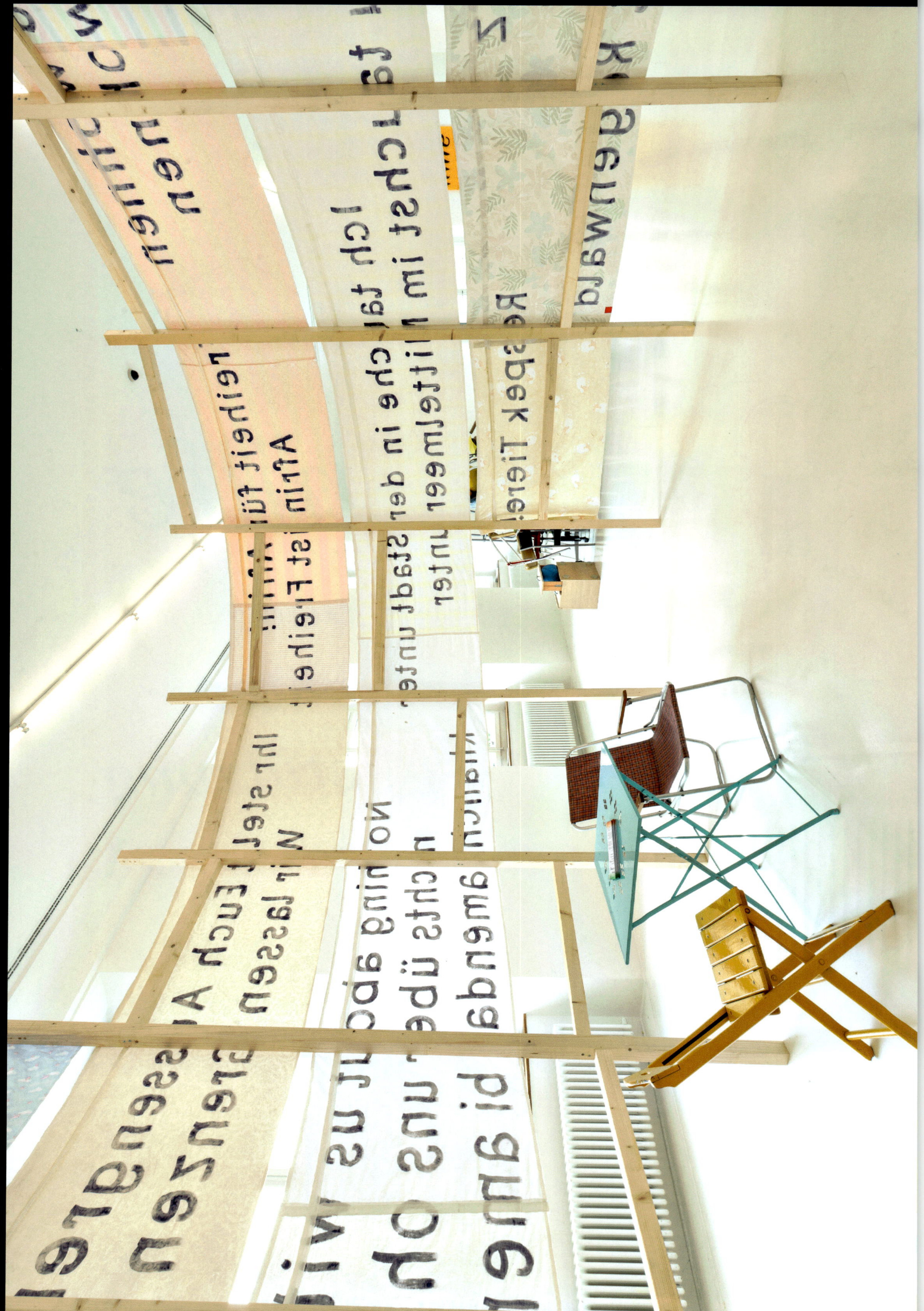

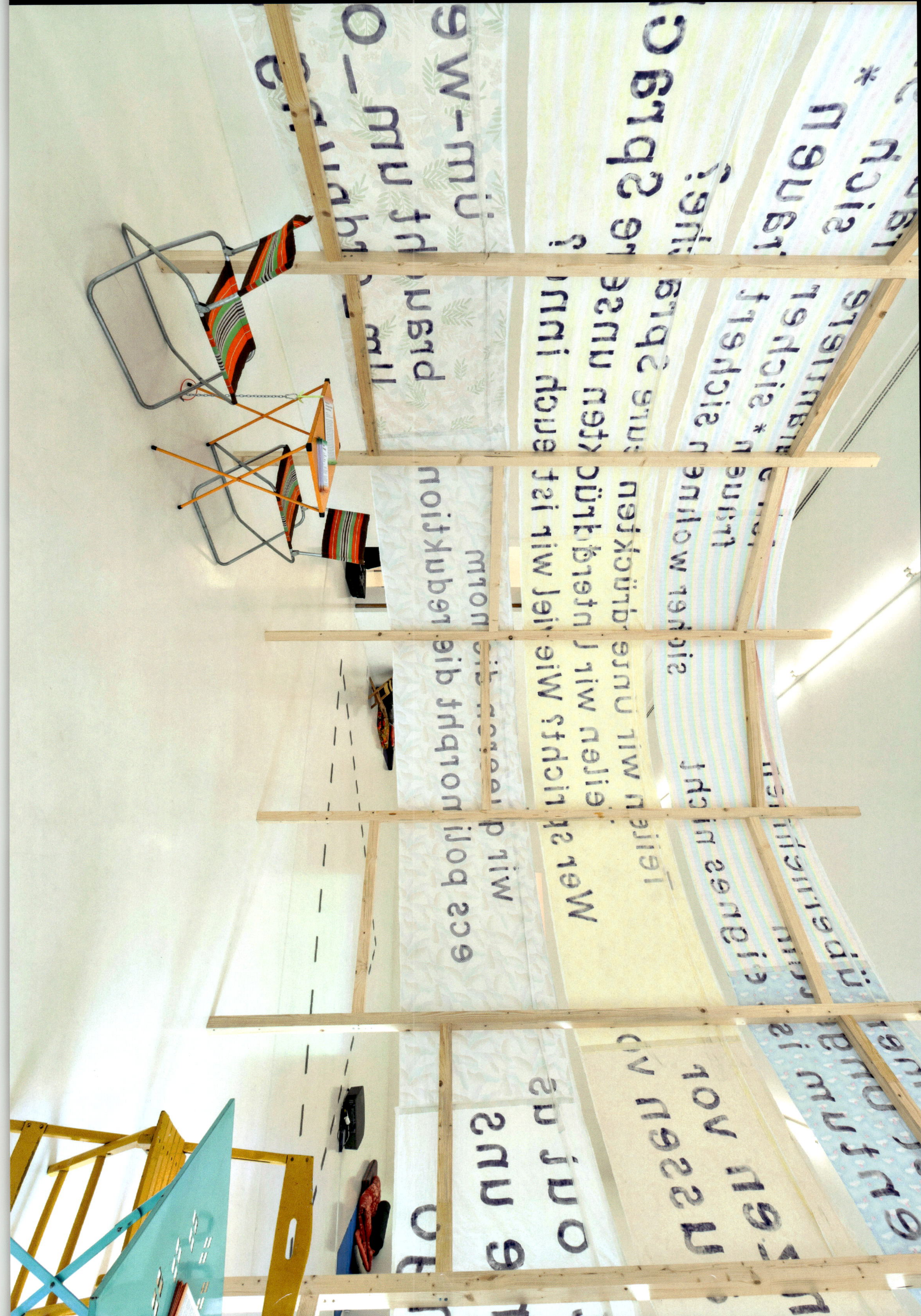

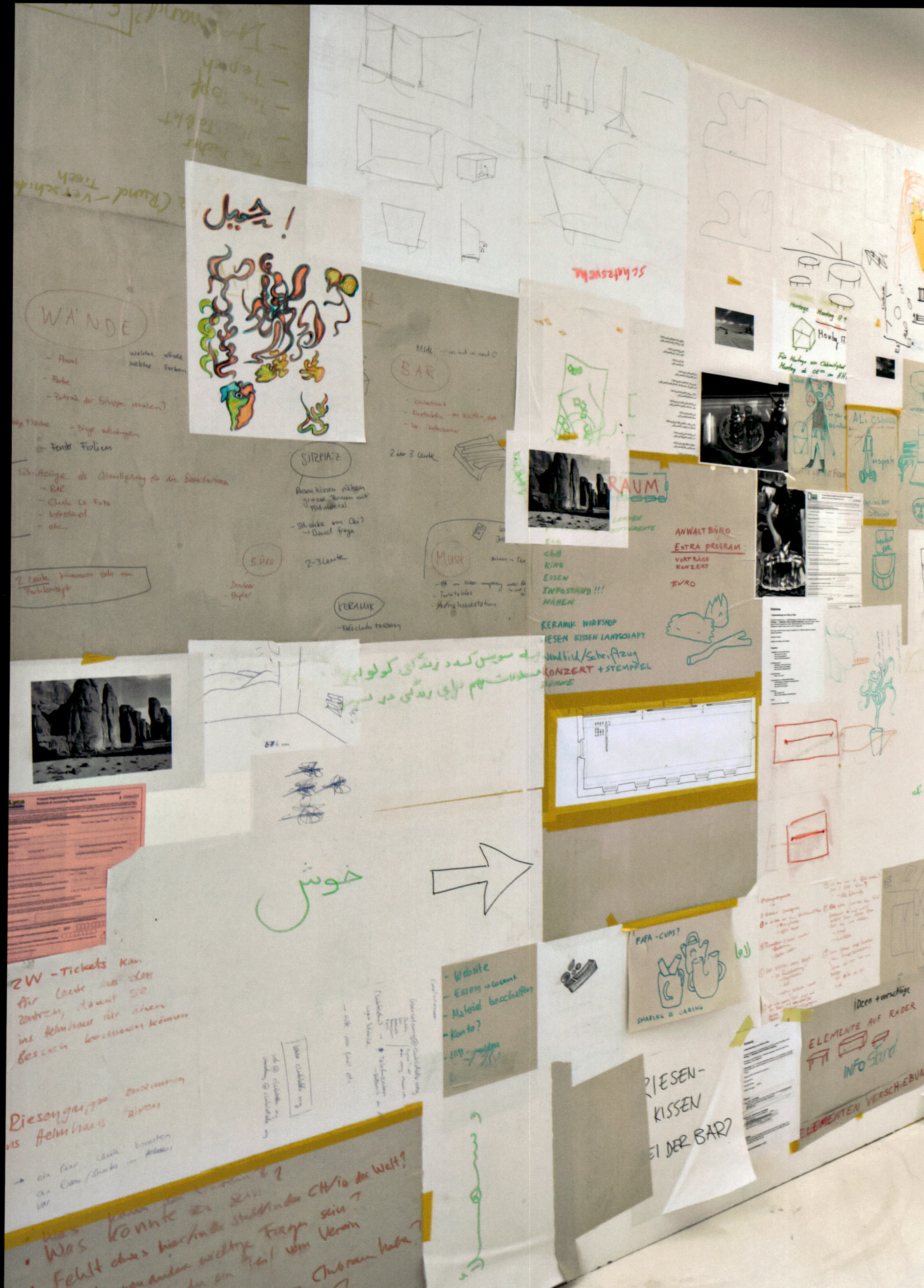
WÄNDE
BAR
KERAMIK
ANWALTBÜRO
EXTRA PROGRAM
KERAMIK WORKSHOP
RIESEN KISSEN LANDSCHAFT
KONZERT + STEMPEL
ZW-Tickets
Website
Essen + Getränk
Material beschaffen
Konto?
SHARING IS CARING
RIESEN-
KISSEN
BEI DER BAR?
Ideen + vorschläge
ELEMENTE AUF RÄDER
INFO STAND
ELEMENTEN VERSCHIEBUNG
Was könnte es sein
Fehlt etwas hier/in der stehenden CH/in der Welt?

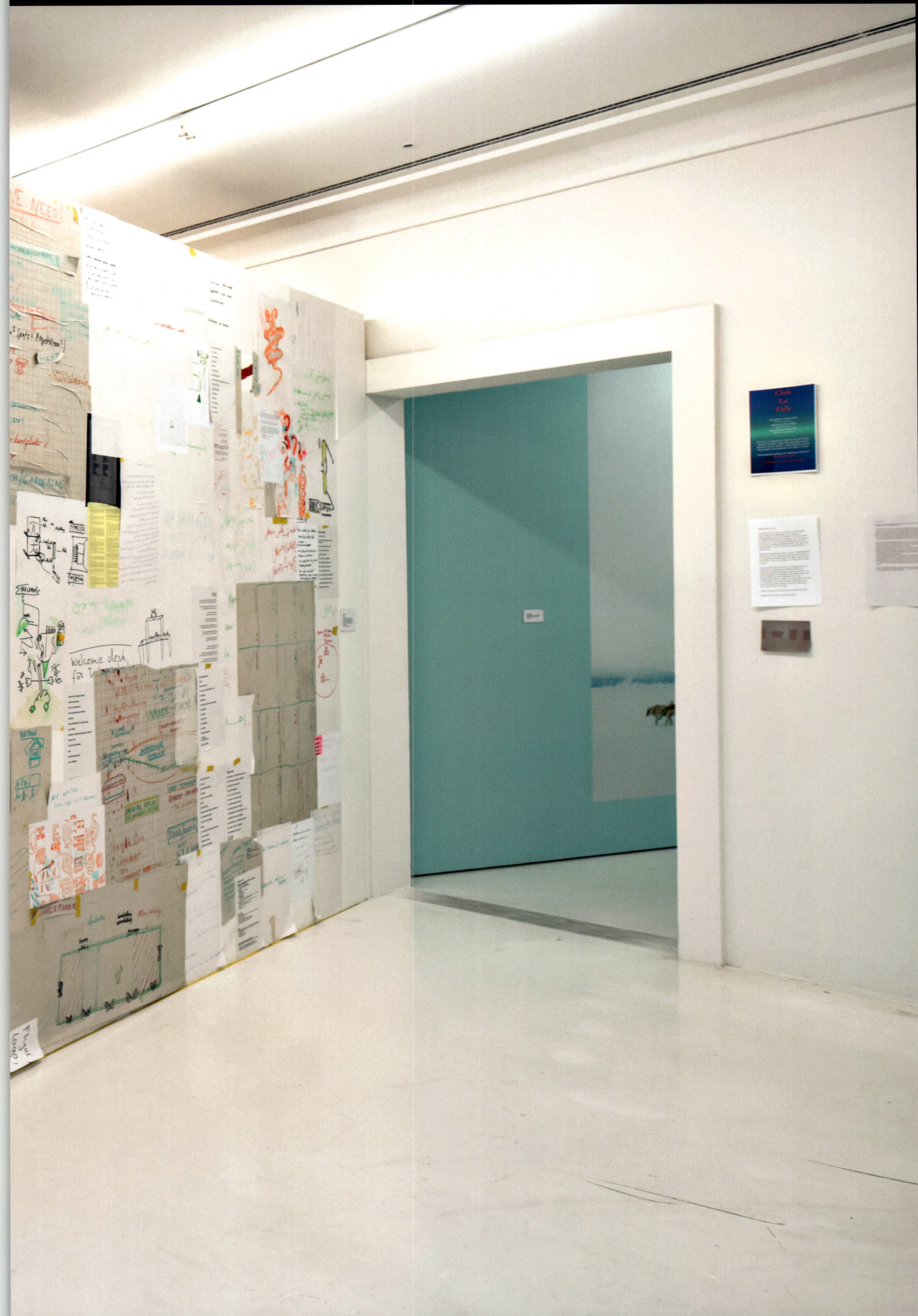
Welcome desk

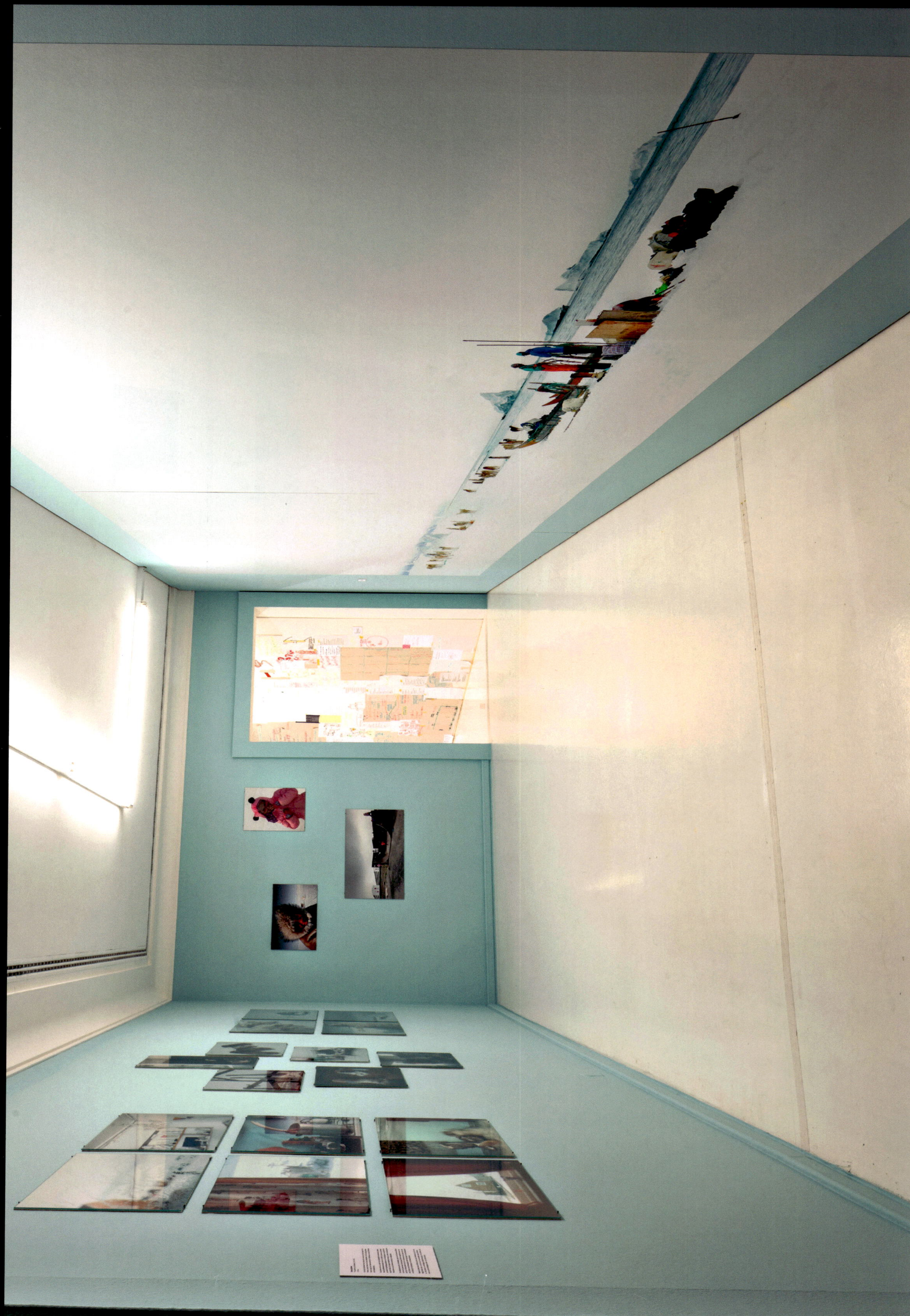

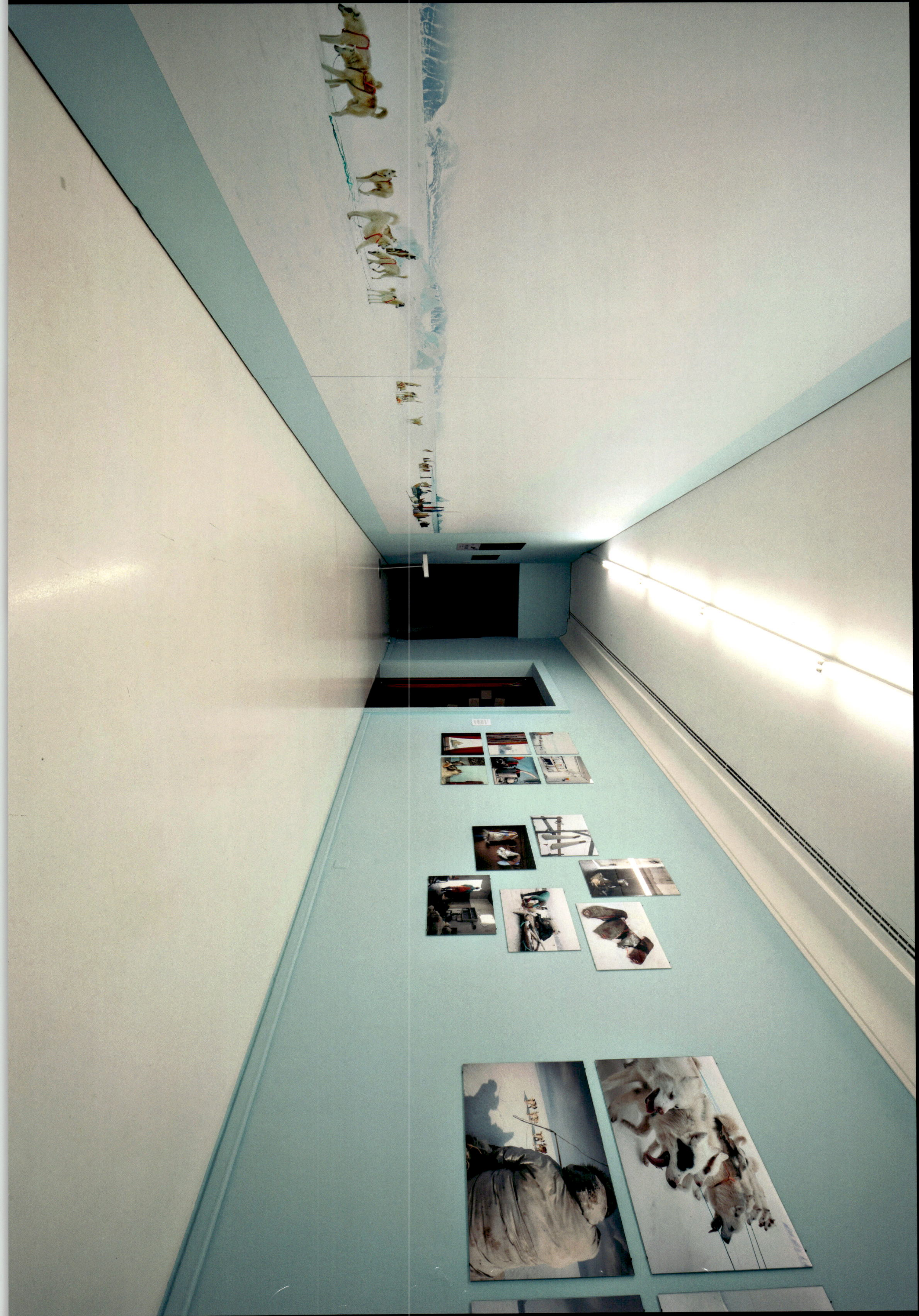

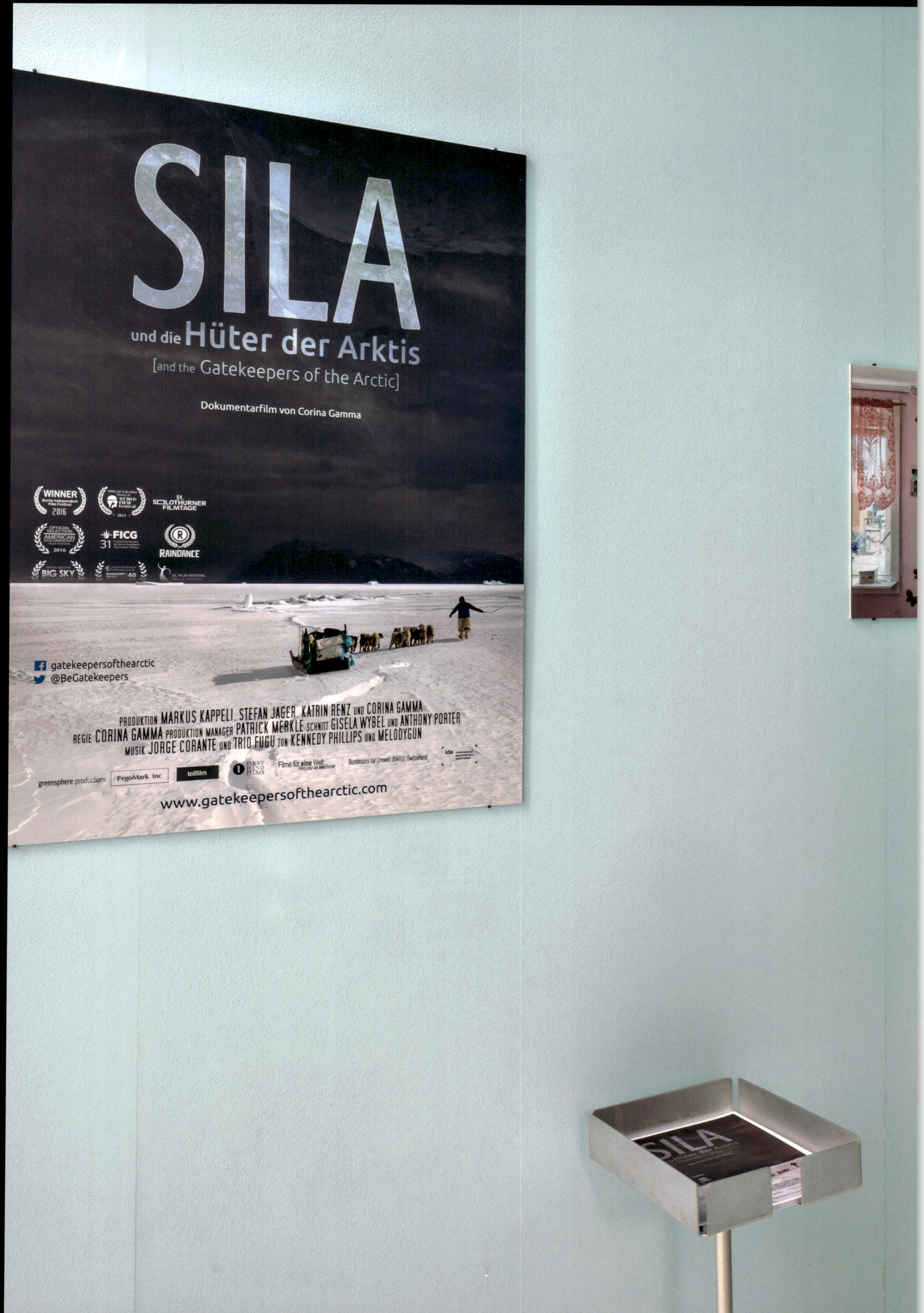
SILA
und die Hüter der Arktis
[and the Gatekeepers of the Arctic]
Dokumentarfilm von Corina Gamma
WINNER 2016
RAINDANCE
BIG SKY
gatekeepersofthearctic
@BeGatekeepers
PRODUKTION MARKUS KAPPELI, STEFAN JAGER, KATRIN RENZ UND CORINA GAMMA
REGIE CORINA GAMMA PRODUKTION MANAGER PATRICK MERKLE SCHNITT GISELA WYBEL UND ANTHONY PORTER
MUSIK JORGE CORANTE UND TRIO FUGU TON KENNEDY PHILLIPS UND MELODYGUN
greensphere productions
PegoMark Inc
tellfilm
www.gatekeepersofthearctic.com
SILA

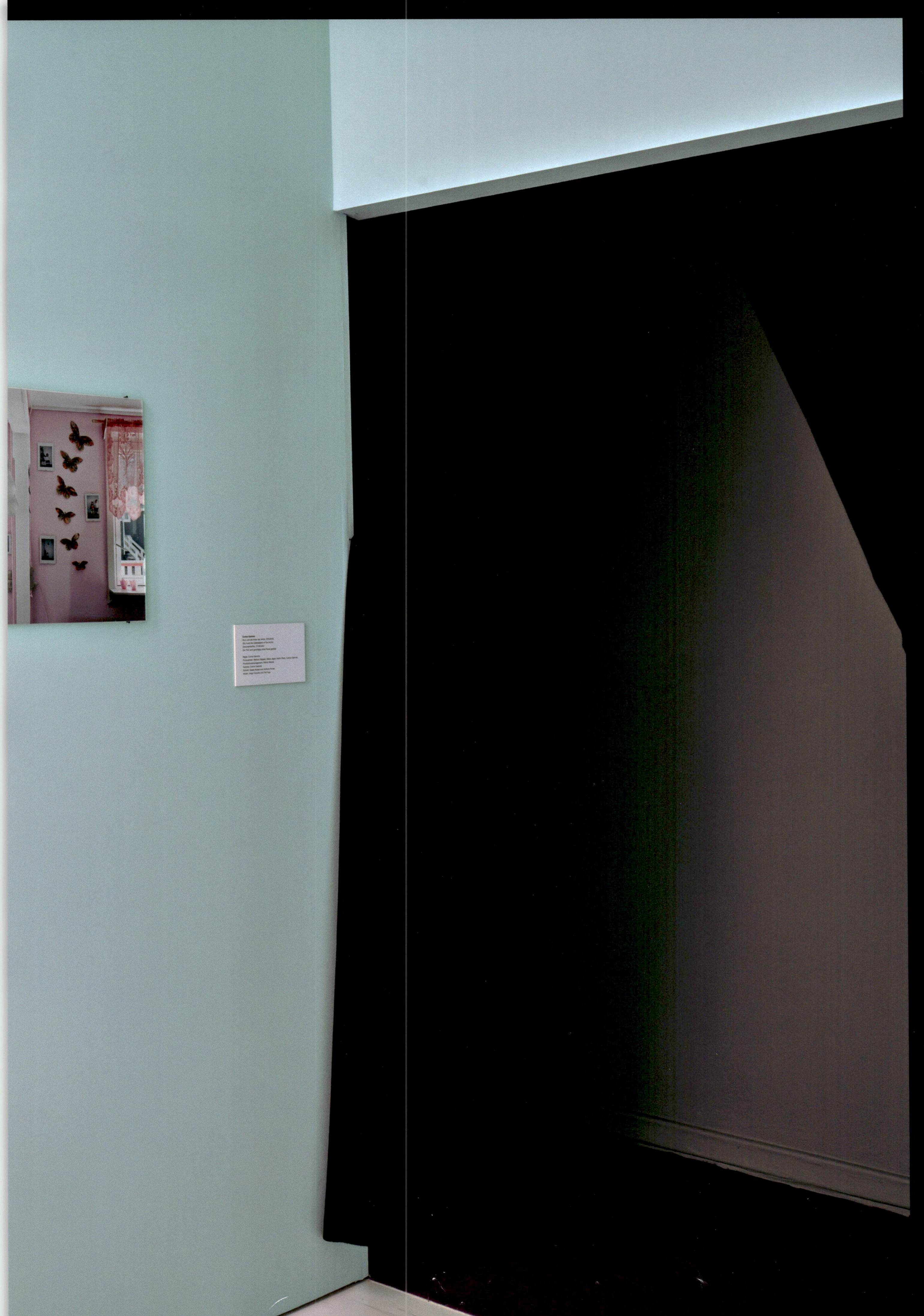

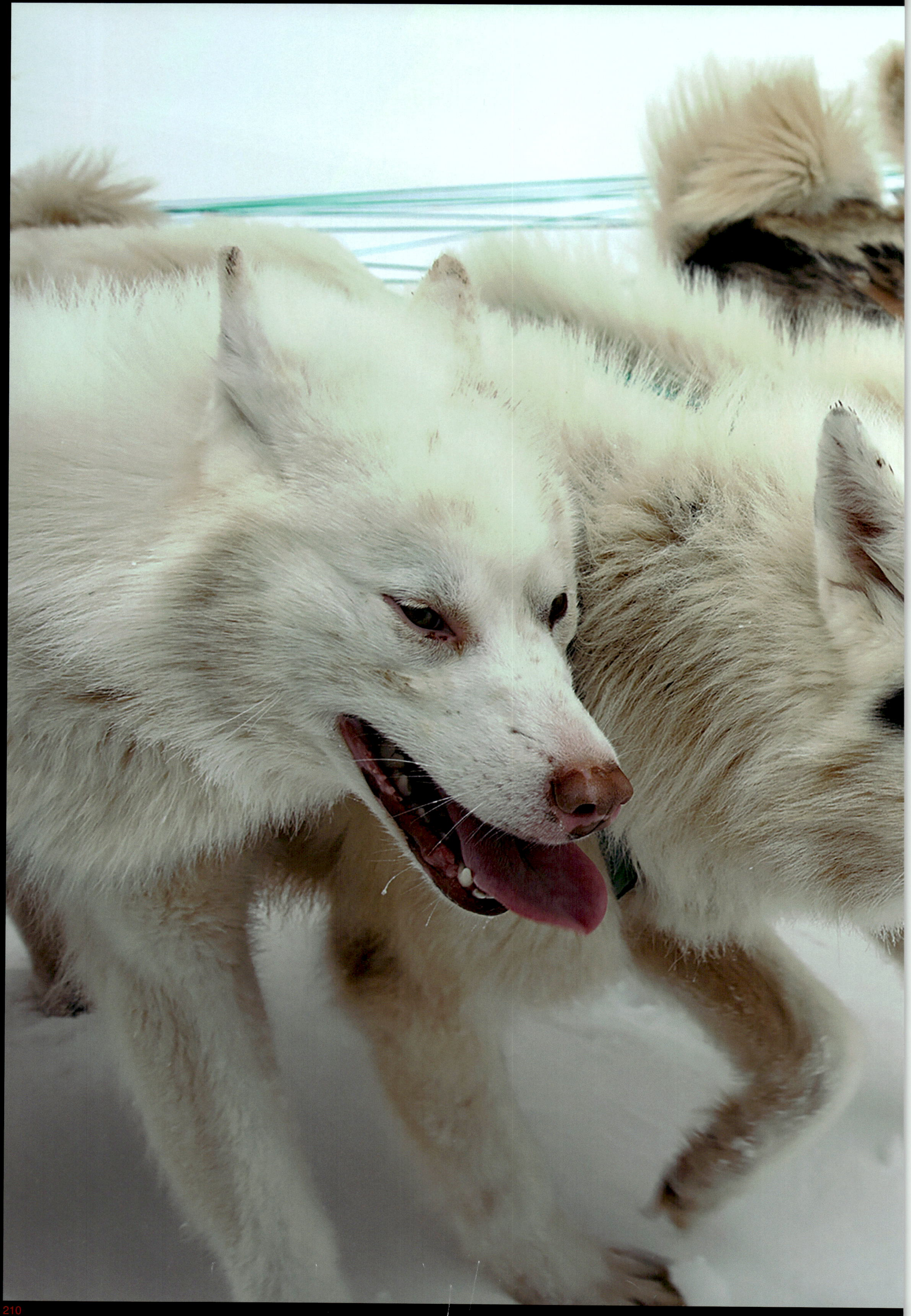

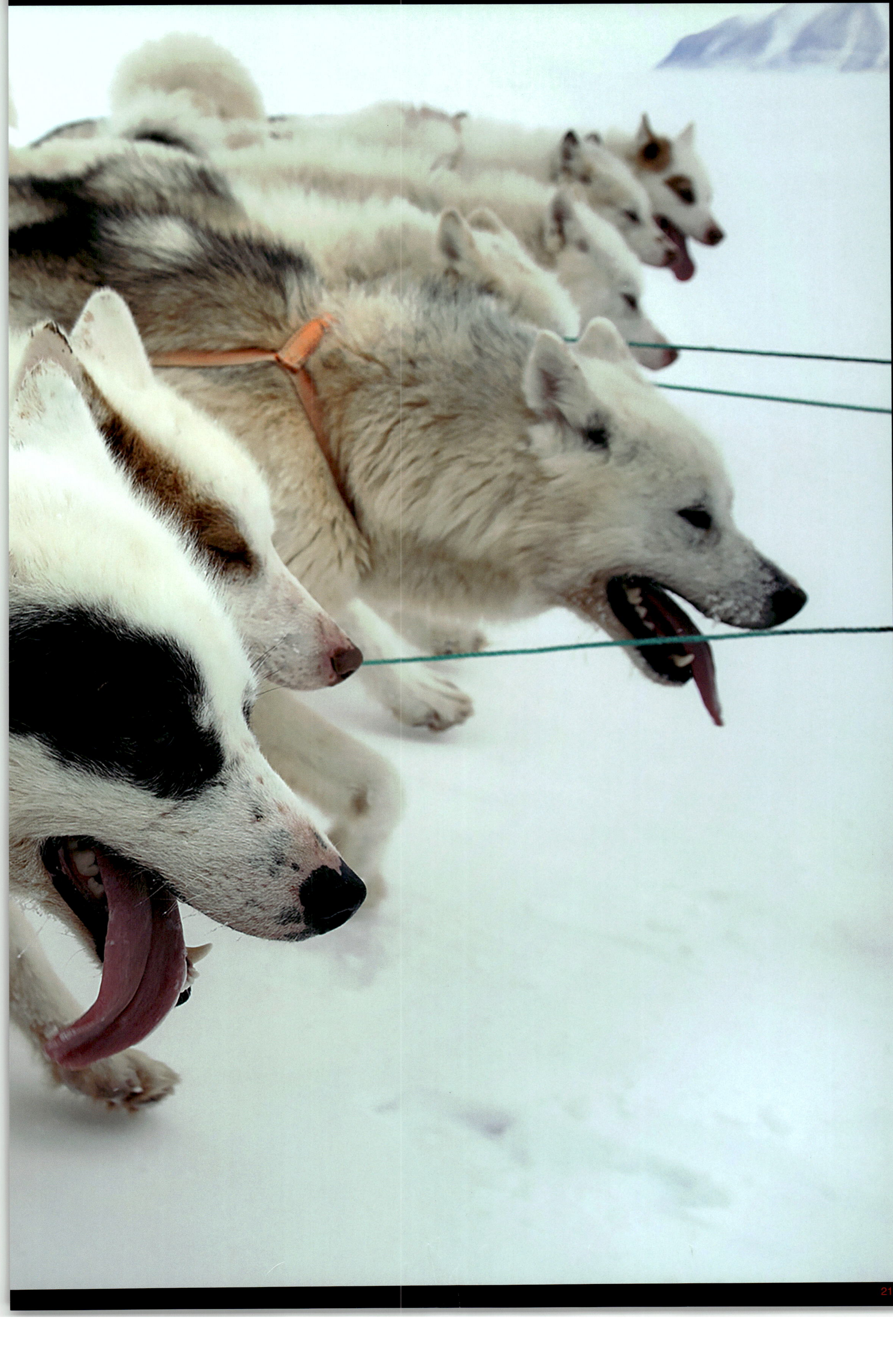

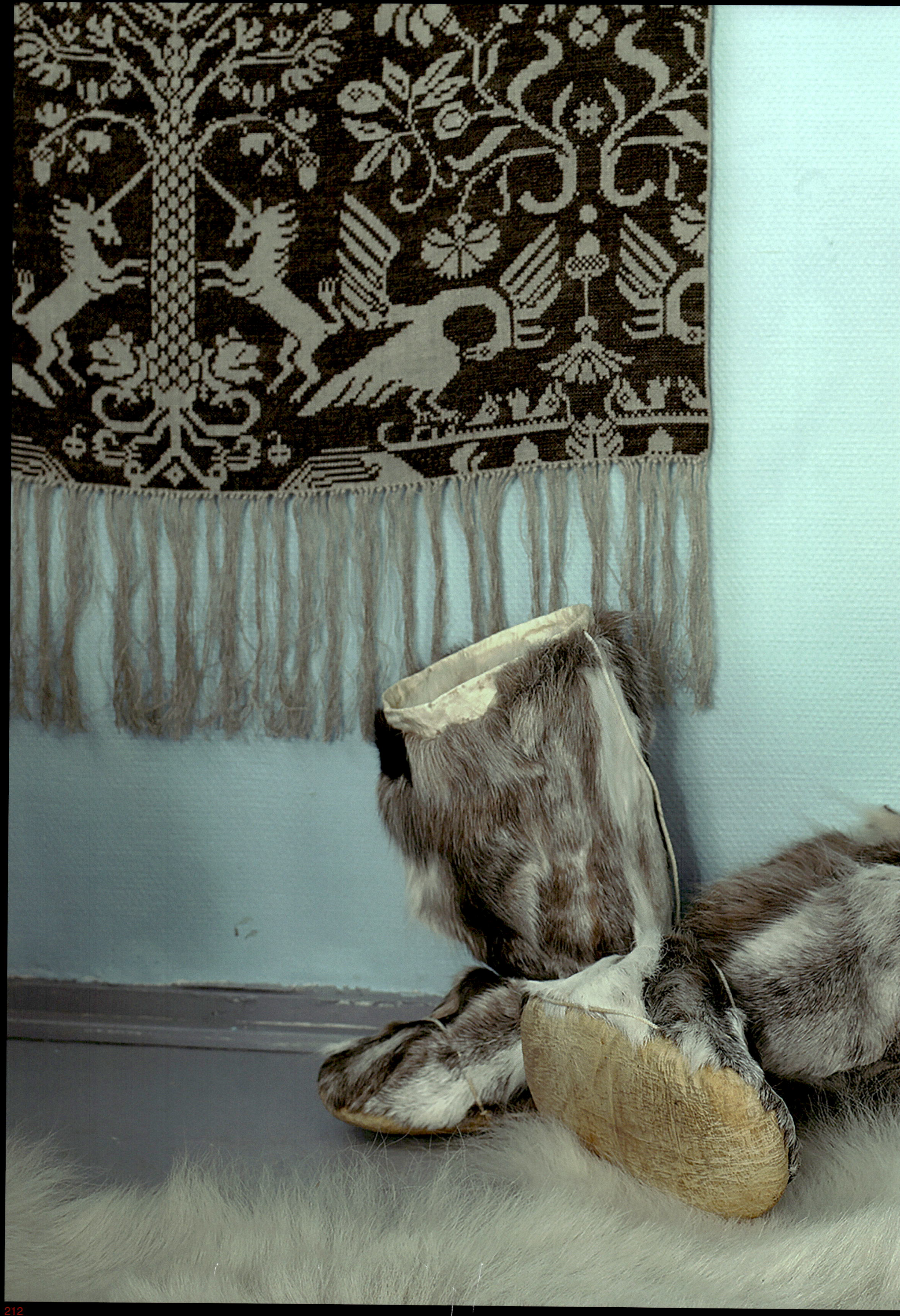

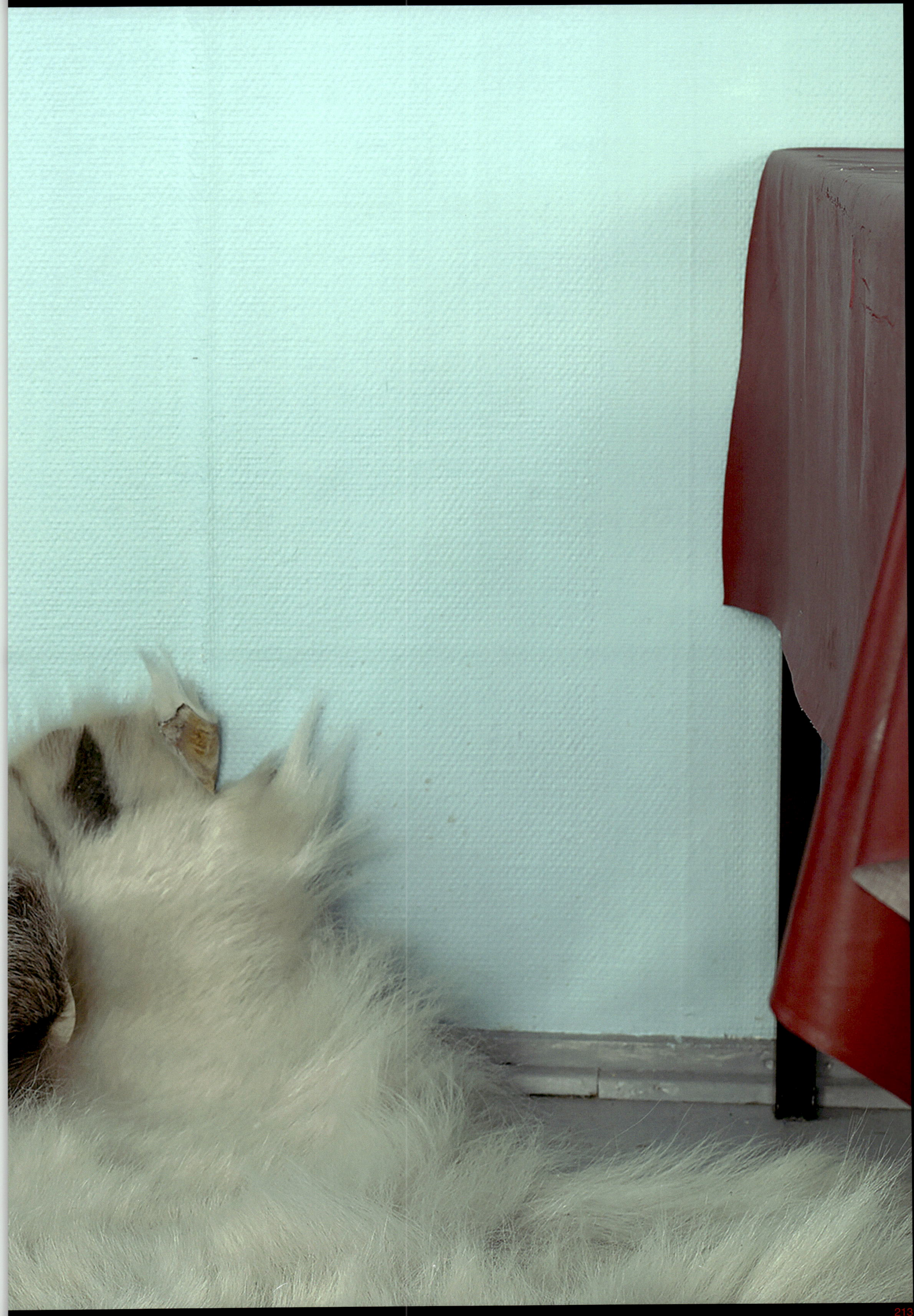

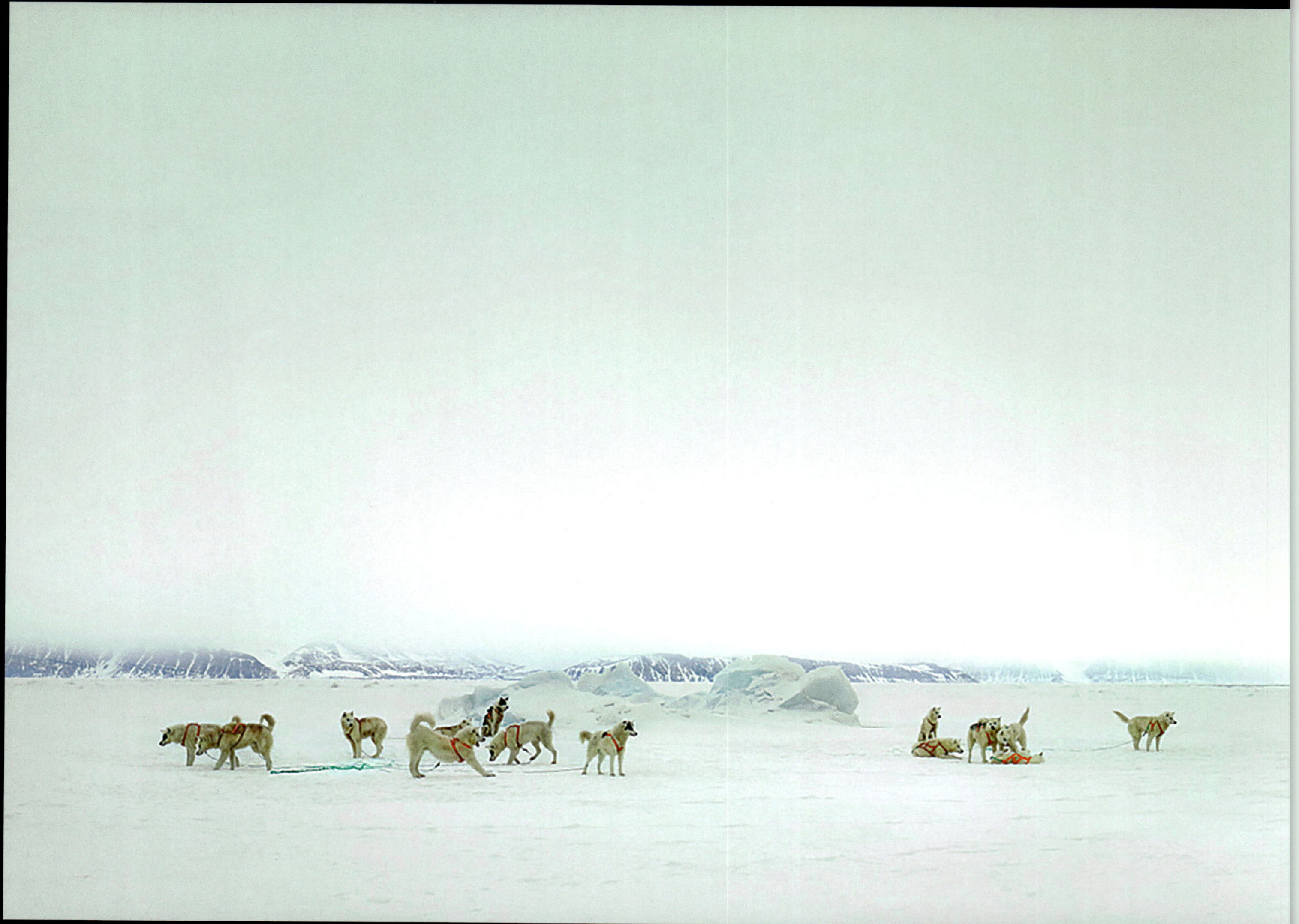

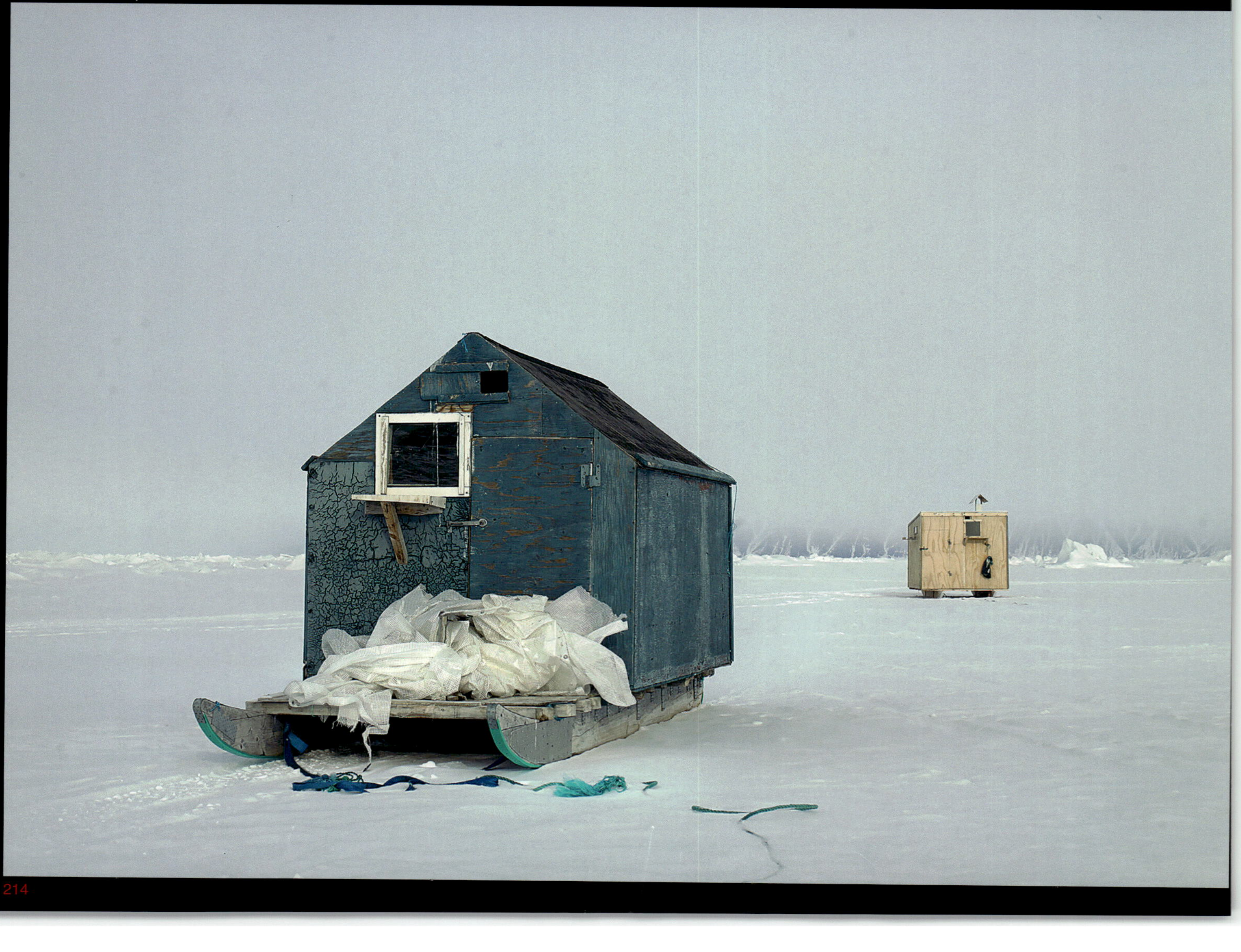

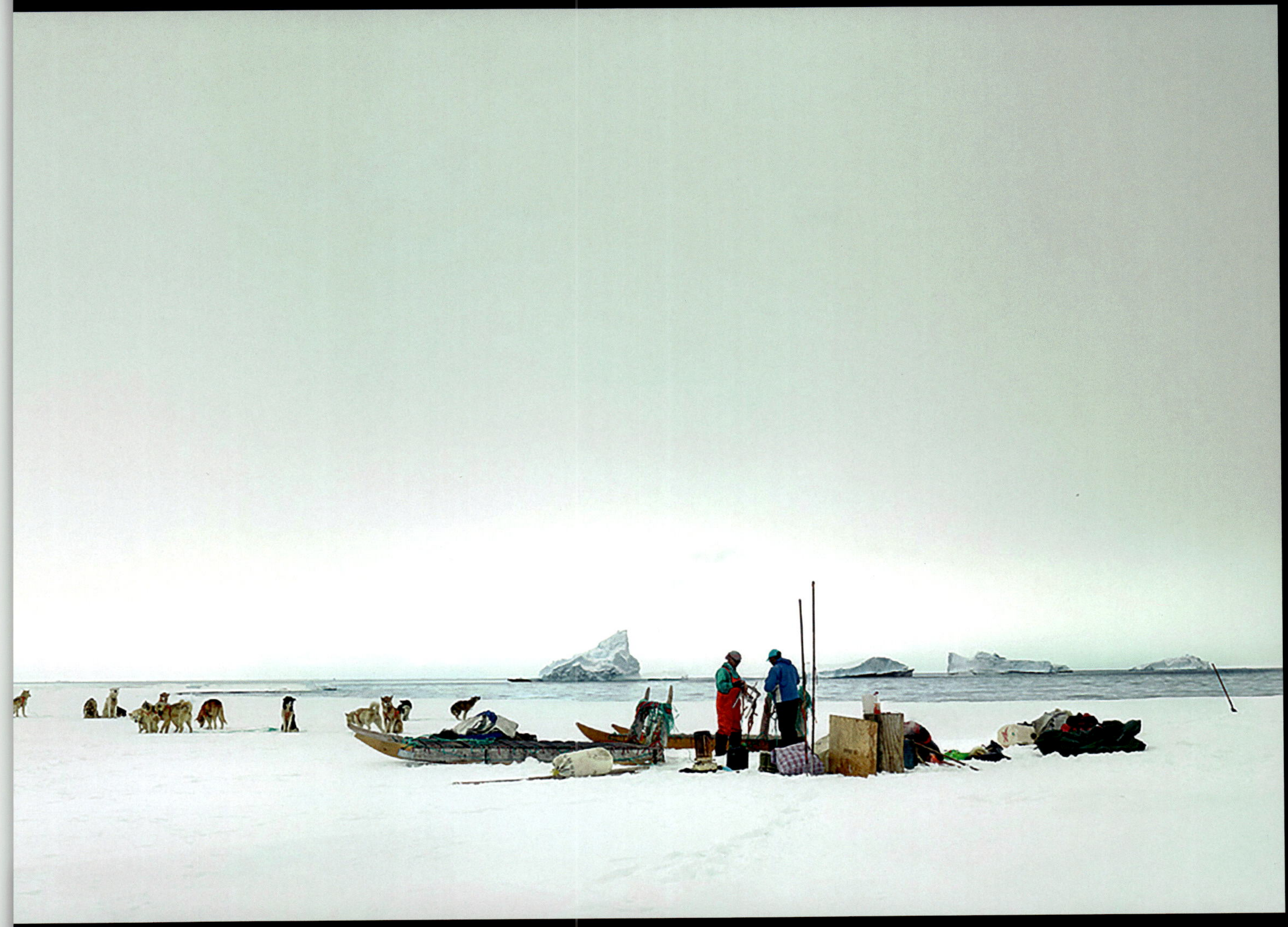

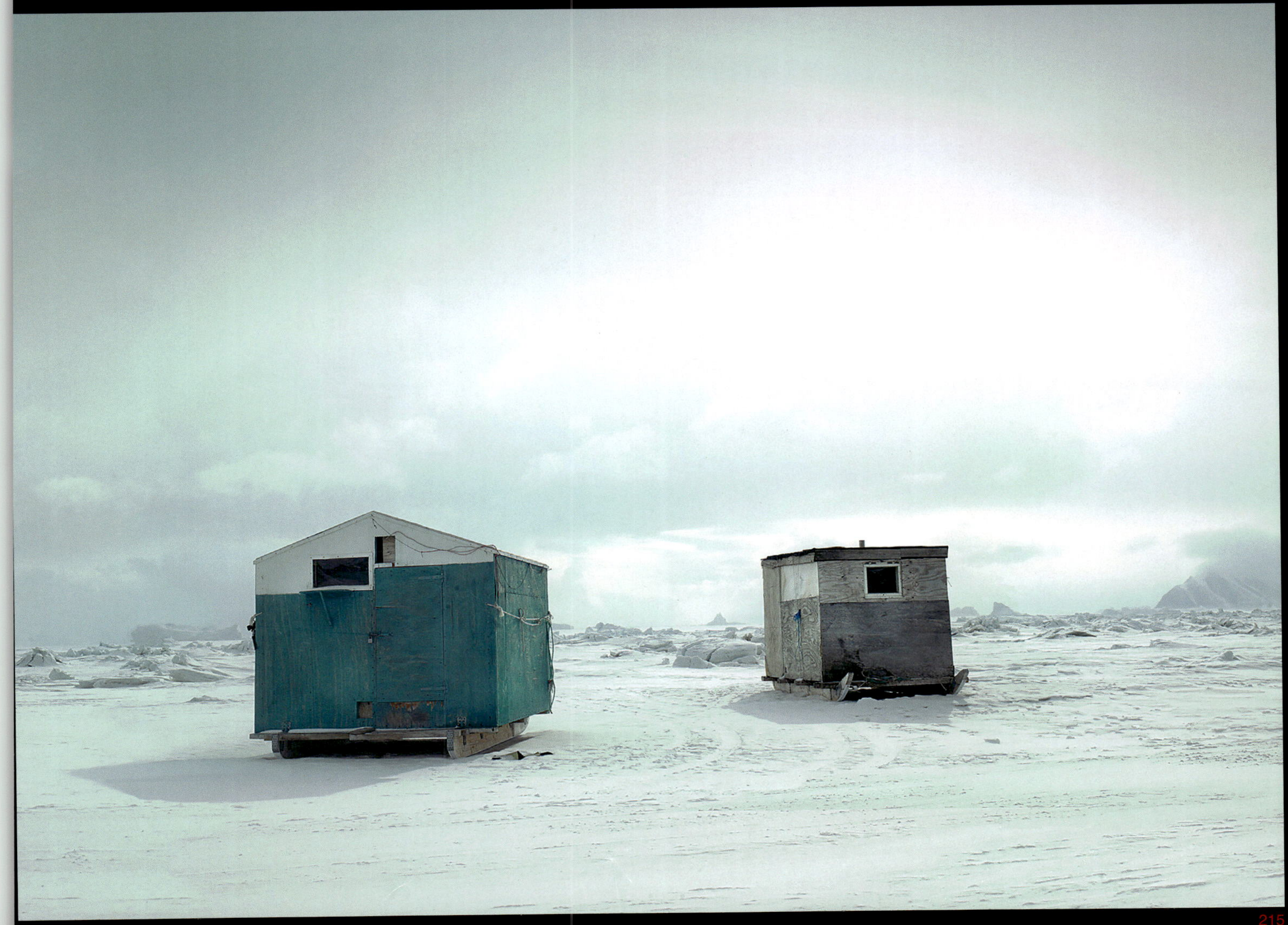

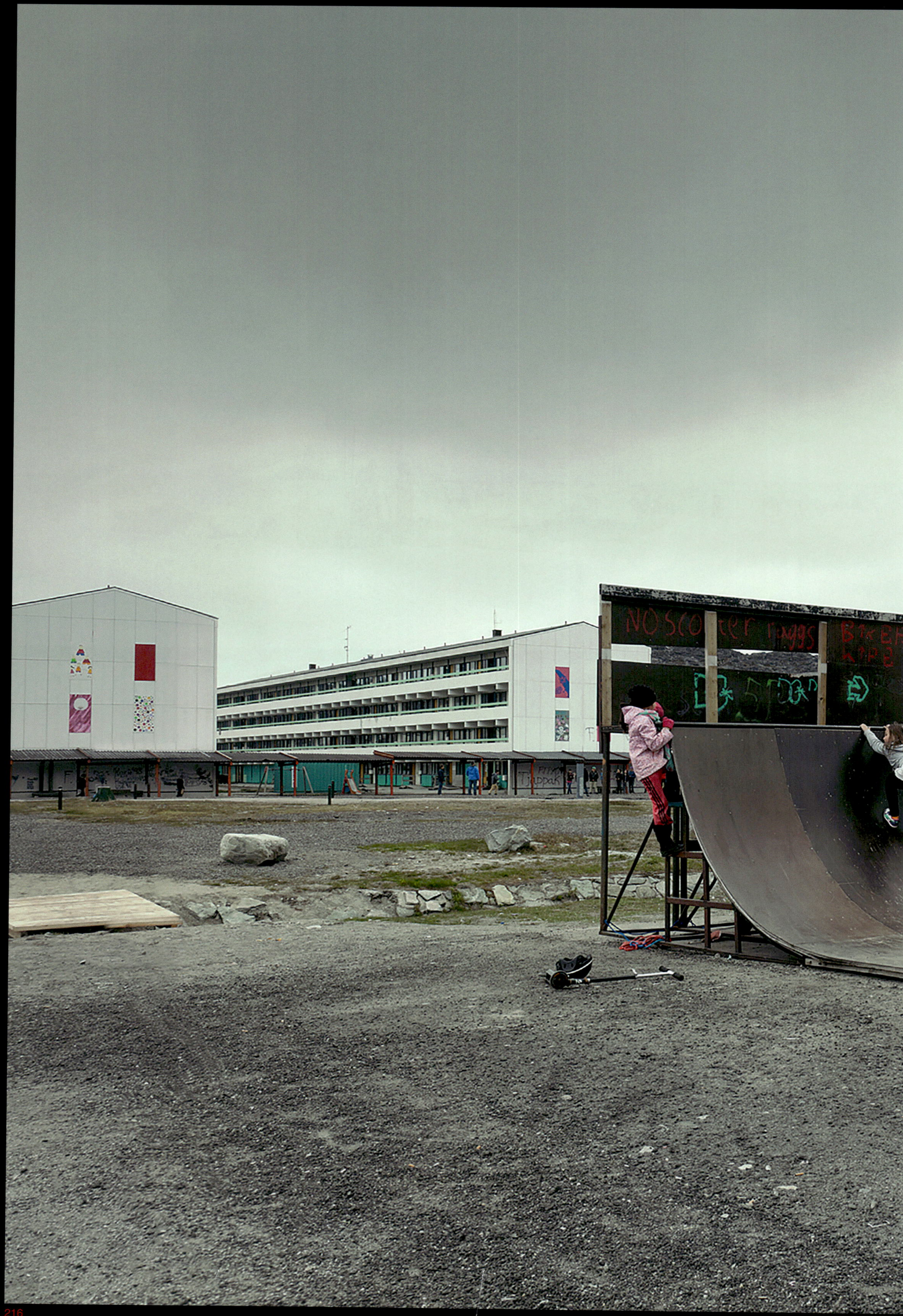

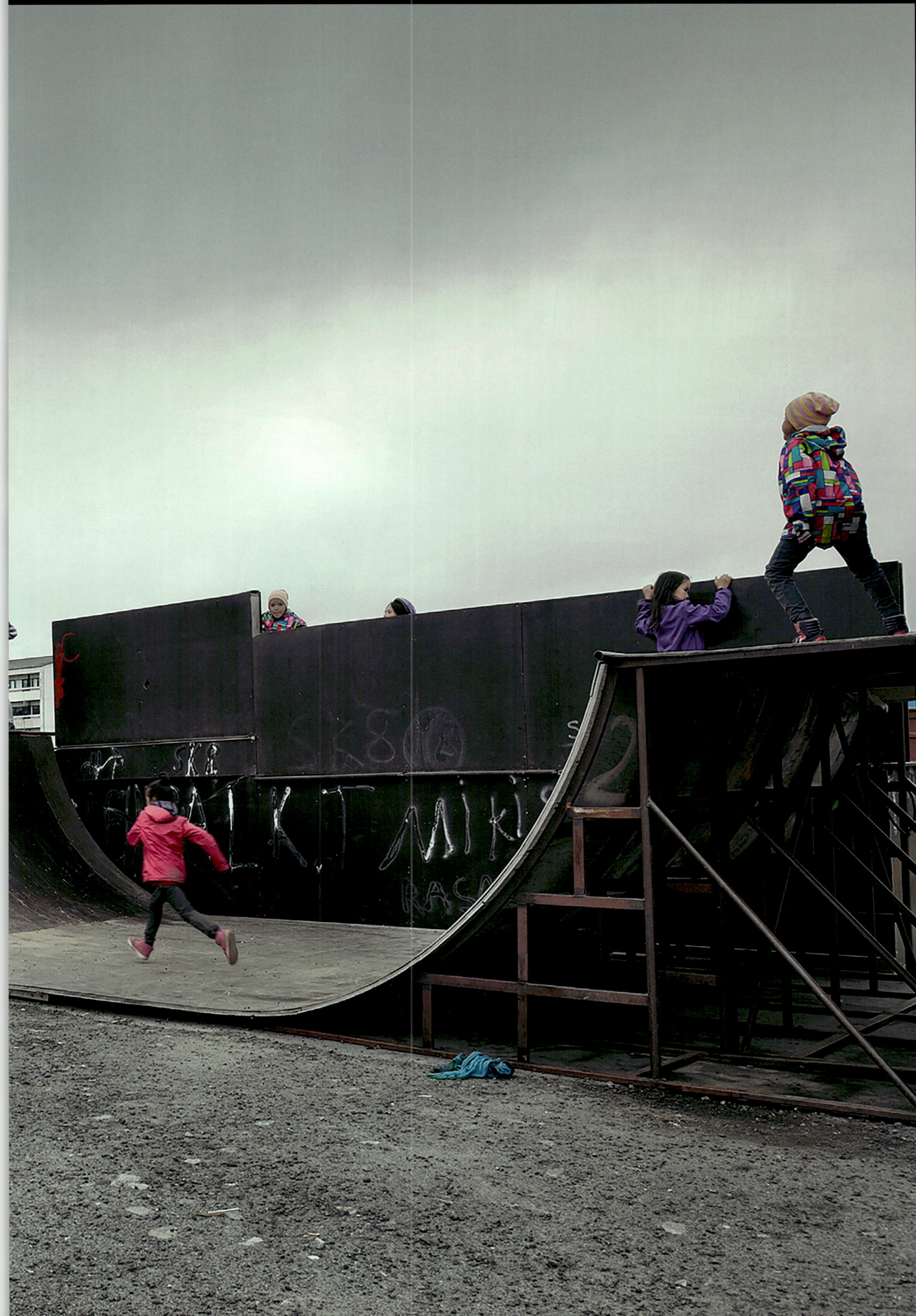

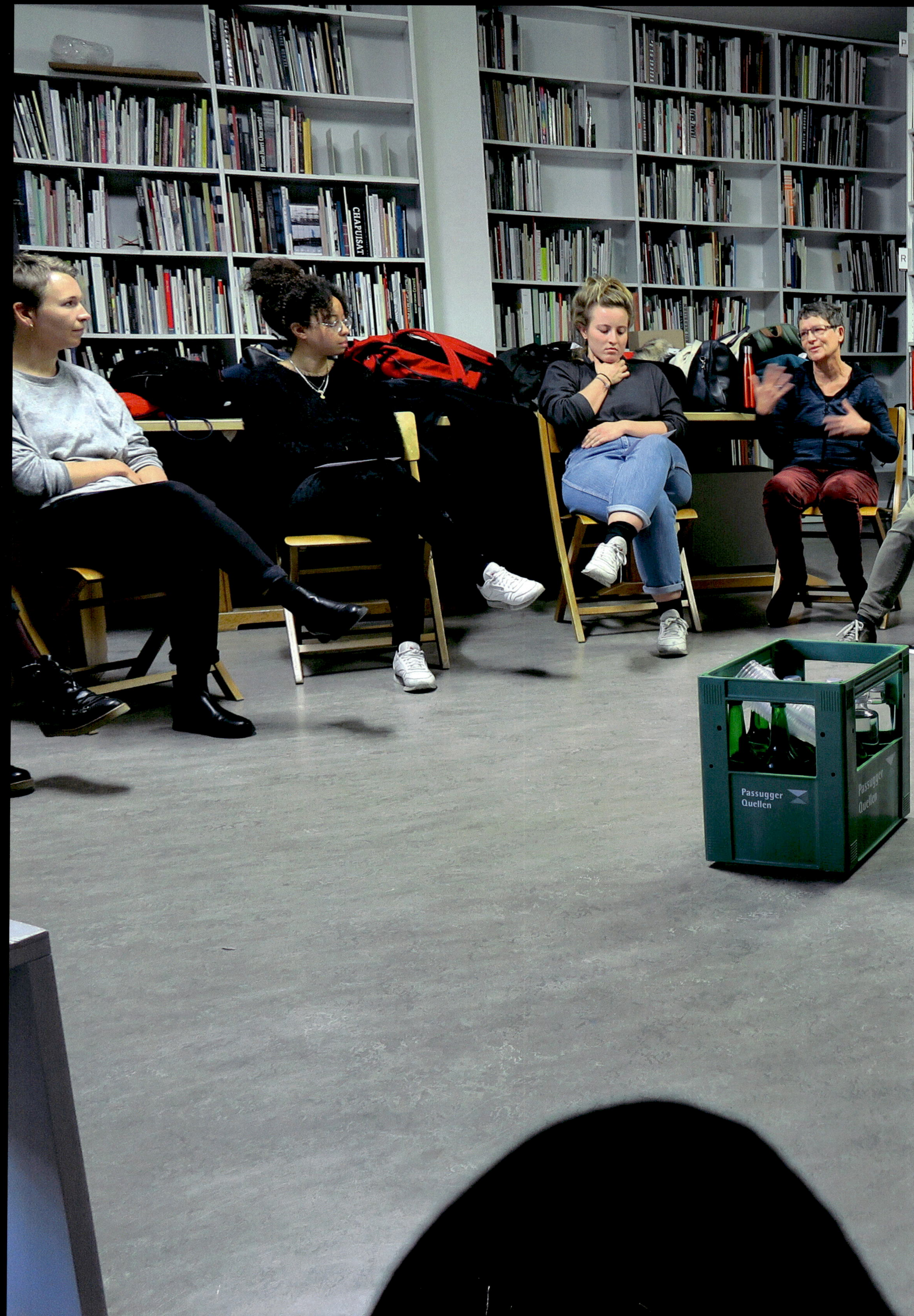
CHAPUISAT
Passugger Quellen
Passugger Quellen

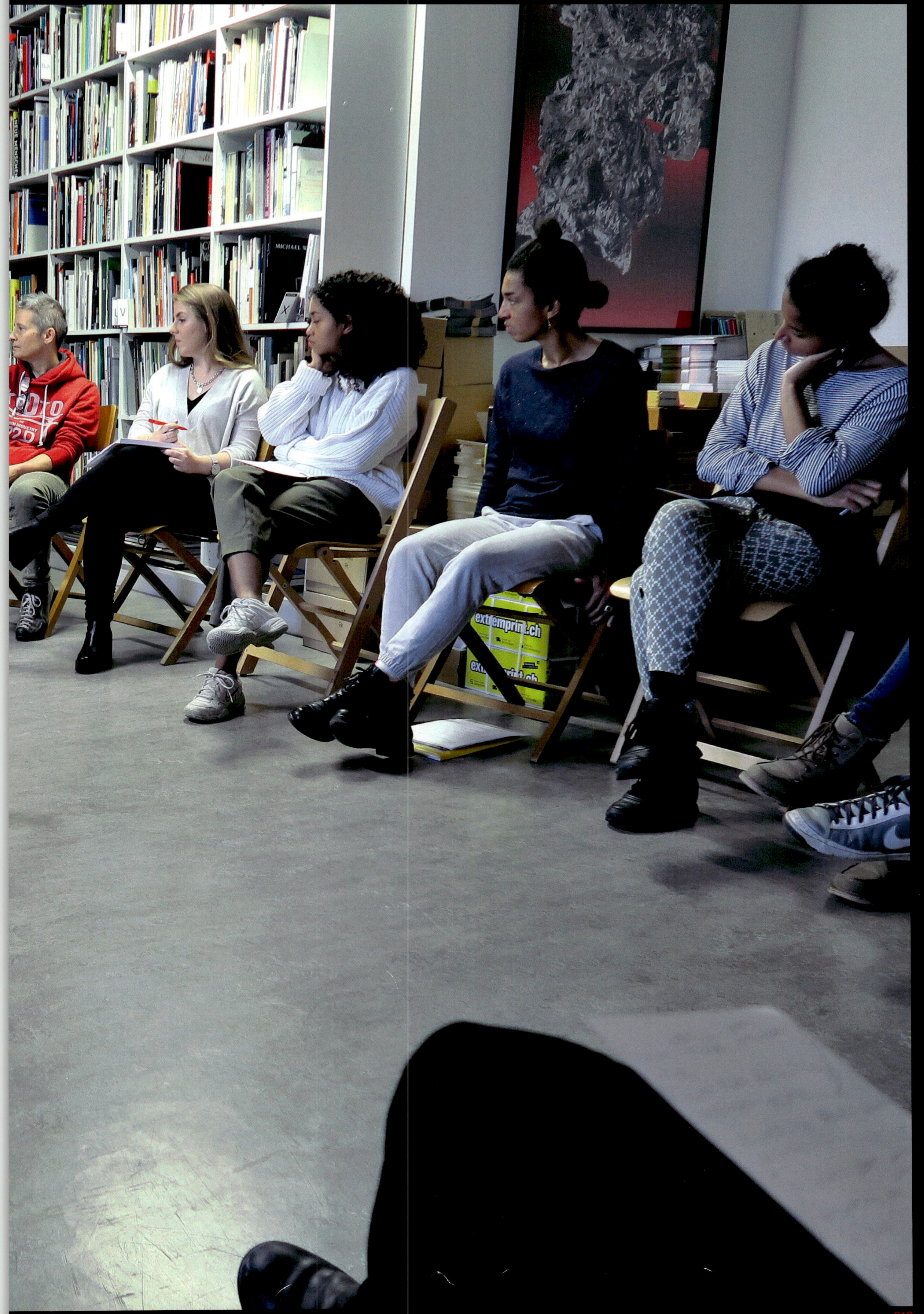

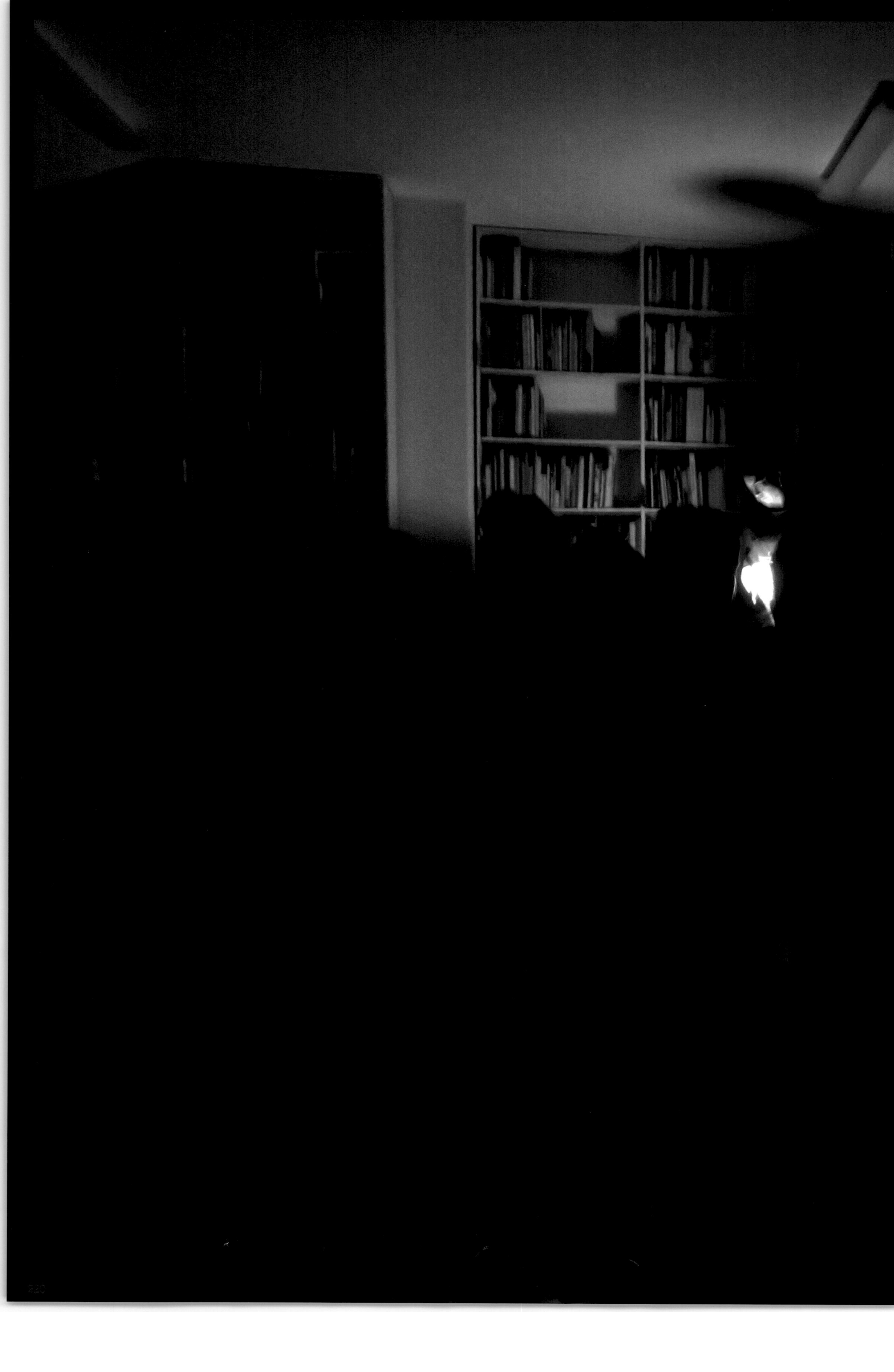

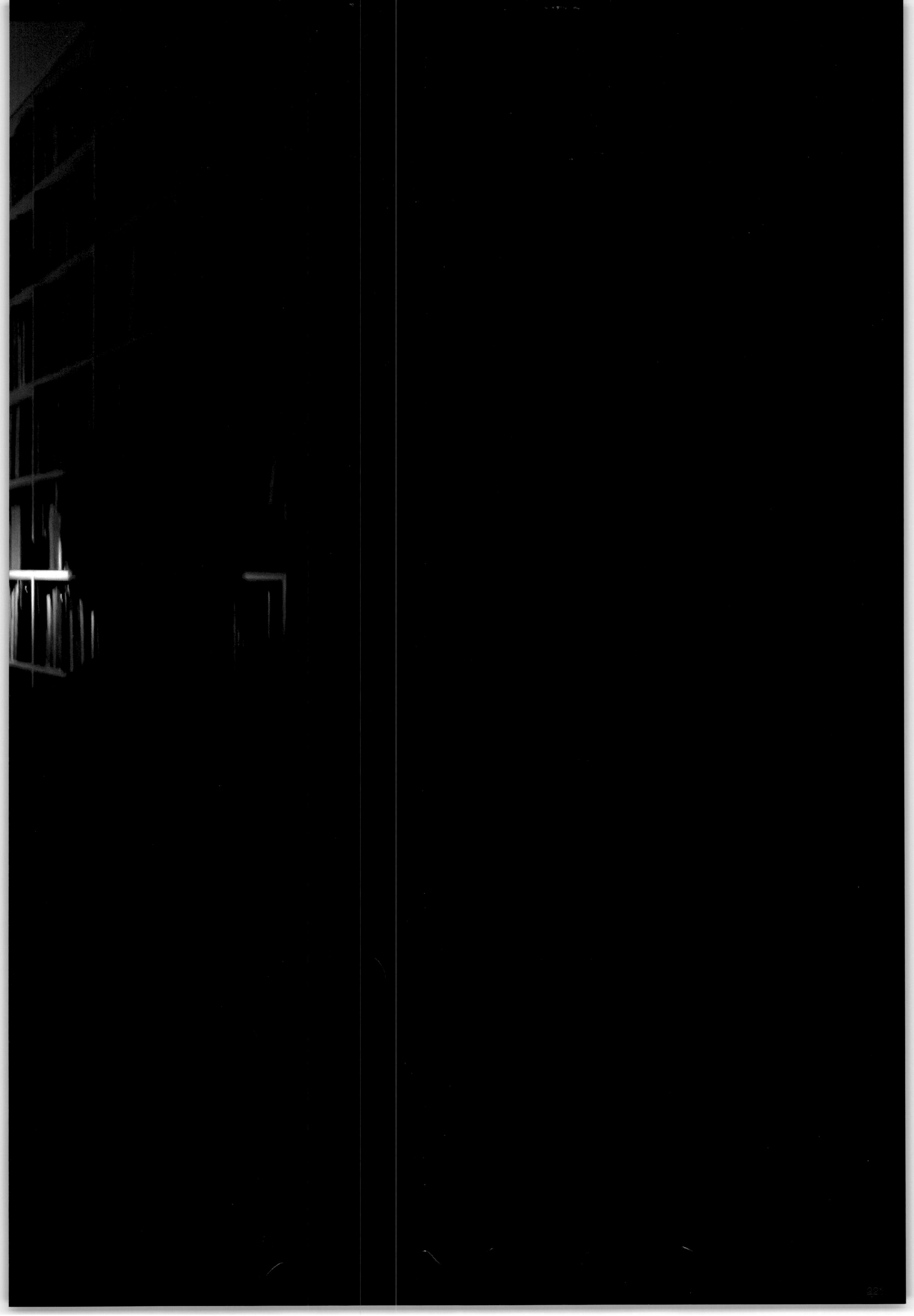

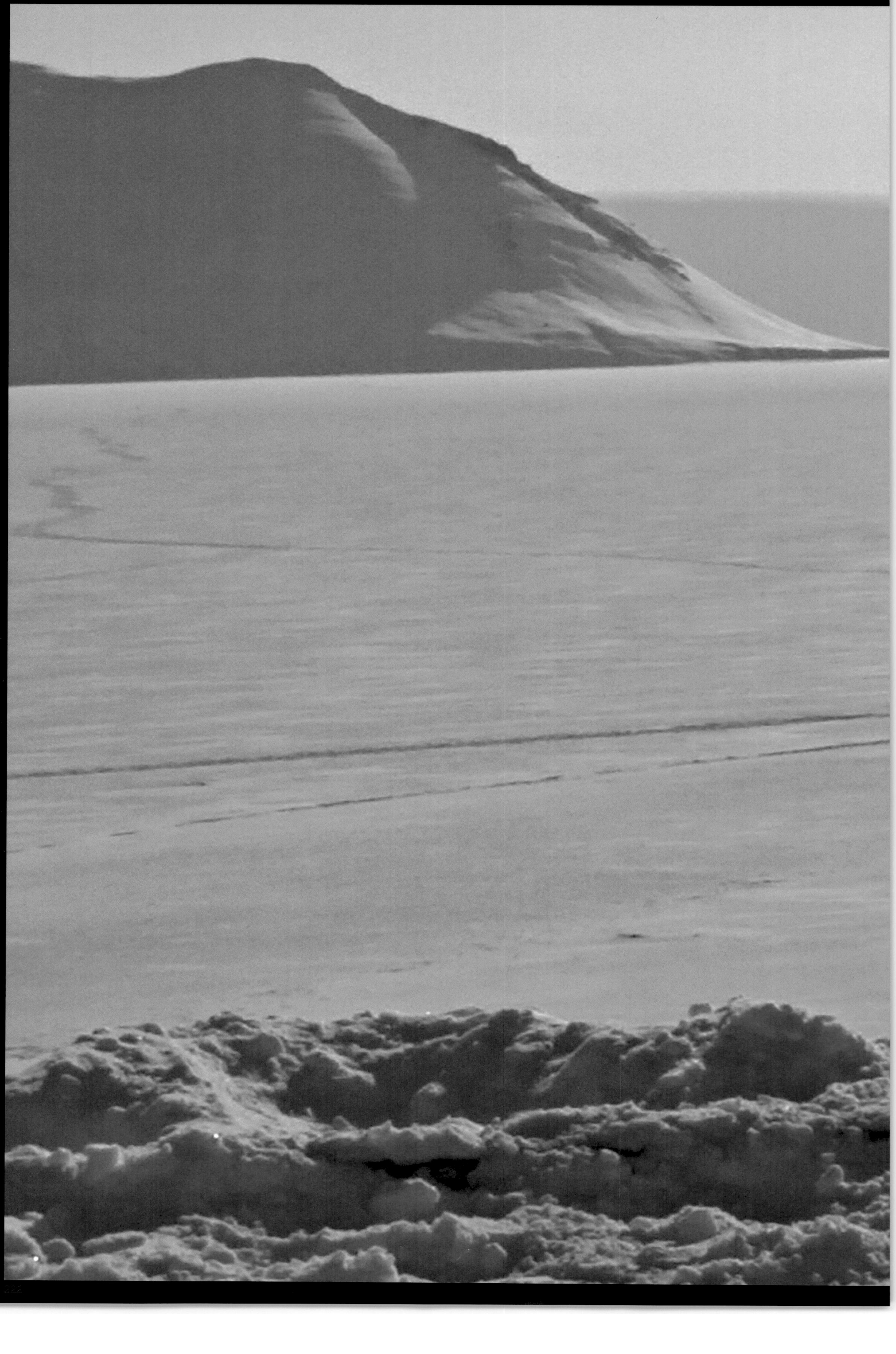

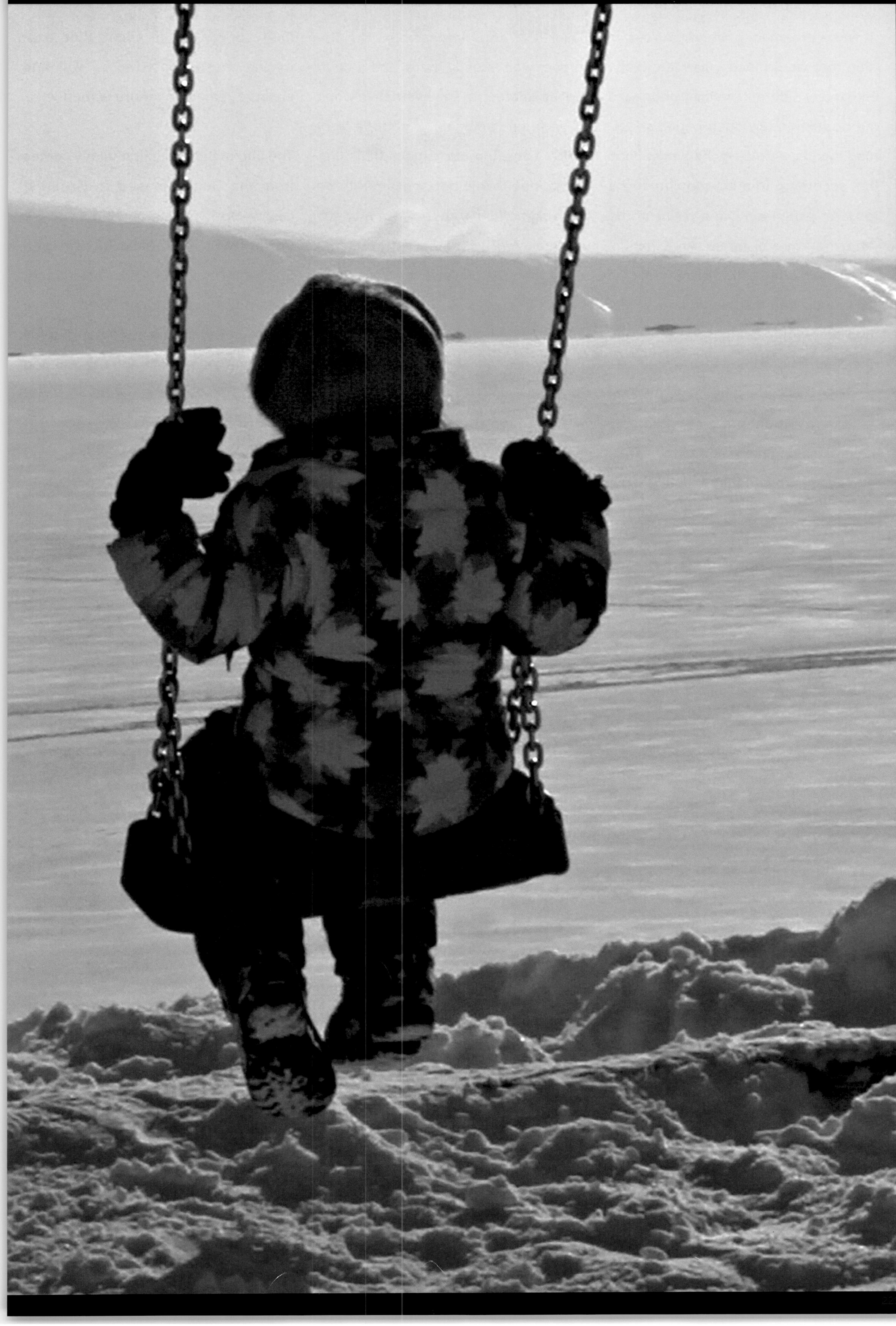

It was a dream long dreamt. An exhibition that would lead – like life itself – into many different, precisely bookended or deliberately open-ended spaces and moods, unfolding chapter by chapter, according to a staged choreography. An exhibition like a piece of theatre, literature or opera. An exhibition that would quite naturally integrate film and music into the fine arts. An exhibition that would bring political art into the aesthetic realm, and where aesthetic art would be political. An exhibition that would put the public at its centre, making them part of the exhibition itself and, with that, an integral part of the art.

An exhibition that faces up to the burning issues of our day: migration and climate change, sustainability and responsibility, solitude and excess communication. An exhibition that constantly leads to the question of just how much we actually want to know. And how much of that we take on board, and how much we let it affect us.

Ultimately, this was an exhibition intended to leave us with a sense of having understood something about the world. Giving us the energy to change the world, and even refashion it anew. Challenging caveats and breaking down prejudices. An exhibition to shake us up, and wake us up. One that would change attitudes. One that would, at least for a moment, and perhaps for some time longer, show the world in a different light.

The demands, of course, were immense. Over the top, impossible. But the dream was already there, and it could not be undreamt. The alternative would have been capitulation: nothing to be done. Lowering our expectations. Instead, one exhibition became three. With some fifty authors from a variety of fields. And a choreography that took eight months to evolve.

What should the world of arts and culture be addressing today? How about the almost unbearable synchronicity of baroque music and the fates of migrants? All with a perception of difference and a difference of perception. Suddenly there are connections between these differences. In baroque music, which once seemed merely almost unbearably beautiful, there is a via dolorosa that equates with migration. And where migration is dealt with on a one-to-one basis, baroque music may reverberate all of a sudden. Not in the exhibition space itself – that would be kitsch. But in the mind. Where the senses and the intellect meet.

The exhibitions were choreographed in such a way that visitors were thrown from one extreme to another. From the extremely personal and private to the social and public. From the global to the local. From the intellectual to the emotional. From politics to culture, from art to film and music. The contrasts are almost unbearably intense. They show us the strength of the forces we confront on an everyday basis as well as the inequalities and equivalences we have to face. Anyone who has ever chosen to spend time examining these coexistences will find encouragement in refaire le monde.

The title of the exhibition trilogy comes from the Geneva-based Italian artist Gianni Motti. On suggesting a reprise of the failed and politically censured 2002 joint project *Capital Affair*, Motti responded promisingly: "Oui – on va refaire le monde." As much a gloomy pessimist as a bright and enlightened visionary, Motti combines humour and earnestness in his work. The second of the three exhibitions was to be devoted to him alone. Motti's EX-POSITION reflects, like a two-sided mirror, not only the first exhibition, refaire le monde * POSITION, which was dedicated to staking out the ground and showing the possibilities, but also the third exhibition refaire le monde * PROPOSITION, which put forward proposals for action to get out of a situation of powerlessness. These proposals were at times more scientific, activistic, documentary and dialogical than we might normally expect of art. But art today offers a broad platform for many ideas. Fortunately. These proposals are also political, even when – perhaps out of political defiance – they are especially artistic.

For almost two decades, the Helmhaus Zürich's exhibition programme has dovetailed the political and the aesthetic. Shortly before the opening of my very first exhibition as newly appointed director, that approach was overtaken by reality: 9/11. That was two months before the opening of the exhibition Forest / Explosions, which posited the thesis that nature and culture, order and chaos, beauty and catastrophe are all ultimately driven by the same forces. The six-part exhibition series WELT – BILDER / WORLD – IMAGES, co-curated with Andreas Fiedler, was dedicated to 49 international positions of politically charged photography, from the war photographer James Nachtwey to the seer Annelies Štrba to the comical abyss of Boris Mikhailov. Exhibitions such as Travelling Through the Eye of History, by Daniel Schwartz, in collaboration with the Martin-Gropius-Bau in Berlin, or Delivery for Mr. Assange by !Mediengruppe Bitnik, curated by Daniel Morgenthaler, Helmhaus curator since 2011, are prime examples of the sociopolitical commitment embraced by Helmhaus Zürich. All based on our insistence that art within the museum must also have something to do with life outside it; that art should either be directly engaged with politics or should provide the space and energy required to reflect on, endure, process and bear this world full of contradictions, and to draw conclusions. Conclusions that lead to other values and worlds, to more mutual respect and kindness, to more solidarity and personal responsibility. An undertaking with such an aim must, necessarily, be an experiment. One that is driven by nothing less than a mission – a cultural activity that is not content merely to be decorative and pleasing – in quest of critical and progressive change, new ideas, new attitudes, and new approaches.

Some 15,000 people visited the three exhibitions in the refaire le monde trilogy. This publication provides an opportunity of making that forward-looking project accessible far beyond the boundaries of the temporary exhibitions, and of widely broadcasting the idea of an open, action-oriented type of exhibition. Perhaps, too, it can help to inspire a new vision of the world, new ways of seeing, and new possibilities of refashioning the world.

“Art should say how the world should be”, wrote Daniel Morgenthaler and I in our editorial for the third exhibition. Admittedly that was somewhat declamatory in tone. A.C. Kupper, who was also artistically involved, having contributed two photographic works to the first and third exhibitions, expanded on that statement, unsolicitedly and charmingly: “Art should say how the world should, could, must or may be.” So we left it that way – because it was quite simply better. Alain Kupper has accompanied us throughout the trilogy and this publication with his harsh and strict, open and flexible graphic design concept. We owe him a debt of gratitude, as we do to all involved, whether from the art world or from other related disciplines. Each one of them made a valuable contribution to this paradisical and at times hellish project. Thanks to an even wider circle of people, the dream of refaire le monde came alive. And lives on?

Simon Maurer

A.C. Kupper

The exhibition **refaire le monde * POSITION** stands under the American flag.

Not.

Or at least, not only. What may look like the American flag is actually the manhole cover for a sewer, surrounded by guide-stripes for the blind, photographed by artist and graphic designer A.C. Kupper on a Zurich street called Militärstrasse. Yet, if anything, what this way of reading the image does is, first and foremost, to reveal our own myopia. Because instead of looking directly at the stark reality of blind people and drug addicts in the city's District 4, we choose to see the symbol of a western nation. In our eyes, even a shithole can be an iconic emblem.

For the group exhibition **Black Magic** at Helmhaus Zürich in 2013, A.C. Kupper photographed people in his circle under perfect lighting conditions and in high definition. But here, he uses a single, grainy photograph to lead us into the dark. The image is, in a way, programmatic for the exhibition series **refaire le monde**. Because, although the Orient even gave us the concept of "orientation", we still orient ourselves towards the west and tend to put "America First". No matter that so many African countries can be reached within hours by plane (without jetlag), they still remain blind spots to us. And no matter how many citizens may come to us from the east as specialists in their respective fields, they still tend to be met with polemical twitter rants, and even segregated, while western expats are lauded. A.C. Kupper's photograph may not spell all this out – but for us as exhibition organisers, it quickly became emblematic of our own blindness.

Images pages 84 to 87, 104/105

Vincent Glanzmann

refaire le monde * POSITION is an exhibition. In other words, it is a show – look! And yet, in the course of creating this show, blindness became a leitmotif. As did music. Musician Vincent Glanzmann regularly embraces blindness as a percussionist who often plays in pitch darkness in his own rehearsal room. That's one reason why he suggested showing his latest compositions – three sound pieces with a total length of about 35 minutes – in a darkened space. Well, "showing" is obviously the wrong word in this context. Because nothing is being shown here – the pieces are not seen, but heard. But perhaps – hopefully – the wildest images might, paradoxically, reveal themselves in the darkness? At times, those images conveyed catastrophe – as when the percussion became an explosion in the piece **Z**. At other times, the music almost took our breath away, as in the piece **Rzw-Shiiiiiii**, whose sounds only gradually become recognisable as human voices and which turns out to be a choral piece, while our eyes gradually become accustomed to the darkness. And finally, the piece **—-the hidden** pays homage to the experimental Greek composer Iannis Xenakis, in which Glanzmann explores how high-frequency tones coexist and how the sounds of nature interact.

Nature? Coexistence? Breathlessmess? Explosion? **refaire le monde** – you can see the world anew, even in the darkness.

Images pages 24 to 29

Maya Homburger & Barry Guy

Heinrich Ignaz Franz Biber's 17th century **Mystery Sonatas** (known in German as **Rosenkranz-Sonaten**) can be heard in the exhibition space, alternating with compositions by Vincent Glanzmann. They typify the heights and depths of life. Originally dedicated to the suffering and redemption that is the bedrock of Christian mysticism, the sonatas also have a universal, abstract significance. Interpreted by Maya Homburger with Camerata Kilkenny & Barry Guy, they speak directly to our emotions in a way that only music can do: "Anticipation, hope, promise, trust, empathy, fear, ambivalence, fury, powerlessness, pain, mortality, redemption and fulfilment" (Maya Homburger). Written for solo violin and basso continuo, the basso continuo is delivered imaginatively by Camerata Kilkenny on six intruments: harp, viola da gamba, theorbo lute, organ, cembalo and double bass. Each of the sonatas has its own scordatura and is not written using conventional musical notation, but in tablature: "The scordatura itself transports us into another world," says Homburger. The intellectual effort and the emotional rollercoaster from sonata to sonata unleash what is "ultimately an almost trance-like release from the self". Together with the ensemble, the soloist interprets the compositional interplay of consonance and dissonance between the five "joyous, dolorous and glorious" sonatas along a spectrum of diverse tonalities, rhythms and rhetorical figures, lending the two-hour work a contemporary feel. Barry Guy, co-founder of the London Jazz Composers Orchestra, and Maya Homburger apply their shared experience of both early music and new music in a way that is mutually enhancing: the early music is enriched by the new music, and the new music, in turn, by the early music. For instance, Guy's composition **Ceremony** (1995) for soloist Maya Homburger is based on Biber's **Mystery Sonatas** as well as on meditation and Navajo song. The seven audio tracks also feature Biber's scordatura.

Like a kind of initiation, the music taps into realms of emotion that stay with us throughout the exhibition.

Images pages 24/25, 178/179

Fabrice Gygi

In the first room, we see nothing. In the second room, we have nothing to say. Nothing at all. We can't even get in. Geneva-based artist Fabrice Gygi has blocked it off in typical fashion. A huge projection illuminates the exhibition space. Maybe there is about to be an important presentation in this windowless Situation Room. Or maybe it has already finished and the decisions have been taken. The first or the last supper.

When we mentioned the exhibition title **refaire le monde** to Fabrice Gygi, he initially responded with the same ferocity that is evident in his works, retorting that the world would have to be destroyed first. But then he proposed an existing work from 2007 called **Meeting Room**. We, in turn, wondered whether a work that was already ten years old could fit in with the concept of **refaire le monde**. But why not? After all, **refaire le monde** can also mean stepping outside the confines of the general compulsion for ever new production. If growth is a fetish of the capitalist system, then **refaire le monde** can also mean preventing further additional growth and looking to the past.

At the same time, **Meeting Room** has grown beyond itself. Today, even more so than ten years ago, we have the feeling of being at the mercy of decisions imposed from above, from left and right. And suddenly there is renewed swaggering with nuclear weapons, and boasting of whose nuclear button is bigger. Does the white picture on the wall perhaps even portray the dense pall following an atomic catastrophe?

That, too, is one of the POSITIONS referred to in the title, to which today's artists can relate. The decisions are constantly being made for us, and we as individuals – both as observers and producers of art – have little say in the matter. The question is: just how much longer are we going to put up with this? What alternatives – PROPOSITIONS – can we suggest?

Meanwhile, on one weekend of the exhibition, Fabrice Gygi is there to sharpen the blade of your pocket knife or breadknife. Another gesture of ferocity. But perhaps, in conversation with Fabrice Gygi, our minds might also be sharpened.

Images pages 1 to 5, 104/105

Pascale Birchler

To begin with, we delved into music with Maya Homburger & Barry Guy. Then Fabrice Gygi led us into the Situation Room to which we have no actual access. And now we suddenly find ourselves in another room, where two larger-than-life figures are already present. They sit impassively on the floor – yet they do seem to register my presence in this overlit room. We share the space. It is not a large space, even artificially diminished. Interpretations, access points and exits run from its tiled walls without trace. It is quiet here. Yet the tension is almost unbearable. Is that due to the challenging passiveness of the two long-limbed blind figures? Both are entirely introspective. And yet they are clearly co-dependent and cannot cope without one another. There are two chairs, larger than normal, welded. They are empty, unoccupied. A window with dark red glazing evokes the notion of escape – escape from this hermetic isolation. But it is just a passing thought. The window is too impenetrable, too blind, too high. And what might be outside?

What Pascale Birchler has created is a completely artificial room. And yet it is real. More real than we might like. I am reminded of Pygmalion, of Dürrenmatt, of Ionesco. Of an abstract absurdity that leads us back into our innermost being. This room is about absence. And presence. About the absence of closeness, of touching, of love. And yet precisely that can also be found here – an invisible tenderness. This room leads inwards. Inwards to the place where we are at our most fragile and vulnerable. To the place where we are constantly refashioning our world. Alone. And with others. This is all about the difficulty of finding ourselves, and about the difficulty of finding others, or the other. It is also about the other that resides within the self. It is about the fluid boundary between me and you, inside and outside, control and loss of control. It is about letting go. "Your heart drives you out of yourself, your heart pursues you, and you stand almost outside yourself and cannot get back again." [Rainer Maria Rilke, The Notebooks of Malte Laurids Brigge, transl. M.D. Herter, (New York, Norton, 1949) p.69] Who am I? What is the self in me? What do you do to me? Am I still myself if there is you? How do I evolve in my engagement with the world? Here we encounter an image of that – in sharpest definition and in vaguest ambiguity. An image that presents itself in all its intimacy and sensuality, simultaneously revealed and concealed. In this alternation between presence and absence, between meeting and fleeing, it is there. And we ourselves determine how we relate to it.

Images pages 16 to 19

Bertold Stallmach

Bertold Stallmach is constantly rethinking not just the world, but his own artistic work as well. He became known for his stop-motion films in which he moulded figures from the depths of the human psyche. For his film **The Mosaic Project**, Stallmach adopted digital animation techniques that opened up entirely new possibilities (cue: refaire) to him. Images of sketchily outlined production processes scurry across the body of a dying protagonist, featuring robots assembling cars and ships delivering cargo. Is this the global economy as we know it, on its deathbed? This creature does not even want to incorporate a start-up any more – "but you must eat something!" urges a human skeleton.

.

The heirs can now do everything anew, perhaps rendering the economy more humane. An unlikely outcome, given that the figures around the deathbed are quite literally defined by what they possess. They are composed of novels, gluesticks, garments, looking for all the world like some online shopping basket from Amazon. One figure, pushed into the abyss by a security guard, is smashed to pieces. When that individual's possessions fall apart, they fall apart too, incapable of functioning in society. Could that happen to us as well? Do we exist only on the basis of our possessions? And how does that relate to the episode in the film **Cahier africain** in the next room of the exhibition, in which the protagonist Amzine and her daughter Fane have to leave everything behind so that they, themselves, at least, can escape the Central African Republic and flee to Chad?

In between, there is a small screen showing an animation by Bertold Stallmach in which civilisations and epochs roil in a nocturnal ocean, so to speak. World history as screensaver. Perhaps something for the decision-makers who are absent from Fabrice Gygi's room…

Images pages 10 to 15, 172/173

Heidi Specogna

An abrupt transition. The documentary film **Cahier africain** by Swiss director Heidi Specogna is based on a small notebook containing the testimonies of some three hundred women, girls and men from the Central African Republic who were abused and raped during the civil war. Specogna had originally travelled to the Central African Republic to work on her film **Carte Blanche** in consultation with investigators looking into war crimes. While she was there she discovered this school excercise notebook – and subsequently recognised some of the people featured in it. Because this homemade piece of evidence had been so important to them, they had even torn their passport photos out of their official documents and pasted them under their statements. In the course of a complex secret mission, the notebook eventually made its way to the International Criminal Court in The Hague as evidence in the trial of warlord Jean-Pierre Bemba.

The Swiss filmmaker spent seven years charting the lives of the war victims Arlette and Amzine. Amzine and her daughter Fane, conceived through rape, recall their suffering. Originally, the film had been meant to show how these women had rebuilt their lives in a country now at peace: **refaire le monde**. But then the next war broke out. 14 years after the fact, Jean-Pierre Bemba became the first person to be convicted in an international court for instrumentalising sexual violence as a war strategy. Shorly afterwards, his conviction was overturned on grounds of procedural irregularities. In the central African region alone, an estimated 100,000 women have been raped during the recent conflicts. It is a crime that can have an enormous impact, given that some women are disowned by their families for it. The Central African Republic – with the world's lowest GDP per capita, yet with an abundance of mineral resources – has bled out into a state with a non-existent middle class ruled by extreme corruption and religion, both of which are instrumentalised in violent ways.

In 2017, the film by Heidi Specogna was lauded in both Switzerland and Germany as Documentary Film of the Year. German broadsheet Frankfurter Allgemeine Zeitung hailed **Cahier africain** as "a great document of humanity", while Swiss weekly newspaper WochenZeitung described it as "an undaunted film about daunting events". Quiet and personal, and almost void of commentary, **Cahier africain** was screened in only a handful of Swiss cinemas and has not so far been broadcast on television. As one of Switzerland's leading film distributors told the director, nobody would pay twenty Francs to see war, rape and death. If this is how today's film industry works, then it is up to museums and art venues to ensure the visibility of this otherwise invisible harsh reality.

Images pages 30 to 47, 110/111

Nakfa Adhanom, Hicham El Khemisi, Filimon Habtom, Fatime Abaka Hadze, Rahimullah Mohammadi, Ali Omar, Raphael Perret, Qurban Ali Rahimi, Sidy Sangare, Jawed Stanikzai

The last room in the exhibition is also about visibility: asylum seekers housed in the transit centre of former trade-fair Hall 9 opposite the Hallenstadion in Zurich's Oerlikon district may well come from the kind of background situation portrayed in the film **Cahier africain**. Most are from Afghanistan, Syria and Eritrea, fleeing war and oppression. As of now, there are some 160 people – children, youths, adults – living in the hall. Initially, in 2015, there were twice as many. Their presence is both highly politicised and at the same time erased from public awareness: who has actually ever spoken to a refugee?

Artist Raphael Perret explores the issues facing a group of asylum seekers in this new world. The refugees tell us about the challenge of rebuilding their lives. They document their everyday existence inside and outside Hall 9 and are asked to comment on what goes well for them and what does not. A detailed reconstruction of one of the wooden shelters built in

Oerlikon during the refugee influx of 2015 gives an insight into how four asylum seekers live together within a confined space. The lack of privacy, without respite, was identified as the main problem according to the asylum seekers of Hall 9. Officially they were to spend a maximum period of one year in this kind of accommodation. Yet one asylum seeker from Hall 9 told of how his own asylum application process had only recently been concluded, after 13 years in an EU country and in Switzerland. The social worker allocated to each asylum seeker is in charge of some 90 individuals and is available on the phone for around half an hour each day. In the Hall itself there are two caseworkers available for the upper floor where families and women are housed. The men on the lower floor are left to their own devices. The political powers that be have not promised any further funding for additional on-site assistance. Very few manage to find work or a home. With social welfare benefits reduced to only emergency support in accordance with a recent referendum, they often find themselves without the means to buy even a tram ticket. Apart from language courses, they face the prospect of spending day after endless day in this unsettling situation.

Raphael Perret speaks to the refugees about their fears and hopes, their concerns and their opportunities. What becomes evident, and compatible with the asylum seekers' right to privacy, is shown in the exhibition: as a rule, things are "done" for the asylum seekers, but Perret would like to see them – as agents of their own lives – being able to get things "done" for themselves. That means not only encouraging dialogue between each other, but also between asylum seekers and the wider public.

Images pages 6 to 9, 48 to 71, 74 to 83, 108/109, 112 to 119, 126, 140/141, 144 to 151, 162/163

refaire le monde * EX-POSITION
Gianni Motti

Between **POSITION** and **PROPOSITION** there has to be a hinge – hard and metallic. There is a stoney path to tread between the findings of **refaire le monde * POSITION** and the ideas of **refaire le monde * PROPOSITION**. And there is a painful barrier to overcome: **refaire le monde * EX-POSITION** abruptly drives a wedge into that gap as the second part of the exhibition trilogy. Unlike Parts 1 and 3, which are both group exhibitions, Part 2 is the preserve of Gianni Motti alone.

Motti, who coined the title of this Helmhaus trilogy in the course of an informal conversation, exposes the conception of exposition, or exhibition-making. Just as he did in 2002, when he and Christoph Büchel invited visitors to find the exhibition budget hidden in the Helmhaus. The exhibition **Capital Affair** was cancelled – and the cheque for CHF 50,000 remains hidden. Now Motti returns to the Helmhaus, fifty years after the tumultuous events of 1968, with works that bring the street into the building and make the border so menacingly tangible that it gets under your skin.

Gianni Motti is the guilty conscience of contemporary art. In the past, he has caged brokers, run for the American presidency, and held an invisible retrospective, heavily protected by security guards, at Zurich's Migros Museum für Gegenwartskunst in 2004. Now he is refashioning our world – and in doing so he is exposing not only the history of art and exhibitions, but ourselves.

The street and the barbed wire in the museum – what does it mean? First of all, it means bringing the outdoors indoors, into the contemplative model space of the art institution – for paving stones and barbed wire are unexpected in interior spaces. The Helmhaus interior, on the other hand, is remarkably open and accessible, because the institution is financed by the city of Zurich and entrance is free. That makes it a truly public cultural institution. And that is why the two works **Think Tank** and **Draft** by Gianni Motti make so much sense here.

Over the years, the Helmhaus has repeatedly hosted radical exhibition concepts – in addition to the exhibition by Christoph Büchel and Gianni Motti mentioned above. Daniele Buetti transformed all the rooms into a scene of catastrophe. Till Velten conducted a religious service. For the World Cup in Japan and South Korea, football was played on circular goals. Peter Regli held a disco for just one dancer. Christian Waldvogel flooded the main first floor exhibition room. And Asia Andrzejka Naveen installed shared accommodation for eleven people. The current exhibition by Gianni Motti continues in this boundary-defying vein – and stands in the art historical tradition of radical artistic initiatives that have brought earth (Walter De Maria), artificial fog (Olafur Eliasson) and even horses (Jannis Kounellis) into the realm of the exhibition space.

The paving stones represent the open, democratic streets and squares that exist throughout central and western Europe. They symbolise the battle for this public, democratic space. The barbed wire symbolises the very opposite. It stands for physically insurmountable boundaries, for separation, for exclusion. Barbed wire is used to secure borders. It surrounds prisons, arms factories and embassies. It protects what is deemed vulnerable. While the people who are actually vulnerable move around freely – and unprotected – in the public sphere, on the paved squares, in the assembly places of the agora.

In an era when borders and freedoms, exclusion and democracy are writ large, the combination of two contrapunctal installations by Gianni Motti on two floors of the Helmhaus pose vital questions about how we coexist and how we wish to coexist. As separate entities or as an open community? The exhibition asks us to reflect on our differences. Do we accept them, or do we have to keep ourselves apart?

The paved square that Gianni Motti has created on the lower floor opens outwards, giving a free view towards the picturesquely paved historic centre of Zurich. It suggests a glimpse of paradise – but that paradise is merely a figment of the imagination. For just a stone's throw away, behind closed and alarm-secured doors, lies the clandestine world of tax evaders and wealth accumulators, whose work and "productivity" lies solely in using money to make even more money. A few years ago, we reached the point at which the economic gain generated by financial transactions actually overtook the economic gain generated by manufactured goods. Zurich remains a bastion of financial wheeling and dealing, to which politicians pander. This financial wheeling and dealing creates and constantly increases inequalities. And those inequalities have to be ensured – if necessary, with barbed wire.

Gianni Motti's **EX-POSITION** exposes the inequalities in Zurich and in the world at large. Within the scope of the exhibition series **refaire le monde** this means that we have to become engaged and fight for our rights to freedom – and against the constraints and barriers to democracy. For the common weal of an open and united society that creates a balance between rich and poor, while understanding and nurturing other qualities than those of the purely economic and mercantilist. Caring and empathetic, warm-hearted and welcoming, playful and creative.

Freedom itself is at stake and indeed on trial. Entrance to the paved spaces is not free, but is dependent on the structural dynamics. The small group that tentatively explores the unsecured paving has the scope to contemplate the value of such freedom: **refaire le monde** is entirely up to us.

Images pages 88 to 103

refaire le monde * PROPOSITION

A.C. Kupper

A.C. Kupper, artist, musician, author, graphic designer and analyst of life, designed the posters and other media communications for the exhibition trilogy **refaire le monde**. His work **Fata Morgana**, created especially for **refaire le monde * PROPOSITION**, also serves as the subject of the exhibition poster.

Kupper found the motif for the first exhibition, **POSITION**, on the Zurich street known as Militärstrasse (the name of the street is no coincidence). In the cast iron cover of a wastewater shaft, surrounded by tactile paving stripes for the blind, he saw the image of an American flag. Photographed with documentary precision, the image represents a political stance that blindly follows superficial impulses. In blatantly demonising others, even hitting below the belt, it is a stance that covers up the sewer of fiscal deficit and, with that, camouflages its own shithole. For the **EX-POSITION** exhibition by Gianni Motti, Kupper recycled and manipulated the visual motif of Motti's work **Motti for President**. The **Motti for President** posters, taking a potshot at Trump, even graced the construction barriers around the Swiss Institute in New York.

The motif for **PROPOSITION** features a razor blade. A tool for both everyday and not so everyday cuts. For beauty and for destruction. For change. The dark void at the centre of the blade, serving as its anchor, is akin to a fata morgana revealing the outlines of a pagoda-like temple architecture. A sharp-edged foreign policy reaps inwardly what it battles outwardly. And so the first motif, the American shithole, connects with the third, the razor blade.

Kupper's razor-sharp rhetoric rips into the dark depths of the profoundly personal (and even suicidal) as well as the political (including mass murder). His visual syntax is cleverly coded; discreet, elegant, stylish and subtle on the one hand, yet painful, incisive and brutal on the other. The substance of this oeuvre emerges in the indissoluble clash of pain and pleasure: its depths are as seductively beautiful as they are destructively cruel. Such an unpredictable shifting of self-camouflaged "black style" is an aesthetically advanced stance in the art world. In the world. In a world teeming with black holes, and traps.

Image pages 106/107

Ursula Biemann

And … cut.

The razer-blade photography by A.C. Kupper is followed by a cut. A cinematic cut. You enter a sluice, dive below, underwater.

The proposition by artist Ursula Biemann – internationally renowned for her video installations addressing the burning geopolitical issues of our day with sharp perspicacity – is that we should listen carefully, precisely in those places where we expect the most profound silence. Her video work **Acoustic Ocean** gives voice to a new kind of superhero – a Sami researcher who uses her scientific instruments to listen to the ocean around the Norwegian Lofoten islands. Other voices that speak, or rather sing, include a blue whale, a dolphin and even prawns and sea-urchins. We woud do well to listen. After all, some threatened whales species, for instance, might be able to tell us a thing or two about being on the verge of extinction.

The same fate is likely to befall us too if we continue to threaten the environment. Research has shown that, the less oxygen we have in the atmosphere due to global warming, the more slowly we think. If it drops to less than its current 21%, our brains will eventually become too slow to read or write these sentences. In the video **Twenty One Percent**, created in collaboration with performance artist Mo Diener, a contemporary superwitch actively combats this development. Working in the forest with cutting-edge technologies and ancient raw materials, she brings her own metabolism into sync with the earth. Or rather: she shows just how interdependent our metabolism is on the balance of the universe. Did you know, for instance, that dead stars actually pump through our veins? The narrator's voice in **Twenty One Percent** explains this towards the end of the film: The iron in our blood originates in the processes unleashed by the death of a star in a supernova explosion.

Superheroes love to fight against underground baddies. The superheroes in Ursula Biemann's films prefer to fight for the creatures and materials of the acquatic world, the earth and the dying stars.

Images pages 120 to 123, 174 to 177, 180 to 186

die grosse um_ordnung

How would you translate **refaire le monde**? Is it about "remaking" or "refashioning" the world?" Or perhaps "re-structuring" or "re-arranging" it? In German, "um_ordnung" [in the looser sense of changing the "order" – i.e. "Ordnung" – of things] sums it up.

die grosse um_ordnung is an activist art project that rails against oppressive mechanisms and stands up for the redistribution of privileges. Initiated by Zurich artist Sabian Baumann and realised in collaboration with Rahel El-Maawi, Tim Zulauf, Diana Bärmann, Simone Aughterlony, niv Acosta and many other artists from diverse fields, **die grosse um_ordnung** was launched in late May 2018 on Zurich's Helvetiaplatz square, with performances and a demonstration that proceeded to the co-producing theatre house Gessnerallee.

A film documentation of this evening can be seen at the Helmhaus. Also, there are discarded items of furniture there, just waiting for their "um-ordnung" (or: rearrangement) by you. A 40-metre long banner lists slogans and demands relating to ways in which the world can be refashioned, remade, rearranged. There is even a pyramid of privilege, demonstrating which privileges you enjoy and asking which you might be willing to give up.

die grosse um_ordnung is not about any specific form of oppression or discrimination. It aims to highlight the many different forms of oppression in our society – whether they relate to gender, disability, race, LGBTQIA+, age etc. Instead of those who are discriminated against having to fight their own solitary battles, **die grosse um_ordnung** seeks to forge a sense of solidarity whereby all those concerned can benefit from the experiences of others and so work and take action together. And that is why it continues – with, for instance, the Soup Discussions in the **PROPOSITION** exhibition, where new relationships are forged and specific interventions can be planned. The **grosse um_ordnung** project seeks to recalibrate the situation so that it is no longer just the case of a super-wealthy minority and their minions calling the shots by dividing the majority and defining which minority is the most worthy of their support.

Images pages 188 to 203. 218 to 221

Roma Jam Session art Kollektiv

Nothing about us without us!

That is the clarion call of the performers and associates of the **Roma Jam Session art Kollektiv** at the opening of the **PROPOSITION** exhibition. It's emblazoned on their T-shirts and on the **die grosse um_ordnung** banner (hung from the scaffolding in the middle of the main Helmhaus space). It's a slogan from the **die grosse um_ordnung** manifesto.

"Nothing about us without us" (Latin: "Nihil de nobis, sine nobis") demands that policies cannot be made by representatives without the full and direct involvement of the groups affected by those policies – be they groups based on nationality, ethnicity, disability or any other criterion, i.e. various groups that are sidelined due to political, social or economic factors. The slogan "Nothing about us without us" has its origins in a central European tradition dating back more than five hundred years. In the English-speaking world, it came into wider use in the 1990s in connection with activism relating to rights for people with disabilities. Later, it was also adopted by a number of other interest groups and activists. **Roma Jam Session** took up the slogan in 2016, following in the footsteps of the Roma artists' and activists' scene in Berlin.

Roma Jam Session art Kollektiv (RJSaK) is the first artists' collective in Switzerland to address and highlight the interests of the Roma minority in our society. The Zurich-based collective works on an interdisciplinary basis and is made up of artists, actors, graphic designers and others from a variety of working spheres.

At their opening performance **Khanchi amendar bi amengo** (Romani for "Nothing about us without us") the participants step out of their comfort zone: everything is about breaking down rigid forms and ingrained habits, exclusion and solitude, by creating a fluidity that encourages a shared sense of future, the potential for new encounters, while having fun and enjoying the aesthetics of constant transformation. All without fear or stress. All decided for us without us? Count us out!

Images pages 128 to 131

Asia Andrzejka Merlin

Refaire le monde? Refaire le nom!

Asia Andrzejka Merlin used to be known as Asia Andrzejka Naveen. It was under this name that she shook up the Helmhaus with her 2015 exhibition **Transformation**, on the first floor of the Helmhaus, where about a dozen artists moved in for two months, sleeping there and having discussions – and changing the institution in the process. It was during the exhibition that the collective changed the name of the show to **Más Cerca**, which means "closer". Three years down the line, Asia Andrzejka Merlin is still producing what might be termed "framed proximity", rather than objects of art. In the exhibition **PROPOSITION**, the artist undertakes a nomadic Sunday discussion round that meanders through the Helmhaus and Wasserkirche buildings. She wants to counter the brainwashing to which we are subjected – and which imposes opinions rather than allowing us to form them ourselves – with brainstorming instead: a collective harvesting of ideas and thoughts, which, like a veritable storm in the brain, might even sweep away some preconceived notions.

Lying on mats covered in canvas – the empty canvas becomes, for once, a comfortable place of repose rather than an uncomfortable void that remains to be filled by painting – you ask yourself "Why don't I share? Why am I not more environmentally aware? Why don't I do more for the common weal?"

Maybe the questions should instead be formulated like this: "Do I share enough? Am I environmentally aware? Do I do enough for the common weal?" The reason they aren't is because, according to

Asia Andrzejka Merlin's proposition, we could all do more, must do more, should do more.

Images page 187

Tanja Roscic

Tanja Roscic's dreamlike, magical, evocative art leads us into times past and hidden rooms. It leaps back into childhood, where the exaggerated emotions of a doll's face meant the world to us. Where barriers seemed insurmountable and made us wonder what really lay behind them. Where such archaically mediaeval concepts as vendetta and blood vengeance still counted. It permeates the present.

Roscic's art is full of such messages. About knowledge both old and new, individual and collective. But the fairytale aspect of this work is also a trap. For Roscic's fairytales are told with an incisive precision that cuts straight to the most vulnerable spot of our innermost life, in all its unpredicability, where powers beyond our control determine the order of things.

Threads hand-dyed by the artist using natural dyes are shaped into woven fabrics. Striking forms, spaces. Cold metal, heated and bent, distorted and welded, harbours faces with a seemingly empty gaze. What is this empty gaze meant to tell us? Is it right or fair to call it empty? Or is there, in this very emptiness, in this mute contemplation, something to be learned? Especially for men? Do they have to learn a language here that is entirely foreign to them? One that they prefer to suppress, because it is a language they do not understand and which fills them with dread?

Roscic's proposition restores the rights of nature, dreams and emotions, leading us into a space that has a precision all its own – one of warmth, feeling, yearning. The contrast between this and the coldly calculating business world that is no stranger to Zurich could not be greater. The artist is a medium, her art an oracle, its effect a tonic. A tonic for the world of business. And for the world of men.

Images pages 20 to 23

Corina Gamma

Nowhere on earth is the effect of climate change as dramatic as at the poles, where the ice caps are melting. In her film **SILA and The Gatekeepers of the Arctic** (2015/2018), Swiss director Corina Gamma shows the impact of climate change in Greenland: on the one hand, how it affects hunting families, while, on the other hand, presenting the work of an international research team. Global warming disturbs the natural food chain: the formation of plankton beneath the ice, which feeds the fish that are, in turn, the prey of creatures such as seals, walrus, polar bears, foxes and hares. The hunting season has been drastically shortened since the 1980s. Directives by the EU, Canada and the USA have also curtailed hunting quotas. As a result, many indigenous Inuit inhabitants have been forced to leave their villages for good and settle in the capital city of Nuuk, where prefabricated accommodation has been built for them. The largest of these buildings has already been demolished. The social tensions were too great – alcoholism, child abuse and other acts of violence were rife.

The international research team headed by Swiss climate scientist Konrad Steffen has been operating a network of weather stations on Greenland since the 1990s, among them the so-called Swiss Camp, whose location was chosen due to the fact that the annual precipitation and snowmelt were about the same. That, however, has since changed. In the meantime, the Swiss Camp has collapsed several times due to the ice sheet melting in spring (when the researchers return) and subsiding by several metres.

In the capital city, the Inuit are losing their culture. Traditionally self-sufficient, they now consume mainly imported food. This, according to Aqqaluk Lynge, former chair of the Inuit Circumpolar Council, is a postcolonial phenomenon. And it looks as though it is only the start of things to come. Major corporations are now setting their sights on oil, gas and minerals.

Aqqaluk Lynge describes the Arctic ice sheet as the earth's barometer. "What happens in the world happens first in the Arctic... we are the canary in the global coal mine." In Greenlandic, SILA stands for a balance, both between the individual and the enviroment, and also between individuals themselves. Global warming disrupts both. The quiet film by Corina Gamma, in which the images speak for themselves, makes that strikingly evident.

Images pages 206 to 217, 222/223

Club La Fafa

A project by Nadja Baldini, Søren Berner, Tawil Bukun Gurdei, Hicham El Khemisi, Maya Hottarek, Jun Kanai, Rahimullah Mohammadi, Ali Omar, Raphael Perret, Levent Pinarci, Juliette Rosset, Arthur Sobrinho, Jawed Stanikzai

In the exhibition **refaire le monde * POSITION** the public encountered a group of refugees living in Hall 9 in Zurich's Oerlikon district and were able to find out more about the issues facing them in their new environment. We have tried to further and sustainably develop this project by Raphael Perret in collaboration with art mediator Nadja Baldini. The subsequent launch of **Club La Fafa** is aimed entirely at creating a sense of solidarity – between people of different cultural backgrounds, different generations, different origins, with and without the experience of being refugees. The club is open to all. Its goal is to benefit mutually from different experiences, abilities and mindsets. Instead of suppressing and denying difference, be it physical or psychological, we seek to make difference fruitful so that something new might grow from it.

The clubroom of **Club La Fafa** in the Helmhaus is a safe yet open space that functions as a base for activities such as debating, dancing, designing, boxing, cooking. It also serves as a starting point for joint activities outside the Helmhaus, such as playing football together, visiting the theatre, or dealing with bureaucracy, and whatever else comes up.

Anyone interested in getting involved is warmly welcome. A number of public meetings are scheduled throughout the duration of the exhibition. We hope that **Club La Fafa** will continue beyond the end of the exhibition, both as the art project that underpins it and, ultimately, as an autonomous entity in its own right.

Fafa is the name of an island in the South Pacific archipelago of Tonga. It is also a resort in Albania, as well as the place serving the best street food in Helsinki. It's the acronym of the Franco-German alliance and that of the financial and administrative framework agreement between the EU and the UN. It's a plant, and also a river in central Africa. And in French slang, it simply means "family". One family.

Images pages 124/125, 132 to 139, 154 to 161, 164 to 171, 204/205

Texts: Simon Maurer, Daniel Morgenthaler, with excerpts from texts by Roma Jam Session art Kollektiv and die grosse um_ordnung

refaire le monde – and We Gatekeepers of the Visual Arts

Social work, activism, science, visual arts – an intersectional approach with the art institution as a safe space

On the first floor, there is a paved agora. On the second floor, however, the sense of freedom that this open, public space conveys is immediately relativised: Gianni Motti has installed military-grade barbed wire to protect something that is evidently very much in need of protection – the empty expanse of the bare white exhibition space.

There are many possible interpretations of the two works presented by Gianni Motti in refaire le monde * EXPOSITION. This solo exhibition by the artist, comprising two individual in-situ installations that also work in combination, forms the centrepiece of our exhibition trilogy. We may interpret them, for instance, as a commentary on the institution itself and thus, by extension, on the role we play as curators. For Gianni Motti's contribution to refaire le monde exposes us mercilessly and even attributes assertions to us that we ourselves would rather not hear: on the first floor, we promise the open and public agora, only to barricade it radically on the second floor. In other words: within these prestigious premises, no matter how much we may preach openness and accessibility, our upper echelons are still impenetrably fenced off by barbed wire. Under the helmet of the Helmhaus, as it were.

In the documentary film SILA and the Gatekeepers of the Arctic **– screened as part of the exhibition refaire le monde * PROPOSITION – Corina Gamma accompanies some Inuit on their travels through Greenland. Nowhere are the effects of pollution and the resulting climate catastrophe more clearly evident than in the Arctic. Corina Gamma sees the indigenous people of Greenland as the gatekeepers and guardians of this region. But whereas Qillaq Danielsen, Peter Avike and Ikuo Oshima are gatekeepers of Greenland's wide white expanses, we are merely the gatekeepers of the white cube.**

The gatekeeping role played by the Inuit as portrayed in the film will become increasingly important, even crucial, over the coming years and decades. In contrast to that, we gatekeepers of the visual arts should be tasked with keeping the barbed wire out of our institutions. Instead of acting as gatekeepers armed with obscure and excluding or exclusive slogans, we should take on a stronger role as caring curators.

But what should we include more – and what should we care for more? The exhibition refaire le monde * PROPOSITION offered a number of hands-on proposals. The representatives of the activist art project die grosse um_ordnung **brought the concept of intersectionality into the Helmhaus with their workshops, soup talks and lectures. Rahel El-Maawi and Pascale Schreibmüller referenced this concept in their presentation by citing the nineteenth century Ohian feminist Sojourner Truth, who repeatedly asked "Ain't I a woman?"** (Image page 189)**. As a women's rights activist, she railed against the fact that she was perceived as a person of colour and as a slave, but not as a woman. British journalist and author Reni Eddo-Lodge picks up this same thread when she accuses feminism of focusing primarily on white women, and points out that there are white feminists who are racist towards her as a feminist of colour: "White feminism is a politics that engages itself with myths such as 'I don't see race'. It is a politics which insists that talking about race fuels racism – thereby denying people of colour the words to articulate our existence."** (1) **That contradicts an intersectional approach in which there is "no hierarchy of oppression", according to poet and essayist Audre Lorde; an approach that acknowledges the discrimination meted out to Reni Eddo-Lodge both as a person of colour and as a woman, and one that unites activists against various forms of oppression instead of fuelling division among them. Just as** die grosse um_ordnung **puts into exemplary practice in the main exhibition space of Helmhaus Zürich.**

Could we transpose this intersectional approach to the visual arts as well? And what form might such an intersectional approach take? In refaire le monde * POSITION, Fabrice Gygi flags up what should – not – be done. His work Meeting Room (Images pages 1 to 5)**, presented in the same space occupied by** die grosse um_ordnung **in the exhibi-**

tion PROPOSITION, consists of a thoroughly impenetrable meeting-room situation with a white wall projection. Either the decision has already been made, or it is to be discussed later. What is clear is that we have no say in it. Like Gianni Motti's installations, this work by Fabrice Gygi could also be read as a comment on our work as curators: that our decisions have already been made, well in advance, by the time you actually enter the Helmhaus, and that all you can do is accept the end result of our convoluted thought processes.

In the third part of the exhibition trilogy, Ursula Biemann's forward-looking PROPOSITION provides a counterpoint to Fabrice Gygi's harsh POSITION. Her video installations Acoustic Ocean and Twenty One Percent feature protagonists dressed as superheroes who act in an extremely gentle and conciliatory way – perhaps their behaviour might even be called intersectional (Images pages 120 to 123, 174 to 177, 180 to 186). They listen, underwater or in the forest, to the diverse voices of ancient nature, albeit using modern-day instruments and knowledge. In their test tubes, they brew up a mix of visual arts, science, and activism. They produce an amalgamation of various raw materials instead of exploiting individual natural resources. In this way, they ensure connections and hybrids – intersections.

Perhaps, seen through the burning-glass of Ursula Biemann's works in refaire le monde * PROPOSITION, there is, in hindsight, an explanation for a strange yet suddenly evident decision, on our part, for the refaire le monde * POSITION episode of the trilogy, in which we had used branches to retrace the architectural structure of the darkened exhibition space where musical works by Maya Homburger & Barry Guy and Vincent Glanzmann could be heard. It was an unusual decision, given that it did not tally with the wishes of the artists, which usually determine such spatial interventions, but instead followed our own wishes as curators. Did we perhaps seek to use those branches to merge nature with the unnatural white of the exhibition space? Did we want to bring something organically growing into the Helmhaus that we might otherwise – perhaps for conservation reasons – have left outside? Did the branches in POSITION perhaps already foreshadow their antithesis in the barbed wire of EX-POSITION?

It would be nice to think of these branches as the harbinger of an intersectional curatorial approach. Or at least as a taste of things to come. For even if we realise that we might benefit from the insights of intersectional activism within an art institution, there is still a long way to go. Nevertheless, we try to define what an intersectionally organised art institution can undertake – or rather, what it has to avoid. First and foremost: it should not play off different protagonists against each other.

It should not play artists off against each other. Obvious as that may sound, one example of this is how the debate, still in its early stages, about the remuneration of artistic work, reveals that the institutional art world profits from an information deficit. It is precisely because there is so little transparency in the art world regarding the remuneration of artists' labour – as indeed in other fields, much to the dismay of women in the wider workforce who are less able to defend their right to equal pay because of this – that some players in art institutions can still get away with not paying the artists they engage.

We should not play off against one another the representatives of different branches of art – visual art, music, dance, theatre – nor those engaged in the related fields of science and political or social activism. That can mean that we do not denigrate a work of art for incorporating, say, science, to the detriment of the purely aesthetic, if that synthesis results in something that is effectively a third option: creating a fusion of both fields. It can also mean accepting that musicians can fill a space otherwise normally reserved for visual artists, just as visual artists can take their place in a concert hall or music venue. And it can also mean making use of the intersections between the institutions rather than pitting them against each other as rivals – which, in turn, only adversely affects the artists.

Instead, we should take seriously the experiences of the various actors and apply them to the benefit of all. We should highlight and address interdependencies, and acknowledge that we, in the visual arts, benefit from science and activism. We should reap the fruits of the intersections between art, science, politics, activism, and between diverse institutions and disciplines. We should make intersectional art.

Of course, that involves us, as curators, acting not so much as gatekeepers, but rather, as agents embracing correlations and connections without succumbing to some unfounded fear of losing out by doing so. After all, as the well-functioning intersectional approaches in activism show, we can only benefit from this – by setting our sights on an inclusive, intersectional programme rather than the pursuit of exclusivity.

But does that mean that we, as curators, will ultimately make our own role redundant? Might we not only cease to be gatekeepers, but even disappear completely?

We do bear a particular responsibility – one that is related to a concept currently as relevant in political activism as intersectionality: the safe space. The safe space defines places where people who feel marginalised can congregate to share their experiences of marginalisation. The very name Helmhaus epitomises this notion. The word "Helm" in German can mean a helmet (not necessarily one worn in war), and the Helmhaus itself is not a former place of arms production. Instead, the building derives its name, historically, from its role as a "helmet" in the sense of a "shelter" for assemblies and markets, and, etymologically, as a "helmet" in the sense of a protective covering.

The possibility that Helmhaus Zürich, along with other institutions of art and culture, might increasingly be viewed as safe spaces on a wider scale is illustrated by the example of Club La Fafa. During the run-up to the refaire le monde * PROPOSITION exhibition, even before the club was actually founded by asylum seekers housed in Hall 9 in the Oerlikon district of Zurich and their collaborators, there were robust discussions as to whether this was an art project or a social work project. Given the intersectional approach that was embraced, we can now state that both of these aspects apply. Rather than posing a problem, however, that offers an opportunity. We are not pitting art and activism and social work against each other, but extracting the most important aspects of each – important not only to us, but also to those involved, be they artists or not. During the PROPOSITION exhibition, it became increasingly evident that a physical environment – a safe space – is crucial for this. It provides a space that alleviates economic pressure. That in itself is a reason to steer the visual arts away from an object-oriented and economy-based market logic. It is a space where exchange is possible without any expectations of evident results. Speaking of results, however: there is a stubbornly held view among members of Club La Fafa (which still exists) that Hall 9 was only closed because the difficult living situation there was so clearly highlighted in the three refaire le monde exhibitions.

The fact that the Helmhaus and we as curators bear the responsibility of offering these agents a safe space is nowhere more evident than when that safe space is called into question. As with Club La Fafa, whose work continues, we have extended and intensified our collaboration with the black women's network Bla*Sh after the refaire le monde trilogy. One journalist, writing in the Swiss daily NZZ, reacted vehemently to an anti-racist Bla*Sh workshop in the exhibition of Color (spring 2019), asserting that the workshop had highlighted something that would never even have crossed her mind – namely, making a distinction between white people and people of Colour – and that it had, in effect, made her a racist for the first time (2). This is just another example of the "I don't see race" attitude which, according to Reni Eddo-Lodge, effectively stymies any discussion about race. It would have been quite constructive if the journalist had voiced her opinions during the workshop and had presented a real opportunity of responding instead of publishing them outside the safe space of the Helmhaus. After all, at the very beginning of the workshop, it had been made clear that the issues discussed among the participants should stay within the workshop, as a safe space for debate.

So do we preach the public space – the agora – while having only barbed wire in mind? We have learned a great deal from the exhibition trilogy refaire le monde: for instance, that we should not defend the institution at all costs as a white cube in which economic

pressure has as much clout as it has beyond those confines. And that we should nevertheless protect the white cube as a safe space where things become possible that might be dismissed or reasoned away in other contexts. We also learned that we must become more than just gatekeepers, and less. That we should not stand in the way, but stand up more for what matters. Let us refaire le monde, out of an intersectional safe space.

Daniel Morgenthaler

(1) Reni Eddo-Lodge, Why I'm No Longer Talking to White People About Race, London: Bloomsbury, 2018, p. 168–9

(2) Judith Sevinç Basad, "Meine drei Stunden als Rassistin", in: Neue Zürcher Zeitung, 11. April 2019, p. 39

Autobiographies

Instead of the usual biographies, we have chosen to let the artists themselves make statements about their work – and how they seek to refashion the world through art.

Ursula Biemann

My art is research oriented and includes fieldwork in remote places where I examine the effects of climate change and the ecologies of forests, oil, ice and water. The multi-layered video essays interweave cinematic landscapes with documentary video material, science fiction, poetry and academic findings to create a narrative about the changing world. When I shifted my focus about ten years ago from migration to ecological topics, I was often asked why I had done so. Given the increasingly obvious ecological crisis, the answer to that question should be obvious. My videos are aimed primarily at contributing to the current discourse surrounding these political topics. They create geographies and filmic environments in which the innovative practicalities of survival come to the fore. That is one reason why I am particularly interested in the indigenous peoples who are being marginalised by the western world's intensive exploitation of the planet and its resources.

In my view, images themselves possess a kind of conceptual, even material, agency. That's why the conservation of the planet can also be recalibrated and reconsidered through experimental aesthetic practices. Speculative and fictional narratives help us to rewrite the past and the future. In **Subatlantic** (2015) I explore how humans and other species adapt to an unstable environment. In **Acoustic Ocean** (2018) I go one step further, with the fictional scientific character embodied by an Arctic performer. The indigenous figure melds with the surroundings and, through her sensory attributes, reveals an ocean of intelligence. The instruments, be they visual, acoustic or digital, define how we can perceive and think about our world. That is something that art and science have in common.

It is important to me to change our relationship with life and the planet, whereby indigenous peoples play a central role through their ethical approach to all species. Artists can contribute to this process by experimenting with a number of different narrative and aesthetic forms. I am also actively involved in founding an indigenous university in southern Colombia. I see it as part of my artistic praxis to help in shaping an institution that promotes and supports indigenous scientists in the region.

Pascale Birchler

It is not the vast, wide, unfathomable world that I explore. I am drawn to another world – an intimate space that has become indispensable to my work. The area of projection, indeed the vessel, for my work relies on imagining that space. And each time there is a different situation in search of a room, a garden or simply a pathway.

I think Siri Hustvedt sums it up perfectly in one of her essays: "It's important to anchor the people or objects you remember or imagine in a mental space – or they begin to float away, or worse, disappear. The idea that memory is rooted in location goes back to the Greeks and exerted a powerful influence on medieval thought. The scholastic philosopher Albertus Magnus wrote, 'Place is something the soul itself makes for laying up images'."

That place is freed from given reality; dimensions can be breached and perspectives shifted. Such a diversion is crucial to a new way of seeing. It is in turning towards an intimate world and in the way we acknowledge objects that we bring them into a new context and suddenly there is movement and language. Is it not poetry and art that are capable of creating a different view of reality? Otherness breaks through our simple, habitual ways of seeing. As though we were unable to recognise anything in the realms of the real because what is true only appears when objects are given a voice.

Club La Fafa

Club La Fafa came into being on 21 September 2018 – at the opening of the exhibition **refaire le monde * PROPOSITION**. However, we already developed the idea for the club in the first part of the trilogy **refaire le monde * POSITION**, where we engaged with people from a refugee background and launched our first shared actions.

As a loose grouping of thirteen individuals, together we turned the museum space into a temporary club room, hosting three months of activities. Together we cooked, sewed, exchanged information, made pottery and played music. The idea was to use the autonomy of art to create a space within the art institution itself that would allow for personal interactions, exchanging information, bonding and sympathising.

In French slang, "fafa" means family. It was this meaning that informed our goal of building a (family-like) community bringing together people from different disciplines and from all different walks of life and work, with and without the experience of being a refugee. Along the line of friendship, love, kindness and empathy, we sought – and still seek – shared interests and possible shared activities. On that basis, we want to send a signal against the adversities and restrictions of current migration policies and explore new forms of "togetherness".

Worldwide migration, the pluralisation of society and the way we treat people with refugee experience are the burning issues of our time. These are the issues that challenge us both as individuals and as institutions. What will it take for the institutions to open up? How does inclusion succeed and what forms of cooperation does that require? These are the questions to which Club La Fafa seeks answers.

Club La Fafa @Helmhaus: Nadja Baldini, Søren Berner, Tawil Bukun Gurdei, Hicham El Khemisi, Maya Hottarek, Jun Kanai, Rahimullah Mohammadi, Ali Omar, Raphael Perret, Levent Pinarci, Juliette Rosset, Arthur Sobrinho, Jawed Stanikzai

Club La Fafa continues to undertake further projects as a constantly evolving team in collaboration with various institutions in the fields of education and the arts.

Corina Gamma

As an artist I am constantly situated within an ongoing dialogue. I use art as the language that describes the world around me. My work is often driven by a curiosity about the things I do not know, but also by a pressing need to process social behaviours and create clarity. When I look at the world through a lens, I act as both artist and viewer, and convey ideas and events. The camera is my eye and also bears witness to what I learn, communicate and construct on the basis of our existing history.

Photography and film reflect reality very subjectively, as any art form does, allowing me to shape my own narratives. It is still an intuitive process, based on an emotional approach to the topic, which often chooses me. The process is an exercise in catharsis, cleansing the conflicts that are not fully resolved or cannot be described objectively.

In many of my projects, I observe changes over time. In this respect, the **SILA** project was very important to me. I experienced a place where local identity and environmental balance are vulnerable to the negative effects of today's society.

Vincent Glanzmann

THE ARTIST IS A COMMENTARY
THE ARTIST IS AUTONOMOUS / TIMELESS
THE ARTIST IS AN ARCHETYPE KIOSK

IN ALL AUTONOMY

~~YES~~

~~THE ARTIST IS AUTONOMOUS~~

CAN BE IS A
~~BUT YES~~ THE ARTIST ~~IS A~~ COMMENTARY GRASPED
~~A COMMENTARY~~ INVITING DISCOURSE ~~INTO THE SPACE~~
DISCOURSE ~~THE PHENOMENON OF THE ARTIST~~ WITHIN SOCIETY ~~SUFFICING~~

THE
EN
INVITING THE PERPETUATION OF MENTAL FLEXIBILITY AND
ASPIRING TO COMPETENCE IN FACING THE UNKNOWN
THE ARCHETYPAL ~~PURE PHENOMENON~~ IS A SOCIAL COMMENTARY
.PROVIDED THERE IS A WILL TO COMMUNICATE

he/she/they, in observing, will bring focus that constitutes a commentary

maintaining mental flexibility / competent handling. This frame of mind that is capable of creating temporary order without shying away from change or integration ~~BUT WILLINGLY~~ MALLEABLY ~~PROPAGATES AN~~ Allows a healthy approach to a constantly changing world . with diverging needs

THE MINDSET OF THE ARCHETYPAL ARTIST IS THE AUSGANG FROM THE NORMATIVE. A NORM NEEDS RENEWAL
.
KNOWING HOW TO EMBRACE CHANGE
Her/his/their role is to represent alternative ways of thought and perception . a ~~MINDS~~ perspective based on a personal construct of reality. Sovereign standpoint.

~~EXCLUDES~~

die grosse um_ordnung

die grosse um_ordnung was a transdisciplinary, intersectional and art-activist project that took place on Zurich's Helvetiaplatz in 2018.

What name could a global majority project carry that takes everyone and everything into consideration and levers out the capitalist, patriarchal, colonial system in all its discriminatory hierarchy? And how can we change this hierarchical agency within ourselves? What shape might the agenda of this movement take? Those were the ideas that emerged from die grosse um_ordnung.

Around 1900, some 80% of the world was colonised. Colonialist – i.e. nationalist, Christian, racist, sexist, heteronormative, capitalist and supposedly "enlightened" – thought continues to permeate individual and global structures. die grosse um_ordnung begins with the individual and the local community and, from there, broadens the view towards the dominance of deregulated capitalism.

Featuring: niv Acosta, choreographer, artist, activist, and the Performance Laboratory with Brandy Butler, Rahel El-Maawi, Meloe Gennai, Eddie Ramirez and Hermes Schneider; Simone Aughterlony, choreographer, performance artist and the Performance Laboratory with Effi Mer Delamaskis, Yael Gesù, Chris Gustafsson, Khadija Makki, Dominic Schibli and Oli Skyler; Diana Bärmann, cultural scientist, Rahel El-Maawi, sociocultural activist, Doro Schürch, performer, Tim Zulauf, artist, theatre impresario, and many others. Initiated by Sabian Baumann. A production by verein für um_ordnung in co-production with Gessnerallee Zürich.

Fabrice Gygi

Faire, refaire, défaire, faire, refaire, défaire, refaire, faire, défaire; c'est assurément le monde qui m'a fait et peut l'inverse!

Maya Homburger & Barry Guy

Maya Homburger was, for many years, a member of John Eliot Gardiner's English Baroque Soloists, before returning to Switzerland after spending much time in England and Ireland. She specialises in performances of H.I.F. Biber's Rosenkranz sonatas and J.S. Bach's chamber music and cantatas. In her concerts with Barry Guy she focuses on the combination of old and new music, with improvisation.

Barry Guy is renowned as one of the most innovative double bass players and composers. His creative diversity and enthusiasm for the experimental have made him a key figure in the revival of musical improvisation. Nevertheless, Barry Guy also gives broad range to composition. In addition to large-scale orchestral works for his jazz ensembles, he has also composed scores for many classical ensembles and soloists. His solo works for violin can be heard on CD recordings by Maya Homburger, framed by sonatas and partitas by J.S. Bach.

To summarise our biographies in just a few words, we'd say: the most important word that comes to mind is DANKE! We are both thankful to have grown up in peace and to have been able to live in countries that are not directly affected by violence. Thankful that we have had the opportunity of experiencing and helping to shape the golden years of the Early Music Scene and the Free Improvisation Scene (Barry) and thankful to have experienced so many inspiring concerts and projects, and continue to do so. Thankful to have such a wonderful audience across the world, which includes many friends who support and inspire us. We know that this is an immense privilege and blessing in the very best sense! THANKS! DANKE!

A.C. Kupper

A simple life surrounded by good people.

Asia Andrzejka Merlin

My work is stripping away biography in order to connect with the higher order and the whole, rather than with a notion of the self.

Gianni Motti

interviewed by Jérôme Sans

You are known for your approach as a hacker of political events, social conditions, sports and nature. Intervening in reality in order to change it seems to be at the core of your mission. How would you describe this approach?

I am a hacker – which means that most politicians are hackers as well. They also change reality, shape our minds, distract from the facts. Nature, too, is a hacker in a sense, with all its catastrophes (earthquakes, storms…). Utlimately, all that is left to me are the in-between spaces. I try to grasp the opportunity of putting the play of everyday life out of kilter.

Can one still be radical today?

It's difficult. The radical has shifted. Today, the radicals are in the stock exchange, in politics. Those are the world's new radicals, the 21st century anarchists. They do whatever they want, to the detriment of the law and of humanity as a whole.

What are the connections between art and politics?

The connections between art and politics are manifold, because art also belongs to the economy. I don't see one single activity that isn't also political. There are also some very curious connections between art and politics. For some time now, I've been finding out that lots of politicians would have liked to be artists, or secretly do art. One even said to me one day that "the statesman is also an artist. To him, the populace is no different than the stone is to the sculptor".

The way the world presents itself today: do you practise something that tends to be humorous, by means of the absurd?

Maybe. I don't know. You know what's absurd? Seven billion human beings spinning around themselves and the sun at the same time, at great speed, on a crust that is cooling down over a firebowl...

Raphael Perret

When I was 16, I visited Madagascar with my parents and I started to understand how the world functions. It was the view from this incredibly rich culture, unique nature, simplicity and poverty, colonial exploitation and a populace rapidly destroying its own existential basis – this view from the other side of the world towards the European environment – that made an impact on me. An environment enclosed in a veil that prevents us from seeing clearly. What I want to do is cut a few holes in that veil.

Stories are the software driving the way society functions – and we desperately need some new ones. Art is all about experimentation, seduction, storytelling, connecting, in many different ways. But I am not interested in pointing fingers, nor in mere aesthetics, but in delivering an emotional punch. Autonomous art has to go beyond the here and now, has to give direction and look towards something new. The artwork emerges in its time and yet rails against it. If art can't do that, advertising takes over.

I often wake up wondering "what is to be done?" Heinrich Böll is supposed to have said that intervention is the only way of staying realistic.

Roma Jam Session art Kollektiv

Roma Jam Session is experimental
Roma Jam Session is performative
Roma Jam Session is community
Roma Jam Session is transformation
Roma Jam Session is art history hacking
Roma Jam Session is Roma Dada Avantgarde
Roma Jam Session is detox and dance
Roma Jam Session is a fluid social sculpture

Roma Jam Session art Kollektiv (http://romajamsession.org) was founded in 2013 at the Shedhalle in Zurich by Mo Diener and RR Marki. It is the first Roma artist collective in Switzerland and in Europe. The Zurich-based group is transdiciplinary, working together in the fields of art, theatre, music and design. In addition to public performances, the collective is also actively involved in activist campaigns with other Roma organisations and NGOs. Given the unrecognised status of the Roma as a transnational minority in Switzerland, the collective has evolved transnationally and intersectionally and has joined forces with die grosse um_ordnung (http://diegrosseumordnung.ch) – a queer-/feminist art project with many alliances. RJSaK is currently collaborating on a follow-up project with these alliances: the Future Archive.

In January 2019, RJSaK was represented at the launch of the RomArchive in the Akademie der Künste, Berlin, with a performative meditation on the situation of Swiss Roma history. In October 2019 the Roma Jam Session was invited by ERIAC to perform in the FutuRoma Pavilion at the Venice Biennale. Together, they presented the performance **CHROMA The Future Is Roma – We pass the Mic to Europe** and exhibited some posters of the **1st Roma Manifesto Zurich**. The performance was accompanied and supported by Roma Community representatives and activists from Milan, Mantua and Venice-Mestre. Roma Jam Session is currently working on the publication **Morphing The Roma Label**.

https://www.romarchive.eu/en
https://eriac.org
http://myartguides.com/collateral-events/futuroma/

Heidi Specogna

From an early stage, I have been more interested in questions than in answers. Questions that put me in touch with places, life histories, and people. Questions that open a window on the other and the unknown. Today, I am alarmed at just how much the fear of the other has increased, and how little curiosity there is about the unknown. In the Amazon, where I recently spent time filming in a small village, I learned that the other is perceived as a welcome extension of the self. It is a beautiful idea, even though – if ethnologists are to be believed – it may have led in earlier times to actually eating the other in order to come closer to perfection.
I work slowly. Often spending several years on a film project, giving it time to reveal itself and taking my time to grasp the subject, by gradually stripping it down to discover all its nuanced shades. Facts, images, analyses, commentaries – the public dissemination of opinion and content in terms of relevant topics has become rapid, superficial and unfocused. My generation has experienced war as a media event. In our minds, we look back on some kind of collective, visual memory of war. What could serve to examine these stored-up images? Where is the enquiring gaze that tears the veil from a news item? Documentary cinema can do that. It can do that thoughtfully and precisely, poetically, playfully, demandingly, loudly, subtly, gently. Equally, a documentary film can trigger thought processes that provoke dialogue and touch viewers deep within the soul.

In every situation, no matter how uncomfortable, my vocation calls for me to take a stance. It does not allow me to simply fall back on "deadlocked opinions". My vocation demands flexibility. It puts obstacles in my path and throws up ever-changing situations that force me to find a new balance, a stance, if only just as far as the next step takes me.

It could therefore be said that my life is like a long trek: from the shores of Lake Biel, where I was born in 1959, and over the Chasseral mountain to Berlin, where I was able to study at the German Film and Television Academy (DFFB) in 1982, and on to the Amazon rainforest, following in the footsteps of a courageous Swiss woman and photographer, then to Addis Ababa to accompany a female Ethiopian singer with my camera.

Bertold Stallmach

Each of my projects begins with a fixed idea: an image, a vision, a fragmentary narrative. Even if I do not always know how close the relationship is and even though the individual ideas may appear to have very little in common at first glance, they do come together to form families and groups that coincide within a story. For me, the work is about creating an aesthetic world where that can happen. A world where these precise figures slot together into these particular scenes with ease. It is, as it were, about combining different parts that don't necessarily fit together. Connecting elements have to be found or invented.

As a kid I used to built soapbox carts out of discarded objects. I'd sometimes rack my brains for hours trying to figure out how to put the pieces together so that they'd be sturdy and so that the cart would roll and could be steered.

Sometimes I think I'm still doing the same thing. Instead of pram components, cupboards and bits of wood found on the street or in skips, now I collect impressions, thoughts and images that I find on my way and put them together in films and exhibitions. I find that very human. Human beings shape their environment, construct realities out of sensory perceptions and thoughts, and fill them with function and meaning. Humans are builders of worlds.

Pages 1 to 5:
rlm*POS
Fabrice Gygi
Meeting Room, 2007
Galvanised steel, thermally bonded steel, wood, projector, DVD
Collection of the artist, on permanent loan to the collection of Kunstmuseum St. Gallen
Views of installation
Photos: FBM Studio
> Text page 227

Pages 6 to 9:
rlm*POS
Nakfa Adhanom, Hicham El Khemisi, Filimon Habtom, Fatime Abakar Hadze, Rahimullah Mohammadi, Ali Omar, Raphael Perret, Qurban Ali Rahimi, Sidy Sangare, Jawed Stanikzai
Fünf Finger sind nicht gleich – im Machen werden sie sich ähnlich [No five fingers are the same – it is what they do that makes them equals], 2018
Various materials
Views of installation (details)
Photos: Raphael Perret
> Text page 229

Pages 10 to 15:
rlm*POS
Bertold Stallmach
Das Mosaikprojekt [The Mosaic Project], 2017
Animated film, 16 Min.
Film stills
> Text page 228

Pages 16 to 19:
rlm*POS
Pascale Birchler
Im Kiefernwald [In the Pine Forest], 2018
Wall painting
Stuhl I [Chair I], 2018
Metal
Die Dichter [The Poets], 2018
Various materials
Ich färbte dir den Himmel brombeer [I Coloured the Sky Blackberry for You], 2018
Metal, acrylic glass
Stuhl II [Chair II], 2018
Metal
Blumen [Flowers], 2018
Metal
Views of installation
Photos: Michel Gilgen
> Text page 227

Pages 20 to 23:
rlm*PROP
Tanja Roscic
Refaire le monde, 2018
Various materials
Views of installation
Photos: Lorenzo Pusterla
> Text page 234

Pages 24/25:
rlm*POS
Exhibition space where the following works can be heard:
Vincent Glanzmann
Z/Rzw-Shiiiiiii/–-thehidden, 2018
Sound installation, percussion, voice, feedbacks
Compositions: Vincent Glanzmann
Recorded and mixed by Vincent Glanzmann
Mastering: Manuel Egger, suburbansound.ch, Winterthur
Mastering Z: Manuel Egger and Jeroen Visser
CD-Design: Dominik Huber, moire.ch
Label: through states of matter (www.throughstatesofmatter.org)
With the kind support of: Popkredit Stadt Zürich, Fachstelle Kultur Kanton Zürich, Fondation Suisa, Stiftung Levedo and Schweizerische Interpreten Stiftung
> Text page 226

Maya Homburger & Barry Guy
Heinrich Ignaz Franz Biber (1644–1704)
The Mystery Sonatas
Maya Homburger, baroque violin
Camerata Kilkenny: Siobhán Armstrong, harp; Sarah Cunningham, viola da gamba; Brian Feehan, Theorbo; Malcolm Proud, organ, cembalo; Barry Guy, double bass
Recorded by Nicholas Parker, 16 to 23 July 2006 at Propstei St. Gerold, Austria
Produced by Nicholas Parker and Maya Homburger
www.maya-recordings.com

Barry Guy
Ceremony, 16:35 Min.
For baroque violin
With beauty I walk
Impervious to pain I walk
Feeling light within I walk
With lively feelings I walk
With beauty before me I walk
With beauty behind me I walk
With beauty below me I walk
With beauty above me I walk
(Navajo song)

Maya Homburger, baroque violin
Barry Guy, double bass
Recorded in April and July 1997 at Propstei St. Gerold, Austria,
and at Rainbow Studio, Oslo, by Peter Laenger and Jan Erik Kongshaug
Produced by Manfred Eicher
Cover photo: Jim Bengston
Further photos: Peter Bastian
Cover design: Sascha Kleis
ECM Production
> Text page 226

View of installation
Photo: FBM Studio

Pages 26 to 29:
rlm*POS
Vincent Glanzmann
–<°>^.°-s-^
Electro-acoustic piece for percussion
17 March 2018, 12, 2, 4, 6 p.m.
Photos: Peter Schneider
> Text page 226

Pages 30/31:
rlm*POS
Heidi Specogna
Röntgenbild [X-ray], PK 12, 2008
C-Print
> Text page 228

Pages 32 to 35:
rlm*POS
Heidi Specogna
Cahier africain [African notebook], Switzerland/Germany, 2016
Documentary film (French, Arabic, Sango)
Colour, 119 min.
Views of installation
Photos: FBM Studio
> Text page 228

Page 36:
rlm*POS
Heidi Specogna
Aus dem Leben von Arlette Walikette [From the Life of Arlette Walikette], PK 12, 2009
C-Print
> Text page 228

Page 37:
rlm*POS
Heidi Specogna
Amzine und Fane [Amzine and Fane], Quartier PK 12, 2008
C-Print
> Text page 228

Pages 38/39:
rlm*POS
Heidi Specogna
Familie Kottaya vor ihrem Haus in Litton Village [The Kottaya Family in Front of Their House in Litton Village], 2008
C-Prints
> Text page 228

Pages 40/41:
rlm*POS
Heidi Specogna
Cahier africain [African notebook], Switzerland/Germany, 2016
Documentary film (French, Arabic, Sango)
Colour, 119 min.
C-Prints
Views of installation
Photos: FBM Studio
> Text page 228

Pages 42/43:
rlm*POS
Heidi Specogna
Cahier africain [African notebook], Switzerland/Germany, 2016
Documentary film (French, Arabic, Sango)
Colour, 119 min.
Fane
Film still
> Text page 228

Pages 44/45:
rlm*POS
Heidi Specogna
Cahier africain [African notebook], Switzerland/Germany, 2016
Documentary film (French, Arabic, Sango)
Colour, 119 min.
Arlette Walikette
Film still
> Text page 228

Pages 46/47:
rlm*POS
Heidi Specogna
Cahier africain [African notebook], Switzerland/Germany, 2016
Documentary film (French, Arabic, Sango)
Colour, 119 min.
Fane
Film still
> Text page 228

Pages 48/49:
rlm*POS
Alltagsbilder [Everyday Images], 2018
Self-documentation by residents of transit centre Hall 9, Zürich-Oerlikon
Self portrait of Hicham El Khemisi, resident of Hall 9 and founding member of Club La Fafa
Photo: Hicham El Khemisi
> Text page 229

Pages 50/51:
rlm*POS
Nakfa Adhanom, Hicham El Khemisi, Filimon Habtom, Fatime Abakar Hadze, Rahimullah Mohammadi, Ali Omar, Raphael Perret, Qurban Ali Rahimi, Sidy Sangare, Jawed Stanikzai
Fünf Finger sind nicht gleich – im Machen werden sie sich ähnlich [No five fingers are the same – it is what they do that makes them equals], 2018
Various materials
View of the reconstruction, at Helmhaus Zürich, of an accommodation unit in transit centre Hall 9, Zürich-Oerlikon
Photo: FBM Studio
> Text page 229

Pages 52/53:
rlm*POS
Sunday meeting with residents of transit centre Halle 9, Zürich-Oerlikon, and guests
25 March 2018, 2 p.m.
Photos: Raphael Perret
> Text page 229

Pages 54/55:
rlm*POS
Nakfa Adhanom, Hicham El Khemisi, Filimon Habtom, Fatime Abakar Hadze, Rahimullah Mohammadi, Ali Omar, Raphael Perret, Qurban Ali Rahimi, Sidy Sangare, Jawed Stanikzai
Fünf Finger sind nicht gleich – im Machen werden sie sich ähnlich [No five fingers are the same – it is what they do that makes them equals], 2018
Various materials
View of the reconstruction, at Helmhaus Zürich, of an accommodation unit in transit centre Hall 9, Zürich-Oerlikon
Photo: FBM Studio
> Text page 229

Page 56:
rlm*POS
Alltagsbilder [Everyday Images], 2018
Self-documentation by residents of transit centre Hall 9, Zürich-Oerlikon
View of an accommodation unit in Hall 9
Photo: anonymous
> Text page 229

Page 57:
rlm*POS
Ali Omar, resident of Hall 9 and founding member of Club La Fafa, in transit centre Hall 9, Zürich-Oerlikon
Photo: Raphael Perret
> Text page 229

Pages 58/59:
rlm*POS
View of transit centre Hall 9, Zürich-Oerlikon
The table from the installation Fünf Finger sind nicht gleich – im Machen werden sie sich ähnlich [No five fingers are the same – it is what they do that makes them equals], 2018, was in use in Hall 9 within two days after the end of the rlm*POS exhibition.
8.5.2018
Photo: Raphael Perret
> Text page 229

Pages 60 to 63:
rlm*POS
Accommodation units in transit centre Hall 9, Zürich-Oerlikon
Photos: Raphael Perret
> Text page 229

Pages 64/65:
rlm*POS
Nakfa Adhanom, Hicham El Khemisi, Filimon Habtom, Fatime Abakar Hadze, Rahimullah Mohammadi, Ali Omar, Raphael Perret, Qurban Ali Rahimi, Sidy Sangare, Jawed Stanikzai
Fünf Finger sind nicht gleich – im Machen werden sie sich ähnlich [No five fingers are the same – it is what they do that makes them equals], 2018
Various materials
View of installation
Photo: FBM Studio
> Text page 229

Pages 66/67:
rlm*POS
View of transit centre Hall 9, Zürich-Oerlikon
Library without books
Photo: Raphael Perret
> Text page 229

Pages 68 to 71:
rlm*POS
Nakfa Adhanom, Hicham El Khemisi, Filimon Habtom, Fatime Abakar Hadze, Rahimullah Mohammadi, Ali Omar, Raphael Perret, Qurban Ali Rahimi, Sidy Sangare, Jawed Stanikzai
Fünf Finger sind nicht gleich – im Machen werden sie sich ähnlich [No five fingers are the same – it is what they do that makes them equals], 2018
Various materials
Views of installation (Details)
Photos: Raphael Perret
> Text page 229

Pages 72/73:
rlm*POS
Questions and comments by visitors on the refaire wall: Refaire le monde? Yes, but how?
Photo: Peter Schneider

Pages 74/75:
rlm*POS
Architecture for Refugees, Switzerland
Mapping the refugee life, 2018
Various materials
Views of installation
Photos: FBM Studio
> Text page 229

Pages 76/77:
rlm*POS
Nakfa Adhanom, Hicham El Khemisi, Filimon Habtom, Fatime Abakar Hadze, Rahimullah Mohammadi, Ali Omar, Raphael Perret, Qurban Ali Rahimi, Sidy Sangare, Jawed Stanikzai
29 Fragen und eine Aussage [29 Questions and One Statement], 2018
Audio and text installation, c. 45 min.
Various materials
View of installation
Photo: FBM Studio
> Text page 229

Pages 78/79:
rlm*POS
Nakfa Adhanom, Hicham El Khemisi, Filimon Habtom, Fatime Abakar Hadze, Rahimullah Mohammadi, Ali Omar, Raphael Perret, Qurban Ali Rahimi, Sidy Sangare, Jawed Stanikzai
Fünf Finger sind nicht gleich – im Machen werden sie sich ähnlich [No five fingers are the same – it is what they do that makes them equals], 2018
Various materials
Views of installation (details)
Photos: Raphael Perret
> Text page 229

Pages 80/81:
rlm*POS
Nakfa Adhanom, Hicham El Khemisi, Filimon Habtom, Fatime Abakar Hadze, Rahimullah Mohammadi, Ali Omar, Raphael Perret, Qurban Ali Rahimi, Sidy Sangare, Jawed Stanikzai
Fünf Finger sind nicht gleich – im Machen werden sie sich ähnlich [No five fingers are the same – it is what they do that makes them equals], 2018
Various materials
View of installation
Photo: FBM Studio
> Text page 229

Pages 82/83:
rlm*POS
Nakfa Adhanom, Hicham El Khemisi, Filimon Habtom, Fatime Abakar Hadze, Rahimullah Mohammadi, Ali Omar, Raphael Perret, Qurban Ali Rahimi, Sidy Sangare, Jawed Stanikzai
Fünf Finger sind nicht gleich – im Machen werden sie sich ähnlich [No five fingers are the same – it is what they do that makes them equals], 2018
Various materials
View of installation (detail)
Photo: Raphael Perret
> Text page 229

Pages 84/85:
rlm*POS
A.C. Kupper
Untitled, 2018
Silver gelatin print on baryta paper
View of installation
Photo: FBM Studio
> Text page 226

Pages 86/87:
rlm*PROP
A.C. Kupper
Posters for the three exhibitions rlm*POS, rlm*EX-POS and rlm*PROP
Photo: Lorenzo Pusterla
> Texts pages 226 and 232

Pages 88 to 91:
rlm*EX-POS
Installing the work Draft, 2015/2018, by Gianni Motti
Barbed wire
Courtesy of the Artist and National Art Museum of China
Photos: Thomas Burla
> Text page 230

Pages 92 to 95:
rlm*EX-POS
Gianni Motti
Draft, 2015/2018
Barbed wire
Courtesy of the Artist and National Art Museum of China
Views of installation
Photos: Gianni Motti
> Text page 230

Pages 96/97:
rlm*EX-POS
Opening of the exhibition rlm*EX-POS by Gianni Motti
17 May 2018, 6 p.m.
Photo: Peter Schneider
> Text page 230

Pages 98 to 101:
rlm*EX-POS
Gianni Motti
Think Tank, 2008/2018
Paving stones
Courtesy Galerie Perrotin
Views of installation
Photos: Gianni Motti
> Text page 230

Pages 102/103:
rlm*EX-POS
Opening of the exhibition rlm*EX-POS by Gianni Motti
17 May 2018, 6 p.m.
Photo: Peter Schneider
> Text page 230

Pages 104/105:
rlm*POS
Fabrice Gygi
Amène ta lame – Aiguisage gratuit [Bring along your blade – free whetting]
Fabrice Gygi sharpening blades carried by visitors in the Helmhaus foyer
24/25 March 2018, 2 p.m.
Photo: Helmhaus Zürich
> Text page 227

Pages 106/107:
rlm*PROP
A.C. Kupper
Fata Morgana, 2018
Silver gelatin print on baryta paper
> Text page 232

Pages 108/109:
rlm*POS
Nakfa Adhanom, Hicham El Khemisi, Filimon Habtom, Fatime Abakar Hadze, Rahimullah Mohammadi, Ali Omar, Raphael Perret, Qurban Ali Rahimi, Sidy Sangare, Jawed Stanikzai
Fünf Finger sind nicht gleich – im Machen werden sie sich ähnlich [No five fingers are the same – it is what they do that makes them equals], 2018
Various materials
Installation
Photo: Raphael Perret
> Text page 229

Pages 110/111:
rlm*POS
Heidi Specogna
Cahier africain [African notebook], Switzerland/Germany, 2016
Documentary film (French, Arabic, Sango)
Colour, 119 min.
Film still
> Text page 228

Pages 112/113:
rlm*POS
Sunday meeting with residents of transit centre Hall 9, Zürich-Oerlikon, and guests
Barbecue in an allotment garden in Zürich-Albisrieden
22 April 2018
Photo: Helmhaus Zürich
> Text page 229

Pages 114/115:
rlm*POS
Sunday meeting with residents of transit centre Hall 9, Zürich-Oerlikon, and guests
Spring festival of the Dunkelhölzli growers' association in the Herrenbergli fruit and berry orchard
29 April 2018
Photo: Monya Pletsch
> Text page 229

Pages 116/117:
rlm*POS
Sunday meeting with residents of transit centre Hall 9, Zürich-Oerlikon, and guests
Spring festival of the Dunkelhölzli growers' association in the Herrenbergli fruit and berry orchard
Fatime Abakar Hadze
29 April 2018
Photo: Raphael Perret
> Text page 229

Pages 118/119:
rlm*POS
Sunday meeting with residents of transit centre Hall 9, Zürich-Oerlikon, and guests
Walk and picnic at Küsnachter Tobel
8 April 2018
Photos: Raphael Perret
> Text page 229

Pages 120/121:
rlm*PROP
Ursula Biemann and Mo Diener
Twenty One Percent, 2016
Video, 18 Min.
Film stills
> Text page 232

Pages 122/123:
rlm*PROP
Ursula Biemann and Mo Diener
Twenty One Percent, 2016
Video, 18 min.
Live performance by Mo Diener
Followed by a discussion with the artists and Yvonne Volkart, curator and lecturer
26 October 2018, 7 p.m.
Photo: Helmhaus Zürich
> Text page 232

Pages 124/125:
rlm*PROP
Fashion shoot with Club La Fafa
Photographer Dan Cermak and stylist Martina Russi used the clubroom at the Helmhaus for a shoot with members of Club La Fafa. Refaire le monde – in clothing by Swiss designers.

Model: Tawil Bukun Gurdei
Jacket: Collective Swallow
T-shirt: The Straight and Narrow
Scarf: Julian Zigerli
Model: Ali Omar
Short-sleeved shirt: Poplin Project
Photos: Dan Cermak
Stylist: Martina Russi
Styling assistant: Ariana Pianca
Hair & make-up: Julia Ritter
> Text page 235

Page 126:
rlm*POS
Events programme Hall 9 at Helmhaus:
"Realitäten erforschen: Perspektivenwechsel mit der Eritrean Diaspora Academy" ["Exploring Realities: Changing Perspectives with the Eritrean Diaspora Academy"] (www.eritrean-diaspora-academy.org)
19 April 2018, 6.30 p.m.
Photo: Peter Schneider
> Text page 229

Page 127:
rlm*PROP
Opening of the exhibition rlm*PROP with surprise concert by Fai Baba
20 September 2018, 6 p.m.
Photo: Helmhaus Zürich

Pages 128 to 131:
rlm*PROP
Opening of the exhibition rlm*PROP
Nothing about us without us
Performative intervention by Roma Jam Session art Kollektiv and accomplices
6 p.m., Paradeplatz: parade to Helmhaus
Sound: Jörg Köppl and Malika Khatir, 4 megaphones, manifesto: die grosse um_ordnung
6.30 p.m., Helmhaus: performative reorganization of the 500-year-old slogan "Nothing about us without us".
Sound and voice: Ilja Komarov plays on a homemade Egyptian string instrument.
Text: Mo Diener; translations: Mustafa Asan (Romanes), Ilja Komarov (Russian), Mo Diener (English)

khanchi amendar bi amengo
Performativno Intervencia, Roma Jam Session art Kollektiv vi Komplizora
18h, Paradeplatz ko Helmhaus
Muzika: Jörg Köppl taj Malika Khatir
18:30h, Helmhaus: performativno reorganizacija e 500 Bershenge Slogans "khanchi amendar bi amengo"
Muzika taj Krlo: Ilja Komarov bashel ko Instrumenti andar o Egipto.
Text: Mo Diener; Romanes: Mustafa Asan; Ruski: Ilja Komarov; Angliski: Mo Diener

20 September 2018, 6 p.m.
Photos: Helmhaus Zürich (Pages 128/129), Mo Diener/Reinard Schmidt (Pages 130/131)
> Text page 233

Pages 132/133:
rlm*PROP
Fashion shoot with Club La Fafa
Photographer Dan Cermak and stylist Martina Russi used the clubroom at the Helmhaus for a shoot with members of Club La Fafa. Refaire le monde – in clothing by Swiss designers.

Model: Nadja Baldini
Dress: After Work Studio
Photos: Dan Cermak
Stylist: Martina Russi
Styling assistant: Ariana Pianca
Hair & make-up: Julia Ritter
> Text page 235

Pages 134/135:
rlm*PROP
Fashion shoot with Club La Fafa
Model: Juliette Rosset
Pullover and trousers: Adrian Reber
Silk scarf: Ikou Tschüss
Photo: Dan Cermak
Stylist: Martina Russi
Styling assistant: Ariana Pianca
Hair & make-up: Julia Ritter
> Text page 235

Pages 136/137:
rlm*PROP
Fashion shoot with Club La Fafa
Model: Søren Berner
Jumpsuit: Kathrin Eckhardt Studio
Shirt: Rafael Kouto
Photo: Dan Cermak
Stylist: Martina Russi
Styling assistant: Ariana Pianca
Hair & make-up: Julia Ritter
> Text page 235

Pages 138/139:
rlm*PROP
Fashion shoot with Club La Fafa
Model: Tawil Bukun Gurdei
Jacket and trousers: Collective Swallow
T-shirt: The Straight and Narrow
Scarf: Julian Zigerli
Photos: Dan Cermak
Stylist: Martina Russi
Styling assistant: Ariana Pianca
Hair & make-up: Julia Ritter
> Text page 235

Pages 140/141:
rlm*POS
Discussion round
Welcome to the problem zone! The pain of exhibition making
"Sind wir jetzt etwa im Menschenzoo oder was?" ["Are we now in a human zoo, or what?"]
Nadja Baldini, curator, Raphael Perret, artist, and other guests (here: Ali Omar) in conversation with Juliette Rosset
26 April 2018, 6.30 p.m.
Photo: Peter Schneider
> Text page 229

Pages 142/143:
rlm*POS
5-o'clock Thesis
"Es braucht Sozialdienst für alle" ["We need social service for all"]
Hans Ruh, social ethicist, in conversation with Daniel Morgenthaler
21 March 2018, 5 p.m.
Photo: Peter Schneider

Pages 144/145:
rlm*POS
Events programme Hall 9 at Helmhaus:
"Realitäten erforschen: Perspektivenwechsel mit der Eritrean Diaspora Academy" ["Exploring Realities: Changing Perspectives with the Eritrean Diaspora Academy"] (www.eritrean-diaspora-academy.org)
19 April 2018, 6.30 p.m.
Photo: Peter Schneider
> Text page 229

Pages 146 to 149:
rlm*POS
Events programme Hall 9 at Helmhaus:
"Kommen – Bleiben – Bauen: Welche Räume braucht die Zukunft?" ["Coming – Staying – Building: what are the spaces the future needs?"]
Thomas Kunz, director of Asyl Organisation Zürich, Lore Mühlbauer, architect and editor of "Flüchtlingsbauten, Handbuch und Planungshilfe", Christoph Oeschger, photographer and artist, and Bruno Vogel, architect, in conversation with Nadja Baldini
5 April 2018, 6.30 p.m.
Photo: Peter Schneider
> Text page 229

Pages 150/151:
rlm*POS
Discussion round
Welcome to the problem zone! The pain of exhibition making
"Sind wir jetzt etwa im Menschenzoo oder was?" ["Are we now in a human zoo, or what?"]
Nadja Baldini, curator, Raphael Perret, artist, and other guests (here: Fatime Abakar Hadze) in conversation with Juliette Rosset
26 April 2018, 6.30 p.m.
Photo: Peter Schneider
> Text page 229

Pages 152/153:
rlm*POS
U5
The Human Crater, 2018
Film screening followed by artists' discussion about temperamental Merapi, gentle Galunggung, wise old Ungaran, superstar Bromo and slightly neurotic Sindoro. The film The Human Crater introduces the personalities of the volcanoes on the Indonesian island of Java.
15 March 2018, 8 p.m.
Photo: Peter Schneider

Pages 154/155:
rlm*PROP
Fashion shoot with Club La Fafa
Model: Ali Omar
Short-sleeved shirt, pouch, trousers: Poplin Project
Photo: Dan Cermak
Stylist: Martina Russi
Styling assistant: Ariana Pianca
Hair & make-up: Julia Ritter
> Text page 235

Page 156:
rlm*PROP
Fashion shoot with Club La Fafa
Model: Hicham El Khemisi
Coat: Kathrin Eckhardt Studio
Trousers: Zurique
Photo: Dan Cermak
Stylist: Martina Russi
Styling assistant: Ariana Pianca
Hair & make-up: Julia Ritter
> Text page 235

Page 157:
lm*PROP
Fashion shoot with Club La Fafa
Model: Jun Kanai
Blazer and trousers: Zurique
Scarf: Ikou Tschüss
Photo: Dan Cermak
Stylist: Martina Russi
Styling assistant: Ariana Pianca
Hair & make-up: Julia Ritter
> Text page 235

Pages 158/159:
rlm*PROP
Fashion shoot with Club La Fafa
Model: Raphael Perret
T-shirt: The Straight and Narrow
Trousers: Zurique
Model: Søren Berner
Jumpsuit: Kathrin Eckhardt Studio
Photos: Dan Cermak
Stylist: Martina Russi
Styling assistant: Ariana Pianca
Hair & make-up: Julia Ritter
> Text page 235

Pages 160/161:
rlm*PROP
Fashion shoot with Club La Fafa
Model: Rahimullah Mohammadi
Pullover: The Straight and Narrow
Cap: Poplin Project
Photo: Dan Cermak
Stylist: Martina Russi
Styling assistant: Ariana Pianca
Hair & make-up: Julia Ritter
> Text page 235

Pages 162/163:
rlm*POS
Nakfa Adhanom, Hicham El Khemisi, Filimon Habtom, Fatime Abakar Hadze, Rahimullah Mohammadi, Ali Omar, Raphael Perret, Qurban Ali Rahimi, Sidy Sangare, Jawed Stanikzai
Fünf Finger sind nicht gleich – im Machen werden sie sich ähnlich [No five fingers are the same – it is what they do that makes them equals], 2018
Various materials
View of installation (detail)
Photo: Raphael Perret
> Text page 229

Pages 164 to 169:
rlm*PROP
Club La Fafa
A project by: Nadja Baldini, Søren Berner, Tawil Bukun Gurdei, Hicham El Khemisi, Maya Hottarek, Jun Kanai, Rahimullah Mohammadi, Ali Omar, Raphael Perret, Levent Pinarci, Juliette Rosset, Arthur Sobrinho, Jawed Stanikzai
Clubroom of Club La Fafa with translation office, music box, tearoom in Helmhaus Zürich
Photos: Lorenzo Pusterla
> Text page 235

Pages 170/171:
rlm*POS
Birthday party for Fatime Abakar Hadze
Involved in the project Fünf Finger sind nicht gleich – im Machen werden sie sich ähnlich [No five fingers are the same – it is what they do that makes them equals], 2018, and founding member of Club La Fafa, at the Lilienberg centre for asylum seekers who are unaccompanied minors (MNA) in Affoltern am Albis
2 May 2018
Photos: Raphael Perret
> Texts pages 229 and 235

Pages 172/173:
rlm*POS
Bertold Stallmach
Das Mosaikprojekt [The Mosaic Project], 2017
Animated film, 16 min.
Film still
> Text page 228

Pages 174/175:
rlm*PROP
Ursula Biemann and Mo Diener
Twenty One Percent, 2016
Video, 18 min.
View of installation
Photo: Lorenzo Pusterla
> Text page 232

Pages 176/177:
rlm*PROP
Ursula Biemann and Mo Diener
Twenty One Percent, 2016
Video, 18 min.
Film still
> Text page 232

Pages 178/179:
rlm*POS
Maya Homburger & Barry Guy
Bach Meditation
An experiment with sounds, colours and transparencies, with Maya Homburger (baroque violin), Barry Guy (double bass) and the audience, coming and going, flowing and meditative – in the Wasserkirche
17 April 2018, 7.30 p.m.
Photo: Peter Schneider
> Text page 226

Pages 180/181:
rlm*PROP
Ursula Biemann
Acoustic Ocean, 2018
Video, 18 min.
View of installation
Photo: Lorenza Pusterla
> Text page 232

Pages 182/183:
rlm*PROP
Ursula Biemann
Acoustic Ocean, 2018
Video, 18 Min.
Film still
> Text page 232

Pages 184/185:
rlm*PROP
Ursula Biemann
Acoustic Ocean, 2018
Video, 18 Min.
Views of installation
Photos: Lorenza Pusterla
> Text page 232

Page 186:
rlm*PROP
Ursula Biemann
Acoustic Ocean, 2018
Video, 18 min.
Installation
Photo: Helmhaus Zürich
> Text page 232

Page 187:
rlm*PROP
Asia Andrzejka Merlin
above:
"Brainstorming the Brainwashing 1: Warum teile ich nicht? [How come I do not share?]"
Sunday talks with Asia Andrzejka Merlin and various guests
23 September 2018, 2 p.m.
Photo: Helmhaus Zürich
> Text page 233

below:
"Brainstorming the Brainwashing 5: Was sind esoterische Gedanken? [What are esoteric thoughts?]"
Sunday talks with Asia Andrzejka Merlin and various guests
21 October 2018, 2 p.m.
Photo: Helmhaus Zürich
> Text page 233

Pages 188/189:
rlm*PROP
"Es gibt (k)eine Hierarchie der Unterdrückung" ["There is(n't) a hierarchy of oppression"]
Lecture on the concept of intersectionality by Pascale Schreibmüller and Rahel El-Maawi
6 November 2018, 6.30 p.m.
Photos: Helmhaus Zürich
> Text page 232

Pages 190 to 193:
rlm*PROP
die grosse um_ordnung –
Intersektionale Suppengespräche [Intersectional Soup Talks]
How do we create communities to recalibrate the prevailing power structures on diverse levels? On three evenings, people from a wide range of political, social and cultural contexts are invited to share soup and conversation while reflecting on intersectional engagement – and planning shared activities.
25 October 2018, 6.30 p.m.
Photos: Helmhaus Zürich
> Text page 232

Pages 194/195:
rlm*PROP
die grosse um_ordnung
Left:
die grosse um_ordnung, 2018
Video documentation of the 26 May 2018 performance on Helvetiaplatz in Zurich, 29 min.
Participants in die grosse um_ordnung:
niv Acosta and the Performance Lab with Brandy Butler, Rahel El-Maawi, Meloe Gennai, Edwin Ramirez and Hermes Schneider
Simone Aughterlony and the Performance Lab with Effi Mer Delamaskis, Yael Gesù, Chris Gustafsson, Khadija Makki, Dominic Schibli and Oli Skyler

Performers and moderators: Mustafa Asan, Firdes Atmaca, Malika Khatir, Jörg Köppl, Doro Schürch
A production by verein für um_ordnung in co-production with Gessnerallee Zürich
Initiated by Sabian Baumann and developed in collaboration with Simone Aughterlony, Diana Bärmann, Rahel El-Maawi, Doro Schürch and Tim Zulauf

Right:
Manifesto, 2018
Banner, Manifesto flyer
In addition to an exhortation to the public, some 80 political organisations were invited to outline their concerns in the form of slogans that could be included in an intersectional manifesto.
The slogans submitted were then processed by the team of die grosse um_ordnung, resulting in the spoken manifesto and the banner, among others. At the event on Helvetiaplatz, everbody was invited to recite the manifesto. In preparation for this, there was a public slogan workshop and rehearsals.
The manifesto flyer contains the text of the manifesto, comprising a selection of the slogans submitted. The text was recited together during the performance on Helvetiaplatz on 26 May 2018.

View of installation
Photo: Lorenzo Pusterla
> Text page 232

Pages 196/197:
rlm*PROP
die grosse um_ordnung
Pyramid of Privilege/Triangle of Privilege, 2018
Floor installation, video, 6 Min.
Views of installation (details)
Photos: Lorenzo Pusterla
> Text page 232

Pages 198/199:
rlm*PROP
die grosse um_ordnung
Screen:
die grosse um_ordnung, 2018
Video documentation of the 26 May 2018 performance on Helvetiaplatz in Zurich, 29 min.

Participants in die grosse um_ordnung:
niv Acosta and the Performance Lab with Brandy Butler, Rahel El-Maawi, Meloe Gennai, Edwin Ramirez and Hermes Schneider
Simone Aughterlony and the Performance Lab with Effi Mer Delamaskis, Yael Gesù, Chris Gustafsson, Khadija Makki, Dominic Schibli and Oli Skyler
Performers and moderators: Mustafa Asan, Firdes Atmaca, Malika Khatir, Jörg Köppl, Doro Schürch
A production by verein für um_ordnung in co-production with Gessnerallee Zürich
Initiated by Sabian Baumann and developed in collaboration with Simone Aughterlony, Diana Bärmann, Rahel El-Maawi, Doro Schürch and Tim Zulauf

Couch with headphones:
Intersectionality and Language, 2018
Abridged audio recording of the discussion at Gessnerallee Zurich on 22 May 2018, 55 min.
A conversation with Peter Fischer and Eleonora Gubler (co-founders and board members of Verein Einfache Sprache), Lann Hornscheidt (authorecs of numerous publications, professorecs of gender studies and linguistics/speech acts; now working with xart splitta e.V., an organisation for anti-discriminatory educational work in Berlin) and Sarah Owens (Head of Design at Zurich University of the Arts (ZHdK), active member of Bla*Sh, the network of black women* in German-speaking Switzerland). Discussion moderated by Rahel El-Maawi (socio-cultural activist and co-initiator of Bla*Sh who launched the "Bla*Sh presents" series of events in addition to many other cultural and political engagements).

Views of installation
Photos: Lorenzo Pusterla
> Text page 232

Pages 200/201:
rlm*PROP
die grosse um_ordnung
Intersectionality and Language, 2018
Abridged audio recording of the discussion at Gessnerallee Zurich on 22 May 2018, 55 min.
A conversation with Peter Fischer and Eleonora Gubler (co-founders and board members of Verein Einfache Sprache), Lann Hornscheidt (authorecs of numerous publications, professorecs of gender studies and linguistics/speech acts; now working with xart splitta e.V., an organisation for anti-discriminatory educational work in Berlin) and Sarah Owens (Head of Design at Zurich University of the Arts (ZHdK), active member of Bla*Sh, the network of black women* in German-speaking Switzerland). Discussion moderated by Rahel El-Maawi (socio-cultural activist and co-initiator of Bla*Sh who launched the "Bla*Sh presents" series of events in addition to many other cultural and political engagements).

Awareness on Helvetiaplatz:
The concept of awareness describes a certain consciousness, quest for knowledge and information, and a sensibility towards problems and issues, particularly when these involve a disregard for physical, psychological and personal boundaries or even spill over into violence in public places. Awareness therefore means challenging sexist, racist, homophobic, transphobic, ableistic, disablist or similarly discriminatory behaviours against entire groups, and also means actively opposing such behaviours. People affected by such behaviours are supported and befriended.
For further information: www.awarenetz.ch

View of installation
Photo: Lorenzo Pusterla
> Text page 232

Pages 202/203:
rlm*PROP
die grosse um_ordnung
Manifesto, 2018
Banner, Manifesto flyer
In addition to an exhortation to the public, some 80 political organisations were invited to outline their concerns in the form of slogans that could be included in an intersectional manifesto.
The slogans submitted were then processed by the team of die grosse um_ordnung, resulting in the spoken manifesto and the banner, among others. At the event on Helvetiaplatz, everbody was invited to recite the manifesto. In preparation for this, there was a public slogan workshop and rehearsals.
The manifesto flyer contains the text of the manifesto, comprising a selection of the slogans submitted. The text was recited together during the performance on Helvetiaplatz on 26 May 2018.

Views of installation
Photos: Lorenzo Pusterla
> Text page 232

Pages 204/205:
rlm*PROP
Club La Fafa
A project by: Nadja Baldini, Søren Berner, Tawil Bukun Gurdei, Hicham El Khemisi, Maya Hottarek, Jun Kanai, Rahimullah Mohammadi, Ali Omar, Raphael Perret, Levent Pinarci, Juliette Rosset, Arthur Sobrinho, Jawed Stanikzai
La Fafa clubroom in Helmhaus Zürich
Photo: Lorenzo Pusterla
> Text page 235

Pages 206 to 209:
rlm*PROP
Corina Gamma
Fotografien aus Grönland [Greenland Photographs], 2011–2018
C-Prints
Views of installation
Photos: Lorenzo Pusterla
> Text page 234

Pages 210 to 217:
rlm*PROP
Corina Gamma
Fotografien aus Grönland [Greenland Photographs], 2011–2018
C-Prints
> Text page 234

Pages 218 to 221:
rlm*PROP
Anti-racist workshop by Bla*Sh
"Vom Nutzen unseres Ärgers – und dem Unbehagen, rassistische Privilegien zu benennen" ["On the Uses of Anger – and the Unease in Speaking Out Against Racist Privilege"]
This workshop is offered to people who want to learn about critical thinking in an anti-racist context. Readings include excerpts from a talk by Audre Lorde, given in 1981 to an audience of white feminists. Through her analysis of exclusion, rage and solidarity, we can learn to question our own assumptions and social positions.
Workshop: Bettina Aremu, Brandy Butler, Rahel El-Maawi, Marilyn Umurungi
Bla*Sh is the network of black women* in German-speaking Switzerland.
3 November 2018, 2–5 p.m.
Photos: Helmhaus Zürich
> Text page 232

Pages 222/223:
rlm*PROP
Corina Gamma
SILA and the Gatekeepers of the Arctic, 2015
Video documentary, 70 min.
Film still
> Text page 234

Colophon

Publication
Edited by: Helmhaus Zürich
Concept: Simon Maurer, Daniel Morgenthaler
Texts: Simon Maurer, Daniel Morgenthaler and the authors named in the autobiographies
Creative director: A.C. Kupper
Photography: the respective photographers named in the credits
English translation: Ishbel Flett
Proofreading: Louise Stein
Printing: Gremper AG, Basel/Pratteln
Paper: LuxoMagic 115 g/m2
Typeface: Berthold Akzidenz Grotesk BE

DIAPHANES, Zürich 2020
www.diaphanes.net

Helmhaus Zürich
Limmatquai 31
CH-8001 Zürich
Switzerland

www.helmhaus.org
info@helmhaus.org
facebook.com/helmhauszuerich
Instagram: @helmhaus_zuerich

English edition
ISBN 978-3-0358-0274-0
German edition
ISBN 978-3-0358-0273-3

Printed in Switzerland

Exhibitions
refaire le monde
Helmhaus Zürich
refaire le monde * POSITION
9 March to 6 May 2018
refaire le monde * EX-POSITION
18 May to 17 June 2018
refaire le monde * PROPOSITION
21 September to 11 November 2018

Director of Helmhaus Zürich: Simon Maurer
Curator: Daniel Morgenthaler
Curators of the exhibitions: Simon Maurer, Daniel Morgenthaler
Coordinators: Peter Schneider, Nathalie Killias, Christoph Eisenring, Juliette Rosset, Bassma El Adisey
Art mediation: Kristina Gersbach, Andrea Huber
Reception: Christoph Eisenring, Sophie Huguenin, Carol May, Nora Schmidt, Corina Simeon, Jana Vanecek
Technical team: Robert Steiner, Sarai Aron, Nino Baumgartner, Miro Aron, Konstantinos Manolakis, Cyril Portmann, Giuliano Scerra
Video: videocompany.ch
Audio: Remo Clematide

Acknowledgments
For their direct and invaluable input into both the exhibition project and the publication, we sincerely thank:

Ursula Biemann
Pascale Birchler

Club La Fafa:
Nadja Baldini
Søren Berner
Tawil Bukun Gurdei
Hicham El Khemisi
Maya Hottarek
Jun Kanai
Rahimullah Mohammadi
Ali Omar
Raphael Perret
Levent Pinarci
Juliette Rosset
Arthur Sobrinho
Jawed Stanikzai

Corina Gamma
Vincent Glanzmann
die grosse um_ordnung, initiated by Sabian Baumann
Fabrice Gygi
Michael Heitz
Maya Homburger & Barry Guy
A.C. Kupper
Asia Andrzejka Merlin
Gianni Motti

Raphael Perret with residents of transit centre Hall 9, Zürich-Oerlikon:
Nakfa Adhanom
Hicham El Khemisi
Filimon Habtom,
Fatime Abakar Hadze
Rahimullah Mohammadi
Ali Omar
Qurban Ali Rahimi
Sidy Sangare
Jawed Stanikzai

Roma Jam Session art Kollektiv, initiated by Mustafa Asan and Mo Diener
Tanja Roscic
Heidi Specogna
Bertold Stallmach

We also wish to express our sincere thanks to the following events participants:

Bettina Aremu
Bruno Baeriswyl
Mirjam Bayerdörfer
Dénètem Touam Bona
Catherine Boss
Daniele Buetti
Maud Châtelet
Mo Diener
Rahel El-Maawi
Eritrean Diaspora Academy
Silvia Federici
Daniel Fink
Sarah Genner
Max Glauner
Marcel Grissmer
Marcel Hänggi
Ilja Komarov
Malika Khatir
Jörg Köppl
Bence Komlosi
Thomas Kunz
Mascha Madörin
Ueli Maurer
Jeanine Meerapfel
Lore Mühlbauer
Andreas Naegeli
Christoph Oeschger
Somos Organicos
Tobias Preisig
Paul Rechsteiner
Carolin Rothmund
Hans Ruh
Pascale Schreibmüller
Marylin Umurungi
U5
Bruno Vogel
Yvonne Volkart
Melanie Wegel
Judith Wittwer

We also gratefully acknowledge all the others, too many to name here, who also participated in the **refaire le monde** project.

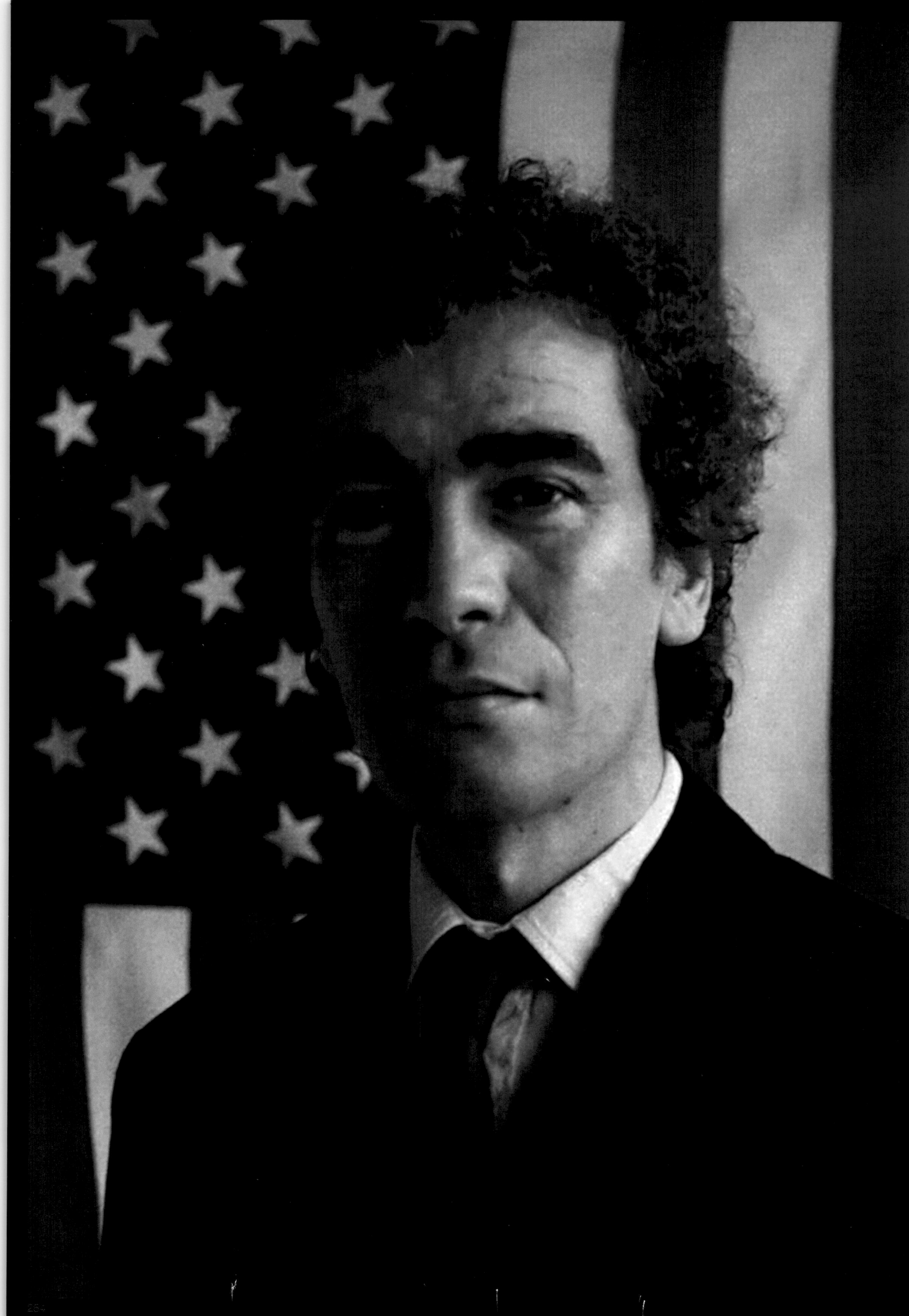

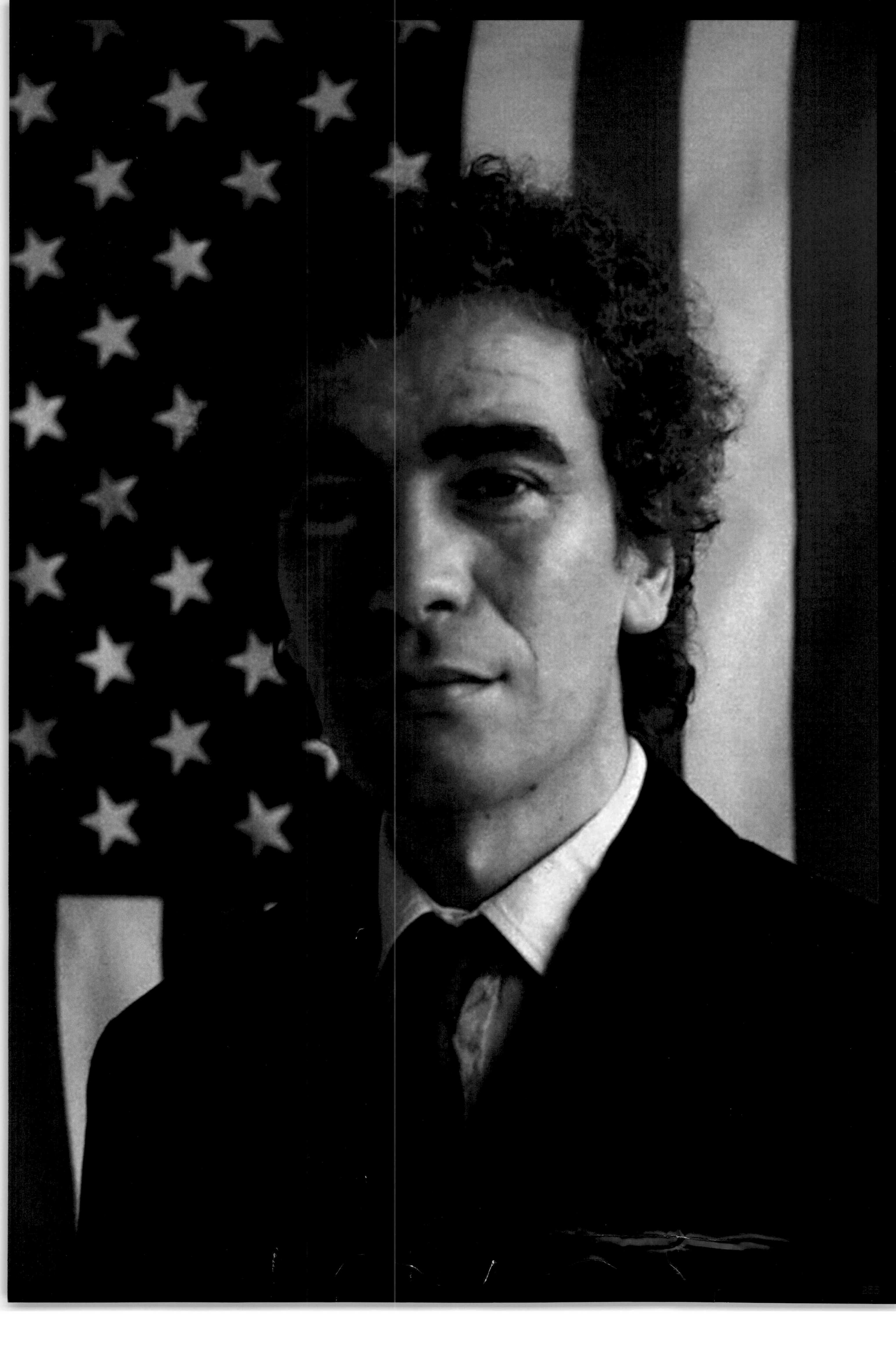